1970

BEST PLAYS OF THE SIXTIES

Books and Plays by Stanley Richards

BOOKS:

BEST PLAYS OF THE SIXTIES

MODERN SHORT COMEDIES FROM BROADWAY
& LONDON

BEST SHORT PLAYS OF THE WORLD THEATRE:
1958–1967

THE BEST SHORT PLAYS 1970

THE BEST SHORT PLAYS 1969

THE BEST SHORT PLAYS 1968

CANADA ON STAGE

PLAYS:

THROUGH A GLASS, DARKLY

AUGUST HEAT

SUN DECK

TUNNEL OF LOVE

JOURNEY TO BAHIA

O DISTANT LAND

MOOD PIECE

MR. BELL'S CREATION

THE PROUD AGE

ONCE TO EVERY BOY

HALF-HOUR, PLEASE

KNOW YOUR NEIGHBOR

GIN AND BITTERNESS

THE HILLS OF BATAAN

DISTRICT OF COLUMBIA

BEST PLAYS OF THE SIXTIES

Edited
*with an introductory note
and prefaces to the plays*

STANLEY RICHARDS

1970
DOUBLEDAY & COMPANY, INC., GARDEN CITY, NEW YORK

DESIGN BY RAYMOND DAVIDSON

Library of Congress Catalog Card Number 73–97684
Copyright © 1970 by Stanley Richards
All Rights Reserved
Printed in the United States of America

for

ELIZABETH LEWIS

and

HEATHER SCOTT

"A double blessing is a double grace"

S.T.

CONTENTS

BECKET   *Jean Anouilh*   1

THE NIGHT OF THE IGUANA   *Tennessee Williams*   119

FIDDLER ON THE ROOF   *Joseph Stein, Jerry Bock,*
Sheldon Harnick   241

PHILADELPHIA, HERE I COME!   *Brian Friel*   329

THE ODD COUPLE   *Neil Simon*   419

THE ROYAL HUNT OF THE SUN   *Peter Shaffer*   523

THE KILLING OF SISTER GEORGE   *Frank Marcus*   623

HADRIAN VII   *Peter Luke*   713

THE BOYS IN THE BAND   *Mart Crowley*   801

THE GREAT WHITE HOPE   *Howard Sackler*   901

PROLOGUE

. . . there is no one kind of theatre, and no one solution to all its problems. That platitude needs to be repeated. The theatre exists by compromise and feeds on contradiction. It exists to explain life and to deny it, to decorate it and to strip it bare. Man goes to the play to understand himself, God, or his neighbours, but he also goes to pass the time. He goes for uplift and amusement, a bit of fun and a moment of catharsis. The theatre is a weapon, a magic, a science; a sedative, an aphrodisiac, a communion service; a holiday and an assize, a dress rehearsal of the here and now and a dream in action. It taxes all senses, holds all worlds in one. It is the most conservative and the most ephemeral, the most opaque and the most transparent, the strongest and the weakest of arts. It is everything and nothing, all or none of these things. The theatre is what you make it. . . .

Richard Findlater

AN INTRODUCTORY NOTE

An editor charged with that distinguished, though often intimidating, descriptive "best" on the spine of his book—and, somehow, that four-letter adjective invariably seems to loom larger and more brilliantly colored than any other word of a title—becomes instant and juicy prey for the stalkers. Even in a society that takes justifiable pride in its freedom of speech and expression, there is, quite curiously, a relatively lower degree of forbearance with, say, freedom of *choice*. Especially for editors of collections. Yet, an editor's first and foremost responsibility is to pursue his task with integrity and to express in his selections a reflection of his own tastes and standards always, of course, hoping that the reader will be in, if not total, at least partial accord with his personal choice of material.

During the 1960s, the Broadway stage presented more than five hundred plays and musicals. (With the exception of one, all of the plays in this anthology were Broadway produced. I should like to add here that this was not to denigrate Off Broadway, a vigorous and significant force in the American theatre, but the subject of another collection.) To select ten "best" plays from the aforementioned total is tantamount to climbing Mt. Everest on water skis. Yet, it was an enormously rewarding, even fascinating assignment, principally because of the pleasurable opportunity of becoming reacquainted with so many plays, some which vividly remained within the scope of memory, others half forgotten.

The 1960s undeniably will be regarded by historians as a decade of enormous and provocative scientific, social and cultural changes. And since the theatre is a respondent (and at its most vital, a mirror of the world in which we live), it, too, exercised its transformative powers during the surging Sixties. Theatrical creators sought and explored new areas for dramatic interpretation and communication, mirroring the attitudes and sweeping changes of the period as well as bringing the pertinence of immediacy to works that were (or may have been) regarded as of classic or traditional design.

If there was a predominant element or factor that motivated my selections, I would say, without hesitation, that it was *dramatic excitement*. The plays set within these pages are pure theatre rather than pure theory. At the root of drama, throughout the centuries, it has been (and I am confident always will be) dramatic excitement, not theory. The great dramatists knew this and respected the value of audience stimulation and involvement. (And why this sudden fuss and rhetoric, particularly in off-beat theatrical circles, about "involving" audiences? From Aeschylus to our own times, serious, thought-provoking plays *always* have demanded emotional and intellectual participation from audiences; otherwise, the theatre would have gone the way of Atlantis.) They had little patience or traffic with turgid, ambiguous or meaningless theorizing. They were thoroughly aware that first and foremost, a dramatist had to have that power to stir the imagination, emotions and intellect of an audience. And whatever transpires in that world of worlds, the theatre, must strike true and be proximate rather than distant. Only then can there be a totally effective rapport between stage and audience.

We read and hear a good deal these days about how the drama is changing, and unquestionably and quite rightly, it is. One principle, however, remains constant. For a play to succeed—and never mind all that jazz about the theatre of isolation, conceptual autonomy and jejune put-ons—it *must* make an audience relate to, or identify with, and care about one or more of its characters who are wholly convincing in their singularity, and then to perceive in them the pattern of all human experience. Shakespeare cut the human carcass so that every tendon, fiber and heartbeat was dissected, revealed to us. If there is no empathy with, or understanding of, the characters and basic situation, there can be no true absorption, concern or response from an audience.

I have selected the plays that follow not as a lofty, dispassionate critic, but as a dedicated involved theatregoer. (I cannot resist the temptation to quote the eighteenth-century poet Alexis Piron's definition of critics: "He is the eunuch in the seraglio, he never creates anything and harms those who do.") And unlike Shakespeare's Henry VIII who uttered: "'Tis ten to one this play can never please all that are here," I voice my hope that the plays I have gathered in this collection will not only please but bring much pleasure and dramatic excitement to all readers.

STANLEY RICHARDS
New York, N.Y.
September, 1969

BEST PLAYS OF THE SIXTIES

Jean Anouilh

The plays of Jean Anouilh, France's most esteemed contemporary dramatist and one of the titans of the modern theatre, have been translated into many languages and have been produced in every conceivable theatrical corner of the world. Yet, in striking contrast to other notables of the international theatre, comparatively little is known about the man personally. Adamantly reticent about private indulgences, M. Anouilh has immunized himself from most journalistic questionings and the granting of interviews: "I shall keep the details of my life to myself."

Nonetheless, some facts have managed to seep through the scrim curtain that separates the man from the dramatist. Jean Anouilh was born on June 23, 1910, in Bordeaux, and while he was still quite young, his family moved to Paris. There he attended the Ecole Colbert and, later, the Collège Chaptal.

After a year and a half of studying law (at the Université de Paris à la Sorbonne), Anouilh washed his hands of briefs and legal documents and joined forces with an advertising firm "where I learned to be ingenious and exact, lessons that took for me the place of literary studies." In one of his rare press interviews, the dramatist reflected: "For three years I wrote copy for products ranging from noodles to automobiles. I consider advertising a great school for playwriting. The precision, conciseness and agility of expression necessary in writing advertisements helped me enormously." Eventually, though, Anouilh and advertising came to a parting of the ways and his passionate interest in the theatre propelled him toward Louis Jouvet, the celebrated actor-manager, and in 1931 he became his secretary.

Whether by destiny or proximity to the great man of the theatre, one year later, Jean Anouilh himself was to become a public figure in France. The occasion: the presentation of his first play, *L'Hermine*, starring Pierre Fresnay. Though it disappeared from the boards after only thirty-seven performances, critics welcomed the young writer as "a promising avant-garde talent," and the play's *succès d'estime* launched him on his life's work.

The next five years were not exactly auspicious ones for M. Anouilh, but in 1937 he scored heavily with *Le Voyageur sans Bagages* (*Traveler Without Luggage*). Performed by the enormously influential theatre couple Georges and Ludmilla Pitoëff, the play transcended Jean Anouilh's erstwhile "avant-garde" status and became the inaugural link in a long chain of successes. To list some, in nonchronological order: *The Waltz of the Toreadors*; *The Lark*; *The Rehearsal*; *Legend of Lovers*; *Antigone*; *Ring Round the Moon*; *Romeo and Jeannette*; *Médée*; *Mademoiselle Colombe*; *Ardèle*; *The Fighting Cock*; *Thieves' Carnival*; *Time Remembered*; *Poor Bitos*; *The Cavern*; and, of course, *Becket*, one of the most provocative and literate plays of the Sixties.

M. Anouilh also has written a number of impressive short plays, including *The Orchestra*; *Madame de . . .* ; *Cécile or The School for Fathers*; *Episode in the Life of an Author*; and his earliest work, *Humulus le Muet*. The latter, known in its English version, as *Augustus*, was written in collaboration with Jean Aurenche, one of France's most distinguished scenarists, and was published for the first time in the United States in this author's collection, *The Best Short Plays 1969*.

The primary function of the theatre is, was and forever will be entertainment. Even the most sublime poetry, the noblest of thoughts, could not exist onstage without a concomitant quota of entertainment. If we strip bare the basic elements of drama, then we are left with nothing more stimulating than disembodied speeches, routine polemics and platitudinous lectures. And Jean Anouilh fully realized this.

After serving two masters, Luigi Pirandello and Jean Giraudoux, Anouilh began to develop and perfect an individualistic style that even in its most bitter moments was eminently entertaining and irresistibly theatrical. The recurring theme of his many plays—the related axis upon which they dazzlingly revolve—is the quest for purity and happiness, deterred or frustrated by either a moral flaw in the central character's own nature or by the corruption of society. A subtle, witty and sardonic writer, Anouilh has classified his plays in two groups: *Pièces roses*, in which the theme is surveyed with illumining wit and comedy, and *Pièces noires*, where it is interpreted through a bitter eye. Whichever mold he happens to select for his interpretation, invariably the dramatist's technical virtuosity and theatrical brilliance give stunning life to his premise, people and plot.

Becket accents Jean Anouilh's mastery of the stage. It is a drama on two closely linked levels—church versus state and the violent emotional relationship of two young men who journeyed from the closest of friendship to deadly antagonism, each implacably convinced that he was right. In *Becket* we have the basic motifs of Anouilh's theatre: the ineluctability of everything that happens in this world and the hopelessness of saving the really human elements —love, friendship, decency—from this fate.

Becket ou L'Honneur de Dieu (directed by M. Anouilh and Roland Piétri) originally was presented in Paris on October 8, 1959. A reigning hit in the French capital, it was translated by Lucienne Hill, whose superb translations of many of the dramatist's works have been widely performed on English-speaking stages.

Hailed by the New York press at its opening, *Becket* later went on to win the Antoinette Perry (Tony) Award as the outstanding play of the 1960–61 season. (In London, it also won the *Evening Standard* Drama Award for 1961.)

How did Jean Anouilh happen to write *Becket?*

In his own words: "I wrote *Becket* by chance. I had bought on the quays of the Seine—where, in curious little stalls set up on the parapet, old gentlemen of another age sell old books to other old gentlemen and to the very young—*The Conquest of England by the Normans*, by Augustin Thierry, an historian of the Romantic school, forgotten today and scrapped; for history, too, has its fashions.

"I did not expect to read this respectable work, which I assumed would be boring. I had bought it because it had a pretty green binding and I needed a spot of green on my shelves. All the same, when I returned home I skimmed through the book (I am well mannered with old books) and I happened upon the chapters that tell the story of Becket, some thirty pages, which one might have taken to be fiction except that the bottom of the pages were jammed with references in Latin from the chroniclers of the twelfth century. . . . I was dazzled. I had expected to find a saint —I am always a trifle distrustful of saints, as I am of great theatre stars—and I found a *man*."

What had gripped M. Anouilh about the story: ". . . this drama of friendship between two men, between the king and his friend, his companion in pleasure and in work, this friend whom he could not cease to love though he became his worst enemy the night he was named Archbishop of Canterbury. . . ."

BECKET

or

The Honor of God

Jean Anouilh

TRANSLATED BY LUCIENNE HILL

Becket was first presented in New York on October 5, 1960, at the St. James Theatre under the auspices of David Merrick. The cast was as follows:

HENRY II	*Anthony Quinn*
HENRY'S PAGE	*Robert Duke*
THOMAS BECKET	*Laurence Olivier*
ARCHBISHOP OF CANTERBURY	*Sydney Walker*
BISHOP OF OXFORD	*Will Hussung*
GILBERT FOLLIOT	*Earl Montgomery*
BISHOP OF YORK	*Victor Thorley*
A SAXON PEASANT	*Robert Weil*
HIS DAUGHTER	*Hilary Beckett*
HIS SON	*Tom Leith*
GWENDOLEN	*Dran Seitz*
1ST ENGLISH BARON	*Louis Zorich*
2ND ENGLISH BARON	*Ronald Weyand*
3RD ENGLISH BARON	*Mel Berger*
4TH ENGLISH BARON	*Ferdi Hoffman*
A FRENCH GIRL	*Madeline Morgan*
A SOLDIER	*Claude Woolman*
A YOUNG MONK	*Brian Crowe*
THE PROVOST MARSHALL	*Victor Thorley*
A FRENCH PRIEST	*Dino Terranova*
WILLIAM OF CORBEIL	*Will Hussung*
A SERVANT	*Peter De Firis*
ANOTHER SERVANT	*Julian Miller*
THE QUEEN MOTHER	*Marie Powers*
THE QUEEN	*Margaret Hall*
HENRY'S ELDER SON	*Dennis Rosa*
HENRY'S YOUNGER SON	*Kit Culkin*
A MONK, SECRETARY TO BECKET	*Tom Leith*
MONKS FROM HASTINGS	*Mel Berger, Ronald Weyand*
LOUIS, KING OF FRANCE	*Robert Eckles*
FRENCH BARONS	*Will Hussung, Sydney Walker*
DUKE OF ARUNDEL	*Claude Woolman*
THE POPE	*Edward Atienza*
CARDINAL ZAMBELLI	*Dino Terranova*
AN OLD FOOTSOLDIER	*Louis Zorich*
A YOUNG FOOTSOLDIER	*Julian Miller*
A PRIEST	*Sydney Walker*

Directed by Peter Glenville
Settings by Oliver Smith
Costumes by Motley
Music by Laurence Rosenthal

The action takes place in England and France between 1155 and 1170 A.D.

ACT ONE

An indeterminate set, with pillars. We are in the cathedral. Center stage: BECKET's tomb; a stone slab with a name carved on it. Two SENTRIES come in and take up their position upstage. Then the KING enters from the back. He is wearing his crown, and is naked under a big cloak. A PAGE follows at a distance. The KING hesitates a moment before the tomb; then removes his cloak with a swift movement and the PAGE takes it away. He falls to his knees on the stone floor and prays, alone, naked, in the middle of the stage. Behind the pillars, in the shadows, one senses the disquieting presence of unseen lookers-on.

KING: Well, Thomas Becket, are you satisfied? I am naked at your tomb and your monks are coming to flog me. What an end to our story! You, rotting in this tomb, larded with my barons' dagger thrusts, and I, naked, shivering in the draughts, and waiting like an idiot for those brutes to come and thrash me. Don't you think we'd have done better to understand each other?

[BECKET *in his Archbishop's robes, just as he was on the day of his death, has appeared on the side of the stage, from behind a pillar. He says softly:*]

BECKET: Understand each other? It wasn't possible.

KING: I said, "In all save the honor of the realm." It was you who taught me that slogan, after all.

BECKET: I answered you, "In all save the honor of God." We were like two deaf men talking.

KING: How cold it was on that bare plain at La Ferté-Bernard, the last time we two met! It's funny, it's always been cold, in our story. Save at the beginning, when we were friends. We had a few fine summer evenings together, with the girls . . .

[*He says suddenly:*]

Did you love Gwendolen, Archbishop? Did you hate me, that night when I said, "I am the King," and took her from you? Perhaps that's what you never could forgive me for?

BECKET: [*Quietly*] I've forgotten.

KING: Yet we were like two brothers, weren't we—you and I? That night it was a childish prank—a lusty lad shouting "I am the King!" . . . I was so young . . . And every thought in my head came from you, you know that.

BECKET: [*Gently, as if to a little boy*] Pray, Henry, and don't talk so much.

KING: [*Irritably*] If you think I'm in the mood for praying at the moment . . .

[BECKET *quietly withdraws into the darkness and disappears during the* KING's *next speech*]

I can see them through my fingers, spying on me from the aisles. Say what you like, they're an oafish lot, those Saxons of yours! To give oneself over naked to those ruffians! With my delicate skin . . . Even you'd be afraid. Besides, I'm ashamed. Ashamed of this whole masquerade. I need them though, that's the trouble. I have to rally them to my cause, against my son, who'll gobble up my kingdom if I let him. So I've come to make my peace with their Saint. You must admit it's funny. You've become a Saint and here am I, the King, desperately in need of that great amorphous mass which could do nothing, up till now, save lie inert beneath its own enormous weight, cowering under blows, and which is all-powerful now. What use are conquests, when you stop to think? They are England now, because of their vast numbers, and the rate

at which they breed—like rabbits, to make good the mas-
sacres. But one must always pay the price—that's another thing
you taught me, Thomas Becket, when you were still advising
me . . . You taught me everything . . . [*Dreamily*] Ah, those
were happy times . . . At the peep of dawn—well, our dawn
that is, around noon, because we always went to bed very
late—you'd come into my room, as I was emerging from the
bathhouse, rested, smiling, debonair, as fresh as if we'd never
spent the entire night drinking and whoring through the town.

[*He says a little sourly:*]

That's another thing you were better at than me . . .

[*The* PAGE *has come in. He wraps a white towel around
the* KING *and proceeds to rub him down. Off stage is heard
for the first time—we will hear it often—the gay, ironical
Scottish marching song which* BECKET *is always whistling.
The lighting changes. We are still in the empty cathedral.
Then, a moment or so later,* BECKET *will draw aside a
curtain and reveal the* KING's *room. Their manner, his and
the* KING's, *faraway at first, like a memory relived, will
gradually become more real.*
THOMAS BECKET, *dressed as a nobleman, elegant, young,
charming, in his short doublet and pointed, upturned shoes,
comes in blithely and greets the* KING]

BECKET: My respects, my Lord!

KING: [*His face brightening*] Oh, Thomas . . . I thought you were
still asleep.

BECKET: I've already been for a short gallop to Richmond and
back, my Lord. There's a divine nip in the air.

KING: [*His teeth chattering*] To think you actually like the cold!
[*To the* PAGE] Rub harder, pig!

[*Smiling,* BECKET *pushes the* PAGE *aside and proceeds to
rub the* KING *himself*]

[*To the* PAGE] Throw a log on the fire and get out. Come
back and dress me later.

BECKET: My prince, I shall dress you myself.

[*The* PAGE *goes*]

KING: Nobody rubs me down the way you do. Thomas, what would I do without you? You're a nobleman, why do you play at being my valet? If I asked my barons to do this, they'd start a civil war!

BECKET: [*Smiling*] They'll come round to it in time, when Kings have learnt to play their role. I am your servant, my prince, that's all. Helping you to govern or helping you get warm again is part of the same thing to me. I like helping you.

KING: [*With an affectionate little gesture*] My little Saxon! At the beginning, when I told them I was taking you into my service, do you know what they all said? They said you'd seize the chance to knife me in the back one day.

BECKET: [*Smiling as he dresses him*] Did you believe them, my prince?

KING: N . . . no. I was a bit scared at first. You know I scare easily . . . But you looked so well brought up, beside those brutes. However did you come to speak French without a trace of an English accent?

BECKET: My parents were able to keep their lands by agreeing to "collaborate," as they say, with the King your father. They sent me to France as a boy to acquire a good French accent.

KING: To France? Not to Normandy?

BECKET: [*Still smiling*] That was their one patriotic conceit. They loathed the Norman accent.

KING: [*Distinctly*] Only the accent?

BECKET: [*Lightly and inscrutably*] My father was a very severe man. I would never have taken the liberty of questioning him on his personal convictions while he was alive. And his death shed no light on them, naturally. He managed, by collaborating, to amass a considerable fortune. As he was also a man of rigid principles, I imagine he contrived to do it in accordance with his conscience. That's a little piece of sleight of hand that men of principle are very skillful at in troubled times.

KING: And you?

BECKET: [*Feigning not to understand the question*] I, my Lord?

KING: [*Putting a touch of contempt into his voice, for despite his admiration for Thomas or perhaps because of it, he would like to score a point against him occasionally*] The sleight of hand, were you adept at it too?

BECKET: [*Still smiling*] Mine was a different problem. I was a frivolous man, you'll agree? In fact, it never came up at all. I adore hunting and only the Normans and their protégés had the right to hunt. I adore luxury and luxury was Norman. I adore life and the Saxons' only birthright was slaughter. I'll add that I adore honor.

KING: [*With faint surprise*] And was honor reconciled with collaboration too?

BECKET: [*Lightly*] I had the right to draw my sword against the first Norman nobleman who tried to lay hands on my sister. I killed him in single combat. It's a detail, but it has its points.

KING: [*A little slyly*] You could always have slit his throat and fled into the forest, as so many did.

BECKET: That would have been uncomfortable, and not a lot of use. My sister would immediately have been raped by some other Norman baron, like all the Saxon girls. Today, she is respected. [*Lightly*] My Lord, did I tell you?—My new gold dishes have arrived from Florence. Will my Liege do me the honor of christening them with me at my house?

KING: Gold dishes! You lunatic!

BECKET: I'm setting a new fashion.

KING: I'm your King and I eat off silver!

BECKET: My prince, your expenses are heavy and I have only my pleasures to pay for. The trouble is I'm told they scratch easily. Still, we'll see. I received two forks as well—

KING: Forks?

BECKET: Yes. It's a new instrument, a devilish little thing to look at—and to use too. It's for pronging meat with and carrying it to your mouth. It saves you dirtying your fingers.

KING: But then you dirty the fork?

BECKET: Yes. But it's washable.

KING: So are your fingers. I don't see the point.

BECKET: It hasn't any, practically speaking. But it's refined, it's subtle. It's very un-Norman.

KING: [*With sudden delight*] You must order me a dozen! I want to see my great fat barons' faces, at the first court banquet, when I present them with that! We won't tell them what they're for. We'll have no end of fun with them.

BECKET: [*Laughing*] A dozen! Easy now, my Lord! Forks are very expensive you know! My prince, it's time for the Privy Council.

KING: [*Laughing too*] They won't make head nor tail of them! I bet you they'll think they're a new kind of dagger. We'll have a hilarious time!

> [*They go out, laughing, behind the curtain, which draws apart to reveal the same set, with the pillars. The Council Chamber. The Councilors stand waiting. The* KING *and* BECKET *come in, still laughing*]

KING: [*Sitting in a chair*] Gentlemen, the Council is open. I have summoned you here today to deal with this refusal of the clergy to pay the absentee tax. We really must come to an understanding about who rules this kingdom, the Church—

> [*The* ARCHBISHOP *tries to speak*]

just a moment, Archbishop!—or me! But before we quarrel, let us take the good news first. I have decided to revive the office of Chancellor of England, keeper of the Triple Lion Seal, and to entrust it to my loyal servant and subject Thomas Becket.

> [BECKET *rises in surprise, the color draining from his face*]

BECKET: My Lord . . . !

KING: [*Roguishly*] What's the matter, Becket? Do you want to

go and piss already? True, we both had gallons to drink
last night!

[*He looks at him with delight*]

Well, that's good! I've managed to surprise you for once,
little Saxon.

BECKET: [*Dropping on one knee, says gravely:*] My Liege, this
is a token of your confidence of which I fear I may not be
worthy. I am very young, frivolous perhaps—

KING: I'm young too. And you know more than all of us put
together. [*To the others*] He's read books, you know. It's
amazing the amount he knows. He'll checkmate the lot of
you! Even the Archbishop! As for his frivolity, don't let
him fool you! He drinks strong wine, he likes to enjoy himself, but he's a lad who thinks every minute of the time!
Sometimes it embarrasses me to feel him thinking away beside
me. Get up, Thomas. I never did anything without your advice
anyway. Nobody knew it, now everybody will, that's all.

[*He bursts out laughing, pulls something out of his pocket.
and gives it to* BECKET]

There. That's the Seal. Don't lose it. Without the Seal, there's
no more England and we'll all have to go back to Normandy.
Now, to work!

[*The* ARCHBISHOP *rises, all smiles, now the first shock is
over*]

ARCHBISHOP: May I crave permission to salute, with my Lord's
approval, my young and learned archdeacon here? For I was
the first—I am weak enough to be proud of pointing it out—
to notice him and take him under my wing. The presence
at this Council, with the preponderant title of Chancellor
of England, of one of our brethren—our spiritual son in a
sense—is a guarantee for the Church of this country, that
a new era of agreement and mutual understanding is dawn-

ing for us all and we must now, in a spirit of confident co-operation—

KING: [*Interrupting*] Etc., etc. . . . Thank you, Archbishop! I knew this nomination would please you. But don't rely too much on Becket to play your game. He is my man.

[*He turns to* BECKET, *beaming*]

Come to think of it, I'd forgotten you were a deacon, little Saxon.

BECKET: [*Smiling*] So had I, my prince.

KING: Tell me—I'm not talking about wenching, that's a venial sin—but on the odd occasions when I've seen you fighting, it seems to me you have a mighty powerful sword arm, for a priest! How do you reconcile that with the Church's commandment forbidding a priest to shed blood?

BISHOP OF OXFORD: [*Prudently*] Our young friend is only a deacon, he has not yet taken all his vows, my Lord. The Church in its wisdom knows that youth must have its day and that—under the sacred pretext of a war—a holy war, I mean, of course, young men are permitted to—

KING: [*Interrupting*] All wars are holy wars, Bishop! I defy you to find me a serious belligerent who doesn't have Heaven on his side, in theory. Let's get back to the point.

ARCHBISHOP: By all means, your Highness.

KING: Our customs demand that every landowner with sufficient acreage to maintain one must send a man-at-arms to the quarterly review of troops, fully armed and shield in hand, or pay a tax in silver. Where is my tax?

BISHOP OF OXFORD: *Distingo*, your Highness.

KING: Distinguish as much as you like. I've made up my mind. I want my money. My purse is open, just drop it in.

[*He sprawls back in his chair and picks his teeth. To* BECKET]

Thomas, I don't know about you, but I'm starving. Have them bring us something to eat.

[BECKET *makes a sign to the* SENTRY *who goes out. A pause. The* ARCHBISHOP *rises*]

ARCHBISHOP: A layman who shirks his duty to the State, which is to assist his Prince with arms, should pay the tax. Nobody will question that.

KING: [*Jovially*] Least of all the clergy!

ARCHBISHOP: [*Continuing*] A churchman's duty to the State is to assist his Prince in his prayers, and in his educational and charitable enterprises. He cannot therefore be liable to such a tax unless he neglects those duties.

BISHOP OF OXFORD: Have we refused to pray?

KING: [*Rising in fury*] Gentlemen! Do you seriously think that I am going to let myself be swindled out of more than two thirds of my revenues with arguments of that sort? In the days of the Conquest, when there was booty to be had, our Norman abbots tucked up their robes all right. And lustily too! Sword in fist, hams in the saddle, at cockcrow or earlier! "Let's go to it, Sire! Out with the Saxon scum! It's God's will! It's God will!" You had to hold them back then! And on the odd occasions when you wasted a little Mass, they never had the time. They'd mislaid their vestments, the churches weren't equipped—any excuse to put it off, for fear they'd miss some of the pickings while their backs were turned!

ARCHBISHOP: Those heroic days are over. It is peacetime now.

KING: Then pay up! I won't budge from that.

[*Turning to* BECKET]

Come on, Chancellor, say something! Has your new title caught your tongue?

BECKET: May I respectfully draw my Lord Archbishop's attention to one small point?

KING: [*Grunting*] Respectfully, but firmly. You're the Chancellor now.

BECKET: [*Calmly and casually*] England is a ship.

KING: [*Beaming*] Why, that's neat! We must use that, sometime.

BECKET: In the hazards of seafaring, the instinct of self-preservation has always told men that there must be one and only one master on board ship. Mutinous crews who drown their captain always end up, after a short interval of anarchy, by entrusting themselves body and soul to one of their number, who then proceeds to rule over them, more harshly sometimes than their drowned captain.

ARCHBISHOP: My Lord Chancellor—my young friend—there is in fact a saying—the captain is sole master after God.

> [*He thunders suddenly, with a voice one did not suspect from that frail body*]

After God!

> [*He crosses himself. All the* BISHOPS *follow suit. The wind of excommunication shivers through the Council. The* KING, *awed, crosses himself too and mumbles, a little cravenly*]

KING: Nobody's trying to question God's authority, Archbishop.

BECKET: [*Who alone has remained unperturbed*] God steers the ship by inspiring the captain's decisions. But I never heard tell that He gave His instructions directly to the helmsman.

> [GILBERT FOLLIOT, *Bishop of London, rises. He is a thin-lipped, venomous man*]

FOLLIOT: Our young Chancellor is only a deacon—but he is a member of the Church. The few years he has spent out in the tumult of the world cannot have made him forget so soon that it is through His Church Militant and more particularly through the intermediary of our Holy Father the Pope and his Bishops—his qualified representatives—that God dictates His decisions to men!

BECKET: There is a chaplain on board every ship, but he is not required to determine the size of the crew's rations, nor to take the vessel's bearings. My Reverend Lord the Bishop of London—who is the grandson of a sailor they tell me—cannot have forgotten that point either.

FOLLIOT: [*Yelping*] I will not allow personal insinuations to compromise the dignity of a debate of this importance! The integrity and honor of the Church of England are at stake!

KING: [*Cheerfully*] No big words, Bishop. You know as well as I do that all that's at stake is its money. I need money for my wars. Will the Church give me any, yes or no?

ARCHBISHOP: [*Cautiously*] The Church of England has always acknowledged that it was its duty to assist the King, to the best of its ability, in all his needs.

KING: There's a fine speech. But I don't like the past tense, Archbishop. There's something so nostalgic about it. I like the present. And the future. Are you going to pay up?

ARCHBISHOP: Your Highness, I am here to defend the privileges which your illustrious forefather William granted to the Church of England. Would you have the heart to tamper with your forefather's work?

KING: May he rest in peace. His work is inviolable. But where he is now he doesn't need money. I'm still on earth unfortunately, and I do.

FOLLIOT: Your Highness, this is a question of principle!

KING: I'm levying troops, Bishop! I have sent for 1,500 German foot soldiers, and three thousand Swiss infantry to help fight the King of France. And nobody has ever paid the Swiss with principles.

BECKET: [*Rises suddenly and says incisively*] I think, your Highness, that it is pointless to pursue a discussion in which neither speaker is listening to the other. The law and custom of the land give us the means of coercion. We will use them.

FOLLIOT: [*Beside himself*] Would you dare—you whom she raised from the obscurity of your base origins—to plunge a dagger in the bosom of your Mother Church?

BECKET: My Lord and King has given me his Seal with the Three Lions to guard. My mother is England now.

FOLLIOT: [*Frothing, and slightly ridiculous*] A deacon! A miserable deacon nourished in our bosom! Traitor! Little viper! Libertine! Sycophant! Saxon!

KING: My Reverend friend, I suggest you respect my Chancellor, or else I'll call my guards.

[*He has raised his voice a little toward the end of this speech. The* GUARDS *come in*]

[*Surprised*] Why, here they are! Oh, no, it's my snack. Excuse me, gentlemen, but around noon I need something to peck at or I tend to feel weak. And a King has no right to weaken, I needn't tell you that. I'll have it in my chapel, then I can pray directly afterwards. Come and sit with me, son.

[*He goes out taking* BECKET *with him. The three prelates have risen, deeply offended. They move away, murmuring to one another, with sidelong glances in the direction in which the* KING *went out*]

FOLLIOT: We must appeal to Rome! We must take a firm line!

YORK: My Lord Archbishop, you are the Primate of England. Your person is inviolate and your decisions on all matters affecting the Church are law in this country. You have a weapon against such intransigence: excommunication.

BISHOP OF OXFORD: We must not use it save with a great deal of prudence, Reverend Bishop. The Church has always triumphed over the centuries, but it has triumphed prudently. Let us bide our time. The King's rages are terrible, but they don't last. They are fires of straw.

FOLLIOT: The little self-seeker he has at his elbow now will make it his business to kindle them. And I think, like the Reverend Bishop, that only the excommunication of that young libertine can reduce him to impotence.

[BECKET *comes in*]

BECKET: My Lords, the King has decided to adjourn his Privy Council. He thinks that a night of meditation will inspire your Lordships with a wise and equitable solution—which he authorizes you to come and submit to him tomorrow.

FOLLIOT: [*With a bitter laugh*] You mean it's time for the hunt.

BECKET: [*Smiling*] Yes, my Lord Bishop, to be perfectly frank with you, it is. Believe me, I am personally most grieved at this difference of opinion and the brutal form it has taken. But I cannot go back on what I said as Chancellor of England. We are all bound, laymen, as well as priests, by the same feudal oath we took to the King as our Lord and Sovereign; the oath to preserve his life, limbs, dignity and honor. None of you, I think, has forgotten the words of that oath?

ARCHBISHOP: [*Quietly*] We have not forgotten it, my son. No more than the other oath we took, before that—the oath to God. You are young, and still uncertain of yourself, perhaps. Yet you have, in those few words, taken a resolution the meaning of which has not escaped me. Will you allow an old man, who is very close to death, and who, in this rather sordid argument, was defending more perhaps than you suspect—to hope, as a father, that you will never know the bitterness of realizing, one day, that you made a mistake.

[*He holds out his ring and* BECKET *kisses it*]

I give you my blessing, my son.

[BECKET *has knelt. Now he rises and says lightly:*]

BECKET: An unworthy son, Father, alas. But when is one worthy? And worthy of what?

[*He pirouettes and goes out, insolent and graceful as a young boy*]

FOLLIOT: [*Violently*] Such insults to your Grace cannot be tolerated! This young rake's impudence must be crushed!

ARCHBISHOP: [*Thoughtfully*] He was with me for a long time. His is a strange, elusive nature. Don't imagine he is the ordinary libertine that outward appearances would suggest. I've had plenty of opportunity to observe him, in the bustle of pleasure and daily living. He is as it were detached. As if seeking his real self.

FOLLIOT: Break him, my Lord, before he finds it! Or the clergy of this country will pay dearly.

ARCHBISHOP: We must be very circumspect. It is our task to see into the hearts of men. And I am not sure that this one will always be our enemy.

[*The* ARCHBISHOP *and the three* BISHOPS *go out. The* KING *is heard calling off stage*]

KING: Well, son, have they gone? Are you coming hunting?

[*Trees come down from the flies. The black velvet curtain at the back opens on a clear sky, transforming the pillars into the leafless trees of a forest in winter. Bugles. The lights have gone down. When they go up again, the* KING *and* BECKET *are on horseback, each with a hawk on his gauntleted wrist. Torrential rain is heard*]

KING: Here comes the deluge [*Unexpectedly*] Do you like hunting this way, with hawks?

BECKET: I don't much care to delegate my errands. I prefer to feel a wild boar on the end of my spear. When he turns and charges there's a moment of delicious personal contact when one feels, at last, responsible for oneself.

KING: It's odd, this craving for danger. Why are you all so hell-bent on risking your necks for the most futile reasons?

BECKET: One has to gamble with one's life to feel alive.

KING: Or dead! You make me laugh.

[*To his hawk*]

Quiet, my pretty, quiet! We'll take your hood off in a minute. You couldn't give much of a performance under all these trees. I'll tell you one creature that loves hawking anyway, and that's a hawk! It seems to me we've rubbed our backsides sore with three hours' riding, just to give them this royal pleasure.

BECKET: [*Smiling*] My Lord, these are Norman hawks. They belong to the master race. They have a right to it.

KING: [*Suddenly, as he reins his horse*] Do you love me, Becket?

BECKET: I am your servant, my prince.

KING: Did you love me when I made you Chancellor? I wonder sometimes if you're capable of love. Do you love Gwendolen?

BECKET: She is my mistress, my prince.

KING: Why do you put labels onto everything to justify your feelings?

BECKET: Because, without labels, the world would have no shape, my prince.

KING: Is it so important for the world to have a shape?

BECKET: It's essential, my prince, otherwise we can't know what we're doing.

[*Bugles in the distance*]

The rain is getting heavier, my Lord! Come, let us shelter in that hut over there.

[*He gallops off. After a second of confused indecision, the* KING *gallops after him, holding his hawk high and shouting:*]

KING: Becket! You didn't answer my question!

[*He disappears into the forest. Bugles again. The four* BARONS *cross the stage, galloping after them, and vanish into the forest. Thunder. Lightning. A hut has appeared to one side of the stage.* BECKET *is heard shouting:*]

BECKET: Hey there! You! Fellow! Can we put the horses under cover in your barn? Do you know how to rub down a horse?

And have a look at the right forefoot of messire's horse. I think the shoe is loose. We'll sit out the storm under your roof.

[*After a second, the* KING *enters the hut, followed by a hairy Saxon who, cap in hand, bows repeatedly, in terrified silence*]

KING: [*Shaking himself*] What a soaking! I'll catch my death!

[*He sneezes*]

All this just to keep the hawks amused!

[*Shouting at the* man]

What are you waiting for? Light a fire, dog! It's freezing cold in this shack.

[*The* MAN, *terror-stricken, does not move. The* KING *sneezes again. To* BECKET]

What is he waiting for?

BECKET: Wood is scarce, my Lord. I don't suppose he has any left.

KING: What—in the middle of the forest?

BECKET: They are entitled to two measures of dead wood. One branch more and they're hanged.

KING: [*Astounded*] Really? And yet people are always complaining about the amount of dead wood in the forests. Still, that's a problem for my intendants, not me.

[*Shouting at the* MAN]

Run and pick up all the wood you can carry and build us a roaring fire! We won't hang you this time, dog!

[*The peasant, terrified, dares not obey.* BECKET *says gently:*]

BECKET: Go, my son. Your King commands it. You've the right.

[*The* MAN *goes out, trembling, bowing to the ground, repeatedly*]

KING: Why do you call that old man your son?

BECKET: Why not? You call him dog, my prince.

KING: It's a manner of speaking. Saxons are always called "dog." I can't think why, really. One could just as well have called them "Saxon"! But that smelly old ragbag your son!

[*Sniffing*]

What on earth can they eat to make the place stink so—dung?

BECKET: Turnips.

KING: Turnips—what are they?

BECKET: Roots.

KING: [*Amused*] Do they eat roots?

BECKET: Those who live in the forests can't grow anything else.

KING: Why don't they move out into the open country then?

BECKET: They would be hanged if they left their area.

KING: Oh, I see. Mark you, that must make life a lot simpler, if you know you'll be hanged at the least show of initiative. You must ask yourself far fewer questions. They don't know their luck! But you still haven't told me why you called the fellow your son?

BECKET: [*Lightly*] My prince, he is so poor and so bereft and I am so strong beside him, that he really is my son.

KING: We'd go a long way with that theory!

BECKET: Besides, my prince, you're appreciably younger than I am and you call me "son" sometimes.

KING: That's got nothing to do with it. It's because I love you.

BECKET: You are our King. We are all your sons and in your hands.

KING: What, Saxons too?

BECKET: [*Lightly, as he strips off his gloves*] England will be fully built, my prince, on the day the Saxons are your sons as well.

KING: You are a bore today! I get the feeling that I'm listening to the Archbishop. And I'm dying of thirst. Hunt around and see if you can't find us something to drink. Go on, it's your son's house!

[BECKET *starts looking, and leaves the room after a while. The* KING *looks around too, examining the hut with curiosity, touching things with grimaces of distaste. Suddenly he notices a kind of trap door at the foot of a wall. He opens it, thrusts his hand in and pulls out a terrified* GIRL. *He shouts:*]

Hey, Thomas! Thomas!

[BECKET *comes in*]

BECKET: Have you found something to drink, Lord?

KING: [*Holding the* GIRL *at arm's length*] No. Something to eat. What do you say to that, if it's cleaned up a bit?

BECKET: [*Coldly*] She's pretty.

KING: She stinks a bit, but we could wash her. Look, did you ever see anything so tiny? How old would you say it was—fifteen, sixteen?

BECKET: [*Quietly*] It can talk, my Lord.

[*Gently, to the* GIRL]

How old are you?

[*The* GIRL *looks at them in terror and says nothing*]

KING: You see? Of course it can't talk!

[*The* MAN *has come back with the wood and stops in the doorway, terrified*]

How old is your daughter, dog?

[*The* MAN *trembles like a cornered animal and says* nothing]

He's dumb as well, that son of yours. How did you get him—with a deaf girl? It's funny the amount of dumb people I meet the second I set foot out of my palace. I rule over a kingdom of the dumb. Can you tell me why?

BECKET: They're afraid, my prince.

KING: I know that. And a good thing too. The populace must live in fear, it's essential. The moment they stop being afraid they have only one thought in mind—to frighten other people instead. And they adore doing that! Just as much as we do! Give them a chance to do it and they catch up fast, those sons of yours! Did you never see a peasants' revolt? I did once in my father's reign, when I was a child. It's not a pretty sight.

[*He looks at the* MAN, *exasperated*]

Look at it, will you? It's tongue-tied, it's obtuse, it stinks and the country is crawling with them!

[*He seizes the* GIRL *who was trying to run away*]

Stay here, you!

[TO BECKET:]

I ask you, what use is it?

BECKET: (*Smiling*) It scratches the soil, it makes bread.

KING: Pooh, the English eat so little of it . . . At the French Court, yes, I daresay—they fairly stuff it down! But here!

BECKET: [*Smiling*] The troops have to be fed. For a King without troops . . .

KING: [*Struck by this*] True enough! Yes, that makes sense. There must be some sort of reason in all these absurdities. Well well, you little Saxon philosopher, you! I don't know how you do it, but you'll turn me into an intelligent man yet! The odd thing is, it's so ugly and yet it makes such pretty daughters. How do you explain that, you who can explain it all?

BECKET: At twenty, before he lost his teeth and took on that indeterminate age the common people have, that man may have been handsome. He may have had one night of love, one minute when he was a King, and shed his fear. Afterwards, his pauper's life went on, eternally the same. And he and his wife no doubt forgot it all. But the seed was sown.

KING: [*Dreamily*] You have such a way of telling things . . .

[*He looks at the* GIRL]

Do you think she'll grow ugly too?

BECKET: For sure.

KING: If we made her a whore and kept her at the palace, would she stay pretty?

BECKET: Perhaps.

KING: Then we'd be doing her a service, don't you think?

BECKET: [*Coldly*] No doubt.

[*The* MAN *stiffens. The* GIRL *cowers, in terror. The* BROTHER *comes in, somber-faced, silent, threatening*]

KING: Would you believe it? They understand every word, you know! Who's that one there?

BECKET: [*Taking in the situation at a glance*] The brother.

KING: How do you know?

BECKET: Instinct, my Lord.

[*His hand moves to his dagger*]

KING: [*Bawling suddenly*] Why are they staring at me like that? I've had enough of this! I told you to get something to drink, dog!

[*Terrified, the* MAN *scuttles off*]

BECKET: Their water will be brackish. I have a gourd of juniper juice in my saddlebag. [*To the* BROTHER] Come and give me a hand, you! My horse is restive.

[*He seizes the boy roughly by the arm and hustles him out into the forest, carelessly whistling his little marching song. Then, all of a sudden, he hurls himself onto him. A short silent struggle.* BECKET *gets the boy's knife away; he escapes into the forest.* BECKET *watches him go for a second, holding his wounded hand. Then he walks around the back of the hut. The* KING *has settled himself on a bench, with his feet up on another, whistling to himself. He lifts the* GIRL's *skirts with his cane and examines her at leisure*]

KING: [*In a murmur*] All my sons! . . .

[*He shakes himself*]

That Becket! He wears me out. He keeps making me think! I'm sure it's bad for the health.

[*He gets up,* BECKET *comes in followed by the* MAN]

What about the water? How much longer do I have to wait?

BECKET: Here it is, my Lord. But it's muddy. Have some of this juniper juice instead.

KING: Drink with me.

[*He notices* BECKET's *hand, wrapped in a bloodstained cloth*]

What's the matter? You're wounded!

BECKET: [*Hiding his hand*] No doubt about it, that horse of mine is a nervous brute. He can't bear his saddle touched. He bit me.

KING: [*With a hearty, delighted laugh*] That's funny! Oh, that's very funny! Milord is the best rider in the Kingdom! Milord can never find a stallion with enough spirit for him! Milord makes us all look silly at the jousts, with his fancy horsemanship, and when he goes to open his saddlebags he gets himself bitten! Like a page!

[*He is almost savagely gleeful. Then suddenly, his gaze softens*]

You're white as a sheet, little Saxon . . . Why do I love you? . . . It's funny, I don't like to think of you in pain. Show me that hand. A horse bite can turn nasty. I'll put some of that juniper gin on it.

BECKET: [*Snatching his hand away*] I already have, my Lord, it's nothing.

KING: Then why do you look so pale? Show me your hand.

BECKET: [*With sudden coldness*] It's an ugly wound and you know you hate the sight of blood.

KING: [*Steps back a little, then exclaims with delight*] All this just to fetch me a drink! Wounded in the service of the King! We'll tell the others you defended me against a wild boar and I'll present you with a handsome gift this evening. What would you like?

BECKET: [*Softly*] This girl.

[*He adds after a pause:*]

I fancy her.

[*A pause*]

KING: [*His face clouding over*] That's tiresome of you. I fancy her too. And where that's concerned, friendship goes by the board.

[*A pause. His face takes on a cunning look*]

All right, then. But favor for favor. You won't forget, will you?

BECKET: No, my prince.

KING: Favor for favor; do you give me your word as a gentleman?

BECKET: Yes, my prince.

KING: [*Draining his glass, suddenly cheerful*] Done! She's yours. Do we take her with us or shall we have her sent?

BECKET: I'll send two soldiers to fetch her. Listen. The others have caught up.

[*A troop of men-at-arms have come riding up behind the shack during the end of the scene*]

KING: [*To the* MAN] Wash your daughter, dog, and kill her fleas. She's going to the palace. For Milord here, who's a Saxon too. You're pleased about that, I hope?

[*To* BECKET *as he goes:*]

Give him a gold piece. I'm feeling generous this morning.

[*He goes out. The* MAN *looks at* BECKET *in terror*]

BECKET: No one will come and take your daughter away. Keep her better hidden in future. And tell your son to join the others, in the forest, he'll be safer there, now. I think one of the soldiers saw us. Here!

[*He throws him a purse and goes out. When he has gone, the* MAN *snatches up the purse, then spits venomously, his face twisted with hate*]

MAN: God rot your guts! Pig!

GIRL: [*Unexpectedly*] He was handsome, that one. Is it true he's taking me to the palace?

MAN: You whore! You Norman's trollop!

[*He hurls himself onto her and beats her savagely. The* KING, BECKET *and the* BARONS *have galloped off, amid the sound of bugles. The hut and the forest backcloth disappear. We are in* BECKET's *palace.*]

FOOTMEN *push on a kind of low bed-couch, with cushions and some stools. Upstage, between two pillars, a curtain behind which can be seen the shadows of banqueting guests. Singing and roars of laughter. Downstage, curled up on the bed,* GWENDOLEN *is playing a string instrument. The curtain is drawn aside.* BECKET *appears. He goes to* GWENDOLEN *while the banqueting and the laughter, punctuated by hoarse incoherent snatches of song, go on upstage.* GWENDOLEN *stops playing*]

GWENDOLEN: Are they still eating?

BECKET: Yes. They have an unimaginable capacity for absorbing food.

GWENDOLEN: [*Softly, beginning to play again*] How can my Lord spend his days and a large part of his nights with such creatures?

BECKET: [*Crouching at her feet and caressing her*] If he spent his time with learned clerics debating the sex of angels, your Lord would be even more bored, my kitten. They are as far from the true knowledge of things as mindless brutes.

GWENDOLEN: [*Gently, as she plays*] I don't always understand everything my Lord condescends to say to me . . . What I do know is that it is always very late when he comes to see me.

BECKET: [*Caressing her*] The only thing I love is coming to you. Beauty is one of the few things which don't shake one's faith in God.

GWENDOLEN: I am my Lord's war captive and I belong to him body and soul. God has willed it so, since He gave the Normans victory over my people. If the Welsh had won the war I would have married a man of my own race, at my father's castle. God did not will it so.

BECKET: [*Quietly*] That belief will do as well as any, my kitten. But, as I belong to a conquered race myself, I have a feeling that God's system is a little muddled. Go on playing.

[GWENDOLEN *starts to play again. Then she says suddenly:*]

GWENDOLEN: I'm lying. You are my Lord, God or no God. And if the Welsh had been victorious, you could just as easily have stolen me from my father's castle. I should have come with you.

[*She says this gravely.* BECKET *rises abruptly and moves away. She looks up at him with anguished eyes and stops playing*]

Did I say something wrong? What is the matter with my Lord?

BECKET: Nothing. I don't like being loved. I told you that.

[*The curtain opens. The* KING *appears*]

KING: [*A little drunk*] Well, son, have you deserted us? It worked! I told you! They've tumbled to it! They're fighting with your forks! They've at last discovered that they're for poking one another's eyes out. They think it's a most ingenious little invention. You'd better go in, son, they'll break them in a minute.

[BECKET *goes behind the curtain to quieten his guests. He can be heard shouting:*]

BECKET: Gentlemen, gentlemen! No, no, they aren't little daggers. No, truly—they're for pronging meat . . . Look, let me show you again.

[*Huge roars of laughter behind the curtain. The* KING *has moved over to* GWENDOLEN. *He stares at her*]

KING: Was that you playing, while we were at table?

GWENDOLEN: [*With a deep curtsy*] Yes, my Lord.

KING: You have every kind of accomplishment, haven't you? Get up.

[*He lifts her to her feet, caressing her as he does so. She moves away, ill at ease. He says with a wicked smile:*]

KING: Have I frightened you, my heart? We'll soon put that right.

[*He pulls the curtain aside*]

Hey there, Becket! That's enough horseplay, my fat lads! Come and hear a little music. When the belly's full, it's good to elevate the mind a bit.

[*To* GWENDOLEN]

Play!

[*The four* BARONS, *bloated with food and drink, come in with* BECKET. GWENDOLEN *has taken up her instrument again. The* KING *sprawls on the bed, behind her. The* BARONS, *with much sighing and puffing, unclasp their belts and sit down on stools, where they soon fall into a stupor.* BECKET *remains standing*]

KING: Tell her to sing us something sad. I like sad music after dinner, it helps the digestion.

[*He hiccups*]

You always feed us far too well, Thomas. Where did you steal that cook of yours?

BECKET: I bought him, Sire. He's a Frenchman.

KING: Really? Aren't you afraid he might poison you? Tell me, how much does one pay for a French cook?

BECKET: A good one, like him, costs almost as much as a horse, my Lord.

KING: [*Genuinely outraged*] It's outrageous! What is the country coming to! No man is worth a horse! If I said "favor for favor" —remember?—and I asked you to give him to me, would you?

BECKET: Of course, my Lord.

KING: [*With a smile, gently caressing* GWENDOLEN] Well, I won't.

I don't want to eat too well every day; it lowers a man's morale.
Sadder, sadder, my little doe.

[*He belches*]

Oh, that venison! Get her to sing that lament they composed
for your mother, Becket. It's my favorite song.

BECKET: I don't like anyone to sing that lament, my Lord.

KING: Why not? Are you ashamed of being a Saracen girl's son?
That's half your charm, you fool! There must be some reason
why you're more civilized than all the rest of us put together! I
adore that song.

[GWENDOLEN *looks uncertainly at* BECKET. *There is a pause.
Then the* KING *says coldly:*]

That's an order, little Saxon.

BECKET: [*Inscrutably, to* GWENDOLEN] Sing.

[*She strikes a few opening chords, while the* KING *makes
himself comfortable beside her, belching contentedly. She
begins:*]

GWENDOLEN: [*Singing*]

> Handsome Sir Gilbert
> Went to the war
> One fine morning in May
> To deliver the heart
> Of Lord Jesus our Saviour,
> From the hands of the Saracens.
> Woe! Woe! Heavy is my heart
> At being without love!
> Woe! Woe! Heavy is my heart
> All the livelong day!

KING: [*Singing*]

> All the livelong day! Go on!

GWENDOLEN:

> As the battle raged
> He swung his mighty sword
> And many a Moor fell dead
> But his trusty charger
> Stumbled in the fray
> And Sir Gilbert fell.
> Woe! Woe! Heavy is my heart!
> At being without love!
> Woe! Woe! Heavy is my heart
> All the livelong day.
>
> Wounded in the head
> Away Gilbert was led
> To the Algiers market
> Chained hand and foot
> And sold there as a slave.

KING: [*Singing, out of tune*]
> All the livelong day!

GWENDOLEN:

> A Saracen's daughter
> Lovely as the night
> Lost her heart to him
> Swore to love him always
> Vowed to be his wife.
>
> Woe! Woe! Heavy is my heart!
> At being without love!
> Woe! Woe! Heavy is my heart
> All the livelong day—

KING: [*Interrupting*] It brings tears to my eyes, you know, that story. I look a brute but I'm soft as swansdown really. One can't change one's nature. I can't imagine why you don't like people to sing that song. It's wonderful to be a love child. When I look at my august parents' faces, I shudder to think what must have gone on. It's marvelous to think of your mother helping your father to escape and then coming to join him in London with you inside her. Sing us the end, girl. I adore the end.

GWENDOLEN: [*Softly*]

> Then he asked the holy Father
> For a priest to baptize her
> And he took her as his wife
> To cherish with his life
> Giving her his soul
> To love and keep alway.
>
> Gay! Gay! Easy is my heart
> At being full of love
> Gay! Gay! Easy is my heart
> To be loved alway.

KING: [*Dreamily*] Did he really love her all his life? Isn't it altered a bit in the song?

BECKET: No, my prince.

KING: [*Getting up, quite saddened*] Funny, it's the happy ending that makes me feel sad . . . Tell me, do you believe in love, Thomas?

BECKET: [*Coldly*] For my father's love for my mother, Sire, yes.

[*The* KING *has moved over to the* BARONS *who are now snoring on their stools. He gives them a kick as he passes*]

KING: They've fallen asleep, the hogs. That's their way of showing their finer feelings. You know, my little Saxon, sometimes I have the impression that you and I are the only sensitive men in England. We eat with forks and we have infinitely distinguished sentiments, you and I. You've made a different man of me, in a way . . . What you ought to find me now, if you loved me, is a girl to give me a little polish. I've had enough of whores.

[*He has come back to* GWENDOLEN. *He caresses her a little and then says suddenly:*]

Favor for favor—do you remember?

[*A pause*]

BECKET: [*Pale*] I am your servant, my prince, and all I have is yours. But you were also gracious enough to say I was your friend.

KING: That's what I mean! As one friend to another it's the thing to do!

[*A short pause. He smiles maliciously, and goes on caressing* GWENDOLEN *who cowers, terrified*]

You care about her then? Can you care for something? Go on, tell me, tell me if you care about her?

[BECKET *says nothing. The* KING *smiles*]

You can't tell a lie. I know you. Not because you're afraid of lies—I think you must be the only man I know who isn't afraid of anything—not even Heaven—but because it's distasteful to you. You consider it inelegant. What looks like morality in you is nothing more than esthetics. Is that true or isn't it?

BECKET: [*Meeting his eyes, says softly*] It's true, my Lord.

KING: I'm not cheating if I ask for her, am I? I said "favor for favor" and I asked you for your word of honor.

BECKET: [*Icily*] And I gave it to you.

[*A pause. They stand quite still. The* KING *looks at* BECKET *with a wicked smile.* BECKET *does not look at him. Then the* KING *moves briskly away*]

KING: Right. I'm off to bed. I feel like an early night tonight.

Delightful evening, Becket. You're the only man in England who knows how to give your friends a royal welcome.

[*He kicks the slumbering* BARONS]

Call my guards and help me wake these porkers.

[*The* BARONS *wake with sighs and belches as the* KING *pushes them about, shouting:*]

Come on, Barons, home! I know you're connoisseurs of good music, but we can't listen to music all night long. Happy evenings end in bed, eh Becket?

BECKET: [*Stiffly*] May I ask your Highness for a brief moment's grace?

KING: Granted! Granted! I'm not a savage. I'll wait for you both in my litter. You can say good night to me downstairs.

[*He goes out, followed by the* BARONS. BECKET *stands motionless for a while under* GWENDOLEN'S *steady gaze. Then he says quietly:*]

BECKET: You will have to go with him, Gwendolen.

GWENDOLEN: [*Composedly*] Did my Lord promise me to him?

BECKET: I gave him my word as a gentleman that I would give him anything he asked for. I never thought it would be you.

GWENDOLEN: If he sends me away tomorrow, will my Lord take me back?

BECKET: No.

GWENDOLEN: Shall I tell the girls to put my dresses in the coffer?

BECKET: He'll send over for it tomorrow. Go down. One doesn't keep the King waiting. Tell him I wish him a respectful good night.

GWENDOLEN: [*Laying her viol on the bed*] I shall leave my Lord my viol. He can almost play it now.

[*She asks, quite naturally:*]

My Lord cares for nothing, in the whole world, does he?

BECKET: No.

GWENDOLEN: [*Moves to him and says gently*] You belong to a conquered race too. But through tasting too much of the honey of life, you've forgotten that even those who have been robbed of everything have one thing left to call their own.

BECKET: [*Inscrutably*] Yes, I daresay I had forgotten. There is a gap in me where honor ought to be. Go now.

> [GWENDOLEN *goes out.* BECKET *stands quite still. Then he goes to the bed, picks up the viol, looks at it, then throws it abruptly away. He pulls off the fur coverlet and starts to unbutton his doublet. A* GUARD *comes in, dragging the* SAXON GIRL *from the forest, whom he throws down in the middle of the room. The* KING *appears*]

KING: [*Hilariously*] Thomas, my son! You'd forgotten her! You see how careless you are! Luckily I think of everything. It seems they had to bully the father and the brother a tiny bit to get her, but anyway, here she is. You see?—I really am a friend to you, and you're wrong not to love me. You told me you fancied her. I hadn't forgotten that, you see. Sleep well, son!

> [*He goes out, followed by the* GUARD. *The* GIRL, *still dazed, looks at* BECKET *who has not moved. She recognizes him, gets to her feet and smiles at him. A long pause, then she asks with a kind of sly coquetry:*]

GIRL: Shall I undress, my Lord?

BECKET: [*Who has not moved*] Of course.

> [*The* GIRL *starts to undress.* BECKET *looks at her coldly, absent-mindedly whistling a few bars of his little march.*

Suddenly he stops, goes to the GIRL, *who stands there dazed and half naked, and seizes her by the shoulders*]

I hope you're full of noble feelings and that all this strikes you as pretty shabby?

[*A* SERVANT *runs in wildly and halts in the doorway speechless. Before he can speak, the* KING *comes stumbling in*]

KING: [*Soberly*] I had no pleasure with her Thomas. She let me lay her down in the litter, limp as a corpse, and then suddenly she pulled out a little knife from somewhere. There was blood everywhere . . . I feel quite sick.

[BECKET *has let go of the* GIRL. *The* KING *adds, haggard:*]

She could easily have killed me instead!

[*A pause. He says abruptly:*]

Send that girl away. I'm sleeping in your room tonight. I'm frightened.

[BECKET *motions to the* SERVANT, *who takes away the half-naked* GIRL. *The* KING *has thrown himself, fully dressed, onto the bed with an animal-like sigh*]

Take half the bed.

BECKET: I'll sleep on the floor, my prince.
KING: No. Lie down beside me. I don't want to be alone tonight.

[*He looks at him and murmurs:*]

You loathe me, I shan't even be able to trust you now . . .
BECKET: You gave me your Seal to keep, my prince. And the

Three Lions of England which are engraved on it keep watch over me too.

[*He snuffs out the candles, all save one. It is almost dark*]

KING: [*His voice already thick with sleep*] I shall never know what you're thinking . . .

[BECKET *has thrown a fur coverlet over the* KING. *He lies down beside him and says quietly:*]

BECKET: It will be dawn soon, my prince. You must sleep. Tomorrow we are crossing to the Continent. In a week we will face the King of France's army and there will be simple answers to everything at last.

[*He has lain down beside the* KING. *A pause, during which the* KING's *snoring gradually increases. Suddenly, the* KING *moans and tosses in his sleep*]

KING: [*Crying out*] They're after me! They're after me! They're armed to the teeth! Stop them! Stop them!

[BECKET *sits up on one elbow. He touches the* KING, *who wakes up with a great animal cry*]

BECKET: My prince . . . my prince . . . sleep in peace. I'm here.
KING: Oh . . . Thomas, it's you . . . They were after me.

[*He turns over and goes back to sleep with a sigh. Gradually he begins to snore again, softly.* BECKET *is still on one elbow. Almost tenderly, he draws the coverlet over the* KING]

BECKET: My prince . . . If you were my true prince, if you were one of my race, how simple everything would be. How tenderly I would love you, my prince, in an ordered world.

Each of us bound in fealty to the other, head, heart and limbs, with no further questions to ask of oneself, ever.

[*A pause. The* KING's *snores grow louder.* BECKET *sighs and says with a little smile:*]

But I cheated my way, a twofold bastard, into the ranks, and found a place among the conquerors. You can sleep peacefully though, my prince. So long as Becket is obliged to improvise his honor, he will serve you. And if one day, he meets it face to face . . .

[*A short pause*]

But where is Becket's honor?

[*He lies down with a sigh, beside the* KING. *The* KING's *snores grow louder still. The candle sputters. The lights grow even dimmer . . .*]

CURTAIN

ACT TWO

The curtain rises on the same set of arching pillars, which now represents a forest in France. The KING's *tent, not yet open for the day, is set up among the trees. A* SENTRY *stands some way off.*

It is dawn. Crouched around a campfire, the four BARONS *are having their morning meal, in silence. After a while, one of them says:*

1ST BARON: This Becket then, who is he?

[*A pause. All four are fairly slow in their reactions*]

2ND BARON: [*Surprised at the question*] The Chancellor of England.

1ST BARON: I know that! But who is he, exactly?

2ND BARON: The Chancellor of England, I tell you! The Chancellor of England is the Chancellor of England! I don't see what else there is to inquire into on that score.

1ST BARON: You don't understand. Look, supposing the Chancellor of England were some other man. Me, for instance . . .

2ND BARON: That's plain idiotic.

1ST BARON: I said supposing. Now, I would be Chancellor of England but I wouldn't be the same Chancellor of England as Becket is. You can follow that, can you?

2ND BARON: [*Guardedly*] Yes . . .

1ST BARON: So, I *can* ask myself the question.

2ND BARON: What question?

1ST BARON: Who is this man Becket?

2ND BARON: What do you mean, who is this man Becket? He's the Chancellor of England.

1ST BARON: Yes. But what I'm asking myself is who is he, as a man?

2ND BARON: [*Looks at him and says sorrowfully*] Have you got a pain?

1ST BARON: No, why?

2ND BARON: A Baron who asks himself questions is a sick Baron. Your sword—what's that?

1ST BARON: My sword?

2ND BARON: Yes.

1ST BARON: [*Putting his hand to the hilt*] It's my sword! And anyone who thinks different—

2ND BARON: Right. Answered like a nobleman. We peers aren't here to ask questions. We're here to give answers.

1ST BARON: Right then. Answer me.

2ND BARON: Not to questions! To orders. You aren't asked to think in the army. When you're face to face with a French man-at-arms, do you ask yourself questions?

1ST BARON: No.

2ND BARON: Does he?

1ST BARON: No.

2ND BARON: You just fall to and fight. If you started asking each other questions like a pair of women, you might as well bring chairs onto the battlefield. If there are any questions to be asked you can be sure they've been asked already, higher up, by cleverer heads than yours.

1ST BARON: [*Vexed*] I meant I didn't like him, that's all.

2ND BARON: Why couldn't you say so then? That we'd have understood. You're entitled not to like him. I don't like him either, come to that. To begin with, he's a Saxon.

1ST BARON: To begin with!

3RD BARON: One thing you can't say though. You can't say he isn't a fighter. Yesterday when the King was in the thick of it, after his squire was killed, he cut his way right through the French, and he seized the King's banner and drew the enemy off and onto himself.

1ST BARON: All right! He's a good fighter!

3RD BARON: [To 2ND BARON] Isn't he a good fighter?

2ND BARON: [Stubbornly] Yes. But he's a Saxon.

1ST BARON: [To the 4TH BARON, who has so far said nothing] How about you, Regnault? What do you think of him?

4TH BARON: [Placidly, swallowing his mouthful of food] I'm waiting.

1ST BARON: Waiting for what?

4TH BARON: Till he shows himself. Some sorts of game are like that: you follow them all day through the forest, by sounds, or tracks, or smell. But it wouldn't do any good to charge ahead with drawn lance; you'd just spoil everything because you don't know for sure what sort of animal it is you're dealing with. You have to wait.

1ST BARON: What for?

4TH BARON: For whatever beast it is to show itself. And if you're patient it always does in the end. Animals know more than men do, nearly always, but a man has something in him that an animal hasn't got: he knows how to wait. With this man Becket—I'll wait.

1ST BARON: For what?

4TH BARON: For him to show himself. For him to break cover.

[He goes on eating]

The day he does, we'll know who he is.

[BECKET's little whistled march is heard off stage. BECKET comes in, armed]

BECKET: Good morning to you, Gentlemen.

[The four BARONS rise politely, and salute]

Is the King still asleep?

1ST BARON: [*Stiffly*] He hasn't called yet.

BECKET: Has the camp marshal presented his list of losses?

1ST BARON: No.

BECKET: Why not?

2ND BARON: [*Surlily*] He was part of the losses.

BECKET: Oh?

1ST BARON: I was nearby when it happened. A lance knocked him off his horse. Once on the ground, the foot soldiers dealt with him.

BECKET: Poor Beaumont. He was so proud of his new armor.

2ND BARON: There must have been a chink in it then. They bled him white. On the ground. French swine!

BECKET: [*With a slight shrug*] That's war.

1ST BARON: War is a sport like any other. There are rules. In the old days, they took you for ransom. A Knight for a Knight. That was proper fighting!

BECKET: [*Smiling*] Since one has taken to sending the foot soldiery against the horses with no personal protection save a cutlass, they're a little inclined to seek out the chink in the armor of any Knight unwise enough to fall off his horse. It's repulsive, but I can understand them.

1ST BARON: If we start understanding the common soldiery war will be butchery plain and simple.

BECKET: The world is certainly tending towards butchery, Baron. The lesson of this battle, which has cost us far too much, is that we will have to form platoons of cutthroats too, that's all.

1ST BARON: And a soldier's honor, my Lord Chancellor, what of that?

BECKET: [*Dryly*] A soldier's honor, Baron, is to win victories. Let us not be hypocritical. The Norman nobility lost no time in teaching those they conquered that little point. I'll wake the King. Our entry into the city is timed for eight o'clock and the *Te Deum* in the cathedral for a quarter past nine. It would be bad policy to keep the French Bishop waiting. We want these people to collaborate with a good grace.

1 ST BARON: [*Grunting*] In my day, we slaughtered the lot and marched in afterwards.

BECKET: Yes, into a dead city! I want to give the King living cities to increase his wealth. From eight o'clock this morning, I am the French people's dearest friend.

1 ST BARON: What about England's honor, then?

BECKET: [*Quietly*] England's honor, Baron, in the final reckoning, has always been to succeed.

[*He goes into the* KING's *tent smiling. The four* BARONS *look at each other, hostile*]

1 ST BARON: [*Muttering*] What a mentality!

4 TH BARON: [*Sententiously*] We must wait for him. One day, he'll break cover.

[*The four* BARONS *move away.* BECKET *lifts the tent flap and hooks it back. The* KING *is revealed, in bed with a girl*]

KING: [*Yawning*] Good morning, son. Did you sleep well?

BECKET: A little memento from the French on my left shoulder kept me awake, Sire. I took the opportunity to do some thinking.

KING: [*Worriedly*] You think too much. You'll suffer for it, you know! It's because people think that there are problems. One day, if you go on like this, you'll think yourself into a dilemma, your big head will present you with a solution and you'll jump feet first into a hopeless mess—which you'd have done far better to ignore, like the majority of fools, who know nothing and live to a ripe old age. What do you think of my little French girl? I must say, I adore France.

BECKET: [*Smiling*] So do I, Sire, like all Englishmen.

KING: The climate's warm, the girls are pretty, the wine is good. I intend to spend at least a month here every winter.

BECKET: The only snag is, it's expensive! Nearly 2,000 casualties yesterday.

KING: Has Beaumont made out his total?

BECKET: Yes. And he added himself to the list.

KING: Wounded?

[BECKET *does not answer. The* KING *shivers. He says somberly:*]

I don't like learning that people I know have died. I've a feeling it may give Death ideas.

BECKET: My prince, shall we get down to work? We haven't dealt with yesterday's dispatches.

KING: Yesterday we were fighting! We can't do everything.

BECKET: That was a holiday! We'll have to work twice as hard today.

KING: Does it amuse you—working for the good of my people? Do you mean to say you love all those folk? To begin with they're too numerous. One can't love them, one doesn't know them. Anyway, you're lying, you don't love anything or anybody.

BECKET: (*Tersely*) There's one thing I do love, my prince, and that I'm sure of. Doing what I have to do and doing it well.

KING: [*Grinning*] Always the es—es . . . What's your word again? I've forgotten it.

BECKET: Esthetics?

KING: Esthetics! Always the esthetic side, eh?

BECKET: Yes, my prince.

KING: [*Slapping the* GIRL'*s rump*] And isn't that esthetic too? Some people go into ecstasies over cathedrals. But this is a work of art too! Look at that—round as an apple . . .

[*Quite naturally, as if he were offering him a sweetmeat:*]

Want her?

BECKET: [*Smiling*] Business, my Lord!

KING: [*Pouting like a schoolboy*] All right. Business. I'm listening. Sit down.

[BECKET *sits down on the bed, beside the* KING, *with the* GIRL *like a fascinated rabbit in between them*]

BECKET: The news is not good, my prince.

KING: [*With a careless wave of the hand*] News never is. That's a known fact. Life is one long web of difficulties. The secret of it—and there is one, brought to perfection by several generations of worldly-wise philosophers—is to give them no importance whatever. In the end one difficulty swallows up the other and you find yourself ten years later still alive with no harm done. Things always work out.

BECKET: Yes. But badly. My prince, when you play tennis, do you simply sit back and let things work out? Do you wait for the ball to hit your racket and say "It's bound to come this way eventually?"

KING: Ah, now just a minute. You're talking about things that matter. A game of tennis is important, it amuses me.

BECKET: And suppose I were to tell you that governing can be as amusing as a game of tennis? Are we going to let the others smash the ball into our court, my prince, or shall we try to score a point, both of us, like two good English sportsmen?

KING: [*Suddenly roused by his sporting instinct*] The point, Begod, the point! You're right! On the court, I sweat and strain, I fall over my feet, I half kill myself, I'll cheat if need be, but I never give up the point!

BECKET: Well then, I'll tell you what the score is, so far. Piecing together all the information I have received from London since we've been on the Continent, one thing strikes me, and that is: that there exists in England a power which has grown until it almost rivals yours, my Lord. It is the power of your clergy.

KING: We did get them to pay the tax. That's something!

BECKET: Yes, it's a small sum of money. And they know that

Princes can always be pacified with a little money. But those men are past masters at taking back with one hand what they were forced to give with the other. That's a little conjuring trick they've had centuries of practice in.

KING: [*To the* GIRL] Pay attention, my little sparrow. Now's your chance to educate yourself. The gentleman is saying some very profound things!

BECKET: [*In the same flippant way*] Little French sparrow, suppose you educate us instead. When you're married—if you do marry despite the holes in your virtue—which would you prefer, to be mistress in your own house or to have your village priest laying down the law there?

[*The* KING, *a little peeved, gets up on his knees on the bed and hides the bewildered* GIRL *under an eiderdown*]

KING: Talk sense, Becket! Priests are always intriguing, I know that. But I also know that I can crush them any time I like.

BECKET: Talk sense, Sire. If you don't do the crushing now, in five years' time there will be two Kings in England, the Archbishop of Canterbury and you. And in ten years' time there will be only one.

KING: [*A bit shamefaced*] And it won't be me?

BECKET: [*Coldly*] I rather fear not.

KING: [*With a sudden shout*] Oh, yes, it will! We Plantagenets hold on to our own! To horse, Becket, to horse! For England's glory! War on the faithful! That will make a change for us!

[*The eiderdown starts to toss. The* GIRL *emerges, disheveled, and red in the face*]

GIRL: [*Pleadingly*] My Lord! I can't breathe!

[*The* KING *looks at her in surprise. He had clearly forgotten her. He bursts out laughing*]

KING: What are you doing there? Spying for the clergy? Be off.

Put your clothes on and go home. Give her a gold piece,
Thomas.

[*The* GIRL *picks up her rags and holds them up in front
of her*]

GIRL: Am I to come back to the camp tonight, my Lord?

KING: [*Exasperated*] Yes. No. I don't know! We're concerned
with the Archbishop now, not you! Be off.

[*The* GIRL *disappears into the back portion of the tent.
The* KING *cries:*]

To horse, Thomas! For England's greatness! With my big
fist and your big brain we'll do some good work, you and
I! [*With sudden concern*] Wait a second. You can never
be sure of finding another one as good in bed.

[*He goes to the rear of the tent and cries:*]

Come back tonight, my angel! I adore you! You have the
prettiest eyes in the world!

[*He comes downstage and says confidentially to* BECKET:]

You always have to tell them that, even when you pay for
it, if you want real pleasure with them. That's high politics,
too!

[*Suddenly anxious, as his childish fear of the clergy returns*]

What will God say to it all, though? After all, they're His
Bishops!

BECKET: [*With an airy gesture*] We aren't children. You know
one can always come to some arrangement with God, on
this earth. Make haste and dress, my prince. We're going to
be late.

KING: [*Hurrying out*] I'll be ready in a second. Do I have to shave?

BECKET: [*Smiling*] It might be as well, after two days' fighting.

KING: What a fuss for a lot of conquered Frenchmen! I wonder sometimes if you aren't a bit too finicky, Thomas.

[*He goes out.* BECKET *closes the tent just as two* SOLDIERS *bring on a* YOUNG MONK, *with his hands tied*]

BECKET: What is it?

SOLDIER: We've just arrested this young monk, my Lord. He was loitering round the camp. He had a knife under his robe. We're taking him to the Provost.

BECKET: Have you got the knife?

[*The* SOLDIER *hands it to him.* BECKET *looks at it, then at the little* MONK]

What use do you have for this in your monastery?

MONK: I cut my bread with it!

BECKET: [*Amused*] Well, well. [*To the* SOLDIERS] Leave him to me. I'll question him.

SOLDIER: He's turbulent, my Lord. He struggled like a very demon. It took four of us to get his knife away and tie him up. He wounded the Sergeant. We'd have finished him there and then, only the Sergeant said there might be some information to be got out of him. That's why we're taking him to the Provost.

[*He adds:*]

That's just to tell you he's a spiteful devil.

BECKET: [*Who has not taken his eyes off the little* MONK] Very well. Stand off.

[*The* SOLDIERS *move out of earshot.* BECKET *goes on looking at the boy, and playing with the knife*]

What are you doing in France? You're a Saxon.

MONK: [*Crying out despite himself*] How do you know?

BECKET: I can tell by your accent. I speak Saxon very well, as well as you speak French. Yes, you might almost pass for a Frenchman—to unpracticed ears. But I'd be careful. In your predicament, you'd do as well to be taken for a Frenchman as a Saxon. It's less unpopular.

[*A pause*]

MONK: [*Abruptly*] I'm prepared to die.

BECKET: [*Smiling*] After the deed. But before, you'll agree it's stupid.

[*He looks at the knife which he is still holding between two fingers*]

Where are you from?

MONK: [*Venomously*] Hastings!

BECKET: Hastings. And who was this kitchen implement intended for?

[*No answer*]

You couldn't hope to kill more than one man with a weapon of this sort. You didn't make the journey for the sake of an ordinary Norman soldier, I imagine.

[*The little* MONK *does not answer*]

[*Tersely*] Listen to me, my little man. They're going to put you to the torture. Have you ever seen that? I'm obliged to attend professionally from time to time. You think you'll have the necessary strength of spirit, but they're terribly ingenious and they have a knowledge of anatomy that our imbecilic doctors would do well to emulate. One always talks.

Believe me, I know. If I can vouch that you've made a full confession, it will go quicker for you. That's worth considering.

[*The* MONK *does not answer*]

Besides, there's an amusing detail to this affair. You are directly under my jurisdiction. The King gave me the deeds and livings of all the abbeys in Hastings when he made me Chancellor.

MONK: [*Stepping back*] Are you Becket?

BECKET: Yes.

[*He looks at the knife with faint distaste*]

You didn't only use it to cut your bread. Your knife stinks of onion, like any proper little Saxon's knife. They're good, aren't they, the Hastings onions?

[*He looks at the knife again with a strange smile*]

You still haven't told me who it was for.

[*The* MONK *says nothing*]

If you meant it for the King, there was no sense in that, my lad. He has three sons. Kings spring up again like weeds! Did you imagine you could liberate your race single-handed?

MONK: No.

[*He adds dully:*]

Not my race. Myself.

BECKET: Liberate yourself from what?

MONK: My shame.

BECKET: [*With sudden gravity*] How old are you?

MONK: Sixteen.

BECKET: [*Quietly*] The Normans have occupied the island for

a hundred years. Shame is an old vintage. Your father and
your grandfather drank it to the dregs. The cup is empty now.

MONK: [*Shaking his head*] No.

[*A shadow seems to cross* BECKET's *eyes. He goes on,
quietly:*]

BECKET: So, one fine morning, you woke in your cell to the
bell of the first offices, while it was still dark. And it was the
bells that told you, a boy of sixteen, to take the whole burden
of shame onto yourself?

MONK: [*With the cry of a cornered animal*] Who told you that?

BECKET: [*Softly*] I told you I was a polyglot. [*Indifferently*]
I'm a Saxon too, did you know that?

MONK: [*Stonily*] Yes.

BECKET: [*Smiling*] Go on. Spit. You're dying to.

[*The* MONK *looks at him, a little dazed, and then spits*]

BECKET: [*Smiling*] That felt good, didn't it? [*Tersely*] The
King is waiting. And this conversation could go on indefinitely.
But I want to keep you alive, so we can continue it one of
these days.

[*He adds lightly:*]

It's pure selfishness, you know. Your life hasn't any sort of
importance for me, obviously, but it's very rare for Fate to
bring one face to face with one's own ghost, when young.
[*Calling*] Soldier!

[*The* SOLDIER *comes back and springs clanking to attention*]

Fetch me the Provost. Run!

[*The* SOLDIER *runs out.* BECKET *comes back to the silent*
YOUNG MONK]

Delightful day, isn't it? This early-morning sun, hot already
under this light veil of mist . . . A beautiful place, France.
But I'm like you, I prefer the solid mists of the Sussex downs.
Sunshine is luxury. And we belong to a race which used to
despise luxury, you and I.

[*The* PROVOST MARSHAL *of the camp comes in, followed
by the* SOLDIER. *He is an important personage, but* BECKET
is inaccessible, even for a PROVOST MARSHAL, *and the man's
behavior shows it*]

Sir Provost, your men have arrested this monk who was loitering
round the camp. He is a lay brother from the convent of
Hastings and he is directly under my jurisdiction. You will
make arrangements to have him sent back to England and
taken to the convent, where his Abbot will keep him under
supervision until my return. There is no specific charge against
him, for the moment. I want him treated without brutality,
but very closely watched. I hold you personally responsible for
him.

PROVOST: Very good, my Lord.

[*He motions to the* SOLDIERS. *They surround the little*
MONK *and take him away without a further glance from*
BECKET. *Left alone,* BECKET *looks at the knife, smiles,
wrinkles his nose and murmurs, with faint distaste:*]

BECKET: It's touching, but it stinks, all the same.

[*He flings the knife away, and whistling his little march
goes toward the tent. He goes in, calling out light-
heartedly:*]

Well, my prince, have you put on your Sunday best? It's
time to go. We mustn't keep the Bishop waiting!

[*A sudden joyful peal of bells. The tent disappears as
soon as* BECKET *has gone in. The set changes. A backcloth
representing a street comes down from the flies. The*

permanent pillars are there, but the SOLDIERS *lining the route have decorated them with standards. The* KING *and* BECKET *advance into the city, on horseback, preceded by two* TRUMPETERS; *the* KING *slightly ahead of* BECKET *and followed by the four* BARONS. *Acclamations from the crowd. Bells, trumpets throughout the scene*]

KING: [*Beaming as he waves*] Listen to that! They adore us, these French!

BECKET: It cost me quite a bit. I had money distributed among the populace this morning. The prosperous classes are at home, sulking, of course.

KING: Patriots?

BECKET: No. But they would have cost too much. There are also a certain number of your Highness' soldiers among the crowd, in disguise, to encourage any lukewarm elements.

KING: Why do you always make a game of destroying my illusions? I thought they loved me for myself! You're an amoral man, Becket. [*Anxiously*] Does one say amoral or immoral?

BECKET: [*Smiling*] It depends what one means.

KING: She's pretty, look—the girl on the balcony to the right there. Suppose we stopped a minute . . .

BECKET: Impossible. The Bishop is waiting in the cathedral.

KING: It would be a lot more fun than going to see a Bishop!

BECKET: My Lord, do you remember what you have to say to him?

KING: [*Waving to the crowd*] Yes, yes, yes! As if it mattered what I say to a French Bishop, whose city I've just taken by force!

BECKET: It matters a great deal. For our future policy.

KING: Am I the strongest or am I not?

BECKET: You are, today. But one must never drive one's enemy to despair. It makes him strong. Gentleness is better politics. It saps virility. A good occupational force must not crush, it must corrupt.

KING: [*Waving graciously*] What about my pleasure then? Where does that enter into your scheme of things? Suppose I charged into this heap of frog-eaters now instead of acting the goat

at their *Te Deum?* I can indulge in a bit of pleasure, can't I?
I'm the conqueror.

BECKET: That would be a fault. Worse, a failing. One can permit
oneself anything, Sire, but one must never indulge.

KING: Yes, Papa, right, Papa. What a bore you are today. Look
at that little redhead there, standing on the fountain! Give
orders for the procession to follow the same route back.

[*He rides on, turning his horse to watch the girl out of
sight. They have gone by, the four* BARONS *bringing up the
rear. Organ music. The standards disappear, together with
the* SOLDIERS. *We are in the cathedral. The stage is empty.
The organ is heard. Swelling chords. The organist is practicing in the empty cathedral. Then a sort of partition is
pushed on, which represents the sacristy.
The* KING, *attired for the ceremony, the* BARONS, *an unknown*
PRIEST *and a* CHOIRBOY *come in. They seem to be waiting
for something. The* KING *sits impatiently on a stool*]

KING: Where's Becket? And what are we waiting for?

1ST BARON: He just said to wait, my Lord. It seems there's
something not quite in order.

KING: [*Pacing about ill-humoredly*] What a lot of fuss for a
French Bishop! What do I look like, I ask you, hanging about
in this sacristy like a village bridegroom!

4TH BARON: I quite agree, my Lord! I can't think why we
don't march straight in. After all, it's your cathedral now.
[*Eagerly*] What do you say, my Lord? Shall we just draw our
swords and charge?

KING: [*Going meekly back to his stool with a worried frown*]
No. Becket wouldn't like it. And he's better than we are at
knowing the right thing to do. If he told us to wait, there must
be a good reason.

[BECKET *hurries in*]

Well, Becket, what's happening? We're freezing to death in
here! What do the French think they're at, keeping us molder-
ing in this sacristy?

BECKET: The order came from me, Sire. A security measure. My police are certain that a French rising was to break out during the ceremony.

[*The* KING *has risen. The* 2ND BARON *has drawn his sword. The other three follow suit*]

2ND BARON: God's Blood!

BECKET: Put up your swords. The King is safe in here. I have put guards on all the doors.

2ND BARON: Have we your permission to go in and deal with it, my Lord? We'll make short work of it!

3RD BARON: Just say the word, Sire! Shall we go?

BECKET: [*Curtly*] I forbid you. There aren't enough of us. I am bringing fresh troops into the city and having the cathedral evacuated. Until that is done, the King's person is in your keeping, gentlemen. But sheathe your swords. No provocation, please. We are at the mercy of a chance incident and I still have no more than the fifty escort men-at-arms in the city.

KING: [*Tugging at* BECKET's *sleeve*] Becket! Is that priest French?

BECKET: Yes. But he is part of the Bishop's immediate entourage. And the Bishop is our man.

KING: You know how reliable English Bishops are! So I leave you to guess how far we can trust a French one! That man has a funny look in his eyes.

BECKET: Who, the Bishop?

KING: No. That priest.

BECKET: [*Glances at the* PRIEST *and laughs*] Of course, my prince, he squints! I assure you that's the only disturbing thing about him! It would be tactless to ask him to leave. Besides, even if he had a dagger, you have your coat of mail and four of your Barons. I must go and supervise the evacuation of the nave.

[*He starts to go. The* KING *runs after him*]

KING: Becket!

[BECKET *stops*]

The choirboy?

BECKET: [*Laughing*] He's only so high!

KING: He may be a dwarf. You never know with the French.

[*Drawing* BECKET *aside*]

Becket, we talked a little flippantly this morning. Are you sure God isn't taking his revenge?

BECKET: [*Smiling*] Of course not. I'm afraid it's simply my police force taking fright and being a little overzealous. Policemen have a slight tendency to see assassins everywhere. They only do it to make themselves important. Bah, what does it matter? We'll hear the *Te Deum* in a deserted church, that's all.

KING: [*Bitterly*] And there was I thinking those folk adored me. Perhaps you didn't give them enough money.

BECKET: One can only buy those who are for sale, my prince. And those are just the ones who aren't dangerous. With the others, it's wolf against wolf. I'll come back straightaway and set your mind at rest.

[*He goes out. The* KING *darts anxious looks on the* PRIEST *as he paces up and down muttering his prayers*]

KING: Baron!

[*The* 4TH BARON *is nearest the* KING. *He steps forward*]

4TH BARON: [*Bellowing as usual*] My Lord?

KING: Shush! Keep an eye on that man, all four of you, and at the slightest move, leap on him.

[*There follows a little comic dumbshow by the* KING

and the PRIEST, *who is beginning to feel uneasy too. A sudden violent knocking on the sacristy door. The* KING *starts]*

Who is it?

[A SOLDIER *comes in*]

SOLDIER: A messenger from London, my Lord. They sent him on here from the camp. The message is urgent.

KING: [*Worried*] I don't like it. Regnault, you go and see.

[*The* 4TH BARON *goes out and comes back again, reassured*]

4TH BARON: It's William of Corbeil, my Lord. He has urgent letters.

KING: You're sure it *is* him? It wouldn't be a Frenchman in disguise? That's an old trick.

4TH BARON: [*Roaring with laughter*] I know him, Sire! I've drained more tankards with him than there are whiskers on his face. And the old goat has plenty!

[*The* KING *makes a sign. The* 4TH BARON *admits the* MESSENGER, *who drops on one knee and presents his letters to the* KING]

KING: Thank you. Get up. That's a fine beard you have, William of Corbeil. Is it well stuck on?

MESSENGER: [*Rising, bewildered*] My beard, Sire?

[*The* 4TH BARON *guffaws and slaps him on the back*]

4TH BARON: You old porcupine you!

[*The* KING *has glanced through the letters*]

KING: Good news, gentlemen! We have one enemy less.

[BECKET *comes in. The* KING *cries joyfully:*]

Becket!

BECKET: Everything is going according to plan, my prince. The troops are on their way. We're only to wait here quietly, until they arrive.

KING: [*Cheerfully*] You're right, Becket, everything is going according to plan. God isn't angry with us. He has just re-called the Archbishop.

BECKET: [*In a murmur*] That little old man . . . How could that feeble body contain so much strength?

KING: Now, now, now! Don't squander your sorrow, my son. I personally consider this an excellent piece of news!

BECKET: He was the first Norman who took an interest in me. He was a true father to me. God rest his soul.

KING: He will! After all the fellow did for Him, he's gone to Heaven, don't worry. Where he'll be definitely more use to God than he was to us. So it's definitely for the best.

[*He pulls* BECKET *to him*]

Becket! My little Becket, I think the ball's in our court now! This is the time to score a point.

[*He seizes his arm, tense and quite transformed*]

An extraordinary idea is just creeping into my mind, Becket. A master stroke! I can't think what's got into me this morning but I suddenly feel extremely intelligent. It probably comes of making love with a French girl last night. I am subtle, Becket, I am profound! So profound it's making my head spin. Are you sure it isn't dangerous to think too hard? Thomas, my little Thomas! Are you listening to me?

BECKET: [*Smiling at his excitement*] Yes, my prince.

KING: [*As excited as a little boy*] Are you listening carefully? Listen, Thomas! You told me once that the best ideas are the stupidest ones, but the clever thing is to think of them! Listen, Thomas! Tradition prevents me from touching the privileges of the Primacy. You follow me so far?

BECKET: Yes, my prince . . .

KING: But what if the Primate is my man? If the Archbishop of Canterbury is for the King, how can his power possibly incommodate me?

BECKET: That's an ingenious idea, my prince, but you forget that his election is a free one.

KING: No! You're forgetting the Royal Hand! Do you know what that is? When the candidate is displeasing to the Throne the King sends his Justicer to the Conclave of Bishops and it's the King who has the final say. That's an old custom too, and for once, it's in my favor! It's fully a hundred years since the the Conclave of Bishops has voted contrary to the wishes of the King!

BECKET: I don't doubt it, my Lord. But we all know your Bishops. Which one of them could you rely on? Once the Primate's miter is on their heads, they grow dizzy with power.

KING: Are you asking me, Becket? I'll tell you. Someone who doesn't know what dizziness means. Someone who isn't even afraid of God. Thomas, my son, I need your help again and this time it's important. I'm sorry to deprive you of French girls and the fun of battle, my son, but pleasure will come later. You are going over to England.

BECKET: I am at your service, my prince.

KING: Can you guess what your mission will be?

[*A tremor of anguish crosses* BECKET's *face at what is to come*]

BECKET: No, my prince.

KING: You are going to deliver a personal letter from me to every Bishop in the land. And do you know what those letters will contain, my Thomas, my little brother? My royal wish to have you elected Primate of England.

[BECKET *has gone deathly white. He says with a forced laugh:*]

BECKET: You're joking, of course, my Lord. Just look at the edifying man, the saintly man whom you would be trusting with these holy functions!

[*He has opened his fine coat to display his even finer doublet*]

Why, my prince, you really fooled me for a second!

[*The* KING *bursts out laughing,* BECKET *laughs too, rather too loudly in his relief*]

A fine Archbishop I'd have made! Look at my new shoes! They're the latest fashion in Paris. Attractive, that little up-turned toe, don't you think? Quite full of unction and compunction, isn't it, Sire?

KING: [*Suddenly stops laughing*] Shut up about your shoes, Thomas! I'm in deadly earnest. I shall write those letters before noon. You will help me.

[BECKET, *deathly pale, stammers:*]

BECKET: But my Lord, I'm not even a priest!

KING: [*Tersely*] You're a deacon. You can take your final vows tomorrow and be ordained in a month.

BECKET: But have you considered what the Pope will say?

KING: [*Brutally*] I'll pay the price!

[BECKET, *after an anguished pause, murmurs:*]

BECKET: My Lord, I see now that you weren't joking. Don't do this.

KING: Why not?

BECKET: It frightens me.

KING: [*His face set and hard*] Becket, this is an order!

[BECKET *stands as if turned to stone. A pause. He murmurs:*]

BECKET: [*Gravely*] If I become Archbishop, I can no longer be your friend.

[*A burst of organ music in the cathedral. Enter an* OFFICER]

OFFICER: The church is now empty, my Lord. The Bishop and his clergy await your Highness' good pleasure.

KING: [*Roughly to* BECKET] Did you hear that, Becket? Pull yourself together. You have an odd way of taking good news. Wake up! They say we can go in now.

[*The procession forms with the* PRIEST *and the* CHOIRBOY *leading.* BECKET *takes his place, almost reluctantly, a pace or so behind the* KING]

BECKET: [*In a murmur*] This is madness, my Lord. Don't do it. I could not serve both God and you.

KING: [*Looking straight ahead, says stonily*] You've never disappointed me, Thomas. And you are the only man I trust. You will leave tonight. Come, let's go in.

[*He motions to the* PRIEST. *The procession moves off and goes into the empty cathedral, as the organ swells. A moment's darkness. The organ continues to play. Then a dim light reveals* BECKET's *room. Open chests into which two* SERVANTS *are piling costly clothes*]

2ND SERVANT: [*Who is the younger of the two*] The coat with the sable trimming as well?

1ST SERVANT: Everything! You heard what he said!

2ND SERVANT: [*Grumbling*] Sables! To beggars! Who'll give them alms if they beg with that on their backs! They'll starve to death!

1ST SERVANT: [*Cackling*] They'll eat the sables! Can't you understand, you idiot! He's going to sell all this and give them the money!

2ND SERVANT: But what will he wear himself? He's got nothing left at all!

[BECKET *comes in, wearing a plain gray dressing gown*]

BECKET: Are the chests full? I want them sent over to the Jew before tonight. I want nothing left in this room but the bare walls. Gil, the fur coverlet!

1ST SERVANT: [*Regretfully*] My Lord will be cold at night.

BECKET: Do as I say.

[*Regretfully, the* 1ST SERVANT *takes the coverlet and puts it in the chest*]

Has the steward been told about tonight's meal? Supper for forty in the great hall.

1ST SERVANT: He says he won't have enough gold plate, my Lord. Are we to mix it with the silver dishes?

BECKET: Tell him to lay the table with the wooden platters and earthenware bowls from the kitchens. The plate has been sold. The Jew will send over for it late this afternoon.

1ST SERVANT: [*Dazed*] The earthenware bowls and the wooden platters. Yes, my Lord. And the steward says could he have your list of invitations fairly soon, my Lord. He only has three runners and he's afraid there won't be time to—

BECKET: There are no invitations. The great doors will be thrown open and you will go out into the street and tell the poor they are dining with me tonight.

1ST SERVANT: [*Appalled*] Very good, my Lord.

[*He is about to go.* BECKET *calls him back*]

BECKET: I want the service to be impeccable. The dishes presented to each guest first, with full ceremony, just as for princes. Go now.

[*The two* SERVANTS *go out.* BECKET, *left alone, casually looks over one or two articles of clothing in the chests. He murmurs:*]

I must say it was all very pretty stuff.

[*He drops the lid and bursts out laughing*]

A prick of vanity! The mark of an upstart. A truly saintly man would never have done the whole thing in one day. Nobody will ever believe it's genuine.

[*He turns to the jeweled crucifix above the bed and says simply:*]

I hope You haven't inspired me with all these holy resolutions in order to make me look ridiculous, Lord. It's all so new to me. I'm setting about it a little clumsily perhaps.

[*He looks at the crucifix and with a swift gesture takes it off the wall*]

And you're far too sumptuous too. Precious stones around your bleeding Body . . . I shall give you to some poor village church.

[*He lays the crucifix on the chest. He looks around the room, happy, lighthearted, and murmurs:*]

It's like leaving for a holiday. Forgive me, Lord, but I never enjoyed myself so much in my whole life. I don't believe You are a sad God. The joy I feel in shedding all my riches must be part of Your divine intentions.

[*He goes behind the curtain into the antechamber where he can be heard gaily whistling an old English marching song. He comes back a second later, his bare feet in sandals, and wearing a monk's coarse woolen robe. He draws the curtain across again and murmurs:*]

BECKET: There. Farewell, Becket. I wish there had been some-thing I had regretted parting with, so I could offer it to You.

[*He goes to the crucifix and says simply:*]

Lord, are You sure You are not tempting me? It all seems far too easy.

[*He drops to his knees and prays*]

CURTAIN

ACT THREE

A room in the KING's *palace. The two* QUEENS, *the* QUEEN
MOTHER *and the* YOUNG QUEEN, *are on stage, working at
their tapestry. The* KING's *two* SONS, *one considerably older
than the other, are playing in a corner, on the floor. The*
KING *is in another corner, playing at cup-and-ball. After
several unsuccessful attempts to catch the ball in the cup,
he throws down the toy and exclaims irritably:*

KING: Forty beggars! He invited forty beggars to dinner!

QUEEN MOTHER: The dramatic gesture, as usual! I always
said you had misplaced your confidence, my son.

KING: [*Pacing up and down*] Madam, I am very particular
where I place my confidence. I only ever did it once in my
whole life and I am still convinced I was right. But there's
a great deal we don't understand! Thomas is ten times more
intelligent than all of us put together.

QUEEN MOTHER: [*Reprovingly*] You are talking about royalty,
my son.

KING: [*Grunting*] What of it? Intelligence has been shared out
on a different basis.

YOUNG QUEEN: It seems he has sold his gold plate and all his
rich clothes to a Jew. He wears an ordinary homespun habit
now.

QUEEN MOTHER: I see that as a sign of ostentation, if nothing
worse! One can become a saintly man, certainly, but not in

a single day. I've never liked the man. You were insane to make him so powerful.

KING: [*Crying out*] He is my friend!

QUEEN MOTHER: [*Acidly*] More's the pity.

YOUNG QUEEN: He is your friend in debauchery. It was he who lured you away from your duty towards me. It was he who first took you to the whorehouses!

KING: [*Furious*] Rubbish, Madam! I didn't need anybody to lure me away from my duty towards you. I made you three children, very conscientiously. Phew! My duty is done for a while.

YOUNG QUEEN: [*Stung*] When that libertine loses the evil influence he has on you, you will come to appreciate the joys of family life again. Pray Heaven he disobeys you!

KING: The joys of family life are limited, Madam. To be perfectly frank, you bore me. You and your eternal backbiting, over your everlasting tapestry, the pair of you! That's no sustenance for a man!

[*He trots about the room, furious, and comes to a halt behind their chairs*]

If at least it had some artistic merit. My ancestress Mathilda, while she was waiting for her husband to finish carving out his kingdom, now *she* embroidered a masterpiece—which they left behind in Bayeux, more's the pity. But that! It's beyond belief it's so mediocre.

YOUNG QUEEN: [*Nettled*] We can only use the gifts we're born with.

KING: Yes. And yours are meager.

[*He glances out of the window once more to look at the time, and says with a sigh:*]

I've been bored to tears for a whole month. Not a soul to talk to. After his nomination, not wanting to seem in too indecent a hurry, I leave him alone to carry out his pastoral tour. Now, back he comes at last, I summon him to the palace and he's late.

[*He looks out of the window again and exclaims:*]

Ah! Someone at the sentry post!

[*He turns away, disappointed*]

No, it's only a monk.

[*He wanders about the room, aimlessly. He goes over to join the children, and watches them playing for a while*]

[*Sourly*] Charming babes. Men in the making. Sly and obtuse already. And to think one is expected to be dewy-eyed over creatures like that, merely because they aren't yet big enough to be hated or despised. Which is the elder of you two?

ELDER BOY: [*Rising*] I am, Sir.

KING: What's your name again?

ELDER BOY: Henry III.

KING: [*Sharply*] Not yet, Sir! Number II is in the best of health. [*To the* QUEEN] You've brought them up well! Do you think of yourself as Regent already? And you wonder that I shun your bedchamber? I don't care to make love with my widow.

[*An* OFFICER *comes in*]

OFFICER: A messenger from the Archbishop, my Lord.

KING: [*Beside himself with rage*] A messenger! A messenger! I summoned the Archbishop Primate in person!

[*He turns to the women, suddenly uneasy, almost touching*]

Perhaps he's ill? That would explain everything.

QUEEN MOTHER: [*Bitterly*] That's too much to hope for.

KING: [*Raging*] You'd like to see him dead, wouldn't you, you females—because he loves me? If he hasn't come, it's because he's dying! Send the man in, quickly! O my Thomas . . .

[*The* OFFICER *goes and admits the* MONK. *The* KING *hurries over to him*]

Who are you? Is Becket ill?

MONK: [*Falling on one knee*] My Lord, I am William son of Etienne, secretary to his Grace the Archbishop.

KING: Is your master seriously ill?

MONK: No, my Lord. His Grace is in good health. He has charged me to deliver this letter with his deepest respects— and to give your Highness this.

[*He bows lower and hands something to the* KING]

KING: [*Stunned*] The Seal? Why has he sent me back the Seal?

[*He unrolls the parchment and reads it in silence. His face hardens. He says curtly, without looking at the* MONK:]

You have carried out your mission. Go.

[*The* MONK *rises and turns to go*]

MONK: Is there an answer from your Highness for his Grace the Archbishop?

KING: [*Harshly*] No!

[*The* MONK *goes out. The* KING *stands still a moment, at a loss, then flings himself onto his throne, glowering. The women exchange a conspiratorial look. The* QUEEN MOTHER *rises and goes to him*]

QUEEN MOTHER: [*Insidiously*] Well, my son, what does you friend say in his letter?

KING: [*Bawling*] Get out! Get out, both of you! And take your royal vermin with you! I am alone!

[*Frightened, the* QUEENS *hurry out with the children. The* KING *stands there a moment, reeling a little, as if stunned by the blow. Then he collapses onto the throne and sobs like a child]*

[*Moaning*] O my Thomas!

[*He remains a moment prostrate, then collects himself and sits up. He looks at the Seal in his hand and says between clenched teeth:*]

You've sent me back the Three Lions of England, like a little boy who doesn't want to play with me any more. You think you have God's honor to defend now! I would have gone to war with all England's might behind me, and against England's interests, to defend you, little Saxon. I would have given the honor of the Kingdom laughingly . . . for you . . . Only I loved you and you didn't love me . . . that's the difference.

[*His face hardens. He adds between clenched teeth:*]

Thanks all the same for this last gift as you desert me. I shall learn to be alone.

[*He goes out. The lights dim.* SERVANTS *remove the furniture. When the lights go up again, the permanent set, with the pillars, is empty. A bare church; a man half hidden under a dark cloak is waiting behind a pillar. It is the* KING. *Closing chords of organ music. Enter* GILBERT FOLLIOT, *Bishop of London, followed by his* CLERGY. *He has just said Mass. The* KING *goes to him*]

Bishop . . .

FOLLIOT: [*Stepping back*] What do you want, fellow?

[*His acolytes are about to step between them, when he exclaims:*]

The King!

KING: Yes.

FOLLIOT: Alone, without an escort, and dressed like a common squire?

KING: The King nevertheless. Bishop, I would like to make a confession.

FOLLIOT: [*With a touch of suspicion*] I am the Bishop of London. The King has his own Confessor. That is an important Court appointment and it has its prerogatives.

KING: The choice of priest for Holy Confession is open, Bishop, even for a King.

[FOLLIOT *motions to his* CLERGY, *who draw away*]

Anway, my confession will be short, and I'm not asking for absolution. I have something much worse than a sin on my conscience, Bishop: a mistake. A foolish mistake.

[FOLLIOT *says nothing*]

I ordered you to vote for Thomas Becket at the Council of Clarendon. I repent of it.

FOLLIOT: [*Inscrutably*] We bowed before the Royal Hand.

KING: Reluctantly, I know. It took me thirteen weeks of authority and patience to crush the small uncrushable opposition of which you were the head, Bishop. On the day the Council met you looked green. They told me you fell seriously ill afterwards.

FOLLIOT: [*Impenetrably*] God cured me.

KING: Very good of Him. But He is rather inclined to look after His own, to the exclusion of anyone else. He let me fall ill without lifting a finger! And I must cure myself without divine intervention. I have the Archbishop on my stomach. A big hard lump I shall have to vomit back. What does the Norman clergy think of him?

FOLLIOT: [*Reserved*] His Grace seems to have the reins of the Church of England well in hand. Those who are in close contact with him even say that he behaves like a holy man.

KING: [*With grudging admiration*] It's a bit sudden, but nothing he does ever surprises me. God knows what the brute is capable of, for good or for evil. Bishop, let us be frank with each other. Is the Church very interested in holy men?

FOLLIOT: [*With the ghost of a smile*] The Church has been wise for so long, your Highness, that she could not have failed to realize that the temptation of saintliness is one of the most insidious and fearsome snares the devil can lay for her priests. The administration of the realm of souls, with the temporal difficulties it carries with it, chiefly demands, as in all administrations, competent administrators. The Roman Catholic Church has its Saints, it invokes their benevolent intercession, it prays to them. But it has no need to create others. That is superfluous. And dangerous.

KING: You seem to be a man one can talk to, Bishop. I misjudged you. Friendship blinded me.

FOLLIOT: [*Still impenetrable*] Friendship is a fine thing.

KING: [*Suddenly hoarse*] It's a domestic animal, a living, tender thing. It seems to be all eyes, forever gazing at you, warming you. You don't see its teeth. But it's a beast with one curious characteristic. It is only after death that it bites.

FOLLIOT: [*Prudently*] Is the King's friendship for Thomas Becket dead, your Highness?

KING: Yes, Bishop. It died quite suddenly. A sort of heart failure.

FOLLIOT: A curious phenomenon, your Highness, but quite frequent.

KING: [*Taking his arm suddenly*] I hate Becket now, Bishop. There is nothing more in common between that man and me than this creature tearing at my guts. I can't bear it any more. I shall have to turn it loose on him. But I am the King; what they conventionally call my greatness stands in my way. I need somebody.

FOLLIOT: [*Stiffening*] I do not wish to serve anything but the Church.

KING: Let us talk like grown men, Bishop. We went in hand in hand to conquer, pillage and ransom England. We quarrel, we try to cheat each other of a penny or two, but Heaven and Earth still have one or two common interests. Do you know what I have just obtained from the Pope? His Blessing to go and murder Catholic Ireland, in the name of the Faith. Yes, a sort of crusade to impose Norman barons and clergy on the Irish, with our swords and standards solemnly blessed as if we were off to give the Turks a drubbing. The only condition: a little piece of silver per household per year, for St. Peter's pence, which the native clergy of Ireland is loath to part with and which I have undertaken to make them pay. It's a mere pittance. But at the end of the year it will add up to a pretty sum. Rome knows how to do her accounts.

FOLLIOT: [*Terror-stricken*] There are some things one should never say, your Highness: one should even try not to know about them, so long as one is not directly concerned with them.

KING: [*Smiling*] We are alone, Bishop, and the church is empty.

FOLLIOT: The church is never empty. A little red lamp burns in front of the High Altar.

KING: [*Impatiently*] Bishop, I like playing games, but only with boys of my own age! Do you take me for one of your sheep, holy pastor? The One whom that little red lamp honors read into your innermost heart and mine a long time ago. Of your cupidity and my hatred, He knows all there is to know.

[FOLLIOT *withdraws into his shell. The* KING *cries irritably:*]

If that's the way you feel you must become a monk, Bishop! Wear a hair shirt on your naked back and go and hide yourself in a monastery to pray! The Bishopric of London, for the purehearted son of a Thames waterman, is too much, or too little!

[*A pause*]

FOLLIOT: [*Impassively*] If, as is my duty, I disregard my private feelings, I must admit that his Grace the Archbishop has so far done nothing which has not been in the interests of Mother Church.

KING: [*Eying him, says jovially*] I can see your game, my little friend. You mean to cost me a lot of money. But I'm rich—

thanks to Becket, who has succeeded in making you pay the Absentee Tax. And it seems to me eminently ethical that a part of the Church's gold should find its way, via you, back to the Church. Besides, if we want to keep this on a moral basis, Holy Bishop, you can tell yourself that as the greatness of the Church and that of the State are closely linked, in serving me, you will in the long run be working for the consolidation of the Catholic Faith.

FOLLIOT: [*Contemplating him with curiosity*] I had always taken your Highness for a great adolescent lout who cared only for his pleasure.

KING: One can be wrong about people, Bishop. I made the same mistake. [*With a sudden cry*] O my Thomas . . .

FOLLIOT: [*Fiercely*] You love him, your Highness! You still love him! You love that mitered hog, that impostor, that Saxon bastard, that little guttersnipe!

KING: [*Seizing him by the throat*] Yes, I love him! But that's my affair, priest! All I confided to you was my hatred. I'll pay you to rid me of him, but don't ever speak ill of him to me. Or we'll fight it out as man to man!

FOLLIOT: Highness, you're choking me!

KING: [*Abruptly releasing him*] We will meet again tomorrow, my Lord Bishop, and we'll go over the details of our enterprise together. You will be officially summoned to the palace on some pretext or other—my good works in your London Diocese, say—where I am your chief parishioner. But it won't be the poor and needy we'll discuss. My poor can wait. The Kingdom they pin their hopes on is eternal.

[*The* KING *goes out.* GILBERT FOLLIOT *remains motionless. His* CLERGY *join him timidly. He takes his crook and goes out with dignity, but not before one of his Canons has discreetly adjusted his miter, which was knocked askew in the recent struggle.*
They have gone out.
The lighting changes. Curtains between the pillars. The episcopal palace.

Morning. A PRIEST *enters, leading two* MONKS *and the* YOUNG MONK *from the convent of Hastings*]

PRIEST: His Grace will receive you here.

[*The two* MONKS *are impressed. They push the* YOUNG MONK *about a little*]

1ST MONK: Stand up straight. Kiss his Grace's ring and try to answer his questions with humility, or I'll tan your backside for you!

2ND MONK: I suppose you thought he'd forgotten all about you? The great never forget anything. And don't you act proud with him or you'll be sorry.

[*Enter* BECKET, *wearing a coarse monk's robe*]

BECKET: Well, brothers, is it fine over in Hastings?

[*He gives them his ring to kiss*]

1ST MONK: Foggy, my Lord.

BECKET: [*Smiling*] Then it's fine in Hastings. We always think fondly of our Abbey there and we intend to visit it soon, when our new duties grant us a moment's respite. How has this young man been behaving? Has he given our Abbot much trouble?

2ND MONK: A proper mule, my Lord. Father Abbot tried kindness, as you recommended, but he soon had to have recourse to the dungeon and bread and water, and even to the whip. Nothing has any effect. The stubborn little wretch is just the same; all defiance and insults. He has fallen into the sin of pride. Nothing I know of will pull him out of that!

1ST MONK: Save a good kick in the rump perhaps—if your Grace will pardon the expression. [*To the boy*] Stand up straight.

BECKET: [*To the boy*] Pay attention to your brother. Stand up straight. As a rule the sin of pride stiffens a man's back. Look me in the face.

[*The* YOUNG MONK *looks at him*]

Good.

[BECKET *looks at the boy for a while, then turns to the* MONKS]

You will be taken to the kitchens where you can refresh yourselves before you leave, brothers. They have orders to treat you well. Don't spurn our hospitality; we relieve you, for today, of your vows of abstinence, and we fondly hope you will do honor to our bill of fare. Greet your father Abbot in Jesus on our behalf.

2ND MONK: [*Hesitantly*] And the lad?

BECKET: We will keep him here.

1ST MONK: Watch out for him, your Grace. He's vicious.

BECKET: [*Smiling*] We are not afraid.

[*The* MONKS *go out.* BECKET *and the* YOUNG MONK *remain, facing each other*]

Why do you hold yourself so badly?

YOUNG MONK: I don't want to look people in the face any more.

BECKET: I'll teach you. That will be your first lesson. Look at me.

[*The boy gives him a sidelong glance*]

Better than that.

[*The boy looks at him*]

Are you still bearing the full weight of England's shame alone? Is it that shame which bends your back like that?

YOUNG MONK: Yes.

BECKET: If I took over half of it, would it weigh less heavy?

[*He motions to the* PRIEST]

Show in their Lordships the Bishops. You'll soon see that being alone is not a privilege reserved entirely for you.

[*The* BISHOPS *come in.* BECKET *leads the* YOUNG MONK *into a corner*]

You stay here in the corner and hold my tablets. I ask only one thing. Don't leap at their throats; you'd complicate everything.

[*He motions to the* BISHOPS *who remain standing*]

FOLLIOT: Your Grace, I am afraid this meeting may be a pointless one. You insisted—against our advice—on attacking the King openly. Even before the three excommunications which you asked us to sanction could be made public, the King has hit back. His Grand Justicer Richard de Lacy has just arrived in your antechamber and is demanding to see you in the name of the King. He is the bearer of an official order summoning you to appear before his assembled Council within twenty-four hours and there to answer the charges made against you.

BECKET: Of what is the King accusing me?

FOLLIOT: Prevarication. Following the examination of accounts by his Privy Council, his Highness demands a considerable sum still outstanding on your administration of the Treasury.

BECKET: When I resigned the Chancellorship I handed over my ledgers to the Grand Justicer who acquitted me of all subsequent dues and claims. What does the King demand?

OXFORD: Forty thousands marks in fine gold.

BECKET: [*Smiling*] I don't believe there was ever as much money in all the coffers of all England in all the time I was Chancellor.

But a clever clerk can soon change that . . . The King has closed his fist and I am like a fly inside it.

[*He smiles and looks at him*]

I have the impression, gentlemen, that you must be feeling something very akin to relief.

YORK: We advised you against open opposition.

BECKET: William of Aynsford, incited by the King, struck down the priest I had appointed to the Parish of his Lordship's See, on the pretext that his Highness disapproved of my choice. Am I to look on while my priests are murdered?

FOLLIOT: It is not for you to appoint a priest to a free fief! There is not a Norman, layman or cleric, who will ever concede that. It would mean reviewing the entire legal system of the Conquest. Everything can be called into question in England except the fact that it was conquered in 1066. England is the land of law and of the most scrupulous respect for the law; but the law begins at that date only, or England as such ceases to exist.

BECKET: Bishop, must I remind you that we are men of God and that we have an Honor to defend, which dates from all eternity?

OXFORD: [*Quietly*] This excommunication was bad policy, your Grace. William of Aynsford is a companion of the King.

BECKET: [*Smiling*] I know him very well. He's a charming man. I have drained many a tankard with him.

YORK: [*Yelping*] And his wife is my second cousin!

BECKET: That is a detail I deplore, my Lord Bishop, but he has killed one of my priests. If I do not defend my priests, who will? Gilbert of Clare has indicted before his court of justice a churchman who was under our exclusive jurisdiction.

YORK: An interesting victim I must say! He deserved the rope a hundred times over. The man was accused of rape and murder. Wouldn't it have been cleverer to let the wretch hang—and have peace?

BECKET: "I bring not peace but the sword." Your Lordship

must I'm sure have read that somewhere. I am not interested in what this man is guilty of. If I allow my priests to be tried by a secular tribunal; if I let Robert de Vere abduct our tonsured clerics from our monasteries, as he has just done, on the grounds that the man was one of his serfs who had escaped land bondage, I don't give much for our freedom and our chances of survival in five years' time, my Lord. I have excommunicated Gilbert of Clare, Robert de Vere and William of Aynsford. The Kingdom of God must be defended like any other Kingdom. Do you think that Right has only to show it's handsome face for everything to drop in its lap? Without Might, its old enemy, Right counts for nothing.

YORK: What Might? Let us not indulge in empty words. The King is Might and he is the law.

BECKET: He is the written law, but there is another, unwritten law, which always makes Kings bend the neck eventually.

[*He looks at them for a moment and smiles*]

I was a profligate, gentlemen, perhaps a libertine, in any case, a worldly man. I loved living and I laughed at all these things. But you passed the burden on to me and now I have to carry it. I have rolled up my sleeves and taken it on my back and nothing will ever make me set it down again. I thank your Lordships. The council is adjourned and I have made my decision. I shall stand by these three excommunications. I shall appear tomorrow before the King's supreme court of Justice.

[*The* BISHOPS *look at one another in surprise, then bow and go out.* BECKET *turns to the* YOUNG MONK]

Well, does the shame weigh less heavy now?

YOUNG MONK: Yes.

BECKET: [*Leading him off and laughing*] Then stand up straight!

[*The drapes close. Distant trumpets. The* KING *comes out from behind the curtains and turns to peep through them*

at something. A pause. Then GILBERT FOLLIOT *comes hurrying in*]

KING: What's happening? I can't see a thing from up here.

FOLLIOT: Legal procedure is taking its course, your Highness.
The third summons has been delivered. He has not appeared.
In a moment he will be condemned in absentia. Once prevarication is established, our Dean the Bishop of Chichester will
go to see him and communicate according to the terms of
the ancient Charter of the Church of England, our corporated
repudiation of allegiance, absolving us of obedience to him—
and our intention to report him to our Holy Father the Pope.
I shall then, as Bishop of London, step forward and publicly
accuse Becket of having celebrated, in contempt of the King,
a sacrilegious Mass at the instigation of the Evil Spirit.

KING: [*Anxiously*] Isn't that going rather far?

FOLLIOT: Of course. It won't fool anyone, but it always works.
The assembly will then go out to vote, in order of precedence,
and return a verdict of imprisonment. The sentence is already
drawn up.

KING: Unanimously?

FOLLIOT: We are all Normans. The rest is your Highness' concern.
It will merely be a matter of carrying out the sentence.

KING : [*Staggering suddenly*] O my Thomas!

FOLLIOT: [*Impassively*] I can still stop the machine, your Highness.

KING: [*Hesitates a second then says*] No. Go.

[FOLLIOT *goes out. The* KING *goes back to his place, be-
hind the curtain*]
The two QUEENS *come into the room, and join the* KING.
All three stand and peer through the curtain. A pause]

YOUNG QUEEN: He's doomed, isn't he?

KING: [*Dully*] Yes.

YOUNG QUEEN: At last!

[*The* KING *turns on her, his face twisted with hate*]

KING: I forbid you to gloat!

YOUNG QUEEN: At seeing your enemy perish—why not?

KING: [*Frothing*] Becket is my enemy, but in the human balance, bastard as he is, and naked as his mother made him, he weighs a hundred times more than you do, Madam, with your crown and all your jewels and your august father the Emperor into the bargain. Becket is attacking me and he has betrayed me. I am forced to fight him and crush him, but at least he gave me, with open hands, everything that is at all good in me. And you have never given me anything but your carping mediocrity, your everlasting obsession with your puny little person and what you thought was due to it. That is why I forbid you to smile as he lies dying!

YOUNG QUEEN: I gave you my youth! I gave you your children!

KING: [*Shouting*] I don't like my children! And as for your youth—that dusty flower pressed in a hymnbook since you were twelve years old, with its watery blood and its insipid scent—you can say farewell to that without a tear. With age, bigotry and malice may perhaps give some spice to your character. Your body was an empty desert, Madam!—which duty forced me to wander in alone. But you have never been a wife to me! And Becket was my friend, red-blooded, generous and full of strength!

[*He is shaken by a sob*]

O my Thomas!

[*The* QUEEN MOTHER *moves over to him*]

QUEEN MOTHER: [*Haughtily*] And I, my son, I gave you nothing either, I suppose?

KING: [*Recovers his composure, glares at her and says dully*] Life. Yes. Thank you. But after that I never saw you save in a passage, dressed for a Ball, or in your crown and ermine mantle, ten minutes before official ceremonies, where you were forced to tolerate my presence. I have always been alone, and no one on this earth has ever loved me except Becket!

QUEEN MOTHER: [*Bitterly*] Well, call him back! Absolve him, since he loves you! Give him supreme power then! But do something!

KING: I am. I'm learning to be alone again, Madam. As usual.

[*A* PAGE *comes in, breathless*]

Well? What's happening? How far have they got?

PAGE: My Liege, Thomas Becket appeared just when everyone had given him up; sick, deathly pale, in full pontifical regalia and carrying his own heavy silver cross. He walked the whole length of the hall without anyone daring to stop him, and when Robert Duke of Leicester, who was to read out his sentence, began the consecrated words, he stopped him with a gesture and forbade him, in God's name, to pronounce judgment against him, his spiritual Father. Then he walked back through the crowd, which parted for him in silence. He has just left.

KING: [*Unable to hide his delight*] Well played, Thomas! One point to you.

[*He checks himself, embarrassed, and then says:*]

And what about my Barons?

PAGE: Their hands flew to their swords with cries of "Traitor! Perjurer! Arrest him! Miserable wretch! Hear your sentence!" But not one of them dared move, or touch the sacred ornaments.

KING: [*With a roar*] The fools! I am surrounded by fools and the only intelligent man in my Kingdom is against me!

PAGE: [*Continuing his story*] Then, on the threshold, he turned, looked at them coldly as they shouted in their impotence, and he said that not so long ago he could have answered their challenge sword in hand. Now he could no longer do it, but he begged them to remember that there was a time when he met strength with strength.

KING: [*Jubilantly*] He could beat them all! All, I tell you! On horseback, on foot, with a mace, with a lance, with a sword! In the lists they fell to him like ninepins!

PAGE: And his eyes were so cold, and so ironic—even though all he had in his hand was his episcopal crook—that one by one, they fell silent. Only then did he turn and go out. They say he has given orders to invite all the beggars of the city to sup at his house tonight.

KING: [*Somberly*] And what about the Bishop of London, who was going to reduce him to powder? What about my busy friend Gilbert Folliot?

PAGE: He had a horrible fit of rage trying to incite the crowd, he let out a screech of foul abuse and then he fainted. They are bringing him round now.

[*The* KING *suddenly bursts into a shout of irrepressible laughter, and, watched by the two outraged* QUEENS, *collapses into the* PAGE's *arms, breathless and helpless with mirth*]

KING: It's too funny! It's too funny!

QUEEN MOTHER: [*Coldly*] You will laugh less heartily tomorrow, my son. If you don't stop him, Becket will reach the coast tonight, ask asylum of the King of France and jeer at you, unpunished, from across the Channel.

[*She sweeps out with the* YOUNG QUEEN. *Suddenly, the* KING *stops laughing and runs out.*
The light changes. Curtains part. We are at the Court of LOUIS, KING OF FRANCE. *He is sitting in the middle of the courtroom, very erect on his throne. He is a burly man with intelligent eyes*]

LOUIS: [*To his* BARONS] Gentlemen, we are in France and a fart on England's King—as the song goes.

1ST BARON: Your Majesty cannot *not* receive his Ambassadors Extraordinary!

LOUIS: Ordinary, or extraordinary, I am at home to all ambassadors. It's my job. I shall receive them.

1ST BARON: They have been waiting in your Majesty's anteroom for over an hour, Sire.

LOUIS: Let them wait. That's *their* job. An ambassador is made for pacing about an antechamber. I know what they are going to ask me.

2ND BARON: The extradition of a felon is a courtesy due from one crowned head to another.

LOUIS: My dear man, crowned heads can play the little game of courtesy but nations owe each other none. My right to play the courteous gentleman stops where France's interests begin. And France's interests consist in making things as difficult as possible for England—a thing England never hesitates to do to us. The Archbishop is a millstone round Henry Plantagenet's neck. Long live the Archbishop! Anyway, I like the fellow.

2ND BARON: My gracious sovereign is master. And so long as our foreign policy permits us to expect nothing of King Henry—

LOUIS: For the time being, it is an excellent thing to stiffen our attitude. Remember the Montmirail affair. We only signed the peace treaty with Henry on condition that he granted to spare the lives of the refugees from Brittany and Poitou whom he asked us to hand over to him. Two months later all of them had lost their heads. That directly touched my personal honor. I was not strong enough at the time, so I had to pretend I hadn't heard of these men's execution. And I continued to lavish smiles on my English cousin. But praise God our affairs have taken a turn for the better. And today *he* needs *us*. So I will now proceed to remember my honor. Show in the ambassadors.

[*Exit* 1ST BARON. *He comes back with* FOLLIOT *and the* DUKE OF ARUNDEL]

1ST BARON: Permit me to introduce to your Majesty the two envoys extraordinary from his Highness Henry of England; his Grace the Bishop of London and the Duke of Arundel.

LOUIS: [*With a friendly wave to the* DUKE] Greetings to you, Milord. I have not forgotten your amazing exploits at the last tournament at Calais. Do you still wield a lance as mightily as you did, Milord?

ARUNDEL: [*With a gratified bow*] I hope so, Sire.

LOUIS: We hope that our friendly relations with your gracious master will allow us to appreciate your jousting skill again before long, on the occasion of the forthcoming festivities.

[FOLLIOT *has unrolled a parchment*]

Bishop, I see you have a letter for us from your master. We are listening.

FOLLIOT: [*Bows again and starts to read*] "To my Lord and friend Louis, King of the French; Henry, King of England, Duke of Normandy, Duke of Aquitaine and Count of Anjou: Learn that Thomas, former Archbishop of Canterbury, after a public trial held at my court by the plenary assembly of the Barons of my realm has been found guilty of fraud, perjury and treason towards me. He has forthwith fled my Kingdom as a traitor, and with evil intent. I therefore entreat you not to allow this criminal, nor any of his adherents, to reside upon your territories, nor to permit any of your vassals to give help, support or counsel to this my greatest enemy. For I solemnly declare that your enemies or those of your Realm would receive none from me or my subjects. I expect you to assist me in the vindication of my honor and the punishment of my enemy, as you would wish me to do for you, should the need arise."

[A *pause.* FOLLIOT *bows very low and hands the parchment to the* KING *who rolls it up casually and hands it to one of the* BARONS]

LOUIS: Gentlemen, we have listened attentively to our gracious cousin's request and we take good note of it. Our chancellery will draft a reply which will be sent to you tomorrow. All we can do at the moment, is express our surprise. No news had reached us of the presence of the Archbishop of Canterbury on our domains.

FOLLIOT: [*Tersely*] Sire, the former Archbishop has taken refuge at the Abbey of St. Martin, near Saint-Omer.

LOUIS: [*Still gracious*] My Lord Bishop, we flatter ourselves that there is some order in our Kingdom. If he were there, we would certainly have been informed.

[*He makes a gesture of dismissal. The Ambassadors bow low and go out backwards, ushered out by the* 1ST BARON. *Immediately,* LOUIS *says to the* 2ND BARON:]

Show in Thomas Becket and leave us.

[*The* 2ND BARON *goes out and a second later admits* THOMAS, *dressed in a monk's robe.* THOMAS *drops onto one knee. The* BARON *goes out*]

[*Kindly*] Rise, Thomas Becket. And greet us as the Primate of England. The bow is enough—and if I know my etiquette, you are entitled to a slight nod of the head from me. There, that's done. I would even be required to kiss your ring, if your visit were an official one. But I have the impression that it isn't, am I right?

BECKET: [*With a smile*] No, Sire. I am only an exile.

LOUIS: [*Graciously*] That too is an important title, in France.

BECKET: I am afraid it is the only one I have left. My property has been seized and distributed to those who served the King against me; letters have been sent to the Duke of Flanders and all his Barons enjoining them to seize my person. John, Bishop of Poitiers, who was suspected of wanting to grant me asylum, has just been poisoned.

LOUIS: [*Smiling*] In fact you are a very dangerous man.

BECKET: I'm afraid so.

LOUIS: [*Unperturbed*] We like danger, Becket. And if the King of France started being afraid of the King of England, there would be something sadly amiss in Europe. We grant you our royal protection on whichever of our domains it will please you to choose.

BECKET: I humbly thank your Majesty. I must, however, tell you that I cannot buy this protection with any act hostile to my country.

LOUIS: You do us injury. That was understood. You may be sure we are practiced enough in the task of Kingship not to make such gross errors in our choice of spies and traitors. The King of France will ask nothing of you. But . . . There is always a but, as I'm sure you are aware, in politics.

[BECKET *looks up. The* KING *rises heavily onto his fat legs, goes to him and says familiarly:*]

I am only responsible for France's interests, Becket. I really can't afford to shoulder those of Heaven. In a month or a year I can summon you back here and tell you, just as blandly, that my dealings with the King of England have taken a different turn and that I am obliged to banish you.

[*He slaps him affably on the back, his eyes sparkling with intelligence and asks, with a smile:*]

I believe you have dabbled in politics too, Archbishop?

BECKET: [*Smiling*] Yes, Sire. Not so very long ago.

LOUIS: [*Jovially*] I like you very much. Mark you, had you been a French Bishop, I don't say I wouldn't have clapped you in prison myself. But in the present circumstances, you have a right to my royal protection. Do you value candor, Becket?

BECKET: Yes, Sire.

LOUIS: Then we are sure to understand each other. Do you intend to go to see the Holy Father?

BECKET: Yes, Sire, if you give me your safe conduct.

LOUIS: You shall have it. But a word in your ear—as a friend. —Keep this to yourself, won't you?—don't go and stir up trou-

ble for me with Rome—Beware of the Pope. He'll sell you
for thirty pieces of silver. The man needs money.

[*The lights dim. A curtain closes. Two small rostrums,
bearing the* POPE *and the* CARDINAL, *are pushed on stage,
to a light musical accompaniment.
The* POPE *is a thin, fidgety little man with an atrocious
Italian accent. The* CARDINAL *is swarthy, and his accent
is even worse. The whole effect is a little grubby, among
the gilded splendor*]

POPE: I don't agree, Zambelli! I don't agree at all! It's a very
bad plan altogether. We will forfeit our honor all for 3,000
silver marks.

CARDINAL: Holy Father, there is no question of forfeiting honor,
but merely of taking the sum offered by the King of England
and thereby gaining time. To lose that sum and give a negative
answer right away would solve neither the problems of the
Curia, nor those of Thomas Becket—nor even, I am afraid,
those of the higher interests of the Church. To accept the
money—the sum is meager, I agree, and cannot be viewed
as a factor in our decision—is merely to make a gesture of
appeasement in the interests of peace in Europe. Which has
always been the supreme duty of the Holy See.

POPE: [*Concerned*] If we take money from the King, I cannot
possibly receive the Archbishop, who has been waiting here
in Rome for a whole month for me to grant him an audience.

CARDINAL: Receive the money from the King, Very Holy Father,
and receive the Archbishop too. The one will neutralize the
other. The money will remove all subversive taint from the
audience you will grant the Archbishop and on the other
hand, the reception of the Archbishop will efface whatever
taint of humiliation there may have been in accepting the
money.

POPE: [*Gloomily*] I don't want to receive him at all. I gather
he is a sincere man. I am always disconcerted by people
of that sort. They leave me with a bad taste in my mouth.

CARDINAL: Sincerity is a form of strategy, just like any other,
Holy Father. In certain very difficult negotiations, when matters

are not going ahead and the usual tactics cease to work, I have been known to use it myself. The great pitfall, of course, if your opponent starts being sincere at the same time as you. Then the game becomes horribly confusing.

POPE: You know what they say Becket's been meaning to ask me?—in the month he's spent pacing about my ante-chamber?

CARDINAL: [*Innocently*] No, Holy Father.

POPE: [*Impatiently*] Zambelli! Don't play the fox with me! It was you who told me!

CARDINAL: [*Caught out*] I beg your pardon, Holy Father, I had forgotten. Or rather, as your Holiness asked me the question, I thought you had forgotten and so I took a chance and—

POPE: [*Irritably*] Zambelli, if we start outmaneuvering each other to no purpose, we'll be here all night!

CARDINAL: [*In confusion*] Force of habit, your Holiness. Excuse me.

POPE: To ask me to relieve him of his rank and functions as Archbishop of Canterbury—that's the reason Becket is in Rome! And do you know why he wants to ask me that?

CARDINAL: [*Candidly for once*] Yes, Holy Father.

POPE: [*Irritably*] No, you do not know! It was your enemy Rapallo who told me!

CARDINAL: [*Modestly*] Yes, but I knew it just the same, because I have a spy in Rapallo's palace.

POPE: [*With a wink*] Culograti?

CARDINAL: No. Culograti is only my spy in his master's eyes. By the man I have spying on Culograti.

POPE: [*Cutting short the digression*] Becket maintains that the election of Clarendon was not a free one, that he owes his nomination solely to the royal whim and that consequently the honor of God, of which he has now decided he is champion, does not allow him to bear his usurped title any longer. He wishes to be nothing more than an ordinary priest.

CARDINAL: [*After a moment's thought*] The man is clearly an abyss of ambition.

POPE: And yet he knows that we know that his title and functions are his only safeguard against the King's anger. I don't give much for his skin wherever he is, when he is no longer Archbishop!

CARDINAL: [*Thoughtfully*] He's playing a deep game. But I have a plan. Your Holiness will pretend to believe in his scruples. You will receive him and relieve him of his titles and functions as Primate, then, immediately after, as a reward for his zeal in defending the Church of England, you will reappoint him Archbishop, in right and due form this time. We thus avert the danger, we score a point against him—and at the same time a point against the King.

POPE: That's a dangerous game. The King has a long arm.

CARDINAL: We can cover ourselves. We will send secret letters to the English court explaining that this new nomination is a pure formality and that we herewith rescind the excommunications pronounced by Becket; on the other hand, we will inform Becket of the existence of these secret letters, swearing him to secrecy and begging him to consider them as null and void.

POPE: [*Getting muddled*] In that case, perhaps there isn't much point in the letters being secret?

CARDINAL: Yes, there is. Because that will allow us to maneuver with each of them as if the other was ignorant of the contents, while taking the precaution of making it known to them both. The main thing is for them not to know that we know they know. It's so simple a child of twelve could grasp it!

POPE: But Archbishop or no, what are we going to do with Becket?

CARDINAL: [*With a lighthearted wave of his hand*] We will send him to a convent. A French convent, since King Louis is protecting him—to the Cistercians say, at Pontigny. The monastic rule is a strict one. It will do that onetime dandy a world of good! Let him learn real proverty! That will teach him to be the comforter of the poor!

POPE: That sounds like good advice, Zambelli. Bread and water and nocturnal prayers are an excellent remedy for sincerity.

[*He muses a moment*]

The only thing that puzzles me, Zambelli, is why you should want to give me a piece of good advice . . .

[*The* CARDINAL *looks a little embarrassed. The little rostra go as they came and the curtain opens revealing a small, bare cell, center stage.* BECKET *is praying before a humble wooden crucifix. Crouching in a corner, the* YOUNG MONK *is playing with a knife*]

BECKET: Yet it would be simple enough. Too simple perhaps. Saintliness is a temptation too. Oh, how difficult it is to get an answer from You, Lord! I was slow in praying to You, but I cannot believe that others, worthier than I, who have spent years asking You questions, have been better than myself at deciphering Your real intentions. I am only a beginner and I must make mistake after mistake, as I did in my Latin translations as a boy, when my riotous imagination made the old priest roar with laughter. But I cannot believe that one learns Your language as one learns any human tongue, by hard studying, with a dictionary, a grammar and a set of idioms. I am sure that to the hardened sinner, who drops to his knees for the first time and murmurs Your name, marveling, You tell him all Your secrets, straightaway, and that he understands. I have served You like a dilettante, surprised that I could still find my pleasure in Your service. And for a long time I was on my guard because of it. I could not believe this pleasure would bring me one step nearer You. I could not believe that the road could be a happy one. Their hair shirts, their fasting, their bells in the small hours summoning one to meet You, on the icy paving stones, in the sick misery of the poor ill-treated human animal—I cannot believe that all these are anything but safeguards for the weak. In power and in luxury, and even in the pleasures of the flesh, I shall not cease to speak to You, I feel this now. You are the God of the rich man and the happy man too, Lord, and therein lies Your profound justice. You do not turn away Your eyes from the man who was given everything from birth. You have not abandoned him, alone in his ensnaring facility. And he may be Your true lost sheep. For Your scheme of things, which we mistakenly call Justice, is secret and profound and You plumb the hidden depths of poor men's puny frames as carefully as those of Kings. And beneath those outward differences, which blind us, but which to You are barely noticeable; beneath the diadem or the grime, You discern the same pride, the same vanity, the same petty, complacent preoccupation with oneself. Lord, I am certain now that You meant to tempt me with this hair shirt, object of so much vapid self-congratulation! this bare cell, this solitude, this absurdly endured winter-cold —and the conveniences of prayer. It would be too easy to buy You like this, at so low a price. I shall leave this convent, where so many precautions hem You round. I shall take up the miter and the golden cope again, and the great silver cross, and I shall go back and fight in the place and with the weapons it has pleased You to give me. It has pleased You to make me Archbishop and to set me, like a solitary pawn, face to face with the King, upon the chessboard. I shall go back to my place, humbly, and let the world accuse me of pride, so that I may do what I believe is my life's work. For the rest, Your will be done.

[*He crosses himself.*
The YOUNG MONK *is still playing with his knife. Suddenly he throws it and watches as it quivers, embedded in the floor*]

CURTAIN

ACT FOUR

The King of France's Court.

KING LOUIS *comes in, holding* BECKET *familiarly by the arm.*

LOUIS: I tell you, Becket, intrigue is an ugly thing. You keep the smell about you for ages afterwards. There is a return of good understanding between the Kingdom of England and Ourselves. Peace in that direction assures me of a great advantage in the struggle which I will shortly have to undertake against the Emperor. I must protect my rear by a truce with Henry Plantagenet, before I march towards the East. And, needless to say, you are one of the items on the King's bill of charges. I can even tell you, that apart from yourself, his demands are negligible. [*Musingly*] Curious man. England's best policy would have been to take advantage of the Emperor's aggressive intentions and close the other jaw of the trap. He is deliberately sacrificing this opportunity for the pleasure of seeing you driven out. He really hates you, doesn't he?

BECKET: [*Simply*] Sire, we loved each other and I think he cannot forgive me for preferring God to him.

LOUIS: Your King isn't doing his job properly, Archbishop. He is giving way to passion. However! He has chosen to score a point against you, instead of against me. You are on his bill, I have to pay his price and banish you. I do not do so without a certain shame. Where are you thinking of going?

BECKET: I am a shepherd who has remained too long away from

his flock. I intend to go back to England. I had already made
my decision before this audience with your Majesty.

LOUIS: [*Surprised*] You have a taste for martyrdom? You disappoint me. I thought you more healthy-minded.

BECKET: Would it be healthy-minded to walk the roads of Europe,
and beg a refuge where my carcass would be safe? Besides,
where would I be safe? I am a Primate of England. That is
a rather showy label on my back. The honor of God and common sense, which for once coincide, dictate that instead of
risking the knife thrust of some hired assassin, on the highway,
I should go and have myself killed—if killed I must be—clad
in my golden cope, with my miter on my head and my silver
cross in my hand, among my flock in my own cathedral. That
place alone befits me.

[*A pause*]

LOUIS: I daresay you're right. [*He sighs*] Ah, what a pity it is to
be a King, sometimes, when one has the surprise of meeting
a man! You'll tell me, fortunately for me, that men are rare.
Why weren't you born on this side of the Channel, Becket?
[*He smiles*] True, you would no doubt have been a thorn in
my side then! The honor of God is a very cumbersome thing.

[*He muses for a moment and then says abruptly:*]

Who cares, I'll risk it! I like you too much. I'll indulge in a
moment's humanity. I am going to try something, even if your
master does seize on the chance to double his bill. After all,
banishing you would merely have cost me a small slice of
honor . . . I am meeting Henry in a day or two, at La
Ferté-Bernard, to seal our agreement. I shall try to persuade
him to make his peace with you. Should he agree, will you be
willing to talk with him?

BECKET: Sire, ever since we stopped seeing each other, I have never
ceased to talk to him.

[*Blackout. Prolonged blare of trumpets. The set is completely removed. Nothing remains but the cyclorama*

*around the bare stage. A vast, arid plain, lashed by the
wind. Trumpets again. Two* SENTRIES *are on stage, watching something in the distance*]

SENTRY: Open those eyes of yours, lad. And drink it all in. You're
new to the job, but you won't see something like this every
day! This is a historic meeting!

YOUNG SENTRY: I daresay, but it's perishing cold! How long
are they going to keep us hanging about?

SENTRY: We're sheltered by the wood here, but you can bet they're
even colder than we are, out there in the plain.

YOUNG SENTRY: Look! They've come up to each other! I wonder what they're talking about?

SENTRY: What do you think they're talking about, muttonhead?
Inquiring how things are at home? Complaining about their
chilblains? The fate of the world, that's what they're arguing
about! Things you and I won't ever understand. Even the
words those bigwigs use—why, you wouldn't even know what
they meant!

[*They go off. The lights go up.* BECKET *and the* KING,
*on horseback, are alone in the middle of the plain, facing
each other. Throughout the scene, the winter blizzard
wails like a shrill dirge beneath their words. And during
their silences, only the wind is heard*]

KING: You look older, Thomas.

BECKET: You too, Highness. Are you sure you aren't too cold?

KING: I'm frozen stiff. You love it of course! You're in your element, aren't you? And you're barefooted as well!

BECKET: [*Smiling*] That's my latest affectation.

KING: Even with these fur boots on, my chilblains are killing me.
Aren't yours, or don't you have any?

BECKET: [*Gently*] Of course.

KING: [*Cackling*] You're offering them up to God, I hope, holy
monk?

BECKET: [*Gravely*] I have better things to offer Him.

KING: [*With a sudden cry*] If we start straightaway, we're sure to quarrel! Let's talk about trivial things. You know my son is fourteen? He's come of age.

BECKET: Has he improved at all?

KING: He's a little idiot and sly like his mother. Becket, don't you ever marry!

BECKET: [*Smiling*] The matter has been taken out of my hands. By you, Highness! It was you who had me ordained!

KING: [*With a cry*] Let's not start yet, I tell you! Talk about something else!

BECKET: [*Lightly*] Has your Highness done much hunting lately?

KING: [*Snarling*] Yes, every day! And it doesn't amuse me any more.

BECKET: Have you any new hawks?

KING: [*Furiously*] The most expensive on the market! But they don't fly straight.

BECKET: And your horses?

KING: The Sultan sent me four superb stallions for the tenth anniversary of my reign. But they throw everyone! Nobody has managed to mount one of them, yet!

BECKET: [*Smiling*] I must see what I can do about that some day.

KING: They'll throw you too! And we'll see your buttocks under your robe! At least, I hope so, or everything would be too dismal.

BECKET: [*After a pause*] Do you know what I miss most, Sire? The horses.

KING: And the women?

BECKET: [*Simply*] I've forgotten.

KING: You hypocrite. You turned into a hypocrite when you became a priest. [*Abruptly*] Did you love Gwendolen?

BECKET: I've forgotten her too.

KING: You did love her! That's the only way I can account for it.

BECKET: [*Gravely*] No, my prince, in my soul and conscience, I did not love her.

KING: Then you never loved anything, that's worse! [*Churlishly*] Why are you calling me your prince, like in the old days?

BECKET: [*Gently*] Because you have remained my prince.

KING: [*Crying out*] Then why are you doing me harm?

BECKET: [*Gently*] Let's talk about something else.

KING: Well, what? I'm cold.

BECKET: I always told you, my prince, that one must fight the cold with the cold's own weapons. Strip naked and splash yourself with cold water every morning.

KING: I used to when you were there to force me into it. I never wash now. I stink. I grew a beard at one time. Did you know?

BECKET: [*Smiling*] Yes. I had a hearty laugh over it.

KING: I cut it off because it itched.

[*He cries out suddenly, like a lost child:*]

Becket, I'm bored!

BECKET: [*Gravely*] My prince. I do so wish I could help you.

KING: Then what are you waiting for? You can see I'm dying for it!

BECKET: [*Quietly*] I'm waiting for the honor of God and the honor of the King to become one.

KING: You'll wait a long time then!

BECKET: Yes. I'm afraid I will.

[*A pause. Only the wind is heard*]

KING: [*Suddenly*] If we've nothing more to say to each other, we might as well go and get warm!

BECKET: We have everything to say to each other, my prince. The opportunity may not occur again.

KING: Make haste, then. Or there'll be two frozen statues on this plain making their peace in a frozen eternity! I am your King, Becket! And so long as we are on this earth you owe me the first move! I'm prepared to forget a lot of things but not the fact that I am King. You yourself taught me that.

BECKET: [*Gravely*] Never forget it, my prince. Even against God. You have a different task to do. You have to steer the ship.

KING: And you—what do you have to do?

BECKET: Resist you with all my might, when you steer against the wind.

KING: Do you expect the wind to be behind me, Becket? No such luck! That's the fairy-tale navigation! God on the King's side? That's never happened yet! Yes, once in a century, at the time of the Crusades, when all Christendom shouts "It's God's will!" And even then! You know as well as I do what private greeds a Crusade covers up, in nine cases out of ten. The rest of the time, it's a head-on wind. And there must be somebody to keep the watch!

BECKET: And somebody else to cope with the absurd wind—and with God. The tasks have been shared out, once and for all. The pity of it is that it should have been between us two, my prince—who were friends.

KING: [*Crossly*] The King of France—I still don't know what he hopes to gain by it—preached at me for three whole days for me to make my peace with you. What good would it do you to provoke me beyond endurance?

BECKET: None.

KING: You know that I am the King, and that I must act like a King! What do you expect of me? Are you hoping I'll weaken?

BECKET: No. That would prostrate me.

KING: Do you hope to conquer me by force then?

BECKET: You are the strong one.

KING: To win me round?

BECKET: No. Not that either. It is not for me to win you round. I have only to say no to you.

KING: But you must be logical, Becket!

BECKET: No. That isn't necessary, my Liege. We must only do—absurdly—what we have been given to do—right to the end.

KING: Yet I know you well enough, God knows. Ten years we spent together, little Saxon! At the hunt, at the whorehouse, at war; carousing all night long the two of us; in the same girl's bed, sometimes . . . and at work in the Council Chamber too. Absurdly. That word isn't like you.

BECKET: Perhaps. I am no longer like myself.

KING: [*Derisively*] Have you been touched by grace?

BECKET: [*Gravely*] Not by the one you think. I am not worthy of it.

KING: Did you feel the Saxon in you coming out, despite Papa's good collaborator's sentiments?

BECKET: No. Not that either.

KING: What then?

BECKET: I felt for the first time that I was being entrusted with something, that's all—there in that empty cathedral, somewhere in France, that day when you ordered me to take up this burden. I was a man without honor. And suddenly I found it —one I never imagined would ever become mine—the honor of God. A frail, incomprehensible honor, vulnerable as a boy-King fleeing from danger.

KING: [*Roughly*] Suppose we talked a little more precisely, Becket, with words I understand? Otherwise we'll be here all night. I'm cold. And the others are waiting for us on the fringes of this plain.

BECKET: I am being precise.

KING: I'm an idiot then! Talk to me like an idiot! That's an order. Will you lift the excommunication which you pronounced on William of Aynsford and others of my liegemen?

BECKET: No, Sire, because that is the only weapon I have to defend this child, who was given, naked, into my care.

KING: Will you agree to the twelve proposals which my Bishops have accepted in your absence at Northampton, and notably to forego the much-abused protection of Saxon clerics who get themselves tonsured to escape land bondage?

BECKET: No, Sire. My role is to defend my sheep. And they are my sheep.

[A *pause*]

Nor will I concede that the Bishops should forego the right to appoint priests in their own dioceses, nor that churchmen should be subject to any but the Church's jurisdiction. These are my duties as a pastor—which it is not for me to relinquish. But I shall agree to the nine other articles in a spirit of peace, and because I know that you must remain King—in all save the honor of God.

[*A pause*]

KING: [*Coldly*] Very well. I will help you defend your God, since that is your new vocation, in memory of the companion you once were to me—in all save the honor of the Realm. You may come back to England, Thomas.

BECKET: Thank you, my prince. I meant to go back in any case and give myself up to your power, for on this earth, you are my King. And in all that concerns this earth, I owe you obedience.

[*A pause*]

KING: [*Ill at ease*] Well, let's go back now. We've finished. I'm cold.

BECKET: [*Dully*] I feel cold too, now.

[*Another pause. They look at each other. The wind howls*]

KING: [*Suddenly*] You never loved me, did you, Becket?

BECKET: In so far as I was capable of love, yes, my prince, I did.

KING: Did you start to love God?

[*He cries out:*]

You mule! Can't you ever answer a simple question?

BECKET: [*Quietly*] I started to love the honor of God.

KING: [*Somberly*] Come back to England. I give you my royal peace. May you find yours. And may you not discover you

were wrong about yourself. This is the last time I shall come
begging to you.

[*He cries out:*]

I should never have seen you again! It hurts too much.

[*His whole body is suddenly shaken by a sob*]

BECKET: [*Goes nearer to him; moved*] My prince—
KING: [*Yelling*] No! No pity! It's dirty. Stand away from me!
Go back to England! It's too cold out here!

[BECKET *turns his horse and moves nearer to the* KING]

BECKET: [*Gravely*] Farewell, my prince. Will you give me the
kiss of peace?
KING: No! I can't bear to come near you! I can't bear to look at
you! Later! Later! When it doesn't hurt any more!
BECKET: I shall set sail tomorrow. Farewell, my prince. I know
I shall never see you again.
KING: [*His face twisted with hatred*] How dare you say that to
me after I gave you my royal word? Do you take me for a
traitor?

[BECKET *looks at him gravely for a second longer, with a
sort of pity in his eyes. Then he slowly turns his horse
and rides away. The wind howls*]

KING: Thomas!

[*But* BECKET *has not heard. The* KING *does not call a
second time. He spurs his horse and gallops off in the
other direction. The lights fade. The wind howls.
The lights change. Red curtains fall.* BECKET'S *whistled
march is heard off stage during the scene change. The curtains open. Royal music. King Henry's palace somewhere in
France. The two* QUEENS, *the* BARONS *and Henry's* SON *are
standing around the dinner table, waiting. The* KING, *his*

*eyes gleaming maliciously, looks at them and then ex-
claims:*]

KING: Today, gentlemen, I shall not be the first to sit down!
[*To his* SON, *with a comic bow*] You are the King, Sir. The
honor belongs to you. Take the high chair. Today I shall wait
on you!

QUEEN MOTHER: [*With slight irritation*] My son!

KING: I know what I'm doing, Madam! [*With a sudden shout*]
Go on, you great loon, look sharp! You're the King, but you're
stupid as ever!

> [*The boy flinches to avoid the blow he was expecting
> and goes to sit in the* KING's *chair, sly and rather ill at
> ease*]

Take your places, gentlemen! I shall remain standing. Barons
of England, here is your second King. For the good of our vast
domains, a kingly colleague had become a necessity. Reviving
an ancient custom, we have decided to have our successor
crowned during our lifetime and to share our responsibilities
with him. We ask you now to give him your homage and to
honor him with the same title as Ourself.

> [*He makes a sign. Two* SERVANTS *have brought in a
> haunch of venison on a silver charger. The* KING *serves his
> son*]

YOUNG QUEEN: [*To her* SON] Sit up straight! And try to eat
properly for once, now that you've been raised to glory!

KING: [*Grunting as he serves him*] He hasn't the face for it!
He's a little slyboots and dim-witted at that. However, he'll be
your King in good earnest one day, so you may as well get
used to him. Besides, it's the best I had to offer.

QUEEN MOTHER: [*Indignantly*] Really, my son! This game is
unworthy of you and of us. You insisted on it—against my
advice—at least play it with dignity!

KING: [*Rounding on her in fury*] I'll play the games that amuse
me, Madam, and I'll play them the way I choose! This mum-

mery, gentlemen, which is, incidentally, without any importance at all—if your new King fidgets, let me know, I'll give
him a good kick up his train—will at the very least have the
appreciable result of showing our new friend, the Archbishop,
that we can do without him. If there was one ancient privilege
the Primacy clung to, tooth and nail, it was its exclusive right
to anoint and consecrate the Kings of this realm. Well, it will
be that old toad the Archbishop of York—with letters from
the Pope authorizing him to do so—I paid the price!—who,
tomorrow, will crown our son in the cathedral! What a joke
that's going to be!

[*He roars with laughter amid the general silence*]

What a tremendous, marvelous joke! I'd give anything to see
that Archbishop's face when he has to swallow that! [*To his*
SON] Get down from there, you imbecile! Go back to the
bottom of the table and take your victuals with you! You
aren't officially crowned until tomorrow.

[*The boy picks up his plate and goes back to his place,
casting a cowed, smoldering look at his father*]

[*Watching him, says jovially:*] What a look! Filial sentiments
are a fine thing to see, gentlemen! You'd like to be the real
King, wouldn't you, you young pig? You'd like that number
III after your name, eh, with Papa good and stiff under his
catafalque! You'll have to wait a bit! Papa is well. Papa is very
well indeed!

QUEEN MOTHER: My son, God knows I criticized your attempts
at reconciliation with that wretch, who has done us nothing
but harm . . . God knows I understand your hatred of him! But
do not let it drag you into making a gesture you will regret,
merely for the sake of wounding his pride. Henry is still a child.
But you were not much older when you insisted on reigning
by yourself, and in opposition to me. Ambitious self-seekers—
and there is never any scarcity of those around Princes—can
advise him, raise a faction against you and avail themselves of
this hasty coronation to divide the Kingdom! Think it over,
there is still time.

KING: We are still alive, Madam, and in control! And nothing can equal my pleasure in imagining my proud friend Becket's face when he sees the fundamental privilege of the Primacy whisked from under his nose! I let him cheat me out of one or two articles the other day, but I had something up my sleeve for him!

QUEEN MOTHER: Henry! I bore the weight of state affairs longer than you ever have. I have been your Queen and I am your mother. You are answerable for the interests of a great Kingdom, not for your moods. You already gave far too much away to the King of France, at La Ferté-Bernard. It is England you must think of, not your hatred—or disappointed love—for that man.

KING: [*In a fury*] Disappointed love—disappointed love? What gives you the right, Madam, to meddle in my loves and hates?

QUEEN MOTHER: You have a rancor against the man which is neither healthy nor manly. The King, your father, dealt with his enemies faster and more summarily than that. He had them killed and said no more about it. If Thomas Becket were a faithless woman whom you still hankered after, you would act no differently. Sweet Jesu, tear him out of your heart once and for all!

[*She bawls suddenly:*]

Oh, if I were a man!

KING: [*Grinning*] Thanks be to God, Madam, he gave you dugs. Which I never personally benefited from. I suckled a peasant girl.

QUEEN MOTHER: [*Acidly*] That is no doubt why you have remained so lumpish, my son.

YOUNG QUEEN: And haven't I a say in the matter? I tolerated your mistresses, Sir, but do you expect me to tolerate everything? Have you ever stopped to think what kind of woman I am? I am tired of having my life encumbered with this man. Becket! Always Becket! Nobody ever talks about anything else here! He was almost less of a hindrance when you loved him. I am a woman. I am your wife and your Queen. I refuse to be treated like this! I shall complain to my father, the Duke of Aquitaine! I shall complain to my uncle, the Emperor! I shall complain to all the Kings of Europe, my cousins! I shall complain to God!

KING: [*Shouting rather vulgarly*] I should start with God! Be off to your private chapel, Madam, and see if He's at home.

[*He turns to his mother, fuming*]

And you, the other Madam, away to your chamber with your secret councilors and go and spin your webs! Get out, both of you! I can't stand the sight of you! I retch with boredom whenever I set eyes on you! And young Henry III too! Go on, get out!

[*He chases him out with kicks, yelling:*]

Here's my royal foot in your royal buttocks! And to the devil with my whole family, if he'll have you! Get out, all of you! Get out! Get out! Get out!

[*The QUEENS scurry out, with a great rustling of silks. He turns to the BARONS who all stand watching him, terror-stricken.*]

[*More calmly*] Let us drink, gentlemen. That's about all one can do in your company. Let us get drunk, like men, all night; until we roll under the table, in vomit and oblivion.

[*He fills their glasses and beckons them closer*]

Ah, my four idiots! My faithful hounds! It's warm beside you, like being in a stable. Good sweat! Comfortable nothingness!

[*He taps their skulls*]

Not the least little glimmer inside to spoil the fun. And to think that before he came I was like you! A good fat machine for belching after drink, for pissing, for mounting girls and punch-

ing heads. What the devil did you put into it, Becket, to
stop the wheels from going round? [*Suddenly to the* 2ND
BARON] Tell me, do you think sometimes, Baron?

2ND BARON: Never, Sire. Thinking has never agreed with an
Englishman. It's unhealthy. Besides, a gentleman has better
things to do.

KING: [*Sitting beside them, suddenly quite calm*] Drink up,
gentlemen. That's always been considered a healthy thing to do.

[*He fills the goblets*]

Has Becket landed? I'm told the sea has been too rough to
cross these last few days.

1ST BARON: [*Somberly*] He has landed, Sire, despite the sea.

KING: Where?

1ST BARON: On a deserted stretch of coast, near Sandwich.

KING: So God did not choose to drown him?

1ST BARON: No.

KING: [*He asks in his sly, brutish way:*] Was nobody there waiting
for him? There must be one or two men in England whom
he can't call his friends!

1ST BARON: Yes. Gervase, Duke of Kent, Regnouf de Broc and
Regnault de Garenne were waiting for him. Gervase had said
that if he dared to land he'd cut off his head with his own
hands. But the native Englishmen from all the coastal towns
had armed themselves to form an escort for the Archbishop.
And the Dean of Oxford went to meet the Barons and charged
them not to cause bloodshed and make you look a traitor,
seeing that you had given the Archbishop a safe conduct.

KING: [*Soberly*] Yes, I gave him a safe conduct.

1ST BARON: All along the road to Canterbury, the peasants, the
artisans and the small shopkeepers came out to meet him,
cheering him and escorting him from village to village. Not
a single rich man, not a single Norman, showed his face.

KING: Only the Saxons?

1ST BARON: Poor people armed with makeshift shields and rusty lances. Riffraff. Swarms of them though, all camping around Canterbury, to protect him. [*Gloomily*] Who would have thought there were so many people in England!

[*The* KING *has remained prostrate without uttering a word. Now he suddenly jumps up and roars:*]

KING: A miserable wretch who ate my bread! A man I raised up from nothing! A Saxon! A man loved! [*Shouting like a madman*] I loved him! Yes, I loved him! And I believe I still do! Enough, O God! Enough! Stop, stop, O God, I've had enough!

[*He flings himself down on the couch, sobbing hysterically; tearing at the horsehair mattress with his teeth, and eating it. The* BARONS, *stupefied, go nearer to him*]

1ST BARON: [*Timidly*] Your Highness . . .

KING: [*Moaning, with his head buried in the mattress*] I can do nothing! Nothing! I'm as limp and useless as a girl! So long as he's alive, I'll never be able to do a thing. I tremble before him astonished. And I am the King! [*With a sudden cry*] Will no one rid me of him? A priest! A priest who jeers at me and does me injury! Are there none but cowards like myself around me? Are there no men left in England? Oh, my heart is beating too fast to bear!

[*He lies, still as death on the torn mattress. The four* BARONS *stand around speechless. Suddenly, on a percussion instrument, there rises a rhythmic beating, a sort of muffled tom-tom which is at first only the agitated heartbeats of the* KING, *but which swells and grows more insistent. The four* BARONS *look at each other. Then they straighten, buckle their sword belts, pick up their helmets and go slowly out, leaving the* KING *alone with the muffled rhythm of the heartbeats, which will continue until the murder. The* KING *lies there prostrate, among the upturned benches, in the deserted hall. A torch splutters and goes out. He sits up, looks around, sees they have gone and suddenly realizes why. A wild, lost look comes into his eyes. A moment's*] *pause then he collapses on the bed with a long broken moan]*

KING: O my Thomas!

[A second torch goes out. Total darkness. Only the steady throb of the heartbeats is heard. A dim light. The forest of pillars again. Canterbury Cathedral. Upstage a small altar, with three steps leading up to it, half screened by a grill. In a corner downstage BECKET, and the YOUNG MONK, who is helping him on with his vestments. Nearby, on a stool, the Archbishop's miter. The tall silver cross is leaning against a pillar]

BECKET: I must look my best today. Make haste.

[The MONK fumbles with the vestments. The muffled tom-tom is heard distantly at first, then closer]

MONK: It's difficult with all those little laces. It wants a girl's hands.

BECKET: *[Softly]* A man's hands are better, today. Never mind the laces. The alb, quickly. And the stole. And then the cope.

MONK: *[Conscientiously]* If it's worth doing it's worth doing well.

BECKET: You're quite right. If it's worth doing it's worth doing well. Do up all the little laces, every one of them. God will give us time.

[A pause. The boy struggles manfully on, putting out his tongue in concentration. The throbbing grows louder]

[Smiling] Don't pull your tongue out like that!

[He watches the boy as he works away]

MONK: *[Sweating but content]* There. That's all done. But I'd rather have cleaned out our pigsty at home! It's not half such hard work!

BECKET: Now the alb.

[A *pause*]

Were you fond of your pigs?

MONK: [*His eyes lighting up*] Yes, I was.

BECKET: At my father's house, we had some pigs too, when I was a child. [*Smiling*] We're two rough lads from Hastings, you and I! Give me the chasuble.

[BECKET *kisses the chasuble and slips it over his head. He looks at the boy and says gently:*]

Do you miss your knife?

MONK: Yes.

[*Pause*]

Will it be today?

BECKET: [*Gravely*] I think so, my son. Are you afraid?

MONK: Oh, no. Not if we have time to fight. All I want is the chance to strike a few blows first; so I shan't have done nothing but receive them all my life. If I can kill one Norman first—just one, I don't want much—one for one, that will seem fair and right enough to me.

BECKET: [*With a kindly smile*] Are you so very set on killing one?

MONK: One for one. After that, I don't much care if I *am* just a little grain of sand in the machine. Because I know that by putting more and more grains of sand in the machine, one day it will come grinding to a stop.

BECKET: [*Gently*] And on that day, what then?

MONK: We'll set a fine, new, well-oiled machine in the place of the old one and this time we'll put the Normans into it instead.

[*He asks, quite without irony:*]

That's what justice means, isn't it?

[BECKET *smiles and does not answer him*]

BECKET: Fetch me the miter.

[*He says quietly, as the boy fetches it:*]

O Lord, You forbade Peter to strike a blow in the Garden of Olives. But I shall not deprive him of that joy. He has had too few joys in his short span on earth. [*To the boy*] Now give me my silver cross. I must hold it.

MONK: [*Passing it to him*] Lord, it's heavy! A good swipe with that and they'd feel it! My word, I wish I could have it!

BECKET: [*Stroking his hair*] Lucky little Saxon! This black world will have been in order to the end, for you.

[*He straightens, grave once more*]

There. I'm ready, all adorned for Your festivities, Lord. Do not, in this interval of waiting, let one last doubt enter my soul.

[*During this scene, the throbbing has grown louder. Now it mingles with a loud knocking on the door. A* PRIEST *runs in wildly*]

PRIEST: Your Grace! There are four armed men outside! They say they must see you on behalf of the King. I've barricaded the door but they're breaking it in! They've got hatchets! Quickly! You must go into the back of the church and have the choir gates closed! They're strong enough, they'll hold!

BECKET: [*Calmly*] It is time for Vespers, William. Does one close the choir gates during Vespers? I never heard of such a thing.

PRIEST: [*Nonplused*] I know, but . . .

BECKET: Everything must be the way it should be. The choir gates will remain open. Come, boy, let us go up to the altar. This is no place to be.

[*He goes toward the altar, followed by the* YOUNG MONK. *A great crash. The door has given way. The four* BARONS *come in, in their helmets. They fling down their hatchets and draw their swords.* BECKET *turns to face them, grave and calm, at the foot of the altar. They stop a moment, uncertain and disconcerted; four statues, huge and threatening. The tom-tom has stopped. There is nothing now but a heavy silence.* BECKET *says simply:*]

Here it comes. The supreme folly. This is its hour.

[*He holds their eyes. They dare not move. He says coldly:*]

One does not enter armed into God's house. What do you want?

1ST BARON: [*Thickly*] Your death.

[*A pause*]

2ND BARON: [*Thickly*] You bring shame to the King. Flee the country or you're a dead man.

BECKET: [*Softly*] It is time for the service.

[*He turns to the altar and faces the tall crucifix without paying any further attention to them. The throbbing starts again, muffled. The four men close in like automata. The* YOUNG MONK *suddenly leaps forward brandishing the heavy silver cross in order to protect* BECKET, *but one of the* BARONS *swings his sword and fells him to the ground.* BECKET *murmurs, as if in reproach:*]

Not even one! It would have given him so much pleasure, Lord. [*With a sudden cry*] Oh how difficult You make it all! And how heavy Your honor is to bear!

[*He adds, very quietly:*]

Poor Henry.

[*The four men hurl themselves onto him. He falls at the
first blow. They hack at his body, grunting like woodcutters.
The* PRIEST *has fled with a long scream, which echoes in
the empty cathedral.
Blackout.
On the same spot. The* KING, *naked, on bended knees at*
BECKET's *tomb, as in the first scene. Four* MONKS *are whip-
ping him with ropes, almost duplicating the gestures of the*
BARONS *as they killed* BECKET]

KING: [*Crying out*] Are you satisfied now, Becket? Does this
settle our account? Has the honor of God been washed clean?

[*The four* MONKS *finish beating him, then kneel down and
bow their heads. The* KING *mutters—one feels it is part of
the ceremony:*]

Thank you. Yes, yes, of course, it was agreed, I forgive you.
Many thanks.

[*The* PAGE *comes forward with a vast cloak, which the*
KING *wraps around himself. The* BARONS *surround the* KING
and help him to dress, while the BISHOPS *and the* CLERGY,
*forming a procession, move away solemnly upstage to the
strains of the organ. The* KING *dresses hurriedly, with evident bad temper, aided by his* BARONS. *He grimaces ill-
humoredly and growls:*]

The pigs! The Norman Bishops just went through the motions,
but those little Saxon monks—my word, they had their money's
worth!

[*A* BARON *comes in. A joyful peal of bells is heard*]

BARON: Sire, the operation has been successful! The Saxon mob
is yelling with enthusiasm outside the cathedral, acclaiming your
Majesty's name in the same breath as Becket's! If the Saxons
are on our side now, Prince Henry's followers look as though
they have definitely lost the day.

KING: [*With a touch of hypocritical majesty beneath his slightly loutish manner*] The honor of God, gentlemen, is a very good thing, and taken all in all, one gains by having it on one's side. Thomas Becket, who was our friend, used to say so. England will owe her ultimate victory over chaos to him, and it is our wish that, henceforward, he should be honored and prayed to in this Kingdom as a saint. Come, gentlemen. We will determine, tonight, in Council, what posthumous honors to render him and what punishment to deal out to his murderers.

1ST BARON: [*Imperturbably*] Sire, they are unknown.

KING: [*Impenetrably*] Our justice will seek them out, Baron, and you will be specially entrusted with this inquiry, so that no one will be in any doubt as to our Royal desire to defend the honor of God and the memory of our friend from this day forward.

> [*The organ swells triumphantly, mingled with the sound of the bells and the cheering of the crowds as they file out*]

CURTAIN

Tennessee Williams

The life and career of Tennessee Williams (born Thomas Lanier Williams in Columbus, Mississippi, in 1911) have been so thoroughly documented in countless periodicals and books, as well as in critical and biographical studies, that there seems little need for reiteration in the pages of this collection. Merely to list Mr. Williams' plays is sufficient for the evocation of many memorable moments in the theatre, for he has peopled the world's stages with characters so durably vibrant that their presences still stalk the corridors of a play-goer's memory.

It is true, perhaps, that the Sixties—with the exception of *The Night of the Iguana*, one of his most powerful and compassionate dramatic statements of the tragic meaning of human frailty—were not particularly kind to the distinguished dramatist. But then, isn't this the rule rather than the exception in the arts: to topple over what one previously has placed on a pedestal? Yet, Tennessee Williams, recipient of two Pulitzer Prizes and four New York Drama Critics' Circle Awards remains, indisputably, a consummate master of theatre. His plays pulsate with the heart's blood of the drama: passion. And although there may be dissenting voices in the wings (stomping perhaps for Arthur Miller, Edward Albee or a half dozen other candidates), this editor (and, assuredly, he is not alone in his belief) contends that Tennessee Williams is the greatest American playwright since Eugene O'Neill. A strong, even debatable, assertion perhaps, but when one re-examines Mr. Williams' predominant works, one cannot but be awed by the dazzling skill of a remarkable dramatist whose major plays no longer tend to be merely plays but, somehow, through the process of creative genius, have transcended into haunting realities.

Tennessee Williams is an electrifying dramatist because, in the main, he creates people who are the sort who breathe fire into scenes, explosively and woundingly. His dialogue reverberates with a lilting eloquence far from the drab, disjunctive patterns of everyday speech and, above all, he is a master of mood. At times, it is hot, oppressive, simmering with catastrophe as in *A Streetcar Named Desire* and *Cat on a Hot Tin Roof*; at other times, it is sad, autumnal, elegiac as in *The Glass Menagerie* and *The Night of the Iguana*. To achieve it, he utilizes the full complement of theatrical instruments: setting, lighting, music, plus that most intangible of gifts, the genius for making an audience forget that any other world exists except the one onstage.

As Mr. Williams often has stated, his special compassion is for "the people who are not meant to win—the lost, the odd, the strange, the difficult people—fragile people who lack talons for the jungle." The clarion call of many, if not most, of his plays is loneliness. Just as the captured iguana in *The Night of the Iguana* symbolizes the bondage to which the people who populate the play are chained, so do his characters in other of his dramas yearn to break loose, out of the cell of the lonely self, to touch and reach another person. "Hell is yourself," Mr. Williams has said. "When you ignore other people completely, that is hell." The revelation toward which all of his plays aspire to is that "moment of self-transcendence, when a person puts himself aside to feel deeply for another person."

The author's enormous talent first won general recognition with the 1945 production of *The Glass Menagerie*, starring Laurette Taylor. Thereafter, he attained world-wide repute with a succession of impressive plays, notably: *A Streetcar Named Desire* (1947); *Summer and Smoke* (1948); *The Rose Tattoo* (1951); *Cat on a Hot Tin Roof* (1955); and *The Night of the Iguana* (1961). Among his other plays, in nonchronological order: *Sweet Bird of Youth*; *Camino Real*; *Orpheus Descending*; *Period of Adjustment*; *The Milk Train Doesn't Stop Here Anymore*; *Kingdom of Earth* (known in its Broadway manifestation as *The Seven Descents of Myrtle*); and most recently, *In the Bar of a Tokyo Hotel*.

Mr. Williams also has written a number of short plays, including *Suddenly Last Summer* and *27 Wagons Full of Cotton*, several volumes of short stories, a book of poetry and a novella, *The Roman Spring of Mrs. Stone.*

A firm disciplinarian where his work is concerned (though, admittedly, not about himself), the dramatist dedicates four hours of each day—"year in, year out"—to writing and about every two years completes a new play. Before settling down to the actual task of writing, however, he "marinates impressions, characters, experiences." *The Night of the Iguana* emerged from a 1940 trip to Acapulco. In 1946, the author's observations and reflections developed into a short story, which in 1959 was transmuted into a short play, produced in Spoleto, Italy. Four separate versions followed before the dramatist was "satisfied" and when *The Night of the Iguana* finally opened on Broadway in December 1961, it was evident that Tennessee Williams possibly was in his finest dramatic form since *A Streetcar Named Desire,* and the play brought him his *fourth* award from the New York Drama Critics' Circle.

THE NIGHT
OF THE IGUANA

Tennessee Williams

The Night of the Iguana was first presented at the Royale Theatre, New York, on December 28, 1961, by Charles Bowden, in association with Violla Rubber. The cast was as follows:

MAXINE FAULK	*Bette Davis*
PEDRO	*James Farentino*
PANCHO	*Christopher Jones*
REVEREND SHANNON	*Patrick O'Neal*
HANK	*Theseus George*
HERR FAHRENKOPF	*Heinz Hohenwald*
FRAU FAHRENKOPF	*Lucy Landau*
WOLFGANG	*Bruce Glover*
HILDA	*Laryssa Lauret*
JUDITH FELLOWES	*Patricia Roe*
HANNAH JELKES	*Margaret Leighton*
CHARLOTTE GOODALL	*Lane Bradbury*
JONATHAN COFFIN (NONNO)	*Alan Webb*
JAKE LATTA	*Louis Guss*

Directed by Frank Corsaro
Setting by Oliver Smith
Lighting by Jean Rosenthal
Costumes by Noel Taylor
Audio Effects by Edward Beyer

Production owned and presented by "The Night of the Iguana" Joint Venture (the joint venture consisting of Charles Bowden and Two Rivers Enterprises, Inc.).

SCENE: *The play takes place in the summer of 1940 in a rather rustic and very Bohemian hotel, the Costa Verde, which, as its name implies, sits on a jungle-covered hilltop overlooking the "caleta," or "morning beach" of Puerto Barrio in Mexico. But this is decidedly not the Puerto Barrio of today. At that time—twenty years ago—the west coast of Mexico had not yet become the Las Vegas and Miami Beach of Mexico. The villages were still predominantly primitive Indian villages, and the still-water morning beach of Puerto Barrio and the rain forests above it were among the world's wildest and loveliest populated places.*

The setting for the play is the wide verandah of the hotel. This roofed verandah, enclosed by a railing, runs around all four sides of the somewhat dilapidated, tropical-style frame structure, but on the stage we see only the front and one side. Below the verandah, which is slightly raised above the stage level, are shrubs with vivid trumpet-shaped flowers and a few cactus plants, while at the sides we see the foliage of the encroaching jungle. A tall coconut palm slants upward at one side, its trunk notched for a climber to chop down coconuts for rum-cocos. In the back wall of the verandah are the doors of a line of small cubicle bedrooms which are screened with mosquito-net curtains. For the night scenes they are lighted from within, so that each cubicle appears as a little interior stage, the curtains giving a misty effect to their dim inside lighting. A path which goes down through the rain forest to the highway and the beach, its opening masked by foliage, leads off from one side of the verandah. A canvas hammock is strung from posts on the verandah and there are a few old wicker rockers and rattan lounging chairs at one side.

ACT ONE

As the curtain rises, there are sounds of a party of excited female tourists arriving by bus on the road down the hill below the Costa Verde Hotel. MRS. MAXINE FAULK, *the proprietor of the hotel, comes around the turn of the verandah. She is a stout, swarthy woman in her middle forties—affable and rapaciously lusty. She is wearing a pair of levis and a blouse that is half unbuttoned. She is followed by* PEDRO, *a Mexican of about twenty—slim and attractive. He is an employee in the hotel and also her casual lover.* PEDRO *is stuffing his shirt under the belt of his pants and sweating as if he had been working hard in the sun.* MRS. FAULK *looks down the hill and is pleased by the sight of someone coming up from the tourist bus below.*

MAXINE: [*Calling out*] Shannon! [*A man's voice from below answers: "Hi!"*] Hah! [MAXINE *always laughs with a single harsh, loud bark, opening her mouth like a seal expecting a fish to be thrown to it*] My spies told me that you were back under the border! [*To* PEDRO] Anda, hombre, anda!

[MAXINE's *delight expands and vibrates in her as* SHANNON *labors up the hill to the hotel. He does not appear on the jungle path for a minute or two after the shouting between them starts*]

MAXINE: Hah! My spies told me you went through Saltillo last week with a busload of women—a whole busload of females, all females, hah! How many you laid so far? Hah!

SHANNON: [*From below, panting*] Great Caesar's ghost . . . stop . . . shouting!

MAXINE: No wonder your ass is draggin', hah!

SHANNON: Tell the kid to help me up with this bag.

MAXINE: [*Shouting directions*] Pedro! Anda—la maléta. Pancho, no seas flojo! Va y trae el equipaje del señor.

> [PANCHO, *another young Mexican, comes around the verandah and trots down the jungle path.* PEDRO *has climbed up a coconut tree with a machete and is chopping down nuts for rum-cocos*]

SHANNON: [*Shouting, below*] Fred? Hey, Fred!

MAXINE: [*With a momentary gravity*] Fred can't hear you, Shannon. [*She goes over and picks up a coconut, shaking it against her ear to see if it has milk in it*]

SHANNON: [*Still below*] Where is Fred—gone fishing?

> [MAXINE *lops the end off a coconut with the machete, as* PANCHO *trots up to the verandah with* SHANNON's *bag—a beat-up Gladstone covered with travel stickers from all over the world. Then* SHANNON *appears, in a crumpled white linen suit. He is panting, sweating and wild-eyed. About thirty-five,* SHANNON *is "black Irish." His nervous state is terribly apparent; he is a young man who has cracked up before and is going to crack up again—perhaps repeatedly*]

MAXINE: Well! Lemme look at you!

SHANNON: Don't look at me, get dressed!

MAXINE: Gee, you look like you had it!

SHANNON: You look like you have been having it, too. Get dressed!

MAXINE: Hell, I'm dressed. I never dress in September. Don't you know I never dress in September?

SHANNON: Well, just, just—button your shirt up.

MAXINE: How long you been off it, Shannon?

SHANNON: Off what?

MAXINE: The wagon . . .

SHANNON: Hell, I'm dizzy with fever. Hundred and three this morning in Cuernavaca.

MAXINE: Watcha got wrong with you?

SHANNON: Fever . . . fever . . . Where's Fred?

MAXINE: Dead.

SHANNON: Did you say *dead?*

MAXINE: That's what I said. Fred is dead.

SHANNON: How?

MAXINE: Less'n two weeks ago, Fred cut his hand on a fish-hook, it got infected, infection got in his blood stream, and he was dead inside of forty-eight hours. [*To* PANCHO] Vete!

SHANNON: Holy smoke. . . .

MAXINE: I can't quite realize it yet.

SHANNON: You don't seem—inconsolable about it.

MAXINE: Fred was an old man, baby. Ten years older'n me. We hadn't had sex together in. . . .

SHANNON: What's that got to do with it?

MAXINE: Lie down and have a rum-coco.

SHANNON: No, no. I want a cold beer. If I start drinking rum-cocos now I won't stop drinking rum-cocos. So Fred is dead? I looked forward to lying is this hammock and talking to Fred.

MAXINE: Well Fred's not talking now, Shannon. A diabetic gets a blood infection, he goes like that without a decent hospital in less'n a week. [*A bus horn is heard blowing from below*] Why don't your busload of women come on up here? They're blowing the bus horn down there.

SHANNON: Let 'em blow it, blow it. . . . [*He sways a little*] I got a fever. [*He goes to the top of the path, divides the flowering bushes and shouts down the hill to the bus*] Hank! Hank! Get them out of the bus and bring 'em up here! Tell 'em the rates are OK. Tell 'em the. . . . [*His voice gives out, and he stumbles back to the verandah, where he sinks down onto the low steps, panting*] Absolutely the worst party I've ever been out with in ten years of conducting tours. For God's sake, help me with 'em because I can't go on. I got to rest here a while. [*She gives him a cold beer*] Thanks. Look and see if they're getting out of the bus. [*She crosses to the masking foilage and separates it to look down the hill*] Are they getting out of the bus or are they staying in it, the stingy— daughters of—bitches. . . . Schoolteachers at a Baptist Female College in Blowing Rock, Texas. Eleven, eleven of them.

MAXINE: A football squad of old maids.

SHANNON: Yeah, and I'm the football. Are they out of the bus?

MAXINE: One's gotten out—she's going into the bushes.

SHANNON: Well, I've got the ignition key to the bus in my pocket—this pocket—so they can't continue without me unless they walk.

MAXINE: They're still blowin' that horn.

SHANNON: Fantastic. I can't lose this party. Blake Tours has put me on probation because I had a bad party last month that tried to get me sacked and I am now on probation with Blake Tours. If I lose this party I'll be sacked for sure . . . Ah, my God, are they still all in the bus? [*He heaves himself off the steps and staggers back to the path, dividing the foliage to look down it, then shouts*] Hank! Get them out of the busssss! Bring them up heeee-re!

HANK'S VOICE: [*From below*] They wanta go back in toooooowwww-n.

SHANNON: They can't go back in toooowwwwn!—Whew—Five years ago this summer I was conducting round-the-world tours for Cook's. Exclusive groups of retired Wall Street financiers. We traveled in fleets of Pierce Arrows and Hispano Suizas.— Are they getting out of the bus?

MAXINE: You're going to pieces, are you?

SHANNON: No! Gone! Gone! [*He rises and shouts down the hill again*] Hank! come up here! Come up here a minute! I wanta talk to you about this situation!—Incredible, fantastic

. . . [*He drops back on the steps, his head falling into his hands*]

MAXINE: They're not getting out of the bus.—Shannon . . . you're not in a nervous condition to cope with this party, Shannon, so let them go and you stay.

SHANNON: You know my situation: I lose this job, what's next? There's nothing lower than Blake Tours, Maxine honey.—Are they getting out of the bus? Are they getting out of it now?

MAXINE: Man's comin' up the hill.

SHANNON: Aw. Hank. You gotta help me with him.

MAXINE: I'll give him a rum-coco.

[HANK *comes grinning onto the verandah*]

HANK: Shannon, them ladies are not gonna come up here, so you better come on back to the bus.

SHANNON: Fantastic.—I'm not going down to the bus and I've got the ignition key to the bus in my pocket. It's going to stay in my pocket for the next three days.

HANK: You can't get away with that, Shannon. Hell, they'll walk back to town if you don't give up the bus key.

SHANNON: They'd drop like flies from sunstrokes on that road. . . . Fantastic, absolutely fantastic . . . [*Panting and sweating, he drops a hand on* HANK's *shoulder*] Hank, I want your co-operation. Can I have it? Because when you're out with a difficult party like this, the tour conductor—me—and the guide—you—have got to stick together to control the situations as they come up against us. It's a test of strength between two men, in this case, and a busload of old wet *hens!* You know that, don't you?

HANK: Well. . . . [*He chuckles*] There's this kid that's crying on the back seat all the time, and that's what's rucked up the deal. Hell, I don't know if you did or you didn't, but they all think that you did 'cause the kid keeps crying.

SHANNON: *Hank? Look!* I don't care what they think. A tour conducted by T. Lawrence Shannon is in his charge, completely—where to go, when to go, every detail of it. Otherwise I resign.

So go on back down there and get them out of that bus before they suffocate in it. Haul them out by force if necessary and herd them up here. Hear me? Don't give me any argument about it. Mrs. Faulk, honey? Give him a menu, give him one of your sample menus to show the ladies. She's got a Chinaman cook here, you won't believe the menu. The cook's from Shanghai, handled the kitchen at an exclusive club there. I got him here for her, and he's a bug, a fanatic about—whew!— continental cuisine . . . can even make beef Strogonoff and thermidor dishes. Mrs. Faulk, honey? Hand him one of those —whew!—one of those fantastic sample menus. [MAXINE *chuckles, as if perpetrating a practical joke, as she hands him a sheet of paper*] Thanks. Now, here. Go on back down there and show them this fantastic menu. Describe the view from the hill, and . . . [HANK *accepts the menu with a chuckling shake of the head*] And have a cold Carta Blanca and. . . .

HANK: You better go down with me.

SHANNON: I can't leave this verandah for at least forty-eight hours. *What in blazes is this?* A little animated cartoon by Hieronymus Bosch?

> [*The German family which is staying at the hotel, the* FAHRENKOPFS, *their daughter and son-in-law, suddenly make a startling, dreamlike entrance upon the scene. They troop around the verandah, then turn down into the jungle path. They are all dressed in the minimal concession to decency and all are pink and gold like baroque cupids in various sizes—Rubensesque, splendidly physical. The bride,* HILDA, *walks astride a big inflated rubber horse which has an ecstatic smile and great winking eyes. She shouts "Horsey, horsey, giddap!" as she waddles astride it, followed by her Wagnerian-tenor bridegroom,* WOLFGANG, *and her father,* HERR FAHRENKOPF, *a tank manufacturer from Frankfurt. He is carrying a portable shortwave radio, which is tuned in to the crackle and guttural voices of a German broadcast reporting the Battle of Britain.* FRAU FAHRENKOPF, *bursting with rich, healthy fat and carrying a basket of food for a picnic at the beach, brings up the rear. They begin to sing a Nazi marching song*]

SHANNON: Aw—Nazis. How come there's so many of them down here lately?

MAXINE: Mexico's the front door to South America—and the back door to the States, that's why.

SHANNON: Aw, and you're setting yourself up here as a receptionist at both doors, now that Fred's dead? [MAXINE *comes over and sits down on him in the hammock*] Get off my pelvis before you crack it. If you want to crack something, crack some ice for my forehead. [*She removes a chunk of ice from her glass and massages his forehead with it*]—Ah, God. . . .

MAXINE: [*Chuckling*] Ha, so you took the young chick and the old hens are squawking about it, Shannon?

SHANNON: The kid asked for it, no kidding, but she's seventeen —less, a month less'n seventeen. So it's serious, it's very serious, because the kid is not just emotionally precocious, she's a musical prodigy, too.

MAXINE: What's that got to do with it?

SHANNON: Here's what it's got to do with it, she's traveling under the wing, the military escort, of this, this—butch vocal teacher who organizes little community sings in the bus. Ah, God! I'm surprised they're not singing now, they must've already suffocated. Or they'd be singing some morale-boosting number like "She's a Jolly Good Fellow" or "Pop Goes the Weasel."—Oh, God. . . . [MAXINE *chuckles up and down the scale*] And each night after supper, after the complaints about the supper and the check-up on the checks by the math instructor, and the vomiting of the supper by several ladies, who have inspected the kitchen—then the kid, the canary, will give a vocal recital. She opens her mouth and out flies Carrie Jacobs Bond or Ethelbert Nevin. I mean after a day of one indescribable torment after another, such as three blowouts, and a leaking radiator in Tierra Caliente. . . . [*He sits up slowly in the hammock as these recollections gather force*] And an evening climb up sierras, through torrents of rain, around hairpin turns over gorges and chasms measureless to man, and with a thermos jug under the driver's seat which the Baptist College ladies think is filled with icewater but which I know is filled with iced tequila—I mean after such a day has finally come to a close, the musical prodigy, Miss Charlotte Goodall, right after supper, before there's a chance to escape, will give a heartbreaking and earsplitting rendition of Carrie Jacobs Bond's "End of a Perfect Day"—with absolutely no humor. . . .

MAXINE: Hah!

SHANNON: Yeah, "Hah!" Last night—no, night before last, the bus burned out its brake linings in Chilpancingo. This town has a hotel . . . this hotel has a piano, which hasn't been tuned since they shot Maximilian. This Texas songbird opens her mouth and out flies "I Love You Truly," and it flies straight at *me*, with *gestures*, all right at *me*, till her chaperone, this Diesel-driven vocal instructor of hers, slams the piano lid down and hauls her out of the mess hall. But as she's hauled out Miss Bird-Girl opens her mouth and out flies, "Larry, Larry, I love you, I love you truly!" That night, when I went to my room, I found that I had a roommate.

MAXINE: The musical prodigy had moved in with you?

SHANNON: The *spook* had moved in with me. In that hot room with one bed, the width of an ironing board and about as hard, the spook was up there on it, sweating, stinking, grinning up at me.

MAXINE: Aw, the spook. [*She chuckles*] So you've got the spook with you again.

SHANNON: That's right, he's the only passenger that got off the bus with me, honey.

MAXINE: Is he here now?

SHANNON: Not far.

MAXINE: On the verandah?

SHANNON: He might be on the other side of the verandah. Oh, he's around somewhere, but he's like the Sioux Indians in the Wild West fiction, he doesn't attack before sundown, he's an after-sundown shadow. . . .

[SHANNON *wriggles out of the hammock as the bus horn gives one last, long protesting blast*]

MAXINE:

> I have a little shadow
> That goes in and out with me,
> And what can be the use of him
> Is more than I can see.

> He's very, very like me,
> From his heels up to his head,
> And he always hops before me
> When I hop into my bed.

SHANNON: That's the truth. He sure hops in the bed with me.

MAXINE: When you're sleeping alone, or . . . ?

SHANNON: I haven't slept in three nights.

MAXINE: Aw, you will tonight, baby.

> [*The bus horn sounds again.* SHANNON *rises and squints down the hill at the bus*]

SHANNON: How long's it take to sweat the faculty of a Baptist Female College out of a bus that's parked in the sun when it's a hundred degrees in the shade?

MAXINE: They're staggering out of it now.

SHANNON: Yeah, I've won *this* round, I reckon. What're they doing down there, can you see?

MAXINE: They're crowding around your pal Hank.

SHANNON: Tearing him to pieces?

MAXINE: One of them's slapped him, he's ducked back into the bus, and she is starting up here.

SHANNON: Oh, Great Caesar's ghost, it's the butch vocal teacher.

MISS FELLOWES: [*In a strident voice, from below*] Shannon! Shannon!

SHANNON: For God's sake, help me with her.

MAXINE: You know I'll help you, baby, but why don't you lay off the young ones and cultivate an interest in normal grown-up women?

MISS FELLOWES: [*Her voice coming nearer*] Shannon!

SHANNON: [*Shouting down the hill*] Come on up, Miss Fellowes, everything's fixed. [*To* MAXINE] Oh, God, here she comes chargin' up the hill like a bull elephant on a rampage!

[MISS FELLOWES *thrashes through the foliage at the top of the jungle path*]

SHANNON: Miss Fellowes, never do that! Not at high noon in a tropical country in summer. Never charge up a hill like you were leading a troop of cavalry attacking an almost impregnable. . . .

MISS FELLOWES: [*Panting and furious*] I don't want advice or instructions, I want the *bus key!*

SHANNON: Mrs. Faulk, this is Miss Judith Fellowes.

MISS FELLOWES: Is this man making a deal with you?

MAXINE: I don't know what you—

MISS FELLOWES: Is this man getting a *kickback* out of you?

MAXINE: Nobody gets any kickback out of me. I turn away more people than—

MISS FELLOWES: [*Cutting in*] This isn't the Ambos Mundos. It says in the brochure that in Puerto Barrio we stay at the Ambos Mundos in the heart of the city.

SHANNON: Yes on the plaza—tell her about the plaza.

MAXINE: What about the plaza?

SHANNON: It's hot, noisy, stinking, swarming with flies. Pariah dogs dying in the—

MISS FELLOWES: How is this place better?

SHANNON: The view from this verandah is equal and I think better than the view from Victoria Peak in Hong Kong, the view from the roof-terrace of the Sultan's palace in—

MISS FELLOWES: [*Cutting in*] I want the view of a clean bed, a bathroom with plumbing that works, and food that is eatable and digestible and not contaminated by filthy—

SHANNON: *Miss Fellowes!*

MISS FELLOWES: Take your hand off my arm.

SHANNON: Look at this sample menu. The cook is a Chinese

imported from Shanghai by *me!* Sent here by *me,* year before last, in nineteen thirty-eight. He was the chef at the Royal Colonial Club in—

MISS FELLOWES: [*Cutting in*] You got a telephone here?

MAXINE: Sure, in the office.

MISS FELLOWES: I want to use it—I'll call collect. Where's the office?

MAXINE: [*To* PANCHO] Llevala al telefono!

[*With* PANCHO *showing her the way,* MISS FELLOWES *stalks off around the verandah to the office,* SHANNON *falls back, sighing desperately, against the verandah wall*]

MAXINE: Hah!

SHANNON: Why did you have to . . . ?

MAXINE: Huh?

SHANNON: Come out looking like this! For you it's funny but for me it's. . . .

MAXINE: This is how I *look.* What's wrong with how I *look?*

SHANNON: I told you to button your shirt. Are you so proud of your boobs that you won't button your shirt up?—Go in the office and see if she's calling Blake Tours to get me fired.

MAXINE: She better not unless she pays for the call.

[*She goes around the turn of the verandah*]

[MISS HANNAH JELKES *appears below the verandah steps and stops short as* SHANNON *turns to the wall, pounding his fist against it with a sobbing sound in his throat*]

HANNAH: Excuse me.

[SHANNON *looks down at her, dazed.* HANNAH *is remarkable-looking—ethereal, almost ghostly. She suggests a Gothic cathedral image of a medieval saint, but animated. She could be thirty, she could be forty: she is totally feminine and yet androgynous-looking—almost timeless. She is wear-*]

ing a cotton print dress and has a bag slung on a strap over her shoulder]

HANNAH: Is this the Costa Verde Hotel?

SHANNON: [*Suddenly pacified by her appearance*] Yes, Yes, it is.

HANNAH: Are you . . . you're not, the hotel manager, are you?

SHANNON: No. She'll be right back.

HANNAH: Thank you. Do you have any idea if they have two vacancies here? One for myself and one for my grandfather who's waiting in a taxi down there on the road. I didn't want to bring him up the hill—till I'd made sure they have rooms for us first.

SHANNON: Well, there's plenty of room here out-of-season—like now.

HANNAH: Good! Wonderful! I'll get him out of the taxi.

SHANNON: Need any help?

HANNAH: No, thank you. We'll make it all right.

[*She gives him a pleasant nod and goes back off down a path through the rain forest. A coconut plops to the ground; a parrot screams at a distance.* SHANNON *drops into the hammock and stretches out. Then* MAXINE *reappears*]

SHANNON: How about the call? Did she make a phone call?

MAXINE: She called a judge in Texas—Blowing Rock, Texas. Collect.

SHANNON: She's trying to get me fired and she is also trying to pin on me a rape charge, a charge of statutory rape.

MAXINE: What's "statutory rape"? I've never known what that was.

SHANNON: That's when a man is seduced by a girl under twenty. [*She chuckles*] It's not funny, Maxine honey.

MAXINE: Why do you want the young ones—or think that you do?

SHANNON: I don't want any, any—regardless of age.

MAXINE: Then why do you take them, Shannon? [*He swallows but does not answer*] Huh, Shannon.

SHANNON: People need human contact, Maxine honey.

MAXINE: What size shoe do you wear?

SHANNON: I don't get the point of that question.

MAXINE: These shoes are shot and if I remember correctly, you travel with only one pair. Fred's estate included one good pair of shoes and your feet look about his size.

SHANNON: I loved ole Fred but I don't want to fill his shoes, honey.

[*She has removed* SHANNON's *beat up, English-made oxfords*]

MAXINE: Your socks are shot. Fred's socks would fit you, too, Shannon. [*She opens his collar*] Aw-aw, I see you got on your gold cross. That's a bad sign, it means you're thinkin' again about goin' back to the Church.

SHANNON: This is my last tour, Maxine. I wrote my old Bishop this morning a complete confession and a complete capitulation.

[*She takes a letter from his damp shirt pocket*]

MAXINE: If this is the letter, baby, you've sweated through it, so the old bugger couldn't read it even if you mailed it to him this time.

[*She has started around the verandah, and goes off as* HANK *reappears up the hill path, mopping his face.* SHANNON's *relaxed position in the hammock aggravates* HANK *sorely*]

HANK: Will you get your ass out of that hammock?

SHANNON: No, I will not.

HANK: Shannon, git out of that hammock! [*He kicks at* SHANNON's *hips in the hammock*]

SHANNON: Hank, if you can't function under rough circumstances, you are in the wrong racket, man. I gave you instructions, the instructions were simple. I said get them out of the bus and. . . .

[MAXINE *comes back with a kettle of water, a towel, and other shaving equipment*]

HANK: Out of the hammock, Shannon! [*He kicks* SHANNON *again, harder*]

SHANNON: [*Warningly*] That's enough, Hank. A little familiarity goes a long way, but not as far as you're going. [MAXINE *starts lathering his face*] What's this, what are you . . . ?

MAXINE: Haven't you ever had a shave-and-haircut by a lady barber?

HANK: The kid has gone into hysterics.

MAXINE: Hold still, Shannon.

SHANNON: Hank, hysteria is a natural phenomenon, the common denominator of the female nature. It's the big female weapon, and the test of a man is his ability to cope with it, and I can't believe you can't. If I believed that you couldn't, I would not be able—

MAXINE: Hold still!

SHANNON: I'm holding still. [*To* HANK] No, I wouldn't be able to take you out with me again. So go on back down there and—

HANK: You want me to go back down there and tell them you're getting a shave up here in a hammock?

MAXINE: Tell them that Reverend Larry is going back to the Church so they can go back to the Female College in Texas.

HANK: I want another beer.

MAXINE: Help yourself, piggly-wiggly, the cooler's in my office right around there. [*She points around the corner of the verandah*]

SHANNON: [*As* HANK *goes off*] It's horrible how you got to bluff and keep bluffing even when hollering "Help!" is all you're up to, Maxine. *You cut me!*

MAXINE: You didn't hold still.

SHANNON: Just trim the beard a little.

MAXINE: I know. Baby, tonight we'll go night swimming, whether it storms or not.

SHANNON: Ah, God. . . .

MAXINE: The Mexican kids are wonderful night swimmers. . . . Hah, when I found 'em they were taking the two-hundred-foot dives off the Quebrada, but the Quebrada Hotel kicked 'em out for being over-attentive to the lady guests there. That's how I got hold of them.

SHANNON: Maxine, you're bigger than life and twice as unnatural, honey.

MAXINE: No one's bigger than life-size, Shannon, or even ever that big, except maybe Fred. [*She shouts "Fred?" and gets a faint answering echo from an adjoining hill*] Little Sir Echo is all that answers for him now, Shannon, but. . . . [*She pats some bay rum on his face*] Dear old Fred was always a mystery to me. He was so patient and tolerant with me that it was insulting to me. A man and a woman have got to challenge each other, y'know what I mean. I mean I hired those diving-boys from the Quebrada six months before Fred died, and did he care? Did he give a damn when I started night swimming with them? No. He'd go night *fishing*, all night, and when I got up the next day, he'd be preparing to go out fishing again, but he just caught the fish and threw them back in the sea.

[HANK *returns and sits drinking his beer on the steps*]

SHANNON: The mystery of old Fred was simple. He was just cool and decent, that's all the mystery of him. . . . Get your pair of night swimmers to grab my ladies' luggage out of the bus before the vocal teacher gets off the phone and stops them.

MAXINE: [*Shouting*] Pedro! Pancho! Muchachos! Trae las maletas al anejo! Pronto! [*The Mexican boys start down the path.* MAXINE *sits in the hammock beside* SHANNON] You I'll put in Fred's old room, next to me.

SHANNON: You want me in his socks and his shoes and in his room next to *you*? [*He stares at her with a shocked surmise*

*of her intentions toward him, then flops back down in the ham-
mock with an incredulous laugh*] Oh no, honey. I've just
been hanging on till I could get in this hammock on this
verandah over the rain forest and the stillwater beach, that's
all that can pull me through this last tour in a condition
to go back to my . . . original . . . vocation.

MAXINE: Hah, you still have some rational moments when you
face the fact that churchgoers don't go to church to hear
atheistical sermons.

SHANNON: Goddamit, I never preached an atheistical sermon
in a church in my life, and. . . .

[MISS FELLOWES *has charged out of the office and rounds
the verandah to bear down on* SHANNON *and* MAXINE,
who jumps up out of the hammock]

MISS FELLOWES: I've completed my call, which I made collect
to Texas.

[MAXINE *shrugs, going by her around the verandah.* MISS
FELLOWES *runs across the verandah*]

SHANNON: [*Sitting up in the hammock*] Excuse me, Miss
Fellowes, for not getting out of this hammock, but I . . .
Miss Fellowes? Please sit down a minute, I want to confess
something to you.

MISS FELLOWES: *That* ought to be int'restin'! *What?*

SHANNON: Just that—well, like everyone else, at some point or
other in life, my life has cracked up on me.

MISS FELLOWES: How does that compensate *us?*

SHANNON: I don't think I know what you mean by *compensate*,
Miss Fellowes. [*He props himself up and gazes at her with
the gentlest bewilderment, calculated to melt a heart of stone.*]
I mean I've just confessed to you that I'm at the end of
my rope, and you say, "How does that compensate *us?*"
Please, Miss Fellowes. Don't make me feel that any adult
human being puts personal compensation before the dreadful,
bare fact of a man at the end of his rope who still has to

try to go on, to continue, as if he'd never been better or stronger in his whole existence. No, don't do that, it would. . . .

MISS FELLOWES: It would *what?*

SHANNON: Shake if not shatter everything left of my faith in essential . . . human . . . *goodness!*

MAXINE: [*Returning, with a pair of socks*] Hah!

MISS FELLOWES: Can you sit there, I mean lie there—yeah, I mean *lie* there . . . ! and talk to me about—

MAXINE: Hah!

MISS FELLOWES: "Essential human goodness"? Why, just plain human decency is beyond your imagination, Shannon, so lie there, lie there and *lie* there, we're *going!*

SHANNON: [*Rising from the hammock*] Miss Fellowes, I thought that I was conducting this party, not you.

MISS FELLOWES: You? You just now *admitted* you're incompetent, as well as. . . .

MAXINE: Hah.

SHANNON: Maxine, will you—

MISS FELLOWES: [*Cutting in with cold, righteous fury*]: *Shannon*, we girls have worked and slaved all year at Baptist Female College for this Mexican tour, and the tour is a cheat!

SHANNON: [*To himself*] Fantastic!

MISS FELLOWES: Yes, *cheat!* You haven't stuck to the schedule and you haven't stuck to the itinerary advertised in the brochure which Blake Tours put out. Now either Blake Tours is cheating us or you are cheating Blake Tours, and I'm putting wheels in motion—I don't care *what* it costs me—I'm. . . .

SHANNON: Oh, Miss Fellowes, isn't it just as plain to you as it is to me that your hysterical insults, which are not at all easy for any born and bred gentleman to accept, are not . . . *motivated, provoked* by . . . anything as *trivial* as the, the . . . the motivations that you're, you're . . . *ascribing* them to? Now can't we talk about the *real, true* cause of . . .

MISS FELLOWES: Cause of *what?*

[CHARLOTTE GOODALL *appears at the top of the hill*]

SHANNON: —Cause of your *rage* Miss Fellowes, your—

MISS FELLOWES: *Charlotte!* Stay down the hill in the *bus!*

CHARLOTTE: Judy, they're—

MISS FELLOWES: *Obey me! Down!*

> [CHARLOTTE *retreats from view like a well-trained dog.* MISS FELLOWES *charges back to* SHANNON *who has gotten out of the hammock. He places a conciliatory hand on her arm*].

MISS FELLOWES: *Take your hand off my arm!*

MAXINE: Hah!

SHANNON: *Fantastic.* Miss Fellowes, please! No more shouting? Please? Now I really must ask you to let this party of ladies come up here and judge the accommodations for themselves and compare them with what they saw passing through town. Miss Fellowes, there is such a thing as charm and beauty in some places, as much as there's nothing but dull, ugly imitation of highway motels in Texas and—

> [MISS FELLOWES *charges over to the path to see if* CHARLOTTE *has obeyed her.* SHANNON *follows, still propitiatory.* MAXINE *says "Hah," but she gives him an affectionate little pat as he goes by her. He pushes her hand away as he continues his appeal to* MISS FELLOWES]

MISS FELLOWES: I've taken a look at those rooms and they'd make a room at the "Y" look like a suite at the Ritz.

SHANNON: Miss Fellowes, I am employed by Blake Tours and so I'm not in a position to tell you quite frankly what mistakes they've made in their advertising brochure. They just don't know Mexico. I do. I know it as well as I know five out of all six continents on the—

MISS FELLOWES: *Continent! Mexico?* You never even studied geography if you—

SHANNON: My degree from Sewanee is *Doctor of Divinity,* but for the past ten years geography's been my *specialty,* Miss

Fellowes, honey! Name any tourist agency I haven't worked for! You couldn't! I'm only, now, with Blake Tours because I—

MISS FELLOWES: Because you *what?* Couldn't keep your hands off innocent, under-age girls in your—

SHANNON: Now, Miss Fellowes. . . . [*He touches her arm again*]

MISS FELLOWES: Take your hand off my arm!

SHANNON: For days I've known you were furious and unhappy, but—

MISS FELLOWES: *Oh!* You think it's just *me* that's unhappy! Hauled in that stifling bus over the byways, off the highways, shook up and bumped up so you could get your rake-off, is that what you—

SHANNON: What I know is, all I know is, that you are the *leader* of the *insurrection!*

MISS FELLOWES: All of the girls in this party have dysentery!

SHANNON: That you can't hold me to blame for.

MISS FELLOWES: I *do* hold you to blame for it.

SHANNON: Before we entered Mexico, at New Laredo, Texas, I called you ladies together in the depot on the Texas side of the border and I passed out mimeographed sheets of instructions on what to eat and what *not* to eat, what to drink, what not to drink in the—

MISS FELLOWES: It's not *what* we ate but *where* we ate that gave us dysentery!

SHANNON: [*Shaking his head like a metronome*] It is not dysentery.

MISS FELLOWES: The result of eating in places that would be condemned by the Board of Health in—

SHANNON: Now wait a minute—

MISS FELLOWES: For disregarding all rules of sanitation.

SHANNON: It is not dysentery, it is not amoebic, it's nothing at all but—

MAXINE: Montezuma's Revenge! That's what we call it.

SHANNON: I even passed out pills. I passed out bottles of Enteroviaform because I knew that some of you ladies would rather be victims of Montezuma's Revenge than spend cinco centavos on bottled water in stations.

MISS FELLOWES: You sold those pills at a profit of fifty cents per bottle.

MAXINE: Hah-hah! [*She knocks off the end of a coconut with the machete, preparing a rum-coco*]

SHANNON: Now fun is fun, Miss Fellowes, but an accusation like that—

MISS FELLOWES: I *priced* them is *pharmacies*, because I suspected that—

SHANNON: Miss Fellowes, I am a gentleman, and as a gentleman I can't be insulted like this. I mean I can't accept insults of that kind even from a member of a tour that I am conducting. And, Miss Fellowes, I think you might also remember, you might try to remember, that you're speaking to an ordained minister of the Church.

MISS FELLOWES: *De*-frocked! But still trying to pass himself off as a minister!

MAXINE: How about a rum-coco? We give a complimentary rum-coco to all our guests here. [*Her offer is apparently unheard. She shrugs and drinks the rum-coco herself*]

SHANNON: —Miss Fellowes? In every party there is always one individual that's discontented, that is not satisfied with all I do to make the tour more . . . unique—to make it different from the ordinary, to give it a personal thing, the Shannon touch.

MISS FELLOWES: The gyp touch, the touch of a defrocked minister.

SHANNON: Miss Fellowes, don't, don't, don't . . . do what . . . you're doing! [*He is on the verge of hysteria, he makes some incoherent sounds, gesticulates with clenched fists, then stumbles wildly across the verandah and leans panting for breath against a post*] Don't! Break! *Human! Pride!*

VOICE FROM DOWN THE HILL: [*A very Texan accent*] Judy? They're taking our luggage!

MISS FELLOWES: [*Shouting down the hill*] Girls! Girls! Don't let those boys touch your luggage. Don't let them bring your luggage in this dump!

GIRL'S VOICE: [*From below*] Judy! We can't stop them!

MAXINE: Those kids don't understand English.

MISS FELLOWES: [*Wild with rage*] Will you please tell those boys to take that luggage back down to the bus? [*She calls to the party below again*] Girls! Hold onto your luggage, don't let them take it away! We're going to drive back to A-cap-ul-co! You *hear?*

GIRL'S VOICE: Judy, they want a swim, first!

MISS FELLOWES: I'll be right back. [*She rushes off, shouting at the Mexican boys*] You! Boys! Muchachos! *You carry that luggage back down!*

[*The voices continue, fading.* SHANNON *moves brokenly across the verandah.* MAXINE *shakes her head*]

MAXINE: Shannon, give 'em the bus key and let 'em go.

SHANNON: And me do what?

MAXINE: Stay here.

SHANNON: In Fred's old bedroom—yeah, in Fred's old bedroom.

MAXINE: You could do worse.

SHANNON: Could I? Well, then, I'll do worse, I'll . . . do worse.

MAXINE: Aw now, baby.

SHANNON: If I could do worse, I'll do worse. . . . [*He grips the section of railing by the verandah steps and stares with wide, lost eyes. His chest heaves like a spent runner's and he is bathed in sweat*]

MAXINE: Give me that ignition key. I'll take it down to the driver while you bathe and rest and have a rum-coco, baby.

[SHANNON *simply shakes his head slightly. Harsh bird cries sound in the rain forest. Voices are heard on the path*]

HANNAH: Nonno, you've lost your sun glasses.

NONNO: No. Took them off. No sun.

[HANNAH *appears at the top of the path, pushing her grandfather,* NONNO, *in a wheelchair. He is a very old man but has a powerful voice for his age and always seems to be shouting something of importance.* NONNO *is a poet and a showman. There is a good kind of pride and he has it, carrying it like a banner wherever he goes. He is immaculately dressed—a linen suit, white as his thick poet's hair; a black string tie; and he is holding a black cane with a gold crook*]

NONNO: Which way is the sea?

HANNAH: Right down below the hill, Nonno. [*He turns in the wheelchair and raises a hand to shield his eyes*] We can't see it from here. [*The old man is deaf, and she shouts to make him hear*]

NONNO: I can feel it and smell it. [*A murmur of wind sweeps through the rain forest*] It's the cradle of life. [*He is shouting, too*] Life began in the sea

MAXINE: These two with your party?

SHANNON: No.

MAXINE: They look like a pair of loonies.

SHANNON: Shut up.

[SHANNON *looks at* HANNAH *and* NONNO *steadily, with a relief of tension almost like that of someone going under hypnosis. The old man still squints down the path, blindly, but* HANNAH *is facing the verandah with a proud person's hope of acceptance when it is desperately needed*]

HANNAH: How do you do.

MAXINE: Hello.

HANNAH: Have you ever tried pushing a gentleman in a wheelchair uphill through a rain forest?

MAXINE: Nope, and I wouldn't even try it *downhill*.

HANNAH: Well, now that we've made it, I don't regret the effort.

What a view for a painter! [*She looks about her, panting, digging into her shoulder-bag for a handkerchief, aware that her face is flushed and sweating*] They told me in town that this was the ideal place for a painter, and they weren't—*whew*—exaggerating!

SHANNON: You've got a scratch on your forehead.

HANNAH: Oh, is that what I felt.

SHANNON: Better put iodine on it.

HANNAH: Yes, I'll attend to that—*whew*—later, thank you.

MAXINE: Anything I can do for you?

HANNAH: I'm looking for the manager of the hotel.

MAXINE: Me—speaking.

HANNAH: Oh, *you're* the manager, *good!* How do you do, I'm Hannah Jelkes, Mrs. . . .

MAXINE: Faulk, Maxine Faulk. What can I do for you folks? [*Her tone indicates no desire to do anything for them*]

HANNAH: [*Turning quickly to her grandfather*] Nonno, the manager is a *lady* from the *States.*

[NONNO *lifts a branch of wild orchids from his lap, ceremonially, with the instinctive gallantry of his kind*]

NONNO: [*Shouting*] Give the lady these—botanical curiosities! —you picked on the way up.

HANNAH: I believe they're wild orchids, isn't that what they are?

SHANNON: Laelia tibicina.

HANNAH: Oh!

NONNO: But tell her, Hannah, tell her to keep them in the icebox till after dark, they draw bees in the sun! [*He rubs a sting on his chin with a rueful chuckle*]

MAXINE: Are you all looking for rooms here?

HANNAH: Yes, we are, but we've come without reservations.

MAXINE: Well, honey, the Costa Verde is closed in September —except for a few special guests, so. . . .

SHANNON: They're special guests, for God's sake.

MAXINE: I thought you said they didn't come with your party.

HANNAH: Please let us be special guests.

MAXINE: *Watch out!*

[NONNO *has started struggling out of the wheelchair.* SHAN-
NON *rushes over to keep him from falling.* HANNAH *has
started toward him, too, then seeing that* SHANNON *has
caught him, she turns back to* MAXINE]

HANNAH: In twenty-five years of travel this is the first time we've
ever arrived at a place without advance reservations.

MAXINE: Honey, that old man ought to be in a hospital.

HANNAH: Oh, no, no, he just sprained his ankle a little in Taxco
this morning. He just needs a good night's rest, he'll be on his
feet tomorrow. His recuperative powers are absolutely amazing
for someone who is ninety-seven years *young.*

SHANNON: Easy, Grampa. Hang on. [*He is supporting the old
man up to the verandah*] Two steps. One! Two! Now you've
made it, Grampa.

[NONNO *keeps chuckling breathlessly as* SHANNON *gets him
onto the verandah and into a wicker rocker*]

HANNAH: [*Breaking in quickly*] I can't tell you how much I
appreciate your taking us in here now. It's—providential.

MAXINE: Well, I can't send that old man back down the hill—
right now—but like I told you the Costa Verde's practically
closed in September. I just take in a few folks as a special
accommodation and we operate on a special basis this month.

NONNO: [*Cutting in abruptly and loudly*] Hannah, tell the lady
that my perambulator is temporary. I will soon be ready to
crawl and then to toddle and before long I will be leaping
around here like an—old—mountain—goat, ha-ha-ha-ha. . . .

HANNAH: Yes, I explained that, Grandfather.

NONNO: I don't like being on wheels.

HANNAH: Yes, my grandfather feels that the decline of the Western world began with the invention of the wheel. [*She laughs heart-ily, but* MAXINE's *look is unresponsive*]

NONNO: And tell the manager . . . the, uh, lady . . . that I know some hotels don't want to take dogs, cats or monkeys and some don't even solicit the patronage of infants in their late nineties who arrive in perambulators with flowers instead of rattles . . . [*He chuckles with a sort of fearful, slightly mad quality.* HANNAH *perhaps has the impulse to clap a hand over his mouth at this moment but must stand there smiling and smiling and smiling*] . . . and a brandy flask instead of a teething ring, but tell her that these, uh, concessions to man's seventh age are only temporary, and. . . .

HANNAH: Nonno, I told her the wheelchair's because of a sprained ankle, Nonno!

SHANNON: [*To himself*] Fantastic.

NONNO: And after my siesta, I'll wheel it back down the hill, I'll kick it back down the hill, right into the sea, and tell her. . . .

HANNAH: Yes? What, Nonno? [*She has stopped smiling now. Her tone and her look are frankly desperate*] What shall I tell her now, Nonno?

NONNO: Tell her that if she'll forgive my disgraceful longevity and this . . . temporary decrepitude . . . I will present her with the last signed . . . compitty [*he means* "copy"] of my first volume of verse, published in . . . when, Hannah?

HANNAH: [*Hopelessly*] The day that President Ulysses S. Grant was inaugurated, Nonno.

NONNO: *Morning Trumpet!* Where is it—you have it, give it to her right now.

HANNAH: Later, a little later! [*Then she turns to* MAXINE *and* SHANNON] My grandfather is the poet Jonathan Coffin. He is ninety-seven years *young* and will be ninety-eight years *young* the fifth of next month, October.

MAXINE: Old folks are remarkable, yep. The office phone's ringing —excuse me, I'll be right back. [*She goes around the veran-dah*]

NONNO: Did I talk too much?

HANNAH: [*Quietly, to* SHANNON] I'm afraid that he did. I don't think she's going to take us.

SHANNON: She'll take you. Don't worry about it.

HANNAH: Nobody would take us in town, and if we don't get in here, I would have to wheel him back down through the rain forest, and then *what*, then *where?* There would just be the road, and no direction to move in, except out to sea—and I doubt that we could make it divide before us.

SHANNON: That won't be necessary. I have a little influence with the patrona.

HANNAH: Oh, then, do use it, please. Her eyes said *no* in big blue capital letters.

[SHANNON *pours some water from a pitcher on the verandah and hands it to the old man*]

NONNO: What is this—libation?

SHANNON: Some icewater, Grampa.

HANNAH: Oh, that's kind of you. Thank you. I'd better give him a couple of salt tablets to wash down with it. [*Briskly she removes a bottle from her shoulder-bag*] Won't you have some? I see you're perspiring, too. You have to be careful not to become dehydrated in the hot seasons under the Tropic of Cancer.

SHANNON: [*Pouring another glass of water*] Are you a little *financially* dehydrated, too?

HANNAH: That's right. Bone-dry, and I think the patrona suspects it. It's a logical assumption, since I pushed him up here myself, and the patrona has the look of a very logical woman. I am sure she knows that we couldn't afford to hire the taxi driver to help us up here.

MAXINE: [*Calling from the back*] Pancho?

HANNAH: A woman's practicality when she's managing something is harder than a man's for another woman to cope with, so if you have influence with her, please do use it. Please try to convince her that my grandfather will be on his feet tomorrow, if not tonight, and with any luck whatsoever, the money situation will be solved just as quickly. Oh, here she comes back, do help us!

[*Involuntarily,* HANNAH *seizes hold of* SHANNON's *wrist as* MAXINE *stalks back onto the verandah, still shouting for* PANCHO. *The Mexican boy reappears, sucking a juicy peeled mango—its juice running down his chin onto his throat*]

MAXINE: Pancho, run down to the beach and tell Herr Fahrenkopf that the German Embassy's waiting on the phone for him. [PANCHO *stares at her blankly until she repeats the order in* Spanish] Dile a Herr Fahrenkopf que la embajada alemana lo llama al telefono. Corre, corre! [PANCHO *starts indolently down the path, still sucking noisily on the mango*] I said *run!* Corre, corre! [*He goes into a leisurely loping pace and disappears through the foliage*]

HANNAH: What graceful people they are!

MAXINE: Yeah, they're graceful like cats, and just as dependable, too.

HANNAH: Shall we, uh, . . . *register* now?

MAXINE: You all can register later but I'll have to collect six dollars from you first if you want to put your names in the pot for supper. That's how I've got to operate here out of season.

HANNAH: Six? Dollars?

MAXINE: Yeah, three each. In season we operate on the continental plan but out of season like this we change to the modified American plan.

HANNAH: Oh, what is the, uh . . . modification of it? [*She gives* SHANNON *a quick glance of appeal as she stalls for time, but his attention has turned inward as the bus horn blows down the hill*]

MAXINE: Just two meals are included instead of all three.

HANNAH: [*Moving closer to* SHANNON *and raising her voice*] Breakfast and dinner?

MAXINE: A continental breakfast and a cold lunch.

SHANNON: [Aside] Yeah, very cold—cracked ice—if you crack it yourself.

HANNAH: [Reflectively] Not dinner.

MAXINE: No! Not dinner.

HANNAH: Oh, I see, uh, but . . . we, uh, operate on a special basis ourselves. I'd better explain it to you.

MAXINE: How do you mean "operate"—on what "basis"?

HANNAH: Here's our card. I think you may have heard of us. [She presents the card to MAXINE] We've had a good many write-ups. My grandfather is the oldest living and practicing poet. And he gives recitations. I . . . paint . . . water colors and I'm a "quick sketch artist." We travel together. We pay our way as we go by my grandfather's recitations and the sale of my water colors and quick character sketches in charcoal or pastel.

SHANNON: [To himself] I have fever.

HANNAH: I usually pass among the tables at lunch and dinner in a hotel. I wear an artist's smock—picturesquely dabbed with paint—wide Byronic collar and flowing silk tie. I don't push myself on people. I just display my work and smile at them sweetly and if they invite me to do so sit down to make a qiuck character sketch in pastel or charcoal. If not? Smile sweetly and go on.

SHANNON: What does Grandpa do?

HANNAH: We pass among the tables together slowly. I introduce him as the world's oldest living and practicing poet. If invited, he gives a recitation of a poem. Unfortunately all of his poems were written a long time ago. But do you know, he has started a new poem? For the first time in twenty years he's started another poem!

SHANNON: Hasn't finished it yet?

HANNAH: He still has inspiration, but his power of concentration has weakened a little, of course.

MAXINE: Right now he's not concentrating.

SHANNON: Grandpa's catchin' forty winks. Grampa? Let's hit the sack.

MAXINE: Now wait a minute. I'm going to call a taxi for these folks to take them back to town.

HANNAH: Please don't do that. We tried every hotel in town and they wouldn't take us. I'm afraid I have to place myself at your . . . mercy.

[*With infinite gentleness* SHANNON *has roused the old man and is leading him into one of the cubicles back of the verandah. Distant cries of bathers are heard from the beach. The afternoon light is fading very fast now as the sun has dropped behind a hilltop out to sea*]

MAXINE: Looks like you're in for one night. Just one.

HANNAH: Thank you.

MAXINE: The old man's in number 4. You take 3. Where's your luggage—no luggage?

HANNAH: I hid it behind some palmettos at the foot of the path.

SHANNON: [*Shouting to* PANCHO] Bring up her luggage. Tu, flojo . . . las maletas. . . . baja las palmas. Vamos! [*The Mexican boys rush down the path*] Maxine honey, would you cash a postdated check for me?

MAXINE: [*Shrewdly*] Yeah—mañana, maybe.

SHANNON: Thanks—generosity is the cornerstone of your nature.

[MAXINE *utters her one-note bark of a laugh as she marches around the corner of the verandah*]

HANNAH: I'm dreadfully afraid my grandfather had a slight stroke in those high passes through the sierras. [*She says this with the coolness of someone saying that it may rain before nightfall. An instant later, a long, long sigh of wind sweeps the hillside. The bathers are heard shouting below*]

SHANNON: Very old people get these little "cerebral accidents," as they call them. They're not regular strokes, they're just little cerebral . . . incidents. The symptoms clear up so quickly that sometimes the old people don't even know they've had them.

[*They exchange this quiet talk without looking at each*

*other. The Mexican boys crash back through the bushes
at the top of the path, bearing some pieces of ancient
luggage fantastically plastered with hotel and travel stickers
indicating a vast range of wandering. The boys deposit the
luggage near the steps*]

SHANNON: How many times have you been around the world?

HANNAH: Almost as many times as the world's been around the
sun, and I feel as if I had gone the whole way on foot.

SHANNON: [*Picking up her luggage*] What's your cell number?

HANNAH: [*Smiling faintly*] I believe she said it was cell number
3.

SHANNON: She probably gave you the one with the leaky roof.
[*He carries the bags into the cubicle.* MAXINE *is visible to the
audience only as she appears outside the door to her office on
the wing of the verandah*] But you won't find out till it rains
and then it'll be too late to do much about it but swim out
of it. [HANNAH *laughs wanly. Her fatigue is now very plain.*
SHANNON *comes back out with her luggage*] Yep, she gave you
the one with the leaky roof so you take mine and. . . .

HANNAH: Oh, no, no, Mr. Shannon, I'll find a dry spot if it rains.

MAXINE: [*From around the corner of the verandah*] Shannon!

[*A bit of pantomime occurs between* HANNAH *and* SHAN-
NON. *He wants to put her luggage in cubicle number 5.
She catches hold of his arm, indicating by gesture toward
the back that it is necessary to avoid displeasing the proprietor.* MAXINE *shouts his name louder.* SHANNON *surren-
ders to* HANNAH's *pleading and puts her luggage back in the
leaky cubicle number 3*]

HANNAH: Thank you so much, Mr. Shannon. [*She disappears behind the mosquito netting.* MAXINE *advances to the verandah
angle as* SHANNON *starts toward his own cubicle*]

MAXINE: [*Mimicking* HANNAH's *voice*] "Thank you so much, Mr.
Shannon."

SHANNON: Don't be bitchy. Some people say thank you sincerely.

[*He goes past her and down the steps from the end of the verandah*] I'm going down for a swim now.

MAXINE: The water's blood temperature this time of day.

SHANNON: Yeah, well, I have a fever so it'll seem cooler to me. [*He crosses rapidly to the jungle path leading to the beach*]

MAXINE : [*Following him*] Wait for me, I'll. . . .

> [*She means she will go down with him, but he ignores her call and disappears into the foliage.* MAXINE *shrugs angrily and goes back onto the verandah. She faces out, gripping the railing tightly and glaring into the blaze of the sunset as if it were a personal enemy. Then the ocean breathes a long cooling breath up the hill, as* NONNO's *voice is heard from his cubicle*]

NONNO:

> How calmly does the orange branch
> Observe the sky begin to blanch,
> Without a cry, without a prayer,
> With no expression of despair. . . .

[*And from a beach cantina in the distance a marimba band is heard playing a popular song of that summer of 1940, "Palabras de Mujer"—which means "Words of Women"*]

SLOW DIM OUT AND SLOW CURTAIN

ACT TWO

Several hours later: near sunset.

The scene is bathed in a deep golden, almost coppery light; the heavy tropical foliage gleams with wetness from a recent rain.

MAXINE comes around the turn of the verandah. To the formalities of evening she has made the concession of changing from levis to clean white cotton pants, and from a blue work shirt to a pink one. She is about to set up the folding cardtables for the evening meal which is served on the verandah. All the while she is talking, she is setting up tables, etc.

MAXINE: Miss Jelkes?

[HANNAH *lifts the mosquito net over the door of cubicle number 3*]

HANNAH: Yes, Mrs. Faulk?

MAXINE: Can I speak to you while I set up these tables for supper?

HANNAH: Of course, you may. I wanted to speak to you, too, [*She comes out. She is now wearing her artist's smock*]

MAXINE: Good.

HANNAH: I just wanted to ask you if there's a tub bath Grandfather could use. A shower is fine for me—I prefer a shower to a tub—but for my grandfather there is some danger of falling down in a shower and at his age, although he says he is made out of India rubber, a broken hipbone would be a very serious matter, so I. . . .

MAXINE: What I wanted to say is I called up the Casa de Huéspedes about you and your Grampa, and I can get you in there.

HANNAH: Oh, but we don't want to *move!*

MAXINE: The Costa Verde isn't the right place for you. Y'see, we cater to folks that like to rough it a little, and—well, frankly, we cater to younger people.

[HANNAH *has started unfolding a cardtable*]

HANNAH: Oh yes . . . uh . . . well . . . the, uh, Casa de Huéspedes, that means a, uh, sort of a rooming house, Mrs. Faulk?

MAXINE: Boarding house. They feed you, they'll even feed you on credit.

HANNAH: Where is it located?

MAXINE: It has a central location. You could get a doctor there quick if the old man took sick on you. You got to think about that.

HANNAH: Yes, I— [*She nods gravely, more to herself than* MAXINE] —I *have* thought about that, but. . . .

MAXINE: What are you doing?

HANNAH: Making myself useful.

MAXINE: Don't do that. I don't accept help from guests here.

[HANNAH *hesitates, but goes on setting the tables*]

HANNAH: Oh, please, let me. Knife and fork on one side, spoon on the . . . ? [*Her voice dies out*]

MAXINE: Just put the plates on the napkins so they don't blow away.

HANNAH: Yes, it is getting breezy on the verandah. [*She continues setting the table*]

MAXINE: Hurricane winds are already hitting up coast.

HANNAH: We've been through several typhoons in the Orient.

Sometimes *outside* disturbances like that are an almost welcome distraction from *inside* disturbances, aren't they? [*This is said almost to herself. She finishes putting the plates on the paper napkins*] When do you want us to leave here, Mrs. Faulk?

MAXINE: The boys'll move you in my station wagon tomorrow —no charge for the service.

HANNAH: That is very kind of you. [MAXINE *starts away*] Mrs. Faulk?

MAXINE: [*turning back to her with obvious reluctance*]: Huh?

HANNAH: Do you know jade?

MAXINE: Jade?

HANNAH: Yes.

MAXINE: Why?

HANNAH: I have a small but interesting collection of jade pieces. I asked if you know jade because in jade it's the craftmanship, the carving of the jade, that's most important about it. [*She has removed a jade ornament from her blouse*] This one, for instance—a miracle of carving. Tiny as it is, it has two figures carved on it—the legendary Prince Ahk and Princess Angh, and a heron flying above them. The artist that carved it probably received for this miraculously delicate workmanship, well, I would say perhaps the price of a month's supply of rice for his family, but the merchant who employed him sold it, I would guess, for at least three hundred pounds sterling to an English lady who got tired of it and gave it to me, perhaps because I painted her not as she was at that time but as I could see she must have looked in her youth. Can you see the carving?

MAXINE: Yeah, honey, but I'm not operating a hock shop here, I'm trying to run a hotel.

HANNAH: I know, but couldn't you just accept it as security for a few days' stay here?

MAXINE: You're completely broke, are you?

HANNAH: Yes, we are—completely.

MAXINE: You say that like you're proud of it.

HANNAH: I'm not proud of it or ashamed of it either. It just

happens to be what's happened to us, which has never happened
before in all our travels.

MAXINE: [*Grudgingly*] You're telling the truth, I reckon, but I
told you the truth, too, when I told you, when you came
here, that I had just lost my husband and he'd left me in such
a financial hole that if living didn't mean more to me than
money, I'd might as well have been dropped in the ocean with
him.

HANNAH: Ocean?

MAXINE: [*Peacefully philosophical about it*] I carried out his
burial instructions exactly. Yep, my husband, Fred Faulk, was
the greatest game fisherman on the west coast of Mexico—
he'd racked up unbeatable records in sailfish, tarpon, kingfish,
barracuda—and on his deathbed, last week, he requested to be
dropped in the sea, yeah, right out there in that bay, not even
sewed up in canvas, just in his fisherman outfit. So now old
Freddie the Fisherman is feeding the fish—fishes' revenge on
old Freddie. How about that, I ask you?

HANNAH: [*Regarding* MAXINE *sharply*] I doubt that he regrets it.

MAXINE: I do. It gives me the shivers.

[*She is distracted by the German party singing a marching
song on the path up from the beach.* SHANNON *appears
at the top of the path, a wet beachrobe clinging to him.*
MAXINE's *whole concentration shifts abruptly to him. She
feeezes and blazes with it like an exposed power line. For
a moment the "hot light" is concentrated on her tense,
furious figure.* HANNAH *provides a visual counterpoint. She
clenches her eyes shut for a moment, and when they open,
it is on a look of stoical despair of the refuge she has
unsuccessfully fought for. Then* SHANNON *approaches the
verandah and the scene is his*]

SHANNON: Here they come up, your conquerors of the world,
Maxine honey, singing "Horst Wessel." [*He chuckles fiercely,
and starts toward the verandah steps*]

MAXINE: Shannon, wash that sand off you before you come on
the verandah.

[*The Germans are heard singing the "Horst Wessel"
marching song. Soon they appear, trooping up from the
beach like an animated canvas by Rubens. They are all
nearly nude, pinked and bronzed by the sun. The women
have decked themselves with garlands of pale green sea-
weed, glistening wet, and the Munich-opera bridegroom
is blowing on a great conch shell. His father-in-law, the
tank manufacturer, has his portable radio, which is still
transmitting a shortwave broadcast about the Battle of
Britain, now at its climax*]

HILDA: [*Capering, astride her rubber horse*] Horsey, horsey,
horsey!

HERR FAHRENKOPF: [*Ecstatically*] London is burning, the
heart of London's on fire! [WOLFGANG *turns a handspring onto
the verandah and walks on his hands a few paces, then tumbles
over with a great whoop.* MAXINE *laughs delightedly with the
Germans*] Beer, beer, beer!

FRAU FAHRENKOPF: Tonight champagne!

[*The euphoric horseplay and shouting continue as they
gambol around the turn of the verandah.* SHANNON *has
come onto the porch.* MAXINE's *laughter dies out a little
sadly, with envy*]

SHANNON: You're turning this place into the Mexican Berch-
tesgaden, Maxine honey?

MAXINE: I told you to wash that sand off. [*Shouts for beer
from the Germans draw her around the verandah corner*]

HANNAH: Mr. Shannon, do you happen to know the Casa de
Huéspedes, or anything about it, I mean? [SHANNON *stares at
her somewhat blankly*] We are, uh, thinking of . . . *moving*
there tomorrow. Do you, uh, recommend it?

SHANNON: I recommend it along with the Black Hole of
Calcutta and the Siberian salt mines.

HANNAH: [*Nodding reflectively*] I suspected as much. Mr. Shannon, in your touring party, do you think there might be

anyone interested in my water colors? Or in my character sketches?

SHANNON: I doubt it. I doubt that they're corny enough to please my ladies. *Oh-oh! Great Caesar's ghost.* . . .

[*This exclamation is prompted by the shrill, approaching call of his 'name.* CHARLOTTE *appears from the rear, coming from the hotel annex, and rushes like a teen-age Medea toward the verandah.* SHANNON *ducks into his cubicle, slamming the door so quickly that a corner of the mosquito netting is caught and sticks out, flirtatiously.* CHARLOTTE *rushes onto the verandah*]

CHARLOTTE: *Larry!*

HANNAH: Are you looking for someone, dear?

CHARLOTTE: Yeah, the man conducting our tour, Larry Shannon.

HANNAH: Oh, Mr. Shannon. I think he went down to the beach.

CHARLOTTE: I just now saw him coming up from the beach. [*She is tense and trembling, and her eyes keep darting up and down the verandah*]

HANNAH: Oh. Well. . . . But. . . .

CHARLOTTE: Larry? Larry! [*Her shouts startle the rain-forest birds into a clamorous moment*]

HANNAH: Would you like to leave a message for him, dear?

CHARLOTTE: No. I'm staying right here till he comes out of wherever he's hiding.

HANNAH: Why don't you just sit down, dear. I'm an artist, a painter. I was just sorting out my water colors and sketches in this portfolio, and look what I've come across. [*She selects a sketch and holds it up*]

SHANNON: [*From inside his cubicle*] Oh, God!

CHARLOTTE: [*Darting to the cubicle*] Larry, let me in there!

[*She beats on the door of the cubicle as* HERR FAHREN-KOPF *comes around the verandah with his portable radio. He is bug-eyed with excitement over the news broadcast in German*]

HANNAH: Guten abend.

[HERR FAHRENKOPF *jerks his head with a toothy grin,
raising a hand for silence.* HANNAH *nods agreeably and
approaches him with her portfolio of drawings. He maintains the grin as she displays one picture after another.*
HANNAH *is uncertain whether the grin is for the pictures
or the news broadcast. He stares at the pictures, jerking
his head from time to time. It is rather like the pantomime
of showing lantern slides*]

CHARLOTTE: [*Suddenly crying out again*] Larry, open this door
and let me in! I know you're in there, Larry!

HERR FAHRENKOPF: Silence, please, for one moment! This is
a recording of Der Führer addressing the Reichstag just . . .
[*He glances at his wristwatch*] . . . eight hours ago, today,
transmitted by Deutsches Nachrichtenbüro to Mexico City.
Please! Quiet, bitte!

[*A human voice like a mad dog's bark emerges from the
static momentarily,* CHARLOTTE *goes on pounding on*
SHANNON's *door.* HANNAH *suggests in pantomime that they
go to the back verandah, but* HERR FAHRENKOPF *despairs
of hearing the broadcast. As he rises to leave, the light
catches his polished glasses so that he appears for a moment
to have electric light bulbs in his forehead. Then he ducks
his head in a genial little bow and goes out beyond the
verandah, where he performs some muscle-flexing movements of a formalized nature, like the preliminary stances
of Japanese Suma wrestlers*]

HANNAH: May I show you my work on the other verandah?

[HANNAH *had started to follow* HERR FAHRENKOPF *with
her portfolio, but the sketches fall out, and she stops to
gather them from the floor with the sad, preoccupied air
of a lonely child picking flowers*]

[SHANNON's *head slowly, furtively, appears through the window of his cubicle. He draws quickly back as* CHARLOTTE

darts that way, stepping on HANNAH's *spilt sketches.* HANNAH
utters a soft cry of protest, which is drowned by CHAR-
LOTTE's *renewed clamor*]

CHARLOTTE: Larry, Larry, Judy's looking for me. Let me come
in, Larry, before she finds me here!

SHANNON: You can't come in. Stop shouting and I'll come out.

CHARLOTTE: All right, come out.

SHANNON: Stand back from the door so I *can*.

[*She moves a little aside and he emerges from his cubicle
like a man entering a place of execution. He leans against
the wall, mopping the sweat off his face with a handkerchief*]

SHANNON: How does Miss Fellowes know what happened that
night? Did you tell her?

CHARLOTTE: I didn't tell her, she guessed.

SHANNON: Guessing isn't knowing. If she is just guessing, that
means she doesn't know—I mean if you're not lying, if you
didn't tell her.

[HANNAH *has finished picking up her drawings and moves
quietly over to the far side of the verandah*]

CHARLOTTE: Don't talk to me like that.

SHANNON: Don't complicate my life now, please, for God's sake,
don't complicate my life now.

CHARLOTTE: Why have you changed like this?

SHANNON: I have a fever. Don't complicate my . . . fever.

CHARLOTTE: You act like you hated me now.

SHANNON: You're going to get me kicked out of Blake Tours,
Charlotte.

CHARLOTTE: Judy is, not me.

SHANNON: Why did you sing "I Love You Truly" at me?

CHARLOTTE: Because I do love you truly!

SHANNON: Honey girl, don't you know that nothing worse could happen to a girl in your, your . . . unstable condition . . . than to get emotionally mixed up with a man in my unstable condition, huh?

CHARLOTTE: No, no, no, I—

SHANNON: [*Cutting through*] Two unstable conditions can set a whole world on fire, can blow it up, past repair, and that is just as true between two people as it's true between. . . .

CHARLOTTE: All I know is you've got to marry me, Larry, after what happened between us in Mexico City!

SHANNON: A man in my condition can't marry, it isn't decent or legal. He's lucky if he can even hold onto his job. [*He keeps catching hold of her hands and plucking them off his shoulders*] I'm almost out of my mind, can't you see that, honey?

CHARLOTTE: I don't believe you don't love me.

SHANNON: Honey, it's almost impossible for anybody to believe they're not loved by someone they believe they love, but honey, I love *nobody*. I'm like that, it isn't my fault. When I brought you home that night I told you goodnight in the hall, just kissed you on the cheek like the little girl that you are, but the instant I opened my door, you rushed into my room and I couldn't get you out of it, not even when I, oh God, tried to scare you out of it by, oh God, don't you remember?

[MISS FELLOWES' *voice is heard from back of the hotel calling, "Charlotte!"*]

CHARLOTTE: Yes, I remember that after making love to me, you hit me, Larry, you struck me in the face, and you twisted my arm to make me kneel on the floor and pray with you for forgiveness.

SHANNON: I do that, I do that always when I, when . . . I don't have a dime left in my nervous emotional bank account— I can't write a check on it, now.

CHARLOTTE: Larry, let me help you!

MISS FELLOWES: [*Approaching*] Charlotte, Charlotte, Charlie!

CHARLOTTE: Help me and let me help you!

SHANNON: The helpless can't help the helpless!

CHARLOTTE: Let me in, Judy's coming!

SHANNON: Let me go. Go away!

[*He thrusts her violently back and rushes into his cubicle, slamming and bolting the door—though the gauze netting is left sticking out. As* MISS FELLOWES *charges onto the verandah,* CHARLOTTE *runs into the next cubicle, and* HANNAH *moves over from where she has been watching and meets her in the center*]

MISS FELLOWES: Shannon, Shannon! Where are you?

HANNAH: I think Mr. Shannon has gone down to the beach.

MISS FELLOWES: Was Charlotte Goodall with him? A young blonde girl in our party—was she with him?

HANNAH: No, nobody was with him, he was completely alone.

MISS FELLOWES: I heard a door slam.

HANNAH: That was mine.

MISS FELLOWES: [*Pointing to the door with the gauze sticking out*] Is this yours?

HANNAH: Yes, mine. I rushed out to catch the sunset.

[*At this moment* MISS FELLOWS *hears* CHARLOTTE *sobbing in* HANNAH's *cubicle. She throws the door open*]

MISS FELLOWES: Charlotte! Come out of there, Charlie! [*She has seized* CHARLOTTE *by the wrist*] What's your word worth—nothing? You promised you'd stay away from him! [CHARLOTTE *frees her arm, sobbing bitterly.* MISS FELLOWES *seizes her again, tighter, and starts dragging her away*] I have talked to your father about this man by long distance and he's getting out a warrant for his arrest, if he dare try coming back to the States after this!

CHARLOTTE: I don't care.

MISS FELLOWES: I do! I'm responsible for you.

CHARLOTTE: I don't want to go back to Texas!

MISS FELLOWES: Yes, you do! And you will!

[*She takes* CHARLOTTE *firmly by the arm and drags her away behind the hotel,* HANNAH *comes out of her cubicle, where she had gone when* MISS FELLOWES *pulled* CHARLOTTE *out of it*]

SHANNON: [*From his cubicle*] Ah, God. . . .

[HANNAH *crosses to his cubicle and knocks by the door*]

HANNAH: The coast is clear now, Mr. Shannon.

[SHANNON *does not answer or appear. She sets down her portfolio to pick up* NONNO's *white linen suit, which she had pressed and hung on the verandah. She crosses to his cubicle with it, and calls in*]

HANNAH: Nonno? It's almost time for supper! There's going to be a lovely, stormy sunset in a few minutes.

NONNO: [*From within*] Coming!

HANNAH: So is Christmas, Nonno.

NONNO: So is the Fourth of July!

HANNAH: We're past the Fourth of July. Hallowe'en comes next and then Thanksgiving. I hope you'll come forth sooner. [*She lifts the gauze net over his cubicle door*] Here's your suit, I've pressed it. [*She enters the cubicle*]

NONNO: It's mighty dark in here, Hannah.

HANNAH: I'll turn the light on for you.

[SHANNON *comes out of his cubicle, like the survivor of a plane crash, bringing out with him several pieces of his clerical garb. The black heavy silk bib is loosely fastened about his panting, sweating chest. He hangs over it a heavy gold cross with an amethyst center and attempts to fasten on a starched round collar. Now* HANNAH *comes back out of*]

NONNO's cubicle, adjusting the flowing silk tie which goes with her "artist" costume. For a moment they both face front, adjusting their two outfits. They are like two actors, in a play which is about to fold on the road, preparing gravely for a performance which may be the last one]

HANNAH: [*Glancing at* SHANNON] Are you planning to conduct church services of some kind here tonight, Mr. Shannon?

SHANNON: Goddamit, please help me with this! [*He means the round collar*]

HANNAH: [*Crossing behind him*] If you're not going to conduct a church service, why get into that uncomfortable outfit?

SHANNON: Because I've been accused of being defrocked and of lying about it, that's why. I want to show the ladies that I'm still a clocked—*frocked!*—minister of the. . . .

HANNAH: Isn't that lovely gold cross enough to convince the ladies?

SHANNON: No, they know I redeemed it from a Mexico City pawnshop, and they suspect that that's where I got it in the first place.

HANNAH: Hold still just a minute. [*She is behind him, trying to fasten the collar*] There now, let's hope it stays on. The button hole is so frayed I'm afraid that it won't hold the button. [*Her fear is instantly confirmed: the button pops out*]

SHANNON: Where'd it go?

HANNAH: Here, right under. . . .

[*She picks it up.* SHANNON *rips the collar off, crumples it and hurls it off the verandah. Then he falls into the hammock, panting and twisting.* HANNAH *quietly opens her sketch pad and begins to sketch him. He doesn't at first notice what she is doing*]

HANNAH: [*As she sketches*] How long have you been inactive in the, uh, Church, Mr. Shannon?

SHANNON: What's that got to do with the price of rice in China?

HANNAH: [*Gently*] Nothing.

SHANNON: What's it got to do with the price of coffee beans in Brazil?

HANNAH: I retract the question. With apologies.

SHANNON: To answer your question politely, I have been inactive in the Church for all but one year since I was ordained a minister of the Church.

HANNAH: [*Sketching rapidly and moving forward a bit to see his face better*] Well, that's quite a sabbatical, Mr. Shannon.

SHANNON: Yeah, that's . . . quite a . . . sabbatical.

[NONNO'S *voice is heard from his cubicle repeating a line of poetry several times*]

SHANNON: Is your grandfather talking to himself in there?

HANNAH: No, he composes out loud. He has to commit his lines to memory because he can't see to write them or read them.

SHANNON: Sounds like he's stuck on one line.

HANNAH: Yes. I'm afraid his memory is failing. Memory failure is his greatest dread. [*She says this almost coolly, as if it didn't matter*]

SHANNON: Are you drawing me?

HANNAH: Trying to. You're a very difficult subject. When the Mexican painter Siqueiros did his portrait of the American poet Hart Crane he had to paint him with closed eyes because he couldn't paint his eyes open—there was too much suffering in them and he couldn't paint it.

SHANNON: Sorry, but I'm not going to close my eyes for you. I'm hypnotizing myself—at least trying to—by looking at the light on the orange tree . . . leaves.

HANNAH: That's all right. I can paint your eyes open.

SHANNON: I had one parish one year and then I wasn't defrocked but I was . . . locked out of my church.

HANNAH: Oh . . . Why did they lock you out of it?

SHANNON: Fornication and heresy . . . in the same week.

HANNAH: [*Sketching rapidly*] What were the circumstances of the . . . uh . . . first offense?

SHANNON: Yeah, the fornication came first, preceded the heresy by several days. A very young Sunday-school teacher asked to see me privately in my study. A pretty little thing—no chance in the world—only child, and both of her parents were spinsters, almost identical spinsters wearing clothes of the opposite sexes. Fooling some of the people some of the time but not me—none of the time. . . . [*He is pacing the verandah with gathering agitation, and the all-inclusive mockery that his guilt produces*] Well, she declared herself to me—wildly.

HANNAH: A declaration of love?

SHANNON: Don't make *fun* of me, honey!

HANNAH: I wasn't.

SHANNON: The natural, or unnatural, attraction of one . . . lunatic for . . . another . . . that's all it was. I was the goddamndest prig in those days that even you could imagine. I said, let's kneel down together and pray and we did, we knelt down, but all of a sudden the kneeling position turned to a reclining position on the rug of my study and . . . When we got up? I struck her. Yes, I did, I struck her in the face and called her a damned little tramp. So she ran home. I heard the next day she'd cut herself with her father's straightblade razor. Yeah, the paternal spinster shaved.

SHANNON: Fatally?

SHANNON: Just broke the skin surface enough to bleed a little, but it made a scandal.

HANNAH: Yes, I can imagine that it . . . provoked some comment.

SHANNON: That it did, it did that. [*He pauses a moment in his fierce pacing as if the recollection still appalled him*] So the next Sunday when I climbed into the pulpit and looked down over all of those smug, disapproving, accusing faces uplifted, I had an impulse to shake them—so I shook them. I had a prepared sermon—meek, apologetic—I threw it away, tossed it into the chancel. Look here, I said, I shouted, I'm tired of conducting services in praise and worship of a senile delinquent —yeah, that's what I said, I shouted! All your Western theologies, the whole mythology of them, are based on the concept of God as a *senile delinquent* and, by God, I will not and cannot continue to conduct services in praise and worship of this, this . . . this. . . .

HANNAH: [*Quietly*] Senile delinquent?

SHANNON: Yeah, this angry, petulant old man. I mean he's represented like a bad-tempered childish old, old, sick, peevish man—I mean like the sort of old man in a nursing home that's putting together a jigsaw puzzle and can't put it together and gets furious at it and kicks over the table. Yes, I tell you they *do* that, all our theologies do it—accuse God of being a cruel, senile delinquent, blaming the world and brutally punishing all he created for his own faults in construction, and then, ha-ha, yeah—a thunderstorm broke that Sunday. . . .

HANNAH: You mean *outside* the church?

SHANNON: Yep, it was wilder than I was! And out they slithered, they slithered out of their pews to their shiny black cockroach sedans, ha-ha, and I shouted after them, hell, I even followed them halfway out of the church, shouting after them as they. . . . [*He stops with a gasp for breath*]

HANNAH: Slithered out?

SHANNON: I shouted after them, go on, go home and close your house windows, all your windows and doors, against the truth about God!

HANNAH: Oh, my heavens. Which is just what they did—poor things.

SHANNON: Miss Jelkes honey, Pleasant Valley, Virginia, was an exclusive suburb of a large city and these poor things were not poor—materially speaking.

HANNAH: [*Smiling a bit*] What was the, uh, upshot of it?

SHANNON: Upshot of it? Well, I wasn't defrocked. I was just locked out of the church in Pleasant Valley, Virginia, and put in a nice little private asylum to recuperate from a complete nervous breakdown as they preferred to regard it, and then, and then I . . . I entered my present line—tours of God's world conducted by a minister of God with a cross and a round collar to prove it. Collecting evidence!

HANNAH: Evidence of what, Mr. Shannon?

SHANNON: [*A touch shyly now*] My personal idea of God, not as a senile delinquent, but as a. . . .

HANNAH: Incomplete sentence.

SHANNON: It's going to storm tonight—a terrific electric storm. Then you will see the Reverend T. Lawrence Shannon's conception of God Almighty paying a visit to the world he created. I want to go back to the Church and preach the gospel of God as Lightning and Thunder . . . and also stray dogs vivisected and . . . and . . . and . . . [*He points out suddenly toward the sea*] That's him! There he is now! [*He is pointing out at a blaze, a majestic apocalypse of gold light, shafting the sky as the sun drops into the Pacific*] His oblivious majesty—and here I am on this . . . dilapidated verandah of a cheap hotel, out of season, in a country caught and destroyed in its flesh and corrupted in its spirit by its gold-hungry Conquistadors that bore the flag of the Inquisition along with the Cross of Christ. Yes . . . and. . . . [*There is a pause*]

HANNAH: Mr. Shannon . . . ?

SHANNON: Yes . . . ?

HANNAH: [*Smiling a little*] I have a strong feeling you will go back to the Church with this evidence you've been collecting, but when you do and it's a black Sunday morning, look out over the congregation, over the smug, complacent faces for a few old, very old faces, looking up at you, as you begin your sermon, with eyes like a piercing cry for something to still look up to, something to still believe in. And then I think you'll not shout what you say you shouted that black Sunday in Pleasant Valley, Virginia. I think you will throw away the violent, furious sermon, you'll toss *it* into the chancel, and talk about . . . no, maybe talk about . . . nothing . . . just . . .

SHANNON: What?

HANNAH: Lead them beside still waters because you know how badly they need the still waters, Mr. Shannon.

[*There is a moment of silence between them*]

SHANNON: Lemme see that thing. [*He seizes the sketch pad from her and is visibly impressed by what he sees. There is another moment which is prolonged to* HANNAH's *embarrassment*]

HANNAH: Where did you say the patrona put your party of ladies?

SHANNON: She had her . . . Mexican concubines put their luggage in the annex.

HANNAH: Where is the annex?

SHANNON: Right down the hill back of here, but all of my ladies except the teen-age Medea and the older Medea have gone out in a glass-bottomed boat to observe the . . . submarine marvels.

HANNAH: Well, when they come back to the annex they're going to observe my water colors with some marvelous submarine prices marked on the mattings.

SHANNON: By God, you're a hustler, aren't you, you're a fantastic cool hustler.

HANNAH: Yes, like *you*, Mr. Shannon. [*She gently removes her sketch pad from his grasp*] Oh, Mr. Shannon, if Nonno, Grandfather, comes out of his cell number 4 before I get back, will you please look out for him for me? I won't be longer than three shakes of a lively sheep's tail. [*She snatches up her portfolio and goes briskly off the verandah*]

SHANNON: Fantastic, absolutely fantastic.

[*There is a windy sound in the rain forest and a flicker of gold light like a silent scattering of gold coins on the verandah; then the sound of shouting voices. The Mexican boys appear with a wildly agitated creature—a captive iguana tied up in a shirt. They crouch down by the cactus clumps that are growing below the verandah and hitch the iguana to a post with a piece of rope.* MAXINE *is attracted by the commotion and appears on the verandah above them*]

PEDRO: Tenemos fiesta!*

PANCHO: Comeremos bien.

* We're going to have a feast! / We'll eat good. / Give it to me! I'll tie it up. / I caught it—*I'll* tie it up! / You'll only let it get away. / Tie it up tight! Ole, ole! Don't let it get away. Give it enough room!

PEDRO: Damela, damela! Yo la ataré.

PANCHO: Yo la cojí—yo la ataré!

PEDRO: Lo que vas a *hacer* es dejarla escapar.

MAXINE: Ammarla fuerte! Ole, ole! No la dejes escapar. Dejala moverse! [*To* SHANNON] They caught an iguana.

SHANNON: I've noticed they did that, Maxine.

[*She is holding her drink deliberately close to him. The Germans have heard the commotion and crowd onto the verandah.* FRAU FAHRENKOPF *rushes over to* MAXINE]

FRAU FAHRENKOPF: What is this? What's going on? A snake? Did they catch a snake?

MAXINE: No. *Lizard.*

FRAU FAHRENKOPF: [*With exaggerated revulsion*] Ouuu . . . lizard! [*She strikes a grotesque attitude of terror as if she were threatened by Jack the Ripper*]

SHANNON: [*To* MAXINE] You like iguana meat, don't you?

FRAU FAHRENKOPF: Eat? *Eat?* A big *lizard?*

MAXINE: Yep, they're mighty good eating—taste like white meat of chicken.

[FRAU FAHRENKOPF *rushes back to her family. They talk excitedly in German about the iguana*]

SHANNON: If you mean Mexican chicken, that's no recommendation. Mexican chickens are scavengers and they taste like what they scavenge.

MAXINE: Naw, I mean Texas chicken.

SHANNON: [*Dreamily*]: Texas . . . chicken. . . .

[*He paces restlessly down the verandah.* MAXINE *divides her attention between his tall, lean figure, that seems incapable of stillness, and the wriggling bodies of the Mexican boys lying on their stomachs half under the verandah—as if she were mentally comparing two opposite attractions to her simple, sensual nature.* SHANNON *turns at the end of the verandah and sees her eyes fixed on him*]

SHANNON: What is the sex of this iguana, Maxine?

MAXINE: Hah, who cares about the sex of an iguana . . . [*He passes close by her*] . . . except another . . . iguana?

SHANNON: Haven't you heard the limerick about iguanas?

[*He removes her drink from her hand and it seems as if he might drink it, but he only sniffs it, with an expression of repugnance. She chuckles*]

There was a young gaucho named Bruno
Who said about love, This I do know:
Women are fine, and sheep are divine,
But iguanas are—*Numero Uno!*

[*On "Numero Uno"* SHANNON *empties* MAXINE's *drink over the railing, deliberately onto the humped, wriggling posterior of* PEDRO, *who springs up with angry protests*]

PEDRO: Me cágo . . . hijo de la . . .

SHANNON: Qué? Qué?

MAXINE: Véte!

[SHANNON *laughs viciously. The iguana escapes and both boys rush shouting after it. One of them dives on it and recaptures it at the edge of the jungle*]

PANCHO: La iguana se escapé.*

MAXINE: Cojela, cojela! La cojíste? Si no la cojes, te morderá el culo. La cojíste?

PEDRO: La cojí.

[*The boys wriggle back under the verandah with the iguana*]

* The iguana's escaped. / Get it, get it, Have you got it? If you don't, it'll bite your behind. Have you got it? / He's got it.

MAXINE: [*Returning to* SHANNON] I thought you were gonna break down and take a drink, Reverend.

SHANNON: Just the odor of liquor makes me feel nauseated.

MAXINE: You couldn't smell it if you got it *in* you. [*She touches his sweating forehead. He brushes her hand off like an insect*] Hah! [*She crosses over to the liquor cart, and he looks after her with a sadistic grin*]

SHANNON: Maxine honey, whoever told you that you look good in tight pants was not a sincere friend of yours.

[*He turns away. At the same instant, a crash and a hoarse, startled outcry are heard from* NONNO'S *cubicle*]

MAXINE: I knew it, I *knew* it! The old man's took a fall!

[SHANNON *rushes into the cubicle, followed by* MAXINE]

[*The light has been gradually, steadily dimming during the incident of the iguana's escape. There is, in effect, a division of scenes here, though it is accomplished without a blackout or curtain. As* SHANNON *and* MAXINE *enter* NONNO'S *cubicle,* HERR FAHRENKOPF *and his party appear on the now twilit verandah. He turns on an outsize light fixture that is suspended from overhead, a full pearly-moon of a light globe that gives an unearthly luster to the scene. The great pearly globe is decorated by night insects, large but gossamer moths that have immolated themselves on its surface: the light through their wings gives them an opalescent color, a touch of fantasy*]

Now SHANNON *leads the old poet out of his cubicle, o'nto the facing verandah. The old man is impeccably dressed in snow-white linen with a black string tie. His leonine mane of hair gleams like silver as he passes under the globe*]

NONNO: No bones broke, I'm made out of India rubber!

SHANNON: A traveler-born falls down many times in his travels.

NONNO: Hannah? [*His vision and other senses have so far deteriorated that he thinks he is being led out by* HANNAH] I'm pretty sure I'm going to finish it here.

SHANNON: [*Shouting, gently*] I've got the same feeling, Grampa.

[MAXINE *follows them out of the cubicle*]

NONNO: I've never been surer of anything in my life.

SHANNON: [*Gently and wryly*] I've never been surer of anything in mine either.

[HERR FAHRENKOPF *has been listening with an expression of entrancement to his portable radio, held close to his ear, the sound unrealistically low. Now he turns it off and makes an excited speech*]

HERR FAHRENKOPF: The London fires have spread all the way from the heart of London to the Channel coast! Goering, Field Marshal Goering, calls it "the new phase of conquest!" *Super-firebombs! Each night!*

[NONNO *catches only the excited tone of this announcement and interprets it as a request for a recitation. He strikes the floor with his cane, throws back his silver-maned head and begins the delivery in a grand, declamatory style*]

NONNO:

Youth must be wanton, youth must be quick,
Dance to the candle while lasteth the wick,

Youth must be foolish and. . . .

[NONNO *falters on the line, a look of confusion and fear on his face. The Germans are amused.* WOLFGANG *goes up to* NONNO *and shouts into his face*]

WOLFGANG: Sir? What is your age? How old?

[HANNAH, *who has just returned to the verandah, rushes up to her grandfather and answers for him*]

HANNAH: He is ninety-seven years *young!*

HERR FAHRENKOPF: How old?

HANNAH: Ninety-seven—almost a *century young!*

[HERR FAHRENKOPF *repeats this information to his beaming wife and* HILDA *in German*]

NONNO: [*Cutting in on the Germans*]

Youth must be foolish and mirthful and blind,
Gaze not before and glance not behind,

Mark not. . . .

[*He falters again*]

HANNAH: [*Prompting him, holding tightly onto his arm*] Mark
not the shadow that darkens the way—

[*They recite the next lines together*]

Regret not the glitter of any lost day,

But laugh with no reason except the red wine,
For youth must be youthful and foolish and blind!

[*The Germans are loudly amused.* WOLFGANG *applauds
directly in the old poet's face.* NONNO *makes a little unsteady bow, leaning forward precariously on his cane.*
SHANNON *takes a firm hold of his arm as* HANNAH *turns
to the Germans, opening her portfolio of sketches and
addressing* WOLFGANG]

HANNAH: Am I right in thinking you are on your honeymoon?
[*There is no response, and she repeats the question in German while* FRAU FAHRENKOPF *laughs and nods vehemently*]
Habe ich recht dass Sie auf Ihrer Hochzeitsreise sind? Was
für eine hübsche junge Braut! Ich mache Pastell-Skizzen . . .

darf ich, würden Sie mir erlauben . . . ? Würden Sie, bitte
. . . bitte. . . .

[HERR FAHRENKOPF *bursts into a Nazi marching song and
leads his party to the champagne bucket on the table at
the left.* SHANNON *has steered* NONNO *to the other table*]

NONNO: [*Exhilarated*] Hannah! What was the *take?*

HANNAH: [*Embarrassed*] Grandfather, sit down, please stop
shouting!

NONNO: Hah? Did they cross your palm with silver or paper,
Hannah?

HANNAH: [*Almost desperately*] Nonno! No more shouting! Sit
down at the table. It's time to *eat!*

SHANNON: Chow time, Grampa.

NONNO: [*Confused but still shouting*] How much did they
come across with?

HANNAH: Nonno! *Please!*

NONNO: Did they, did you . . . sell 'em a . . . water color?

HANNAH: No sale, Grandfather!

MAXINE: Hah!

[HANNAH *turns to* SHANNON, *her usual composure shattered, or nearly so*]

HANNAH: He won't sit down or stop shouting.

NONNO: [*Blinking and beaming with the grotesque suggestion
of an old coquette*] Hah? How rich did we strike it, Hannah?

SHANNON: *You* sit down, Miss Jelkes. [*He says it with gentle
authority, to which she yields. He takes hold of the old man's
forearm and places in his hand a crumpled Mexican bill*]
Sir? Sir? [*He is shouting*] Five! Dollars! I'm putting it in
your pocket.

HANNAH: We can't accept . . . gratuities, Mr. Shannon.

SHANNON: Hell, I gave him five pesos.

NONNO: Mighty good for one poem!

SHANNON: Sir? Sir? The *pecuniary rewards* of a *poem* are *grossly inferior* to its *merits, always!*

> [*He is being fiercely, almost mockingly tender with the old man—a thing we are when the pathos of the old, the ancient, the dying is such a wound to our own [savagely beleaguered] nerves and sensibilities that this outside demand on us is beyond our collateral, our emotional reserve. This is as true of* HANNAH *as it is of* SHANNON, *of course. They have both overdrawn their reserves at this point of the encounter between them*]

NONNO: Hah? Yes. . . . [*He is worn out now, but still shouting*] We're going to clean up in this place!

SHANNON: You bet you're going to clean up here!

> [MAXINE *utters her one-note bark of a laugh.* SHANNON *throws a hard roll at her. She wanders amiably back toward the German table*]

NONNO: [*Tottering, panting, hanging onto* SHANNON's *arm, thinking it is* HANNAH's] Is the, the . . . dining room . . . crowded? [*He looks blindly about with wild surmise*]

SHANNON: Yep, it's filled to capacity! There's a big crowd at the door! [*His voice doesn't penetrate the old man's deafness*]

NONNO: If there's a cocktail lounge, Hannah, we ought to . . . work that . . . first. Strike while the iron is hot, ho, ho, while it's hot. . . . [*This is like a delirium—only as strong a woman as* HANNAH *could remain outwardly impassive*]

HANNAH: He thinks you're me, Mr. Shannon. Help him into a chair. Please stay with him a minute, I. . . .

> [*She moves away from the table and breathes as if she has just been dragged up half-drowned from the sea.* SHANNON *eases the old man into a chair. Almost at once* NONNO's *feverish viality collapses and he starts drifting back toward half sleep*]

SHANNON: [*Crossing to* HANNAH]: What you breathing like that for?

HANNAH: Some people take a drink, some take a pill. I just take a few deep breaths.

SHANNON: You're making too much out of this. It's a natural thing in a man as old as Grampa.

HANNAH: I know, I know. He's had more than one of these little "cerebral accidents" as you call them, and all in the last few months. He was amazing till lately. I had to show his passport to prove that he was the oldest living and practicing poet on earth. We did well, we made expenses and *more!* But . . . when I saw he was failing, I tried to persuade him to go back to Nantucket, but he conducts our tours. He said, "No, *Mexico!*" So here we are on this windy hilltop like a pair of scarecrows. . . . The bus from Mexico City broke down at an altitude of 15,000 feet above sea level. That's when I think the latest cerebral incident happened. It isn't so much the loss of hearing and sight but the . . . dimming out of the mind that I can't bear, because until lately, just lately, his mind was amazingly clear. But yesterday? In Taxco? I spent nearly all we had left on the wheelchair for him and still he insisted that we go on with the trip till we got to the sea, the . . . cradle of life as he calls it. . . . [*She suddenly notices* NONNO, *sunk in his chair as if lifeless. She draws a sharp breath, and goes quietly to him*]

SHANNON: [*To the Mexican boys*] Servicio! Aqui! [*The force of his order proves effective: they serve the fish course*]

HANNAH: What a kind man you are. I don't know how to thank you, Mr. Shannon. I'm going to wake him up now. Nonno! [*She claps her hands quietly at his ear. The old man rouses with a confused, breathless chuckle*] Nonno, linen napkins. [*She removes a napkin from the pocket of her smock*] I always carry one with me, you see, in case we run into paper napkins as sometimes happens, you see. . . .

NONNO: Wonderful place here. . . . I hope it is à la carte, Hannah, I want a very light supper so I won't get sleepy. I'm going to work after supper. I'm going to finish it here.

HANNAH: Nonno? We've made a friend here. Nonno, this is the Reverend Mr. Shannon.

NONNO: [*Struggling out of his confusion*]: Reverend?

HANNAH: [*Shouting to him*] Mr. Shannon's an Episcopal clergyman, Nonno.

NONNO: A man of God?

HANNAH: A man of God, on vacation.

NONNO: Hannah, tell him I'm too old to baptize and too young to bury but on the market for marriage to a rich widow, fat, fair and forty.

> [NONNO *is delighted by all of his own little jokes. One can see him exchanging these pleasantries with the rocking chair brigades of summer hotels at the turn of the century—and with professors' wives at little colleges in New England. But now it has become somewhat grostesque in a touching way, this desire to please, this playful manner, these venerable jokes.* SHANNON *goes along with it. The old man touches something in him which is outside of his concern with himself. This part of the scene, which is played in a "scherzo" mood, has an accompanying windy obligato on the hilltop—all through it we hear the wind from the sea gradually rising, sweeping up the hill through the rain forest, and there are fitful glimmers of lightning in the sky*]

NONNO: But very few ladies ever go past forty if you believe 'em, ho, ho! Ask him to . . . give the blessing. Mexican food needs blessing.

SHANNON: Sir, you give the blessing. I'll be right with you. [*He has broken one of his shoe laces*]

NONNO: Tell him I will oblige him on one condition.

SHANNON: What condition, sir?

NONNO: That you'll keep my daughter company when I retire after dinner. I go to bed with the chickens and get up with the roosters, ho, ho! So you're a man of God. A benedict or a bachelor?

SHANNON: Bachelor, sir. No sane and civilized woman would have me, Mr. Coffin.

NONNO: What did he say, Hannah?

HANNAH: [*Embarrassed*] Nonno, give the blessing.

NONNO: [*Not hearing this*] I call her my daughter, but she's my daughter's daughter. We've been in charge of each other since she lost both her parents in the very first automobile crash on the island of Nantucket.

HANNAH: Nonno, give the blessing.

NONNO: She isn't a modern flapper, she isn't modern and she— doesn't flap but she was brought up to be a wonderful wife and mother. But . . . I'm a selfish old man so I've kept her all to myself.

HANNAH: [*Shouting into his ear*] Nonno, Nonno, the blessing!

NONNO: [*Rising with an effort*] Yes, the blessing. Bless this food to our use, and ourselves to Thy service. Amen. [*He totters back into his chair*]

SHANNON: Amen.

[NONNO's *mind starts drifting, his head drooping forward. He murmurs to himself*]

SHANNON: How good is the old man's poetry?

HANNAH: My grandfather was a fairly well-known minor poet before the First World War and for a little while after.

SHANNON: In the minor league, huh?

HANNAH: Yes, a minor league poet with a major league spirit. I'm proud to be his granddaughter. . . . [*She draws a pack of cigarettes from her pocket, then replaces it immediately without taking a cigarette*]

NONNO: [*Very confused*] Hannah, it's too hot for . . . hot cereals this . . . morning. . . . [*He shakes his head several times with a rueful chuckle*]

HANNAH: He's not quite back, you see, he thinks it's morning. [*She says this as if making an embarrassing admission, with a quick, frightened smile at* SHANNON]

SHANNON: Fantastic—*fantastic.*

HANNAH: That word "fantastic" seems to be your favorite word, Mr. Shannon.

SHANNON: [*Looking out gloomily from the verandah*] Yeah, well, you know we—live on two levels, Miss Jelkes, the realistic level and the fantastic level, and which is the real one, really. . . .

HANNAH: I would say both, Mr. Shannon.

SHANNON: But when you live on the fantastic level as I have lately but have got to operate on the realistic level, that's when you're spooked, that's the spook. . . . [*This is said as if it were a private reflection*] I thought I'd shake the spook here but conditions have changed here. I didn't know the patrona had turned to a widow, a sort of bright widow spider. [*He chuckles almost like* NONNO]

[MAXINE *has pushed one of those gay little brass-and-glass liquor carts around the corner of the verandah. It is laden with an ice bucket, coconuts and a variety of liquors. She hums gaily to herself as she pushes the cart close to the table*]

MAXINE: Cocktails, anybody?

HANNAH: No, thank you, Mrs. Faulk, I don't think we care for any.

SHANNON: People don't drink cocktails between the fish and the entrée, Maxine honey.

MAXINE: Grampa needs a toddy to wake him up. Old folks need a toddy to pick 'em up. [*She shouts into the old man's ear*] Grampa! How about a toddy? [*Her hips are thrust out at* SHANNON]

SHANNON: Maxine, your ass—excuse me, Miss Jelkes—your hips, Maxine, are too fat for this verandah.

MAXINE: Hah! Mexicans like 'em, if I can judge by the pokes and pinches I get in the busses to town. And so do the Germans. Ev'ry time I go near Herr Fahrenkopf he gives me a pinch or a goose.

SHANNON: Then go near him again for another goose.

MAXINE: Hah! I'm mixing Grampa a Manhattan with two cherries in it so he'll live through dinner.

SHANNON: Go on back to your Nazis, I'll mix the Manhattan for him. [*He goes to the liquor cart*]

MAXINE: [*To* HANNAH] How about you, honey, a little soda with lime juice?

HANNAH: Nothing for me, thank you.

SHANNON: Don't make nervous people more nervous, Maxine.

MAXINE: You better let me mix that toddy for Grampa, you're making a mess of it, Shannon.

[*With a snort of fury, he thrusts the liquor cart like a battering ram at her belly. Some of the bottles fall off it; she thrusts it right back at him*]

HANNAH: Mrs. Faulk, Mr. Shannon, this is childish, please stop it!

[*The Germans are attracted by the disturbance. They cluster around, laughing delightedly.* SHANNON *and* MAXINE *seize opposite ends of the rolling liquor cart and thrust it toward each other, both grinning fiercely as gladiators in mortal combat. The Germans shriek with laughter and chatter in German*]

HANNAH: Mr. Shannon, stop it! [*She appeals to the Germans*] Bitte! Nehmen Sie die Spirituosen weg. Bitte, nehmen Sie sie weg.

[SHANNON *has wrested the cart from* MAXINE *and pushed it at the Germans. They scream delightedly. The cart crashes into the wall of the verandah.* SHANNON *leaps down the steps and runs into the foliage. Birds scream in the rain forest. Then sudden quiet returns to the verandah as the Germans go back to their own table*]

MAXINE: Crazy, black Irish Protestant son of a . . . Protestant!

HANNAH: Mrs. Faulk, he's putting up a struggle not to drink.

MAXINE: Don't interfere. You're an interfering woman.

HANNAH: Mr. Shannon is dangerously . . . disturbed.

MAXINE: I know how to handle him, honey—you just met him today. Here's Grampa's Manhattan cocktail with two cherries in it.

HANNAH: Please don't call him Grampa.

MAXINE: Shannon calls him Grampa.

HANNAH: [*Taking the drink*] He doesn't make it sound condescending, but you *do*. My grandfather is a gentleman in the true sense of the word, he is a *gentle man*.

MAXINE: What are you?

HANNAH: I am his granddaughter.

MAXINE: Is that all you are?

HANNAH: I think it's enough to be.

MAXINE: Yeah, but you're also a deadbeat, using that dying old man for a front to get in places without the cash to pay even one day in advance. Why, you're dragging him around with you like Mexican beggars carry around a sick baby to put the touch on the tourists.

HANNAH: I told you I had no money.

MAXINE: Yes, and I told you that I was a widow—recent. In such a financial hole they might as well have buried me with my husband.

[SHANNON *reappears from the jungle foilage but remains unnoticed by* HANNAH *and* MAXINE]

HANNAH: [*With forced calm*] Tomorrow morning, at daybreak, I will go in town. I will set up my easel in the plaza and peddle my water colors and sketch tourists. I am not a weak person, my failure here isn't typical of me.

MAXINE: I'm not a weak person either.

HANNAH: No. By no means, no. Your strength is awe-inspiring.

MAXINE: You're goddam right about that, but how do you think you'll get to Acapulco without the cabfare or even the busfare there?

HANNAH: I will go on shanks' mare, Mrs. Faulk—islanders are good walkers. And if you doubt my word for it, if you really think I came here as a deadbeat, then I will put my grandfather back in his wheelchair and push him back down this hill to the road and all the way back into town.

MAXINE: Ten miles, with a storm coming up?

HANNAH: Yes, I would—I will. [*She is dominating* MAXINE *in this exchange. Both stand beside the table.* NONNO's *head is drooping back into sleep*]

MAXINE: I wouldn't let you.

HANNAH: But you've made it clear that you don't want us to stay here for one night even.

MAXINE: The storm would blow that old man out of his wheelchair like a dead leaf.

HANNAH: He would prefer that to staying where he's not welcome, and I would prefer it for him, and for myself, Mrs. Faulk. [*She turns to the Mexican boys*] Where is his wheelchair? Where is my grandfather's wheelchair?

[*This exchange has roused the old man. He struggles up from his chair, confused, strikes the floor with his cane and starts declaiming a poem*]

NONNO:

Love's an old remembered song
A drunken fiddler plays,
Stumbling crazily along
Crooked alleyways.

When his heart is mad with music
He will play the—

HANNAH: Nonno, not now, Nonno! He thought someone asked for a poem. [*She gets him back into the chair.* HANNAH *and* MAXINE *are still unaware of* SHANNON]

MAXINE: Calm down, honey.

HANNAH: I'm perfectly calm, Mrs. Faulk.

MAXINE: I'm *not*. That's the trouble.

HANNAH: I understand that, Mrs. Faulk. You lost your husband just lately. I think you probably miss him more than you know.

MAXINE: No, the trouble is Shannon.

HANNAH: You mean his nervous state and his . . . ?

MAXINE: No, I just mean Shannon. I want you to lay off him, honey, You're not for Shannon and Shannon isn't for you.

HANNAH: Mrs. Faulk, I'm a New England spinster who is pushing forty.

MAXINE: I got the vibrations between you—I'm very good at catching vibrations between people—and there sure was a vibration between you and Shannon the moment you got here. That, just that, believe me, nothing but that has made this . . . misunderstanding between us. So if you just don't mess with Shannon, you and your Grampa can stay on here as long as you want to, honey.

HANNAH: Oh, Mrs. Faulk, do I look like a *vamp*?

MAXINE: They come in all types. I've had all types of them here.

[SHANNON *comes over to the table*]

SHANNON: Maxine, I told you don't make nervous people more nervous, but you wouldn't listen.

MAXINE: What you need is a drink.

SHANNON: Let me decide about that.

HANNAH: Won't you sit down with us, Mr. Shannon, and eat something? Please. You'll feel better.

SHANNON: I'm not hungry right now.

HANNAH: Well, just sit down with us, won't you?

[SHANNON *sits down with* HANNAH]

MAXINE: [*Warningly to* HANNAH] O.K. O.K. . . .

NONNO: [*Rousing a bit and mumbling*] Wonderful . . . wonderful place here.

[MAXINE *retires from the table and wheels the liquor cart over to the German party*]

SHANNON: Would you have gone through with it?

HANNAH: Haven't you ever played poker, Mr. Shannon?

SHANNON: You mean you were bluffing?

HANNAH: Let's say I was drawing to an inside straight. [*The wind rises and sweeps up the hill like a great waking sigh from the ocean*] It *is* going to storm. I hope your ladies aren't still out in that, that . . . glass-bottomed boat, observing the, uh, submarine . . . marvels.

SHANNON: That's because you don't know these ladies. However, they're back from the boat trip. They're down at the cantina, dancing together to the jukebox and hatching new plots to get me kicked out of Blake Tours.

HANNAH: What would you do if you. . . .

SHANNON: Got the sack? Go back to the Church or take the long swim to China. [HANNAH *removes a crumpled pack of cigarettes from her pocket. She discovers only two left in the pack and decides to save them for later. She returns the pack to her pocket*] May I have one of your cigarettes, Miss Jelkes? [*She offers him the pack. He takes it from her and crumples it and throws it off the verandah*] Never smoke those, they're made out of tobacco from cigarette stubs that beggars pick up off sidewalks and out of gutters in Mexico city. [*He produces a tin of English cigarettes*] Have these—Benson and Hedges, imported, in an airtight tin, my luxury in my life.

HANNAH: Why—thank you, I will, since you have thrown mine away.

SHANNON: I'm going to tell you something about yourself. You are a lady, a *real* one and a *great* one.

HANNAH: What have I done to merit that compliment from you?

SHANNON: It isn't a compliment, it's just a report on what I've noticed about you at a time when it's hard for me to notice anything outside myself. You took out those Mexican cigarettes, you found you just had two left, you can't afford to buy a new pack of even that cheap brand, so you put them away for later. Right?

HANNAH: Mercilessly accurate, Mr. Shannon.

SHANNON: But when I asked you for one, you offered it to me without a sign of reluctance.

HANNAH: Aren't you making a big point out of a small matter?

SHANNON: Just the opposite, honey, I'm making a small point out of a very large matter. [SHANNON *has put a cigarette in his lips but has no matches.* HANNAH *has some and she lights his cigarette for him*] How'd you learn how to light a match in the wind?

HANNAH: Oh, I've learned lots of useful little things like that. I wish I'd learned some *big* ones.

SHANNON: Such as what?

HANNAH: How to help you, Mr. Shannon. . . .

SHANNON: Now I know why I came here!

HANNAH: To meet someone who can light a match in the wind?

SHANNON: [*Looking down at the table, his voice choking*] To meet someone who wants to *help* me, Miss Jelkes. . . . [*He makes a quick, embarrassed turn in the chair, as if to avoid her seeing that he has tears in his eyes. She regards him steadily and tenderly, as she would her grandfather*]

HANNAH: Has it been so long since anyone has wanted to help you, or have you just. . . .

SHANNON: Have I—what?

HANNAH: Just been so much involved with a struggle in yourself that you haven't noticed when people have wanted to help you, the little they can? I know people torture each other many times like devils, but sometimes they do see and know each other, you know, and then, if they're decent, they do want to help each other all that they can. Now will you please help *me*? Take care of Nonno while I remove my water colors from the annex verandah because the storm is coming up by leaps and bounds now.

[*He gives a quick, jerky nod, dropping his face briefly into the cup of his hands. She murmurs "Thank you" and springs up, starting along the verandah. Halfway across, as the storm closes in upon the hilltop with a thunderclap and a sound of rain coming,* HANNAH *turns to look back at the table.* SHANNON *has risen and gone around the table to* NONNO]

SHANNON: Grampa? Nonno? Let's get up before the rain hits us, Grampa.

NONNO: What? What?

[SHANNON *gets the old man out of his chair and shepherds him to the back of the verandah as* HANNAH *rushes toward the annex. The Mexican boys hastily clear the table, fold it up and lean it against the wall.* SHANNON *and* NONNO *turn and face toward the storm, like brave men facing a firing squad.* MAXINE *is excitedly giving orders to the boys*]

MAXINE: Pronto, pronto, muchachos! Pronto, pronto!* Llevaros todas las cosas! Pronto, pronto! Recoje los platos! Apurate con el mantel!

PEDRO: Nos estamos dando prisa!

PANCHO: Que el chubasco lave los platos!

[*The German party look on the storm as a Wagnerian climax. They rise from their table as the boys come to clear it, and start singing exultantly. The storm, with its white convulsions of light, is like a giant white bird attacking the hilltop of the Costa Verde.* HANNAH *reappears with her water colors clutched against her chest*]

SHANNON: Got them?

HANNAH: Yes, just in time. Here is your God, Mr. Shannon.

* Hurry, hurry, boys! Pick everything up! Get the plates! Hurry with the table cloth! / We *are* hurrying! / Let the storm wash the plates!

SHANNON: [*Quietly*] Yes, I see him, I hear him, I know him. And if he doesn't know that I know him, let him strike me dead with a bolt of his lightning.

[*He moves away from the wall to the edge of the verandah as a fine silver sheet of rain descends off the sloping roof, catching the light and dimming the figures behind it. Now everything is silver, delicately lustrous.* SHANNON *extends his hands under the rainfall, turning them in it as if to cool them. Then he cups them to catch the water in his palms and bathes his forehead with it. The rainfall increases. The sound of the marimba band at the beach cantina is brought up the hill by the wind.* SHANNON *lowers his hands from his burning forehead and stretches them out through the rain's silver sheet as if he were reaching for something outside and beyond himself. Then nothing is visible but these reaching-out hands. A pure white flash of lightning reveals* HANNAH *and* NONNO *against the wall, behind* SHANNON, *and the electric globe suspended from the roof goes out, the power extinguished by the storm. A clear shaft of light stays on* SHANNON's *reaching out hands till the stage curtain has fallen, slowly*]*

* Note: In staging, the plastic elements should be restrained so that they don't take precedence over the more important human values. It should not seem like an "effect curtain." The faint, windy music of the marimba band from the cantina should continue as the houselights are brought up for the intermission.

INTERMISSION

ACT THREE

*The verandah, several hours later. Cubicles number 3, 4,
and 5 are dimly lighted within. We see* HANNAH *in number 3, and* NONNO *in number 4.* SHANNON, *who has taken
off his shirt, is seated at a table on the verandah, writing
a letter to his Bishop. All but this table have been folded
and stacked against the wall and* MAXINE *is putting the
hammock back up which had been taken down for dinner.
The electric power is still off and the cubicles are lighted
by oil lamps. The sky has cleared completely, the moon
is making for full and it bathes the scene in an almost
garish silver which is intensified by the wetness from the
recent rainstorm. Everything is drenched—there are pools
of silver here and there on the floor of the verandah. At
one side a smudgepot is burning to repel the mosquitoes,
which are particularly vicious after a tropical downpour
when the wind is exhausted.*

SHANNON *is working feverishly on the letter to the Bishop,
now and then slapping at a mosquito on his bare torso.
He is shiny with perspiration, still breathing like a spent
runner, muttering to himself as he writes and sometimes
suddenly drawing a loud deep breath and simultaneously
throwing back his head to stare up wildly at the night sky.*
HANNAH *is seated on a straight-back chair behind the
mosquito netting in her cubicle—very straight herself, holding a small book in her hands but looking steadily over
it at* SHANNON, *like a guardian angel. Her hair has been
let down.* NONNO *can be seen in his cubicle rocking back
and forth on the edge of the narrow bed as he goes over*

and over the lines of his first new poem in "twenty-some years"—which he knows is his last one.

Now and then the sound of distant music drifts up from the beach cantina.

MAXINE: Workin' on your sermon for next Sunday, Rev'rend?

SHANNON: I'm writing a very important letter, Maxine. [*He means don't disturb me*]

MAXINE: Who to, Shannon?

SHANNON: The Dean of the Divinity School at Sewanee. [MAXINE *repeats* "Sewanee" *to herself, tolerantly*] Yes, and I'd appreciate it very much, Maxine honey, if you'd get Pedro or Pancho to drive into town with it tonight so it will go out first thing in the morning.

MAXINE: The kids took off in the station wagon already—for some cold beers and hot whores at the cantina.

SHANNON: "Fred's dead"—he's lucky. . . .

MAXINE: Don't misunderstand me about Fred, baby. I miss him, but we'd not only stopped sleeping together, we'd stopped talking together except in grunts—no quarrels, no misunderstandings, but if we exchanged two grunts in the course of a day, it was a long conversation we'd had that day between us.

SHANNON: Fred knew when I was spooked—wouldn't have to tell him. He'd just look at me and say, "Well, Shannon, you're spooked."

MAXINE: Yeah, well, Fred and me'd reached the point of just grunting.

SHANNON: Maybe he thought you'd turned into a pig, Maxine.

MAXINE: Hah! You know damn well that Fred respected me, Shannon, like I did Fred. We just, well, you know . . . age difference. . . .

SHANNON: Well, you've got Pedro and Pancho.

MAXINE: Employees. They don't respect me enough. When you let employees get too free with you, personally, they stop

respecting you, Shannon. And it's well, it's . . . humiliating—
not to be . . . respected.

SHANNON: Then take more bus trips to town for the Mexican
pokes and the pinches, or get Herr Fahrenkopf to "respect"
you, honey.

MAXINE: Hah! You kill me. I been thinking lately of selling
out here and going back to the States, to Texas, and operating
a tourist camp outside some live town like Houston or Dallas,
on a highway, and renting out cabins to business executives
wanting a comfortable little intimate little place to give a
little after-hours dictation to their cute little secretaries that
can't type or write shorthand. Complimentary rum-cocos-bath-
rooms with bidets. I'll introduce the bidet to the States.

SHANNON: Does everything have to wind up on that level with
you, Maxine?

MAXINE: Yes and no, baby. I know the difference between loving
someone and just sleeping with someone—even I know about
that. [*He starts to rise*] We've both reached a point where
we've got to settle for something that works for us in our lives
—even if it isn't on the highest kind of level.

SHANNON: I don't want to rot.

MAXINE: You wouldn't. I wouldn't let you! I know your psycholog-
ical history. I remember one of your conversations on this
verandah with Fred. You was explaining to him how your
problems first started. You told him that Mama, your mama,
used to send you to bed before you was ready to sleep—so
you practiced the little boy's vice, you amused yourself with
yourself. And once she caught you at it and whaled your backside with the back side of a hairbrush because she said she had
to punish you for it because it made God mad as much as it
did Mama, and she had to punish you for it so God wouldn't
punish you for it harder than she would.

SHANNON: I was talking to Fred.

MAXINE: Yeah, but I heard it, all of it. You said you loved
God and Mama and so you quit it to please them, but it was
your secret pleasure and you harbored a secret resentment against
Mama and God for making you give it up. And so you got
back at God by preaching atheistical sermons and you got
back at Mama by starting to lay young girls.

SHANNON: I have never delivered an atheistical sermon, and never would or could when I go back to the Church.

MAXINE: You're not going back to no Church. Did you mention the charge of statutory rape to the Divinity Dean?

SHANNON: [*Thrusting his chair back so vehemently that it topples over*] Why don't you *let up* on me? You haven't let up on me since I got here this morning! *Let up on me!* Will you please *let up* on me?

MAXINE: [*Smiling serenely into his rage*] Aw baby. . . .

SHANNON: What do you mean by "aw baby"? What do you want out of me, Maxine honey?

MAXINE: Just to do this, [*She runs her fingers through his hair. He thrusts her hand away*]

SHANNON: Ah, God. [*Words fail him. He shakes his head with a slight, helpless laugh and goes down the steps from the verandah*]

MAXINE: The Chinaman in the kitchen says, "No sweat." . . . "No sweat." He says that's all his philosophy. All the Chinese philosophy in three words, "Mei yoo guanchi"—which is Chinese for "no sweat." . . . With your record and a charge of statutory rape hanging over you in Texas, how could you go to a church except to the Holy Rollers with some lively young female rollers and a bushel of hay on the church floor?

SHANNON: I'll drive into town in the bus to post this letter tonight. [*He has started toward the path. There are sounds below. He divides the masking foliage with his hands and looks down the hill*]

MAXINE: [*Descending the steps from the verandah*] Watch out for the spook, he's out there.

SHANNON: My ladies are up to something. They're all down there on the road, around the bus.

MAXINE: They're running out on you, Shannon.

[*She comes up beside him. He draws back and she looks down the hill. The light in number 3 cubicle comes on and HANNAH rises from the little table that she had cleared for letter writing. She removes her Kabuki robe from a hook*]

*and puts it on as an actor puts on a costume in his dressing
room.* NONNO'S *cubicle is also lighted dimly. He sits on the
edge of his cot, rocking slightly back and forth, uttering
an indistinguishable mumble of lines from his poem*]

MAXINE: Yeah. There's a little fat man down there that looks
like Jake Latta to me. Yep, that's Jake, that's Latta. I reckon
Blake Tours has sent him here to take over your party, Shannon. [SHANNON *looks out over the jungle and lights a cigarette
with jerky fingers*] Well, let him do it. No sweat! He's coming
up here now. Want me to handle it for you?

SHANNON: I'll handle it for myself. You keep out of it, please.

[*He speaks with a desperate composure.* HANNAH *stands
just behind the curtain of her cubicle, motionless as a
painted figure, during the scene that follows.* JAKE LATTA
comes puffing up the verandah steps, beaming genially]

LATTA: Hi there, Larry.

SHANNON: Hello, Jake. [*He folds his letter into an envelope*]
Mrs. Faulk honey, this goes air special.

MAXINE: First you'd better address it.

SHANNON: Oh!

[SHANNON *laughs and snatches the letter back, fumbling
in his pocket for an address book, his fingers shaking
uncontrollably.* LATTA *winks at* MAXINE. *She smiles tolerantly*]

LATTA: How's our boy doin', Maxine?

MAXINE: He'd feel better if I could get him to take a drink.

LATTA: Can't you get a drink down him?

MAXINE: Nope, not even a rum-coco.

LATTA: Let's have a rum-coco, Larry.

SHANNON: You have a rum-coco, Jake. I have a party of ladies
to take care of. And I've discovered that situations come up
in this business that call for cold, sober judgment. How about

you? Haven't you ever made that discovery, Jake? What're you doing here? Are you here with a party?

LATTA: I'm here to pick up your party, Larry boy.

SHANNON: That's interesting! On whose authority, Jake?

LATTA: Blake Tours wired me in Cuernavaca to pick up your party here and put them together with mine cause you'd had this little nervous upset of yours and. . . .

SHANNON: Show me the wire! Huh?

LATTA: The bus driver says you took the ignition key to the bus.

SHANNON: That's right. I have the ignition key to the bus and I have this party and neither the bus or the party will pull out of here till I say so.

LATTA: Larry, you're a sick boy. Don't give me trouble.

SHANNON: What jail did they bail you out of, you fat zero?

LATTA: Let's have the bus key, Larry.

SHANNON: Where did they dig you up? You've got no party in Cuernavaca, you haven't been out with a party since thirty-seven.

LATTA: Just give me the bus key, Larry.

SHANNON: In a pig's—snout!—like yours!

LATTA: Where is the reverend's bedroom, Mrs. Faulk?

SHANNON: The bus key is in my pocket. [He slaps his pants pocket fiercely] Here, right here, in my pocket! Want it? Try and get it, Fatso!

LATTA: What language for a reverend to use, Mrs. Faulk. . . .

SHANNON: [Holding up the key] See it? [He thrusts it back into his pocket] Now go back wherever you crawled from. My party of ladies is staying here three more days because several of them are in no condition to travel and neither—neither am I.

LATTA: They're getting in the bus now.

SHANNON: How are you going to start it?

LATTA: Larry, don't make me call the bus driver up here to hold you down while I get that key away from you. You want to see the wire from Blake Tours? Here. [*He produces the wire*] Read it.

SHANNON: You sent that wire to yourself.

LATTA: From Houston?

SHANNON: You had it sent you from Houston. What's that prove? Why, Blake Tours was nothing, *nothing!*—till they got me. You think they'd let me go?—Ho, ho! Latta, it's caught up with you, Latta, all the whores and tequila have hit your brain now, Latta. [LATTA *shouts down the hill for the bus driver*] Don't you realize what I mean to Blake Tours? Haven't you seen the brochure in which they mention, they brag, that special parties are conducted by the Reverend T. Lawrence Shannon, D.D., noted world traveler, lecturer, son of a minister and grandson of a bishop, and the direct descendant of two colonial governors? [MISS FELLOWES *appears at the verandah steps*] Miss Fellowes has read the brochure, she's memorized the brochure. She knows what it says about me.

MISS FELLOWES: [*To* LATTA] Have you got the bus key?

LATTA: Bus driver's going to get it away from him, lady. [*He lights a cigar with dirty, shaky fingers*]

SHANNON: Ha-ha-ha-ha-ha! [*His laughter shakes him back against the verandah wall*]

LATTA: He's gone. [*He touches his forehead*]

SHANNON: Why, those ladies . . . have had . . . some of them, most of them if not all of them . . . for the first time in their lives the advantage of contact, social contact, with a gentleman born and bred, whom under no other circumstances they could have possibly met . . . let alone be given the chance to insult and accuse and. . . .

MISS FELLOWES: Shannon! The girls are in the bus and we want to go now, so give up that key. Now!

[HANK, *the bus driver, appears at the top of the path, whistling casually: he is not noticed at first*]

SHANNON: If I didn't have a decent sense of responsibility to these parties I take out, I would gladly turn over your party—

because I don't like your party—to this degenerate here, this
Jake Latta of the gutter-rat Lattas. Yes, I would—I would surrender the bus key in my pocket, even to Latta, but I am not
that irresponsible, no, I'm not, to the parties that I take out,
regardless of the party's treatment of me. I still feel responsible
for them till I get them back wherever I picked them up.
[HANK *comes onto the verandah*] Hi, Hank. Are you friend
or foe?

HANK: Larry, I got to get that ignition key now so we can get
moving down there.

SHANNON: Oh! Then *foe!* I'm disappointed, Hank. I thought you
were friend, not foe. [HANK *puts a wrestler's armlock on*
SHANNON *and* LATTA *removes the key from his pocket.* HAN-
NAH *raises a hand to her eyes*] O.K., O.K., you've got the
bus key. By force. I feel exonerated now of all responsibility.
Take the bus and the ladies in it and go. Hey, Jake, did you
know they had lesbians in Texas—without the dikes the plains
of Texas would be engulfed by the Gulf. [*He nods his head
violently toward* MISS FELLOWES, *who springs forward and slaps
him*] Thank you, Miss Fellowes. Latta, hold on a minute. I
will not be stranded here. I've had unusual expenses on this trip.
Right now I don't have my fare back to Houston or even to
Mexico City. Now if there's any truth in your statement that
Blake Tours have really authorized you to take over my party,
then I am sure they have . . . [*He draws a breath, almost
gasping*] . . . I'm sure they must have given you something in
the . . . the nature of . . . *severance* pay? Or at least enough
to get me back to the States?

LATTA: I got no money for you.

SHANNON: I hate to question your word, but. . . .

LATTA: We'll drive you back to Mexico City. You can sit up
front with the driver.

SHANNON: *You would do that, Latta. I'd* find it *humiliating.*
Now! Give me my severance pay!

LATTA: Blake Tours is having to refund those ladies half the
price of the tour. That's your severance pay. And Miss Fellowes
tells me you got plenty of money out of this young girl you
seduced in. . . .

SHANNON: Miss Fellowes, did you really make such a . . . ?

MISS FELLOWES: When Charlotte returned that night, she'd cashed two traveler's checks.

SHANNON: After I had spent all my own cash.

MISS FELLOWES: On what? Whores in the filthy places you took her through?

SHANNON: Miss Charlotte cashed two ten-dollar traveler's checks because I had spent all the cash I had on me. And I've never had to, I've certainly never desired to, have relations with whores.

MISS FELLOWES: You took her through ghastly places, such as. . . .

SHANNON: I showed her what she wanted me to show her. Ask her! I showed her San Juan de Letran, I showed her Tenampa and some other places not listed on the Blake Tours brochure. I showed her more than the floating gardens at Xochimilco, Maximilian's Palace, and the mad Empress Carlotta's little homesick chapel, Our Lady of Guadalupe, the monument to Juarez, the relics of the Aztec civilization, the sword of Cortez, the headdress of Montezuma. I showed her what she told me she wanted to see. Where is she? Where is Miss . . . oh, down there with the ladies. [*He leans over the rail and shouts down*] Charlotte! Charlotte! [MISS FELLOWES *seizes his arm and thrusts him away from the verandah rail*]

MISS FELLOWES: Don't you dare!

SHANNON: Dare what?

MISS FELLOWES: Call her, speak to her, go near her, you, you . . . *filthy!*

[MAXINE *reappears at the corner of the verandah, with the ceremonial rapidity of a cuckoo bursting from a clock to announce the hour. She just stands there with an incongruous grin, her big eyes unblinking, as if they were painted on her round beaming face.* HANNAH *holds a gold-lacquered Japanese fan motionless but open in one hand; the other hand touches the netting at the cubicle door as if she were checking an impulse to rush to* SHANNON'S *defense. Her*

attitude has the style of a Kabuki dancer's pose. SHANNON's
manner becomes courtly again]

SHANNON: Oh, all right, I won't. I only wanted her to confirm
my story that I took her out that night at her request, not at
my . . . suggestion. All that I did was offer my services to her
when *she* told *me* she'd like to see things not listed in the
brochure, not usually witnessed by ordinary tourists such as. . . .

MISS FELLOWES: Your hotel bedroom? Later? That too? She
came back *flea*-bitten!

SHANNON: Oh, now, don't exaggerate, please. Nobody ever got any
fleas off Shannon.

MISS FELLOWES: Her clothes had to be fumigated!

SHANNON: I understand your annoyance, but you are going too
far when you try to make out that I gave Charlotte fleas. I don't
deny that. . . .

MISS FELLOWES: Wait till they get my *report!*

SHANNON: I don't deny that it's possible to get fleabites on
a tour of inspection of what lies under the public surface
of cities, off the grand boulevards, away from the nightclubs,
even away from Diego Sivera's murals, but. . . .

MISS FELLOWES: Oh, preach that in a pulpit, Reverend Shannon *de*-frocked!

SHANNON: [*Ominously*] You've said that once too often. [*He
seizes her arm*] This time before witnesses. Miss Jelkes? Miss
Jelkes!

[HANNAH *opens the curtain of her cubicle*]

HANNAH: Yes, Mr. Shannon, what is it?

SHANNON: You heard what this. . . .

MISS FELLOWES: Shannon! Take your hand off my arm!

SHANNON: Miss Jelkes, just tell me, did you hear what she . . .
[*His voice stops oddly with a choked sobbing sound. He runs
at the wall and pounds it with his fists*]

MISS FELLOWES: I spent this entire afternoon and over twenty dollars checking up on this impostor, with long-distance phone calls.

HANNAH: Not impostor—you mustn't say things like that.

MISS FELLOWES: You were locked out of your church!—for atheism and seducing of girls!

SHANNON: [*Turning about*] In front of God and witnesses, you are lying, *lying!*

LATTA: Miss Fellowes, I want you to know that Blake Tours was deceived about this character's background and Blake Tours will see that he is blacklisted from now on at every travel agency in the States.

SHANNON: How about Africa, Asia, Australia? The whole world, Latta, God's world, has been the range of my travels. I haven't stuck to the schedules of the brochures and I've always allowed the ones that were willing to see, to *see!*—the underworlds of all places, and if they had hearts to be touched, feelings to feel with, I gave them a priceless chance to feel and be touched. And none will ever forget it, none of them, ever, never! [*The passion of his speech imposes a little stillness*]

LATTA: Go on, lie back in your hammock, that's all you're good for, Shannon. [*He goes to the top of the path and shouts down the hill*] O.K., let's get cracking. Get that luggage strapped on top of the bus, we're moving! [*He starts down the hill with* MISS FELLOWES]

NONNO: [*Incongruously, from his cubicle*]

How calmly does the orange branch
Observe the sky begin to blanch. . . .

[SHANNON *sucks in his breath with an abrupt, fierce sound. He rushes off the verandah and down the path toward the road.* HANNAH *calls after him, with a restraining gesture.* MAXINE *appears on the verandah. Then a great commotion commences below the hill, with shrieks of outrage and squeals of shocked laughter*]

MAXINE: [*Rushing to the path*] Shannon! Shannon! Get back up here, get back up here. Pedro, Pancho, traerme a Shannon.

Que está haciendo allí? Oh, my God! Stop him, for God's sake, somebody stop him!

[SHANNON *returns, panting and spent. He is followed by* MAXINE]

MAXINE: Shannon, go in your room and stay there until that party's gone.

SHANNON: Don't give me orders.

MAXINE: You do what I tell you to do or I'll have you removed —you know where.

SHANNON: Don't push me, don't pull at me, Maxine.

MAXINE: All right, do as I say.

SHANNON: Shannon obeys only Shannon.

MAXINE: You'll sing a different tune if they put you where they put you in 'thirty-six. Remember 'thirty-six, Shannon?

SHANNON: O.K., Maxine, just . . . let me breathe alone, please. I won't go but I will lie in the . . . hammock.

MAXINE: Go into Fred's room where I can watch you.

SHANNON: Later, Maxine, not yet.

MAXINE: Why do you always come here to crack up, Shannon?

SHANNON: It's the hammock, Maxine, the hammock by the rain forest.

MAXINE: Shannon, go in your room and stay there until I get back. Oh, my God, the money. They haven't paid the mother-grabbin' bill. I got to go back down there and collect their goddam bill before they. . . . Pancho, vijilalo, entiendes? [*She rushes back down the hill, shouting* "Hey! Just a minute down there!"]

SHANNON: What did I do? [*He shakes his head, stunned*] I don't know what I did.

[HANNAH *opens the screen of her cubicle but doesn't come out. She is softly lighted so that she looks, again, like a medieval sculpture of a saint. Her pale gold hair catches the soft light. She has let it down and still holds the silver-backed brush with which she was brushing it*]

SHANNON: God almighty, I . . . what did I do? I don't know what I did. [*He turns to the Mexican boys who have come back up the path*] Que hice? Que hice?

[*There is breathless, spasmodic laughter from the boys as* PANCHO *informs him that he pissed on the ladies' luggage*]

PANCHO: Tú measte en las maletas de las señoras!

[SHANNON *tries to laugh with the boys, while they bend double with amusement.* SHANNON'*s laughter dies out in little choked spasms. Down the hill,* MAXINE'*s voice is raised in angry altercation with* JAKE LATTA. MISS FELLOWES' *voice is lifted and then there is a general rhubarb to which is added the roar of the bus motor*]

SHANNON: There go my ladies, ha, ha! There go my . . . [*He turns about to meet* HANNAH'*s grave, compassionate gaze. He tries to laugh again. She shakes her head with a slight restraining gesture and drops the curtain so that her softly luminous figure is seen as through a mist*] . . . ladies, the last of my—ha, ha!—ladies. [*He bends far over the verandah rail, then straightens violently and with an animal outcry begins to pull at the chain suspending the gold cross about his neck.* PANCHO *watches indifferently as the chain cuts the back of* SHANNON'*s neck.* HANNAH *rushes out to him*]

HANNAH: Mr. Shannon, stop that! You're cutting yourself doing that. That isn't necessary, so stop it! [*To* PANCHO] Agarrale las manos! [PANCHO *makes a halfhearted effort to comply, but* SHANNON *kicks at him and goes on with the furious self-laceration*] Shannon, let me do it, let me take it off you. Can I take it off you? [*He drops his arms. She struggles with the clasp of the chain but her fingers are too shaky to work it*]

SHANNON: No, no, it won't come off, I'll have to break it off me.

HANNAH: No, no, wait—I've got it. [*She has now removed it*]

SHANNON: Thanks. Keep it. Goodbye! [*He starts toward the path down to the beach*]

HANNAH: Where are you going? What are you going to do?

SHANNON: I'm going swimming. I'm going to swim out to China!

HANNAH: No, no, not tonight, Shannon! Tomorrow . . . tomorrow, Shannon!

> [*But he divides the trumpet-flowered bushes and passes through them.* HANNAH *rushes after him, screaming for "Mrs. Faulk."* MAXINE *can be heard shouting for the Mexican boys*]

MAXINE: Muchachos, cojerlo! Atarlo! Está loco. Traerlo acqui. Catch him, he's crazy. Bring him back and tie him up!

> [*In a few moments* SHANNON *is hauled back through the bushes and onto the verandah by* MAXINE *and the boys. They rope him into the hammock. His struggle is probably not much of a real struggle—histrionics mostly. But* HANNAH *stands wringing her hands by the steps as* SHANNON, *gasping for breath, is tied up*]

HANNAH: The ropes are too tight on his chest!

MAXINE: No, they're not. He's acting, acting. He likes it! I know this black Irish bastard like nobody ever knowed him, so you keep out of it, honey. He cracks up like this so regular that you can set a calendar by it. Every eighteen months he does it, and twice he's done it here and I've had to pay for his medical care. Now I'm going to call in town to get a doctor to come out here and give him a knockout injection, and if he's not better tomorrow he's going into the Casa de Locos again like he did the last time he cracked up on me!

> [*There is a moment of silence*]

SHANNON: Miss Jelkes?

HANNAH: Yes.

SHANNON: Where are you?

HANNAH: I'm right here behind you. Can I do anything for you?

SHANNON: Sit here where I can see you. Don't stop talking. I have to fight this panic.

[*There is a pause. She moves a chair beside his hammock. The Germans troop up from the beach. They are delighted by the drama that* SHANNON *has provided. In their scanty swimsuits they parade onto the verandah and gather about* SHANNON's *captive figure as if they were looking at a funny animal in a zoo. Their talk is in German except when they speak directly to* SHANNON *or* HANNAH. *Their heavily handsome figures gleam with oily wetness and they keep chuckling lubriciously*]

HANNAH: Please! Will you be so kind as to leave him alone?

[*They pretend not to understand her.* FRAU FAHRENKOPF *bends over* SHANNON *in his hammock and speaks to him loudly and slowly in English*]

FRAU FAHRENKOPF: Is this true you make pee-pee all over the suitcases of the ladies from Texas? Hah? Hah? You run down there to the bus and right in front of the ladies you pees all over the luggage of the ladies from Texas?

[HANNAH's *indignant protest is drowned in the Rabelaisian laughter of the Germans*]

HERR FAHRENKOPF: Thees is vunderbar, vunderbar! Hah? Thees is a *epic gesture!* Hah? Thees is the way to demonstrate to ladies that you are a American *gentleman!* Hah?

[*He turns to the others and makes a ribald comment. The two women shriek with amusement,* HILDA *falling back into the arms of* WOLFGANG, *who catches her with his hands over her almost nude breasts*]

HANNAH: [*Calling out*] Mrs. Faulk! Mrs. Faulk! [*She rushes to the verandah angle as* MAXINE *appears there*] Will you please ask these people to leave him alone. They're tormenting him like an animal in a trap.

[*The Germans are already trooping around the verandah, laughing and capering gaily*]

SHANNON: [*Suddenly, in a great shout*] Regression to infantilism, ha, ha, regression to infantilism . . . The infantile protest, ha, ha, ha, the infantile expression of rage at Mama and rage at God and rage at the goddam crib, and rage at the everything, rage at the . . . everything. . . . Regression to infantilism. . . .

[*Now all have left but* HANNAH *and* SHANNON]

SHANNON: Untie me.

HANNAH: Not yet.

SHANNON: I can't stand being tied up.

HANNAH: You'll have to stand it a while.

SHANNON: It makes me panicky.

HANNAH: I know.

SHANNON: A man can die of panic.

HANNAH: Not if he enjoys it as much as you, Mr. Shannon.

[*She goes into her cubicle directly behind his hammock. The cubicle is lighted and we see her removing a small teapot and a tin of tea from her suitcase on the cot, then a little alcohol burner. She comes back out with these articles*]

SHANNON: What did you mean by that insulting remark?

HANNAH: What remark, Mr. Shannon?

SHANNON: That I enjoy it.

HANNAH: Oh . . . that.

SHANNON: Yes. That.

HANNAH: That wasn't meant as an insult, just an observation. I don't judge people, I draw them. That's all I do, just draw them, but in order to draw them I have to observe them, don't I?

SHANNON: And you've observed, you think you've observed, that I like being tied in this hammock, trussed up in it like a hog being hauled off to the slaughter house, Miss Jelkes.

HANNAH: Who wouldn't like to suffer and atone for the sins of himself and the world if it could be done in a hammock with ropes instead of nails, on a hill that's so much lovelier than Golgotha, the Place of the Skull, Mr. Shannon? There's something almost voluptuous in the way that you twist and groan in that hammock—no nails, no blood, no death. Isn't that a comparatively comfortable, almost voluptuous kind of crucifixion to suffer for the guilt of the world, Mr. Shannon?

[*She strikes a match to light the alcohol burner. A pure blue jet of flame springs up to cast a flickering, rather unearthly glow on their section of the verandah. The glow is delicately refracted by the subtle, faded colors of her robe—a robe given to her by a Kabuki actor who posed for her in. Japan*]

SHANNON: Why have you turned against me all of a sudden, when I need you the most?

HANNAH: I haven't turned against you at all, Mr. Shannon. I'm just attempting to give you a character sketch of yourself, in words instead of pastel crayons or charcoal.

SHANNON: You're certainly suddenly very sure of some New England spinsterish attitudes that I didn't know you had in you. I thought that you were an *emancipated* Puritan, Miss Jelkes.

HANNAH: Who is . . . ever . . . completely?

SHANNON: I thought you were sexless but you've suddenly turned into a woman. Know how I know that? Because you, not me—not me—are taking pleasure in my tied-up condition. All women, whether they face it or not, want to see a man in a tied-up situation. They work at it all their lives, to get a man in a tied-up situation. Their lives are fulfilled, they're satisfied at last, when they get a man, or as many men as they can, in the tied-up situation. [HANNAH *leaves the alcohol burner and teapot and moves to the railing where she grips a verandah post and draws a few deep breaths*] You don't like this observation of you? The shoe's too tight for comfort when it's on your own foot, Miss Jelkes? Some deep breaths again— feeling panic?

HANNAH: [*Recovering and returning to the burner*] I'd like to untie you right now, but let me wait till you've passed through your present disturbance. You're still indulging yourself in your . . . your Passion Play performance. I can't help observing this self-indulgence in you.

SHANNON: What rotten indulgence?

HANNAH: Well, your busload of ladies from the female college in Texas. I don't like those ladies any more than you do, but after all, they did save up all year to make this Mexican tour, to stay in stuffy hotels and eat the food they're used to. They want to be at home away from home, but you . . . you indulged yourself, Mr. Shannon. You did conduct the tour as if it was just for you, for your own pleasure.

SHANNON: Hell, what pleasure—going through hell all the way?

HANNAH: Yes, but comforted, now and then, weren't you, by the little musical prodigy under the wing of the college vocal instructor?

SHANNON: Funny, ha-ha funny! Nantucket spinsters have their wry humor, don't they?

HANNAH: Yes, they do. They have to.

SHANNON: [*Becoming progressively quieter under the cool influence of her voice behind him*] I can't see what you're up to, Miss Jelkes honey, but I'd almost swear you're making a pot of tea over there.

HANNAH: That is just what I'm doing.

SHANNON: Does this strike you as the right time for a tea party?

HANNAH: This isn't plain tea, this is poppyseed tea.

SHANNON: Are you a slave to the poppy?

HANNAH: It's a mild, sedative drink that helps you get through nights that are hard for you to get through and I'm making it for my grandfather and myself as well as for you, Mr. Shannon. Because, for all three of us, this won't be an easy night to get through. Can't you hear him in his cell number 4, mumbling over and over and over the lines of his new poem? It's like a blind man climbing a staircase that goes to nowhere, that just falls off into space, and I hate to say what it is. . . . [*She draws a few deep breaths behind him*]

SHANNON: Put some hemlock in his poppyseed tea tonight so he won't wake up tomorrow for the removal to the Casa de Huéspedes. Do that act of mercy. Put in the hemlock and I will consecrate it, turn it to God's blood. Hell, if you'll get me out of this hammock I'll serve it to him myself, I'll be your accomplice in this act of mercy. I'll say, "Take and drink this, the blood of our—

HANNAH: Stop it! Stop being childishly cruel! I can't stand for a person that I respect to talk and behave like a small, cruel boy, Mr. Shannon.

SHANNON: What've you found to respect in me, Miss . . . Thin-Standing-Up-Female-Buddha?

HANNAH: I respect a person that has had to fight and howl for his decency and his—

SHANNON: *What* decency?

HANNAH: Yes, for his decency and his bit of goodness, much more than I respect the lucky ones that just had theirs handed out to them at birth and never afterwards snatched away from them by . . . unbearable . . . torments, I. . . .

SHANNON: You *respect* me?

HANNAH: I do.

SHANNON: But you just said that I'm taking pleasure in a . . . voluptuous crucifixion without nails. A . . . what? . . . painless atonement for the—

HANNAH: [*Cutting in*] Yes, but I think—

SHANNON: Untie me!

HANNAH: Soon, soon. Be patient.

SHANNON: Now!

HANNAH: Not quite yet, Mr. Shannon. Not till I'm reasonably sure that you won't swim out to China, because, you see, I think you think of the . . . "the long swim to China" as another painless atonement. I mean I don't think you think you'd be intercepted by sharks and barracudas before you got far past the barrier reef. And I'm afraid you *would be*. It's as simple as that, if that is simple.

SHANNON: What's simple?

HANNAH: Nothing, except for simpletons, Mr. Shannon.

SHANNON: Do you believe in people being tied up?

HANNAH: Only when they might take the long swim to China.

SHANNON: All right, Miss Thin-Standing-Up-Female-Buddha, just light a Benson & Hedges cigarette for me and put it in my mouth and take it out when you hear me choking on it—if that doesn't seem to you like another bit of voluptuous self-crucifixion.

HANNAH: [*Looking about the verandah*] I will, but . . . where did I put them?

SHANNON: I have a pack of my own in my pocket.

HANNAH: Which pocket?

SHANNON: I don't know which pocket, you'll have to frisk me for it. [*She pats his jacket pocket*]

HANNAH: They're not in your coat pocket.

SHANNON: Then look for them in my pants pockets.

[*She hesitates to put her hand in his pants pockets, for a moment.* HANNAH *has always had a sort of fastidiousness, a reluctance, toward intimate physical contact. But after the momentary fastidious hesitation, she puts her hands in his pants pocket and draws out the cigarette pack*]

SHANNON: Now light it for me and put it in my mouth.

[*She complies with these directions. Almost at once he chokes and the cigarette is expelled*]

HANNAH: You've dropped it on you—where is it?

SHANNON: [*Twisting and lunging about in the hammock*] It's under me, under me, burning. Untie me, for God's sake, will you—it's burning me through my pants!

HANNAH: Raise your hips so I can—

SHANNON: I can't, the ropes are too tight. Untie me, untieeeee meeeeee!

HANNAH: I've found it, I've found it!

> [*But* SHANNON'S *shout has brought* MAXINE *out of her office. She rushes onto the verandah and sits on* SHANNON'S *legs*]

MAXINE: Now hear this, you crazy black Irish mick, you! You Protestant black Irish looney, I've called up Lopez, Doc Lopez. Remember him—the man in the dirty white jacket that come here the last time you cracked up here? And hauled you off to the Casa de Locos? Where they threw you into that cell with nothing in it but a bucket and straw and a water pipe? That you crawled up the water pipe? And dropped head-down on the floor and got a concussion? Yeah, and I told him you were back here to crack up again and if you didn't quiet down here tonight you should be hauled out in the morning.

SHANNON: [*Cutting in, with the honking sound of a panicky goose*] Off, off, off, off, off!

HANNAH: Oh, Mrs. Faulk, Mr. Shannon won't quiet down till he's left alone in the hammock.

MAXINE: Then why don't *you* leave him alone?

HANNAH: I'm not sitting on him and he . . . has to be cared for by someone.

MAXINE: And the someone is *you?*

HANNAH: A long time ago, Mrs. Faulk, I had experience with someone in Mr. Shannon's condition, so I know how necessary it is to let them be quiet for a while.

MAXINE: He wasn't quiet, he was shouting.

HANNAH: He will quiet down again. I'm preparing a sedative tea for him, Mrs. Faulk.

MAXINE: Yeah, I see. Put it out. Nobody cooks here but the Chinaman in the kitchen.

HANNAH: This is just a little alcohol burner, a spirit lamp, Mrs. Faulk.

MAXINE: I know what it is. It goes out! [*She blows out the flame under the burner*]

SHANNON: Maxine honey? [*He speaks quietly now*] Stop persecuting this lady. You can't intimidate her. A bitch is no match for a lady except in a brass bed, honey, and sometimes not even there.

[*The Germans are heard shouting for beer—a case of it to take down to the beach*]

WOLFGANG: Eine Kiste Carta Blanca.

FRAU FARHRENKOPF: Wir haben genug gehabt . . . vielleicht nicht.

HERR FAHRENKOPF: Nein! Niemals genung.

HILDA: Mutter du bist dick . . . aber wir sind es nicht.

SHANNON: Maxine, you're neglecting your duties as a beerhall waitress. [*His tone is deceptively gentle*] They want a case of Carta Blanca to carry down to the beach, so give it to 'em . . . and tonight, when the moon's gone down, if you'll let me out of this hammock, I'll try to imagine you as a . . . as a nympth in her teens.

MAXINE: A fat lot of good you'd be in your present condition.

SHANNON: Don't be a sexual snob at your age, honey.

MAXINE: Hah! [*But the unflattering offer has pleased her realistically modest soul, so she goes back to the Germans*]

SHANNON: Now let me try a bit of your poppyseed tea, Miss Jelkes.

HANNAH: I ran out of sugar, but I had some ginger, some sugared ginger. [*She pours a cup of tea and sips it*] Oh, it's not well brewed yet, but try to drink some now and the—[*She lights the burner again*]—the second cup will be better. [*She crouches by the hammock and presses the cup to his lips. He raises his head to sip it, but he gags and chokes*]

SHANNON: *Caesar's ghost!*—it could be chased by the witches' brew from Macbeth.

HANNAH: Yes, I know, it's still bitter.

[*The Germans appear on the wing of the verandah and go trooping down to the beach, for a beer festival and a moonlight swim. Even in the relative dark they have a luminous color, an almost phosphorescent pink and gold color of skin. They carry with them a case of Carta Blanca beer and the fantastically painted rubber horse. On their faces are smiles of euphoria as they move like a dream-image, starting to sing a marching song as they go*]

SHANNON: Fiends out of hell with the . . . voices of . . . angels.

HANNAH: Yes, they call it "the logic of contradictions," Mr. Shannon.

SHANNON: [*Lunging suddenly forward and undoing the loosened ropes*] Out! Free! Unassisted!

HANNAH: Yes, I never doubted that you could get loose, Mr. Shannon.

SHANNON: Thanks for your help, anyhow.

HANNAH: Where are you going?

[*He has crossed to the liquor cart*]

SHANNON: Not far. To the liquor cart to make myself a rum-coco.

HANNAH: Oh. . . .

SHANNON: [*At the liquor cart*] Coconut? Check. Machete? Check. Rum? Double check! Ice? The ice bucket's empty. O.K., it's a night for warm drinks. Miss Jelkes? Would you care to have your complimentary rum-coco?

HANNAH: No thank you, Mr. Shannon.

SHANNON: You don't mind me having mine?

HANNAH: Not at all, Mr. Shannon.

SHANNON: You don't disapprove of this weakness, this self-indulgence?

HANNAH: Liquor isn't your problem, Mr. Shannon.

SHANNON: What is my problem, Miss Jelkes?

HANNAH: The oldest one in the world—the need to believe in something or in someone—almost anyone—almost anything . . . something.

SHANNON: Your voice sounds hopeless about it.

HANNAH: No, I'm not hopeless about it. In fact, I've discovered something to believe in.

SHANNON: Something like . . . God?

HANNAH: No.

SHANNON: What?

HANNAH: Broken gates between people so they can reach each other, even if it's just for one night only.

SHANNON: One night stands, huh?

HANNAH: One night . . . communication between them on a verandah outside their . . . separate cubicles, Mr. Shannon.

SHANNON: You don't mean physically, do you?

HANNAH: No.

SHANNON: I didn't think so. Then what?

HANNAH: A little understanding exchanged between them, a wanting to help each other through nights like this.

SHANNON: Who was the someone you told the widow you'd helped long ago to get through a crack-up like this one I'm going through?

HANNAH: Oh . . . that. Myself.

SHANNON: You?

HANNAH: Yes. I can help you because I've been through what you are going through now. I had something like your spook— I just had a different name for him. I called him the blue devil, and . . . oh . . . we had quite a battle, quite a contest between us.

SHANNON: Which you obviously won.

HANNAH: I couldn't afford to lose.

SHANNON: How'd you beat your blue devil?

HANNAH: I showed him that I could endure him and I made him respect my endurance.

SHANNON: How?

HANNAH: Just by, just by . . . enduring. Endurance is something that spooks and blue devils respect. And they respect all the tricks that panicky people use to outlast and outwit their panic.

SHANNON: Like poppyseed tea?

HANNAH: Poppyseed tea or rum-cocos or just a few deep breaths. Anything, everything, that we take to give them the slip, and so to keep on going.

SHANNON: To where?

HANNAH: To somewhere like this, perhaps. This verandah over the rain forest and the still-water beach, after long, difficult travels. And I don't mean just travels about the world, the earth's surface. I mean . . . subterranean travels, the . . . the journey's that the spooked and bedevilled people are forced to take through the . . . the *unlighted* sides of their natures.

SHANNON: Don't tell me you have a dark side to your nature. [*He says this sardonically*]

HANNAH: I'm sure I don't have to tell a man as experienced and knowledgeable as you, Mr. Shannon, that everything has its shadowy side?

[*She glances up at him and observes that she doesn't have his attention. He is gazing tensely at something off the verandah. It is the kind of abstraction, not vague but fiercely concentrated, that occurs in madness. She turns to look where he's looking. She closes her eyes for a moment and draws a deep breath, then goes on speaking in a voice like a hypnotist's, as if the words didn't matter, since he is not listening to her so much as to the tone and the cadence of her voice*]

HANNAH: Everything in the whole solar system has a shadowy

side to it except the sun itself—the sun is the single exception.
You're not listening, are you?

SHANNON: [*As replying to her*] The spook is the rain forest.
[*He suddenly hurls his coconut shell with great violence off
the verandah, creating a commotion among the jungle birds*]
Good shot—it caught him right on the kisser and his teeth
flew out like popcorn from a popper.

HANNAH: Has he gone off—to the dentist?

SHANNON: He's retreated a little way away for a little while,
but when I buzz for my breakfast tomorrow, he'll bring it in
to me with a grin that'll curdle the milk in the coffee and he'll
stink like a . . . a gringo drunk in a Mexican jail who's slept
all night in his vomit.

HANNAH: If you wake up before I'm out, I'll bring your coffee
in to you . . . if you call me.

SHANNON: [*His attention returns to her*] No, you'll be gone,
God help me.

HANNAH: Maybe and maybe not. I might think of something
tomorrow to placate the widow.

SHANNON: The widow's implacable, honey.

HANNAH: I think I'll think of something because I have to.
I can't let Nonno be moved to the Casa de Huéspedes, Mr.
Shannon. Not any more than I could let you take the long swim
out to China. You know that. Not if I can prevent it, and when
I have to be resourceful, I can be very resourceful.

SHANNON: How'd you get over your crack-up?

HANNAH: I never cracked up, I couldn't afford to. Of course,
I nearly did once. I was young once, Mr. Shannon, but I was
one of those people who can be young without really having
their youth, and not to have your youth when you are young is
naturally very disturbing. But I was lucky. My work, this
occupational therapy that I gave myself—painting and doing
quick character sketches—made me look out of myself, not in,
and gradually, at the far end of the tunnel that I was stuggling
out of I began to see this faint, very faint gray light—the light
of the world outside me—and I kept climbing toward it. I had
to.

SHANNON: Did it stay a gray light?

HANNAH: No, no, it turned white.

SHANNON: Only white, never gold?

HANNAH: No, it stayed only white, but white is a very good light to see at the end of a long black tunnel you thought would be neverending, that only God or Death could put a stop to, especially when you . . . since I was . . . far from sure about God.

SHANNON: You'll still unsure about him?

HANNAH: Not as unsure as I was. You see, in my profession I have to look hard and close at human faces in order to catch something in them before they get restless and call out, "Waiter, the check, we're leaving." Of course sometimes, a few times, I just see blobs of wet dough that pass for human faces, with bits of jelly for eyes. Then I cue in Nonno to give a recitation, because I can't draw such faces. But those aren't the usual faces, I don't think they're even real. Most times I *do* see something, and I can catch it—I *can*, like I caught something in your face when I sketched you this afternoon with your eyes open. Are you still listening to me? [*He crouches beside her chair, looking up at her intently*] In Shanghai, Shannon, there is a place that's called the House for the Dying—the old and penniless dying, whose younger, penniless living children and grandchildren take them there for them to get through with their dying on pallets, on straw mats. The first time I went there it shocked me I ran away from it. But I came back later and I saw that their children and grandchildren and the custodians of the place had put little comforts beside their death-pallets, little flowers and opium candies and religious emblems. That made me able to stay to draw their dying faces. Sometimes only their eyes were still alive, but, Mr. Shannon, those eyes of the penniless dying with those last little comforts beside them, I tell you, Mr. Shannon, those eyes looked up with their last dim life left in them as clear as the stars in the Southern Cross, Mr. Shannon. And now . . . now I am going to say something to you that will sound like something that only the spinster granddaughter of a minor romantic poet is likely to say. . . . Nothing I've ever seen has seemed as beautiful to me, not even the view from this verandah between the sky and the still-water beach, and lately . . . lately my grandfather's eyes have looked up at me like that. . . . [*She rises abruptly and crosses to the front of the verandah*] Tell me, what is that sound I keep hearing down there?

SHANNON: There's a marimba band at the cantina on the beach.

HANNAH: I don't mean that, I mean that scraping, scuffling sound that I keep hearing under the verandah.

SHANNON: Oh, that. The Mexican boys that work here have caught an iguana and tied it up under the verandah, hitched it to a post, and naturally of course it's trying to scramble away. But it's got to the end of its rope, and get any further it cannot. Ha-ha—that's it. [*He quotes from* NONNO's *poem:* "And still the orange," etc.] Do you have any life of your own—besides your water colors and sketches and your travels with Grampa?

HANNAH: We make a home for each other, my grandfather and I. Do you know what I mean by a home? I don't mean a regular home. I mean I don't mean what other people mean when they speak of a home, because I don't regard a home as a . . . well, as a place, a building . . . a house . . . of wood, bricks, stone. I think of a home as being a thing that two people have between them in which each can . . . well, nest—rest—live in, emotionally speaking. Does that make any sense to you, Mr. Shannon?

SHANNON: Yeah, complete. But. . . .

HANNAH: Another incomplete sentence.

SHANNON: We better leave it that way. I might've said something to hurt you.

HANNAH: I'm not thin skinned, Mr. Shannon.

SHANNON: No, well, then, I'll say it. . . . [*He moves to the liquor cart*] When a bird builds a nest to rest in and live in, it doesn't build it in a . . . a falling-down tree.

HANNAH: I'm not a bird, Mr. Shannon.

SHANNON: I was making an analogy, Miss Jelkes.

HANNAH: I thought you were making yourself another rum-coco, Mr. Shannon.

SHANNON: Both. When a bird builds a nest, it builds it with an eye for . . . the relative permanence of the location, and also for the purpose of mating and propagating its species.

HANNAH: I still say that I'm not a bird, Mr. Shannon, I'm a human being and when a member of that fantastic species builds a nest in the heart of another, the question of permanence isn't the first or even the last thing that's considered . . . necessarily? . . . always? Nonno and I have been continually reminded of the impermanence of things lately. We go back to a hotel where we've been many times before and it isn't there any more. It's been demolished and there's one of those glassy, brassy new ones. Or if the old one's still there, the manager or the Maitre D who always welcomed us back so cordially before has been replaced by someone new who looks at us with suspicion.

SHANNON: Yeah, but you still had each other.

HANNAH: Yes. We did.

SHANNON: But when the old gentleman goes?

HANNAH: Yes?

SHANNON: What will you do? Stop?

HANNAH: Stop or go on . . . probably go on.

SHANNON: Alone? Checking into hotels alone, eating alone at tables for one in a corner, the tables waiters call aces.

HANNAH: Thank you for your sympathy, Mr. Shannon, but in my profession I'm obliged to make quick contacts with strangers who turn to friends very quickly.

SHANNON: Customers aren't friends.

HANNAH: They turn to friends, if they're friendly.

SHANNON: Yeah, but how will it seem to be traveling alone after so many years of traveling with. . . .

HANNAH: I will know how it feels when I feel it—and don't say alone as if nobody had ever gone on alone. For instance, you.

SHANNON: I've always traveled with trainloads, planeloads and busloads of tourists.

HANNAH: That doesn't mean you're still not really alone.

SHANNON: I never fail to make an intimate connection with someone in my parties.

HANNAH: Yes, the youngest young lady, and I was on the verandah this afternoon when the latest of these young ladies gave a demonstration of how lonely the intimate connection has always been for you. The episode in the cold, inhuman hotel room, Mr. Shannon, for which you despise the lady almost as much as you despise yourself. Afterwards you are so polite to the lady that I'm sure it must chill her to the bone, the scrupulous little attentions that you pay her in return for your little enjoyment of her. The gentleman-of-Virginia act that you put on for her, your noblesse oblige treatment of her . . . Oh no, Mr. Shannon, don't kid yourself that you ever travel with someone. You have always traveled alone except for your spook, as you call it. He's your traveling companion. Nothing, nobody else has traveled with you.

SHANNON: Thank you for your sympathy, Miss Jelkes.

HANNAH: You're welcome, Mr. Shannon. And now I think I had better warm up the poppyseed tea for Nonno. Only a good night's sleep could make it possible for him to go on from here tomorrow.

SHANNON: Yes, well, if the conversation is over—I think I'll go down for a swim now.

HANNAH: To China?

SHANNON: No, not to China, just to the little island out here with the sleepy bar on it . . . called the Cantina Serena.

HANNAH: Why?

SHANNON: Because I'm not a nice drunk and I was about to ask you a not nice question.

HANNAH: Ask it. There's no set limit on questions here tonight.

SHANNON: And no set limit on answers?

HANNAH: None I can think of between you and me, Mr. Shannon.

SHANNON: That I will take you up on.

HANNAH: Do.

SHANNON: It's a bargain.

HANNAH: Only do lie back down in the hammock and drink a full cup of the poppyseed tea this time. It's warmer now and the sugared ginger will make it easier to get down.

SHANNON: All right. The question is this: have you never had in your life any kind of a love life? [HANNAH *stiffens for a moment*] I thought you said there was no limit set on questions.

HANNAH: We'll make a bargain—I will answer your question *after* you've had a full cup of the poppyseed tea so you'll be able to get the good night's sleep you need, too. It's fairly warm now and the sugared ginger's made it much more— [*She sips the cup*]—palatable.

SHANNON: You think I'm going to drift into dreamland so you can welch on the bargain? [*He accepts the cup from her*]

HANNAH: I'm not a welcher on bargains. Drink it all. All. *All!*

SHANNON: [*With a disgusted grimace as he drains the cup*] Great Caesar's ghost. [*He tosses the cup off the verandah and falls into the hammock, chuckling*] The oriental idea of a Mickey Finn, huh? Sit down where I can see you, Miss Jelkes honey. [*She sits down in a straight-back chair, some distance from the hammock*] Where I can *see* you! I don't have an x-ray eye in the back of my head, Miss Jelkes. [*She moves the chair alongside the hammock*] Further, further, up further. [*She complies*] There now. Answer the question now, Miss Jelkes honey.

HANNAH: Would you mind repeating the question.

SHANNON: [*Slowly, with emphasis*] Have you never had in all of your life and your travels any experience, any encounter, with what Larry-the-crackpot Shannon thinks of as a love life?

HANNAH: There are . . . worse things than chastity, Mr. Shannon.

SHANNON: Yeah, lunacy and death are both a little worse, *maybe!* But chastity isn't a thing that a beautiful woman or an attractive man falls into like a booby trap or an overgrown gopher hole, is it? [*There is a pause*] I still think you are welching on the bargain and I. . . . [*He starts out of the hammock*]

HANNAH: Mr. Shannon, this night is just as hard for me to get through as it is for you to get through. But it's you that are welching on the bargain, you're not staying in the hammock.

Lie back down in the hammock. Now. Yes. Yes, I have had two experiences, well, encounters, with. . . .

SHANNON: *Two*, did you say?

HANNAH: Yes, I said two. And I wasn't exaggerating and don't you say "fantastic" before I've told you both stories. When I was sixteen, your favorite age, Mr. Shannon, each Saturday afternoon my grandfather Nonno would give me thirty cents, my allowance, my pay for my secretarial and housekeeping duties. Twenty-five cents for admission to the Saturday matinee at the Nantucket movie theatre and five cents extra for a bag of popcorn, Mr. Shannon. I'd sit at the almost empty back of the movie theatre so that the popcorn munching wouldn't disturb the other movie patrons. Well . . . one afternoon a young man sat down beside me and pushed his . . . knee against mine and . . . I moved over two seats but he moved over beside me and continued this . . . pressure! I jumped up and screamed, Mr. Shannon. He was arrested for molesting a minor.

SHANNON: Is he still in the Nantucket jail?

HANNAH: No. I got him out. I told the police that it was a Clara Bow picture—it *was* a Clara Bow picture—and I was just overexcited.

SHANNON: Fantastic.

HANNAH: Yes, very! The second experience is much more recent, only two years ago, when Nonno and I were operating at the Raffles Hotel in Singapore, and doing very well there, making expenses and more. One evening in the Palm Court of the Raffles we met this middle-aged, sort of nondescript Australian salesman. You know—plump, bald-spotted, with a bad attempt at speaking with an upper-class accent and terribly overfriendly. He was alone and looked lonely. Grandfather said him a poem and I did a quick character sketch that was shamelessly flattering of him. He paid me more than my usual asking price and gave my grandfather five Malayan dollars, yes, and he even purchased one of my water colors. Then it was Nonno's bedtime. The Aussie salesman asked me out in a sampan with him. Well, he'd been so generous . . . I accepted. I did, I accepted. Grandfather went up to bed and I went out in the sampan with this ladies' underwear salesman. I noticed that he became more and more. . . .

SHANNON: What?

HANNAH: Well . . . *agitated* . . . as the afterglow of the sunset faded out on the water. [*She laughs with a delicate sadness*] Well, finally, eventually, he leaned toward me . . . we were vis-à-vis in the sampan . . . and he looked intensely, passionately into my eyes. [*She laughs again*] And he said to me: "Miss Jelke? Will you do me a favor? Will you do something for me?" "What?" said I. "Well," said he, "if I turn my back, if I look the other way, will you take off some piece of your clothes and let me hold it, just hold it?"

SHANNON: Fantastic!

HANNAH: Then he said, "It will just take a few seconds." "Just a few seconds for what?" I asked him. [*She gives the same laugh again*] He didn't say for what, but. . . .

SHANNON: His satisfaction?

HANNAH: Yes.

SHANNON: What did you do—in a situation like that?

HANNAH: I . . . gratified his request, I did! And he kept his promise. He did keep his back turned till I said ready and threw him . . . the part of my clothes.

SHANNON: What did he do with it?

HANNAH: He didn't move, except to seize the article he'd requested. I looked the other way while his satisfaction took place.

SHANNON: Watch out for commercial travelers in the Far East. Is that the moral, Miss Jelkes honey?

HANNAH: Oh, no, the moral is oriental. Accept whatever situation you cannot improve.

SHANNON: When it's inevitable, lean back and enjoy it—is that it?

HANNAH: He'd bought a water color. The incident was embarrassing, not violent. I left and returned unmolested. Oh,

and the funniest part of all is that when we got back to the
Raffles Hotel, he took the piece of apparel out of his pocket
like a bashful boy producing an apple for his schoolteacher and
tried to slip it into my hand in the elevator. I wouldn't accept
it. I whispered, "Oh, please keep it, Mr. Willoughby!" He'd
paid the asking price for my water color and somehow the little
experience had been rather touching, I mean it was so *lonely*,
out there in the sampan with violet streaks in the sky and this
little middle-aged Australian making sounds like he was dying
of asthma! And the planet Venus coming serenely out of a
fair-weather cloud, over the Straits of Malacca. . . .

SHANNON: And that experience . . . you call that a. . .

HANNAH: A love experience? Yes. I do call it one.

[*He regards her with incredulity, peering into her face so
closely that she is embarrassed and becomes defensive*]

SHANNON: That, that . . . sad, dirty little episode, you call it
a . . . ?

HANNAH: [*Cutting in sharply*] Sad it certainly was—for the
odd little man—but why do you call it "dirty"?

SHANNON: How did you feel when you went into your bedroom?

HANNAH: Confused, I . . . a little confused, I suppose. . . . I'd
known about loneliness—but not that degree or . . . depth of
it.

SHANNON: You mean it didn't *disgust you?*

HANNAH: Nothing human disgusts me unless it's unkind, violent.
And I told you how gentle he was—apologetic, shy, and really
very, well, *delicate* about it. However, I do grant you it was on
the rather fantastic level.

SHANNON: You're. . . .

HANNAH: I am *what?* "Fantastic"?

[*While they have been talking, NONNO's voice has been
heard now and then, mumbling, from his cubicle. Suddenly it becomes loud and clear*]

NONNO:

And finally the broken stem,
The plummeting to earth and then. . . .

[*His voice subsides to its mumble.* SHANNON, *standing behind* HANNAH, *places his hand on her throat*]

HANNAH: What is that for? Are you about to strangle me, Mr. Shannon?

SHANNON: You can't stand to be touched?

HANNAH: Save it for the widow. It isn't for me.

SHANNON: Yes, you're right. [*He removes his hand*] I could do it with Mrs. Faulk, the inconsolable widow, but I couldn't with you.

HANNAH: [*Dryly and lightly*] Spinster's loss, widow's gain, Mr. Shannon.

SHANNON: Or widow's loss, spinster's gain. Anyhow it sounds like some old parlor game in a Virginia or Nantucket Island parlor. But . . . I wonder something. . . .

HANNAH: What do you wonder?

SHANNON: If we couldn't . . . *travel* together, I mean just *travel* together?

HANNAH: Could we? In your opinion?

SHANNON: Why not, I don't see why not.

HANNAH: I think the impracticality of the idea will appear much clearer to you in the morning, Mr. Shannon. [*She folds her dimly gold-lacquered fan and rises from her chair*] Morning can always be counted on to bring us back to a more realistic level. . . . Good night, Mr. Shannon. I have to pack before I'm too tired to.

SHANNON: Don't leave me out here alone yet.

HANNAH: I have to pack now so I can get up at daybreak and try my luck in the plaza.

SHANNON: You won't sell a water color or sketch in that blazing hot plaza tomorrow. Miss Jelkes honey, I don't think you're operating on the realistic level.

HANNAH: Would I be if I thought we could travel together?

SHANNON: I still don't see why we couldn't.

HANNAH: Mr. Shannon, you're not well enough to travel anywhere with anybody right now. Does that sound cruel of me?

SHANNON: You mean that I'm stuck here for good? Winding up with the . . . inconsolable widow?

HANNAH: We all wind up with something or with someone, and if it's someone instead of just something, we're lucky, perhaps . . . unusually lucky. [*She starts to enter her cubicle, then turns to him again in the doorway*] Oh, and tomorrow. . . . [*She touches her forehead as if a little confused as well as exhausted*]

SHANNON: What about tomorrow?

HANNAH: [*With difficulty*] I think it might be better, tomorrow, if we avoid showing any particular interest in each other, because Mrs. Faulk is a morbidly jealous woman.

SHANNON: *Is* she?

HANNAH: Yes, she seems to have misunderstood our . . . sympathetic interest in each other. So I think we'd better avoid any more long talks on the verandah. I mean till she's thoroughly reassured it might be better if we just say good morning or good night to each other.

SHANNON: We don't even have to say that.

HANNAH: I will, but you don't have to answer.

SHANNON: [*Savagely*] How about wall-tappings between us by way of communication? You know, like convicts in separate cells communicate with each other by tapping on the walls of the cells? One tap: I'm here. Two taps: are you there? Three taps: yes, I am. Four taps: that's good, we're together. *Christ!* . . . Here, take this. [*He snatches the gold cross from his pocket*] Take my gold cross and hock it, it's 22-carat gold.

HANNAH: What do you, what are you . . . ?

SHANNON: There's a fine amethyst in it, it'll pay your travel expenses back to the States.

HANNAH: Mr. Shannon, you're making no sense at all now.

SHANNON: Neither are you, Miss Jelkes, talking about tomorrow, and. . . .

HANNAH: All I was saying was. . . .

SHANNON: You won't *be* here tomorrow! Had you forgotten you won't be here tomorrow?

HANNAH: [*With a slight, shocked laugh*] Yes, I *had*, I'd forgotten!

SHANNON: The widow wants you out and you'll go, even if you sell your water colors like hotcakes to the pariah dogs in the plaza. [*He stares at her, shaking his head hopelessly*]

HANNAH: I suppose you're right, Mr. Shannon. I must be too tired to think or I've contracted your fever. . . . It had actually slipped my mind for a moment that—

NONNO: [*Abruptly, from his cubicle*] Hannah!

HANNAH: [*Rushing to his door*] Yes, what is it, Nonno? [*He doesn't hear her and repeats her name louder*] Here I am, I'm here.

NONNO: Don't come in yet, but stay where I can call you.

HANNAH: Yes, I'll *hear* you, Nonno. [*She turns toward* SHANNON, *drawing a deep breath*]

SHANNON: Listen, if you don't take this gold cross that I never want on me again, I'm going to pitch it off the verandah at the spook in the rain forest. [*He raises an arm to throw it, but she catches his arm to restrain him*]

HANNAH: All right, Mr. Shannon, I'll take it, I'll hold it for you.

SHANNON: Hock it, honey, you've got to.

HANNAH: Well, if I do, I'll mail the pawn ticket to you so you can redeem it, because you'll want it again, when you've gotten over your fever. [*She moves blindly down the verandah and starts to enter the wrong cubicle*]

SHANNON: That isn't your cell, you went past it. [*His voice is gentle again*]

HANNAH: I did, I'm sorry. I've never been this tired in all my life. [*She turns to face him again. He stares into her face. She looks blindly out, past him*] Never! [*There is a slight pause*]

What did you say is making that constant, dry, scuffling sound beneath the verandah?

SHANNON: I told you.

HANNAH: I didn't hear you.

SHANNON: I'll get my flashlight, I'll show you. [*He lurches rapidly into his cubicle and back out with a flashlight*] It's an iguana. I'll show you. . . . See? The iguana? At the end of its rope? Trying to go on past the end of its goddam rope? Like *you!* Like *me!* Like Grampa with his last poem!

[*In the pause which follows singing is heard from the beach*]

HANNAH: What is a—what—iguana?

SHANNON: It's a kind of lizard—a big one, a giant one. The Mexican kids caught it and tied it up.

HANNAH: Why did they tie it up?

SHANNON: Because that's what they do. They tie them up and fatten them up and then eat them up, when they're ready for eating. They're a delicacy. Taste like white meat of chicken. At least the Mexicans think so. And also the kids, the Mexican kids, have a lot of fun with them, poking out their eyes with sticks and burning their tails with matches. You know? Fun? Like that?

HANNAH: Mr. Shannon, please go down and cut it loose!

SHANNON: I can't do that.

HANNAH: Why can't you?

SHANNON: Mrs. Faulk wants to eat it. I've got to please Mrs. Faulk, I am at her mercy. I am at her disposal.

HANNAH: I don't understand. I mean I don't understand how anyone could eat a big lizard.

SHANNON: Don't be so critical. If you got hungry enough you'd eat it too. You'd be surprised what people will eat if hungry. There's a lot of hungry people still in the world. Many have died of starvation, but a lot are still living and hungry, believe you me, if you will take my word for it. Why, when I was conducting a party of—*ladies?*—yes, ladies . . . through a country that shall be nameless but in this world, we were passing by rubberneck bus along a tropical coast when we saw a great mound of . . . well, the smell was unpleasant. One of my ladies said, "Oh, Larry, what is that?" My name being Lawrence, the most familiar ladies sometimes call me Larry. I didn't use the four letter word for what the great mound was. I didn't think it was necessary to say it. Then she noticed, and I noticed too, a pair of very old natives of this nameless country, practically naked except for a few filthy rags, creeping and crawling about this mound of . . . and . . . occasionally stopping to pick something out of it, and pop it into their mouths. What? Bits of undigested . . . food particles, Miss Jelkes. [*There is silence for a moment. She makes a gagging sound in her throat and rushes the length of the verandah to the wooden steps and disappears for a while.* SHANNON *continues, to himself and the moon*] Now why did I tell her that? Because it's true? That's no reason to tell her, because it's true. Yeah. Because it's true was a good reason not to tell her. Except . . . I think I first *faced* it in that nameless country. The gradual, rapid, natural, unnatural—predestined, accidental—cracking up and going to pieces of young Mr. T. Lawrence Shannon, yes, still *young* Mr. T. Lawrence Shannon, by which rapid-slow process . . . his final tour of ladies through tropical countries. . . . Why did I say "tropical"? Hell! Yes! It's always been tropical countries I took ladies through. Does that, does that—huh?—signify something, I wonder? Maybe. Fast decay is a thing of hot climates, steamy, hot, wet climates, and I run back to them like a. . . . Incomplete sentence. . . . Always seducing a lady or two, or three or four or five ladies in the party, but really ravaging her first by pointing out to her the—what?—horrors? Yes, horrors!—of the tropical country being conducted a tour through. My . . . brain's going out now, like a failing—power. . . . So I stay here, I reckon, and live off la patrona for the rest of my life. Well, she's old enough to predecease me. She could check out of here first, and I imagine that after a couple of years of having to satisfy her I might be prepared for the shock of her passing on. . . . Cruelty . . . pity. What is it? . . . Don't know, all I know is. . . .

HANNAH: [*From below the verandah*] You're talking to yourself.

SHANNON: No, To you. I knew you could hear me out there, but not being able to see you I could say it easier, you know . . . ?

NONNO:

A chronicle no longer gold,
A bargaining with mist and mould. . . .

HANNAH: [*Coming back onto the verandah*] I took a closer look at the iguana down there.

SHANNON: You did? How did you like it? Charming? Attractive?

HANNAH: No, it's not an attractive creature. Nevertheless I think it should be cut loose.

SHANNON: Iguanas have been known to bite their tails off when they're tied up by their tails.

HANNAH: This one is tied by its throat. It can't bite its own head off to escape from the end of the rope, Mr. Shannon. Can you look at me and tell me truthfully that you don't know it's able to feel pain and panic?

SHANNON: You mean it's one of God's creatures?

HANNAH: If you want to put it that way, yes, it is. Mr. Shannon, will you please cut it loose, set it free? Because if you don't, I will.

SHANNON: Can you look at *me* and tell *me* truthfully that this reptilian creature, tied up down there, doesn't mostly disturb you because of its parallel situation to your Grampa's dying-out effort to finish one last poem, Miss Jelkes?

HANNAH: Yes, I. . . .

SHANNON: Never mind completing that sentence We'll play God tonight like kids play house with old broken crates and boxes. All right? Now Shannon is going to go down there with his machete and cut the damn lizard loose so it can run back to its bushes because God won't do it and we are going to play God here.

HANNAH: I knew you'd do that. And I thank you.

[SHANNON *goes down the two steps from the verandah with the machete. He crouches beside the cactus that hides the iguana and cuts the rope with a quick, hard stroke of the machete. He turns to look after its flight, as the low,*

excited mumble in cubicle 3 grows louder. Then NONNO's
voice turns to a sudden shout]

NONNO: *Hannah! Hannah!* [*She rushes to him, as he wheels himself out of his cubicle onto the verandah*]

HANNAH: Grandfather! What is it?

NONNO: I! believe! it! is! *finished!* Quick, before I forget it—
pencil, paper! Quick! please! Ready?

HANNAH: Yes. All ready, Grandfather.

NONNO: [*In a loud, exalted voice*]

> How calmly does the orange branch
> Observe the sky begin to blanch
> Without a cry, without a prayer,
> With no betrayal of despair.
>
> Sometime while night obscures the tree
> The zenith of its life will be
> Gone past forever, and from thence
> A second history will commence.
>
> A chronicle no longer gold,
> A bargaining with mist and mould,
> And finally the broken stem
> The plummeting to earth; and then
>
> An intercourse not well designed
> For beings of a golden kind
> Whose native green must arch above
> The earth's obscene, corrupting love.
>
> And still the ripe fruit and the branch
> Observe the sky begin to blanch
> Without a cry, without a prayer,
> With no betrayal of despair.
>
> O Courage, could you not as well
> Select a second place to dwell,
> Not only in that golden tree
> But in the frightened heart of me?

Have you got it?

HANNAH: Yes!

NONNO: All of it?

HANNAH: Every word of it.

NONNO: It is *finished?*

HANNAH: Yes.

NONNO: Oh! God! Finally finished?

HANNAH: Yes, finally finished. [*She is crying. The singing voices flow up from the beach*]

NONNO: After waiting so long!

HANNAH: Yes, we waited so long.

NONNO: And it's good! It is *good?*

HANNAH: It's—it's. . . .

NONNO: What?

HANNAH: Beautiful, Grandfather! [*She springs up, a fist to her mouth*] Oh, Grandfather, I am so happy for you. Thank you for writing such a lovely poem! It was worth the long wait. Can you sleep now, Grandfather?

NONNO: You'll have it typewritten tomorrow?

HANNAH: Yes. I'll have it typed up and send it off to *Harper's.*

NONNO: Hah? I didn't hear that, Hannah.

HANNAH: [*Shouting*] I'll have it typed up tomorrow, and mail it to *Harper's* tomorrow! They've been waiting for it a long time, too! You know!

NONNO: Yes, I'd like to pray now.

HANNAH: Good night. Sleep now, Grandfather. You've finished your loveliest poem.

NONNO: [*Faintly, drifting off*] Yes, thanks and praise . . .

[MAXINE *comes around the front of the verandah, followed by* PEDRO *playing a harmonica softly. She is prepared for a night swim, a vividly striped towel thrown over her shoulders. It is apparent that the night's progress has mellowed her spirit: her face wears a faint smile which is suggestive of those cool, impersonal, all-comprehending smiles on the carved heads of Egyptian or Oriental deities. Bearing a rum-coco, she approaches the hammock, discovers it empty, the ropes on the floor, and calls softly to* PEDRO]

MAXINE: Shannon ha escapado [PEDRO *goes on playing dreamily. She throws back her head and shouts*] SHANNON! [*The call is echoed by the hill beyond.* PEDRO *advances a few steps and points under the verandah*]

PEDRO: Miré. Allé 'hasta Shannon.

[SHANNON *comes into view from below the verandah, the severed rope and machete dangling from his hands*]

MAXINE: What are you doing down there, Shannon?

SHANNON: I cut loose one of God's creatures at the end of the rope.

[HANNAH, *who has stood motionless with closed eyes behind the wicker chair, goes quietly toward the cubicles and out of the moon's glare*]

MAXINE: [*Tolerantly*] What'd you do that for, Shannon?

SHANNON: So that one of God's creatures could scramble home safe and free. . . . A little act of grace, Maxine.

MAXINE: [*Smiling a bit more definitely*] C'mon up here, Shannon. I want to talk to you.

SHANNON: [*Starting to climb onto the verandah, as* MAXINE *rattles the ice in the coconut shell*] What d'ya want to talk about, Widow Faulk?

MAXINE: Let's go down and swim in that liquid moonlight.

SHANNON: Where did you pick up that poetic expression?

[MAXINE *glances back at* PEDRO *and dismisses him with,* "Vamos." *He leaves with a shrug, the harmonica fading out*]

MAXINE: Shannon, I want you to stay with me.

SHANNON: [*Taking the rum-coco from her*] You want a drinking companion?

MAXINE: No, I just want you to stay here, because I'm alone here now and I need somebody to help me manage the place.

[HANNAH *strikes a match for a cigarette*]

SHANNON: [*Looking toward her*] I want to remember that face. I won't see it again.

MAXINE: Let's go down to the beach.

SHANNON: I can make it down the hill, but not back up.

MAXINE: I'll get you back up the hill. [*They have started off now, toward the path down through the rain forest*] I've got five more years, maybe ten, to make this place attractive to the male clientele, the middle-aged ones at least. And you can take care of the women that are with them. That's what you can do, you know that, Shannon.

[*He chuckles happily. They are now on the path,* MAXINE *half leading half supporting him. Their voices fade as* HANNAH *goes into* NONNO's *cubicle and comes back with a shawl, her cigarette left inside. She pauses between the door and the wicker chair and speaks to herself and the sky*]

HANNAH: Oh, God, can't we stop now? Finally? Please let us. It's so quiet here, now.

[*She starts to put the shawl about* NONNO, *but at the same moment his head drops to the side. With a soft intake of breath, she extends a hand before his mouth to see if he is still breathing. He isn't. In a panicky moment, she looks right and left for someone to call to. There's no one. Then she bends to press her head to the crown of* NONNO's *and the curtain starts to descend*]

THE END

Heute wollen wir ein Liedlein singen,
Trinken wollen wir den kuehlen Wein;
Und die Glaeser sollen dazu klingen,
Denn es muss, es muss geschieden sein.

Gib' mir deine Hand,
Deine weisse Hand,
Leb'wohl, mein Schatz, leb'wohl, mein Schatz
Lebe wohl, lebe wohl,
Denn wir fahren. Boom! Boom!
Denn wir fahren. Boom! Boom!
Denn wir fahren gegen Engelland. Boom! Boom!

Let's sing a little song today,
And drink some cool wine;
The glasses should be ringing
Since we must, we must part.

Give me your hand,
Your white hand,
Farewell, my love, farewell,
Farewell, farewell,
Since we're going—
Since we're going—
Since we're going against England.

Joseph Stein—Jerry Bock—Sheldon Harnick

A luminous musical, *Fiddler on the Roof* not only irradiated the theatre of the Sixties, it also added to the canon of great works of the American musical stage. Based on the stories of Sholom Alei-chem—the most beloved and perhaps the greatest Jewish writer and humorist of modern times—the musical play has transcended areal and language differentiations and has impressively traveled its way to global success. At the time this is being written, *Fiddler on the Roof* is entering its sixth consecutive year on The Broadway stage; the London company is in its third year at Her Majesty's Theatre; and other troupes performing the Joseph Stein-Jerry Bock-Sheldon Harnick musical are current in Australia, New Zealand, Switzerland, Norway, Finland, Iceland, Yugoslavia, South Africa, Czechoslovakia, West Germany, Argentina and Austria. In 1970, the musical will be seen for the initial time in France, Poland, Belgium, Spain, Turkey, Mexico and East Germany while return engagements are scheduled for Israel, Holland and Japan.

As this collection of BEST PLAYS OF THE SIXTIES goes to press, *Fiddler on the Roof* (with 2100 performances) ranks as the fourth longest running musical in Broadway history. The record presently is held by *My Fair Lady* (2717 performances), but it is not in-conceivable that *Fiddler on the Roof*, with its audience popularity undiminished at the close of the Sixties, might well surpass that figure.

At its opening in 1964, *Fiddler on the Roof* was lavishly hailed by the press. Henry Hewes, writing in the *Saturday Review*, de-scribed it as "a remarkably effective mixture that thoroughly enter-tains without ever losing a sense of connection with the more painful realities that underlie its humor, its beauty, and its ritual celebrations." John Chapman, first-night arbiter for the New York *Daily News* termed it "one of the great works of the American musical theatre" while his colleague Howard Taubman of the New York *Times* joyously reported that "it catches the essence of a moment in history with sentiment and radiance . . . an exceptional accomplishment."

The acclaimed presentation won innumerable awards, including the New York Drama Critics' Circle Award as best musical of 1964–65; the Page One Award of the American Newspaper Guild; and nine Antoinette Perry (Tony) Awards, notably the citation for best musical of the year. The production also scored "bests" in four leading categories in *Variety's* annual Poll of New York's Drama Critics and in London, sixteen critics named *Fiddler on the Roof* the best foreign musical of the season.

In transmitting the Sholom Aleichem stories from the printed page to the musical stage, Joseph Stein noted that: ". . . the problem of adaptation was to remain true to the spirit, the feeling of Sholom Aleichem and transmute it for a contemporary audience . . . to tell the story of Tevye, his family and his community in terms which would have meaning for today."

Utilizing some of the important episodes and, of course, certain of the main characters from the progenitor's works, Mr. Stein created a fresh story that dealt with "the gradual breakdown of the traditional cultural forms and beliefs of the *shtetl*, the village community, under the buffeting of social change and hostile forces, finally leading to disintegration of that society. We decided to make this crumbling of tradition, illustrated by the daughters' love stories and other developments, the theme of our play."

To endow the story with a further significance for our times, Mr. Stein and his collaborators "brought to the foreground an element implicit in the Tevye tales . . . the hostility, the violence, the injustice practiced by a ruling majority against a weak minority. We wanted in this to point up the internal strength, the dignity, the humor of that people and, like minorities today, their unique talent for survival."

Joseph Stein (book) was born in New York City, and educated at James Monroe High School, City College and Columbia University's School of Social Work. He was employed as a psychiatric social worker when he wrote his first material, in 1946, for radio's

"Chamber Music Society of Lower Basin Street." Subsequent writing assignments began to crowd his slate and he was compelled to relinquish social work. In the two years that followed, Mr. Stein became a leading writer in radio and, later, television. In 1948, he began writing for the theatre, contributing sketches (written in collaboration with Will Glickman) to various revues, principally, *Inside U.S.A.* and *Lend an Ear*. Between sketches the coauthors fashioned a comedy, *Mrs. Gibbon's Boys*, produced by George Abbott in 1949. With that fleeting experience behind them, the Messrs. Stein and Glickman rejoined the world of revue by providing material for *Alive and Kicking*, which tarried rather briefly at the Winter Garden Theatre.

In 1955, however, the team surfaced to substantial success with the book for the musical *Plain and Fancy*. This was followed by the Sammy Davis, Jr. vehicle *Mr. Wonderful* (1956) and *The Body Beautiful* (1958).

In 1959, Mr. Stein coadapted (with Robert Russell) the musical book for *Take Me Along* (from Eugene O'Neill's nostalgic comedy, *Ah, Wilderness*) and, individually, *Juno* (derived from Sean O'Casey's modern classic, *Juno and the Paycock*). And in 1963, his comedy, *Enter Laughing* (based on Carl Reiner's autobiographical novel) established a Broadway run of 419 performances.

During the 1968–69 season, Joseph Stein was represented on the New York stage by the book for *Zorbá* and as coproducer of Joseph Heller's drama, *We Bombed in New Haven*.

Jerry Bock (music) and Sheldon Harnick (lyrics) first came into joint view with the 1958 production of the aforementioned *The Body Beautiful*. Although that musical hardly could be classified as a success, it was an important (and catalytical) event for the songwriting duo, for their work so impressed producer Harold Prince, his late partner, Robert Griffith, and the doyen director George Abbott that they commissioned the collaborators to take on the assignment of creating the songs and musical numbers for *Fiorello!* The 1959 presentation ran for 795 performances, garnered a New York Drama Critics' Circle Award and the Pulitzer Prize and propelled the team of Bock and Harnick to the forefront of the American musical theatre. It also was the harbinger of their most celebrated success, *Fiddler on the Roof*, and the start of their long and successful association with Harold Prince under whose managerial banner they also collaborated on *Tenderloin* (1960) and *She Loves Me* (1963).

With their 1966 Broadway musical, *The Apple Tree* (based on stories by Mark Twain, Frank R. Stockton and Jules Feiffer), Bock and Harnick entered a new phase of collaboration: in addition to creating the words and music, they also functioned as coauthors of the book.

Jerry Bock was born in New Haven, Connecticut, in 1928, raised in Flushing, New York, and attended Flushing High School (where he began his composing career) and the University of Wisconsin. He received his baptism as a "professional" composer at Camp Tamiment in the Poconos, later wrote much of the music for television's "Your Show of Shows." He also contributed songs (with Larry Holofcener as lyricist) to the revue *Catch a Star* and an edition of *The Ziegfeld Follies*. His first full Broadway score was written for *Mr. Wonderful* (1956).

Born in Chicago in 1924, Sheldon Harnick was inspired by his mother's passion for commemorating all occasions in verse and while still at grammar school picked up the thread and commenced to write poems himself, "mostly doggerel and mostly nonsense." In 1943, he entered the Army and it was while in service that he first started seriously to write songs which he performed at various USO shows, sandwiching them in between his violin solos.

In 1946, he returned to Chicago and enrolled at Northwestern University where he contributed songs to the annual student musicals and doubled as a fiddle player with the show's orchestra. After graduation from Northwestern, he worked with the Compass (an improvisational group which advanced the careers of Mike Nichols, Barbara Harris, Elaine May, Alan Arkin, the Second City troupe and others) and, for a while, as a violinist with Xavier Cugat's orchestra, then after being fired for "swaying to the left instead of the right," he headed for New York and a career as a song writer.

Prior to teaming up with Jerry Bock, Mr. Harnick contributed his talents to *New Faces of 1952* (notably, with the number "The Boston Beguine"). During this period (the 1950s), some other revues that included his work were *Two's Company; The Littlest Revue; Take Five; Kaleidoscope;* and *John Murray Anderson's Almanac*.

FIDDLER ON THE ROOF
Book by Joseph Stein
Music by Jerry Bock
Lyrics by Sheldon Harnick

Based on Sholom Aleichem's stories

Fiddler on the Roof was first presented by Harold Prince at the Imperial Theatre, New York, on September 22, 1964. The cast was as follows:

TEVYE, *a dairyman*	Zero Mostel
GOLDE, *his wife*	Maria Karnilova
TZEITEL	Joanna Merlin
HODEL	Julia Migenes
CHAVA — *their daughters*	Tanya Everett
SHPRINTZE	Marilyn Rogers
BIELKE	Linda Ross
YENTE, *a matchmaker*	Beatrice Arthur
MOTEL KAMZOIL, *a tailor*	Austin Pendelton
SHANDEL, *his mother*	Helen Verbit
PERCHIK, *a student*	Bert Convy
LAZAR WOLF, *a butcher*	Michael Granger
MORDCHA, *an innkeeper*	Zvee Scooler
RABBI	Gluck Sandor
MENDEL, *his son*	Leonard Frey
AVRAM, *a bookseller*	Paul Lipson
NAHUM, *a beggar*	Maurice Edwards
GRANDMA TZEITEL, *Golde's grandmother*	Sue Babel
FRUMA-SARAH, *Lazar Wolf's first wife*	Carol Sawyer
YUSSEL, *a hatter*	Mitch Thomas
CONSTABLE	Joseph Sullivan
FYEDKA, *a young man*	Joe Ponazecki
SASHA, *his friend*	Robert Berdeen

and

THE FIDDLER   Gino Conforti

VILLAGERS: Tom Abbott, John C. Attle, Sue Babel, Sammy Bayes, Robert Berdeen, Lorenzo Bianco, Duane Bodin, Robert Currie, Sarah Felcher, Tony Gardell, Louis Genevrino, Ross Gifford, Dan Jasin, Sandra Kazan, Thom Koutsoukos, Sharon Lerit, Sylvia Mann, Peff Modelski, Irene Paris, Charles Rule, Carol Sawyer, Roberta Senn, Mitch Thomas, Helen Verbit

Entire production directed and choreographed
by JEROME ROBBINS

Settings by Boris Aronson
Costumes by Patricia Zipprodt
Lighting by Jean Rosenthal
Orchestrations by Don Walker
Musical Direction & Vocal Arrangements by Milton Greene
Dance Music arranged by Betty Walberg
Production Stage Manager, Ruth Mitchell

THE PLACE: *Anatevka, a village in Russia.*

THE TIME: *1905, on the eve of the revolutionary period.*

PROLOGUE

The exterior of TEVYE's *house. A* FIDDLER *is seated on the roof, playing.* TEVYE *is outside the house.*

TEVYE: A fiddler on the roof. Sounds crazy, no? But in our little village of Anatevka, you might say every one of us is a fiddler on the roof, trying to scratch out a pleasant, simple tune without breaking his neck. It isn't easy. You may ask, why do we stay up here if it's so dangerous? We stay because Anatevka is our home. And how do we keep our balance? That I can tell you in a word—tradition!

VILLAGERS: [*Enter, singing*]

Tradition, tradition—Tradition.
Tradition, tradition—Tradition.

TEVYE: Because of our traditions, we've kept our balance for many, many years. Here in Anatevka we have traditions for everything—how to eat, how to sleep, how to wear clothes. For instance, we always keep our heads covered and always wear a little prayer shawl. This shows our constant devotion to God. You may ask, how did this tradition start? I'll tell you—I don't know! But it's a tradition. Because of our traditions, everyone knows who he is and what God expects him to do.

TEVYE *and* PAPAS: [*Sing*]

["Tradition"]
Who, day and night,
Must scramble for a living,

Feed a wife and children,
Say his daily prayers?
And who has the right,
As master of the house,
To have the final word at home?

ALL:

The papa, the papa—Tradition.
The papa, the papa—Tradition.

GOLDE *and* MAMAS:

Who must know the way to make a proper home,
A quiet home, a kosher home?
Who must raise a family and run the home
So Papa's free to read the Holy Book?

ALL:

The mama, the mama—Tradition.
The mama, the mama—Tradition.

SONS:

At three I started Hebrew school,
At ten I learned a trade.
I hear they picked a bride for me.
I hope she's pretty.

ALL:

The sons, the sons—Tradition.
The sons, the sons—Tradition.

DAUGHTERS:

And who does Mama teach
To mend and tend and fix,
Preparing me to marry
Whoever Papa picks?

ALL:

The daughters, the daughters—Tradition.
The daughters, the daughters—Tradition.

[*They repeat the song as a round*]

PAPAS:

The papas.

MAMAS:

The mamas.

SONS:

The sons.

DAUGHTERS:

The daughters.

ALL:

Tradition.

PAPAS:

The papas.

MAMAS:

The mamas.

SONS:

The sons.

DAUGHTERS:

The daughters.

ALL:

Tradition.

TEVYE: And in the circle of our little village, we have always had our special types. For instance, Yente, the matchmaker . . .

YENTE: Avram, I have a perfect match for your son. A wonderful girl.

AVRAM: Who is it?

YENTE: Ruchel, the shoemaker's daughter.

AVRAM: Ruchel? But she can hardly see. She's almost blind.

YENTE: Tell the truth, Avram, is your son so much to look at? The way she sees and the way he looks, it's a perfect match.

[*All dance*]

TEVYE: And Reb Nahum, the beggar . . .

NAHUM: Alms for the poor, alms for the poor.

LAZAR: Here, Reb Nahum, is one kopek.

NAHUM: One kopek? Last week you gave me two kopeks.

LAZAR: I had a bad week.

NAHUM: So if you had a bad week, why should I suffer?

[*All dance*]

TEVYE: And, most important, our beloved rabbi . . .

MENDEL: Rabbi, may I ask you a question?

RABBI: Certainly, my son.

MENDEL: Is there a proper blessing for the Tsar?

RABBI: A blessing for the Tsar? Of course. May God bless and keep the Tsar—far away from us!

[*All dance*]

TEVYE: Then, there are the others in our village. They make a much bigger circle.

[*The* PRIEST, *the* CONSTABLE, *and other* RUSSIANS *cross the stage. The two groups nod to each other*]

TEVYE: His Honor the Constable, his Honor the Priest, and his Honor—many others. We don't bother them, and, so far, they don't bother us. And among ourselves we get along perfectly well. Of course, there was the time [*Pointing to the* TWO MEN] when he sold him a horse and he delivered a mule, but that's all settled now. Now we live in simple peace and harmony and—

[*The* TWO MEN *begin an argument, which is taken up by the entire group*]

FIRST MAN: It was a horse.

SECOND MAN: It was a mule.

FIRST MAN: It was a horse!

SECOND MAN: It was a mule, I tell you!

VILLAGERS: Horse!

VILLAGERS: Mule!

VILLAGERS: Horse!

VILLAGERS: Mule!

VILLAGERS: Horse!

VILLAGERS: Mule!

VILLAGERS: Horse!

VILLAGERS: Mule!

EVERYONE:

> Tradition, tradition—Tradition.
> Tradition, tradition—Tradition.

TEVYE: [*Quieting them*] Tradition. Without our traditions, our lives would be as shaky as—as a fiddler on the roof!

> [*The* VILLAGERS *exit, and the house opens to show its interior*]

SCENE ONE

The kitchen of TEVYE'S *house.* GOLDE, TZEITEL, *and* HODEL *are preparing for the Sabbath.* SHPRINTZE *and* BIELKE *enter from outside, carrying logs.*

SHPRINTZE: Mama, where should we put these?

GOLDE: Put them on my head! By the stove, foolish girl. Where is Chava?

HODEL: She's in the barn, milking.

BIELKE: When will Papa be home?

GOLDE: It's almost Sabbath and he worries a lot when he'll be home! All day long riding on top of his wagon like a prince.

TZEITEL: Mama, you know that Papa works hard.

GOLDE: His horse works harder! And you don't have to defend your papa to me. I know him a little longer than you. He could drive a person crazy. [*Under her breath*] He should only live and be well. [*Out loud*] Shprintze, bring me some more potatoes.

[CHAVA *enters, carrying a basket, with a book under her apron*]

Chava, did you finish milking?

CHAVA: Yes, Mama. [*She drops the book*]

GOLDE: You were reading again? Why does a girl have to read? Will it get her a better husband? Here. [*Hands* CHAVA *the book*]

[CHAVA *exits into the house.* SHPRINTZE *enters with basket of potatoes*]

SHPRINTZE: Mama, Yente's coming. She's down the road.

HODEL: Maybe she's finally found a good match for you, Tzeitel.

GOLDE: From your mouth to God's ears.

TZEITEL: Why does she have to come now? It's almost Sabbath.

GOLDE: Go finish in the barn. I want to talk to Yente alone.

SHPRINTZE: Mama, can I go out and play?

GOLDE: You have feet? Go.

BIELKE: Can I go too?

GOLDE: Go too.

[SHPRINTZE *and* BIELKE *exit*]

TZEITEL: But Mama, the men she finds. The last one was so old and he was bald. He had no hair.

GOLDE: A poor girl without a dowry can't be so particular. You want hair, marry a monkey.

TZEITEL: After all, Mama, I'm not yet twenty years old, and—

GOLDE: Shah! [*Spits between her fingers*] Do you have to boast about your age? Do you want to tempt the Evil Eye? Inside.

[TZEITEL *leaves the kitchen as* YENTE *enters from outside*]

YENTE: Golde darling, I had to see you because I have such news for you. And not just every-day-in-the-week news—once-in-a-lifetime news. And where are your daughters? Outside, no? Good. Such diamonds, such jewels. You'll see, Golde, I'll find every one of them a husband. But you shouldn't be so picky. Even the worst husband, God forbid, is better than no husband, God forbid. And who should know better than me? Ever since my husband died I've been a poor widow, alone, nobody to talk to, nothing to say to anyone. It's no life. All I do at night is think of him, and even thinking of him gives me no pleasure, because you know as well as I, he was not much of a person. Never made a living, everything he touched turned to mud, but better than nothing.

MOTEL: [*Entering*] Good evening. Is Tzeitel in the house?

GOLDE: But she's busy. You can come back later.

MOTEL: There's something I'd like to tell her.

GOLDE: Later.

TZEITEL: [*Entering*] Oh, Motel, I thought I heard you.

GOLDE: Finish what you were doing. [TZEITEL *goes out. To* MOTEL] I said later.

MOTEL: [*Exiting*] All right!

YENTE: What does that poor little tailor, Motel, want with Tzeitel?

GOLDE: They have been friends since they were babies together. They talk, they play . . .

YENTE: [*Suspiciously*] They play? What do they play?

GOLDE: Who knows? They're just children.

YENTE: From such children, come other children.

GOLDE: Motel, he's a nothing. Yente, you said—

YENTE: Ah, children, children! They are your blessing in your old age. But my Aaron, may he rest in peace, couldn't give me children. Believe me, he was good as gold, never raised his voice to me, but otherwise he was not much of a man, so what good is it if he never raised his voice? But what's the use complaining. Other women enjoy complaining, but not Yente. Not every woman in the world is a Yente. Well, I must prepare my poor Sabbath table, so goodbye, Golde, and it was a pleasure talking our hearts out to each other. [*She starts to exit*]

GOLDE: Yente, you said you had news for me.

YENTE: [*Returning*] Oh, I'm losing my head. One day it will fall off altogether, and a horse will kick it into the mud, and goodbye, Yente. Of course, the news. It's about Lazar Wolf, the butcher. A good man, a fine man. And I don't have to tell you that he's well off. But he's lonely, the poor man. After all, a widower . . . You understand? Of course you do. To make it short, out of the whole town, he's cast his eye on Tzeitel.

GOLDE: My Tzeitel?

YENTE: No, the Tsar's Tzeitel! Of course your Tzeitel.

GOLDE: Such a match, for my Tzeitel. But Tevye wants a learned man. He doesn't like Lazar.

YENTE: Fine. So he won't marry him. Lazar wants the daughter, not the father. Listen to me, Golde, send Tevye to him. Don't tell him what it's about. Let Lazar discuss it himself. He'll win him over. He's a good man, a wealthy man—true? Of course true! So you'll tell me how it went, and you don't have to thank me, Golde, because aside from my fee—which anyway Lazar will pay—it gives me satisfaction to make people happy— what better satisfaction is there? So goodbye, Golde, and you're welcome.

[*She goes out. Enter* TZEITEL]

TZEITEL: What did she want, Mama?

GOLDE: When I want you to know, I'll tell you. Finish washing the floor.

[*She exits.* HODEL *and* CHAVA *enter with wash mop and bucket*]

HODEL: I wonder if Yente found a husband for you?

TZEITEL: I'm not anxious for Yente to find me a husband.

CHAVA: [*Teasing*] Not unless it's Motel, the tailor.

TZEITEL: I didn't ask you.

HODEL: Tzeitel, you're the oldest. They have to make a match for you before they can make one for me.

CHAVA: And then after her, one for me.

HODEL: So if Yente brings—

TZEITEL: Oh, Yente! Yente!

HODEL: Well, somebody has to arrange the matches. Young people can't decide these things for themselves.

CHAVA: She might bring someone wonderful—

HODEL: Someone interesting—

CHAVA: And well off—

HODEL: And important—[*Sings*]

["Matchmaker, Matchmaker"]
                Matchmaker, Matchmaker,
                    Make me a match,
                    Find me a catch.
                    Catch me a catch.
                Matchmaker, Matchmaker,
                    Look through your book
                And make me a perfect match.

CHAVA:

                Matchmaker, Matchmaker,
                    I'll bring the veil,
                    You bring the groom,
                    Slender and pale.
                Bring me a ring for I'm longing to be
                    The envy of all I see.

HODEL:

                    For Papa,
                Make him a scholar.

CHAVA:

                    For Mama,
                Make him rich as a king.

CHAVA *and* HODEL:

                    For me, well,
                    I wouldn't holler
                If he were as handsome as anything.

                Matchmaker, Matchmaker,
                    Make me a match,

Find me a find,
Catch me a catch.
Night after night in the dark I'm alone,
So find me a match
Of my own.

TZEITEL: Since when are you interested in a match, Chava? I thought you just had your eye on your books. [HODEL *chuckles*] And you have your eye on the rabbi's son.

HODEL: Why not? We only have one rabbi and he only has one son. Why shouldn't I want the best?

TZEITEL: Because you're a girl from a poor family. So whatever Yente brings, you'll take. Right? Of course right. [*Sings*]

Hodel, oh Hodel,
Have I made a match for you!
He's handsome, he's young!
All right, he's sixty-two,
But he's a nice man, a good catch—true? True.

I promise you'll be happy.
And even if you're not,
There's more to life than that—
Don't ask me what.

Chava, I found him.
Will you be a lucky bride!
He's handsome, he's tall—
That is, from side to side.
But he's a nice man, a good catch—right? Right.

You heard he has a temper.
He'll beat you every night,
But only when he's sober,
So you're all right.

Did you think you'd get a prince?
Well, I do the best I can.
With no dowry, no money, no family background
Be glad you got a man.

CHAVA:

Matchmaker, Matchmaker,
You know that I'm

Still very young.
Please, take your time.

HODEL:

Up to this minute
I misunderstood
That I could get stuck for good.

CHAVA *and* HODEL:

Dear Yente,
See that he's gentle.
Remember,
You were also a bride.
It's not that
I'm sentimental.

CHAVA, HODEL, *and* TZEITEL:

It's just that I'm terrified!

Matchmaker, Matchmaker,
Plan me no plans,
I'm in no rush.
Maybe I've learned
Playing with matches
A girl can get burned.
So,
Bring me no ring,
Groom me no groom,
Find me no find,
Catch me no catch,
Unless he's a matchless match.

SCENE TWO

The exterior of TEVYE'S *house.* TEVYE *enters, pulling his cart.
He stops, and sits on the wagon seat, exhausted.*

TEVYE: Today I am a horse. Dear God, did you have to make my
poor old horse lose his shoe just before the Sabbath? That
wasn't nice. It's enough you pick on me, Tevye, bless me with
five daughters, a life of poverty. What have you got against my

horse? Sometimes I think when things are too quiet up there,
You say to Yourself: "Let's see, what kind of mischief can I
play on my friend Tevye?"

GOLDE: [*Entering from house*] You're finally here, my bread-
winner.

TEVYE: [*To heaven*] I'll talk to You later.

GOLDE: Where's your horse?

TEVYE: He was invited to the blacksmith's for the Sabbath.

GOLDE: Hurry up, the sun won't wait for you. I have something
to say to you. [*Exits into the house*]

TEVYE: As the Good Book says, "Heal us, O Lord, and we shall
be healed." In other words, send us the cure, we've got the
sickness already. [*Gestures to the door*] I'm not really complaining—after all, with Your help, I'm starving to death. You
made many, many poor people. I realize, of course, that it's no
shame to be poor, but it's no great honor either. So what would
have been so terrible if I had a small fortune? [*Sings*]

["If I Were a Rich Man"]

> If I were a rich man,
> Daidle deedle daidle
> Digguh digguh deedle daidle dum,
> All day long I'd biddy biddy bum,
> If I were a wealthy man.
>
> Wouldn't have to work hard,
> Daidle deedle daidle
> Digguh digguh deedle daidle dum,
> If I were a biddy biddy rich
> Digguh digguh deedle daidle man.

> I'd build a big, tall house with rooms by the dozen
> Right in the middle of the town,
> A fine tin roof and real wooden floors below.
> There would be one long staircase just going up,
> And one even longer coming down,
> And one more leading nowhere just for show.

> I'd fill my yard with chicks and turkeys and geese
> And ducks for the town to see and hear,
> Squawking just as noisily as they can.

And each loud quack and cluck and gobble and honk
Will land like a trumpet on the ear,
As if to say, here lives a wealthy man.

[*Sighs*]

If I were a rich man,
Daidle deedle daidle
Digguh digguh deedle daidle dum,
All day long I'd biddy biddy bum,
If I were a wealthy man.

Wouldn't have to work hard,
Daidle deedle daidle
Digguh digguh deedle daidle dum,
If I were a biddy biddy rich
Digguh digguh deedle daidle man.

I see my wife, my Golde, looking like a rich man's wife,
With a proper double chin,
Supervising meals to her heart's delight.
I see her putting on airs and strutting like a peacock,
Oi! what a happy mood she's in,
Screaming at the servants day and night.

The most important men in town will come to fawn on me.
They will ask me to advise them like a Solomon the Wise,
"If you please, Reb Tevye. Pardon me, Reb Tevye,"
Posing problems that would cross a rabbi's eyes.

[*He chants*]

And it won't make one bit of diff'rence
If I answer right or wrong.
When you're rich they think you really know!

If I were rich I'd have the time that I lack
To sit in the synagogue and pray,
And maybe have a seat by the eastern wall,
And I'd discuss the Holy Books with the learned men
Seven hours every day.
That would be the sweetest thing of all.

[*Sighs*]

If I were a rich man,
Daidle deedle daidle
Digguh digguh deedle daidle dum,
All day long I'd biddy biddy bum,
If I were a wealthy man.

Wouldn't have to work hard,
Daidle deedle daidle
Digguh digguh deedle daidle dum,
Lord, who made the lion and the lamb,
You decreed I should be what I am,
Would it spoil some vast, eternal plan—
If I were a wealthy man?

[As *the song ends,* MORDCHA, MENDEL, PERCHIK, AVRAM, *and other* TOWNSPEOPLE *enter*]

MORDCHA: There he is! You forgot my order for the Sabbath!

TEVYE: Reb Mordcha, I had a little accident with my horse.

MENDEL: Tevye, you didn't bring the Rabbi's order.

TEVYE: I know, Reb Mendel.

AVRAM: Tevye, you forgot my order for the Sabbath.

TEVYE: This is bigger news than the plague in Odessa.

AVRAM: [*Waving the newspaper that he holds*] Talking about news, terrible news in the outside world—terrible!

MORDCHA: What is it?

MENDEL: What does it say?

AVRAM: In a village called Rajanka, all the Jews were evicted, forced to leave their homes.

[*They all look at each other*]

MENDEL: For what reason?

AVRAM: It doesn't say. Maybe the Tsar wanted their land. Maybe a plague . . .

MORDCHA: May the Tsar have his own personal plague.

ALL: Amen.

MENDEL: [*To* AVRAM] Why don't you ever bring us some good news?

AVRAM: I only read it. It was an edict from the authorities.

MORDCHA: May the authorities start itching in places that they can't reach.

ALL: Amen.

PERCHIK: [*Has quietly entered during above and sat down to rest*] Why do you curse them? What good does your cursing do? You stand around and curse and chatter and don't do anything. You'll all chatter your way into the grave.

MENDEL: Excuse me, you're not from this village.

PERCHIK: No.

MENDEL: And where are you from?

PERCHIK: Kiev. I was a student in the university there.

MORDCHA: Aha! The university. Is that where you learned to criticize your elders?

PERCHIK: That's where I learned that there is more to life than talk. You should know what's going on in the outside world.

MORDCHA: Why should I break my head about the outside world? Let them break their own heads.

TEVYE: He's right. As the Good Book says, "If you spit in the air, it lands in your face."

PERCHIK: That's nonsense. You can't close your eyes to what's happening in the world.

TEVYE: He's right.

AVRAM: He's right and he's right? How can they both be right?

TEVYE: You know, you're also right.

MORDCHA: He's right! He's still wet behind the ears! Good Sabbath, Tevye.

VILLAGERS: Good Sabbath, Tevye.

[*They take their orders and leave.* MENDEL *remains*]

MENDEL: Tevye, the rabbi's order. My cheese!

TEVYE: Of course. So you're from Kiev, Reb . . .

PERCHIK: Perchik.

TEVYE: Perchik. So, you're a newcomer here. As Abraham said, "I am a stranger in a strange land."

MENDEL: Moses said that.

TEVYE: [To MENDEL] Forgive me. As King David put it, "I am slow of speech and slow of tongue."

MENDEL: That was also Moses.

TEVYE: For a man with a slow tongue, he talked a lot.

MENDEL: And the cheese!

[TEVYE *notices that* PERCHIK *is eying the cheese hungrily*]

TEVYE: Here, have a piece.

PERCHIK: I have no money. And I am not a beggar.

TEVYE: Here—it's a blessing for me to give.

PERCHIK: Very well—for your sake! [*He takes the cheese and devours it*]

TEVYE: Thank you. You know, it's no crime to be poor.

PERCHIK: In this world, it's the rich who are the criminals. Some day their wealth will be ours.

TEVYE: That would be nice. If they would agree, I would agree.

MENDEL: And who will make this miracle come to pass?

PERCHIK: People. Ordinary people.

MENDEL: Like you?

PERCHIK: Like me.

MENDEL: Nonsense!

TEVYE: And until your golden day comes, Reb Perchik, how will you live?

PERCHIK: By giving lessons to children. Do you have children?

TEVYE: I have five daughters.

PERCHIK: Five?

TEVYE: Daughters.

PERCHIK: Girls should learn too. Girls are people.

MENDEL: A radical!

PERCHIK: I would be willing to teach them. Open their minds to great thoughts.

TEVYE: What great thoughts?

PERCHIK: Well, the Bible has many lessons for our times.

TEVYE: I am a very poor man. Food for lessons? [PERCHIK *nods*] Good. Stay with us for the Sabbath. Of course, we don't eat like kings, but we don't starve, either. As the Good Book says, "When a poor man eats a chicken, one of them is sick."

MENDEL: Where does the Book say that?

TEVYE: Well, it doesn't exactly say that, but someplace it has something about a chicken. Good Sabbath.

MENDEL: Good Sabbath.

PERCHIK: Good Sabbath.

[MENDEL *exits as* TEVYE *and* PERCHIK *enter the house*]

SCENE THREE

The interior of TEVYE'*s house.* TEVYE'*s daughters are there.* TEVYE *and* PERCHIK *enter.*

TEVYE: Good Sabbath, children.

DAUGHTERS: [*Running to him*] Good Sabbath, Papa.

TEVYE: Children! [*They all stop*] This is Perchik. Perchik, this is my oldest daughter.

PERCHIK: Good Sabbath.

TZEITEL: Good Sabbath.

PERCHIK: You have a pleasant daughter.

TEVYE: I have five pleasant daughters. [*He beckons to the girls, and they run into his arms, eagerly, and* TEVYE *kisses each*]

This is mine . . . this is mine . . . this is mine . . . this is mine
. . . this is mine . . .

[MOTEL *enters.* TEVYE *almost kisses him in sequence*]

This is not mine. Perchik, this is Motel Kamzoil and he is—

GOLDE: [*Entering*] So you did me a favor and came in.

TEVYE: This is also mine. Golde, this is Perchik, from Kiev, and
he is staying the Sabbath with us. He is a teacher. [*To*
SHPRINTZE *and* BIELKE] Would you like to take lessons from
him? [*They giggle*]

PERCHIK: I am really a good teacher, a very good teacher.

HODEL: I heard once, the rabbi who must praise himself has a
congregation of one.

PERCHIK: Your daughter has a quick and witty tongue.

TEVYE: The wit she gets from me. As the Good Book says—

GOLDE: The Good Book can wait. Get washed!

TEVYE: The tongue she gets from her mother.

GOLDE: Motel, you're also eating with us? [MOTEL *gestures, "Yes,
if I may"*] Of course, another blessing. Tzeitel, two more.
Shprintze, Bielke, get washed. Get the table.

TZEITEL: Motel can help me.

GOLDE: All right. Chava, you go too. [*To* PERCHIK] You can
wash outside at the well.

[*Exit the* DAUGHTERS, PERCHIK, *and* MOTEL]

Tevye, I have something to say to you.

TEVYE: Why should today be different? [*He starts to pray*]

GOLDE: Tevye, I have to tell you—

TEVYE: Shhh. I'm praying. [*Prays*]

GOLDE: [*Having waited a moment*] Lazar Wolf wants to see you.

[TEVYE *begins praying again, stopping only to respond to*
GOLDE, *then returning to prayer*]

TEVYE: The butcher? About what? [*Prays*]

GOLDE: I don't know. Only that he says it is important.

TEVYE: What can be important? I have nothing for him to slaughter. [*Prays*]

GOLDE: After the Sabbath, see him and talk to him.

TEVYE: Talk to him about what? If he is thinking about buying my new milk cow [*Prays*] he can forget it. [*Prays*]

GOLDE: Tevye, don't be an ox. A man sends an important message, at least you can talk to him.

TEVYE: Talk about what? He wants my new milk cow! [*Prays*]

GOLDE: [*Insisting*] Talk to him!

TEVYE: All right. After the Sabbath, I'll talk to him.

[TEVYE *and* GOLDE *exit. He is still praying.* MOTEL, TZEITEL, *and* CHAVA *bring in the table.* CHAVA *exits*]

TZEITEL: Motel, Yente was here.

MOTEL: I saw her.

TZEITEL: If they agree on someone, there will be a match and then it will be too late for us.

MOTEL: Don't worry, Tzeitel. I have found someone who will sell me his used sewing machine, so in a few weeks I'll have saved up enough to buy it, and then your father will be impressed with me and . . .

TZEITEL: But, Motel, a few weeks may be too late.

MOTEL: But what else can we do?

TZEITEL: You could ask my father for my hand tonight. Now!

MOTEL: Why should he consider me now? I'm only a poor tailor.

TZEITEL: And I'm only the daughter of a poor milkman. Just talk to him.

MOTEL: Tzeitel, if your father says no, that's it, it's final. He'll yell at me.

TZEITEL: Motel!

MOTEL: I'm just a poor tailor.

TZEITEL: Motel, even a poor tailor is entitled to some happiness.

MOTEL: That's true.

TZEITEL: [*Urgently*] Will you talk to him? Will you talk to him?

MOTEL: All right, I'll talk to him.

TEVYE: [*Entering*] It's late! Where is everybody? Late.

MOTEL: [*Following him*] Reb Tevye—

TEVYE: [*Disregarding him*] Come in, children, we're lighting the candles.

MOTEL: Reb Tevye. [*Summoning courage*] Reb Tevye, Reb Tevye.

TEVYE: Yes? What is it? [*Loudly*] Well, Motel, what is it?

MOTEL: [*Taken aback*] Good Sabbath, Reb Tevye.

TEVYE: [*Irritated with him*] Good Sabbath, Good Sabbath. Come, children, come.

[TEVYE's *family,* PERCHIK, *and* MOTEL *gather around the table.* GOLDE *lights the candles and says a prayer under her breath*]

TEVYE *and* GOLDE: [*Sing to* DAUGHTERS]
["Sabbath Prayer"]
May the Lord protect and defend you,
May He always shield you from shame,
May you come to be
In Yisroel a shining name.
May you be like Ruth and like Esther,
May you be deserving of praise.
Strengthen them, O Lord,
And keep them from the stranger's ways.

May God bless you
And grant you long lives.

[*The lights go up behind them, showing other families, behind a transparent curtain, singing over Sabbath candles*]

GOLDE:
> May the Lord fulfill our Sabbath prayer for you.

TEVYE *and* GOLDE:
> May God make you
> Good mothers and wives.

TEVYE:
> May He send you husbands who will care for you.

TEVYE *and* GOLDE:
> May the Lord protect and defend you
> May the Lord preserve you from pain.
> Favor them, O Lord,
> With happiness and peace.
> O hear our Sabbath prayer.
> Amen.

SCENE FOUR

The Inn, the following evening. AVRAM, LAZAR, MENDEL, *and several other people are sitting at tables.* LAZAR *is waiting impatiently, drumming on the tabletop, watching the door.*

LAZAR: Reb Mordcha.

MORDCHA: Yes, Lazar Wolf.

LAZAR: Please bring me a bottle of your best brandy and two glasses.

AVRAM: "Your best brandy," Reb Lazar?

MORDCHA: What's the occasion? Are you getting ready for a party?

LAZAR: There might be a party. Maybe even a wedding.

MORDCHA: A wedding? Wonderful. And I'll be happy to make the wedding merry, lead the dancing, and so forth. For a little fee, naturally.

LAZAR: Naturally, a wedding is no wedding without you—and your fee.

[FYEDKA *enters with several other* RUSSIANS]

FIRST RUSSIAN: Good evening, Innkeeper.

MORDCHA: Good evening.

FIRST RUSSIAN: We'd like a drink. Sit down, Fyedka.

MORDCHA: Vodka? Schnapps?

FYEDKA: Vodka.

MORDCHA: Right away.

[TEVYE *enters.* LAZAR, *who has been watching the door, turns away, pretending not to be concerned*]

TEVYE: Good evening.

MORDCHA: Good evening, Tevye.

MENDEL: What are you doing here so early?

TEVYE: [*Aside to* MENDEL] He wants to buy my new milk cow. Good evening, Reb Lazar.

LAZAR: Ah, Tevye. Sit down. Have a drink. [*Pours a drink*]

TEVYE: I won't insult you by saying no. [*Drinks*]

LAZAR: How goes it with you, Tevye?

TEVYE: How should it go?

LAZAR: You're right.

TEVYE: And you?

LAZAR: The same.

TEVYE: I'm sorry to hear that.

LAZAR: [*Pours a drink*] So how's your brother-in-law in America?

TEVYE: I believe he is doing very well.

LAZAR: He wrote you?

TEVYE: Not lately.

LAZAR: Then how do you know?

TEVYE: If he was doing badly, he would write. May I? [*Pours himself another drink*]

LAZAR: Tevye, I suppose you know why I wanted to see you.

TEVYE: [*Drinks*] Yes, I do, Reb Lazar, but there is no use talking about it.

LAZAR: [*Upset*] Why not?

TEVYE: Why yes? Why should I get rid of her?

LAZAR: Well, you have a few more without her.

TEVYE: I see! Today you want one. Tomorrow you may want two.

LAZAR: [*Startled*] Two? What would I do with two?

TEVYE: The same as you do with one!

LAZAR: [*Shocked*] Tevye! This is very important to me.

TEVYE: Why is it so important to you?

LAZAR: Frankly, because I am lonesome.

TEVYE: [*Startled*] Lonesome? What are you talking about?

LAZAR: You don't know?

TEVYE: We're talking about my new cow. The one you want to buy from me.

LAZAR: [*Stares at* TEVYE, *then bursts into laughter*] A milk cow! So I won't be lonesome! [*He howls with laughter.* TEVYE *stares at him*]

TEVYE: What's so funny?

LAZAR: I was talking about your daughter. Your daughter, Tzeitel! [*Bursts into laughter.* TEVYE *stares at him, upset*]

TEVYE: My daughter, Tzeitel?

LAZAR: Of course, your daughter, Tzeitel! I see her in my butcher shop every Thursday. She's made a good impression on me. I like her. And as for me, Tevye, as you know, I'm pretty well off. I have my own house, a good store, a servant. Look, Tevye, why do we have to try to impress each other? Let's shake hands and call it a match. And you won't need a dowry for her. And maybe you'll find something in your own purse, too.

TEVYE: [*Shouting*] Shame on you! Shame! [*Hiccups*] What do you mean, my purse? My Tzeitel is not the sort that I would sell for money!

LAZAR: [*Calming him*] All right! Just as you say. We won't talk about money. The main thing is, let's get it done with. And I will be good to her, Tevye. [*Slightly embarrassed*] I like her. What do you think?

TEVYE: [*To the audience*] What do I think? What do I think? I never liked him! Why should I? You can have a fine conversation with him, if you talk about kidneys and livers. On the other hand, not everybody has to be a scholar. If you're wealthy enough, no one will call you stupid. And with a butcher, my daughter will surely never know hunger. Of course, he has a problem—he's much older than her. That's her problem. But she's younger. That's his problem. I always thought of him as a butcher, but I misjudged him. He is a good man. He likes her. He will try to make her happy. [*Turns to* LAZAR] What do I think? It's a match!

LAZAR: [*Delighted*] You agree?

TEVYE: I agree.

LAZAR: Oh, Tevye, that's wonderful. Let's drink on it.

TEVYE: Why not? To you.

LAZAR: No, my friend, to you.

TEVYE: To the both of us.

LAZAR: To our agreement.

TEVYE: To our agreement. To our prosperity. To good health and happiness. [*Enter* FIDDLER] And, most important—[*Sings*]

["To Life"]
To Life, to Life, L'Chaim.

TEVYE *and* LAZAR:
L'Chaim, L'Chaim, To Life.

TEVYE:
Here's to the father I've tried to be.

LAZAR:
Here's to my bride to be.

TEVYE *and* LAZAR:

Drink, L'Chaim,
To Life, to Life, L'Chaim.
L'Chaim, L'Chaim, to Life.

TEVYE:

Life has a way of confusing us,

LAZAR:

Blessing and bruising us,

TEVYE *and* LAZAR:

Drink, L'Chaim, to Life.

TEVYE:

God would like us to be joyful,
Even when our hearts lie panting on the floor.

LAZAR:

How much more can we be joyful
When there's really something
To be joyful for!

TEVYE *and* LAZAR:

To Life, to Life, L'Chaim.

TEVYE:

To Tzeitel, my daughter.

LAZAR:

My wife.
It gives you something to think about,

TEVYE:

Something to drink about,

TEVYE *and* LAZAR:

Drink, L'Chaim, to Life.

LAZAR: Reb Mordcha.

MORDCHA: Yes, Lazar Wolf.

LAZAR: Drinks for everybody.

MENDEL: What's the occasion?

LAZAR: I'm taking myself a bride.

VILLAGERS: Who? Who?

LAZAR: Tevye's eldest, Tzeitel.

VILLAGERS: Mazeltov. . . . Wonderful. . . . Congratulations. . . . [*Sing*]

To Lazar Wolf.

TEVYE:

To Tevye.

VILLAGERS:

To Tzeitel, your daughter.

LAZAR:

My wife.

ALL:

May all your futures be pleasant ones,
Not like our present ones.
Drink, L'Chaim, to Life,
To Life, L'Chaim,
L'Chaim, L'Chaim, to Life.
It takes a wedding to make us say,
"Let's live another day,"
Drink, L'Chaim, to Life.

We'll raise a glass and sip a drop of schnapps
In honor of the great good luck
That favored you.

We know that
When good fortune favors two such men
It stands to reason we deserve it, too.
To us and our good fortune.
Be happy, be healthy, long life!
And if our good fortune never comes,
Here's to whatever comes.
Drink, L'Chaim, to Life.
Dai-dai-dai-dai-dai-dai-dai.

[*They begin to dance. A* RUSSIAN *starts to sing, and they stop, uncomfortable*]

RUSSIAN:

Za va sha, Zdarovia,
Heaven bless you both, Nazdrovia,
To your health, and may we live together in peace.

Za va sha, Zdarovia,
Heaven bless you both, Nazdrovia,
To your health, and may we live together in peace.

OTHER RUSSIANS:
May you both be favored with the future of your choice.
May you live to see a thousand reasons to rejoice.

Za va sha, Zdarovia,
Heaven bless you both, Nazdrovia,
To your health, and may we live together in peace.
Hey!

[*The* RUSSIANS *begin to dance, the* OTHERS *join in and they dance to a wild finale pileup on the bar*]

TEVYE: [*From the pileup*]
To Life!

[*Blackout*]

SCENE FIVE

The street outside the Inn. Entering through the inn door are the FIDDLER, LAZAR, TEVYE, *the other* VILLAGERS, *and the* RUSSIANS, *singing "To Life."*

LAZAR: You know, Tevye, after the marriage, we will be related. You will be my papa.

TEVYE: Your papa! I always wanted a son, but I wanted one a little younger than myself.

[*The* CONSTABLE *enters*]

CONSTABLE: Good evening.

FIRST RUSSIAN: Good evening, Constable.

CONSTABLE: What's the celebration?

FIRST RUSSIAN: Tevye is marrying off his oldest daughter.

CONSTABLE: May I offer my congratulations, Tevye?

TEVYE: Thank you, your Honor.

[*All but* TEVYE *and the* CONSTABLE *exit*]

CONSTABLE: Oh, Tevye, I have a piece of news that I think I should tell you, as a friend.

TEVYE: Yes, your Honor?

CONSTABLE: And I'm giving you this news because I like you. You are a decent, honest person, even though you are a Jewish dog.

TEVYE: How often does a man get a compliment like that? And your news?

CONSTABLE: We have received orders that sometime soon this district is to have a little unofficial demonstration.

TEVYE: [*Shocked*] A pogrom? Here?

CONSTABLE: No—just a little unofficial demonstration.

TEVYE: How little?

CONSTABLE: Not too serious—just some mischief, so that if an inspector comes through, he will see that we have done our duty. Personally, I don't know why there has to be this trouble between people, but I thought I should tell you, and you can tell the others.

TEVYE: Thank you, your Honor. You're a good man. If I may say so, it's too bad you're not a Jew.

CONSTABLE: [*Amused*] That's what I like about you, Tevye, always joking. And congratulations again, for your daughter.

TEVYE: Thank you, your Honor. Goodbye. [*The* CONSTABLE *exits.* TEVYE *turns to heaven*] Dear God, did You have to send me news like that, today of all days? It's true that we are the Chosen People. But once in a while can't You choose someone else? Anyway, thank You for sending a husband for my Tzeitel. L'Chaim.

[*The* FIDDLER *enters, he circles* TEVYE, *and they dance off together*]

SCENE SIX

Outside TEVYE's *house.* PERCHIK *is teaching* SHPRINTZE *and* BIELKE *while they peel potatoes at a bench.* HODEL *is cleaning pails at the pump.*

PERCHIK: Now, children, I will tell you the story from the Bible, of Laban and Jacob, and then we will discuss it together. All right? [*They nod*] Good. Now Laban had two daughters, Leah and the beautiful Rachel. And Jacob loved the younger, Rachel, and he asked Laban for her hand. Laban agreed, if Jacob would work for him for seven years.

SHPRINTZE: Was Laban a mean man?

PERCHIK: [*Dryly*] He was an employer! Now, after Jacob worked seven years, do you know what happened? Laban fooled him, and gave him his ugly daughter, Leah. So, to marry Rachel, Jacob was forced to work another seven years. You see, children, the Bible clearly teaches us, you must never trust an employer. Do you understand?

SHPRINTZE: Yes, Perchik.

BIELKE: Yes, Perchik.

PERCHIK: Good, now—

GOLDE: [*Entering from the barn*] Papa isn't up yet?

HODEL: No, Mama.

GOLDE: Then enough lessons. We have to do Papa's work today. How long can he sleep? He staggered home last night and fell into bed like a dead man. I couldn't get a word out of him. Put that away and clean the barn. [SHPRINTZE *and* BIELKE *exit into the barn. To* HODEL] Call me when Papa gets up. [GOLDE *exits.* HODEL *pumps a bucket of water*]

HODEL: That was a very interesting lesson, Perchik.

PERCHIK: Do you think so?

HODEL: Although I don't know if the rabbi would agree with your interpretation.

PERCHIK: And neither, I suppose, would the rabbi's son.

HODEL: My little sisters have big tongues.

PERCHIK: And what do you know about him, except that he is the rabbi's son? Would you be interested in him if he were the shoemaker's son, or the tinsmith's son?

HODEL: At least I know this, he does not have any strange ideas about turning the world upside down.

PERCHIK: Certainly. Any new idea would be strange to you. Remember, the Lord said, "Let there be light."

HODEL: Yes, but He was not talking to you personally. Good day. [Starts off]

PERCHIK: You have spirit. Even a little intelligence, perhaps.

HODEL: Thank you.

PERCHIK: But what good is your brain? Without curiosity it is a rusty tool. Good day, Hodel.

HODEL: We have an old custom here. A boy acts respectfully to a girl. But, of course, that is too traditional for an advanced thinker like you.

PERCHIK: Our traditions! Nothing must change! Everything is perfect exactly the way it is!

HODEL: We like our ways.

PERCHIK: Our ways are changing all over but here. Here men and women must keep apart. Men study. Women in the kitchen. Boys and girls must not touch, should not even look at each other.

HODEL: I am looking at you!

PERCHIK: You are very brave! Do you know that in the city boys and girls can be affectionate without permission of a matchmaker? They hold hands together, they even dance together— new dances—like this. [He seizes her and starts dancing, humming] I learned it in Kiev. Do you like it?

HODEL: [Startled] It's very nice.

PERCHIK: [Stops dancing] There. We've just changed an old custom.

HODEL: [Bewildered] Yes. Well, you're welcome—I mean, thank you—I mean, good day.

PERCHIK: Good day!

[TEVYE *enters, suffering from a headache*]

TEVYE: Bielke, Shprintze, what's your name?

HODEL: Hodel, Papa.

TEVYE: Where is Tzeitel?

HODEL: She's in the barn.

TEVYE: Call her out. [HODEL *exits into the barn*] Reb Perchik.
How did the lesson go today?

PERCHIK: [*Watching* HODEL'*s exit*] I think we made a good beginning.

[*Enter* GOLDE]

GOLDE: Ah, he's finally up. What happened last night, besides
your drinking like a peasant? Did you see Lazar Wolf? What
did he say? What did you say? Do you have news?

TEVYE: Patience, woman. As the Good Book says, "Good news
will stay and bad news will refuse to leave." And there's another saying that goes—

GOLDE: [*Exasperated*] You can die from such a man!

[TZEITEL *enters from the barn.* HODEL *and* CHAVA *follow her*]

TEVYE: Ah, Tzeitel, my lamb, come here. Tzeitel, you are to be
congratulated. You are going to be married!

GOLDE: Married!

TZEITEL: What do you mean, Papa?

TEVYE: Lazar Wolf has asked for your hand.

GOLDE: [*Thrilled*] I knew it!

TZEITEL: [*Bewildered*] The butcher?

GOLDE: [*Enraptured*] My heart told me this was our lucky day.
O dear God, I thank Thee, I thank Thee.

TEVYE: And what do you say, Tzeitel?

GOLDE: What can she say? My first-born, a bride! May you grow old with him in fortune and honor, not like Fruma-Sarah, that first wife of his. She was a bitter woman, may she rest in peace. Not like my Tzeitel. And now I must thank Yente. My Tzeitel, a bride! [*She hurries off*]

HODEL *and* CHAVA: [*Subdued*] Mazeltov, Tzeitel.

TEVYE: You call that a Mazeltov? [HODEL *and* CHAVA *exit*] And you, Reb Perchik, aren't you going to congratulate her?

PERCHIK: [*Sarcastic*] Congratulations, Tzeitel, for getting a rich man.

TEVYE: Again with the rich! What's wrong with being rich?

PERCHIK: It is no reason to marry. Money is the world's curse.

TEVYE: May the Lord smite me with it! And may I never recover! Tzeitel knows I mean only her welfare. Am I right, Tzeitel?

TZEITEL: Yes, Papa.

TEVYE: You see.

PERCHIK: I see. I see very well. [*He exits*]

TEVYE: Well, Tzeitel, my child, why are you so silent? Aren't you happy with this blessing?

TZEITEL: [*Bursts into tears*] Oh, Papa, Papa.

TEVYE: What is it? Tell me.

TZEITEL: Papa, I don't want to marry him. I can't marry him. I can't—

TEVYE: What do you mean, you can't? If I say you will, you will.

TZEITEL: Papa, if it's a matter of money, I'll do anything. I'll hire myself out as a servant. I'll dig ditches, I'll haul rocks, only don't make me marry him, Papa, please.

TEVYE: What's wrong with Lazar? He likes you.

TZEITEL: Papa, I will be unhappy with him. All my life will be unhappy. I'll dig ditches, I'll haul rocks.

TEVYE: But we made an agreement. With us an agreement is an agreement.

TZEITEL: [*Simply*] Is that more important than I am, Papa? Papa, don't force me. I'll be unhappy all my days.

TEVYE: All right. I won't force you.

FIDDLER ON THE ROOF

TZEITEL: Oh, thank you, Papa.

TEVYE: It seems it was not ordained that you should have all the comforts of life, or that we should have a little joy in our old age after all our hard work.

[*Enter* MOTEL, *breathless*]

MOTEL: Reb Tevye, may I speak to you?

TEVYE: Later, Motel. Later.

MOTEL: I would like to speak to you.

TEVYE: Not now, Motel. I have problems.

MOTEL: That's what I want to speak to you about. I think I can help.

TEVYE: Certainly. Like a bandage can help a corpse. Goodbye, Motel. Goodbye.

TZEITEL: At least listen to him, Papa.

TEVYE: All right. You have a tongue, talk.

MOTEL: Reb Tevye, I hear you are arranging a match for Tzeitel.

TEVYE: He also has ears.

MOTEL: I have a match for Tzeitel.

TEVYE: What kind of match?

MOTEL: A perfect fit.

TEVYE: A perfect fit.

MOTEL: Like a glove.

TEVYE: Like a glove.

MOTEL: This match was made exactly to measure.

TEVYE: A perfect fit. Made to measure. Stop talking like a tailor and tell me who it is.

MOTEL: Please, don't shout at me.

TEVYE: All right. Who is it?

MOTEL: Who is it?

TEVYE: [*Pauses*] Who is it?

MOTEL: Who is it?

TEVYE: Who is it?

MOTEL: It's me—myself.

TEVYE: [*Stares at him, then turns to the audience, startled and amused*] Him? Himself? [*To* MOTEL] Either you're completely out of your mind or you're crazy. [*To the audience*] He must be crazy. [*To* MOTEL] Arranging a match for yourself. What are you, everything? The bridegroom, the matchmaker, the guests all rolled into one? I suppose you'll even perform the ceremony. You must be crazy!

MOTEL: Please don't shout at me, Reb Tevye. As for being my own matchmaker, I know it's a little unusual.

TEVYE: Unusual? It's crazy.

MOTEL: Times are changing, Reb Tevye. The thing is, your daughter Tzeitel and I gave each other our pledge more than a year ago that we would marry.

TEVYE: [*Stunned*] You gave each other your pledge?

TZEITEL: Yes, Papa, we gave each other our pledge.

TEVYE: [*Looks at them, turns to the audience. Sings*]

["Tradition" Reprise]

They gave each other a pledge.
Unheard of, absurd.
You gave each other a pledge?
Unthinkable.
Where do you think you are?
In Moscow?
In Paris?
Where do they think they are?
America?
What do you think you're doing?
You stitcher, you nothing!
Who do you think you are?
King Solomon?
This isn't the way it's done,
Not here, not now.
Some things I will not, I cannot, allow.
Tradition—
Marriages must be arranged by the papa.

This should never be changed.
One little time you pull out a prop,
And where does it stop?
Where does it stop?

[*Speaks*]

Where does it stop? Do I still have something to say about my
daughter, or doesn't anyone have to ask a father any more?

MOTEL: I have wanted to ask you for some time, Reb Tevye, but
first I wanted to save up for my own sewing machine.

TEVYE: Stop talking nonsense. You're just a poor tailor.

MOTEL: [*Bravely*] That's true, Reb Tevye, but even a poor tailor
is entitled to some happiness. [*Looks at* TZEITEL, *triumphantly*] I promise you, Reb Tevye, your daughter will not
starve.

TEVYE: [*Impressed, turns to the audience*] He's beginning to
talk like a man. On the other hand, what kind of match would
that be, with a poor tailor? On the other hand, he's an honest,
hard worker. On the other hand, he has absolutely nothing.
On the other hand, things could never get worse for him, they
could only get better. [*Sings*]

They gave each other a pledge—
Unheard of, absurd.
They gave each other a pledge—
Unthinkable.
But look at my daughter's face—
She loves him, she wants him—
And look at my daughter's eyes,
So hopeful.

[*Shrugs. To the audience*]

Tradition!

[*To* TZEITEL *and* MOTEL]

Well, children, when shall we make the wedding?

TZEITEL: Thank you, Papa.

MOTEL: Reb Tevye, you won't be sorry.

TEVYE: I won't be sorry? I'm sorry already!

TZEITEL: Thank you, Papa.

MOTEL: Thank you, Papa.

TEVYE: Thank you, Papa! They pledged their troth! [*Starts to exit, then looks back at them*] Modern children! [*Has a sudden thought*] Golde! What will I tell Golde? What am I going to do about Golde? [*To heaven*] Help! [*Exits*]

TZEITEL: Motel, you were wonderful!

MOTEL: It was a miracle! It was a miracle. [*Sings*]

["Miracle of Miracles"]

Wonder of wonders, miracle of miracles,
God took a Daniel once again,
Stood by his side, and miracle of miracles,
Walked him through the lion's den.

Wonder of wonders, miracle of miracles,
I was afraid that God would frown.
But, like He did so long ago in Jericho,
God just made a wall fall down.

When Moses softened Pharaoh's heart,
That was a miracle.
When God made the waters of the Red Sea part,
That was a miracle, too.

But of all God's miracles large and small,
The most miraculous one of all
Is that out of a worthless lump of clay
God has made a man today.

Wonder of wonders, miracle of miracles,
God took a tailor by the hand,
Turned him around, and, miracle of miracles,
Led him to the Promised Land.

When David slew Goliath, yes!
That was a miracle.

When God gave us manna in the wilderness,
That was a miracle, too.

But of all God's miracles, large and small,
The most miraculous one of all
Is the one I thought could never be—
God has given you to me.

SCENE SEVEN

TEVYE'S *bedroom. The room is in complete darkness. A* *groan is heard, then another, then a scream.*

TEVYE: Aagh! Lazar! Motel! Tzeitel!

GOLDE: What is it? What?

TEVYE: Help! Help! Help!

GOLDE: Tevye, wake up! [GOLDE *lights the lamp. The light reveals* TEVYE *asleep in bed*]

TEVYE: [*In his sleep*] Help! Help!

GOLDE: [*Shaking him*] Tevye! What's the matter with you? Why are you howling like that?

TEVYE: [*Opening his eyes, frightened*] Where is she? Where is she?

GOLDE: Where is who? What are you talking about?

TEVYE: Fruma-Sarah. Lazar Wolf's first wife, Fruma-Sarah. She was standing here a minute ago.

GOLDE: What's the matter with you, Tevye? Fruma-Sarah has been dead for years. You must have been dreaming. Tell me what you dreamt, and I'll tell you what it meant.

TEVYE: It was terrible.

GOLDIE: Tell me.

TEVYE: All right—only don't be frightened!

GOLDE: [*Impatiently*] Tell me!

TEVYE: All right, this was my dream. In the beginning I dreamt that we were having a celebration of some kind. Everybody we knew was there, and musicians too.

[*As he speaks,* MEN, *including a* RABBI, WOMEN *and* MUSICIANS *enter the bedroom.* TEVYE, *wearing a nightshirt, starts to get out of bed to join the dream*]

TEVYE: In the middle of the dream, in walks your Grandmother Tzeitel, may she rest in peace.

GOLDE: [*Alarmed*] Grandmother Tzeitel? How did she look?

TEVYE: For a woman who is dead thirty years, she looked very good. Naturally, I went up to greet her. She said to me—

[GRANDMA TZEITEL *enters, and* TEVYE *approaches her and greets her in pantomime.* GRANDMA *sings*]

["The Tailor, Motel Kamzoil"]

GRANDMA TZEITEL:
            A blessing on your head,

RABBI:
            Mazeltov, Mazeltov.

GRANDMA TZEITEL:
            To see a daughter wed.

RABBI:
            Mazeltov, Mazeltov.

GRANDMA TZEITEL:
            And such a son-in-law,
            Like no one ever saw,
            The tailor Motel Kamzoil.

GOLDE: [*Bewildered*] Motel?

GRANDMA TZEITEL:
            A worthy boy is he,

RABBI:
            Mazeltov, Mazeltov.

GRANDMA TZEITEL:
            Of pious family.

RABBI:

Mazeltov, Mazeltov.

GRANDMA TZEITEL:

They named him after my
Dear Uncle Mordecai,
The tailor Motel Kamzoil.

GOLDE: A tailor! She must have heard wrong. She meant a butcher.

[TEVYE, *who has returned to* GOLDE, *listens to this, then
runs back to* GRANDMA TZEITEL]

TEVYE:

You must have heard wrong, Grandma,
There's no tailor,
You mean a butcher, Grandma,
By the name of Lazar Wolf.

GRANDMA TZEITEL: [*Flies into the air, screaming angrily*]
No!! [*Sings*]

I mean a tailor, Tevye.
My great grandchild,
My little Tzeitel, who you named for me,
Motel's bride was meant to be.
For such a match I prayed.

CHORUS:

Mazeltov, Mazeltov,

GRANDMA TZEITEL:

In heaven it was made.

CHORUS:

Mazeltov, Mazeltov,

GRANDMA TZEITEL:

A fine upstanding boy,
A comfort and a joy,
The tailor Motel Kamzoil.

GOLDE: [*From bed*] But we announced it already. We made
a bargain with the butcher.

TEVYE:

But we announced it, Grandma,
To our neighbors.
We made a bargain, Grandma,
With the butcher, Lazar Wolf.

GRANDMA TZEITEL: [*Again flies into the air, screaming angrily*] No!! [*Sings*]

So you announced it, Tevye,
That's your headache.
But as for Lazar Wolf, I say to you,
Tevye, that's your headache, too.

CHORUS:

A blessing on your house, Mazeltov, Mazeltov,
Imagine such a spouse, Mazeltov, Mazeltov,
And such a son-in-law,
Like no one ever saw,
The tailor Motel Kamzoil.

TEVYE: [*Speaks*] It was a butcher!

CHORUS:

The tailor Motel Kamzoil.

TEVYE: [*Speaks*] It was Lazar Wolfe! [*Sings*]

The tailor Motel Kam . . .

CHORUS:

Shah! shah!
Look!
Who is this?
Who is this?
Who comes here?
Who? who? who? who? who?
What woman is this
By righteous anger shaken?

SOLO VOICES:

Could it be?
Sure!
Yes, it could!
Why not?
Who could be mistaken?

CHORUS:
> It's the butcher's wife come from beyond the grave.
> It's the butcher's dear, darling, departed wife,
> Fruma-Sarah, Fruma-Sarah
> Fruma-Sarah, Fruma-Sarah, Fruma-Sarah.

FRUMA-SARAH:
> Tevye! Tevye!
> What is this about your daughter marrying my husband?

CHORUS:
> Yes, her husband.

FRUMA-SARAH:
> Would you do this to your friend and neighbor,
> Fruma-Sarah?

CHORUS:
> Fruma-Sarah.

FRUMA-SARAH:
> Have you no consideration for a woman's feelings?

CHORUS:
> Woman's feelings.

FRUMA-SARAH:
> Handing over my belongings to a total stranger.

CHORUS:
> Total stranger.

FRUMA-SARAH:
> How can you allow it, how?
> How can you let your daughter take my place?
> Live in my house, carry my keys,
> And wear my clothes, pearls—how?

CHORUS:
> How can you allow your daughter
> To take her place?

FRUMA-SARAH:
> Pearls!

CHORUS:
> House!

FRUMA-SARAH:

Pearls!

CHORUS:

Keys!

FRUMA-SARAH:

Pearls!

CHORUS:

Clothes!

FRUMA-SARAH:

Pearls!

CHORUS:

How?

FRUMA-SARAH:

Tevye!!

CHORUS:

Tevye!!

FRUMA-SARAH:
Such a learned man as Tevye wouldn't let it happen.

CHORUS:

Let it happen.

FRUMA-SARAH:
Tell me that it isn't true, and then I wouldn't worry.

CHORUS:

Wouldn't worry.

FRUMA-SARAH:
Say you didn't give your blessing to your daughter's
Marriage.

CHORUS:
Daughter's marriage.

FRUMA-SARAH:
Let me tell you what would follow such a fatal wedding.

CHORUS:
Fatal wedding.
Shh!

FRUMA-SARAH:
> If Tzeitel marries Lazar Wolf,
> I pity them both.
> She'll live with him three weeks,
> And when three weeks are up,
> I'll come to her by night,
> I'll take her by the throat, and . . .
> This I'll give your Tzeitel,
> That I'll give your Tzeitel,
> This I'll give your Tzeitel,

[*Laughs wildly*]

Here's my wedding present if she marries Lazar Wolfe!

[*She starts choking Tevye. The* CHORUS *exits screaming*]

GOLDE: [*While* TEVYE *is being choked*] It's an evil spirit; May it fall into the river; may it sink into the earth. Such a dark and horrible dream! And to think it was brought on by that butcher. If my Grandmother Tzeitel, may she rest in peace, took the trouble to come all the way from the other world to tell us about the tailor, all we can say is that it is all for the best, and it couldn't possibly be any better. Amen.

TEVYE: Amen.

GOLDE: [*Sings*]
> A blessing on my head, Mazeltov, Mazeltov,
> Like Grandma Tzeitel said, Mazeltov, Mazeltov.
> We'll have a son-in-law,
> Like no one eve saw,
> The tailor Motel Kamzoil.

TEVYE:
> We haven't got the man,

GOLDE:
> Mazeltov, Mazeltov.

TEVYE:
> We had when we began.

GOLDE:
> Mazeltov, Mazeltov.

TEVYE:

> But since your Grandma came,
> She'll marry what's his name?

GOLDE:

> The tailor Motel Kamzoil.

TEVYE *and* GOLDE:

> The tailor Motel Kamzoil,
> The tailor Motel Kamzoil,
> The tailor Motel Kamzoil.

[GOLDE *goes back to sleep.* TEVYE *mouths the words "Thank You" to God, and goes to sleep*]

SCENE EIGHT

The village street and the interior of MOTEL's *tailor shop.* MOTEL *and* CHAVA *are in the shop.* VILLAGERS *pass by.*

MAN: Bagels, fresh bagels.

WOMAN: [*Excited*] Did you hear? Did you hear? Tevye's Tzeitel is marrying Motel, not Lazar Wolf.

VILLAGERS: No!

WOMAN: Yes.

MENDEL: Tzeitel is marrying Motel?

WOMAN: Yes!

VILLAGERS: No! [*They rush into the shop and surround* MOTEL. MORDCHA *enters the street*] Mazeltov, Motel. Congratulations.

MORDCHA: What's all the excitement?

AVRAM: Tevye's Tzeitel is going to marry—

MORDCHA: I know. Lazar Wolf, the butcher. It's wonderful.

AVRAM: No. Motel, the tailor.

MORDCHA: Motel, the tailor, that's terrible! [*Rushes into the shop*] Mazeltov, Motel.

WOMAN: [*To* SHANDEL, *exiting from the shop*] Imagine! Tzeitel is marrying Motel. I can't believe it!

SHANDEL: [*Outraged*] What's wrong with my son, Motel?

WOMAN: Oh, excuse me, Shandel. Mazeltov.

VILLAGERS: [*Inside the shop*] Mazeltov, Mazeltov.

MOTEL: Yussel, do you have a wedding hat for me?

YUSSEL: Lazar Wolf ordered a hat but it's not cheap.

MOTEL: I got his bride, I can get his hat!

YUSSEL: Then come, Motel, come.

MOTEL: Chava, can you watch the shop for a few minutes? I'll be back soon.

CHAVA: Of course.

MOTEL: Thank you, Chava. [*They all exit from the shop, calling Mazeltovs*]

VILLAGERS: [*To* CHAVA] We just heard about your sister. . . . Mazeltov, Chava. . . . Mazeltov, Chava.

CHAVA: Thanks—thank you very much.

[*All but* CHAVA *exit.* FYEDKA, SASHA *and another* RUSSIAN *enter at the same time. They cross to* CHAVA, *blocking her way into the shop*]

SASHA *and* RUSSIAN: [*Mockingly, imitiating others, with a slight mispronunciation*] Mazeltov, Chava. Mazeltov, Chava.

CHAVA: Please may I pass.

SASHA: [*Getting in her way*] Why? We're congratulating you.

RUSSIAN: Mazeltov, Chava.

FYEDKA: [*Calmly*] All right, stop it.

SASHA: What's wrong with you?

FYEDKA: Just stop it.

SASHA: Now listen here, Fyedka—

FYEDKA: Goodbye, Sasha. [SASHA *and the* RUSSIAN *hesitate*] I said goodbye! [*They look at* FYEDKA *curiously, then exit*] I'm sorry about that. They mean no harm.

CHAVA: Don't they? [*She enters shop. He follows her*] Is there something you want?

FYEDKA: Yes. I'd like to talk to you.

CHAVA: I'd rather not. [*She hesitates*]

FYEDKA: I've often noticed you at the bookseller's. Not many girls in this village like to read. [*A sudden thought strikes him. He extends the book he is holding*] Would you like to borrow this book? It's very good.

CHAVA: No, thank you.

FYEDKA: Why? Because I'm not Jewish? Do you feel about us the way they feel about you? I didn't think you would. And what do you know about me? Let me tell you about myself. I'm a pleasant fellow, charming, honest, ambitious, quite bright, and very modest.

CHAVA: I don't think we should be talking this way.

FYEDKA: I often do things I shouldn't. Go ahead, take the book. It's by Heinrich Heine. Happens to be Jewish, I believe.

CHAVA: That doesn't matter.

FYEDKA: You're quite right. [*She takes the book*] Good. After you return it, I'll ask you how you like it, and we'll talk about it for a while. Then we'll talk about life, how we feel about things, and it can all turn out quite pleasant.

[CHAVA *puts the book on the table as* MOTEL *enters.*]

MOTEL: Oh, Fyedka! Can I do something for you?

FYEDKA: No, thank you. [*Starts to leave*]

MOTEL: Oh, you forgot your book.

CHAVA: No, it's mine.

MOTEL: Thank you, Chava. [CHAVA *takes the book and leaves the shop with* FYEDKA]

FYEDKA: [*Outside*] Good day, Chava.

CHAVA: Good day.

FYEDKA: [*Pleasantly*] Fyedka.

CHAVA: Good day, Fyedka. [*They exit.* MOTEL *puts on his wedding hat*]

SCENE NINE

Part of TEVYE's *yard. Night.* TZEITEL, *in a bridal gown, enters, followed by* TEVYE, GOLDE, HODEL, BIELKE, CHAVA, SHPRINTZE, *and* RELATIONS. MOTEL *enters, followed by his* PARENTS *and* RELATIONS. *Many* GUESTS *enter, carrying lit candles. The men take their places on the right, as a group, the women on the left;* TZEITEL *and* MOTEL *stand in the center.* MOTEL *places a veil over* TZEITEL's *head.* FOUR MEN *enter, carrying a canopy. They are followed by the* RABBI. *The canopy is placed over* MOTEL *and* TZEITEL. GUESTS *start singing.*

["Sunrise, Sunset"]

TEVYE:

Is this the little girl I carried?
Is this the little boy at play?

GOLDE:

I don't remember growing older.
When did they?

TEVYE:

When did she get to be a beauty?
When did he grow to be so tall?

GOLDE:

Wasn't it yesterday when they were small?

MEN:

Sunrise, sunset,
Sunrise, sunset,
Swiftly flow the days.
Seedlings turn overnight to sunflowers,
Blossoming even as we gaze.

WOMEN:

Sunrise, sunset,
Sunrise, sunset,
Swiftly fly the years.
One season following another,
Laden with happiness and tears.

TEVYE:
>
> What words of wisdom can I give them?
> How can I help to ease their way?

GOLDE:
>
> Now they must learn from one another
> Day by day.

PERCHIK:
>
> They look so natural together.

HODEL:
>
> Just like two newlyweds should be.

PERCHIK *and* HODEL:
>
> Is there a canopy in store for me?

ALL:
>
> Sunrise, sunset,
> Sunrise, sunset,
> Swiftly fly the years.
> One season following another,
> Laden with happiness and tears.

[*During the song, the following mime is performed. The* RABBI *lifts* TZEITEL's *veil. He prays over a goblet of wine and hands it to the bride and groom. They each sip from it.* TZEITEL *slowly walks in a circle around* MOTEL. MOTEL *places a ring on* TZEITEL's *finger. The* RABBI *places a wine-glass on the floor. The song ends. A moment's pause.* MOTEL *treads on the glass*]

ALL: [*At the moment the glass breaks*] Mazeltov!

SCENE TEN

The set opens to show the entire yard of TEVYE's *house. Part of it is divided down the center by a short partition. Several tables are set up at the rear of each section. The* MUSICIANS *play, and all dance and then seat themselves on benches at the tables. The women are on the left, the men on the right. As the dance concludes,* MORDCHA *mounts a stool and signals for silence. The noise subsides.*

ALL: Shah. Shah. Quiet. Reb Mordcha. Shah. Shah.

MORDCHA: My friends, we are gathered here to share the joy of the newlyweds, Motel and Tzeitel. May they live together in peace to a ripe old age. Amen.

ALL: Amen.

[*The* RABBI *slowly makes his way to the table, assisted by* MENDEL]

MORDCHA: Ah, here comes our beloved rabbi. May he be with us for many, many years.

RABBI: [*Ahead of the others*] Amen.

ALL: Amen.

MORDCHA: I want to announce that the bride's parents are giving the newlyweds the following: a new featherbed, a pair of pillows—

GOLDE: [*Shouting from the women's side*] Goose pillows.

MORDCHA: Goose pillows. And this pair of candlesticks.

ALL: Mazeltov!

MORDCHA: Now let us not in our joy tonight forget those who are no longer with us, our dear departed, who lived in pain and poverty and hardship and who died in pain and poverty and hardship. [*All sob. He pauses a moment*] But enough tears. [*The mourning stops immediately*] Let's be merry and content, like our good friend, Lazar Wolf, who has everything in the world, except a bride. [*Laughter*] But Lazar has no ill feelings. In fact, he has a gift for the newlyweds that he wants to announce himself. Come, Lazar Wolf.

LAZAR: [*Rising*] Like he said, I have no ill feelings. What's done is what's done. I am giving the newlyweds five chickens, one for each of the first five Sabbaths of their wedded life. [*Murmurs of appreciation from all*]

TEVYE: [*Rising*] Reb Lazar, you are a decent man. In the name of my daughter and her new husband, I accept your gift. There is a famous saying that—

LAZAR: Reb Tevye, I'm not marrying your daughter. I don't have to listen to your sayings.

TEVYE: If you would listen a second, I was only going to say—

LAZAR: Why should I listen to you? A man who breaks an agreement!

[*Murmurs by the assemblage*]

MENDEL: Not now, Lazar, in the middle of a wedding.

LAZAR: I have a right to talk.

TEVYE: [*Angry*] What right? This is not your wedding.

LAZAR: It should have been!

[*Murmurs by the assemblage*]

MENDEL: Reb Lazar, don't shame Reb Tevye at his daughter's wedding.

LAZAR: But he shamed me in front of the whole village!

[*An argument breaks out. Everyone takes sides*]

ALL: That's true . . . The rabbi said . . . It was a shame . . . He has no feelings . . . This is not the place—

MENDEL: Shah. Shah. Quiet. The rabbi. The rabbi, the rabbi.

RABBI: [*Rising, as the noise subsides*] I say—Let's sit down. [*Sits*]

TEVYE: We all heard the wise words of the rabbi.

[*Everyone returns to his seat*]

MORDCHA: Now, I'd like to sing a little song that—

TEVYE: [*Bursting out*] You can keep your diseased chickens!

LAZAR: Leave my chickens out of this. We made a bargain.

TEVYE: The terms weren't settled.

LAZAR: We drank on it—

FIRST MAN: I saw them, they drank on it.

SECOND MAN: But the terms weren't settled.

SHANDEL: What's done is done.

TEVYE: Once a butcher, always a butcher.

GOLDE: I had a sign. My own grandmother came to us from the grave.

YENTE: What sign? What grandmother? My grandfather came to me from the grave and told me that her grandmother was a big liar.

LAZAR: We drank on it.

[*Bedlam.* MORDCHA *tries to quiet the guests.* PERCHIK *climbs onto a stool, banging two tin plates together*]

MORDCHA: Quiet, I'm singing.

TEVYE: The terms weren't settled.

GOLDE: I had a sign.

YENTE: An agreement is an agreement.

PERCHIK: [*Silences them*] Quiet! Quiet! What's all the screaming about? "They drank on it—" "An agreement—" "A sign." It's all nonsense. Tzeitel wanted to marry Motel and not Lazar.

MENDEL: A young girl decides for herself?

PERCHIK: Why not? Yes! They love each other.

AVRAM: Love!

LAZAR: Terrible!

MENDEL: He's a radical!

YENTE: What happens to the matchmaker?

[*Another violent argument breaks out*]

RABBI: I say—I say— [*They all turn to him*]

TEVYE: Let's sit down? [*Rabbi nods*]

MORDCHA: Musicians, play. A dance, a dance! [*The music starts, but no one dances*] Come on, dance. It's a wedding.

YENTE: Some wedding!

[PERCHIK *crosses to the women's side*]

AVRAM: What's he doing?

TEVYE: Perchik!

FIRST MAN: Stop him!

PERCHIK: [To HODEL] Who will dance with me?

MENDEL: That's a sin!

PERCHIK: It's no sin to dance at a wedding.

AVRAM: But with a girl?

LAZAR: That's what comes from bringing a wild man into your house.

TEVYE: [Signaling PERCHIK to return to the men's side] He's not a wild man. His ideas are a little different, but—

MENDEL: It's a sin.

PERCHIK: It's no sin. Ask the rabbi. Ask him. [They all gather around the RABBI]

TEVYE: Well, Rabbi?

RABBI: [Thumbs through a book, finds the place] Dancing— Well, it's not exactly forbidden, but—

TEVYE: There, you see? It's not forbidden.

PERCHIK: [To HODEL] And it's no sin. Now will someone dance with me? [HODEL rises to dance]

GOLDE: Hodel!

HODEL: It's only a dance, Mama.

PERCHIK: Play! (PERCHIK and HODEL dance]

LAZAR: Look at Tevye's daughter.

MENDEL: She's dancing with a man.

TEVYE: I can see she's dancing [Starts toward them as if to stop them. Changes his mind] And I'm going to dance with my wife. Golde! [GOLDE hesitates, then dances with him]

SHANDEL: Golde! [MOTEL crosses to TZEITEL] Motel!

[TZEITEL dances with MOTEL. Others join them. They all dance, except for LAZAR and YENTE, who storm off. As the dance reaches a wild climax, the CONSTABLE and his MEN enter, carrying clubs. The dancers see them and slowly stop]

CONSTABLE: I see we came at a bad time, Tevye. I'm sorry, but the orders are for tonight. For the whole village. [*To the* MUSICIANS] Go on, play, play. All right, men.

[*The* RUSSIANS *begin their destruction, turning over tables, throwing pillows, smashing dishes and the window of the house. One of them throws the wedding-gift candlesticks to the ground, and* PERCHIK *grapples with him. But he is hit with a club and falls to the ground. The* GUESTS *leave*]

HODEL: [*Rushes to* PERCHIK] No, Perchik!

[*The* GUESTS *have left during the above action*]

CONSTABLE: [*To his* MEN] All right, enough! [*To* TEVYE] I am genuinely sorry. You understand. [TEVYE *does not answer. To his* MEN] Come. [*The* CONSTABLE *and his* MEN *exit*]

GOLDE: Take him in the house. [HODEL *helps* PERCHIK *into the house*]

TEVYE: [*Quietly*] What are you standing around for? Clean up. Clean up.

[*They start straightening up, picking up broken dishes, bringing bedding back to the house.* TZEITEL *picks up the candlesticks, one of which is broken. They freeze at sudden sounds of destruction in a nearby house, then continue straightening up as:*]

THE CURTAIN FALLS

PROLOGUE

The exterior of TEVYE'S *house.* TEVYE *is sitting on a bench.*

TEVYE: [*To heaven*] That was quite a dowry You gave my daughter Tzeitel at her wedding. Was that necessary? Anyway, Tzeitel and Motel have been married almost two months now. They work very hard, they are as poor as squirrels in winter. But they are both so happy they don't know how miserable they are. Motel keeps talking about a sewing machine. I know You're very busy—wars and revolutions, floods, plagues, all those little things that bring people to You—couldn't You take a second away from Your catastrophes and get it for him? How much trouble would it be? Oh, and while You're in the neighborhood, my horse's left leg—Am I bothering You too much? I'm sorry. As the Good Book says—Why should I tell You what the Good Book says? [*Exits*]

SCENE ONE

The exterior of TEVYE'S *house. Afternoon.* HODEL *enters, petulantly, followed by* PERCHIK.

PERCHIK: Please don't be upset, Hodel.

HODEL: Why should I be upset? If you must leave, you must.

PERCHIK: I do have to. They expect me in Kiev tomorrow morning.

HODEL: So you told me. Then goodbye.

PERCHIK: Great changes are about to take place in this country. Tremendous changes. But they can't happen by themselves.

HODEL: So naturally you feel that you personally have to—

PERCHIK: Not only me. Many people. Jews, Gentiles, many people hate what is going on. Don't you understand?

HODEL: I understand, of course. You want to leave. Then goodbye.

PERCHIK: Hodel, your father, the others here, think what happened at Tzeitel's wedding was a little cloudburst and it's over and everything will now be peaceful again. It won't. Horrible things are happening all over the land—pogroms, violence—whole villages are being emptied of their people. And it's reaching everywhere, and it will reach here. You understand?

HODEL: Yes, I—I suppose I do.

PERCHIK: I have work to do. The greatest work a man can do.

HODEL: Then goodbye, Perchik.

PERCHIK: Before I go [He hesitates, then summons up courage], there is a certain question I wish to discuss with you.

HODEL: Yes?

PERCHIK: A political question.

HODEL: What is it?

PERCHIK: The question of marriage.

HODEL: This is a political question?

PERCHIK: [Awkwardly] In a theoretical sense, yes. The relationship between a man and woman known as marriage is based on mutual beliefs, a common attitude and philosophy towards society—

HODEL: And affection.

PERCHIK: And affection. This relationship has positive social values. It reflects a unity and solidarity—

HODEL: And affection.

PERCHIK: Yes. And I personally am in favor it it. Do you understand?

HODEL: I think you are asking me to marry you.

PERCHIK: In a theoretical sense, yes, I am.

HODEL: I was hoping you were.

PERCHIK: Then I take it you approve? And we can consider ourselves engaged, even though I am going away? [*She nods*] I am very happy, Hodel. Very happy.

HODEL: So am I, Perchik.

PERCHIK: [*Sings*]

["Now I Have Everything"]

I used to tell myself
That I had everything,
But that was only half true.
I had an aim in life,
And that was everything,
But now I even have you.

I have something that I would die for,
Someone that I can live for, too.

Yes, now I have everything—
Not only everything,
I have a little bit more—
Besides having everything,
I know what everything's for.

I used to wonder,
Could there be a wife
To share such a difficult, wand'ring kind of life.

HODEL:

I was only out of sight,
Waiting right here.

PERCHIK:

Who knows tomorrow
Where our home will be?

HODEL:

I'll be with you and that's
Home enough for me.

PERCHIK:
> Everything is right at hand.

HODEL *and* PERCHIK:
> Simple and clear.

PERCHIK:
> I have something that I would die for,
> Someone that I can live for, too.

> Yes, now I have everything—
> Not only everything,
> I have a little bit more—
> Besides having everything,
> I know what everything's for.

HODEL: And when will we be married, Perchik?

PERCHIK: I will send for you as soon as I can. It will be a hard life, Hodel.

HODEL: But it will be less hard if we live it together.

PERCHIK: Yes.

[TEVYE *enters*]

TEVYE: Good evening.

PERCHIK: Good evening. Reb Tevye, I have some bad news. I must leave this place.

TEVYE: When?

PERCHIK: Right away.

TEVYE: I'm sorry, Perchik. We will all miss you.

PERCHIK: But I also have some good news. You can congratulate me.

TEVYE: Congratulations. What for?

PERCHIK: We're engaged.

TEVYE: Engaged?

HODEL: Yes, Papa, we're engaged. [*Takes* PERCHIK's *hand*]

TEVYE: [*Pleasantly, separating them*] No, you're not. I know, you like him, and he likes you, but you're going away, and you're staying here, so have a nice trip, Perchik. I hope you'll be very happy, and my answer is no.

HODEL: Please, Papa, you don't understand.

TEVYE: I understand. I gave my permission to Motel and Tzeitel, so you feel that you also have a right. I'm sorry, Perchik. I like you, but you're going away, so go in good health and my answer is still no.

HODEL: You don't understand, Papa.

TEVYE: [*Patiently*] You're not listening. I say no. I'm sorry, Hodel, but we'll find someone else for you, here in Anatevka.

PERCHIK: Reb Tevye.

TEVYE: What is it?

PERCHIK: We are not asking for your permission, only for your blessing. We are going to get married.

TEVYE: [*To* HODEL] You're not asking for my permission?

HODEL: But we would like your blessing, Papa.

TEVYE:

["Tradition" Reprise]

I can't believe my own ears. My blessing? For what?
For going over my head? Impossible.
At least with Tzeitel and Motel, they asked me,
They begged me.
But now, if I like it or not,
She'll marry him.
So what do you want from me? Go on, be wed.
And tear out my beard and uncover my head.
Tradition!
They're not even asking permission
From the papa.
What's happening to the tradition?
One little time I pulled out a thread
And where has it led? Where has it led?

Where has it led? To this! A man tells me he is getting married. He doesn't ask me, he tells me. But first, he abandons her.

HODEL: He is not abandoning me, Papa.

PERCHIK: As soon as I can, I will send for her and marry her. I love her.

TEVYE: [*Mimicking him*] "I love her." Love. It's a new style. On the other hand, our old ways were once new, weren't they? On the other hand, they decided without parents, without a matchmaker. On the other hand, did Adam and Eve have a matchmaker? Yes, they did. Then it seems these two have the same matchmaker. [*Sings*]

> They're going over my head—
> Unheard of, absurd.
> For this they want to be blessed?—
> Unthinkable.
> I'll lock her up in her room.
> I couldn't—I should!—
> But look at my daughter's eyes.
> She loves him.
> Tradition!

[*Shrugs*]

Very well, children, you have my blessing and my permission.

HODEL: Oh, thank you, Papa. You don't know how happy that makes me.

TEVYE: [*To the audience*] What else could I do?

PERCHIK: Thank you, Papa.

TEVYE: [*Worried*] "Thank you, Papa." What will I tell your mother? Another dream?

PERCHIK: Perhaps if you tell her something—that I am going to visit a rich uncle—something like that.

TEVYE: Please, Perchik. I can handle my own wife. [PERCHIK *and* HODEL *exit. He calls aggressively*] Golde! Golde! [*She enters from the house. He speaks timidly*] Hello, Golde. I've just been talking to Perchik and Hodel.

GOLDE: Well?

TEVYE: They seem to be very fond of each other—

GOLDE: Well?

TEVYE: Well, I have decided to give them my permission to become engaged. [*Starts into the house*]

GOLDE: [*Stopping him*] What? Just like this? Without even asking me?

TEVYE: [*Roaring*] Who asks you? I'm the father.

GOLDE: And who is he? A pauper. He has nothing, absolutely nothing!

TEVYE: [*Hesitating*] I wouldn't say that. I hear he has a rich uncle, a very rich uncle. [*Changes the subject*] He is a good man, Golde. I like him. He is a little crazy, but I like him. And what's more important, Hodel likes him. Hodel loves him. So what can we do? It's a new world, a new world. Love. [*Starts to go, then has a sudden thought*] Golde— [*Sings*]

["Do You Love Me?"]
Do you love me?

GOLDE:
Do I what?

TEVYE:
Do you love me?

GOLDE:
Do I love you?
With our daughters getting married
And this trouble in the town,
You're upset, you're worn out,
Go inside, go lie down.
Maybe it's indigestion.

TEVYE: Golde, I'm asking you a question—
Do you love me?

GOLDE:
You're a fool.

TEVYE: I know—
But do you love me?

GOLDE:
Do I love you?
For twenty-five years I've washed your clothes,
Cooked your meals, cleaned your house,
Given you children, milked the cow.
After twenty-five years, why talk about
Love right now?

TEVYE:

> Golde, the first time I met you
> Was on our wedding day.
> I was scared.

GOLDE:

> I was shy.

TEVYE:

> I was nervous.

GOLDE:

> So was I.

TEVYE:

> But my father and my mother
> Said we'd learn to love each other.
> And now I'm asking, Golde,
> Do you love me?

GOLDE:

> I'm your wife.

TEVYE: I know—

> But do you love me?

GOLDE:

> Do I love him?
> For twenty-five years I've lived with him,
> Fought with him, starved with him.
> Twenty-five years my bed is his.
> If that's not love, what is?

TEVYE:

> Then you love me?

GOLDE:

> I suppose I do.

TEVYE:

> And I suppose I love you, too.

TEVYE *and* GOLDE:

> It doesn't change a thing,
> But even so,
> After twenty-five years,
> It's nice to know.

SCENE TWO

The village street. YENTE, TZEITEL, *and other villagers cross.* YENTE *and* TZEITEL *meet.*

FISH SELLER: Fish! Fresh fish!

YENTE: Oh, Tzeitel, Tzeitel darling. Guess who I just saw! Your sister Chava with that Fyedka! And it's not the first time I've seen them together.

TZEITEL: You saw Chava with Fyedka?

YENTE: Would I make it up? Oh, and Tzeitel, I happened to be at the post office today and the postman told me there was a letter there for your sister Hodel.

TZEITEL: Wonderful, I'll go get it. [*Starts off*]

YENTE: I got it! It's from her intended, Perchik. [*Hands letter to* TZEITEL]

TZEITEL: Hodel will be so happy, she's been waiting—But it's open.

YENTE: It happened to be open. [TZEITEL *exits.* YENTE *watches her leave, then turns to a group of* VILLAGERS] Rifka, I have such news for you. [*Sings*]

["I Just Heard"]
Remember Perchik, that crazy student?
Remember at the wedding,
When Tzeitel married Motel
And Perchik started dancing
With Tevye's daughter Hodel?
Well, I just learned
That Perchik's been arrested, in Kiev.

VILLAGERS:

No!

YENTE:

Yes!

[YENTE *and the* FIRST GROUP *exit. A* WOMAN *crosses to a* SECOND GROUP]

FIRST WOMAN: Shandel, Shandel! Wait till I tell you—
> Remember Perchik, that crazy student?
> Remember at the wedding.
> He danced with Tevye's Hodel?
> Well,
> I just heard
> That Hodel's been arrested, in Kiev.

VILLAGERS:
> No! Terrible, terrible!

[*The* SECOND GROUP *exits. A* SECOND WOMAN *crosses to a* THIRD GROUP]

SECOND WOMAN: Mirila!
> Do you remember Perchik,
> That student, from Kiev?
> Remember how he acted
> When Tzeitel married Motel?
> Well, I just heard
> That Motel's been arrested
> For dancing at the wedding.

VILLAGERS:
> No!

SECOND WOMAN:
> In Kiev!

[*The* THIRD GROUP *exits.* MENDEL *crosses to a* FOURTH GROUP]

MENDEL: Rabbi! Rabbi!
> Remember Perchik, with all his strange ideas?
> Remember Tzeitel's wedding
> Where Tevye danced with Golde?
> Well I just heard
> That Tevye's been arrested
> And Golde's gone to Kiev.

VILLAGERS:
> No!

MENDEL:
God forbid.

VILLAGERS:
She didn't.

MENDEL:
She did.

[*The* FOURTH GROUP *exits.* AVRAM *crosses to the* FIFTH GROUP. YENTE *enters and stands at the edge of the* GROUP *to listen*]

AVRAM: Listen, everybody, terrible news—terrible—
Remember Perchik,
Who started all the trouble?
Well, I just heard, from someone who should know,
That Golde's been arrested,
And Hodel's gone to Kiev.
Motel studies dancing,
And Tevye's acting strange.
Shprintze has the measles,
And Bielke has the mumps.

YENTE: And that's what comes from men and women dancing!

SCENE THREE

The exterior of the railroad station. Morning. HODEL *enters and walks over to a bench.* TEVYE *follows, carrying her suitcase.*

HODEL: You don't have to wait for the train, Papa. You'll be late for your customers.

TEVYE: Just a few more minutes. Is he in bad trouble, that hero of yours? [*She nods*] Arrested? [*She nods*] And convicted?

HODEL: Yes, but he did nothing wrong. He cares nothing for himself. Everything he does is for humanity.

TEVYE: But if he did nothing wrong, he wouldn't be in trouble.

HODEL: Papa, how can you say that, a learned man like you? What wrongs did Joseph do, and Abraham, and Moses? And they had troubles.

TEVYE: But why won't you tell me where he is now, this Joseph of yours?

HODEL: It is far, Papa, terribly far. He is in a settlement in Siberia.

TEVYE: Siberia! And he asks you to leave your father and mother and join him in that frozen wasteland, and marry him there?

HODEL: No, Papa, he did not ask me to go. I *want* to go. I don't want him to be alone. I want to help him in his work. It is the greatest work a man can do.

TEVYE: But, Hodel, baby—

HODEL: Papa— [*Sings*]

["Far From the Home I Love"]

How can I hope to make you understand
Why I do what I do,
Why I must travel to a distant land
Far from the home I love?

Once I was happily content to be
As I was, where I was,
Close to the people who are close to me
Here in the home I love.

Who could see that a man would come
Who would change the shape of my dreams?
Helpless, now, I stand with him
Watching older dreams grow dim.

Oh, what a melancholy choice this is,
Wanting home, wanting him,
Closing my heart to every hope but his,
Leaving the home I love.

There where my heart has settled long ago
I must go, I must go.
Who could imagine I'd be wand'ring so
Far from the home I love?
Yet, there with my love, I'm home.

TEVYE: And who, my child, will there be to perform a marriage, there in the wilderness?

HODEL: Papa, I promise you, we will be married under a canopy.

TEVYE: No doubt a rabbi or two was also arrested. Well, give him my regards, this Moses of yours. I always thought he was a good man. Tell him I rely on his honor to treat my daughter well. Tell him that.

HODEL: Papa, God alone knows when we shall see each other again.

TEVYE: Then we will leave it in His hands. [*He kisses* HODEL, *starts to go, stops, looks back, then looks to heaven*] Take care of her. See that she dresses warm. [*He exits, leaving* HODEL *seated on the station platform*]

SCENE FOUR

The village street, some months later. The VILLAGERS *enter.*

AVRAM: Reb Mordcha, did you hear the news? A new arrival at Motel and Tzeitel's.

MORDCHA: A new arrival at Motel and Tzeitel's? I must congratulate him.

AVRAM: Rabbi, did you hear the news? A new arrival at Motel and Tzeitel's.

RABBI: Really?

MENDEL: Mazeltov.

FIRST MAN: Mazeltov.

SECOND MAN: Mazeltov.

[SHANDEL *crosses quickly, meeting a* WOMAN]

WOMAN: Shandel, where are you running?

SHANDEL: To my boy, Motel. There's a new arrival there.

VILLAGERS: Mazeltov, Mazeltov, Mazeltov, Shandel.

SCENE FIVE

MOTEL's *tailor shop*. MOTEL *and* CHAVA *are in the shop.* GOLDE *and the* VILLAGERS *crowd around* MOTEL, *congratulating him. They fall back, revealing a used sewing machine.*

VILLAGERS: Mazeltov, Motel. We just heard. Congratulations. Wonderful.

MOTEL: Thank you, thank you, very much.

[TZEITEL *enters*]

AVRAM: Mazeltov, Tzeitel.

TZEITEL: [*Ecstatic*] You got it!

MOTEL: I got it!

TZEITEL: It's beautiful.

MOTEL: I know!

TZEITEL: Have you tried it yet?

MOTEL: [*Holds up two different-colored pieces of cloth sewn together*] Look.

TZEITEL: Beautiful.

MOTEL: I know. And in less than a minute. And see how close and even the stitches are.

TZEITEL: Beautiful.

MOTEL: I know. From now on, my clothes will be perfect, made by machine. No more handmade clothes.

[*The* RABBI *enters*]

MORDCHA: The rabbi, the rabbi.

MOTEL: Look, Rabbi, my new sewing machine.

RABBI: Mazeltov.

TZEITEL: Rabbi, is there a blessing for a sewing machine?

RABBI: There is a blessing for everything. [*Prays*] Amen.

VILLAGERS: Amen. . . . Mazeltov. [VILLAGERS, RABBI *exit*]

GOLDE: And the baby? How is the baby?

TZEITEL: He's wonderful, Mama.

[FYEDKA *enters. There is an awkward pause*]

FYEDKA: Good afternoon.

MOTEL: Good afternoon, Fyedka.

FYEDKA: I came for the shirt.

MOTEL: It's ready.

TZEITEL: See, it's my new sewing machine.

FYEDKA: I see. Congratulations.

MOTEL: Thank you.

FYEDKA: [*After another awkward moment*] Good day. [*Leaves the shop*]

MOTEL: Good day.

GOLDE: How does it work?

MOTEL: See, it's an amazing thing. You work it with your foot and your hand.

[CHAVA *exits from the shop and meets* FYEDKA *outside*]

FYEDKA: They still don't know about us? [*She shakes her head*] You must tell them.

CHAVA: I will, but I'm afraid.

FYEDKA: Chava, let me talk to your father.

CHAVA: No, that would be the worst thing, I'm sure of it.

FYEDKA: Let me try.

CHAVA: No, I'll talk to him. I promise.

[TEVYE *enters*]

FYEDKA: [*Extending his hand*] Good afternoon.

TEVYE: [*Takes the hand limply*] Good afternoon.

FYEDKA: [*Looks at* CHAVA] Good day. [*Exits*]

TEVYE: Good day. What were you and he talking about?

CHAVA: Nothing, we were just talking. [TEVYE *turns to go into* MOTEL's *shop*] Papa, Fyedka and I have known each other for a long time and and—

TEVYE: [*Turning back*] Chava, I would be much happier if you would remain friends from a distance. You must not forget who you are and who that man is.

CHAVA: He has a name, Papa.

TEVYE: Of course. All creatures on earth have a name.

CHAVA: Fyedka is not a creature, Papa. Fyedka is a man.

TEVYE: Who says that he isn't? It's just that he is a different kind of man. As the Good Book says, "Each shall seek his own kind." Which, translated, means, "A bird may love a fish, but where would they build a home together?" [*He starts toward the shop, but* CHAVA *seizes his arm*]

CHAVA: The world is changing, Papa.

TEVYE: No. Some things do not change for us. Some things will never change.

CHAVA: We don't feel that way.

TEVYE: We?

CHAVA: Fyedka and I. We want to be married.

TEVYE: Are you out of your mind? Don't you know what this means, marrying outside of the faith?

CHAVA: But, Papa—

TEVYE: No, Chava! I said no! Never talk about this again! Never mention his name again! Never see him again! Never! Do you understand me?

CHAVA: Yes, Papa. I understand you.

[GOLDE *enters from the shop, followed by* SHPRINTZE *and* BIELKE]

GOLDE: You're finally here? Let's go home. It's time for supper.

TEVYE: I want to see Motel's new machine.

GOLDE: You'll see it some other time. It's late.

TEVYE: Quiet, woman, before I get angry. And when I get angry, even flies don't dare to fly.

GOLDE: I'm very frightened of you. After we finish supper, I'll faint. Come home.

TEVYE: [*Sternly*] Golde. I am the man in the family. I am head of the house. I want to see Motel's new machine, now! [*Strides to the door of the shop, opens it, looks in, closes the door, turns to* GOLDE] Now, let's go home! [*They exit.* CHAVA *remains looking after them*]

SCENE SIX

A road. Late afternoon. TEVYE *is pushing his cart.*

TEVYE: [*Sinks down on the cart*] How long can that miserable horse of mine complain about his leg? [*Looks up*] Dear God, if I can walk on two legs, why can't he walk on three? I know I shouldn't be too upset with him. He is one of Your creatures and he has the same rights as I have: the right to be sick, the right to be hungry, the right to work like a horse. And, dear God, I'm sick and tired of pulling this cart. I know, I know, I should push it a while. [*He starts pushing the cart*]

GOLDE: [*Offstage*] Tevye! [*She enters, upset*] Tevye!

TEVYE: [*Struck by her manner*] What? What is it?

GOLDE: It's Chava. She left home this morning. With Fyedka.

TEVYE: What?

GOLDE: I looked all over for her. I even went to the priest. He told me—they were married.

TEVYE: Married! [*She nods*] Go home, Golde. We have other children at home. Go home, Golde. You have work to do. I have work to do.

GOLDE: But, Chava—

TEVYE: Chava is dead to us! We will forget her. Go home.
[GOLDE *exits*. TEVYE *sings*]

["Chavaleh"]

TEVYE:

Little bird, little Chavaleh,
I don't understand what's happening today.
Everything is all a blur.
All I can see is a happy child,
The sweet little bird you were,
Chavaleh, Chavaleh.

Little bird, little Chavaleh,
You were always such a pretty little thing.
Everybody's fav'rite child,
Gentle and kind and affectionate,
What a sweet little bird you were,
Chavaleh, Chavaleh.

[CHAVA *enters*]

CHAVA: Papa, I want to talk with you. Papa, stop. At least listen
to me. Papa, I beg you to accept us.

TEVYE: [*To heaven*] Accept them? How can I accept them.
Can I deny everything I believe in? On the other hand, can
I deny my own child? On the other hand, how can I turn
my back on my faith, my people? If I try to bend that far,
I will break. On the other hand . . . there is no other hand.
No Chava. No—no—no!

CHAVA: Papa. Papa.

VILLAGERS: [*Seen behind a transparent curtain, sing as* CHAVA
exits slowly]

Tradition. Tradition. Tradition.

SCENE SEVEN

TEVYE's *barn*. YENTE *enters with two* BOYS, *teenage students,
who are obviously uncomfortable in the situation.*

YENTE: Golde, are you home? I've got the two boys, the boys I told you about.

[GOLDE *enters, followed by* SHPRINTZE *and* BIELKE]

Golde darling, here they are, wonderful boys, both learned boys, Golde, from good families, each of them a prize, a jewel. You couldn't do better for your girls—just right. From the top of the tree.

GOLDE: I don't know, Yente. My girls are still so young.

YENTE: So what do *they* look like, grandfathers? Meanwhile they'll be engaged, nothing to worry about later, no looking around, their future all signed and sealed.

GOLDE: Which one for which one?

YENTE: What's the difference? Take your pick.

GOLDE: I don't know, Yente. I'll have to talk with—

[*Enter* LAZAR WOLF, AVRAM, MENDEL, MORDCHA, *and other* VILLAGERS]

AVRAM: Golde, is Reb Tevye home?

GOLDE: Yes, but he's in the house. Why, is there some trouble?

AVRAM: [*To* BIELKE *and* SHPRINTZE] Call your father. [*They exit*]

YENTE: [*To the boys*] Go home. Tell your parents I'll talk to them. [*They exit*]

GOLDE: What is it? Why are you all gathered together like a bunch of goats? What's—

[TEVYE *enters*]

AVRAM: Reb Tevye, have you seen the constable today?

TEVYE: No. Why?

LAZAR: There are some rumors in town. We thought because you knew him so well, maybe he told you what is true and what is not.

TEVYE: What rumors?

AVRAM: Someone from Zolodin told me that there was an edict issued in St. Petersburg that all—shh. Shh.

[*He stops as the* CONSTABLE *enters with* TWO MEN]

TEVYE: Welcome, your Honor. What's the good news in the world?

CONSTABLE: I see you have company.

TEVYE: They are my friends.

CONSTABLE: It's just as well. What I have to say is for their ears also. Tevye, how much time do you need to sell your house and all your household goods? [*There is a gasp from the* VILLAGERS. *They are stunned. They look to* TEVYE]

TEVYE: Why should I sell my house? Is it in anybody's way?

CONSTABLE: I came here to tell you that you are going to have to leave Anatevka.

TEVYE: And how did I come to deserve such an honor?

CONSTABLE: Not just you, of course, but all of you. At first I thought you might be spared, Tevye, because of your daughter Chava, who married—

TEVYE: My daughter is dead!

CONSTABLE: I understand. At any rate, it affects all of you. You have to leave.

TEVYE: But this corner of the world has always been our home. Why should we leave?

CONSTABLE: [*Irritated*] I don't know why. There's trouble in the world. Troublemakers.

TEVYE: [*Ironically*] Like us!

CONSTABLE: You aren't the only ones. Your people must leave all the villages—Zolodin, Rabalevka. The whole district must be emptied. [*Horrified and amazed exclamations from the* VILLAGERS] I have an order here, and it says that you must sell your homes and be out of here in three days.

VILLAGERS: Three days! . . . Out in three days!

TEVYE: And you who have known us all your life, you'd carry out this order?

CONSTABLE: I have nothing to do with it, don't you understand?

TEVYE: [*Bitterly*] We understand.

FIRST MAN: And what if we refuse to go?

CONSTABLE: You will be forced out.

LAZAR: We will defend ourselves.

VILLAGERS: Stay in our homes . . . Refuse to leave . . . Keep our land.

SECOND MAN: Fight!

CONSTABLE: Against our army? I wouldn't advise it!

TEVYE: I have some advice for you. Get off my land! [*The* VILLAGERS *crowd toward the* CONSTABLE *and his* MEN] This is still my home, my land. Get off my land! [*The* CONSTABLE *and his* MEN *start to go. The* CONSTABLE *turns*]

CONSTABLE: You have three days! [*Exits*]

FIRST MAN: After a lifetime, a piece of paper and get thee out.

MORDCHA: We should get together with the people of Zolodin. Maybe they have a plan.

FIRST MAN: We should defend ourselves. An eye for an eye, a tooth for a tooth.

TEVYE: Very good. And that way, the whole world will be blind and toothless.

MENDEL: Rabbi, we've been waiting for the Messiah all our lives. Wouldn't this be a good time for him to come?

RABBI: We'll have to wait for him someplace else. Meanwhile, let's start packing. [*The* VILLAGERS *start to go, talking together*]

VILLAGERS: He's right. . . . I'll see you before I go.

FIRST MAN: Three days!

MORDCHA: How will I be able to sell my shop? My merchandise?

THIRD MAN: Where can I go with a wife, her parents, and three children? [*Exits all but* YENTE, GOLDE, AVRAM, LAZAR, MENDEL, *and* TEVYE]

YENTE: Well, Anatevka hasn't been exactly the Garden of Eden.

AVRAM: That's true.

GOLDE: After all, what've we got here? [*Sings*]
["Anatevka"]
A little bit of this,
A little bit of that,

YENTE:
A pot,

LAZAR:
A pan,

MENDEL:
A broom,

AVRAM:
A hat.

TEVYE: [*Speaks*] Someone should have set a match to this place long ago.

MENDEL:
A bench,

AVRAM:
A tree,

GOLDE:
So what's a stove?

LAZAR:
Or a house?

MENDEL: [*Speaks*] People who pass through Anatevka don't even know they've been here.

GOLDE:
A stick of wood,

YENTE:
A piece of cloth.

ALL:
What do we leave?
Nothing much,
Only Anatevka. . . .

Anatevka, Anatevka,
Underfed, overworked Anatevka,
Where else could Sabbath be so sweet?

Anatevka, Anatevka,
Intimate, obstinate Anatevka,
Where I know everyone I meet.

Soon I'll be a stranger in a strange new place,
Searching for an old familiar face
From Anatevka.

I belong in Anatevka,
Tumbledown, workaday Anatevka,
Dear little village, little town of mine.

GOLDE: Eh, it's just a place.

MENDEL: And our forefathers have been forced out of many, many places at a moment's notice.

TEVYE: [*Shrugs*] Maybe that's why we always wear our hats.

SCENE EIGHT

Outside TEVYE's *house.* MOTEL *and* TZEITEL *are packing baggage into a cart and a wagon.* SHPRINTZE *and* BIELKE *enter with bundles.*

SHPRINTZE: Where will we live in America?

MOTEL: With Uncle Abram, but he doesn't know it yet.

SHPRINTZE: I wish you and the baby were coming with us.

TZEITEL: We'll be staying in Warsaw until we have enough money to join you.

GOLDE: [*Entering, with goblets*] Motel, be careful with these. My mother and father, may they rest in peace, gave them to us on our wedding day.

TZEITEL: [*To* BIELKE *and* SHPRINTZE] Come, children, help me pack the rest of the clothes. [*They exit into house*]

YENTE: [*Enters*] Golde darling, I had to see you before I left because I have such news for you. Golde darling, you remember I told you yesterday I didn't know where to go, what to do with these old bones? Now I know! You want to hear? I'll tell you. Golde darling, all my life I've dreamed of going to one place and now I'll walk, I'll crawl, I'll get there. Guess where. You'll never guess. Every year at Passover, what do we say? "Next year in Jerusalem, next year in the Holy Land."

GOLDE: You're going to the Holy Land!

YENTE: You guessed! And you know why? In my sleep, my husband, my Aaron, came to me and said, "Yente, go to the Holy Land." Usually, of course, I wouldn't listen to him, because, good as he was, too much brains he wasn't blessed with. But in my sleep it's a sign. Right? So, somehow or other, I'll get to the Holy Land. And you want to know what I'll do there? I'm a matchmaker, no? I'll arrange marriages, yes? Children come from marriages, no? So I'm going to the Holy Land to help our people increase and multiply. It's my mission. So goodbye, Golde.

GOLDE: Goodbye, Yente. Be well and go in peace. [*They embrace*]

YENTE: [*Exiting*] Maybe next time, Golde, we will meet on happier occasions. Meanwhile, we suffer, we suffer, we suffer in silence! Right? Of course, right. [*She exits.* GOLDE *sits on a large straw trunk, sadly wrapping a pair of silver goblets.* TEVYE *enters, carrying a bundle of books, and puts them on the wagon*]

TEVYE: We'll have to hurry, Golde. [*She is looking at the goblets*] Come, Golde, we have to leave soon.

GOLDE: Leave. It sounds so easy.

TEVYE: We'll all be together soon. Motel, Tzeitel and the baby, they'll come too, you'll see. That Motel is a person.

GOLDE: And Hodel and Perchik? When will we ever see them?

TEVYE: Do they come visiting us from Siberia every Sabbath? You know what she writes. He sits in prison, and she works, and soon he will be set free and together they will turn the world upside down. She couldn't be happier. And the other children will be with us.

GOLDE: [*Quietly*] Not all.

TEVYE: [*Sharply*] All. Come, Golde, we have to get finished.

GOLDE: I still have to sweep the floor.

TEVYE: Sweep the floor?

GOLDE: I don't want to leave a dirty house. [*She exits behind the house as* LAZAR *enters, carrying a large suitcase*]

LAZAR: Well, Tevye, I'm on my way.

TEVYE: Where are you going?

LAZAR: Chicago. In America. My wife, Fruma-Sarah, may she rest in peace, has a brother there.

TEVYE: That's nice.

LAZAR: I hate him, but a relative is a relative! [*They embrace*] Goodbye, Tevye. [LAZAR *exits.* TEVYE *enters the house, passing* TZEITEL, *who enters with a blanket and a small bundle*]

TEVYE: Tzeitel, are they finished inside?

TZEITEL: Almost, Papa. [TZEITEL *puts the blanket on* MOTEL's *wagon, kneels down, and begins rummaging in the bundle.* CHAVA *and* FYEDKA *enter.* TZEITEL *turns to enter the house, and sees them*] Chava! [CHAVA *runs to her. They embrace.* TZEITEL *looks toward the house*] Papa will see you.

CHAVA: I want him to. I want to say goodbye to him.

TZEITEL: He will not listen.

CHAVA: But at least he will hear.

TZEITEL: Maybe it would be better if I went inside and told Mama that—

[GOLDE *comes round the side of the house*]

GOLDE: Chava!

[*She starts toward her as* TEVYE *enters from the house with a length of rope. He sees them, turns, re-enters house, returns, and bends down to tie up the straw trunk, his back to* CHAVA *and* FYEDKA]

CHAVA: Papa, we came to say goodbye. [TEVYE *does not respond, but goes on working*] We are also leaving this place. We are going to Cracow.

FYEDKA: We cannot stay among people who can do such things to others.

CHAVA: We wanted you to know that. Goodbye, Papa, Mama. [*She waits for an answer, gets none, and turns to go*]

FYEDKA: Yes, we are also moving. Some are driven away by edicts, others by silence. Come, Chava.

TZEITEL: Goodbye, Chava, Fyedka.

TEVYE: [*To* TZEITEL, *prompting her under his breath as he turns to another box*] God be with you!

TZEITEL: [*Looks at him, then speaks to Chava, gently*] God be with you!

CHAVA: We will write to you in America. If you like.

GOLDE: We will be staying with Uncle Abram.

CHAVA: Yes, Mama. [CHAVA *and* FYEDKA *exit.* TEVYE *turns and watches them leave. There is a moment of silence; then he turns on* GOLDE]

TEVYE: [*With mock irritation*] We will be staying with Uncle Abram! We will be staying with Uncle Abram! The whole world has to know our business!

GOLDE: Stop yelling and finish packing. We have a train to catch.

[MOTEL, SHPRINTZE, *and* BIELKE *enter from the house*]

TEVYE: I don't need your advice, Golde. Tzeitel, don't forget the baby. We have to catch a train, and a boat. Bielke, Shprintze, put the bundles on the wagon.

[TEVYE *moves the wagon to the center of the stage, and* MOTEL *puts the trunk on it.* TZEITEL *brings the baby out of the house. They turn to one another for goodbyes*]

TZEITEL: Goodbye, Papa. [*They embrace*]

GOLDE: Goodbye, Motel.

MOTEL: Goodbye, Mama.

[TZEITEL *and* GOLDE *embrace*]

TEVYE: Work hard, Motel. Come to us soon.

MOTEL: I will, Reb Tevye. I'll work hard. [TEVYE *takes one last look at the baby, then* TZEITEL *and* MOTEL *exit with their cart. When they are gone,* TEVYE *turns to the wagon*]

TEVYE: [*Picking up pots*] Come, children. Golde, we can leave these pots.

GOLDE: No, we can't.

TEVYE: All right, we'll take them. [*Puts them back*]

BIELKE: [*Childishly, swinging around with* SHPRINTZE] We're going on a train and a boat. We're going on a—

GOLDE: [*Sharply*] Stop that! Behave yourself! We're not in America yet!

TEVYE: Come, children. Let's go.

[*The stage begins to revolve, and* TEVYE *begins to pull the wagon in the opposite direction. The other* VILLAGERS, *including the* FIDDLER, *join the circle. The revolve stops. There is a last moment together, and the* VILLAGERS *exit, at different times and in opposite directions, leaving the family on stage.* TEVYE *begins to pull his wagon upstage, revealing the* FIDDLER, *playing his theme.* TEVYE *stops, turns, beckons to him. The* FIDDLER *tucks his violin under his arm and follows the family upstage as the curtain falls*]

Brian Friel

Brian Friel, who was born on January 9, 1929, outside Omagh, a market town in County Tyrone, Northern Ireland, recently told an interviewer: "There are two kinds of Irishmen. There is the garrulous swashbuckling Brendan Behan type and then there is the black morose kind. I am not of the first sort." Whatever their personality differences, however, there is little doubt that both Friel and Behan are Ireland's most valued and prominent export dramatists of recent times.

With the New York première of *Philadelphia, Here I Come!* (Mr. Friel's first sortie in the American theatre), it was immediately apparent that a rare and genuine talent had been sent us from the Emerald Isle. The chorus of professional hosannas began with drama critic Walter Kerr's paean: "This morning the sun shines brighter . . . *Philadelphia, Here I Come!* is a funny play, a prickly play, finally a most affecting play, and the pleasure it gives is of a most peculiar kind. Author Brian Friel has set all of his cranky, fond, and obstinately shy people to searching for the one word that is everlastingly on the tip of everyone's tongue, and everlastingly not spoken. He has written a play about an ache, and he has written it so simply and so honestly that the ache itself becomes a warming-fire." At season's end, the David Merrick presentation of the play won five nominations for Antoinette Perry (Tony) Awards—the New York theatre's highest honor—and *Variety's* Poll of New York's Drama Critics cited the author as the year's "most promising new Broadway playwright."

Until 1960, Mr. Friel (who lives in Derry City with his wife and four daughters) taught in sundry public schools "around the

Irish countryside," then declared he'd had enough of pedagoguery and turned an avocation (writing) into a full-time profession. Although his short stories frequently have appeared in *The New Yorker* magazine and two collections of stories (*The Saucer of Larks* and *The Gold in the Sea*) have been published in the United States, his primary recognition has come through the stage.

In the autumn of 1966, while *Philadelphia, Here I Come!* was still delighting New York theatregoers, Mr. Friel was again represented on the Broadway stage with *The Loves of Cass McGuire*. Though the latter was a short-lived effort, the author soon was due to resume success with his double bill, *Lovers*. As the inaugural attraction of the 1968–69 New York theatre season, the critics once again acclaimed him as "a lovely writer, funny and compassionate" while *Life* magazine reported that "although Friel's dialogue is not in verse, he writes so beautifully and his ear for Irish speech is so faultless that he has written a kind of poem, touching and often hilarious." The success of *Lovers* was immediate, and following its engagement at the Vivian Beaumont Theatre (as part of the Lincoln Center Festival '68), it was transferred to the Music Box Theatre for an extended run, then toured nationally.

Mr. Friel's previous plays, produced in Belfast and Dublin, are *This Doubtful Paradise*, *The Blind Mice* and *The Enemy Within*, the last named at the Abbey Theatre.

As this is being written, Brian Friel is scheduled to have two Broadway premières during the 1969–70 season. The first, *The Mundy Scheme*, a comedy dealing with Irish politics and corruption in high office, originally opened at the Olympia Theatre, Dublin, on June 10, 1969. It was staged there by Donal Donnelly who starred in the Broadway presentation of *Philadelphia, Here I Come!* (Mr. Donnelly will also direct the American production of *The Mundy Scheme*).

Mr. Friel's second entry of the season, *Crystal and Fox*, is concerned with itinerant actors in the hinterlands of present-day Ireland. This enterprise will reunite the dramatist and director Hilton Edwards, whose initial staging of *Philadelphia, Here I Come!* at the Dublin Theatre Festival (1964) originated its (and the author's) journey to international prominence.

PHILADELPHIA,
HERE I COME!

Brian Friel

Philadelphia, Here I Come! was first presented at the Gaiety Theatre, Dublin, on September 28, 1964, by Edwards-MacLiammóir: Dublin Gate Theatre Production Ltd., in association with the Dublin Theatre Festival and Oscar Lewenstein Ltd.

The first American performance of *Philadelphia, Here I Come!* was presented at the Helen Hayes Theatre, New York, on February 16, 1966, by the David Merrick Arts Foundation, by arrangement with Oscar Lewenstein and Michael White.

The cast was as follows:

MADGE		*Mairin O'Sullivan*
GARETH O'DONNELL	{ *in Public*	*Patrick Bedford*
	{ *in Private*	*Donal Donnelly*
S. B. O'DONNELL		*Eamon Kelly*
KATE DOOGAN		*Louise Sorel*
SENATOR DOOGAN		*William Griffis*
MASTER BOYLE		*Joseph Boland*
LIZZY SWEENEY		*Mavis Villiers*
CON SWEENEY		*Joseph Warren*
BEN BURTON		*John Cecil Holm*
NED		*Thomas Connolly*
TOM		*Dermot McNamara*
JOE		*Michael Berkson*
CANON MICK O'BYRNE		*Donald Marye*

Directed by Hilton Edwards
Setting by Lloyd Burlingame

TIME: *The present in the small village of Ballybeg in County Donegal, Ireland. The action takes place on the night before, and on the morning of, GAR's departure for Philadelphia.*

When the curtain rises the only part of the stage that is lit is the kitchen, i.e., the portion on the left from the point of view of the audience. It is sparsely and comfortlessly furnished—a bachelor's kitchen. There are two doors; one left which leads to the shop, and one upstage leading to the scullery [off]. Beside the shop door is a large deal table, now set for tea without cloth and with rough cups and saucers. Beside the scullery door is an old-fashioned dresser. On the scullery wall is a large school-type clock.

Stage right, now in darkness, is GAR's bedroom. Both bedroom and kitchen should be moved upstage, leaving a generous apron. GAR's bedroom is furnished with a single bed, a wash-hand-basin [crockery jug and bowl], a table with a record-player and records, and a small chest of drawers.

These two areas—kitchen and GAR's bedroom—occupy more than two-thirds of the stage. The remaining portion is fluid: in Episode I for example, it represents a room in SENATOR DOOGAN's home.

The two GARS, PUBLIC GAR and PRIVATE GAR, are two views of the one man. PUBLIC GAR is the GAR that people see, talk to, talk about. PRIVATE GAR is the unseen man, the man within, the conscience, the alter ego, the secret thoughts, the id.

PRIVATE GAR, the spirit, is invisible to everybody, always. Nobody except PUBLIC GAR hears him talk. But even PUBLIC GAR, although he talks to PRIVATE GAR occasionally, never sees him and never looks at him. One cannot look at one's alter ego.

EPISODE I

Kitchen in the home of County Councillor S. B. O'DONNELL *who owns a general shop. As the curtain rises,* MADGE, *the housekeeper, enters from the scullery with a tray in her hands and finishes setting the table. She is a woman in her sixties. She walks as if her feet were precious. She pauses on her way past the shop door.*

MADGE: Gar! Your tea!

PUBLIC: [*Off*] Right!

[*She finishes setting the table and is about to go to the scullery door when* PUBLIC GAR *marches on stage. He is ecstatic with joy and excitement: tomorrow morning he leaves for Philadelphia*]

GAR: [*Singing*] 'Philadelphia, here I come, right back where I started from . . .' [*Breaks off and catches* MADGE] Come on, Madge! What about an old-time waltz!

MADGE: Agh, will you leave me alone.

[*He holds on to her and forces her to do a few steps as he sings in waltz time*]

PUBLIC: 'Where bowers of flowers bloom in the spring'—

MADGE: [*Struggling*] Stop it! Stop it! You brat you!

PUBLIC: Madge, you dance like an angel. [*Suddenly lets her go and springs away from her*] Oh, but you'd give a fella bad thoughts very quick!

MADGE: And the smell of fish of you, you dirty thing!

[*He grabs her again and puts his face up to hers, very confidentially*]

PUBLIC: Will you miss me?

MADGE: Let me on with my work!

PUBLIC: The truth!

MADGE: Agh, will you quit it, will you?

PUBLIC: I'll tickle you till you squeal for mercy.

MADGE: Please, Gar . . .

PUBLIC: [*Tickling her*] Will you miss me, I said?

MADGE: I will—I will—I will—I——

PUBLIC: That's better. Now tell me: What time is it?

MADGE: Agh, Gar——

PUBLIC: What time is it?

MADGE: [*Looking at clock*] Ten past seven.

PUBLIC: And what time do I knock off at?

MADGE: At seven.

PUBLIC: Which means that on my last day with him he got ten minutes overtime out of my hide. [*He releases* MADGE] Instead of saying to me: [*Grandly*] 'Gar, my son, since you are leaving me forever, you may have the entire day free,' what does he do? Lines up five packs of flour and says: [*In flat dreary tones*] 'Make them up into two-pound pokes.'

MADGE: He's losing a treasure, indeed!

PUBLIC: So d'you know what I said to him? I just drew myself up and looked him straight in the eye and said to him: 'Two-pound pokes it will be'—just like that.

MADGE: That flattened him.

[*She goes off to the scullery. He stands at the door and talks in to her*]

PUBLIC: And that wasn't it all. At six o'clock he remembered about the bloody pollock, and him in the middle of the Angelus [*Stands in imitation of the father: head bowed, hands on chest. In flat tones*] 'Behold-the-handmaid-of-the-Lord-Gut-and-salt-them-fish.' So by God I lashed so much salt on those bloody fish that any poor bugger that eats them will die of thirst. But when the corpses are strewn all over Ballybeg, where will I be? In the little old U.S.A.! Yip-eeeeee! [*He swings away from the scullery door and does a few exuberant steps as he sings*] 'Philadelphia, here I come, rightah backah where Ah started from—' [*He goes into his bedroom, flings himself down on his bed, rests his head on his hands, and looks at the ceiling. Sings alternate lines of 'Philadelphia'—first half—with* PRIVATE [*off*]]

PUBLIC: It's all over.

PRIVATE: [*Off, in echo-chamber voice*] And it's all about to begin. It's all over.

PUBLIC: And all about to begin.

PRIVATE: [*Now on*] Just think, Gar.

PUBLIC: Think . . .

PRIVATE: Think. . . . Up in that big bugger of a jet, with its snout pointing straight for the States, and its tail belching smoke over Ireland; and you sitting up at the front [PUBLIC *acts this*] with your competent fingers poised over the controls; and then away down below in the Atlantic you see a bloody bugger of an Irish boat out fishing for bloody pollock and——

[PUBLIC *nose-dives, engines screaming, machine guns stuttering*]

PUBLIC: Rat-tat-tat-tat-tat-tat-tat-tat-tat-tat.

PRIVATE: Abandon ship! Make for the life-boats! Send for Canon Mick O'Byrne!

[PUBLIC *gains altitude and nose-dives again*]

PUBLIC: Rat-tat-tat-tat-tat-tat-tat-tat-tat.

PRIVATE: To hell with women and children! Say an Act of Contrition!

PUBLIC: Yip-eeeee!

[*He finishes taking off the shop coat, rolls it into a bundle, and places it carefully on the floor*]

PRIVATE: It looks as if—I can't see very well from the distance—but it looks as if—yes!—yes!—the free is being taken by dashing Gar O'Donnell [PUBLIC *gets back from the coat, poises himself to kick it*] pride of the Ballybeg team. [*In commentator's hushed voice*] O'Donnell is now moving back, taking a slow, calculating look at the goal, I've never seen this boy in the brilliant form he's in today—absolute magic in his feet. He's now in position, running up, and——

[PUBLIC *kicks the shop coat into the air*]

PUBLIC: Ya-hoooo! [*Sings and gyrates at same time*] 'Philahdelph-yah, heah Ah come, rightah backah weah Ah stahted from, boom-boom-boom-boom——'

[*He breaks off suddenly when* PRIVATE *addresses him in sombre tones of a judge*]

PRIVATE: Gareth Mary O'Donnell.

[PUBLIC *springs to attention, salutes, and holds this absurd military stance. He is immediately inside his bedroom door, facing it*]

PUBLIC: Sir.

PRIVATE: You are full conscious of all the consequences of your decision?

PUBLIC: Yessir.

PRIVATE: Of leaving the country of your birth, the land of the curlew and the snipe, the Aran sweater and the Irish Sweepstakes?

PUBLIC: [*With fitting hesitation*] I-I-I-I have considered all these, Sir.

PRIVATE: Of going to a profane, irreligious, pagan country of gross materialism?

PUBLIC: I am fully sensitive to this, Sir.

PRIVATE: Where the devil himself holds sway, and lust—abhorrent lust—is everywhere indulged in shamelessly?

[PUBLIC *winks extravagantly and nudges an imaginary man beside him*]

PUBLIC: Who are you tellin'? [*Poker-stiff again*] Shamelessly, Sir, shamelessly.

[MADGE *has entered from the scullery, carrying an old suitcase and a bundle of clothes*]

PRIVATE: And yet you persist in exposing yourself to these frightful dangers?

PUBLIC: I would submit, Sir, that these stories are slightly exaggerated, Sir. For every door that opens——[MADGE *opens the bedroom door*]

MADGE: Oh! You put the heart across me there! Get out of my road, will you, and quit eejiting about!

PUBLIC: Madge, you're an aul duck.

MADGE: Aye, so. There's the case. And there's a piece of rope for I see the clasp's all rusted. And there's your shirts and your winter vests and your heavy socks. And you'll need to air them shirts before you—Don't put them smelly hands on them!

PUBLIC: Sorry!

MADGE: See that they're well aired before you put them on. He's said nothing since, I suppose?

PUBLIC: Not a word.

PRIVATE: The bugger.

MADGE: But he hasn't paid you your week's wages?

PUBLIC: £3 15s—that'll carry me far.

MADGE: He'll have something to say then, you'll see. And maybe he'll slip you a couple of extra pounds.

PUBLIC: Whether he says good-bye to me or not, or whether he slips me a few miserable quid or not, it's a matter of total indifference to me, Madge.

MADGE: Aye, so. Your tea's on the table—but that's a matter of total indifference to me.

PUBLIC: Give me time to wash, will you?

MADGE: And another thing: just because he doesn't say much doesn't mean that he hasn't feelings like the rest of us.

PUBLIC: Say much? He's said nothing!

MADGE: He said nothing either when your mother died. It must have been near daybreak when he got to sleep last night. I could hear his bed creaking.

PUBLIC: Well to hell with him——

MADGE: [Leaving] Don't come into your tea smelling like a lobster-pot.

PUBLIC: If he wants to speak to me he knows where to find me! But I'm damned if I'm going to speak to him first!

[MADGE goes off to the scullery]

[Calling after her] And you can tell him I said that if you like!

PRIVATE: What the hell do you care about him. Screwballs! Skinflint! Skittery Face! You're free of him and his stinking bloody shop. And tomorrow morning, boy, when that little ole plane gets up into the skies, you'll stick your head out the window [PUBLIC acts this] and spit down on the lot of them!

[S.B. appears at the shop door. He is in his late sixties. Wears a hat, a good dark suit, collar and tie, black apron. S. B. O'DONNELL is a responsible, respectable citizen] s.b.: Gar!

[PUBLIC *reacts instinctively.* PRIVATE *keeps calm*]

PRIVATE: Let the bugger call.

s.b.: [*Louder*] Gar!

[*Instinct is stronger than reason:* PUBLIC *rushes to his door and opens it. But as soon as he opens it and looks out at his father he assumes in speech and gesture a surly, taciturn gruffness. He always behaves in this way when he is in his father's company*]

PUBLIC: Aye?

s.b.: How many coils of barbed-wire came in on the mail-van this evening?

PUBLIC: Two. Or was it three?

s.b.: That's what I'm asking you. It was you that carried them into the yard.

PUBLIC: There were two—no, no, no, three—yes, three—or maybe it was . . . was it two?

s.b.: Agh!

[s.b. *retires to the shop.* PUBLIC *and* PRIVATE *come back into the bedroom*]

PRIVATE: What sort of a stupid bugger are you? Think, man! You went out and stood yarning to Joe the Post; then you carried one coil into the yard and came out with the sack of spuds for the parochial; then you carried in the second coil . . . and put it in the corner . . . and came out again to the van . . . and. . . . [PUBLIC *skips into the air*] Ah, what the hell odds! That's his headache, old Nicodemus! After to-morrow a bloody roll of barbed-wire will be a mere bagatelle to you. [*In cowboy accent*] Yeah, man. You see tham thar plains stretchin' 's far th'eye can see, man? Well, tham thar plains belongs to Garry the Kid. An' Garry the Kid he don't go in for none of your fancy fencin'. No siree. [*His eye lights on the fresh laundry* MADGE *brought in*] And what'll you wear on the plane tomorrow, old rooster, eh?

[PUBLIC *picks up a clean shirt, holds it to his chest, and surveys himself in the small mirror above his wash-hand-basin*]

Pretty smart, eh?

PUBLIC: Pretty smart.

PRIVATE: Pretty sharp?

PUBLIC: Pretty sharp.

PRIVATE: Pretty ou-la-la?

PUBLIC: Mais oui.

PRIVATE: And not a bad looker, if I may say so.

PUBLIC: You may. You may.

PRIVATE: [*In heavy U.S. accent*] I'm Patrick Palinakis, president of the biggest chain of biggest hotels in the world. We're glad to have you, Mr. O'Donnell.

PUBLIC: [*Sweet, demure*] And I'm glad to be here, Sir.

PRIVATE: Handsomely said, young man. I hope you'll be happy with us and work hard and one day maybe you'll be president of the biggest chain of biggest hotels in the world.

PUBLIC: That's my ambition, Sir.

PRIVATE: You are twenty-five years of age, Mr. O'Donnell?

PUBLIC: Correct.

PRIVATE: And you spent one year at University College Dublin?

PUBLIC: Yes, Sir.

PRIVATE: Would you care to tell me why you abandoned your academic career, Mr. O'Donnell?

PUBLIC: [*With disarming simplicity*] Well, just before I sat my First Arts exam, Sir, I did an old Irish *turas*, or pilgrimage, where I spent several nights in devout prayer, Sir.

PRIVATE: St. Patrick's Pilgrimage—on Lough——?

PUBLIC: St. Harold's Cross, Sir. And it was there that I came to realize that a life of scholarship was not for me. So I returned to my father's business.

PRIVATE: Yeah. You mentioned that your father was a businessman. What's his line?

PUBLIC: Well, Sir, he has—what you would call—his finger in many pies—retail mostly—general dry goods—assorted patent drugs—hardware—ah—ah—dehydrated fish—men's king-size hose —snuffs from the exotic East . . . of Donegal—a confection for gourmets, known as Peggy's Leg—weedkiller—[*Suddenly breaking off: in his normal accent: rolling on the bed*] Yahoooooo! It is now sixteen or seventeen years since I saw the Queen of France, then the Dauphiness, at Versailles——

PRIVATE: Let's git packin', boy. Let's git that li'l ole saddle bag opened and let's git packin'. But first let's have a li'l ole music on the li'l ole phonograph. Yeah man. You bet. Ah reckon. Yessir.

> [PUBLIC *puts a record on the player: First Movement, Mendelssohn's Violin Concerto.* PUBLIC *is preening himself before his performance, and while he is flexing his fingers and adjusting his bow-tie,* PRIVATE *announces in the reverential tones of a radio announcer*]

The main item in tonight's concert is the first movement of the Violin Concerto in E Minor, Opus 64, by Jacob Ludwig Felix Mendelssohn. The orchestra is conducted by Gareth O'Donnell and the soloist is the Ballybeg half-back, Gareth O'Donnell. Music critics throughout the world claim that O'Donnell's simultaneous wielding of baton and bow is the greatest thing since Leather Ass died. Mendelssohn's Violin Concerto, 3rd movement.

> [PRIVATE *sits demurely on the chair.* PUBLIC *clears his throat. Now* PUBLIC *plays the violin, conducts, plays the violin, conducts, etc., etc. This keeps up for some time. Then* PRIVATE *rises from his chair*]

Agh, come on, come on, come on! Less aul foolin'. To work, old rooster, to work. [PUBLIC *stops. Turns player down low and changes from the first to the second movement. Takes a look at the case* MADGE *brought in*] Ah, hell, how can any bloody bugger head into a jet plane with aul cardboard rubbish like that! [PUBLIC *examines the surface*] Damnit, maybe you could give it a lick of paint! Or wash it! [PUBLIC *spits on the lid and rubs it with his finger*] God, you'll rub a hole in the damn thing if you're not careful! Maybe aul Screwballs'll slip you a fiver tonight and you can get a new one in Dublin.

PUBLIC: What a hope!

[PUBLIC *opens the case and sniffs the inside*]

PRIVATE: Oh! Stinks of cat's pee!

[PUBLIC *lifts out a sheet of faded newspaper*]

PUBLIC: [*Reads*] The *Clarion*—1st January 1937.

PRIVATE: Precious medieval manuscript . . . my God, was it? . . . By God it was—the day they were married—and it [*The case*] hasn't been opened since their honeymoon . . . she and old Screwballs off on a side-car to Bundoran for three days. . . .

PUBLIC: O God, the Creator and Redeemer of all the faithful give to the soul of Maire, my mother, the remission of all her sins, that she may obtain. . . .

PRIVATE: She was small, Madge says, and wild, and young, Madge says, from a place called Bailtefree beyond the mountains; and her eyes were bright, and her hair was loose, and she carried her shoes under her arm until she came to the edge of the village, Madge says, and then she put them on. . . .

PUBLIC: Eternal rest grant unto her, O Lord, and let perpetual light shine. . . .

PRIVATE: She was nineteen and he was forty, and he owned a shop, and he wore a soft hat, and she thought he was the grandest gentleman that ever lived, Madge says; and he—he couldn't take his eyes off her, Madge says. . . .

PUBLIC: O God, O God the Creator and Redeemer. . . .

PRIVATE: And sometime in that first year, when she was pregnant with you, laddybuck, the other young girls from Bailtefree would call in here to dress up on their way to a dance, Madge says, and her face would light up too, Madge says. . . . [PUBLIC *puts the newspaper carefully inside the folds of a shirt*] . . . And he must have known, old Screwballs, he must have known, Madge says, for many a night he must have heard her crying herself to sleep . . . and maybe it was good of God to take her away three days after you were born. . . . [*Suddenly boisterous*] Damn you, anyhow, for a bloody stupid bastard! It is now sixteen or seventeen years since I saw the Queen of France, then the Dauphiness, at Versailles! And to hell with that bloody mushy fiddler!

[PUBLIC *goes quickly to the record-player and sings boisterously as he goes*]

PUBLIC: 'Philadelphia, here I come——'

PRIVATE: Watch yourself, nut-head. If your let yourself slip that way, you might find that——

PUBLIC: '—right back where I started from.'

[PUBLIC *has taken off the Mendelssohn and is now searching for another*]

PRIVATE: Something lively! Something bloody animal! A bit of aul thumpety-thump! [PUBLIC *puts on the record*] An' you jist keep atalkin' to you'self all the time, Mistah, 'cos once you stop atalkin' to you'self ah reckon then you jist begin to think kinda crazy things—[*The record begins any lively piece of Ceilidh Band music*] Ahhhhh!

PUBLIC: Yipeeeeeeeee!

[PUBLIC *dances up and down the length of his bedroom. Occasionally he leaps high into the air or does a neat bit of foot-work. Occasionally he lilts. Occasionally he talks to different people he meets on the dance floor*]

Righ-too-del-loo-del-oo-del-oo-del-oo-del-oo-del-ah,
Rum-ta-del-ah-del-ah-del-agh-del-ah-del-ah-del-agh.

Hell of a crowd here the night, eh? Yah-ho! Man, you're looking powerful! Great!

[PRIVATE *sits on the chair and watches. When he speaks his voice is soft.* PUBLIC *pretends not to hear him*]

PRIVATE: Remember—that was Katie's tune. You needn't pretend you have forgotten. And it reminds you of the night the two of you made all the plans, and you thought your heart would burst with happiness.

PUBLIC: [*Louder*] Tigh-righ-tigh-righ-scal-del-de-da-del-ah, Come on! A dirty big swing! Yaaaaaaaaaaah!

PRIVATE: [*Quietly, rapidly insisting*] Are you going to take her photograph to the States with you? When are you going to say good-bye to her? Will you write to her? Will you send her cards and photographs? You loved her once, old rooster; you wanted so much to marry her that it was a bloody sickness. Tell me, randy boy; tell me the truth: have you got over that sickness? Do you still love her? Do you still lust after her? Well, do you? Do you? Do you?

PUBLIC: Bugger!

[PUBLIC *suddenly stops dancing, switches—almost knocks —off the record-player, pulls a wallet out of his hip pocket and produces a snap. He sits and looks at it*]

PRIVATE: Shhhhhhhhhhhhh. . . .

PUBLIC: [*Softly*] Kate . . . sweet Katie Doogan . . . my darling Kathy Doogan. . . .

PRIVATE: [*In same soft tone*] Aul bitch. [*Loudly*] Rotten aul snobby bitch! Just like her stinking rotten father and mother —a bugger and a buggeress—a buggeroo and a buggerette!

PUBLIC: No, no; my fault—all my fault——

PRIVATE: [*Remembering and recalling tauntingly*] By God, that was a night, boy, eh? By God, you made a right bloody cow's ass of yourself. [PUBLIC *goes off right*] Remember—when was it?—ten months ago?—you had just come back from a walk out the Mill Road, and the pair of you had the whole thing planned: engaged at Christmas, married at Easter, and fourteen of a family—seven boys and seven girls. Cripes, you make me laugh! You bloody-well make me die laughing. You were going to 'develop' the hardware lines and she was going to take charge of the 'drapery!' The drapery! The fishy socks and the shoebox of cotton spools and rusted needles! And you—you were to ask Screwballs for a rise in pay—'in view of your increased responsibilities!' And you were so far gone that night, laddybuck,—[PUBLIC *and* KATE *enter from the left and walk very slowly across the front of the stage. They stop and kiss. Then they move on again*]—So bloody-well astray in the head with 'love' that you went and blabbed about your secret egg deals that nobody knew anything about—not even Madge! Stupid bloody get! O my God, how you stick yourself I'll never know!

PUBLIC: Kate—Kathy—I'm mad about you! I'll never last till Easter! I'll—I'll—I'll bloody-well burst! [*He catches her again and kisses her*]

PRIVATE: Steady, boy, steady. You know what the Canon says: long passionate kisses in lonely places. . . .

PUBLIC: Our daughters'll all be gentle and frail and silly, like you; and our sons—they'll be thick bloody louts, sexy goats, like me, and by God I'll beat the tar out of them!

KATE: But £3 15s Gar! We could never live on that.

PUBLIC: [*Kissing her hair*] Mmmm.

KATE: Gar! Listen! Be sensible.

PUBLIC: Mmm?

KATE: How will we *live?*

PRIVATE: [*Imitating*] 'How will we *live?*'

PUBLIC: Like lords—free house, free light, free fuel, free groceries! And every night at seven when we close—except Saturday; he stays open till damn near midnight on Saturdays, making out bloody bills; and sure God and the world knows that sending out bills here is as hopeless as peeing against the wind. . . .

KATE: Gar! No matter what you say we just couldn't live on that much money. It—it's not possible. We'll need to have more security than that.

PUBLIC: Maybe he'll die—tonight—of galloping consumption!

KATE: Gar. . . .

PUBLIC: What's troubling you?

[*He tries to kiss her again and she avoids him*]

KATE: Please. This is serious.

PRIVATE: 'Please. This is serious.'

PUBLIC: [*Irritably*] What is it?

KATE: You'll have to see about getting more money.

PUBLIC: Of course I'll see about getting more money! Haven't I
told you I'm going to ask for a rise?

KATE: But will he——?

PUBLIC: I'll get it; don't you worry; I'll get it. Besides: [*With
dignity*] I have a—a-a source of income that he knows nothing
about—that nobody knows nothing about—knows anything
about.

KATE: [*With joy*] Investments? Like Daddy?

PUBLIC: Well . . . sort of . . . [*Quickly*] You know when I go
round the country every Tuesday and Thursday in the lorry?

KATE: Yes?

PUBLIC: Well, I buy eggs direct from the farms and sell them
privately to McLaughlin's Hotel—[*Winks*]—for a handsome
profit—[*Quickly*]—but he knows nothing about it.

KATE: And how much do you make?

PUBLIC: It varies—depending on the time of year.

KATE: Roughly.

PUBLIC: Oh, anything from 12s 6d to £1.

KATE: Every Tuesday and Thursday?

PUBLIC: Every month. [*Grabs her again*] God, Kate, I can't
even wait till Christmas!

KATE: Shhhhh.

PUBLIC: But I can't. We'll have to get married sooner—next
month—next week——

PRIVATE: Steady, steady. . . .

PUBLIC: Kate . . . my sweet Katie . . . my darling Kathy. . . .

[*They kiss. Suddenly* KATE *breaks off. Her voice is urgent*]

KATE: We'll go now, rightaway, and tell them.

PUBLIC: Who?

KATE: Mammy and Daddy. They're at home tonight. [*She catches his arm and pulls him towards the left*] Come on. Quickly. Now, Gar, now.

PUBLIC: [*Adjusting his tie*] God, Kathy, I'm in no—look at the shoes—the trousers——

KATE: What matter. It must be now, Gar, now!

PUBLIC: What—what—what'll I say?

KATE: That you want their permission to marry me next week.

PUBLIC: God, they'll wipe the bloody floor with me!

KATE: Gar!

[*She kisses him passionately, quickly, then breaks off and goes. Stage right, now lit. A room in* DOOGAN's *house*]

PUBLIC: God, my legs are trembling! Kathy. . . .

KATE: Anybody at home? Mammy! Daddy!

[PUBLIC *hesitates before entering* DOOGAN's *house.* PRIVATE *is at his elbow, prompting him desperately*]

PRIVATE: Mr. Doogan . . . —Senator Doogan—I want to ask your permission. . . . O my God! . . .

KATE: Yo-ho!

PRIVATE: Mrs. Doogan, Kate and I have to get married rightaway —Cripes, no!——

KATE: Where is everybody! Yo-ho-yo-ho!

PRIVATE: If the boys could see you now!

[KATE *comes back to him, gives him a quick kiss on the cheek*]

KATE: Don't look so miserable. Here . . . [*Fixes his tie*]

PUBLIC: Kathy, maybe we should wait until—until—until next Sunday——

KATE: [*Earnestly*] Remember, it's up to you, entirely up to you.

DOOGAN: [*Off*] That you, Kate?

KATE: [*Rapidly*] You have £20 a week and £5,000 in the bank and your father's about to retire. [*Turning and smiling at* DOOGAN—*Lawyer, Senator, middle forties—who has now entered*] Just Gar and I, Daddy.

DOOGAN: Hello, Gareth. You're a stranger.

PRIVATE: Speak, you dummy you!

KATE: [*Filling in*] Where's Mammy?

DOOGAN: She's watching TV. [*To* GAR] And how are things with you, Gareth?

PUBLIC: Mr. Doogan, I want——

PRIVATE: Go on.

PUBLIC: I won't be staying long.

DOOGAN: [*To* KATE] Francis arrived when you were out. Took a few days off and decided to come north.

PRIVATE: Cripes!

KATE: He—he's—he's here—now?

DOOGAN: Inside with your mother. Ask them to join us, will you?

[KATE *gives* PUBLIC *a last significant look*]

KATE: You talk to Daddy, Gar.

PRIVATE: God, I will, I will.

[KATE *goes off right*]

DOOGAN: You've met Francis King, haven't you, Gareth?

PUBLIC: Yes—yes——

PRIVATE: King of the bloody fairies!

DOOGAN: We don't want to raise Kate's hopes unduly, but strictly between ourselves there's a good chance that he'll get the new dispensary job here.

PUBLIC: Kate's hopes?

DOOGAN: Didn't she tell you? No, I can see she didn't. Of course there's nothing official yet; not even what you might call an understanding. But if this post does fall into his lap, well, her mother and I . . . let's say we're living in hope. A fine boy, Francis; and we've known the Kings, oh, since away back. As a matter of fact his father and I were class-fellows at school. . . .

[DOOGAN *goes on and on. We catch an occasional word. Meantime* PRIVATE *has moved up to* PUBLIC's *elbow*]

PRIVATE: Cripes, man!

DOOGAN: . . . and then later at university when he did medicine and I did law, we knocked about quite a bit. . . .

PRIVATE: O God, the aul bitch! Cripes, you look a right fool standing there—the father of fourteen children!—Get out, you eejit you! Get out! Get out quick before the others come in and die laughing at you! And all the time she must have known—the aul bitch!—And you promised to give her breakfast in bed every morning! And you told her about the egg money!

DOOGAN: . . . your father, Gareth?

PRIVATE: He's talking to you, thick-skull.

PUBLIC: What—what—what's that?

DOOGAN: Your father—how is he?

PUBLIC: Oh he—he—he's grand, thanks.

PRIVATE: Get out! Get out!

PUBLIC: Look Mr. Doogan, if you'll excuse me, I think I'd better move on——

DOOGAN: Aren't you waiting for supper? The others will be along in a moment for——

PUBLIC: No, I must run. I've got to make up half-a-hundredweight of sugar bags.

PRIVATE: Brilliant!

PUBLIC: Say good-bye to——

DOOGAN: Certainly—certainly. Oh, Gareth—[PUBLIC *pauses. Awkwardly, with sincerity*] Kate is our only child, Gareth, and her happiness is all that is important to us——

PRIVATE: [*Sings*] 'Give the woman in the bed more porter——'

DOOGAN: What I'm trying to say is that any decision she makes will be her own—

PRIVATE: '—Give the man beside her water, Give the woman in the bed more porter,——'

DOOGAN: Just in case you should think that her mother or I were . . . in case you might have the idea. . . .

PUBLIC: [*Rapidly*] Good night, Mr. Doogan.

[PUBLIC *rushes off*]

DOOGAN: Good-bye. . . . Gareth.

[DOOGAN *stands lighting his pipe*]

KATE: [*Enters down right of* DOOGAN *and sees that* GAR *is no longer there*] Where's Gar?

DOOGAN: He didn't seem anxious to stay.

KATE: But didn't he—did he——?

DOOGAN: No, he didn't. [*He crosses* KATE *to exit down right as light fades to blackout on* DOOGAN's *room.* PUBLIC *and* PRIVATE *move back to the bedroom where* PUBLIC *is putting away the photograph and begins washing*]

PRIVATE: [*Wearily*] Mrs. Doctor Francis King. September 8th. In harvest sunshine. Red carpet and white lilies and Sean Horgan singing 'Bless This House'—and him whipped off to Sligo jail two days later for stealing turf. Honeymoon in Mallorca and you couldn't have afforded to take her to Malahide. By God, Gar, aul sod, it was a sore hoke on the aul prestige, eh? Between ourselves, aul son, in the privacy of the bedroom, between you and me and the wall, as the fella says, has it left a deep scar on the aul skitter of a soul, eh? What I mean to say like, you took it sort of bad, between you and me and the wall, as the fella says——

PUBLIC: [*Sings*] 'Philadelphia, here I come, right back——'

PRIVATE: But then there's more fish in the sea, as the fella says, and they're all the same when they're upside down; and between you and me and the wall, the first thing you would have had to do would have been to give the boot to Daddy Senator. And I'm thinking, Gar, aul rooster, that wouldn't have made you his pet son-in-law. Mister Fair-play Lawyer Senator Doogan—'her happiness is all that is important to us!' You know, of course, that he carries one of those wee black cards in the inside pocket of his jacket, privately printed for him: 'I am a Catholic. In case of accident send for a bishop.' And you know, too, that in his spare time he travels for maternity corsets; and that he's a double spy for the Knights and the Masons; and that he takes pornographic photographs of Mrs. D. and sends them anonymously to reverend mothers. And when you think of a bugger like that, you want to get down on your knees and thank God for aul Screwballs. [*Imitating his father's slow speech*] So you're going to America in the morning, son?

[PUBLIC *carries on with his washing and dressing and at the same time does this dialogue*]

PUBLIC: Yes, Father.

PRIVATE: Nothing like it to broaden the mind. Man, how I'd love to travel. But there's some it doesn't agree with—like me, there.

PUBLIC: In what way, Father?

PRIVATE: The bowels, son. Let me move an inch from the house here—and they stall.

PUBLIC: No!

PRIVATE: Like the time I went to Lough Derg, away back in '35. Not a budge. The bare feet were nothing to the agonies I went through. I was bound up for two full weeks afterwards.

PUBLIC: It taught you a lesson.

PRIVATE: Didn't it just? Now I wouldn't even think of travelling.

PUBLIC: Anchored by the ass.

PRIVATE: Bound by the bowels.

PUBLIC: Tethered by the toilet. Tragic.

[PUBLIC *has now finished dressing. He surveys himself in the mirror*]

PRIVATE: Not bad. Not bad at all. And well preserved for a father of fourteen children.

PUBLIC: [*In absurd Hollywood style*] Hi, gorgeous! You live in my block?

PRIVATE: [*matching the accent*] Yeah, big handsome boy. Sure do.

PUBLIC: Mind if I walk you past the incinerator, to the elevator?

PRIVATE: You're welcome, slick operator.

[PUBLIC *is facing the door of his bedroom.* MADGE *enters the kitchen from the scullery*]

PUBLIC: What'ya say, li'l chick, you and me—you know—I'll spell it out for ya ifya like. [*Winks, and clicks his tongue*]

PRIVATE: You say the cutest things, big handsome boy!

PUBLIC: A malted milk at the corner drug-store?

PRIVATE: Wow!

PUBLIC: A movie at the downtown drive-in?

PRIVATE: Wow-wow!

PUBLIC: Two hamburgers, two cokes, two slices of blueberry pie?

PRIVATE: Wow-wow-wow.

PUBLIC: And then in my apartment——

[MADGE *enters the bedroom*]

MADGE: Gee, Mary, and Jay! Will you quit them antics!

PUBLIC: Well, you should knock anyway before you enter a man's room!

MADGE: Man! I bathed you every Saturday night till you were a big lout of fourteen! Your tea's cold waiting.

[*She goes into the kitchen.* PUBLIC *and* PRIVATE *follow her*]

PUBLIC: How was I to know that?

MADGE: Amn't I hoarse calling you? Dear, but you're in for a cooling when you go across! [*As she passes through the shop door on way to scullery*] Boss!

PRIVATE: [*in imitation*] 'Boss!'

MADGE: [*She pauses at the scullery door. With shy delight*] I forgot to tell you. Nelly had a wee baby this morning.

PUBLIC: Go on!

MADGE: A wee girl. 7 lb. 4 oz.

PUBLIC: How many's that you have now?

MADGE: Four grandnieces and three grandnephews. [*Pause*] And they're going to call this one Madge—at least so she *says*.

PUBLIC: I'll send it a—a—a—an elephant out of my first wages! An elephant for wee Madge!

MADGE: I had a feeling it would be a wee girl this time. Maybe I'll take a run over on Sunday and square the place up for her. She could do with some help, with seven of them.

PUBLIC: You're a brick, Madge.

MADGE: Aye, so. [*As she goes to scullery*] Wee Madge, maybe.
. . .

[PUBLIC *sits at the table.* PRIVATE *leans against the wall beside him*]

PRIVATE: And now what are you sad about? Just because she lives for those Mulhern children, and gives them whatever few half-pence she has? Madge, Madge, I think I love you more than any of them. Give me a piece of your courage, Madge.

[S.B. *enters from the shop and goes through his nightly routine. He hangs up the shop keys. He looks at his pocket watch and checks its time with the clock on the wall. He takes off his apron, folds it carefully, and leaves it on the back of his chair. Then he sits down to eat. During all these ponderous jobs* PRIVATE *keeps up the following chatter:*]

And here comes your pleasure, your little ray of sunshine. Ladies and Gentlemen, I give you—the one and only—the inimitable—the irrepressible—the irresistible—County Councillor —S—B—O'Donnell! [*Trumpet—hummed—fanfare. Continues in the smooth, unctuous tones of the commentator at a mannequin parade*] And this time Marie Celeste is wearing a cheeky little head-dress by Pamela of Park Avenue, eminently suitable for cocktail parties, morning coffee, or just casual shopping. It is of brown Viennese felt, and contrasts boldly with the attractive beach ensemble, created by Simon. The pert little apron is detachable—[S.B. *removes apron*]—thank you, Marie Celeste—and underneath we have the tapered Italian-line slacks in ocelot. I would draw your attention to the large collar stud which is highly decorative and can be purchased separately at our boutique. We call this seductive outfit 'Indiscretion.' It can be worn six days a week, in or out of bed. [*In polite tone*] Have a seat Screwballs. [S.B. *sits down at the table*] Thank you. Remove the hat. [S.B. *takes off the hat to say grace. He blesses himself*] On again. [*Hat on*] Perfectly trained; the most obedient father I ever had. And now for our nightly lesson in the English language. Repeat slowly after me: Another day over.

S.B.: Another day over.

PRIVATE: Good. Next phrase. I suppose we can't complain.

S.B.: I suppose we can't complain.

PRIVATE: Not bad. Now for a little free conversation. But no obscenities, Father dear; the child is only twenty-five. [S.B. *eats in silence. Pause*] Well, come on, come on! Where's that old rapier wit of yours, the toast of the Ballybeg coffee houses?

S.B.: Did you set the rat-trap in the store?

PUBLIC: Aye.

PRIVATE: [*Hysterically*] Isn't he a riot! Oh my God, that father of yours just kills me! But wait—wait—shhh-shhh——

S.B.: I didn't find as many about the year.

PRIVATE: Oooooh God! Priceless! Beautiful! Delightful! 'I didn't find as many about the year!' Did you ever hear the beat of that? Wonderful! But isn't he in form tonight? But isn't he? You know, it's not every night that jewels like that, pearls of wisdom on rodent reproduction, drop from those lips! But hold it—hold it——!

[S.B. *takes out a handkerchief, removes his teeth, wraps them in the handkerchief, and puts them in his pocket*]

PRIVATE: [*Exhales with satisfaction*] Ah! That's what we were waiting for; complete informality; total relaxation between intimates. Now we can carry on. Screwballs. [*Pause*] I'm addressing you, Screwballs.

[S.B. *clears his throat*]

Thank you. [*As the following speech goes on all trace of humour fades from* PRIVATE's *voice. He becomes more and more intense and it is with an effort that he keeps his voice under control*] Screwballs, we've eaten together like this for the past twenty-odd years, and never once in all that time have you made as much as one unpredictable remark. Now, even though you refuse to acknowledge the fact, Screwballs, I'm leaving you forever. I'm going to Philadelphia, to work in an hotel. And you know why I'm going, Screwballs, don't you. Because I'm twenty-five, and you treat me as if I were five—I can't order even a dozen loaves without getting your permission. Because you pay me less than you pay Madge. But worse, far worse than that, Screwballs, because—*we embarrass one another*. If one of us were to say, 'You're looking tired' or 'That's a bad cough you have,' the other would fall over backways with embarrassment. So tonight d'you know what I want you to do? I want you to make one unpredictable remark, and even though I'll still be on that plane tomorrow morning, I'll have doubts: Maybe I should have stuck it out; maybe the old codger did have feelings; maybe I have maligned the old bastard. So now, Screwballs, say . . . [*Thinks*] . . . 'Once upon a time a rainbow ended in our garden' . . . say, 'I like to walk across the White Strand when there's a misty rain falling' . . . say, 'Gar, son—' say, 'Gar, you bugger you, why don't you stick it out here with me for it's not such a bad aul bugger of a place.' Go on. Say it! Say it! Say it!

S.B.: True enough. . . .

PUBLIC: [*Almost inaudibly*] Aye?

S.B.: I didn't find as many about the year.

PUBLIC: [*Roars*] Madge! Madge!

S.B.: No need to roar like that.

PUBLIC: The—the—the—bread's done. We need more bread.

S.B.: You know where it's kept, don't you?

[MADGE *at scullery door*]

PUBLIC: Can we have more bread, Madge . . . please. . . .

MADGE: Huh! Pity you lost the power of your legs.

PUBLIC: I'll—I'll get it myself—it doesn't matter. . . .

[MADGE *comes over to the table and takes the plate from* PUBLIC. *She gives* S.B. *a hard look*]

MADGE: [*Irony*] The chatting in this place would deafen a body. Won't the house be quiet soon enough—long enough?

[*She shuffles off with the plate*]

PRIVATE: Tick-tock-tick-tock-tick-tock. It is now sixteen or seventeen years since I saw the Queen of France, then the Dauphiness, at Versailles. . . . Go on! What's the next line?

[S.B. *produces a roll of money from his pocket and puts it on the table*] s.b.: I suppose you'll be looking for your pay.

public: I earned it.

s.b.: I'm not saying you didn't. It's all there—you needn't count it.

public: I didn't say I was going to count it, did I?

private: Tick-tock-tick-tock-tick-tock——

public: More tea?

s.b.: Sure you know I never take a second cup.

private: [Imitating] 'Sure you know I never take a second cup.' [Brittle and bright again] Okay, okay, okay, it's better this way, Screwballs, isn't it? You can't teach new tricks to two old dogs like us. In the meantime there's a little matter I'd like to discuss with you, Screwballs . . . [With exaggerated embarrassment] it's—it's nothing really . . . it's just something I'm rather hesitant to bring up, but I'm advised by the very best Church authorities that you'll be only too glad to discuss it with your son. Admittedly we're both a bit late in attacking the issue now, but—ha—you see——

[MADGE enters with a plate of bread. PRIVATE makes a very obvious show of changing the subject]

Oh marvellous weather—truly wonderful for the time of year— a real heat wave—all things considered——

MADGE: A body couldn't get a word in edgeways with you two!

PRIVATE: Madge has such a keen sense of humour, don't you agree? I love people with a sense of humour, don't you? It's the first thing I look for in a person. I seize them by the throat and say to them, 'Have you a sense of humour?' And then, if they have, I feel—I feel at home with them immediately. . . . But where was I? Oh, yes—our little talk—I'm beginning to wonder, Screwballs—I suspect—I'm afraid—[In a rush, ashamed]—I think I'm a sex-maniac! [Throws his hands up] Please, please don't cry, Screwballs; please don't say anything; and above all please don't stop eating. Just—just let me talk a bit more—let me communicate with someone—that's what they all advise—communicate—pour out your pent-up feelings into a sympathetic ear. So all I ask for the moment is that you listen—just listen to me. As I said, I suspect that—that I'm an s.-m. [*Rapidly, in self-defence*] But I'm not the only one, Screwballs; oh indeed I am not; and all the boys around—some of them are far worse than I am. [*As if he had been asked the question*] Why? Why do I think we're all s.-m.s? Well, because none of us is married. Because we're never done boasting about the number of hot courts we know—and the point is we're all virgins. Because——

[*Voices off*]

Shhhh! Someone's coming. Not a word to anybody. This is our secret. Scouts' honour.

[*Enter* MASTER BOYLE *from the scullery. He is around sixty, white-haired, handsome, defiant. He is shabbily dressed; his eyes, head, hands, arms are constantly moving —he sits for a moment and rises again—he puts his hands in his pocket and takes them out again—his eyes roam around the room but see nothing.* S.B. *is barely courteous to him*]

S.B.: Oh, good night, Master Boyle. How are you doing?

PUBLIC: Master.

BOYLE: Sean. Gar. No, no, don't stir. I only dropped in for a second.

PUBLIC: Sit over and join us.

BOYLE: No. I'm not stopping.

S.B.: Here's a seat for you. I was about to go out to the shop anyway to square up a bit.

BOYLE: Don't let me hold you back.

S.B.: I'll be in again before you leave, Master.

BOYLE: If you have work to do. . . .

PRIVATE: [*To* S.B.] Ignorant bastard! [*Looking at Boyle*] On his way to the pub! God, but he's a sorry wreck too, arrogant and pathetic. And yet whatever it is about you. . . .

BOYLE: Tomorrow morning, isn't it?

PUBLIC: Quarter past seven. I'm getting the mail van the length of Strabane.

BOYLE: You're doing the right thing, of course. You'll never regret it. I gather it's a vast restless place that doesn't give a curse about the past; and that's the way things should be. Impermanence and anonymity—it offers great attractions. You've heard about the latest to-do?

PUBLIC: Another row with the Canon? I really hadn't heard——

BOYLE: But the point is he can't sack me! The organization's behind me and he can't budge me. Still, it's a . . . a bitter victory to hold on to a job when your manager wants rid of you.

PUBLIC: Sure everybody knows the kind of the Canon, Master.

BOYLE: I didn't tell you, did I, that I may be going out there myself?

PRIVATE: Poor bastard.

BOYLE: I've been offered a big post in Boston, head of education in a reputable university there. They've given me three months to think it over. What are you going to do?

PUBLIC: Work in an hotel.

BOYLE: You have a job waiting for you?

PUBLIC: In Philadelphia.

BOYLE: You'll do all right. You're young and strong and of average intelligence.

PRIVATE: Good old Boyle. Get the dig in.

BOYLE: Yes, it was as ugly and as squalid as all the other to-dos—before the whole school—the priest and the teacher—dedicated moulders of the mind. You're going to stay with friends?

PUBLIC: With Aunt Lizzy.

BOYLE: Of course.

PRIVATE: Go on. Try him.

PUBLIC: You knew her, didn't you, Master?

BOYLE: Yes, I knew all the Gallagher girls: Lizzy, Una, Rose, Agnes. . . .

PRIVATE: And Maire, my mother, did you love her?

BOYLE: A long, long time ago . . . in the past. . . . He comes in to see your father every night, doesn't he?

PUBLIC: The Canon? Oh, it's usually much later than this——

BOYLE: I think so much about him that—ha—I feel a peculiar attachment for him. Funny, isn't it? Do you remember the Christmas you sent me the packet of cigarettes? And the day you brought me a pot of jam to the digs? It was you, wasn't it?

PRIVATE: Poor Boyle——

BOYLE: All children are born with generosity. Three months they gave me to make up my mind.

PUBLIC: I remember very well——

BOYLE: By the way—[*Producing a small book*] a—little something to remind you of your old teacher—my poems——

PUBLIC: Thank you very much.

BOYLE: I had them printed privately last month. Some of them are a bit mawkish but you'll not notice any distinction.

PUBLIC: I'm very grateful, Master.

BOYLE: I'm not going to give you advice, Gar. Is that clock right? Not that you would heed it even if I did; you were always obstinate——

PRIVATE: Tch, tch.

BOYLE: But I would suggest that you strike out on your own as soon as you find your feet out there. Don't keep looking back over your shoulder. Be 100 per cent American.

PUBLIC: I'll do that.

BOYLE: There's an inscription on the fly-leaf. By the way, Gar, you couldn't lend me 10s until—ha—I was going to say until next week but you'll be gone by then.

PUBLIC: Surely, surely.

BOYLE: I seem to have come out without my wallet. . . .

PRIVATE: Give him the quid.

[PUBLIC *gives over a note.* BOYLE *does not look at it*]

BOYLE: Fine. I'll move on now. Yes, I knew all the Gallagher girls from Bailtefree, long, long ago. Maire and Una and Rose and Lizzy and Agnes and Maire, your mother. . . .

PRIVATE: You might have been my father.

BOYLE: Oh, another thing I meant to ask you: should you come across any newspapers or magazines over there that might be interested in an occasional poem, perhaps you would send me some addresses——

PUBLIC: I'll keep an eye out.

BOYLE: Not that I write as much as I should. You know how you get caught up in things. But you have your packing to do, and I'm talking too much as usual.

[*He holds out his hand and they shake hands. He does not release* PUBLIC'*s hand*]

Good luck, Gareth.

PUBLIC: Thanks, Master.

BOYLE: Forget Ballybeg and Ireland.

PUBLIC: It's easier said.

BOYLE: Perhaps you'll write me.

PUBLIC: I will indeed.

BOYLE: Yes, the first year. Maybe the second. I'll—I'll miss you, Gar.

PRIVATE: For God's sake get a grip on yourself.

PUBLIC: Thanks for the book and for——

[BOYLE *embraces* PUBLIC *briefly*]

PRIVATE: Stop it! Stop it! Stop it!

[BOYLE *breaks away and goes quickly off through the scullery. He bumps into* MADGE *who is entering*]

MADGE: Lord, the speed of him! His tongue out for a drink!

PRIVATE: Quick! Into your room!

MADGE: God knows I don't blame the Canon for wanting rid of that——

[PUBLIC *rushes to the bedroom.* PRIVATE *follows*]

Well! The manners about this place!

[*She gathers up the tea things.* PUBLIC *stands inside the bedroom door, his hands up to his face.* PRIVATE *stands at his elbow, speaking urgently into his ear*]

PRIVATE: Remember—you're going! At 7:15. You're still going! He's nothing but a drunken aul schoolmaster—a conceited, arrogant wash-out!

PUBLIC: O God, the Creator and Redeemer of all the faithful——

PRIVATE: Get a grip on yourself! Don't be a damned sentimental fool! [*Sings*] 'Philadelphia, here I come——'

PUBLIC: Maire and Una and Rose and Agnes and Lizzy and Maire——

PRIVATE: Yessir, you're going to cut a bit of a dash in them thar States! Great big sexy dames and night clubs and high living and films and dances and——

PUBLIC: Kathy, my own darling Kathy——

PRIVATE: [*Sings*] 'Where bowers of flowers bloom in the spring'

PUBLIC: I don't—I can't.

PRIVATE: [*Sings*] 'Each morning at dawning, everything is bright and gay/A sun-kissed miss says Don't be late—' Sing up, man!

PUBLIC: I—I—I——

PRIVATE: [*Sings*] 'That's why I can hardly wait.'

PUBLIC: [*Sings limply*] 'Philadelphia, here I come.'

PRIVATE: That's it, laddybuck!

TOGETHER: 'Philadelphia, here I come.'

CURTAIN

EPISODE II

A short time later. PUBLIC *is lying on the bed, his hands behind his head.* PRIVATE *is slumped in the chair, almost as if he were dozing.* PUBLIC *sings absently.*

PUBLIC: [*Sings*]

Last night she came to me, she came softly in,
So softly she came that her feet made no din,
And laid her hand on me, and this she did say,
'It will not be long till our wedding day.'

[*When the singing stops there is a moment of silence. Then, suddenly,* PRIVATE *springs to his feet*]

PRIVATE: What the bloody hell are you at, O'Donnell? Snap out of it, man! Get up and keep active! The devil makes work for idle hands! It is now sixteen or seventeen years since I saw the Queen of France, then the Dauphiness, at Versailles.

[PUBLIC *goes off the bed and begins taking clothes from the chest of drawers and putting them into his case*]

PRIVATE: [*Lilting to a mad air of his own making*] Ta-ra-del-oo-del-ah-dol-de-dol-de-dol-del-ah—[*Continuing as rapidly as he can speak*]—Tell me this and tell me no more: Why does a hen cross the road?

PUBLIC: Why?

PRIVATE: To get to the other side. Ha-ha! Why does a hen lay an egg?

PUBLIC: Why?

PRIVATE: Because it can't lay a brick. Yo-ho. Why does a sailor wear a round hat?

PUBLIC: Why?

PRIVATE: To cover his head. Hee-hee-hee. Nought out of three; very bad for a man of average intelligence. That's the style. Keep working; keep the mind active and well stretched by knowing the best that is thought and written in the world, and you wouldn't call Daddy Senator your father-in-law. [*Sings*]

> Give the woman in the bed more porter
> Give the man beside her water
> Give the woman in the bed more porter
> More porter for the woman in the bed.

[*Confidentially*] D'you know what I think laddie; I mean, just looking at you there.

PUBLIC: What?

PRIVATE: You'd make a hell of a fine President of the United States.

[PUBLIC *straightens up and for a second surveys the room with the keen eye of a politician. Relaxes again*]

PUBLIC: Agh!

PRIVATE: But you would!

PUBLIC: You need to be born an American citizen.

PRIVATE: True for you. What about Chairman of General Motors?

[PUBLIC *shrugs indifferently*]

Boss of the Teamsters' Union?

[PUBLIC *shrugs his indifference*]

PRIVATE: Hollywood—what about Hollywood?

PUBLIC: Not what it was.

PRIVATE: Dammit but you're hard to please too. Still, there must be something great in store for you. [*Cracks his fingers at his brainwave*] The U. S. Senate! Senator Gareth O'Donnell, Chairman of the Foreign Aid Committee!

[*He interviews* PUBLIC *who continues packing his clothes busily*]

Is there something you would like to say, Senator, before you publish the findings of your committee?

PUBLIC: Nothing to say.

PRIVATE: Just a few words.

PUBLIC: No comment.

PRIVATE: Isn't it a fact that suspicion has fallen on Senator Doogan?

PUBLIC: Nothing further to add.

PRIVATE: Did your investigators not discover that Senator Doogan is the grandfather of fourteen unborn illegitimate children? That he sold his daughter to the king of the fairies for a crock of gold? That a Chinese spy known to the FBI as Screwballs——

PUBLIC: Screwballs?

PRIVATE: Screwballs.

PUBLIC: Describe him.

PRIVATE: Tall, blond, athletic-looking——

PUBLIC: Military moustache?

PRIVATE: —very handsome; uses a diamond-studded cigarette-holder.

PUBLIC: Usually accompanied by a dark seductive woman in a low-cut evening gown?

PRIVATE: —wears a monocle, fluent command of languages——

PUBLIC: But seldom speaks? A man of few words?

PRIVATE: —drives a cream convertible, villas in Istanbul, Cairo and Budapest——

PUBLIC: [*Declaims*] Merchant Prince, licensed to deal in tobacco——

PRIVATE: An' sowl! That's me man! To a T! The point is—what'll we do with him?

PUBLIC: Sell him to a harem?

PRIVATE: Hide his cascara sagrada?

[MADGE *comes into the kitchen to lift the tablecloth*]

PUBLIC: [*Serious*] Shhh!

PRIVATE: The boys? Is it the boys? To say good-bye?

PUBLIC: Shhhh!

PRIVATE: It's Madge—aul fluke-feet Madge.

[*They both stand listening to the sound of* MADGE *flapping across the kitchen and out to the scullery*]

PUBLIC: [*Calls softly*] Madge.

[PRIVATE *drops into the armchair.* PUBLIC *stands listening until the sound has died away*]

PRIVATE: [*Wearily*] Off again! You know what you're doing, don't you, laddybuck? Collecting memories and images and impressions that are going to make you bloody miserable; and in a way that's what you want, isn't it?

PUBLIC: Bugger!

[PRIVATE *springs to his feet again. With forced animation*]

PRIVATE: Bugger's right! Bugger's absolutely correct! Back to the job! Keep occupied. Be methodical.
               Eanie-meanie-minie-mow
               Catch-the-baby-by-the-toe.
Will all passengers holding immigration visas please come this way.

[PUBLIC *produces documents from a drawer. He checks them*]

PRIVATE: Passport?

PUBLIC: Passport.

PRIVATE: Visa?

PUBLIC: Visa.

PRIVATE: Vaccination cert.?

PUBLIC: Vaccination cert.

PRIVATE: Currency?

PUBLIC: Eighty dollars.

PRIVATE: Sponsorship papers?

PUBLIC: Signed by Mr. Conal Sweeney.

PRIVATE: Uncle Con and Aunt Lizzy. Who made the whole thing possible. Read her letter again—strictly for belly-laughs.

PUBLIC: [*Reads*] Dear Nephew Gar: Just a line to let you know that your Uncle Con and me have finalized all the plans——

PRIVATE: Uncle Con and *I.*

PUBLIC: —and we will meet you at the airport and welcome you and bring you to our apartment which you will see is located in a pretty nice locality and you will have the spare room which has TV and air-conditioning and window meshes and your own bathroom with a shower——

PRIVATE: Adjacent to RC church. No children. Other help kept.

PUBLIC: You will begin at the Emperor Hotel on Monday 23rd which is only about twenty minutes away.

PRIVATE: Monsieur, madam.

PUBLIC: Con says it is a fine place for to work in and the owner is Mr. Patrick Palinakis who is half Irish——

PRIVATE: Patrick.

PUBLIC: —and half Greek.

PRIVATE: Palinakis.

PUBLIC: His grandfather came from County Mayo.

PRIVATE: By the hokey! The Greek from Belmullet!

PUBLIC: We know you will like it here and work hard.

PRIVATE: [*Rapidly*] Monsieur-madam-monsieur-madam-monsieur-madam——

PUBLIC: We remember our short trip to Ireland last September with happy thoughts and look forward to seeing you again. Sorry we missed your father that day. We had Ben Burton in to dinner last evening. He sends his regards.

PRIVATE: Right sort, Ben.

PUBLIC: Until we see you at the airport, all love, Elise.

PRIVATE: *Elise!* Damnit, Lizzy Gallagher, but you came on in the world.

PUBLIC: P.S. About paying back the passage money which you mentioned in your last letter—desist!—no one's crying about it.

PRIVATE: Aye, Ben Burton was a right skin.

PUBLIC: [*Remembering*] September 8th.

PRIVATE: By God, Lizzy was in right talking form that day——

PUBLIC: 'You are invited to attend the wedding of Miss Kathleen Doogan of Gortmore House——'

PRIVATE: [*Snaps*] Shut up, O'Donnell! You've got to quit this moody drivelling! [*Coaxing*] They arrived in the afternoon; remember? A beautiful quiet harvest day, the sun shining, not a breath of wind; and you were on your best behaviour. And Madge—remember? Madge was as huffy as hell with the carry-on of them, and you couldn't take your eyes off Aunt Lizzy, your mother's sister—so this was your mother's sister—remember?

[*Three people have moved into the kitchen:* CON SWEENEY, LIZZY SWEENEY, *and* BEN BURTON. *All three are in the fifty-five to sixty region.* BURTON *is American, the* SWEENEYS *Irish-American.* CON SWEENEY *sits at the kitchen table with* BEN BURTON. LIZZY *moves around in the centre of the kitchen.* PUBLIC *stands at the door of his bedroom.* PRIVATE *hovers around close to* PUBLIC. *The three guests have glasses in their hands. None of them is drunk, but* LIZZY *is more than usually garrulous. She is a small energetic woman, heavily made-up, impulsive.* CON, *her husband, is a quiet, patient man.* BURTON, *their friend, sits smiling at his glass most of the time. As she talks,* LIZZY *moves from one to the other, and she has the habit of putting her arm around, or catching the elbow of, the person she is addressing. This constant physical touching is new and disquieting to* PUBLIC. *A long laugh from* LIZZY:]

LIZZY: Anyhow, there we are, all sitting like stuffed ducks in the front seat—Una and Agnes and Rose and Mother and me—you know—and mother dickied up in her good black shawl and everything—and up at the altar rails there's Maire all by herself and her shoulders are sorta working—you know—and you couldn't tell whether she was crying or giggling—she was a helluva one for giggling—but maybe she was crying that morning—I don't know——

CON: Get on with the story, honey.

LIZZY: [*With dignity*] Would you please desist from bustin' in on me?

[CON *spreads his hands in resignation*]

LIZZY: But listen to this—this'll kill you—Mother's here, see? And Agnes is here and I'm here. And Agnes leans across Mother to me—you know—and she says in this helluva loud voice—she says—[*Laughs*]—this really does kill me—she says —in this whisper of hers—and you know the size of Bailtefree chapel; couldn't swing a cat in that place—[*Suddenly anxious*] That chapel's still there, isn't it? It hasn't fell down or nothing, has it?

CON: [*Dryly*] Unless it fell down within the last couple of hours. We drove up there this morning. Remember?

LIZZY: [*Relieved*] Yeah. So we did. Fine place. Made me feel kinda—you know—what the hell was I talking about?

BEN: Agnes leaned over to you and said——

[LIZZY *puts her arm around him and kisses the crown of his head*]

LIZZY: Thanks, Ben. A great friend with a great memory! I'll tell you, Gar, Ben Burton's one hundred per cent. The first and best friend we made when we went out. [*To* CON] Right, honey?

CON: Right.

LIZZY: Way back in '37.

CON: '38.

LIZZY: [*Loudly*] October 23rd, 19 and 37 we sailed for the United States of America. [CON *spreads his hands*] Nothing in our pockets. No job to go to. And what does Ben do?

CON: A guy in a million.

LIZZY: He gives us this apartment. He gives us dough. He gives us three meals a day—until bonzo finally gets himself this job. Looks after us like we were his own skin and bone. Right, honey?

CON: Right.

LIZZY: So don't let nobody say nothing against Ben Burton. Then when he gets this job in this downtown store——

CON: First job was with the construction company.

LIZZY: Would you *please* desist? [CON *spreads hands*] His first job was with Young and Pecks, hauling out them packing cases and things; and then he moved to the construction company, and *then* we got a place of our own.

PUBLIC: You were telling us about that morning.

LIZZY: What's he talking about?

PUBLIC: The day my father and mother got married.

LIZZY: That day! Wasn't that something? With the wind howling and the rain slashing about! And Mother, poor Mother, may God be good to her, she thought that just because Maire got this guy with a big store we should all of got guys with big stores. And poor Maire—we were so alike in every way, Maire and me. But he was good to her. I'll say that for S. B. O'Donnell —real good to her. *Where the hell is he anyhow?* Why will S. B. O'Donnell, my brother-in-law, not meet me?

CON: Gar told you—he's away at a wedding.

LIZZY: *What wedding?*

CON: Some local girl and some Dublin doc.

LIZZY: What local girl? You think I'm a stranger here or something?

CON: [To PUBLIC] What local girl?

PUBLIC: Senator Doogan's daughter.

PRIVATE: Kathy.

LIZZY: Never heard of him. Some Johnny-hop-up. When did they start having Senators about this place for Gawds sakes?

BEN: [To PUBLIC] You have a senate in Dublin, just like our Senate, don't you?

LIZZY: Don't you start telling me nothing about my own country, Ben. You got your own problems to look after. Just you leave me to manage this place, okay?

BEN: Sorry, Elise.

LIZZY: Ben! [She kisses the top of his head] Only that I'm a good Irish-American Catholic—[To PUBLIC] and believe me, they don't come much better than that—and only that I'm stuck with Rudolph Valentino, I'd take a chance with Ben Burton any day [Kisses him again] black Lutheran and all that he is.

> [MADGE appears at the door of the shop. She refuses to look at the visitors. Her face is tight with disapproval. Her accent is very precise]

MADGE: Are there any Clarions to spare or are they all ordered?

PUBLIC: They're all ordered, Madge.

LIZZY: Doing big deals there, honey, huh?

MADGE: Thank you, Gareth.

> [MADGE withdraws]

LIZZY: 'Thank you, Gareth!' [She giggles to herself]

CON: Honey! [To PUBLIC] You'll think about what we were discussing?

PUBLIC: I will, Uncle Con.

CON: The job's as good as you'll get and we'd be proud to have you.

LIZZY: Don't force him.

CON: I'm not forcing him. I'm only telling him.

LIZZY: Well now, you've told him—a dozen times. So now desist, will you?

[CON *spreads his hands*]

PUBLIC: I will think about it. Really.

LIZZY: Sure! Sure! Typical Irish! He will think about it! And while he's thinking about it the store falls in about his head! What age are you? Twenty-four? Twenty-five? What are you waiting for? For S.B. to run away to sea? Until the weather gets better?

CON: Honey!

LIZZY: I'm talking straight to the kid! He's Maire's boy and I've got an interest in him—the only nephew I have. [*To* BEN] Am I right or am I wrong?

BEN: I'm still up in Bailtefree chapel.

LIZZY: Where? [*Confidentially to* CON] Give him no more to drink. [*Patiently to* BEN] You're sitting in the home of S. B. O'Donnell and my deceased sister, Maire, Ben.

CON: You were telling us a story about the morning they got married, honey, in Bailtefree chapel.

LIZZY: Yeah, I know, I know, but you keep busting in on me.

PUBLIC: You were about to tell us what Agnes whispered to you.

LIZZY: [*Crying*] Poor Aggie—dead. Maire—dead. Rose, Una, Lizzy—dead—all gone—all dead and gone. . . .

CON: Honey, *you're* Lizzy.

LIZZY: So *what*?

CON: Honey, you're not dead.

LIZZY: [*Regarding* CON *cautiously*] You gone senile all of a sudden? [*Confidentially to* BEN] Give him no more to drink. [*To* CON] For Gawds sakes who says I'm dead?

BEN: You're very much alive, Elise.

[*She goes to him and gives him another kiss*]

LIZZY: Thank you, Ben. A great friend with a great intellect. Only one thing wrong with Ben Burton: he's a black Baptist.

BEN: Just for the record, Gar, I'm Episcopalian.

LIZZY: Episcopalian—Lutheran—Baptist—what's the difference? As our pastor, Father O'Flaherty, says—'My dear brethren,' he says, 'Let the whole cart-load of them, and the whole zoo of them, be to thee as the Pharisee and the publican.'

CON: Honey!

LIZZY: But he's still the best friend we have. And we have many good, dear, kind friends in the U.S. Right, honey?

CON: Right.

LIZZY: But when it comes to holding a candle to Ben Burton— look—comparisons are—he's not in the halfpenny place with them!

BEN: [*Laughing*] Bang on, Elise!

LIZZY: Am I right or am I wrong?

CON: Honey!

LIZZY: [*To* PUBLIC] And that's why I say to you: America's Gawd's own country. Ben?

BEN: Don't ask me. I was born there.

LIZZY: What d'ya mean—'Don't ask me?' I *am* asking you. He should come out or he should not—which is it?

BEN: It's just another place to live, Elise. Ireland—America—what's the difference?

LIZZY: You tell him, honey. You tell him the set-up we have. [*Now with growing urgency, to* PUBLIC] We have this ground-floor apartment, see, and a car that's air-conditioned, and colour TV, and this big collection of all the Irish records you ever heard, and 15,000 bucks in Federal Bonds—

CON: Honey.

LIZZY: —and a deep freezer and—and—and a back yard with this great big cherry tree, and squirrels and night-owls and the smell of lavender in the spring and long summer evenings and snow at Christmas and a Christmas tree in the parlour and—and—and——

CON: Elise. . . .

LIZZY: And it's all so Gawd-awful because we have no one to share it with us. . . . [*She begins to sob*]

CON: [*Softly*] It's okay, honey, okay. . . .

LIZZY: He's my sister's boy—the only child of five girls of us——

BEN: I'll get the car round the front.

[BEN *goes off through the scullery*]

LIZZY: —and we spent a fortune on doctors, didn't we, Connie, but it was no good, and then I says to him, 'We'll go home to Ireland,' I says, 'and Maire's boy, we'll offer him everything we have——'

PRIVATE: [*Terrified*] No. No.

LIZZY: '—everything, and maybe we could coax him—you know——' maybe it was sorta bribery—I dunno—but he would have everything we ever gathered——

PRIVATE: Keep it! Keep it!

LIZZY: —and all the love we had in us——

PRIVATE: No! No!

CON: Honey, we've a long drive back to the hotel.

LIZZY: [*Trying to control herself*] That was always the kind of us Gallagher girls, wasn't it . . . either laughing or crying . . . you know, sorta silly and impetuous, shooting our big mouths off, talking too much, not like the O'Donnells—you know— kinda cold——

PRIVATE: Don't man, don't.

CON: Your gloves, honey. It's been a heavy day.

LIZZY: [*To* PUBLIC, *with uncertain dignity*] Tell your father that we regret we did not have the opportunity for to make his acquaintance again after all these——

PUBLIC: [*Impetuously*] I want to go to America—if you'll have me——

PRIVATE: Laddy!

CON: Sure. You think about it, son. You think about it.

PUBLIC: Now—as soon as I can, Aunt Lizzy—I mean it—

LIZZY: Gar? [*To* CON, *as if for confirmation*] Honey?

CON: Look son——

LIZZY: To us, Gar? To come to us? To our home?

CON: Ben's waiting, Elise.

PUBLIC: If you'll have me. . . .

LIZZY: If we'll have him, he says; he says if we'll have him! That's why I'm here! That's why I'm half-shot-up!

[*She opens her arms and approaches him*]

Oh Gar, my son——

PRIVATE: Not yet! Don't touch me yet!

[LIZZY *throws her arms around him and cries happily*]

LIZZY: My son, Gar, Gar, Gar. . . .

PRIVATE: [*Softly, with happy anguish*] God . . . my God . . . Oh my God. . . .

BLACKOUT

When the bedroom light goes up PUBLIC *and* PRIVATE *are there. The kitchen is empty.* PUBLIC *bangs the lid of his case shut and* PRIVATE *stands beside him, jeering at him. While this taunting goes on* PUBLIC *tries to escape by fussing about the room.*

PRIVATE: September 8th, the sun shining, not a breath of wind—and this was your mother's sister—remember. And that's how you were got! Right, honey? Silly and impetuous like a Gallagher! Regrets?

PUBLIC: None.

PRIVATE: Uncertainties?

PUBLIC: None.

PRIVATE: Little tiny niggling reservations?

PUBLIC: None.

PRIVATE: Her grammar?

PUBLIC: Shut up!

PRIVATE: But, honey, wasn't it something?

PUBLIC: Go to hell.

PRIVATE: Her vulgarity?

PUBLIC: Bugger off.

PRIVATE: She'll tuck you into your air-conditioned cot every night.

[PUBLIC, *so that he won't hear, begins to whistle 'Phila-delphia, Here I Come'*]

PRIVATE: And croon, 'Sleep well, my li'l honey child.'

[PUBLIC *whistles determinedly*]

She got you soft on account of the day it was, didn't she?

[PUBLIC *whistles louder*]

And because she said you were an O'Donnell—'cold like.'

PUBLIC: It is now sixteen or seventeen years since I saw the Queen of France——

PRIVATE: But of course when she threw her arms around you—well, well, well!

PUBLIC: —then the Dauphiness, at Versailles——

PRIVATE: Poor little orphan boy!

PUBLIC: Shut up! Shut up!

PRIVATE: [*In child's voice*] Ma-ma. . . . Maa-ma.

[PUBLIC *flings open the bedroom door and dashes into the kitchen.* PRIVATE *follows behind*]

PUBLIC: Madge!

PRIVATE: [*Quietly, deliberately*] You don't want to go, laddy-buck. Admit it. You don't want to go.

[MADGE *enters from the scullery*]

PUBLIC: [*Searching for an excuse*] I can't find my coat. I left it in my room.

[MADGE *gives him a long, patient look, goes to the nail below the school clock, lifts down the coat, and hands it to him. He takes it from her and goes towards the scullery door*]

PUBLIC: If you would only learn to leave things where you find them you wouldn't be such a bad aul nuisance.

[PUBLIC *and* PRIVATE *go off*]

MADGE: [*Calls*] Don't you dare come home drunk!

[PUBLIC's *head appears round the door*]

PUBLIC: [*Softly*] I'm going to say good-bye to the boys over a quiet drink or two. And how I spend my nights is a matter entirely for myself.

MADGE: 'The Boys!' Couldn't even come here to say good-bye to you on your last night.

PRIVATE: Straight to the bone!

PUBLIC: Just you mind your business and I'll mind mine.

MADGE: How many of them are getting the pension now?

PUBLIC: And in case you're in bed when I get back I want a call at half-six.

MADGE: The clock'll be set. If you hear it well and good.

[PUBLIC *disappears.* MADGE *fusses about the kitchen until* S.B. *enters from the shop. He has a newspaper in his hand*

and sits at the head of the table. She watches him as he
reads. She adjusts a few things. She looks back at him,
then suddenly, on the point of tears, she accuses him]

MADGE: You sit there, night after night, year after year, reading
that aul paper, and not a tooth in your head! If you had any
decency in you at all, you would keep them plates in while
there's a lady in your presence!

S.B.: [*Puzzled*] Eh?

MADGE: I mean it. It—it—it—it just drives me mad, the sight of
you! [*The tears begin to come*] And I have that much work to
do: the stairs have to be washed down, and the store's to be
swept, and your room has to be done out—and—and—I'm telling you I'll be that busy for the next couple of weeks that I
won't have time to lift my head!

[*She dashes off.* S.B. *stares after her, then out at the audi-*
ence. Then, very slowly, he looks down at the paper again
—it has been upside down—and turns it right side up. But
he can't read. He looks across at GAR's *bedroom, sighs,*
rises, and exits very slowly to the shop. Silence for a second
after S.B. *leaves. The silence is suddenly shattered by the*
boisterous arrival of the boys and GAR. *We hear their exag-*
gerated laughter and talk outside before they burst in. When
they enter they take over the kitchen, sprawling on chairs,
hunting for tumblers for the stout they produce from their
pockets, taking long, deep pulls on their cigarettes, giving
the impression that they are busy, purposeful, randy gents
about to embark on some exciting adventure. But their
bluster is not altogether convincing. There is something
false about it. Tranquility is their enemy: they fight it
valiantly. At the beginning of this scene GAR *is flattered*
that the boys have come to him. When they consistently
refuse to acknowledge his leaving—or perhaps because he
is already spiritually gone from them—his good humour de-
serts him. He becomes apart from the others. NED *is the*
leader of the group. TOM *is his feed-man, subserviently*
watching for every cue. JOE, *the youngest of the trio, and*
not yet fully committed to the boys' way of life, is torn

between fealty to NED *and* TOM *and a spontaneous and simple loneliness over* GAR's *departure. Nothing would suit him better than a grand loud send-off party. But he cannot manage this, and his loyalty is divided. He is patently gauche, innocent, obvious]*

NED: There's only one way to put the fear of God up them bastards—[*Points to his boot*]—every time—you know where.

JOE: Who's the ref, Ned?

TOM: Jimmy Pat Barney from Bunmornan. [*Guardedly to* PUBLIC] Where's the aul fella?

PUBLIC: Haven't a bloody clue. Probably in the shop. Relax, man.

NED: That [*The boot*] or the knee—it's the only game them gets can play; and we can play it too.

TOM: [*Relaxing*] They've a hell of a forward line all the same, Ned.

NED: They'll be in crutches this day week. By God, I can hardly wait to get the studs planted in wee Bagser Doran's face! [*He crashes his fist into the palm of his hand*]

TOM: All the same, Jimmy Pat Barney's the get would put you off very quick.

NED: He won't say a word to me. He knows his match when he meets it.

[TOM *laughs appreciatively.* MADGE *appears at the scullery door*]

MADGE: [*Coldly*] Just thought I heard somebody whispering. So youse finally made it.

JOE: [*Holding up glass*] True to our word, Madge, that's us!

PUBLIC: [*Happily*] They were on their way here when I ran into them.

MADGE: Aye, so. [NED *belches*] Mister Sweeney, too; gentlemanly as ever.

NED: [*Slapping his knee*] Come on away over here and I'll take some of the starch out of you, Madge Mulhern. How long is since a fella gripped your knee? Haaaaaaaaaaa!

MADGE: None of your smutty talk here, Mister Sweeney. And if the boss comes in and finds them bottles——

PUBLIC: I'll keep them in order, Madge.

MADGE: 'Boys!' How are you!

[*She goes out*]

TOM: [*Calling*] You're jealous because you're past it—that's what's wrong with you. Right, Ned?

PUBLIC: [*Raising glass*] Well, boys, when you're lining out on the pitch, you can think of me, because I'll be thinking of you.

JOE: [*Earnestly*] Lucky bloody man, Gar. God, I wish I was in your——

NED: [*Quickly*] By the way, lads, who's the blondie thing I seen at the last Mass on Sunday?

TOM: A big redhead?

NED: Are you bloody-well deaf! A blondie! She wouldn't be Maggie Hanna's niece, would she?

TOM: There was two of them, sitting over near the box?

NED: I seen one.

TOM: 'Cos they're English. Staying at the hotel. But the big red thing—she's one of Neil McFadden's girls.

NED: Annie? Is Annie home?

JOE: Aye, she is. So I heard the mammy saying.

NED: Bloody great! That's me fixed up for the next two weeks! Were any of youse ever on that job?

JOE: No, I wasn't, Ned.

TOM: For God's sake, she wouldn't spit on you!

NED: Game as they're going, big Annie. But you need the constitution of a horse. I had her for the fortnight she was home last year and she damned near killed me.

PUBLIC: Big Annie from up beyond the quarry?

JOE: You know, Gar—the one with the squint.

NED: [*With dignity*] Annie McFadden has no squint.

PUBLIC: Away and take a running race to yourself, Ned.

NED: [*With quiet threat*] What do you mean?

PUBLIC: You were never out with big Annie McFadden in your puff, man.

NED: Are you calling me a liar?

PRIVATE: [*Wearily*] What's the point.

TOM: [*Quickly*] Oh, by God, Ned was there, Gar, many's and many's the time. Weren't you, Ned?

PUBLIC: Have it your own way.

JOE: [*Nervously*] And maybe she got the squint straightened out since I saw her last. All the women get the squints straightened out nowadays. Damnit, you could walk from here to Cork nowadays and you wouldn't see a woman with a——

NED: I just don't like fellas getting snottery with me, that's all.

[*There follows an uneasy silence during which* PRIVATE *surveys the group*]

PRIVATE: The boys. . . . They weren't always like this, were they? There was a hell of a lot of crack, wasn't there? There was a hell of a lot of laughing, wasn't there?

TOM: [*Briskly*] Bit of life about the place next week, lads—the Carnival. Too bad you'll miss it, Gar. By God, it was a holy fright last year, night after night. [*To* NED] Remember?

NED: [*Sulkily*] Bloody cows, the whole bloody lot of them!

TOM: Mind the night with the two wee Greenock pieces?

NED: [*Thawing*] Aw, stop, stop!

TOM: Talk about hot things!

NED: Liveliest wee tramps I ever laid!

TOM: And the fat one from Dublin you picked up at the dance that night—the one that hauled you down into the ditch!

NED: I was never the same since.

TOM: [*To* PUBLIC] Whatever it is about him, if there's a fast woman in the country, she'll go for Ned first thing. Lucky bugger! [*Pause*] Aye, lucky bugger!

[*Another brief silence. These silences occur like regular cadences. To defeat them someone always introduces a fresh theme*]

PUBLIC: I'm for off tomorrow, boys.

NED: [*Indifferently*] Aye, so, so. . . .

TOM: Brooklyn, isn't it?

PUBLIC: Philadelphia.

TOM: Philadelphia. That's where Jimmy Crerand went to, isn't it? Philadelphia. . . .

NED: [*Quickly*] Mind the night Jimmy and us went down to the caves with them Dublin skivvies that was working up at the Lodge? [*To* PUBLIC] Were you?—No, you weren't with us that night.

JOE: Was *I* there, Ned?

NED: You mind the size of Jimmy?—five foot nothing and scared of his shadow.

PUBLIC: Best goalie we ever had.

NED: One of the women was Gladys and the other was Emmy or something——

TOM: Damnit, I mind now! Gladys and Emmy—that was it, Ned!

NED: Anyhow the rest of us went in for a swim——

TOM: In the bloody pelt!

NED: —and your man Jimmy was left in the cave with the women; and what the hell do they do but whip the trousers off him!

JOE: No, I *wasn't* there that night.

NED: And the next thing we see is wee Jimmy coming shouting across the White Strand and the two Dublin cows haring after him.

TOM: Not a stab on him!

NED: —and him squealing at the top of his voice, 'Save me, boys, save me!'

TOM: Never drew breath till he reached home!

NED: [*To* GAR] You missed that night.

TOM: 'Save me, boys, save me!'

NED: I don't think we went to bed that night at all.

TOM: You may be sure we didn't.

NED: Powerful.

[*Another silence descends. After a few seconds* PRIVATE *speaks*]:

PRIVATE: We were *all* there that night, Ned. And the girls' names were Gladys and Susan. And they sat on the rocks dangling their feet in the water. And we sat in the cave, peeping out at them. And then Jimmy Crerand suggested that we go in for a swim; and we all ran to the far end of the shore; and we splashed about like schoolboys. Then we came back to the cave, and wrestled with one another. And then out of sheer boredom, Tom, you suggested that we take the trousers off Crerand—just to prove how manly we all were. But when Ned started towards Jimmy—five foot nothing, remember?—wee Jimmy squared up and defied not only the brave Ned but the whole lot of us. So we straggled back home, one behind the other, and left the girls dangling their feet in the water. And that was that night.

PUBLIC: If the ground's not too hard, you'll do well on Sunday.

NED: Hard or soft—[*Examining his boot*]—I've a couple of aul scores to settle.

PUBLIC: You'll never get as good a half-back as the one you're losing.

NED: [*Quickly, with pretended interest*] D'you know what I'm thinking? We'd better see about transport.

TOM: Damnit, you're right. I'll get the aul fella's van easy enough. Can you get your Charlie's lorry?

NED: Just maybe. I'd better try him the night.

JOE: What about a song from Gar, boys, before we break up?

NED: What time is it?

JOE: It's early in the night yet.

TOM: Twenty past nine.

NED: We'd better move then; Charlie was talking about going to a dance in Ardmore.

TOM: Damnit, that's an idea!

JOE: We'll all go—a big last night for Gar!

NED: Ardmore? Are you mad? Bloody women in that place don't know what they're for!

TOM: True for you. Scream their heads off if you laid a hand on them.

NED: But I'll tell you what we'll do—call in home first to see Charlie and then go on to the hotel for a dirty big booze-up.

JOE: I don't like drinking in that place.

NED: Them two English bits—what's their name?

TOM: Them strangers? Agh you wouldn't have a chance there. They do nothing but walk and look at weeds and stuff——

NED: Who wouldn't have a chance?

TOM: I know, Ned. But them two—they're sort of stiff-looking—like—like they worked in a post-office or something.

NED: They're women, aren't they?

TOM: Damnit, we might! . . . Still I don't know. . . . They knit a lot. . . . [*To* PUBLIC] What d'you think?

JOE: I vote we stay here.

PUBLIC: And you can count me out. I've an early start.

NED: £10 to a shilling I click with one or other of them!

PUBLIC: I won't be here to collect my winnings.

NED: Come on! Any takers? Never clapped eyes on them and I'm offering ten notes to a bob!

TOM: Cripes, I know that look in his eyes!

NED: Wise bloody men! The blood's up, lads! Off to the front! Any volunteers for a big booze-up and a couple of women?

TOM: Did he say women? Sign me on!

JOE: I don't think I'm in form the night, boys——

NED: We'll show them a weed or two, eh?

TOM: Out to the sand-banks! Get them in the bloody bent!

NED: We're away—Wait! Wait!—How much money have you?

[*They both produce their money—a fistful of small coins*]

TOM: 2s 6d . . . 2s 11d . . . 3s 3d . . . 3s 5½d.

NED: And I have 6s 2d. It'll have to do. Say a prayer they're fast and thrifty.

TOM: Dirty aul brute! Lead the way, Bull!

NED: I'm telling you—the blood's up!

TOM: Coming, lads?

PUBLIC: I'm getting up at half-six.

NED: [*Casually from the door*] So long, Gar. You know the aul rule—If you can't be good. . . .

TOM: Send us a pack of them playing cards—the ones with the dirty pictures on the back!

NED: And if the women are as easy as the money out there, we might think of joining you. [*To* TOM] Right, old cock?

TOM: Bull on regardless! Yaaaaaaaaaaah!

[*They open the door.* NED *hesitates and begins taking off the broad leather belt with the huge brass buckle that supports his trousers*]

NED: [*Shyly, awkwardly*] By the way, Gar, since I'll not see you again before you go——

TOM: Hi! What are you at? At least wait till you're sure of the women?

NED: [*Impatiently to* TOM] Agh, shut up! [*To* PUBLIC] If any of them Yankee scuts try to beat you up some dark night, you can . . . [*Now he is very confused and flings the belt across the room to* PUBLIC] . . . you know . . . there's a bloody big buckle on it . . . many's a get I scutched with it. . . .

TOM: Safe enough, lads: he has braces on as well!

NED: I meant to buy you something good, but the aul fella didn't sell the calf to the jobbers last Friday . . . and he could have, the stupid bastard, such a bloody stupid bastard of an aul fella!

PUBLIC: [*Moved*] Thanks, Ned . . . thanks. . . .

JOE: Damnit, I have nothing for you, Gar.

TOM: [*Quickly*] Are we for the sandbanks or are we not?

NED: You'll make out all right over there . . . have a. . . .

TOM: I know that look in his eyes!

[NED *wheels rapidly on* TOM, *gives him a more than playful punch, and says savagely*]

NED: Christ, if there's one get I hate, it's you!

[*He goes off quickly,* TOM *looks uncertainly after him, looks back at* PUBLIC, *and says with dying conviction*]

TOM: The blood's up. . . . Oh by God, when he goes on like that, the . . . the blood's up all right. . . .

[TOM *looks after* NED, *then back to* JOE *and* GAR, *as if he can't decide which to join, then impetuously he dashes off after* NED, *calling*]

Hi! Ned, Ned, wait for me. . . .

[*There is a silence.* PUBLIC *is looking at the belt.* JOE *begins to fidget. Now* PUBLIC *becomes aware of him*]

PUBLIC: What the hell are you waiting for?

JOE: Damnit, man, like it's your last night and all, and I thought——

PUBLIC: Get to hell and run after them.

JOE: Sure you know yourself they'll hang about the gable of the hotel and chat and do nothing.

PUBLIC: For God's sake, man, those English women will be swept off their feet!

JOE: [*Uncertainly*] You're taking a hand at me now.

PUBLIC: I'm telling you, you're missing the chance of a lifetime.

JOE: Maybe—eh?—what d'you think?

PUBLIC: Go on! Go on!

JOE: God, maybe you're right. You never know what'll happen, eh? You finish that [Drink] for me! God, maybe we'll click the night! Say a wee prayer we do! Cripes, my blood's up too! Where's my cap?

[*He grabs the cap, dashes to the door, remembers he won't see* GAR *again*]

JOE: Send us a card, Gar, sometimes, eh?

PUBLIC: Surely, Joe.

JOE: Lucky bloody man. I wish I was you.

PUBLIC: There's nothing stopping you, is there?

JOE: Only that the mammy planted sycamore trees last year, and she says I can't go till they're tall enough to shelter the house.

PUBLIC: You're stuck for another couple of days, then. Away off with you, man.

JOE: Good luck, Gar. And tell Madge that the next time she asks us up for tea we'd bloody well better get it.

PUBLIC: She *asked* you?

JOE: That's why I was joking her about us keeping our word. As if we wanted tea, for God's sake! But I'd better catch up with the stirks before they do damage . . . So long, aul cock!

[*He runs off*]

PUBLIC: Madge. . . . Oh God. . . .

[PRIVATE *moves over beside him. He speaks quickly, savagely at first, spitting out the first three lines. Gradually he softens, until the speech ends almost in a whisper*]

PRIVATE: They're louts, ignorant bloody louts, and you've always known it! And don't pretend you're surprised; because you're not. And you know what they'll do tonight, don't you? They'll shuffle around the gable of the hotel and take an odd furtive peep into the lounge at those English women who won't even look up from their frigid knitting! Many a time you did it yourself, bucko! Aye, and but for Aunt Lizzy and the grace of God, you'd be there tonight, too, watching the lights go out over the village, and hearing the front doors being bolted, and seeing the blinds being raised; and you stamping your feet to keep the numbness from spreading, not wanting to go home, not yet for another while, wanting to hold on to the night although nothing can happen now, nothing at all. . . . Joe and Tom and big, thick, generous Ned. . . . No one will ever know or understand the fun there was; for there *was* fun and there *was* laughing—foolish, silly fun and foolish, silly laughing; but what it was all about you can't remember, can you? Just the memory of it—that's all you have now—*just the memory*; and even now, even so soon, it is being distilled of all its coarseness; and what's left is going to be precious, precious gold. . . .

[*There is a knock at the door.* PUBLIC *goes off to answer it*]

KATE: [*Off*] Hello, Gar.

PRIVATE: Kate!

KATE: [*On*] This isn't a healthy sign, drinking by yourself.

PRIVATE: Talk! Talk!

PUBLIC: What—what are you doing here?

KATE: I hear you're off to America.

PUBLIC: First thing in the morning.

KATE: You wouldn't think of calling to say good-bye to your friends, I suppose?

PUBLIC: I was going to, but I——

PRIVATE: Careful!

PUBLIC: —it went clean out of my mind. You know how it is, getting ready. . . .

KATE: I understand, Gar.

PRIVATE: She's a married woman, you bugger!

KATE: Philadelphia?

PUBLIC: Yes. Take a seat.

KATE: To an aunt, isn't it?

PUBLIC: That's right. A sister of mother's.

KATE: And you're going to work in a hotel.

PUBLIC: You know as much about it as I do.

KATE: You know Baile Beag—Small Town.

PUBLIC: I'll probably go to night-school as well—you know, at night——

PRIVATE: Brilliant.

PUBLIC: —do law or medicine or something——

PRIVATE: Like hell! First Arts stumped you!

KATE: You'll do well, Gar; make a lot of money, and come back here in twenty years' time, and buy the whole village.

PUBLIC: Very likely. That's my plan anyhow.

PRIVATE: Kate . . . Kathy. . . .

PUBLIC: How's your father and mother?

KATE: Fine, thanks. And Mr. O'Donnell?

PUBLIC: Grand, grand. Is Dr. King well?

KATE: I hear no complaints.

PRIVATE: Then the Dauphiness of Versailles. And surely never lighted on this orb, which she hardly seemed to touch, a more delightful vision. I saw her just above the horizon, decorating and cheering the elevated sphere she just began to move in——

PUBLIC: [A shade louder than necessary] I'll come home when I make my first million, driving a Cadillac and smoking cigars and taking movie-films.

KATE: I hope you're very happy there and that life will be good to you.

PUBLIC: [Slightly louder] I'll make sure life's good to me from now on.

KATE: You father'll miss you.

PUBLIC: [Rapidly, aggressively] That's his look out! D'you know something? If I had to spend another week in Ballybeg, I'd go off my bloody head! This place would drive anybody crazy! Look around you, for God's sake! Look at Master Boyle! Look at my father! Look at the Canon! Look at the boys! Asylum cases, the whole bloody lot of them!

PRIVATE: [*Pained*] Shhhhhhh!

PUBLIC: Listen, if someone were to come along to me tonight and say, 'Ballybeg's yours—lock, stock, and barrel,' it wouldn't make that [*Cracks his fingers*] much difference to me. If you're not happy and content in a place—then—then—then you're not happy and content in a place! It's as simple as that. I've stuck around this hole far too long. I'm telling you: it's a bloody quagmire, a backwater, a dead-end! And everybody in it goes crazy sooner or later! Everybody!

PRIVATE: Shhhhhhh. . . .

PUBLIC: There's nothing about Ballybeg that I don't know already. I hate the place, and every stone, and every rock, and every piece of heather around it! Hate it! Hate it! And the sooner that plane whips me away, the better I'll like it!

KATE: It isn't as bad as that, Gar.

PUBLIC: You're stuck here! What else can you say!

PRIVATE: That'll do!

PUBLIC: And you'll die here! But I'm not stuck! I'm free! Free as the bloody wind!

KATE: All I meant was——

PUBLIC: Answerable to nobody! All this bloody yap about father and son and all this sentimental rubbish about 'homeland' and 'birthplace'—yap! Bloody yap! Impermanence—anonymity —that's what I'm looking for; a vast restless place that doesn't give a damn about the past. To hell with Ballybeg, that's what I say!

PRIVATE: Oh, man. . . .

KATE: I'd better go. Francis'll be wondering what's keeping me.

PUBLIC: [*Recklessly*] Tell him I was asking for him.

KATE: Good-bye, Gar.

PUBLIC: [*In same tone*] Enjoy yourself, Kate. And if you can't be good—you know?

[*As* PUBLIC *goes off with* KATE]

Be sure to call the first one after me.

[*She is gone.* PUBLIC *returns and immediately buries his face in his hands*]

PRIVATE: Kate . . . sweet Katie Doogan . . . my darling Kathy Doogan. . . .

[PUBLIC *uncovers his face and with trembling fingers lights a cigarette and takes a drink. As he does*]

PRIVATE: [*Very softly*] Oh my God, steady man, steady—it is now sixteen or seventeen years since I saw the Queen of France, then the Dauphiness, at Versailles, and surely never lighted on this orb—Oh God, Oh my God, those thoughts are sinful—[*Sings*] 'As beautiful Kitty one morning was tripping with a pitcher of milk——'

[PUBLIC *attempts to whistle his song 'Philadelphia, Here I Come.' He whistles the first phrase and the notes die away.* PRIVATE *keeps on talking while* PUBLIC *attempts to whistle*]

PRIVATE: We'll go now, right away, and tell them—Mammy and Daddy—they're at home tonight—now, Gar, now—it must be *now*—remember, it's up to you—entirely up to you—gut and salt them fish—and they're going to call this one Madge, at least so she *says*——

[PUBLIC *makes another attempt to whistle*]

—a little something to remind you of your old teacher—don't keep looking back over your shoulder, be 100 per cent American

—a packet of cigarettes and a pot of jam—seven boys and seven girls—and our daughters'll be all gentle and frail and silly like you—and I'll never wait till Christmas—I'll burst, I'll bloody-well burst—good-bye, Gar, it isn't as bad as that—good-bye, Gar, it isn't as bad as that—good-bye, Gar, it isn't as bad as that——

PUBLIC: [*In whispered shout*] Screwballs, say something! Say *something,* Father!

QUICK CURTAIN

EPISODE III

PART ONE

A short time later. The rosary is being said. PUBLIC *is kneeling with his back to the audience.* S.B. *is kneeling facing the audience.* MADGE *is facing the shop door.* PRIVATE *kneels beside* PUBLIC. MADGE *is saying her decade, and the other three—*S.B., PUBLIC *and* PRIVATE*—are answering. The words are barely distinct, a monotonous, somnolent drone. After a few moments* PRIVATE *lowers his body until his rear is resting on the backs of his legs. We cannot see* PUBLIC's *face. While* PRIVATE *talks, the rosary goes on.*

PRIVATE: [*Relaxing, yawning*] Ah-ho-ho-ho-ho-ho. This time to-morrow night, bucko, you'll be saying the rosary all by yourself —unless Lizzy and Con say it [*Joins in a response in American accent*]—Holy Mairy, Mother of Gawd, pray for us sinners now and at the hour . . . [*He tails off as his mind wanders again*] No, not this time tomorrow. It's only about half-four in Philadelphia now, and when it's half-nine there it'll be the wee hours of the morning here; and Screwballs'll be curled up and fast asleep in his wee cot—[*To* S.B.]—right, honey? And when he's dreaming, you'll be swaggering down 56th Street on Third at the junction of 29th and Seventh at 81st with this big blonde nuzzling up to you—[*Suddenly kneels erect again and responds in unison with* PUBLIC. *Keeps this up for two or three responses and slowly subsides again*] You'd need to be careful out there, boy; some of those Yankee women are dynamite. But you'll never marry; never; bachelor's written all over you. Fated to be alone, a man without intimates; something of an enigma. Who is he, this silent one? Where is he from? Where does he go? Every night we see him walking beneath the trees along the bank of the canal, his black cloak swinging behind him, his eyes lost in thought, his servant following him at a respectful distance. [*In reply*] Who is he? I'll tell you who he is: The Bachelor. All the same, laddybuck, there are compensations in being a bachelor. You'll age slowly and graciously, and then, perhaps, when you're quite old—about forty-three—you'll meet this beautiful girl of nineteen, and you'll fall madly in love. Karin—that's her name—no—ah—ah—Tamara—[*Caressing the word*] Tamara—granddaughter of an exiled Russian prince, and you'll be consumed by a magnificent passion; and this night you'll invite her to dinner in your penthouse, and you'll be dressed in a deep blue velvet jacket, and the candles will discover magic fairy lights in her hair, and you'll say to her, 'Tamara,' and she'll incline her face towards you, and close her eyes, and whisper——

[*From a few seconds back the droning prayers have stopped. Now* MADGE *leans over to* PUBLIC *and gives him a rough punch*]

MADGE: Your decade!

[PRIVATE *and* PUBLIC *jump erect again and in perfect unison give out their decade. Gradually, as the prayers continue, they relax into their slumped position*]

PRIVATE: When you're curled up in your wee cot, Screwballs, do you dream? Do you ever dream of the past, Screwballs, of that wintry morning in Bailtefree, and the three days in Bundoran? . . .

[PUBLIC *stays as he is.* PRIVATE *gets slowly to his feet and moves over to* S.B. *He stands looking down at him*]

. . . and of the young, gay girl from beyond the mountains who sometimes cried herself to sleep? [*Softly, nervously, with growing excitement*] God—maybe—Screwballs—behind those dead eyes and that flat face are there memories of precious moments in the past? My God, have I been unfair to you? Is it possible that you have hoarded in the back of that mind of yours—do you remember—it was an afternoon in May—oh, fifteen years ago—I don't remember every detail but some things are as vivid as can be: the boat was blue and the paint was peeling and there was an empty cigarette packet floating in the water at the bottom between two trout and the left rowlock kept slipping and you had given me your hat and had put your jacket round my shoulders because there had been a shower of rain. And you had the rod in your left hand—I can see the cork nibbled away from the butt of the rod—and maybe we had been chatting—I don't remember—it doesn't matter—but between us at that moment there was this great happiness, this great joy—you must have felt it too—it was so much richer than a content—it was a great, great happiness, and active, bubbling joy—although nothing was being said—just the two of us fishing on a lake on a showery day—and young as I was I felt, I knew, that this was precious, and your hat was soft on the top of my ears—I can feel it—and I shrank down into your coat—and then, then for no reason at all except that you were happy too, you began to sing: [*Sings*]

All round my hat I'll wear a green coloured ribbono,
All round my hat for a twelve month and a day.
And if anybody asks me the reason why I wear it,
It's all because my true love is far, far away.

[*The rosary is over.* MADGE *and* S.B. *get slowly to their feet.* PUBLIC *and* PRIVATE *are not aware that the prayers are finished.* S.B. *does the nightly job of winding the clock*]

MADGE: Will you take your supper now?
S.B.: Any time suits you.

[MADGE *goes to* PUBLIC, *still kneeling*]

MADGE: And what about St. Martin de Porres?

PUBLIC: Mm?

[*He blesses himself hurriedly, in confusion, and gets to his feet*]

MADGE: Supper.

PUBLIC: Yes—yes—please, Madge——

MADGE: [*Going off*] I suppose even the saints must eat now and again, too.

[*Pause.* S.B. *consults his pocket watch*]

S.B.: What time do you make it?

PUBLIC: Quarter to ten.

S.B.: It's that anyhow.

PRIVATE: Go on! Ask him! He must remember!

S.B.: The days are shortening already. Before we know we'll be burning light before closing time.

PRIVATE: Go on! Go on!

PUBLIC: [*In the churlish, off-hand tone he uses to* S.B.] What ever happened to that aul boat on Lough na Cloc Cor.

S.B.: What's that?

PRIVATE: Again!

PUBLIC: That aul boat that used to be up on Lough na Cloc Cor—an aul blue thing—d'you remember it?

S.B.: A boat? Eh? [*Voices off*] The Canon!

PRIVATE: Bugger the Canon!

[*The* CANON *enters; a lean, white man with alert eyes and a thin mouth. He is talking back to* MADGE *in the scullery*]

CANON: Hee-hee-hee—you're a terrible woman.

S.B.: Well, Canon!

CANON: That Madge . . . hee-hee-hee.

PUBLIC: Good night, Canon.

CANON: She says I wait till the rosary's over and the kettle's on . . . hee-hee-hee.

S.B.: She's a sharp one, Madge.

CANON: 'You wait,' says she, 'till the rosary's over and the kettle's on!'

PRIVATE: Hee-hee-hee.

S.B.: Pay no heed to Madge, Canon.

PRIVATE: And how's the O'Donnell family tonight?

CANON: And how's the O'Donnell family tonight?

[PUBLIC *sits when the* CANON *sits*]

S.B.: Living away as usual. Not a thing happening.

PRIVATE: Liar!

CANON: Just so, now, just so.

S.B.: Will we have a game now or will we wait till the supper comes in?

CANON: We may as well commence, Sean. I see no reason why we shouldn't commence.

S.B.: [*Setting the board*] Whatever you say, Canon.

CANON: Hee-hee-hee. 'You wait,' says she, 'till the rosary's over and the kettle's on.'

PRIVATE: She's a sharp one, Madge.

S.B.: She's a sharp one, Madge.

CANON: It'll be getting near your time, Gareth.

PUBLIC: Tomorrow morning, Canon.

CANON: Just so, now. Tomorrow morning.

PRIVATE: Tomorrow morning.

CANON: Tomorrow morning.

S.B.: Here we are.

CANON: Powerful the way time passes, too.

S.B.: Black or white, Canon?

CANON: [*Considering the problem*] Black or white. . . .

PRIVATE: Black for the crows and white for the swans.

CANON: Black for the crows and white for the swans.

PRIVATE: Ha-ha! [*He preens himself at his skill in prophecy*]

S.B.: Have a shot at the black the night.

CANON: Maybe I will then.

PRIVATE: Can't take the money off you every night.

CANON: Can't take the trousers off you every night. Hee-hee-hee.

PRIVATE: [*Shocked*] Canon O'Byrne!

S.B.: You had a great streak of luck last night, I'll grant you that.

CANON: [*A major announcement*] D'you know what?

S.B.: What's that, Canon?

CANON: You'll have rain before morning.

S.B.: D'you think so?

CANON: It's in the bones. The leg's giving me the odd jab.

S.B.: We could do without the rain then.

CANON: Before the morning you'll have it.

S.B.: Tch-tch-tch. We get our fill of it here.

CANON: The best barometer I know.

S.B.: Aye. No want of rain.

CANON: Before the morning.

S.B.: As if we don't get enough of it.

CANON: The jabs are never wrong.

PRIVATE: [*Wildly excited*] Stop press! News flash! Sensation! We interrupt our programmes to bring you the news that Canon Mick O'Byrne, of Ballybeg, Ireland, has made the confident prediction that *you'll* have rain before the morning! Stand by for further bulletins!

CANON: 'You wait,' says she, 'till the rosary's over and the kettle's on!'

S.B.: Usual stakes, Canon?

CANON: I see no reason to alter them.

S.B.: What about putting them up—just for the first game?

CANON: The thin end of the wedge, eh, as the Bishop says?

No, Sean, the way I see it, a half-penny a game'll neither make nor break either of us.

[*Enter* MADGE *with cups of tea and a plate of biscuits*]

MADGE: Have you begun already?

S.B.: Shh!

MADGE: If it was turkeys or marble clocks they were playing for they couldn't be more serious!

S.B.: Quiet!

MADGE: Agh!

[*She leaves their tea beside them and brings a cup over to* PUBLIC. *They talk in undertones*]

MADGE: Wouldn't you love to throw it round them!

PUBLIC: Scalding hot!

MADGE: And raise blisters on their aul bald pates!—God forgive me!

PUBLIC: Madge.

MADGE: What?

PUBLIC: Why don't you take a run over to see the new baby?

MADGE: I've more on my mind than that.

PUBLIC: I'll put up the jars and wash up these few things.

MADGE: And this the last night we'll have you to torment us?

PUBLIC: Go on. Go on. We won't start swopping the dirty stories till we get you out of the road.

S.B.: Shhhhhhh!

PUBLIC: Hurry up. Nelly'll be wondering why you didn't show up.

MADGE: Aye, so.

PUBLIC: Your own namesake, isn't it?

MADGE: So she *says*.

PUBLIC: Get a move on. You'll be back before bedtime.

MADGE: What d'you think?

PUBLIC: Quick!

MADGE: I'm away! [*She takes a few steps away and comes back*] Don't forget: them shirts isn't right aired. [*Just when she is at the scullery door*]

PUBLIC: Madge.

MADGE: What is it?

PRIVATE: Don't! Don't!

PUBLIC: Why did my mother marry him instead of Master Boyle?

MADGE: What?

PUBLIC: She went with both of them, didn't she?

MADGE: She married the better man by far.

PUBLIC: But she went with Boyle first, didn't she?

MADGE: I've told you before: she went with a dozen—that was the kind of her—she couldn't help herself.

PUBLIC: But is that what started Boyle drinking?

MADGE: If it was, more fool he. And any other nosing about you want to do, ask the Boss. For you're not going to pump me.

[*She goes off*]

PRIVATE: What the hell had you to go and ask that for! Snap, boy, snap! We want no scenes tonight. Get up and clear out of this because you're liable to get over-excited watching these two dare-devils dicing with death. [PUBLIC *takes his cup and goes towards his bedroom*] Into your survival shelter and brood, brood, brood. [*As if replying to the draught players—who have not noticed his exit*] No, no, I'm not leaving. Just going in here to have a wee chat with my Chinese mistress.

[PUBLIC *goes into his bedroom, leaving the door open.* PRIVATE *stays in the kitchen.* PUBLIC *in the bedroom mimes the actions of* PRIVATE *in the following sequence.* PRIVATE *stands at the table between* S.B. *and* CANON]

PRIVATE: Canon battling tooth and nail for another half-penny; Screwballs fighting valiantly to retain his trousers! Gripped in mortal combat! County Councillor versus Canon! Screwballs versus Canonballs! [*Stares intently at them*] Hi, kids! Having fun, kids? [*Gets to his feet, leans his elbow on the table, and talks confidentially into their faces*] Any chance of a game, huh? Tell me, boys, strictly between ourselves, will you miss me? You will? You really will? But now I want you both to close your eyes—please, my darlings—don't, don't argue—just do as I say—just close your eyes and think of all the truly wonderful times we've had together. Now! What'll we chat about, eh? Let's—chat—about—what? No, Screwballs, not women; not before you-know-who. [*Looking at the* CANON] Money? Agh, sure, Canon, what interest have you in money? Sure as long as you get to Tenerife for five weeks every winter what interest have you in money? But I'm wasting my time with you, Canon—Screwballs here is different; there's an affinity between Screwballs and me that no one, literally, no one could understand—except you, Canon [*Deadly serious*], because you're warm and kind and soft and sympathetic—all things to all men —because you could translate all this loneliness, this groping, this dreadful bloody buffoonery into Christian terms that will make life bearable for us all. And yet you don't say a word. Why, Canon? Why, arid Canon? Isn't this your job?—to translate? Why don't you speak, then? Prudence arid Canon? Prudence be damned! Christianity isn't prudent—it's insane! Or maybe this just happens to be one of your bad nights—[*Suddenly bright and brittle again*]—A pound to a shilling I make you laugh! [*Dancing around, singing to the tune of 'Daisy'*] 'Screwballs, Screwballs, give me your answer do. I'm half crazy all for the love of you. I'm off to Philadelphey, and I'll leave you on the shelfey——'

[S.B. *gives a short dry laugh*]

PRIVATE: A pound you owe me! Money for aul rope! And you, Canon, what about giving us a bar or two?

CANON: Aye.

PRIVATE: You will? Wonderful! What'll it be? A pop number? An aul Gregorian come-all-ye? A whack out of an aul aria?

CANON: I had you cornered.

PRIVATE: 'I had you cornered'—I know it! I know it! I know it!

Okay. [*Sings in the style of a modern crooner*] 'I had you cornered/That night in Casablanca/That night you said you loved me—' all set? Boys and girls, that top, pop recording star, Kenny O'Byrne and the Ballybeg Buggers in their latest fabulous release, 'I Had You Cornered.'

> PRIVATE *stands with head lowered, his foot tapping, his fingers clicking in syncopated rhythm, waiting for the* CANON *to begin. He keeps this up for a few seconds. Then in time to his own beat he sings very softly, as he goes to the bedroom*]

> Should aul acquaintance be forgot
> And never brought to min'?
> Should aul acquaintance be forgot
> And days o' lang-syne?
> Yah—ooooo.

> [PUBLIC *suddenly sits up in bed*]

Mendelssohn! That's the bugger'll tear the guts out of you! [PUBLIC *puts on a recording of the Second Movement of the Violin Concerto.* PRIVATE, *now almost frenzied, dashes back to the kitchen*] Give us a bar or two, Mendelssohn, aul fella. Come on, lad; resin the aul bow and spit on your hands and give us an aul bar!

> [*The record begins.* PRIVATE *runs to the table and thrusts his face between the players*]

Listen! Listen! Listen! D'you hear it? D'you know what the music says? [*To* S.B.] It says that once upon a time a boy and his father sat in a blue boat on a lake on an afternoon in May, and on that afternoon a great beauty happened, a beauty that has haunted the boy ever since, because he wonders now did it really take place or did he imagine it. There are only the two of us, he says; each of us is all the other has; and why can we not even look at each other? Have pity on us, he says; have goddam pity on every goddam bloody man jack of us!

[*He comes away from the table and walks limply back to the bedroom. When he gets to the bedroom door he turns, surveys the men*]

To hell with all strong silent men!

[*He goes into the bedroom, drops into the chair, and sits motionless.* PUBLIC *sinks back on to the bed again. Silence*]

CANON: What's that noise?

S.B.: What's that, Canon?

CANON: A noise of some sort.

S.B.: Is there?

[*They listen*]

S.B.: I don't hear——

CANON: Wait.

S.B.: Is it——

CANON: It's music—is it?

S.B.: Music?

CANON: Aye. It's music.

S.B.: That'll be Gar then.

CANON: Oh.

S.B.: Playing them records of his.

CANON: Thought I heard something.

S.B.: All he asks is to sit in there and play them records all day.

CANON: It makes him happy.

S.B.: Terrible man for the records.

CANON: Just so, now. It'll be getting near his time, he tells me.

S.B.: Tomorrow morning.

CANON: Tomorrow morning.

S.B.: Aye, tomorrow morning. Powerful the way time passes, too.

CANON: 'You wait,' says she, 'till the rosary's over and the kettle's on.'

S.B.: A sharp one, Madge.

CANON: Ah-hah. There's hope for you yet.

S.B.: I don't know, is there?

CANON: No. You're not too late yet.

S.B.: Maybe . . . maybe. . . .

CANON: No, I wouldn't say die yet—not yet I wouldn't.

SLOW CURTAIN

PART TWO

The small hours of the morning. The kitchen is dimly lit. In the kitchen, just outside the bedroom door, are GAR's *cases, and lying across them are his coat, his cap, and a large envelope containing his X-ray and visa. The bedroom is in darkness: just enough light to see* PUBLIC *on the bed and* PRIVATE *in the chair.* S.B. *comes in from the scullery carrying a cup of tea in his hand. He is dressed in long trousers, a vest, a hat, socks. He moves slowly towards the table, sees the cases, goes over to them, touches the coat, goes back towards the table, and sits there, staring at the bedroom door. He coughs. Immediately* PRIVATE *is awake and* PUBLIC *sits up sleepily in bed.*

PRIVATE: What—what—what's that? [*Relaxing*] Madge probably. Looking to see is the door bolted.

[PUBLIC *gets out of bed and switches on the light. Looks at his watch*]

You'll not sleep again tonight, laddo.

PUBLIC: Bugger.

[PUBLIC *looks at himself in the mirror and then sits on edge of bed*]

PRIVATE: Four more hours. This is the last time you'll lie in this bed, the last time you'll look at that pattern [*On the floor*], the last time you'll listen to the silence of Ballybeg, the last time you'll——

PUBLIC: Agh, shut up!

PRIVATE: It is now sixteen or seventeen years since I saw the Queen of France. Go into the shop, man, and get yourself a packet of aspirin; that'll do the trick. [*Looking up at ceiling*] Mind if I take a packet of aspirin, Screwballs? Send the bill to the U.S.A., okay? Out you go, boy, and get a clatter of pills!

[*They both go into the kitchen.* PUBLIC *stops dead when he sees* S.B. *staring at him*]

PRIVATE: My God! Lady Godiva!

PUBLIC: Is this where you are?

S.B.: Aye—I—I—I—I wasn't sleeping. What has you up?

[PUBLIC *goes to where the key of the shop is hung up*]

PUBLIC: I—I wasn't sleeping either. I'll get some aspirins inside.

S.B.: It's hard to sleep sometimes. . . .

PUBLIC: It is, aye . . . sometimes. . . .

S.B.: There's tea in the pot.

PUBLIC: Aye?

S.B.: If it's a headache you have.

PUBLIC: It'll make me no worse anyway.

[PUBLIC *goes into the scullery.* PRIVATE *stands at the door and talks into him*]

PRIVATE: Now's your time, boy. The small hours of the morning. Put your head on his shoulder and say, 'How's my wee darling Daddy?'

[PUBLIC *puts his head round the door*]

PUBLIC: You take some?

s.b.: Sure you know I never take a second cup.

private: Playing hard to get. Come on, bucko; it's your place to make the move—the younger man. Say—say—say—say, 'Screwballs, with two magnificent legs like that, how is it you were never in show biz?' Say, 'It is now sixteen or seventeen—'—Say —oh my God—say—say something.

[PUBLIC *enters with a cup of tea*]

public: You'll need a new tyre for the van.

s.b.: What one's that?

public: The back left-hand one. I told you. It's done.

s.b.: Aye. So you did.

public: And—and——

private: What else?

public: —and don't forget the fencing posts for McGuire next Wednesday.

s.b.: Fencing posts.

public: Twelve dozen. The milk lorry'll take them. I spoke to Packey.

s.b.: Aye. . . . right. . . .

private: Go on! Keep talking!

public: And if you're looking for the pliers, I threw them into the tea chest under the counter.

s.b.: Which tea chest?

public: The one near the window.

s.b.: Oh, I see—I see. . . .

private: You're doing grand. Keep at it. It's the silence that's the enemy.

public: You'll be wanting more plug tobacco. The traveller'll be here this week.

s.b.: More plug.

public: It's finished. The last of it went up to Curran's wake.

s.b.: I'll—I'll see about that.

PUBLIC: And you'll need to put a new clasp on the lower window —the tinkers are about again.

S.B.: Aye?

PUBLIC: They were in at dinner time. I got some cans off them.

S.B.: I just thought I noticed something shining from the ceiling.

PUBLIC: It's the cans then.

S.B.: Aye.

PUBLIC: That's what it is. I bought six off them.

S.B.: They'll not go to loss.

PUBLIC: They wanted me to take a dozen but I said six would do us.

S.B.: Six is plenty. They don't go as quick as they used to—them cans.

PUBLIC: They've all got cookers and ranges and things.

S.B.: What's that?

PUBLIC: I say they don't buy them now because the open fires are nearly all gone.

S.B.: That's it. All cookers and ranges and things these times.

PUBLIC: That's why I wouldn't take the dozen.

S.B.: You were right, too. Although I mind the time when I got through a couple of dozen a week.

PUBLIC: Aye?

S.B.: All cans it was then. Maybe you'd sell a kettle at turf-cutting or if there'd be a Yank coming home. . . .

[Pause]

PUBLIC: Better get these pills and then try to get a couple of hours sleep——

S.B.: You're getting the mail van to Strabane?

[PUBLIC *gives him a quick, watchful look*]

PUBLIC: At a quarter past seven.

S.B.: [*Awkwardly*] I was listening to the weather forecast there . . . moderate westerly winds and occasional showers, it said.

PUBLIC: Aye?

S.B.: I was thinking it—it—it—it would be a fair enough day for going up in thon plane.

PUBLIC: It should be, then.

S.B.: Showers—just like the Canon said. . . . And I was meaning to tell you that you should sit at the back. . . .

PRIVATE: It is now sixteen or seventeen years—the longest way round's the shortest way home——

S.B.: So *he* was saying, too . . . you know there—if there was an accident or anything—it's the front gets it hardest—

PUBLIC: I suppose that's true enough.

S.B.: So *he* was saying . . . not that I would know—just that he was saying it there. . . .

PRIVATE: [*Urgently, rapidly*] Now! Now! He might remember —he might. But if he does, my God, laddo—what if he does?

PUBLIC: [*With pretended carelessness*] D'you know what kept coming into my mind the day?

S.B.: Eh?

PUBLIC: The fishing we used to do on Lough na Cloc Cor.

S.B.: [*Confused, on guard*] Oh, aye, Lough na Cloc Cor—aye —aye——

PUBLIC: We had a throw on it every Sunday during the season.

S.B.: That's not the day nor yesterday.

PUBLIC: [*More quickly*] There used to be a blue boat on it— d'you remember it?

S.D.: Many's the fish we took off that same lake.

PUBLIC: D'you remember the blue boat?

S.B.: A blue one, eh?

PUBLIC: I don't know who owned it. But it was blue. And the paint was peeling.

S.B.: [*Remembering*] I mind a brown one the doctor brought from somewhere up in the——

PUBLIC: [*Quickly*] It doesn't matter who owned it. It doesn't even matter that it was blue. But d'you remember one afternoon in May—we were up there—the two of us—and it must have rained because you put your jacket round my shoulders and gave me your hat——

S.B.: Aye?

PUBLIC: —and it wasn't that we were talking or anything—but suddenly—suddenly you sang 'All Round My Hat I'll Wear a Green Coloured Ribbono'——

S.B.: Me?

PUBLIC: —for no reason at all except that we—that you were happy. D'you remember? D'you remember?

[*There is a pause while* S.B. *tries to recall*]

S.B.: No . . . no, then, I don't. . . .

[PRIVATE *claps his hands in nervous mockery*]

PRIVATE: [*Quickly*] There! There! There!

S.B.: 'All Round My Hat?' No, I don't think I ever knew that one. It wasn't 'The Flower of Sweet Strabane,' was it? That was my song.

PUBLIC: It could have been. It doesn't matter.

PRIVATE: So now you know: it never happened! Ha-ha-ha-ha-ha.

S.B.: 'All Round My Hat?'—that was never one of mine. What does it go like?

PUBLIC: I couldn't tell you. I don't know it either.

PRIVATE: Ha-ha-ha-ha-ha-ha-ha-ha.

S.B.: And you say the boat was blue?

PUBLIC: It doesn't matter. Forget it.

S.B.: [*Justly, reasonably*] There was a brown one belonging to the doctor, and before that there was a wee flat-bottom—but it was green—or was it white? I'll tell you, you wouldn't be thinking of a punt—it could have been blue—one that the curate had down the pier last summer——

[PRIVATE's *mocking laughter increases.* PUBLIC *rushes quickly into the shop.* PRIVATE, *still mocking, follows*]

—a fine sturdy wee punt it was, too, and it could well have been the. . . .

[*He sees that he is alone and tails off. Slowly he gets to his feet and goes towards the scullery door. He meets* MADGE *entering. She is dressed in outside clothes. She is very weary*]

MADGE: What has you up?

S.B.: Me? Aw, I took medicine and the cramps wouldn't let me sleep. I thought you were in bed?

MADGE: I was over at Nelly's. The place was upside down.

S.B.: There's nothing wrong, is there?

MADGE: Not a thing.

S.B.: The baby's strong and healthy?

MADGE: Grand—grand.

S.B.: That's all that matters.

MADGE: They're going to call it Brigid.

S.B.: Brigid—that's a grand name . . . Patrick, Brigid, and Colmcille. . . .

[MADGE *takes off her hat and coat.* S.B. *hesitates*]

Madge. . . .

MADGE: You'll get a cold padding about in yon rig.

S.B.: Madge, I'll manage rightly, Madge, eh?

MADGE: Surely you will.

S.B.: I'll get one of Charley Bonner's boys to do the van on Tuesdays and Thursdays and I'll manage rightly?

MADGE: This place is cold. Away off to bed.

S.B.: It's not like in the old days when the whole countryside did with me; I needed the help then. But it's different now. I'll manage by myself now. Eh? I'll manage fine, eh?

MADGE: Fine.

s.b.: D'you mind the trouble we had keeping him at school just after he turned ten. D'you mind nothing would do him but he'd get behind the counter. And he had this wee sailor suit on him this morning——

MADGE: A sailor suit? He never had a sailor suit.

s.b.: Oh, he had, Madge. Oh, Madge, he had. I can see him, with his shoulders back, and the wee head up straight, and the mouth, aw, man, as set, and says he this morning, I can hear him saying it, says he, 'I'm not going to school. I'm going into my daddy's business'—you know—all important—and, d'you mind, you tried to coax him to go to school, and not a move you could get out of him, and him as manly looking, and this wee sailor suit as smart looking on him, and—and—and at the heel of the hunt I had to go with him myself, the two of us, hand in hand, as happy as larks—we were that happy, Madge—and him dancing and chatting beside me—mind?—you couldn't get a word in edge-ways with all the chatting he used to go through. . . . Maybe, Madge, maybe it's because I could have been his grandfather, eh?

MADGE: I don't know.

s.b.: I was too old for her, Madge, eh?

MADGE: I don't know. They're a new race—a new world.

s.b.: [Leaving] In the wee sailor suit—all the chatting he used to go through. . . . I don't know either. . . .

MADGE: [Looking at GAR's case] Tomorrow'll be sore on him: his heart'll break tomorrow, and all next week, and the week after maybe. . . . Brigid—aye, it's all right—[Trying out the sound of the name] Brigid—Biddy—Biddy Mulhern—Brigid Mulhern—aye—like Madge Mulhern doesn't sound right—[Trying it out]—Madge Mulhern—Madge Mulhern—I don't know —it's too aul fashioned or something. . . . Has he his cap? [Finds it in the pocket of the coat. Also finds an apple] . . . Aye, he has. And an apple, if you don't mind—for all his grief. He'll be all right. That Lizzy one'll look after him well, I suppose, if she can take time off from blatherin'. Garden front and back, and a TV in the house of lords—I'll believe them things when I see them! Never had much time for blatherin' women. . . . [Remembering] An envelope. . . . [She takes

two notes from her pocket, goes to the dresser, and finds an
envelope. She puts the money into the envelope, and slips
the envelope into the coat pocket] That'll get him a cup of
tea on the plane. I had put them two pounds by me to get my
feet done on the fair day. But I can wait till next month.
From what I hear, there's no big dances between now and
then. . . . [*She stands looking at the bedroom door*] So. I
think that's everything. . . . [*She raises her hand in a sort of*
vague Benediction, then shuffles towards the scullery] When
the Boss was his age, he was the very same as him: leppin, and
eejitin' about and actin' the clown; as like as two peas. And
when he's the age the Boss is now, he'll turn out just the same.
And although I won't be here to see it, you'll find that he's
learned nothin' in-between times. That's people for you—they'd
put you astray in the head if you thought long enough about
them.

[PUBLIC *and* PRIVATE *enter from the shop*]

PUBLIC: You down too? Turning into a night club, this place.

MADGE: I'm only getting back.

PUBLIC: Well, how's the new Madge?

MADGE: Strong and healthy—and that's all that matters. Were you
and the Boss chatting there?

PUBLIC: When's the christening?

MADGE: Sunday. After last Mass.

PUBLIC: Madge Mulhern. Are you proud?

MADGE: I'm just tired, son. Very tired.

PUBLIC: You're sure there's nothing wrong, Madge?

MADGE: If there was something wrong, wouldn't I tell you?

PRIVATE: Of course she would. Who else has she?

PUBLIC: Did you tell her she's getting an elephant out of my
first wages?

MADGE: Aye, so. The jars are up?

PUBLIC: They are.

MADGE: And the dishes washed?

PUBLIC: All done.

MADGE: I'll give you a call at half-six, then.

PUBLIC: Madge—Madge, you'd let me know if—if he got sick or anything?

MADGE: Who else would there be?

PUBLIC: Just in case . . . not that it's likely—he'll outlive the whole of us. . . .

MADGE: Good night.

PUBLIC: Sleep well, Madge.

MADGE: Sleep well yourself.

[MADGE *goes off.* PUBLIC *and* PRIVATE *watch her shuffle off*]

PRIVATE: Watch her carefully, every movement, every gesture, every little peculiarity: keep the camera whirring; for this is a film you'll run over and over again—Madge Going to Bed On My Last Night At Home. . . . Madge. . . . [PUBLIC *and* PRIVATE *go into bedroom*] God, Boy, why do you have to leave? Why? Why?

PUBLIC: I don't know. I—I—I don't know.

QUICK CURTAIN

Neil Simon

In the decade of the Sixties, Neil Simon rose to the theatrical summit as America's foremost writer of contemporary comedies. The roseate series of events began on February 22, 1961, with his initial Broadway play, *Come Blow Your Horn*, which ran for 677 performances. This was followed by the book for the musical *Little Me* (1962); *Barefoot in the Park* (1963); *The Odd Couple* (1965); the musical *Sweet Charity* (1966) and *The Star-Spangled Girl* (1966).

In 1968, Mr. Simon provided the Broadway theatre with two of its reigning successes of the year: *Plaza Suite*, a trio of short comedies that transpire at different intervals in the identical suite at the Hotel Plaza, New York, and the book for the musical *Promises, Promises*. The latter, based on the Billy Wilder film *The Apartment*, had music by Burt Bacharach and lyrics by Hal David.

Mr. Simon was born in the Bronx, New York, on July 4, 1927. He attended New York University and the University of Denver. His first theatrical affiliation came as a sketch writer (in collaboration with his brother Danny) for resort revues at Camp Tamiment, Pennsylvania. From there he moved on to television, supplying comedy material for such personalities as Phil Silvers, Jackie Gleason, Red Buttons, Tallulah Bankhead and, notably, for Sid Caesar and Imogene Coca in "Your Show of Shows."

An accomplished hand at pointed comedy, Mr. Simon later contributed sketches to two Broadway revues, *Catch a Star* (1955) and *New Faces of 1956*.

In 1965, the dramatist won an Antoinette Perry (Tony) Award as the year's best author for *The Odd Couple*, which appears in this collection, and in 1968, he was the recipient of the Sam S. Shubert

Award in recognition of his outstanding contribution to the American theatre.

An acknowledged master of comedy technique, Mr. Simon recently was asked for his "prescription" for successful comedy writing. "The idea of a prescription for comedy," he replied, "is obviously ridiculous. What works for one playwright rarely works for another, and even the fact that a certain approach succeeded for a writer before does not mean that it will surely produce an amusing play for that same scribe a second time."

Mr. Simon, however, would be the first to agree that comedy, as with all forms of drama, must originate with the characters, for valid and appreciable humor only can emerge from their involvements in, and reactions to, a situation. "In the first of 112 versions of *Come Blow Your Horn*, the opening five minutes of the play were crammed with good jokes . . . in fact, some of the best I had ever written . . . and the scene was terrible. The audience, knowing nothing of the characters or situation, could not have cared less. Now I know enough to *start* with the *characters*."

And where do they come from? "In the case of *The Odd Couple*, from a party I attended in California. All the men there were divorced, all their dates were their new girl friends. Most of these men were sharing apartments with other divorced men because alimony payments forced them to save money."

The basic conflict in *The Odd Couple* stems from two people of "completely opposite nature and temperament"—the meticulously neat man and his roommate, the compulsively untidy slob. "I put them in an intolerable situation, and let the sparks fly. The extra ingredient, and very important, is that they must both emphatically *believe* that their way of life is the right one. . . ."

While Neil Simon's plays may be regarded by some as merely lighthearted entertainments, there is, if one digs deeply enough beyond the surface of laughter, an underlying element of human truths, particularly in *The Odd Couple*. Quite recently, London's respected drama critic Herbert Kretzmer wrote in *The Daily Express* that Mr. Simon's "genius has been not only to write some of the funniest one-line gags now being spoken on the English-speaking stage, but to suggest also something of the pain, aspiration and panic behind all those flip phrases."

Not only did *The Odd Couple* chalk up a Broadway run of 964 performances, as a film it became one of Paramount's all-time high grossers and as the 1960s draw to a close, the play still is touring and being performed in many corners of the world.

The author recently completed an original screenplay, *The Out-of-Towners* (which was filmed in New York with Jack Lemmon and Sandy Dennis), and in December 1969, his newest comedy, *Last of the Red Hot Lovers*, will open in New York under the auspices of Saint Subber, whose production of Mr. Simon's *Barefoot in the Park* ran for 1530 performances, making it the seventh longest-running comedy in Broadway history.

THE
ODD COUPLE

Neil Simon

The Odd Couple was first presented by Saint Subber on March 10, 1965, at the Plymouth Theatre, New York. The cast was as follows:

SPEED	*Paul Dooley*
MURRAY	*Nathaniel Frey*
ROY	*Sidney Armus*
VINNIE	*John Fiedler*
OSCAR MADISON	*Walter Matthau*
FELIX UNGAR	*Art Carney*
GWENDOLYN PIGEON	*Carole Shelley*
CECILY PIGEON	*Monica Evans*

Directed by Mike Nichols
Setting by Oliver Smith
Lighting by Jean Rosenthal
Costumes by Ann Roth

SYNOPSIS OF SCENES

The action takes place in an apartment on Riverside Drive in New York City.

ACT ONE

A hot summer night.

ACT TWO

SCENE 1: *Two weeks later, about eleven at night.*
SCENE 2: *A few days later, about eight P.M.*

ACT THREE

The next evening, about seven-thirty.

ACT ONE

It is a warm summer night in OSCAR MADISON's *apartment. This is one of those large eight-room affairs on Riverside Drive in the upper eighties. The building is about thirty-five years old and still has vestiges of its glorious past—high ceilings, walk-in closets and thick walls. We are in the living room with doors leading off to the kitchen, a bedroom and a bathroom, and a hallway to the other bedrooms.*

Although the furnishings have been chosen with extreme good taste, the room itself, without the touch and care of a woman these past few months, is now a study in slovenliness. Dirty dishes, discarded clothes, old newspapers, empty bottles, glasses filled and unfilled, opened and unopened laundry packages, mail and disarrayed furniture abound. The only cheerful note left in this room is the lovely view of the New Jersey Palisades through its twelfth-floor window. Three months ago this was a lovely apartment.

As the curtain rises, the room is filled with smoke. A poker game is in progress. There are six chairs around the table but only four men are sitting. They are MURRAY, ROY, SPEED *and* VINNIE. VINNIE, *with the largest stack of chips in front of him, is nervously tapping his foot; he keeps checking his watch.* ROY *is watching* SPEED *and* SPEED *is glaring at* MURRAY *with incredulity and utter fascination.* MURRAY *is the dealer. He slowly and methodically tries to shuffle. It is a ponderous and painful business.* SPEED *shakes his head in disbelief. This is all done wordlessly.*

SPEED: [*Cups his chin in his hand and looks at* MURRAY] Tell me, Mr. Maverick, is this your first time on the riverboat?

MURRAY: [*With utter disregard*] You don't like it, get a machine.

[*He continues to deal slowly*]

ROY: Geez, it stinks in here.

VINNIE: [*Looks at his watch*] What time is it?

SPEED: Again what time is it?

VINNIE: [*Whining*] My watch is slow. I'd like to know what time it is.

SPEED: [*Glares at him*] You're winning ninety-five dollars, that's what time it is. Where the hell are you running?

VINNIE: I'm not running anywhere. I just asked what time it was. Who said anything about running?

ROY: [*Looks at his watch*] It's ten-thirty.

[*There is a pause.* MURRAY *continues to shuffle*]

VINNIE: [*After the pause*] I got to leave by twelve.

SPEED: [*Looks up in despair*] Oh, Christ!

VINNIE: I told you that when I sat down. I got to leave by twelve. Murray, didn't I say that when I sat down? I said I got to leave by twelve.

SPEED: All right, don't talk to him. He's dealing. [*To* MURRAY] Murray, you wanna rest for a while? Go lie down, sweetheart.

MURRAY: You want speed or accuracy, make up your mind.

[*He begins to deal slowly.* SPEED *puffs on his cigar angrily*]

ROY: Hey, you want to do me a really big favor? Smoke toward New Jersey.

[SPEED *blows smoke at* ROY]

MURRAY: No kidding, I'm really worried about Felix. [*Points to an empty chair*] He's never been this late before. Maybe somebody should call. [*Yells off*] Hey, Oscar, why don't you call Felix?

ROY: [*Waves his hand through the smoke*] Listen, why don't we chip in three dollars apiece and buy another window. How the hell can you breathe in here?

MURRAY: How many cards you got, four?

SPEED: Yes, Murray, we all have four cards. When you give us one more, we'll all have five. If you were to give us two more, we'd have six. Understand how it works now?

ROY: [*Yells off*] Hey, Oscar, what do you say? In or out?

[*From offstage we hear* OSCAR'*s voice*]

OSCAR: [*Offstage*] Out, pussycat, out!

[SPEED *opens and the others bet*]

VINNIE: I told my wife I'd be home by one the latest. We're making an eight o'clock plane to Florida. I told you that when I sat down.

SPEED: Don't cry, Vinnie. You're forty-two years old. It's embarrassing. Give me two . . .

[*He discards*]

ROY: Why doesn't he fix the air conditioner? It's ninety-eight degrees, and it sits there sweating like everyone else. I'm out.

[*He goes to the window and looks out*]

MURRAY: Who goes to Florida in July?

VINNIE: It's off-season. There's no crowds and you get the best room for one-tenth the price. No cards . . .

SPEED: Some vacation. Six cheap people in an empty hotel.

MURRAY: Dealer takes four . . . Hey, you think maybe Felix is sick? [*He points to the empty chair*] I mean he's never been this late before.

ROY: [*Takes a laundry bag from an armchair and sits*] You know, it's the same garbage from last week's game. I'm beginning to recognize things.

MURRAY: [*Throwing his cards down*] I'm out . . .

SPEED: [*Showing his hand*] Two kings . . .

VINNIE: Straight . . .

[*He shows his hand and takes in the pot*]

MURRAY: Hey, maybe he's in his office locked in the john again. Did you know Felix was once locked in the john overnight? He wrote out his entire will on a half a roll of toilet paper! Heee, what a nut!

[VINNIE *is playing with his chips*]

SPEED: [*Glares at him as he shuffles the cards*] Don't play with your chips. I'm asking you nice; don't play with your chips.

VINNIE: [*To* SPEED] I'm not playing. I'm counting. Leave me alone. What are you picking on me for? How much do you think I'm winning? Fifteen dollars!

SPEED: Fifteen dollars? You dropped more than that in your cuffs!

[SPEED *deals a game of draw poker*]

MURRAY: [*Yells off*] Hey, Oscar, what do you say?

OSCAR: [*Enters carrying a tray with beer, sandwiches, a can of peanuts, and opened bags of pretzels and Fritos*] I'm in! I'm in! Go ahead. Deal!

[OSCAR MADISON *is forty-three. He is a pleasant, appealing man who seems to enjoy life to the fullest. He enjoys his weekly poker game, his friends, his excessive drinking and his cigars. He is also one of those lucky creatures in life who even enjoys his work—he's a sportswriter for the New York* Post. *His carefree attitude is evident in the sloppiness of his household, but it seems to bother others more than it does* OSCAR. *This is not to say that* OSCAR *is without cares or worries. He just doesn't seem to have any*]

VINNIE: Aren't you going to look at your cards?

OSCAR: [*Sets the tray on a side chair*] What for? I'm gonna bluff anyway. [*Opens a bottle of Coke*] Who gets the Coke?

MURRAY: I get a Coke.

OSCAR: My friend Murray the policeman gets a warm Coke.

[*He gives him the bottle*]

ROY: [*Opens the betting*] You still didn't fix the refrigerator? It's been two weeks now. No wonder it stinks in here.

OSCAR: [*Picks up his cards*] Temper, temper. If I wanted nagging I'd go back with my wife. [*Throws them down*] I'm out. Who wants food?

OSCAR: [*Looks under the bread*] I got brown sandwiches and green sandwiches. Well, what do you say?

MURRAY: What's the green?

OSCAR: It's either very new cheese or very old meat.

MURRAY: I'll take the brown.

[OSCAR *gives* MURRAY *a sandwich*]

ROY: [*Glares at* MURRAY] Are you crazy? You're not going to eat that, are you?

MURRAY: I'm hungry.

ROY: His refrigerator's been broken for two weeks. I saw milk standing in there that wasn't even in the bottle.

OSCAR: [*To* ROY] What are you, some kind of a health nut? Eat, Murray, eat!

ROY: I've got six cards . . .

SPEED: That figures—I've got three aces. Misdeal.

[*They all throw their cards in.* SPEED *begins to shuffle*]

VINNIE: You know who makes very good sandwiches? Felix. Did you ever taste his cream cheese and pimento on date-nut bread?

SPEED: [*To* VINNIE] All right, make up your mind poker or

menus. [OSCAR *opens a can of beer, which sprays in a geyser over the players and the table. There is a hubbub as they all yell at* OSCAR. *He hands* ROY *the overflowing can and pushes the puddle of beer under the chair. The players start to go back to the game only to be sprayed again as* OSCAR *opens another beer can. There is another outraged cry as they try to stop* OSCAR *and mop up the beer on the table with a towel which was hanging on the standing lamp.* OSCAR, *undisturbed, gives them the beer and the bags of refreshments, and they finally sit back in their chairs.* OSCAR *wipes his hands on the sleeve of* ROY's *jacket which is hanging on the back of the chair*] Hey, Vinnie, tell Oscar what time you're leaving.

VINNIE: [*Like a trained dog*] Twelve o'clock.

SPEED: [*To the others*] You hear? We got ten minutes before the next announcement. All right, this game is five card stud. [*He deals and ad libs calling the cards, ending with* MURRAY's *card*] . . . And a bullet for the policeman. All right, Murray, it's your bet. [*No answer*] Do something, huh.

OSCAR: [*Getting a drink at the bar*] Don't yell at my friend Murray.

MURRAY: [*Throwing in a coin*] I'm in for a quarter.

OSCAR: [*Proudly looks in* MURRAY's *eyes*] Beautiful, baby, beautiful.

[*He sits down and begins to open the can of peanuts*]

ROY: Hey, Oscar, let's make a rule. Every six months you have to buy fresh potato chips. How can you live like this? Don't you have a maid?

OSCAR: [*Shakes his head*] She quit after my wife and kids left. The work got to be too much for her. [*He looks on the table*] The pot's shy. Who didn't put in a quarter?

MURRAY: [*To* OSCAR] You didn't.

OSCAR: [*Puts in money*] You got a big mouth, Murray. Just for that, lend me twenty dollars.

[SPEED *deals another round*]

MURRAY: I just loaned you twenty dollars ten minutes ago.

[*They all join in a round of betting*]

OSCAR: You loaned me *ten* dollars *twenty* minutes ago. Learn to count, pussycat.

MURRAY: Learn to play poker, chicken licken! Borrow from somebody else. I keep winning my own money back.

ROY: [*To* OSCAR] You owe everybody in the game. If you don't have it, you shouldn't play.

OSCAR: All right, I'm through being the nice one. You owe me six dollars apiece for the buffet.

SPEED: [*Dealing another round of cards*] Buffet? Hot beer and two sandwiches left over from when you went to high school?

OSCAR: What do you want at a poker game, a tomato surprise? Murray, lend me twenty dollars or I'll call your wife and tell her you're in Central Park wearing a dress.

MURRAY: You want money, ask Felix.

OSCAR: He's not here.

MURRAY: Neither am I.

ROY: [*Gives him money*] All right, here. You're on the books for another twenty.

OSCAR: How many times are you gonna keep saying it?

[*He takes the money*]

MURRAY: When are you gonna call Felix?

OSCAR: When are we gonna play poker?

MURRAY: Aren't you even worried? It's the first game he's missed in over two years.

OSCAR: The record is fifteen years set by Lou Gehrig in 1939! I'll call! I'll call!

ROY: How can you be so lazy?

[*The phone rings*]

OSCAR: [*Throwing his cards in*] Call me irresponsible, I'm funny that way.

[*He goes to the phone*]

SPEED: Pair of sixes . . .

VINNIE: Three deuces . . .

SPEED: [*Throws up his hands in despair*] This is my last week. I get all the aggravation I need at home.

[OSCAR *picks up the phone*]

OSCAR: Hello! Oscar the Poker Player!

VINNIE: [*To* OSCAR] If it's my wife tell her I'm leaving at twelve.

SPEED: [*To* VINNIE] You look at your watch once more and you get the peanuts in your face. [*To* ROY] Deal the cards!

[*The game continues during* OSCAR's *phone conversation, with* ROY *dealing a game of stud*]

OSCAR: [*Into the phone*] Who? Who did you want, please? *Dabby?* Dabby who? No, there's no Dabby here. Oh, *Daddy!* [*To the others*] For crise sakes, it's my kid. [*Back into the phone, he speaks with great love and affection*] Brucey, hello, baby. Yes, it's Daddy! [*There is a general outburst of ad libbing from the poker players. To the others*] Hey, come on, give me a break, willya? My five-year-old kid is calling from California. It must be costing him a fortune. [*Back into the phone*] How've you been, sweetheart? Yes, I finally got your letter. It took three weeks. Yes, but next time you tell Mommy to give you a stamp. I know, but you're not supposed to draw it on. [*He laughs. To the others*] You hear?

SPEED: We hear. We hear. We're all thrilled.

OSCAR: [*Into the phone*] What's that, darling? What goldfish? Oh, in your room! Oh, sure. Sure, I'm taking care of them. [*He holds the phone over his chest*] Oh, God, I killed my kid's goldfish! [*Back into the phone*] Yes, I feed them every day.

ROY: Murderer!

OSCAR: Mommy wants to speak to me? Right. Take care of yourself, soldier. I love you.

VINNIE: [*Beginning to deal a game of stud*] Ante a dollar . . .

SPEED: [*To* OSCAR] Cost you a dollar to play. You got a dollar?

OSCAR: Not after I get through talking to this lady. [*Into the phone with false cheerfulness*] Hello, Blanche. How are you? Err, yes, I have a pretty good idea why you're calling. I'm a week behind with the check, right? *Four* weeks? That's not possible. Because it's not possible. Blanche, I keep a record of every check and I *know* I'm only *three* weeks behind! Blanche, I'm trying the best I can. Blanche, don't threaten me with jail because it's not a threat. With my expenses and my alimony, a prisoner takes home more pay than I do! Very nice, in front of the kids. Blanche, don't tell me you're going to have my salary attached, just say good-bye! Good-bye! [*He hangs up. To the players*] I'm eight hundred dollars behind in alimony so let's up the stakes.

[*He gets his drink from the poker table*]

ROY: She can do it, you know.

OSCAR: What?

ROY: Throw you in jail. For nonsupport of the kids.

OSCAR: Never. If she can't call me once a week to aggravate me, she's not happy.

[*He crosses to the bar*]

MURRAY: It doesn't bother you? That you can go to jail? Or that maybe your kids don't have enough clothes or enough to eat?

OSCAR: Murray, *Poland* could live for a year on what my kids leave over from lunch! Can we play cards?

[*He refills his drink*]

ROY: But that's the point. You shouldn't *be* in this kind of trouble. It's because you don't know how to manage anything. I should know; I'm your accountant.

OSCAR: [*Crossing to the table*] If you're my accountant, how come I need money?

ROY: If you need money, how come you play poker?

OSCAR: Because I need money.

ROY: But you always lose.

OSCAR: That's why I need the money! Listen, *I'm* not complaining. *You're* complaining. I get along all right. I'm living.

ROY: Alone? In eight dirty rooms?

OSCAR: If I win tonight, I'll buy a broom.

> [MURRAY *and* SPEED *buy chips from* VINNIE, *and* MURRAY *begins to shuffle the deck for a game of draw*]

ROY: That's not what you need. What you need is a wife.

OSCAR: How can I afford a wife when I can't afford a broom?

ROY: Then don't play poker.

OSCAR: [*Puts down his drink, rushes to* ROY *and they struggle over the bag of potato chips, which rips, showering everyone. They all begin to yell at one another*] Then don't come to my house and eat my potato chips!

MURRAY: What are you yelling about? We're playing a friendly game.

SPEED: Who's *playing?* We've been sitting here talking since eight o'clock.

VINNIE: Since *seven.* That's why I said I was going to quit at *twelve.*

SPEED: How'd you like a stale banana right in the mouth?

MURRAY: [*The peacemaker*] All right, all right, let's calm down. Take it easy. I'm a cop, you know. I could arrest the whole lousy game. [*He finishes dealing the cards*] Four . . .

OSCAR: [*Sitting at the table*] My friend Murray the Cop is right. Let's just play cards. And please hold them up; I can't see where I marked them.

MURRAY: You're worse than the kids from the PAL.

OSCAR: But you still love me, Roy, sweety, right?

ROY: [*Petulant*] Yeah, yeah.

OSCAR: That's not good enough. Come on, say it. In front of the whole poker game. "I love you, Oscar Madison."

ROY: You don't take any of this seriously, do you? You owe money to your wife, your government, your friends . . .

OSCAR: [*Throws his cards down*] What do you want me to do, Roy, jump in the garbage disposal and grind myself to death? [*The phone rings. He goes to answer it*] Life goes on even for those of us who are divorced, broke and sloppy. [*Into the phone*] Hello? Divorced, Broke and Sloppy. Oh, hello, sweetheart. [*He becomes very seductive, pulls the phone to the side and talks low, but he is still audible to the others, who turn and listen*] I told you not to call me during the game. I can't talk to you now. You *know* I do, darling. All right, just a minute. [*He turns*] Murray, it's your wife.

[*He puts the phone on the table and sits on the sofa*]

MURRAY: [*Nods disgustedly as he crosses to the phone*] I wish you *were* having an affair with her. Then she wouldn't bother *me* all the time. [*He picks up the phone*] Hello, Mimi, what's wrong?

[SPEED *gets up, stretches and goes into the bathroom*]

OSCAR: [*In a woman's voice, imitating* MIMI] What time are you coming home? [*Then imitating* MURRAY] I don't know, about twelve, twelve-thirty.

MURRAY: [*Into the phone*] I don't know, about twelve, twelve-thirty! [ROY *gets up and stretches*] Why, what did you want, Mimi? "A corned beef sandwich and a strawberry malted!"

OSCAR: Is she pregnant again?

MURRAY: [*Holds the phone over his chest*] No, just fat! [*There is the sound of a toilet flushing, and after* SPEED *comes out of the bathroom,* VINNIE *goes in. Into the phone again*] What? How could you hear that, I had the phone over my chest? Who? Felix? No, he didn't show up tonight. What's wrong? You're kidding! How should I know? All right, all right, good-bye. [*The toilet flushes again, and after* VINNIE *comes out of the bathroom,* ROY *goes in*] Good-bye, Mimi. Good-bye. [*He hangs up. To the others*] Well, what did I tell you? I knew it!

ROY: What's the matter?

MURRAY: [*Pacing by the couch*] Felix is missing!

OSCAR: Who?

MURRAY: Felix! Felix Ungar! The man who sits in that chair every week and cleans ashtrays. I told you something was up.

SPEED: [*At the table*] What do you mean, missing?

MURRAY: He didn't show up for work today. He didn't come home tonight. No one knows where he is. Mimi just spoke to his wife.

VINNIE: [*In his chair at the poker table*] Felix?

MURRAY: They looked everywhere. I'm telling you he's missing.

OSCAR: Wait a minute. No one is missing for one day.

VINNIE: That's right. You've got to be missing for forty-eight hours before you're missing. The worst he could be is lost.

MURRAY: How could he be lost? He's forty-four years old and lives on West End Avenue. What's the matter with you?

ROY: [*Sitting in an armchair*] Maybe he had an accident.

OSCAR: They would have heard.

ROY: If he's laying in a gutter somewhere? Who would know who he is?

OSCAR: He's got ninety-two credit cards in his wallet. The minute something happens to him, America lights up.

VINNIE: Maybe he went to a movie. You know how long those pictures are today.

SPEED: [*Looks at* VINNIE *contemptuously*] No wonder you're going to Florida in July! Dumb, dumb, dumb!

ROY: Maybe he was mugged?

OSCAR: For thirty-six hours? How much money could he have on him?

ROY: Maybe they took his clothes. I knew a guy who was mugged in a doctor's office. He had to go home in a nurse's uniform.

[OSCAR *throws a pillow from the couch at* ROY]

SPEED: Murray, you're a cop. What do you think?

MURRAY: I think it's something real bad.

SPEED: How do you know?

MURRAY: I can feel it in my bones.

SPEED: [*To the others*] You hear? Bulldog Drummond.

ROY: Maybe he's drunk. Does he drink?

OSCAR: Felix? On New Year's Eve he has Pepto-Bismal. What are we guessing? I'll call his wife.

[*He picks up the phone*]

SPEED: Wait a minute! Don't start anything yet. Just 'cause we don't know where he is doesn't mean somebody else doesn't. Does he have a girl?

VINNIE: A what?

SPEED: A girl? You know. Like when you're through work early.

MURRAY: Felix? Playing around? Are you crazy? He wears a vest and galoshes.

SPEED: [*Gets up and moves toward* MURRAY] You mean you automatically know who has and who hasn't got a girl on the side?

MURRAY: [*Moves to* SPEED] Yes, I automatically know.

SPEED: All right, you're so smart. Have I got a girl?

MURRAY: No, you haven't got a girl. What you've got is what *I've* got. What you *wish* you got and what you *got* is a whole different civilization! *Oscar* maybe has a girl on the side.

SPEED: That's different. He's divorced. That's not on the side. That's in the middle.

[*He moves to the table*]

OSCAR: [*To them both as he starts to dial*] You through? 'Cause one of our poker players is missing. I'd like to find out about him.

VINNIE: I thought he looked edgy the last couple of weeks. [*To* SPEED] Didn't you think he looked edgy?

SPEED: No. As a matter of fact, I thought *you* looked edgy.

[*He moves down to the right*]

OSCAR: [*Into the phone*] Hello? Frances? Oscar. I just heard.

ROY: Tell her not to worry. She's probably hysterical.

MURRAY: Yeah, you know women.

[*He sits down on the couch*]

OSCAR: [*Into the phone*] Listen, Frances, the most important thing is not to worry. Oh! [*To the others*] She's not worried.

MURRAY: Sure.

OSCAR: [*Into the phone*] Frances, do you have *any* idea where he could be? He what? You're kidding? Why? No, I didn't know. Gee, that's too bad. All right, listen, Frances, you just sit tight and the minute I hear anything I'll let you know. Right. G'bye.

[*He hangs up. They all look at him expectantly. He gets up wordlessly and crosses to the table, thinking. They all watch him a second, not being able to stand it any longer*]

MURRAY: Ya gonna tell us or do we hire a private detective?

OSCAR: They broke up!

ROY: Who?

OSCAR: Felix and Frances! They broke up! The entire marriage is through.

VINNIE: You're kidding!

ROY: I don't believe it.

SPEED: After twelve years?

[OSCAR *sits down at the table*]

VINNIE: They were such a happy couple.

MURRAY: Twelve years doesn't mean you're a *happy* couple. It just means you're a *long* couple.

SPEED: Go figure it. Felix and Frances.

ROY: What are you surprised at? He used to sit there every Friday night and tell us how they were fighting.

SPEED: I know. But who believes Felix?

VINNIE: What happened?

OSCAR: She wants out, that's all.

MURRAY: He'll go to pieces. I know Felix. He's going to try something crazy.

SPEED: That's all he ever used to talk about. "My beautiful wife. My wonderful wife." What happened?

OSCAR: His beautiful, wonderful wife can't stand him, that's what happened.

MURRAY: He'll kill himself. You hear what I'm saying? He's going to go out and try to kill himself.

SPEED: [*To* MURRAY] Will you shut up, Murray? Stop being a cop for two minutes. [*To* OSCAR] Where'd he go, Oscar?

OSCAR: He went out to kill himself.

MURRAY: What did I tell you?

ROY: [*To* OSCAR] Are you serious?

OSCAR: That's what she said. He was going out to kill himself. He didn't want to do it at home 'cause the kids were sleeping.

VINNIE: Why?

OSCAR: Why? Because that's Felix, that's why. [*He goes to the bar and refills his drink*] You know what he's like. He sleeps on the window sill. "Love me or I'll jump." 'Cause he's a nut, that's why.

MURRAY: That's right. Remember he tried something like that in the army? She wanted to break off the engagement so he started cleaning guns in his mouth.

SPEED: I don't believe it. Talk! That's all Felix is, talk.

VINNIE: [*Worried*] But is that what he said? In those words? "I'm going to kill myself?"

OSCAR: [*Pacing about the table*] I don't know in what words. She didn't read it to me.

ROY: You mean he left her a note?

OSCAR: No, he sent a telegram.

MURRAY: A *suicide telegram*? Who sends a suicide telegram?

OSCAR: Felix, the nut, that's who! Can you imagine getting a thing like that? She even has to tip the kid a quarter.

ROY: I don't get it. If he wants to kill himself, why does he send a telegram?

OSCAR: Don't you see how his mind works? If he sends a note, she might not get it till Monday and he'd have no excuse for not being dead. This way, for a dollar ten, he's got a chance to be saved.

VINNIE: You mean he really doesn't want to kill himself? He just wants sympathy.

OSCAR: What he'd really like is to go to the funeral and sit in the back. He'd be the biggest crier there.

MURRAY: He's right.

OSCAR: Sure I'm right.

MURRAY: We get these cases every day. All they want is attention. We got a guy who calls us every Saturday afternoon from the George Washington Bridge.

ROY: I don't know. You never can tell what a guy'll do when he's hysterical.

MURRAY: Nahhh. Nine out of ten times they don't jump.

ROY: What about the tenth time?

MURRAY: They jump. He's right. There's a possibility.

OSCAR: Not with Felix. I know him. He's too nervous to kill himself. He wears his seatbelt in a drive-in movie.

VINNIE: Isn't there someplace we could look for him?

SPEED: Where? Where would you look? Who knows where he is?

[*The doorbell rings. They all look at* OSCAR]

OSCAR: Of course! If you're going to kill yourself, where's the safest place to do it? With your friends!

[VINNIE *starts for the door*]

MURRAY: [*Stopping him*] Wait a minute! The guy may be hysterical. Let's play it nice and easy. If *we're* calm, maybe *he'll* be calm.

ROY: [*Getting up and joining them*] That's right. That's how they do it with those guys out on the ledge. You talk nice and soft.

[SPEED *rushes over to them, and joins in the frenzied discussion*]

VINNIE: What'll we say to him?

MURRAY: We don't say nothin'. Like we never heard a thing.

OSCAR: [*Trying to get their attention*] You through with this discussion? Because he already could have hung himself out in the hall. [*To* VINNIE] Vinnie, open the door!

MURRAY: Remember! Like we don't know nothin'.

[*They all rush back to their seats and grab up cards, which they concentrate on with the greatest intensity.* VIN-NIE *opens the door.* FELIX UNGAR *is there. He's about forty-four. His clothes are rumpled as if he had slept in them, and he needs a shave. Although he tries to act matter-of-fact, there is an air of great tension and nervousness about him*]

FELIX: [*Softly*] Hi, Vin! [VINNIE *quickly goes back to his seat and studies his cards.* FELIX *has his hands in his pockets, trying to be very nonchalant. With controlled calm*] Hi, fellas. [*They all mumble hello, but do not look at him. He puts his coat over the railing and crosses to the table*] How's the game going? [*They all mumble appropriate remarks, and continue staring at their cards*] Good! Good! Sorry I'm late. [FELIX *looks a little disappointed that no one asks "What?" He starts to pick up a sandwich, changes his mind and makes a gesture of distaste. He vaguely looks around*] Any Coke left?

OSCAR: [*Looking up from his cards*] Coke? Gee, I don't think so. I got a Seven-Up!

FELIX: [*Bravely*] No, I felt like a Coke. I just don't feel like Seven-Up tonight!

[*He stands watching the game*]

OSCAR: What's the bet?

SPEED: You bet a quarter. It's up to Murray. Murray, what do you say? [MURRAY *is staring at* FELIX] Murray! Murray!

ROY: [*To* VINNIE] Tap his shoulder.

VINNIE: [*Taps* MURRAY'S *shoulder*] Murray!

MURRAY: [*Startled*] What? What?

SPEED: It's up to you.

MURRAY: Why is it always up to me?

SPEED: It's not always up to you. It's up to you now. What do you do?

MURRAY: I'm in. I'm in.

[*He throws in a quarter*]

FELIX: [*Moves to the bookcase*] Anyone call about me?

OSCAR: Er, not that I can remember. [*To the others*] Did anyone call for Felix? [*They all shrug and ad lib "No"*] Why? Were you expecting a call?

FELIX: [*Looking at the books on the shelf*] No! No! Just asking.

[*He opens a book and examines it*]

ROY: Er, I'll see his bet and raise it a dollar.

FELIX: [*Without looking up from the book*] I just thought someone might have called.

SPEED: It costs me a dollar and a quarter to play, right?

OSCAR: Right!

FELIX: [*Still looking at the book, in a sing song*] But, if no one called, no one called.

> [*He slams the book shut and puts it back. They all jump at the noise*]

SPEED: [*Getting nervous*] What does it cost me to play again?

MURRAY: [*Angry*] A dollar and a quarter! A *dollar and a quarter!* Pay attention, for crise sakes!

ROY: All right, take it easy. Take it easy.

OSCAR: Let's calm down, everyone, heh?

MURRAY: I'm sorry. I can't help it. [*Points to* SPEED] He makes me nervous.

SPEED: I make *you* nervous. You make *me* nervous. You make *everyone* nervous.

MURRAY: [*Sarcastic*] I'm sorry. Forgive me. I'll kill myself.

OSCAR: Murray!

> [*He motions with his head to* FELIX]

MURRAY: [*Realizes his error*] Oh! Sorry.

> [SPEED *glares at him. They all sit in silence a moment, until* VINNIE *catches sight of* FELIX, *who is now staring out an upstage window. He quickly calls the others' attention to* FELIX]

FELIX: [*Looking back at them from the window*] Gee, it's a pretty view from here. What is it, twelve floors?

OSCAR: [*Quickly crossing to the window and closing it*] No. It's only eleven. That's all. Eleven. It says twelve but it's really only eleven. [*He then turns and closes the other window*

as FELIX *watches him.* OSCAR *shivers slightly*] Chilly in here.
[*To the others*] Isn't it chilly in here?

[*He crosses back to the table*]

ROY: Yeah, that's much better.

OSCAR: [*To* FELIX] Want to sit down and play? It's still early.

VINNIE: Sure. We're in no rush. We'll be here till three, four
in the morning.

FELIX: [*Shrugs*] I don't know; I just don't feel much like
playing now.

OSCAR: [*Sitting at the table*] Oh! Well, what *do* you feel
like doing?

FELIX: [*Shrugs*] I'll find something. [*He starts to walk toward
the other room*] Don't worry about me.

OSCAR: Where are you going?

FELIX: [*Stops in the doorway. He looks at the others who
are all staring at him*] To the john.

OSCAR: [*Looks at the others, worried, then at* FELIX] Alone?

FELIX: [*Nods*] I always go alone! Why?

OSCAR: [*Shrugs*] No reason. You gonna be in there long?

FELIX: [*Shrugs, then says meaningfully, like a martyr*] As long
as it takes.

[*Then he goes into the bathroom and slams the door
shut behind him. Immediately they all jump up and crowd
about the bathroom door, whispering in frenzied anxiety*]

MURRAY: Are you crazy? Letting him go to the john alone?

OSCAR: What did you want me to do?

ROY: Stop him! Go in with him!

OSCAR: Suppose he just has to go to the john?

MURRAY: Supposing he does? He's better off being embarrassed
than dead!

OSCAR: How's he going to kill himself in the john?

SPEED: What do you mean, how? Razor blades, pills. Anything that's in there.

OSCAR: That's the kids' bathroom. The worst he could do is brush his teeth to death.

ROY: He could jump.

VINNIE: That's right. Isn't there a window in there?

OSCAR: It's only six inches wide.

MURRAY: He could break the glass. He could cut his wrists.

OSCAR: He could also flush himself into the East River. I'm telling you he's not going to try anything!

[*He moves to the table*]

ROY: [*Goes to the doorway*] Shhh! Listen! He's crying. [*There is a pause as all listen as* FELIX *sobs*] You hear that. He's crying.

MURRAY: Isn't that terrible? For God's sakes, Oscar, do something! Say something!

OSCAR: What? What do you say to a man who's crying in your bathroom?

[*There is the sound of the toilet flushing and* ROY *makes a mad dash back to his chair*]

ROY: He's coming!

[*They all scramble back to their places.* MURRAY *gets mixed up with* VINNIE *and they quickly straighten it out.* FELIX *comes back into the room. But he seems calm and collected, with no evident sign of having cried*]

FELIX: I guess I'll be running along.

[*He starts for the door.* OSCAR *jumps up. So do the others*]

OSCAR: Felix, wait a second.

FELIX: No! No! I can't talk to you. I can't talk to anyone.

[*They all try to grab him, stopping him near the stairs*]

MURRAY: Felix, please. We're your friends. Don't run out like this.

[FELIX *struggles to pull away*]

OSCAR: Felix, sit down. Just for a minute. Talk to us.

FELIX: There's nothing to talk about. There's nothing to say. It's over. Over. Everything is over. Let me go!

[*He breaks away from them and dashes into the stage-right bedroom. They start to chase him and he dodges from the bedroom through the adjoining door into the bathroom*]

ROY: Stop him! Grab him!

FELIX: [*Looking for an exit*] Let me out! I've got to get out of here!

OSCAR: Felix, you're hysterical.

FELIX: Please let me out of here!

MURRAY: The john! Don't let him get in the john!

FELIX: [*Comes out of the bathroom with* ROY *hanging onto him, and the others trailing behind*] Leave me alone. Why doesn't everyone leave me alone?

OSCAR: All right, Felix, I'm warning you. Now cut it out!

[*He throws a half-filled glass of water, which he has picked up from the bookcase, into* FELIX's *face*]

FELIX: It's *my* problem. I'll work it out. Leave me alone. Oh, my stomach.

[*He collapses in* ROY's *arms*]

MURRAY: What's the matter with your stomach?

VINNIE: He looks sick. Look at his face.

[*They all try to hold him as they lead him over to the couch*]

FELIX: I'm not sick. I'm all right. I didn't take anything, I swear. Ohh, my stomach.

OSCAR: What do you mean you didn't take anything? What did you take?

FELIX: [*Sitting on the couch*] Nothing! Nothing! I didn't take anything. Don't tell Frances what I did, please! Oohh, my stomach.

MURRAY: He took something! I'm telling you he took something.

OSCAR: What, Felix? *What?*

FELIX: Nothing! I didn't take anything.

OSCAR: Pills? Did you take pills?

FELIX: No! No!

OSCAR: [*Grabbing* FELIX] Don't lie to me, Felix. Did you take pills?

FELIX: No, I didn't. I didn't take anything.

MURRAY: Thank God he didn't take pills.

[*They all relax and take a breath of relief*]

FELIX: Just a few, that's all.

[*They all react in alarm and concern over the pills*]

OSCAR: He took pills.

MURRAY: How many pills?

OSCAR: What kind of pills?

FELIX: I don't know what kind. Little green ones. I just grabbed anything out of her medicine cabinet. I must have been crazy.

OSCAR: Didn't you look? Didn't you see what kind?

FELIX: I couldn't see. The light's broken. Don't call Frances. Don't tell her. I'm so ashamed. So ashamed.

OSCAR: Felix, how many pills did you take?

FELIX: I don't know. I can't remember.

OSCAR: I'm calling Frances.

FELIX: [*Grabs him*] No! Don't call her. Don't call her. If she hears I took a whole bottle of pills . . .

MURRAY: A whole bottle? A *whole bottle of pills?* [*He turns to* VINNIE] My God, call an ambulance!

[VINNIE *runs to the front door*]

OSCAR: [*To* MURRAY] You don't even know what *kind!*

MURRAY: What's the difference! He took a whole bottle!

OSCAR: Maybe they were vitamins. He could be the healthiest one in the room! Take it easy, will you?

FELIX: Don't call Frances. Promise me you won't call Frances.

MURRAY: Open his collar. Open the window. Give him some air.

SPEED: Walk him around. Don't let him go to sleep.

[SPEED *and* MURRAY *pick* FELIX *up and walk him around, while* ROY *rubs his wrists*]

ROY: Rub his wrists. Keep his circulation going.

VINNIE: [*Running to the bathroom to get a compress*] A cold compress. Put a cold compress on his neck.

[*They sit* FELIX *in the armchair, still chattering in alarm*]

OSCAR: One doctor at a time, heh? All the interns shut the hell up!

FELIX: I'm all right. I'll be all right. [*To* OSCAR *urgently*] You didn't call Frances, did you?

MURRAY: [*To the others*] You just gonna stand here? No one's gonna do anything? I'm calling a doctor.

[*He crosses to the phone*]

FELIX: No! No doctor.

MURRAY: You *gotta* have a doctor.

FELIX: I don't need a doctor.

MURRAY: You gotta get the pills out.

FELIX: I got them out. I threw up before! [*He sits back weakly.* MURRAY *hangs up the phone*] Don't you have a root beer or a ginger ale?

[VINNIE *gives the compress to* SPEED]

ROY: [*To* VINNIE] Get him a drink.

OSCAR: [*Glares angrily at* FELIX] He threw them up!

VINNIE: Which would you rather have, Felix, the root beer or the ginger ale?

SPEED: [*To* VINNIE] Get him the drink! Just get him the drink.

[VINNIE *runs into the kitchen as* SPEED *puts the compress on* FELIX's *head*]

FELIX: Twelve years. Twelve years we were married. Did you know we were married twelve years, Roy?

ROY: [*Comforting him*] Yes, Felix. I knew.

FELIX: [*With great emotion in his voice*] And now it's over. Like that, it's over. That's hysterical, isn't it?

SPEED: Maybe it was just a fight. You've had fights before, Felix.

FELIX: No, it's over. She's getting a lawyer tomorrow. *My* cousin. She's using *my* cousin! [*He sobs*] Who am *I* going to get?

[VINNIE *comes out of the kitchen with a glass of root beer*]

MURRAY: [*Patting his shoulder*] It's okay, Felix. Come on. Take it easy.

VINNIE: [*Gives the glass to* FELIX] Here's the root beer.

FELIX: I'm all right, honestly. I'm just crying.

[*He puts his head down. They all look at him helplessly*]

MURRAY: All right, let's not stand around looking at him. [*Pushes* SPEED *and* VINNIE *away*] Let's break it up, heh?

FELIX: Yes, don't stand there looking at me. Please.

OSCAR: [*To the others*] Come on, he's all right. Let's call it a night.

> [MURRAY, SPEED *and* ROY *turn in their chips at the poker table, get their coats and get ready to go*]

FELIX: I'm so ashamed. Please, fellas, forgive me.

VINNIE: [*Bending to* FELIX] Oh, Felix, we—we understand.

FELIX: Don't say anything about this to anyone, Vinnie. Will you promise me?

VINNIE: I'm going to Florida tomorrow.

FELIX: Oh, that's nice. Have a good time.

VINNIE: Thanks.

FELIX: [*Turns away and sighs in despair*] We were going to go to Florida next winter. [*He laughs, but it's a sob*] Without the kids! Now they'll go without me.

> [VINNIE *gets his coat and* OSCAR *ushers them all to the door*]

MURRAY: [*Stopping at the door*] Maybe one of us should stay?

OSCAR: It's all right, Murray.

MURRAY: Suppose he tries something again?

OSCAR: He won't try anything again.

MURRAY: How do you *know* he won't try anything again?

FELIX: [*Turns to* MURRAY] I won't try anything again. I'm very tired.

OSCAR: [*To* MURRAY] You hear? He's very tired. He had a busy night. Good night, fellows.

> [*They all ad lib good-byes and leave. The door closes, but opens immediately and* ROY *comes back in*]

ROY: If anything happens, Oscar, just call me.

[*He exits, and as the door starts to close, it reopens and* SPEED *comes in*]

SPEED: I'm three blocks away. I could be here in five minutes.

[*He exits, and as the door starts to close, it reopens and* VINNIE *comes back in*]

VINNIE: If you need me I'll be at the Meridian Motel in Miami Beach.

OSCAR: You'll be the first one I'll call, Vinnie.

[VINNIE *exits. The door closes and then reopens as* MURRAY *comes back*]

MURRAY: [*To* OSCAR] You're sure?

OSCAR: I'm sure.

MURRAY: [*Loudly to* FELIX, *as he gestures to* OSCAR *to come to the door*] Good night, Felix. Try to get a good night's sleep. I guarantee you things are going to look a lot brighter in the morning. [*To* OSCAR, *sotto voce*] Take away his belt and his shoe laces.

[*He nods and exits.* OSCAR *turns and looks at* FELIX *sitting in the armchair and slowly moves across the room. There is a moment's silence*]

OSCAR: [*He looks at* FELIX *and sighs*] Ohh, Felix, Felix, Felix, Felix!

FELIX: [*Sits with his head buried in his hands. He doesn't look up*] I know, I know, I know, I know! What am I going to do, Oscar?

OSCAR: You're gonna wash down the pills with some hot, black coffee. [*He starts for the kitchen, then stops*] Do you think I could leave you alone for two minutes?

FELIX: No, I don't think so! Stay with me, Oscar. Talk to me.

OSCAR: A cup of black coffee. It'll be good for you. Come on in the kitchen. I'll sit on you.

FELIX: Oscar, the terrible thing is, I think I still love her. It's a lousy marriage but I still love her. I didn't want this divorce.

OSCAR: [*Sitting on the arm of the couch*] How about some Ovaltine? You like Ovaltine? With a couple of fig newtons or chocolate mallomars?

FELIX: All right, so we didn't get along. But we had two wonderful kids, and a beautiful home. Didn't we, Oscar?

OSCAR: How about vanilla wafers? Or Vienna fingers? I got everything.

FELIX: What more does she want? What does *any* woman want?

OSCAR: I want to know what *you* want. Ovaltine, coffee or tea. Then we'll get to the divorce.

FELIX: It's not fair, damn it! It's just not fair! [*He bangs his fist on the arm of the chair angrily, then suddenly winces in great pain and grabs his neck*] Oh! Ohh, my neck. My neck!

OSCAR: What? What?

FELIX: [*He gets up and paces in pain. He is holding his twisted neck*] It's a nerve spasm. I get it in the neck. Oh! Ohh, that hurts.

OSCAR: [*Rushing to help*] Where? Where does it hurt?

FELIX: [*Stretches out an arm like a halfback*] Don't touch me! Don't touch me!

OSCAR: I just want to see where it hurts.

FELIX: It'll go away. Just let me alone a few minutes. Ohh! Ohh!

OSCAR: [*Moving to the couch*] Lie down; I'll rub it. It'll ease the pain.

FELIX: [*In wild contortions*] You don't know how. It's a special way. Only Frances knows how to rub me.

OSCAR: You want me to ask her to come over and rub you?

FELIX: [*Yells*] No! No! We're getting divorced. She wouldn't want to rub me any more. It's tension. I get it from tension. I must be tense.

OSCAR: I wouldn't be surprised. How long does it last?

FELIX: Sometimes a minute, sometimes hours. I once got it while I was driving. I crashed into a liquor store. Ohhh! Ohhh!

[*He sits down, painfully, on the couch*]

OSCAR: [*Getting behind him*] You want to suffer or do you want me to rub your stupid neck?

[*He starts to massage it*]

FELIX: Easy! Easy!

OSCAR: [*Yells*] Relax, damn it: relax!

FELIX: [*Yells back*] Don't yell at me! [*Then quietly*] What should I do? Tell me nicely.

OSCAR: [*Rubbing the neck*] Think of warm jello!

FELIX: Isn't that terrible? I can't do it. I can't relax. I sleep in one position all night. Frances says when I die on my tombstone it's going to say, "Here Stands Felix Ungar." [*He winces*] Oh! Ohh!

OSCAR: [*Stops rubbing*] Does that hurt?

FELIX: No, it feels good.

OSCAR: Then say so. You make the same sound for pain or happiness.

[*Starts to massage his neck again*]

FELIX: I know. I know. Oscar—I think I'm crazy.

OSCAR: Well, if it'll make you feel any better, I think so too.

FELIX: I mean it. Why else do I go to pieces like this? Coming up here, scaring you to death. Trying to kill myself. What is that?

OSCAR: That's panic. You're a panicky person. You have a low threshold for composure.

[*He stops rubbing*]

FELIX: Don't stop. It feels good.

OSCAR: If you don't relax I'll break my fingers. [*Touches his hair*] Look at this. The only man in the world with clenched hair.

FELIX: I do terrible things, Oscar. You know I'm a cry baby.

OSCAR: Bend over.

[FELIX *bends over and* OSCAR *begins to massage his back*]

FELIX: [*Head down*] I tell the whole world my problems.

OSCAR: [*Massaging hard*] Listen, if this hurts just tell me, because I don't know what the hell I'm doing.

FELIX: It just isn't nice, Oscar, running up here like this, carrying on like a nut.

OSCAR: [*Finishes massaging*] How does your neck feel?

FELIX: [*Twists his neck*] Better. Only my back hurts.

[*He gets up and paces, rubbing his back*]

OSCAR: What you need is a drink.

[*He starts for the bar*]

FELIX: I can't drink. It makes me sick. I tried drinking last night.

OSCAR: [*At the bar*] Where *were* you last night?

FELIX: Nowhere. I just walked.

OSCAR: All night?

FELIX: All night.

OSCAR: In the rain?

FELIX: No. In a hotel. I couldn't sleep. I walked around the room all night. It was over near Times Square. A dirty, depressing room. Then I found myself looking out the window. And suddenly, I began to think about jumping.

OSCAR: [*He has two glasses filled and crosses to* FELIX] What changed your mind?

FELIX: Nothing. I'm still thinking about it.

OSCAR: Drink this.

[*He hands him a glass, crosses to the couch and sits*]

FELIX: I don't want to get divorced, Oscar. I don't want to suddenly change my whole life. [*He moves to the couch and sits next to* OSCAR] Talk to me, Oscar. What am I going to do? What am I going to do?

OSCAR: You're going to pull yourself together. And then you're going to drink that Scotch, and then you and I are going to figure out a whole new life for you.

FELIX: Without Frances? Without the kids?

OSCAR: It's been done before.

FELIX: [*Paces around*] You don't understand, Oscar. I'm nothing without them. I'm—*nothing!*

OSCAR: What do you mean, nothing? You're something! [FELIX *sits in the armchair*] A person! You're flesh and blood and bones and hair and nails and ears. You're not a fish. You're not a buffalo. You're *you!* You walk and talk and cry and complain and eat little green pills and send suicide telegrams. No one else does that, Felix. I'm telling you, *you're the only one of its kind in the world!* [*He goes to the bar*] Now drink that.

FELIX: Oscar, you've been through it yourself. What did you do? How did you get through those first few nights?

OSCAR: [*Pours a drink*] I did exactly what you're doing.

FELIX: Getting hysterical!

OSCAR: No, drinking! *Drinking!* [*He comes back to the couch with the bottle and sits*] I drank for four days and four nights. And then I fell through a window. I was bleeding but I was forgetting.

[*He drinks again*]

FELIX: How can you forget your kids? How can you wipe out twelve years of marriage?

OSCAR: You can't. When you walk into eight empty rooms every night it hits you in the face like a wet glove. But those are the facts, Felix. You've got to face it. You can't spend the rest of your life crying. It annoys people in the movies! Be a good boy and drink your Scotch.

[*He stretches out on the couch with his head near* FELIX]

FELIX: I can imagine what Frances must be going through.

OSCAR: What do you mean, what *she's* going through?

FELIX: It's much harder on the woman, Oscar. She's all alone with the kids. Stuck there in the house. She can't get out like me. I mean where is she going to find someone now at her age? With two kids. Where?

OSCAR: I don't know. Maybe someone'll come to the door! Felix, there's a hundred thousand divorces a year. There must be *something* nice about it. [FELIX *suddenly puts both his hands over his ears and hums quietly*] What's the matter now?

[*He sits up*]

FELIX: My ears are closing up. I get it from the sinus. It must be the dust in here. I'm allergic to dust.

[*He hums. Then he gets up and tries to clear his ears by hopping first on one leg then the other as he goes to the window and opens it*]

OSCAR: [*Jumping up*] What are you doing?

FELIX: I'm not going to jump. I'm just going to breathe. [*He takes deep breaths*] I used to drive Frances crazy with my allergies. I'm allergic to perfume. For a while the only thing she could wear was my after-shave lotion. I was impossible to live with. It's a wonder she took it this long.

[*He suddenly bellows like a moose. He makes this strange sound another time.* OSCAR *looks at him dumbfounded*]

OSCAR: What are you doing?

FELIX: I'm trying to clear my ears. You create a pressure inside and then it opens it up.

[*He bellows again*]

OSCAR: Did it open up?

FELIX: A little bit. [*He rubs his neck*] I think I strained my throat.

[*He paces about the room*]

OSCAR: Felix, why don't you leave yourself alone? Don't tinker.

FELIX: I can't help myself. I drive everyone crazy. A marriage counselor once kicked me out of his office. He wrote on my chart, "Lunatic!" I don't blame her. It's impossible to be married to me.

OSCAR: It takes two to make a rotten marriage.

[*He lies back down on the couch*]

FELIX: You don't know what I was like at home. I bought her a book and made her write down every penny we spent. Thirty-eight cents for cigarettes; ten cents for a paper. Everything had to go in the book. And then we had a big fight because I said she forgot to write down how much the book was. Who could live with anyone like that?

OSCAR: An accountant! What do I know? We're not perfect. We all have faults.

FELIX: Faults? Heh! Faults. We have a maid who comes in to clean three times a week. And on the other days, Frances does the cleaning. And at night, after they've both cleaned up, I go in and clean the whole place again. I can't help it. I like things clean. Blame it on my mother. I was toilet-trained at five months old.

OSCAR: How do you remember things like that?

FELIX: I loused up the marriage. Nothing was ever right. I used to recook everything. The minute she walked out of the kitchen I would add salt or pepper. It's not that I didn't trust her, it's just that I was a better cook. Well, I cooked myself out of a marriage. [*He bangs his head with the palm of his hand three times*] God damned idiot!

[*He sinks down in the armchair*]

OSCAR: Don't do that; you'll get a headache.

FELIX: I can't stand it, Oscar. I hate me. Oh, boy, do I hate me.

OSCAR: You don't hate you. You love you. You think no one has problems like you.

FELIX: Don't give me that analyst jazz. I happen to know I hate my guts.

OSCAR: Come on, Felix; I've never *seen* anyone so in love.

FELIX: [*Hurt*] I thought you were my friend.

OSCAR: That's why I can talk to you like this. Because I love you almost as much as *you* do.

FELIX: Then help me.

OSCAR: [*Up on one elbow*] How can I help you when I can't help myself? You think *you're* impossible to live with? Blanche used to say, "What time do you want dinner?" And I'd say, "I don't know. I'm not hungry." Then at three o'clock in the morning I'd wake her up and say, "Now!" I've been one of the highest paid sportswriters in the East for the past fourteen years, and we saved eight and a half dollars— in pennies! I'm never home, I gamble, I burn cigar holes in the furniture, drink like a fish and lie to her every chance I get. And for our tenth wedding anniversary, I took her to see the New York Rangers-Detroit Red Wings hockey game where she got hit with a puck. And I *still* can't understand why she left me. That's how impossible *I* am!

FELIX: I'm not like you, Oscar. I couldn't take it living all alone. I don't know how I'm going to work. They've got to fire me. How am I going to make a living?

OSCAR: You'll go on street corners and cry. They'll throw nickels at you! You'll work, Felix; you'll work.

[*He lies back down*]

FELIX: You think I ought to call Frances?

OSCAR: [*About to explode*] What for?

[*He sits up*]

FELIX: Well, talk it out again.

OSCAR: You've *talked* it all out. There are no words left in your entire marriage. When are you going to face up to it?

FELIX: I can't help it, Oscar; I don't know what to do.

OSCAR: Then listen to me. Tonight you're going to sleep here. And tomorrow you're going to get your clothes and your electric toothbrush and you'll move in with me.

FELIX: No, no. It's your apartment. I'll be in the way.

OSCAR: There's eight rooms. We could go for a year without seeing each other. Don't you understand? I *want* you to move in.

FELIX: Why? I'm a pest.

OSCAR: I *know* you're a pest. You don't have to keep telling me.

FELIX: Then why do you want me to live with you?

OSCAR: Because I can't stand living alone, that's why! For crying out loud, I'm proposing to you. What do you want, a ring?

FELIX: [*Moves to* OSCAR] Well, Oscar, if you really mean it, there's a lot I can do around here. I'm very handy around the house. I can fix things.

OSCAR: You don't have to fix things.

FELIX: I want to do *something*, Oscar. Let me do something.

OSCAR: [*Nods*] All right, you can take my wife's initials off the towels. Anything you want.

FELIX: [*Beginning to tidy up*] I can cook. I'm a terrific cook.

OSCAR: You don't have to cook. I eat cold cuts for breakfast.

FELIX: Two meals a day at home, we'll save a fortune. We've got to pay alimony, you know.

OSCAR: [*Happy to see* FELIX's *new optimism*] All right, you can cook.

[*He throws a pillow at him*]

FELIX: [*Throws the pillow back*] Do you like leg of lamb?

OSCAR: Yes, I like leg of lamb.

FELIX: I'll make it tomorrow night. I'll have to call Frances. She has my big pot.

OSCAR: *Will you forget Frances!* We'll get our own pots. Don't drive me crazy before you move in. [*The phone rings.* OSCAR *picks it up quickly*] Hello? Oh, hello, Frances!

FELIX: [*Stops cleaning and starts to wave his arms wildly. He whispers screamingly*] I'm not here! I'm not here! You didn't see me. You don't know where I am. I didn't call. I'm not here. I'm not here.

OSCAR: [*Into the phone*] Yes, he's here.

FELIX: [*Pacing back and forth*] How does she sound? Is she worried? Is she crying? What is she saying? Does she want to speak to me? I don't want to speak to her.

OSCAR: [*Into the phone*] Yes, he is!

FELIX: You can tell her I'm not coming back. I've made up my mind. I've had it there. I've taken just as much as she has. You can tell her for me if she thinks I'm coming back she's got another think coming. Tell her. Tell her.

OSCAR: [*Into the phone*] Yes! Yes, he's fine.

FELIX: Don't tell her I'm fine! You heard me carrying on before. What are you telling her that for? I'm not fine.

OSCAR: [*Into the phone*] Yes, I understand, Frances.

FELIX: [*Sits down next to* OSCAR] Does she want to speak to me? Ask her if she wants to speak to me?

OSCAR: [*Into the phone*] Do you want to speak to him?

FELIX: [*Reaches for the phone*] Give me the phone. I'll speak to her.

OSCAR: [*Into the phone*] Oh. You don't want to speak to him.

FELIX: She doesn't want to speak to me?

OSCAR: [*Into the phone*] Yeah, I see. Right. Well, good-bye.

[*He hangs up*]

FELIX: She didn't want to speak to me?

OSCAR: No!

FELIX: Why did she call?

OSCAR: She wants to know when you're coming over for your clothes. She wants to have the room repainted.

FELIX: Oh!

OSCAR: [*Pats* FELIX *on the shoulder*] Listen, Felix, it's almost one o'clock.

[*He gets up*]

FELIX: Didn't want to speak to me, huh?

OSCAR: I'm going to bed. Do you want a cup of tea with Fruitanos or Raisinettos?

FELIX: She'll paint it pink. She always wanted it pink.

OSCAR: I'll get you a pair of pajamas. You like stripes, dots, or animals?

[*He goes into the bedroom*]

FELIX: She's really heartbroken, isn't she? I want to kill myself, and she's picking out colors.

OSCAR: [*In the bedroom*] Which bedroom do you want? I'm lousy with bedrooms.

FELIX: [*Gets up and moves toward the bedroom*] You know, I'm glad. Because she finally made me realize—it's over. It didn't sink in until just this minute.

OSCAR: [*Comes back with pillow, pillowcase, and pajamas*] Felix, I want you to go to bed.

FELIX: I don't think I believed her until just now. My marriage is *really* over.

OSCAR: Felix, go to bed.

FELIX: Somehow it doesn't seem so bad now. I mean, I think I can live with this thing.

OSCAR: Live with it tomorrow. Go to bed tonight.

FELIX: In a little while. I've got to think. I've got to start re-arranging my life. Do you have a pencil and paper?

OSCAR: Not in a little while. Now! It's my house; I make up the bedtime.

[*He throws the pajamas to him*]

FELIX: Oscar, please. I have to be alone for a few minutes. I've got to get organized. Go on, you go to bed. I'll—I'll clean up.

[*He begins picking up debris from the floor*]

OSCAR: [*Putting the pillow into the pillowcase*] You don't have to clean up. I pay a dollar fifty an hour to clean up.

FELIX: It's all right, Oscar. I wouldn't be able to sleep with all this dirt around anyway. Go to bed. I'll see you in the morning.

[*He puts the dishes on the tray*]

OSCAR: You're not going to do anything big, are you, like rolling up the rugs?

FELIX: Ten minutes, that's all I'll be.

OSCAR: You're sure?

FELIX: [*Smiles*] I'm sure.

OSCAR: No monkey business?

FELIX: No monkey business. I'll do the dishes and go right to bed.

OSCAR: Yeah.

[*Crosses up to his bedroom, throwing the pillow into the downstage bedroom as he passes. He closes his bedroom door behind him*]

FELIX: [*Calls him*] Oscar! [OSCAR *anxiously comes out of his bedroom and crosses to* FELIX] I'm going to be all right! It's going to take me a couple of days, but I'm going to be all right.

OSCAR: [*Smiles*] Good! Well, good night, Felix.

[*He turns to go toward the bedroom as* FELIX *begins to plump up a pillow from the couch*]

FELIX: Good night, Frances.

[OSCAR *stops dead.* FELIX, *unaware of his error, plumps another pillow as* OSCAR *turns and stares at* FELIX *with a troubled expression*]

CURTAIN

ACT TWO

SCENE 1

Two weeks later, about eleven at night. The poker game
is in session again. VINNIE, ROY, SPEED, MURRAY *and* OSCAR
are all seated at the table. FELIX's *chair is empty.*

  There is one major difference between this scene and
the opening poker-game scene. It is the appearance of the
room. It is immaculately clean. No, not clean. Sterile!
Spotless! Not a speck of dirt can be seen under the ten
coats of Johnson's Glo-Coat that have been applied to the
floor in the last three weeks. No laundry bags, no dirty
dishes, no half-filled glasses.

  Suddenly FELIX *appears from the kitchen. He carries a*
tray with glasses and food—and napkins. After putting the
tray down, he takes the napkins one at a time, flicks them
out to full length and hands one to every player. They
take them with grumbling and put them on their laps. He
picks up a can of beer and very carefully pours it into a tall
glass, measuring it perfectly so that not a drop spills or over-
flows. With a flourish he puts the can down.

FELIX: [*Moves to* MURRAY] An ice-cold glass of beer for Murray.

[MURRAY *reaches up for it*]

MURRAY: Thank you, Felix.

FELIX: [*Holds the glass back*] Where's your coaster?

MURRAY: My what?

FELIX: Your coaster. The little round thing that goes under the glass.

MURRAY: [*Looks around on the table*] I think I bet it.

OSCAR: [*Picks it up and hands it to* MURRAY] I knew I was winning too much. Here!

FELIX: Always try to use your coasters, fellows. [*He picks up another drink from the tray*] Scotch and a little bit of water?

SPEED: [*Raises his hand*] Scotch and a little bit of water. [*Proudly*] And I have my coaster.

[*He holds it up for inspection*]

FELIX: [*Hands him the drink*] I hate to be a pest but you know what wet glasses do?

[*He goes back to the tray and picks up and wipes a clean ashtray*]

OSCAR: [*Coldly and deliberately*] They leave little rings on the table.

FELIX: [*Nods*] Ruins the finish. Eats right through the polish.

OSCAR: [*To the others*] So let's watch those little rings, huh?

FELIX: [*Takes an ashtray and a plate with a sandwich from the tray and crosses to the table*] And we have a clean ashtray for Roy [*Handing* ROY *the ashtray*] Aaaaand—a sandwich for Vinnie.

[*Like a doting headwaiter, he skillfully places the sandwich in front of* VINNIE]

VINNIE: [*Looks at* FELIX, *then at the sandwich*] Gee, it smells good. What is it?

FELIX: Bacon, lettuce and tomato with mayonnaise on pumpernickel toast.

VINNIE: [*Unbelievingly*] Where'd you get it?

FELIX: [*Puzzled*] I made it. In the kitchen.

VINNIE: You mean you put in toast and cooked bacon? Just for me?

OSCAR: If you don't like it, he'll make you a meat loaf. Takes him five minutes.

FELIX: It's no trouble. Honest. I love to cook. Try to eat over the dish. I just vacuumed the rug. [*He goes back to the tray, then stops*] Oscar!

OSCAR: [*Quickly*] Yes, sir?

FELIX: I forgot what you wanted. What did you ask me for?

OSCAR: Two three-and-a-half-minute eggs and some petit fours.

FELIX: [*Points to him*] A double gin and tonic. I'll be right back. [FELIX *starts out, then stops at a little box on the bar*] Who turned off the Pure-A-Tron?

MURRAY: The what?

FELIX: The Pure-A-Tron! [*He snaps it back on*] Don't play with this, fellows. I'm trying to get some of the grime out of the air.

[*He looks at them and shakes his head disapprovingly, then exits. They all sit in silence a few seconds*]

OSCAR: Murray, I'll give you two hundred dollars for your gun.

SPEED: [*Throws his cards on the table and gets up angrily*] I can't take it any more. [*With his hand on his neck*] I've had it up to here. In the last three hours we played four minutes of poker. I'm not giving up my Friday nights to watch cooking and housekeeping.

ROY: [*Slumped in his chair, head hanging down*] I can't breathe. [*He points to the Pure-A-Tron*] That lousy machine is sucking everything out of the air.

VINNIE: [*Chewing*] Gee, this is delicious. Who wants a bite?

MURRAY: Is the toast warm?

VINNIE: Perfect. And not too much mayonnaise. It's really a well-made sandwich.

MURRAY: Cut me off a little piece.

VINNIE: Give me your napkin. I don't want to drop any crumbs.

SPEED: [*Watches them, horrified, as* VINNIE *carefully breaks the sandwich over* MURRAY's *napkin. Then he turns to* OSCAR] Are you listening to this? Martha and Gertrude at the Automat. [*Almost crying in despair*] What the hell happened to our poker game?

ROY: [*Still choking*] I'm telling you that thing could kill us. They'll find us here in the morning with our tongues on the floor.

SPEED: [*Yells at* OSCAR] Do something! Get him back in the game.

OSCAR: [*Rises, containing his anger*] Don't bother me with your petty little problems. You get this one stinkin' night a week. I'm cooped up here with Dione Lucas twenty-four hours a day.

[*He moves to the window*]

ROY: It was better before. With the garbage and the smoke, it was better before.

VINNIE: [*To* MURRAY] Did you notice what he does with the bread?

MURRAY: What?

VINNIE: He cuts off the crusts. That's why the sandwich is so light.

MURRAY: And then he only uses the soft, green part of the lettuce. [*Chewing*] It's really delicious.

SPEED: [*Reacts in amazement and disgust*] I'm going out of my mind.

OSCAR: [*Yells toward the kitchen*] Felix! Damn it, Felix!

SPEED: [*Takes the kitty box from the bookcase, puts it on the table, and puts the money in*] Forget it. I'm going home.

OSCAR: Sit down!

SPEED: I'll buy a book and I'll start to read again.

OSCAR: Siddown! Will you siddown! [*Yells*] Felix!

SPEED: Oscar, it's all over. The day his marriage busted up was the end of our poker game. [*He takes his jacket from the back of the chair and crosses to the door*] If you find some real players next week, call me.

OSCAR: [*Following him*] You can't run out now. I'm a big loser.

SPEED: [*With the door open*] You got no one to blame but yourself. Its all your fault. You're the one who stopped him from killing himself.

[*He exits and slams the door*]

OSCAR: [*Stares at the door*] He's right! The man is absolutely right.

[*He moves to the table*]

MURRAY: [*To* VINNIE] Are you going to eat that pickle?

VINNIE: I wasn't thinking of it. Why? Do you want it?

MURRAY: Unless you want it. It's your pickle.

VINNIE: No, no. Take it. I don't usually eat pickle.

[VINNIE *holds the plate with the pickle out to* MURRAY. OSCAR *slaps the plate, which sends the pickle flying through the air*]

OSCAR: Deal the cards!

MURRAY: What did you do that for?

OSCAR: Just deal the cards. You want to play poker, deal the cards. You want to eat, go to Schrafft's. [*To* VINNIE] Keep your sandwich and your pickles to yourself. I'm losing ninety-two dollars and everybody's getting fat! [*He screams*] Felix!

[FELIX *appears in the kitchen doorway*]

FELIX: What?

OSCAR: Close the kitchen and sit down. It's a quarter to twelve. I still got an hour and a half to win this month's alimony.

ROY: [*Sniffs*] What is the smell? Disinfectant! [*He smells the cards*] It's the cards. *He washed the cards!*

> [*He throws down the cards, takes his jacket from the chair and moves past the table to put his money into the kitty box*]

FELIX: [*Comes to the table with* OSCAR's *drink, which he puts down; then he sits in his own seat*] Okay. What's the bet?

OSCAR: [*Hurrying to his seat*] I can't believe it. We're gonna play cards again. [*He sits*] It's up to Roy. Roy, baby, what are you gonna do?

ROY: I'm going to get in a cab and go to Central Park. If I don't get some fresh air, you got yourself a dead accountant.

> [*He moves toward the door*]

OSCAR: [*Follows him*] What do you mean? It's not even twelve o'clock.

ROY: [*Turns back to* OSCAR] Look, I've been sitting here breathing Lysol and ammonia for four hours! Nature didn't intend for poker to be played like that. [*He crosses to the door*] If you wanna have a game next week [*He points to* FELIX] either Louis Pasteur cleans up *after* we've gone, or we play in the Hotel Dixie! Good night!

> [*He goes and slams the door. There is a moment's silence.* OSCAR *goes back to the table and sits*]

OSCAR: We got just enough for handball!

FELIX: Gee, I'm sorry. Is it my fault?

VINNIE: No, I guess no one feels like playing much lately.

MURRAY: Yeah. I don't know what it is, but something's happening to the old gang.

> [*He goes to a side chair, sits and puts on his shoes*]

OSCAR: Don't you know what's happening to the old gang? It's breaking up. Everyone's getting divorced. I swear, we used to have better games when we couldn't get out at night.

VINNIE: [*Getting up and putting on his jacket*] Well, I guess I'll be going too. Bebe and I are driving to Asbury Park for the weekend.

FELIX: Just the two of you, heh? Gee, that's nice! You always do things like that together, don't you?

VINNIE: [*Shrugs*] We have to. I don't know how to drive! [*He takes all the money from the kitty box and moves to the door*] You coming, Murray?

MURRAY: [*Gets up, takes his jacket and moves toward the door*] Yeah, why not? If I'm not home by one o'clock with a hero sandwich and a frozen éclair, she'll have an all-points out on me. Ahhh, you guys got the life.

FELIX: Who?

MURRAY: [*Turns back*] Who? You! The Marx Brothers! Laugh, laugh, laugh. What have you got to worry about? If you suddenly want to go to the Playboy Club to hunt Bunnies, who's gonna stop you?

FELIX: I don't belong to the Playboy Club.

MURRAY: I know you don't, Felix, it's just a figure of speech. Anyway, it's not such a bad idea. Why don't you join?

FELIX: Why?

MURRAY: Why! Because for twenty-five dollars they give you a key—and you walk into Paradise. *My* keys cost thirty cents—and you walk into corned beef and cabbage. [*He winks at him*] Listen to me.

[*He moves to the door*]

FELIX: What are you talking about, Murray? You're a happily married man.

MURRAY: [*Turns back on the landing*] I'm not talking about *my* situation. [*He puts on his jacket*] I'm talking about *yours!* Fate has just played a cruel and rotten trick on you, so enjoy it! [*He turns to go, revealing "PAL" letters sewn on the back of his jacket*] C'mon, Vinnie.

[VINNIE *waves good-bye and they both exit*]

FELIX: [*Staring at the door*] That's funny, isn't it, Oscar? They think we're happy. They really think we're enjoying this. [*He gets up and begins to straighten up the chairs*] They don't know, Oscar. They don't know what it's like.

[*He gives a short, ironic laugh, tucks the napkins under his arm and starts to pick up the dishes from the table*]

OSCAR: I'd be immensely grateful to you, Felix, if you didn't clean up just now.

FELIX: [*Puts dishes on the tray*] It's only a few things. [*He stops and looks back at the door*] I can't get over what Murray just said. You know I think they really envy us. [*He clears more stuff from the table*]

OSCAR: Felix, leave everything alone. I'm not through dirtying-up for the night.

[*He drops some poker chips on the floor*]

FELIX: [*Putting stuff on the tray*] But don't you see the irony of it? Don't you see it, Oscar?

OSCAR: [*Sighs heavily*] Yes, I see it.

FELIX: [*Clearing the table*] No, you don't. I really don't think you do.

OSCAR: Felix, I'm telling you I see the irony of it.

FELIX: [*Pauses*] Then tell me. What is it? What's the irony?

OSCAR: [*Deep breath*] The irony is—unless we can come to some other arrangement, I'm gonna kill you! That's the irony.

FELIX: What's wrong?

[*He crosses back to the tray and puts down all the glasses and other things*]

OSCAR: There's something wrong with this system, that's what's wrong. I don't think that two single men living alone in a big eight-room apartment should have a cleaner house than my mother.

FELIX: [*Gets the rest of the dishes, glasses and coasters from the table*] What are you talking about? I'm just going to put the dishes in the sink. You want me to leave them here all night?

OSCAR: [*Takes his glass, which* FELIX *has put on the tray, and crosses to the bar for a refill*] I don't care if you take them to bed with you. You can play Mr. Clean all you want. But don't make *me* feel guilty.

FELIX: [*Takes the tray into the kitchen, leaving the swinging door open*] I'm not asking you to do it, Oscar. You don't have to clean up.

OSCAR: [*Moves up to the door*] That's why you make me feel guilty. You're always in my bathroom hanging up my towels. Whenever I smoke you follow me around with an ashtray. Last night I found you washing the kitchen floor, shaking your head and moaning, "Footprints, footprints!"

[*He paces around the room*]

FELIX: [*Comes back to the table with a silent butler. He dumps the ashtrays, then wipes them carefully*] I didn't say they were yours.

OSCAR: [*Angrily sits down in the wing chair*] Well, they *were* mine, damn it. I have feet and they make prints. What do you want me to do, climb across the cabinets?

FELIX: No! I want you to walk on the floor.

OSCAR: I appreciate that! I really do.

FELIX: [*Crosses to the telephone table and cleans the ashtray there*] I'm just trying to keep the place livable. I didn't realize I irritated you that much.

OSCAR: I just feel I should have the right to decide when my bathtub needs a going over with Dutch Cleanser. It's the democratic way!

FELIX: [*Puts the silent butler and his rag down on the coffee table and sits down glumly on the couch*] I was wondering how long it would take.

OSCAR: How long *what* would take?

FELIX: Before I got on your nerves.

OSCAR: I didn't say you get on my nerves.

FELIX: Well, it's the same thing. You said I irritated you.

OSCAR: *You* said you irritated me. I didn't say it.

FELIX: Then what *did* you say?

OSCAR: I don't know *what* I said. What's the difference what I said?

FELIX: It doesn't make any difference. I was just repeating what I thought you said.

OSCAR: Well, don't repeat what you *thought* I said. Repeat what I *said!* My God, that's irritating!

FELIX: You see! You *did* say it!

OSCAR: I don't believe this whole conversation.

[*He gets up and paces by the table*]

FELIX: [*Pawing with a cup*] Oscar, I'm—I'm sorry. I don't know what's wrong with me.

OSCAR: [*Still pacing*] And don't pout. If you want to fight, we'll fight. But don't pout! Fighting *I* win. Pouting *you* win!

FELIX: You're right. Everything you say about me is absolutely right.

OSCAR: [*Really angry, turns to* FELIX] And don't give in so easily. I'm *not* always right. Sometimes *you're* right.

FELIX: You're right. I do that. I always figure I'm in the wrong.

OSCAR: Only this time you *are* wrong. And I'm right.

FELIX: Oh, leave me alone.

OSCAR: And don't sulk. That's the same as pouting.

FELIX: I know. I know. [*He squeezes his cup with anger*] Damn me, why can't I do one lousy thing right?

[*He suddenly stands up and cocks his arm back, about to hurl the cup angrily against the front door. Then he thinks better of it, puts the cup down and sits*]

OSCAR: [*Watching this*] Why didn't you throw it?

FELIX: I almost did. I get so insane with myself sometimes.

OSCAR: Then why don't you throw the cup?

FELIX: Because I'm trying to control myself.

OSCAR: Why?

FELIX: What do you mean, why?

OSCAR: Why do you have to control yourself? You're angry, you felt like throwing the cup, why don't you throw it?

FELIX: Because there's no point to it. I'd still be angry and I'd have a broken cup.

OSCAR: How do you *know* how you'd feel? Maybe you'd feel *wonderful*. Why do you have to control every single thought in your head? Why don't you let loose *once* in your life? Do something that you *feel* like doing—and not what you *think* you're supposed to do. Stop keeping books, Felix. Relax. Get drunk. Get angry. C'mon, *break the goddamned cup!*

[FELIX *suddenly stands up and hurls the cup against the door, smashing it to pieces. Then he grabs his shoulder in pain*]

FELIX: Oww! I hurt my arm!

[*He sinks down on the couch, massaging his arm*]

OSCAR: [*Throws up his hands*] You're hopeless! You're a hopeless mental case!

[*He paces around the table*]

FELIX: [*Grimacing with pain*] I'm not supposed to throw with that arm. What a stupid thing to do.

OSCAR: Why don't you live in a closet? I'll leave your meals outside the door and slide in the papers. Is that safe enough?

FELIX: [*Rubbing his arm*] I used to have bursitis in this arm. I had to give up golf. Do you have a heating pad?

OSCAR: How can you hurt your arm throwing a cup? If it had coffee in it, that's one thing. But an empty cup . . .

[*He sits in the wing chair*]

FELIX: All right, cut it out, Oscar. That's the way I am. I get hurt easily. I can't help it.

OSCAR: You're not going to cry, are you? I think all those tears dripping on the arm is what gave you bursitis.

FELIX: [*Holding his arm*] I once got it just from combing my hair.

OSCAR: [*Shaking his head*] A world full of room-mates and I pick myself the Tin Man. [*He sighs*] Oh, well, I suppose I could have done worse.

FELIX: [*Moves the rag and silent butler to the bar. Then he takes the chip box from the bar and crosses to the table*] You're darn right, you could have. A *lot* worse.

OSCAR: How?

FELIX: What do you mean, how? How'd you like to live with ten-thumbs Murray or Speed and his complaining? [*He gets down on his knees, picks up the chips and puts them into the box*] Don't forget I cook and clean and take care of this house. I save us a lot of money, don't I?

OSCAR: Yeah, but then you keep me up all night counting it.

FELIX: [*Goes to the table and sweeps the chips and cards into the box*] Now wait a minute. We're not always going at each other. We have some fun too, don't we?

OSCAR: [*Crosses to the couch*] Fun? Felix, getting a clear picture on Channel Two isn't my idea of whoopee.

FELIX: What are you talking about?

OSCAR: All right, what do you and I do every night?

[*He takes off his sneakers and drops them on the floor*]

FELIX: What do we do? You mean after dinner?

OSCAR: That's right. After we've had your halibut steak and the dishes are done and the sink has been Brillo'd and the pans have been S.O.S.'d and the leftovers have been Saran-Wrapped —what do we do?

FELIX: [*Finishes clearing the table and puts everything on top of the bookcase*] Well, we read, we talk . . .

OSCAR: [*Takes off his pants and throws them on the floor*] No, no. *I* read and *you* talk! I try to work and you talk. I take a bath and you talk. I go to sleep and you talk. We've got your life arranged pretty good but I'm still looking for a little entertainment.

FELIX: [*Pulling the kitchen chairs away from the table*] What are you saying? That I talk too much?

OSCAR: [*Sits on the couch*] No, no. I'm not complaining. You have a lot to say. What's worrying me is that I'm beginning to listen.

FELIX: [*Pulls the table into the alcove*] Oscar, I told you a hundred times, just tell me to shut up. I'm not sensitive.

[*He pulls the love seat down into the room, and centers the table between the windows in the alcove*]

OSCAR: I don't think you're getting my point. For a husky man, I think I've spent enough evenings discussing tomorrow's menu. The night was made for other things.

FELIX: Like what?

[*He puts two dining chairs neatly on one side of the table*]

OSCAR: Like unless I get to touch something soft in the next two weeks, I'm in big trouble.

FELIX: You mean women?

[*He puts the two other dining chairs neatly on the other side of the table*]

OSCAR: If you want to give it a name, all right, women!

FELIX: [*Picks up the two kitchen chairs and starts toward the landing*] That's funny. You know I haven't even *thought* about women in weeks.

OSCAR: I fail to see the humor.

FELIX: [*Stops*] No, that's really strange. I mean when Frances and I were happy, I don't think there was a girl on the street I didn't stare at for ten minutes. [*He crosses to the kitchen door and pushes it open with his back*] I used to take the wrong subway home just following a pair of legs. But since we broke up, I don't even know what a woman looks like.

[*He takes the chairs into the kitchen*]

OSCAR: Well, either I could go downstairs and buy a couple of magazines—or I could make a phone call.

FELIX: [*From the kitchen, as he washes the dishes*] What are you saying?

OSCAR: [*Crosses to a humidor on a small table and takes out a cigar*] I'm saying let's spend one night talking to someone with higher voices than us.

FELIX: You mean go out on a date?

OSCAR: Yah . . .

FELIX: Oh, well, I—I can't.

OSCAR: Why not?

FELIX: Well, it's all right for you. But I'm still married.

OSCAR: [*Paces toward the kitchen door*] You can *cheat* until the divorce comes through!

FELIX: It's not that. It's just that I have no—no *feeling* for it. I can't explain it.

OSCAR: Try!

FELIX: [*Comes to the doorway with a brush and dish in his hand*] Listen, I intend to go out. I get lonely too. But I'm just separated a few weeks. Give me a little time.

[*He goes back to the sink*]

OSCAR: There isn't any time left. I saw *TV Guide* and there's nothing on this week! [*He paces into and through the kitchen and out the kitchen door onto the landing*] What am I asking you? All I want to do is have dinner with a couple of girls. You just have to eat and talk. It's not hard. You've eaten and talked before.

FELIX: Why do you need me? Can't you go out yourself?

OSCAR: Because I may want to come back here. And if we walk in and find you washing the windows, it puts a damper on things.

[*He sits down*]

FELIX: [*Pokes his head out of the kitchen*] I'll take a pill and go to sleep.

[*He goes back into the kitchen*]

OSCAR: Why take a pill when you can take a girl?

FELIX: [*Comes out with an aerosol bomb held high over his head and circles around the room, spraying it*] Because I'd feel guilty, that's why. Maybe it doesn't make any sense to you, but that's the way I feel.

[*He puts the bomb on the bar and takes the silent butler and rag into the kitchen. He places them on the sink and busily begins to wipe the refrigerator*]

OSCAR: Look, for all I care you can take her in the kitchen and make a blueberry pie. But I think it's a lot healthier than sitting up in your bed every night writing Frances' name all through the crossword puzzles. Just for one night, talk to another girl.

FELIX: [*Returns, pushes the love seat carefully into position and sits, weakening*] But who would I call? The only single girl I know is my secretary and I don't think she likes me.

OSCAR: [*Jumps up and crouches next to* FELIX] Leave that to me. There's two sisters who live in this building. English girls. One's a widow; the other's a divorcée. They're a barrel of laughs.

FELIX: How do you know?

OSCAR: I was trapped in the elevator with them last week. [*Runs to the telephone table, puts the directory on the floor, and gets down on his knees to look for the number*] I've been meaning to call them but I didn't know which one to take out. This'll be perfect.

FELIX: What do they look like?

OSCAR: Don't worry. Yours is very pretty.

FELIX: I'm not worried. Which one is mine?

OSCAR: [*Looking in the book*] The divorcée.

FELIX: [*Goes to* OSCAR] Why do I get the divorcée?

OSCAR: I don't care. You want the widow?

[*He circles a number on the page with a crayon*]

FELIX: [*Sitting on the couch*] No, I don't want the widow. I don't even want the divorcée. I'm just doing this for you.

OSCAR: Look, take whoever you want. When they come in the door, point to the sister of your choice. [*Tears the page out of the book, runs to the bookcase and hangs it up*] I don't care. I just want to have some laughs.

FELIX: All right. All right.

OSCAR: [*Crosses to the couch and sits next to* FELIX] Don't say all right. I want you to promise me you're going to try to have a good time. Please, Felix. It's important. Say, "I promise."

FELIX: [*Nods*] I promise.

OSCAR: Again!

FELIX: I promise!

OSCAR: And no writing in the book, a dollar thirty for the cab.

FELIX: No writing in the book.

OSCAR: No one is to be called Frances. It's Gwendolyn and Cecily.

FELIX: No Frances.

OSCAR: No crying, sighing, moaning or groaning.

FELIX: I'll smile from seven to twelve.

OSCAR: And this above all, no talk of the past. Only the present.

FELIX: And the future.

OSCAR: That's the new Felix I've been waiting for. [*Leaps up and prances around*] Oh, is this going to be a night. Hey, where do you want to go?

FELIX: For what?

OSCAR: For dinner. Where'll we eat?

FELIX: You mean a restaurant? For the four of us? It'll cost a fortune.

OSCAR: We'll cut down on laundry. We won't wear socks on Thursdays.

FELIX: But that's throwing away money. We can't afford it, Oscar.

OSCAR: We have to eat.

FELIX: [*Moves to* OSCAR] We'll have dinner here.

OSCAR: *Here?*

FELIX: I'll cook. We'll save thirty, forty dollars.

[*He goes to the couch, sits and picks up the phone*]

OSCAR: What kind of a double date is that? You'll be in the kitchen all night.

FELIX: No, I won't. I'll put it up in the afternoon. Once I get my potatoes in, I'll have all the time in the world.

[*He starts to dial*]

OSCAR: [*Pacing back and forth*] What happened to the new Felix? Who are you calling?

FELIX: Frances. I want to get her recipe for London broil. The girls'll be crazy about it.

[*He dials as* OSCAR *storms off toward his bedroom*]

CURTAIN

SCENE 2

It is a few days later, about eight o'clock.

No one is on stage. The dining table looks like a page out of House and Garden. It is set for dinner for four, complete with linen tablecloth, candles and wine glasses. There is a floral centerpiece and flowers about the room, and crackers and dip on the coffee table. There are sounds of activity in the kitchen.

The front door opens and OSCAR *enters with a bottle of wine in a brown paper bag, his jacket over his arm. He looks about gleefully as he listens to the sounds from the kitchen. He puts the bag on the table and his jacket over a chair.*

OSCAR: [*Calls out in a playful mood*] I'm home, dear! [*He goes into his bedroom, taking off his shirt, and comes skipping out shaving with a cordless razor, with a clean shirt and a tie over his arm. He is joyfully singing as he admires the table*] Beautiful! Just beautiful! [*He sniffs, obviously catching the aroma from the kitchen*] Oh, yeah. Something wonderful is going on in that kitchen. [*He rubs his hands gleefully*] No, sir. There's no doubt about it. I'm the luckiest man on earth. [*He puts the razor into his pocket and begins to put on the shirt.* FELIX *enters slowly from the kitchen. He's wearing a small dish towel as an apron. He has a ladle in one hand. He looks silently and glumly at* OSCAR, *crosses to the armchair and sits*] I got the wine. [*He takes the bottle out of the bag and puts it on the table*] Batard Montrachet. Six and a quarter. You don't mind, do you, pussycat? We'll walk to work this week. [FELIX *sits glumly and silently*] Hey, no kidding, Felix, you did a great job. One little suggestion? Let's come down a little with the lights [*He switches off the wall brackets*]—and up very softly with the music. [*He crosses to the stereo set in the bookcase and picks up some record albums*] What do you think goes better with London broil, Mancini or Sinatra? [FELIX *just stares ahead*] Felix? What's the matter? [*He puts the albums down*] Something's wrong. I can tell by your conversation. [*He goes into the bathroom, gets a bottle of after-shave lotion and comes out putting it on*] All right, Felix, what is it?

FELIX: [*Without looking at him*] What is it? Let's start with what time do you think it is?

OSCAR: What time? I don't know. Seven thirty?

FELIX: Seven thirty? Try eight o'clock.

OSCAR: [*Puts the lotion down on the small table*] All right, so it's eight o'clock. So?

[*He begins to fix his tie*]

FELIX: So? You said you'd be home at seven.

OSCAR: Is that what I said?

FELIX: [*Nods*] That's what you said. "I will be home at seven" is what you said.

OSCAR: Okay, I said I'd be home at seven. And it's eight. So what's the problem?

FELIX: If you knew you were going to be late, why didn't you call me?

OSCAR: [*Pauses while making the knot in his tie*] I couldn't call you. I was busy.

FELIX: Too busy to pick up a phone? Where were you?

OSCAR: I was in the office, working.

FELIX: Working? Ha!

OSCAR: Yes. Working!

FELIX: I called your office at seven o'clock. You were gone.

OSCAR: [*Tucking in his shirt*] It took me an hour to get home. I couldn't get a cab.

FELIX: Since when do they have cabs in Hannigan's Bar?

OSCAR: Wait a minute. I want to get this down on a tape recorder, because no one'll believe me. You mean now I have to call you if I'm coming home late for dinner?

FELIX: [*Crosses to* OSCAR] Not *any* dinner. Just the ones I've been slaving over since two o'clock this afternoon—to help save *you* money to pay your wife's alimony.

OSCAR: [*Controlling himself*] Felix, this is no time to have a domestic quarrel. We have two girls coming down any minute.

FELIX: You mean you told them to be here at eight o'clock?

OSCAR: [*Takes his jacket and crosses to the couch, then sits and takes some dip from the coffee table*] I don't remember what I said. Seven thirty, eight o'clock. What difference does it make?

FELIX: [*Follows* OSCAR] I'll tell you what difference. You told me they were coming at seven thirty. You were going to be here at seven to help me with the hors d'oeuvres. At seven thirty they arrive and we have cocktails. At eight o'clock we have dinner. It is now eight o'clock. *My London broil is finished!* If we don't eat now the whole damned thing'll be *dried out!*

OSCAR: Oh, God, help me.

FELIX: Never mind helping *you*. Tell Him to save the meat. Because we got nine dollars and thirty-four cents worth drying up in there right now.

OSCAR: Can't you keep it warm?

FELIX: [*Pacing*] What do you think I am, the Magic Chef? I'm lucky I got it to come out at eight o'clock. What am I going to do?

OSCAR: I don't know. Keep pouring gravy on it.

FELIX: What gravy?

OSCAR: Don't you have any gravy?

FELIX: [*Storms over to* OSCAR] Where the hell am I going to get gravy at eight o'clock?

OSCAR: [*Getting up*] I thought it comes when you cook the meat.

FELIX: [*Follows him*] When you *cook the meat?* You don't know the first thing you're talking about. You have to make gravy. It doesn't come!

OSCAR: You asked my advice, I'm giving it to you.

[*He puts on his jacket*]

FELIX: Advice? [*He waves the ladle in his face*] You didn't know where the kitchen was till I came here and showed you.

OSCAR: You wanna talk to me, put down the spoon.

FELIX: [*Exploding in rage, again waving the ladle in his face*] Spoon? You dumb ignoramus. It's a ladle. You don't even know it's a ladle.

OSCAR: All right, Felix, get a hold of yourself.

FELIX: [*Pulls himself together and sits on the love seat*] You think it's so easy? Go on. The kitchen's all yours. Go make a London broil for four people who come a half hour late.

OSCAR: [*To no one in particular*] Listen to me. I'm arguing with him over gravy.

[*The bell rings*]

FELIX: [*Jumps up*] Well, they're here. Our dinner guests. I'll get a saw and cut the meat.

[*He starts for the kitchen*]

OSCAR: [*Stopping him*] Stay where you are!

FELIX: I'm not taking the blame for this dinner.

OSCAR: Who's blaming you? Who even *cares* about the dinner?

FELIX: [*Moves to* OSCAR] I care. I take *pride* in what I do. And you're going to explain to them exactly what happened.

OSCAR: All right, you can take a Polaroid picture of me coming in at eight o'clock! Now take off that stupid apron because I'm opening the door.

[*He rips the towel off* FELIX *and goes to the door*]

FELIX: [*Takes his jacket from a dining chair and puts it on*] I just want to get one thing clear. This is the last time I ever cook for you. Because people like you don't even appreciate a decent meal. That's why they have TV dinners.

OSCAR: You through?

FELIX: I'm through!

OSCAR: Then smile. [OSCAR *smiles and opens the door. The girls poke their heads through the door. They are in their young thirties and somewhat attractive. They are undoubtedly British*] Well, hello.

GWENDOLYN: [*To* OSCAR] Hallo.

CECILY: [*To* OSCAR] Hallo.

GWENDOLYN: I do hope we're not late.

OSCAR: No, no. You timed it perfectly. Come on in. [*He points to them as they enter*] Er, Felix, I'd like you to meet two very good friends of mine, Gwendolyn and Cecily . . .

CECILY: [*Pointing out his mistake*] Cecily and Gwendolyn.

OSCAR: Oh, yes. Cecily and Gwendolyn . . . er [*Trying to remember their last name*] Er . . . Don't tell me. Robin? No, no. Cardinal?

GWENDOLYN: Wrong both times. It's Pigeon!

OSCAR: Pigeon. Right. Cecily and Gwendolyn Pigeon.

GWENDOLYN: [*To* FELIX] You don't spell it like Walter Pidgeon. You spell it like "Coo-Coo" Pigeon.

OSCAR: We'll remember that if it comes up. Cecily and Gwendolyn, I'd like you to meet my room-mate, and our chef for the evening, Felix Ungar.

CECILY: [*Holding her hand out*] Heh d'yew dew?

FELIX: [*Moving to her and shaking her hand*] How do you do?

GWENDOLYN: [*Holding her hand out*] Heh d'yew dew?

FELIX: [*Stepping up on the landing and shaking her hand*] How do you do you?

[*This puts him nose to nose with* OSCAR, *and there is an awkward pause as they look at each other*]

OSCAR: Well, we did that beautifully. Why don't we sit down and make ourselves comfortable?

[FELIX *steps aside and ushers the girls down into the room. There is ad libbing and a bit of confusion and milling about as they all squeeze between the armchair and the couch, and the* PIGEONS *finally seat themselves on the couch.* OSCAR *sits in the armchair, and* FELIX *sneaks past him to the love seat. Finally all have settled down*]

CECILY: This is ever so nice, isn't it, Gwen?

GWENDOLYN: [*Looking around*] Lovely. And much nicer than our flat. Do you have help?

OSCAR: Er, yes. I have a man who comes in every night.

CECILY: Aren't you the lucky one?

[CECILY, GWENDOLYN *and* OSCAR *all laugh at her joke.* OSCAR *looks over at* FELIX *but there is no response*]

OSCAR: [*Rubs his hands together*] Well, isn't this nice? I was telling Felix yesterday about how we happened to meet.

GWENDOLYN: Oh? Who's Felix?

OSCAR: [*A little embarrassed, he points to* FELIX] He is!

GWENDOLYN: Oh, yes, of course. I'm so sorry.

[FELIX *nods that it's all right*]

CECILY: You know it happened to us again this morning.

OSCAR: What did?

GWENDOLYN: Stuck in the elevator again.

OSCAR: Really? Just the two of you?

CECILY: And poor old Mr. Kessler from the third floor. We were in there half an hour.

OSCAR: No kidding? What happened?

GWENDOLYN: Nothing much, I'm afraid.

[CECILY *and* GWENDOLYN *both laugh at her latest joke, joined by* OSCAR. *He once again looks over at* FELIX, *but there is no response*]

OSCAR: [*Rubs his hands again*] Well, this really is nice.

CECILY: And ever so much cooler than our place.

GWENDOLYN: It's like equatorial Africa on our side of the building.

CECILY: Last night it was so bad Gwen and I sat there in nature's own cooling ourselves in front of the open fridge. Can you imagine such a thing?

OSCAR: Er, I'm working on it.

GWENDOLYN: Actually, it's impossible to get a night's sleep. Cec and I really don't know what to do.

OSCAR: Why don't you sleep with an air conditioner?

GWENDOLYN: We haven't got one.

OSCAR: I know. But we have.

GWENDOLYN: Oh, you! I told you about that one, didn't I, Cec?

FELIX: They say it may rain Friday.

[*They all stare at* FELIX]

GWENDOLYN: Oh?

CECILY: That should cool things off a bit.

OSCAR: I wouldn't be surprised.

FELIX: Although sometimes it gets hotter after it rains.

GWENDOLYN: Yes, it does, doesn't it?

[*They continue to stare at* FELIX]

FELIX: [*Jumps up and, picking up the ladle, starts for the kitchen*] Dinner is served!

OSCAR: [*Stopping him*] No, it isn't!

FELIX: Yes, it is!

OSCAR: No, it isn't! I'm sure the girls would like a cocktail first. [*To the girls*] Wouldn't you, girls?

GWENDOLYN: Well, I wouldn't put up a struggle.

OSCAR: There you are. [*To* CECILY] What would you like?

CECILY: Oh, I really don't know. [*To* OSCAR] What have you got?

FELIX: London broil.

OSCAR: [*To* FELIX] She means to drink. [*To* CECILY] We have everything. And what we don't have, I mix in the medicine cabinet. What'll it be?

> [*He crouches next to her*]

CECILY: Oh, a double vodka.

GWENDOLYN: Cecily, not before dinner.

CECILY: [*To the men*] My sister. She watches over me like a mother hen. [*To* OSCAR] Make it a *small* double vodka.

OSCAR: A small double vodka! And for the beautiful mother hen?

GWENDOLYN: Oh, I'd like something cool. I think I would like to have a double Drambuie with some crushed ice, unless you don't have the crushed ice.

OSCAR: I was up all night with a sledge hammer. I shall return!

> [*He goes to the bar and gets bottles of vodka and Drambuie*]

FELIX: [*Going to him*] Where are you going?

OSCAR: To get the refreshments.

FELIX: [*Starting to panic*] Inside? What'll I do?

OSCAR: You can finish the weather report.

> [*He exits into the kitchen*]

FELIX: [*Calls after him*] Don't forget to look at my meat! [*He turns and faces the girls. He crosses to a chair and sits. He crosses his legs nonchalantly. But he is ill at ease and he crosses them again. He is becoming aware of the silence and he can no longer get away with just smiling]* Er, Oscar tells me you're sisters.

CECILY: Yes. That's right.

[She looks at GWENDOLYN]

FELIX: From England.

GWENDOLYN: Yes. That's right.

[She looks at CECILY]

FELIX: I see. *[Silence. Then, his little joke]* We're not brothers.

CECILY: Yes. We know.

FELIX: Although I am a brother. I have a brother who's a doctor. He lives in Buffalo. That's upstate in New York.

GWENDOLYN: *[Taking a cigarette from her purse]* Yes, we know.

FELIX: You know my brother?

GWENDOLYN: No. We know that Buffalo is upstate in New York.

FELIX: Oh!

[He gets up, takes a cigarette lighter from the side table and moves to light GWENDOLYN's cigarette]

CECILY: We've been there! Have you?

FELIX: No! Is it nice?

CECILY: Lovely.

[FELIX closes the lighter on GWENDOLYN's cigarette and turns to go back to his chair, taking the cigarette, now caught in the lighter, with him. He notices the cigarette and hastily gives it back to GWENDOLYN, stopping to light it once again. He puts the lighter back on the table and sits down nervously. There is a pause]

FELIX: Isn't that interesting? How long have you been in the United States of America?

CECILY: Almost four years now.

FELIX: [*Nods*] Uh huh. Just visiting?

GWENDOLYN: [*Looks at* CECILY] No! We live here.

FELIX: And you work here too, do you?

CECILY: Yes. We're secretaries for Slenderama.

GWENDOLYN: You know. The health club.

CECILY: People bring us their bodies and we do wonderful things with them.

GWENDOLYN: Actually, if you're interested, we can get you ten per cent off.

CECILY: Off the price, not off your body.

FELIX: Yes, I see. [*He laughs. They all laugh. Suddenly he shouts toward the kitchen*] Oscar, where's the drinks?

OSCAR: [*Offstage*] Coming! Coming!

CECILY: What field of endeavor are you engaged in?

FELIX: I write the news for CBS.

CECILY: Oh! Fascinating!

GWENDOLYN: Where do you get your ideas from?

FELIX: [*He looks at her as though she's a Martian*] From the news.

GWENDOLYN: Oh, yes, of course. Silly me . . .

CECILY: Maybe you can mention Gwen and I in one of your news reports.

FELIX: Well, if you do something spectacular, maybe I will.

CECILY: Oh, we've done spectacular things but I don't think we'd want it spread all over the telly, do you, Gwen?

[*They both laugh*]

FELIX: [*He laughs too, then cries out almost for help*] Oscar!

OSCAR: [*Offstage*] Yeah, yeah!

FELIX: [*To the girls*] It's such a large apartment, sometimes you have to shout.

GWENDOLYN: Just you two baches live here?

FELIX: Baches? Oh, bachelors! We're not bachelors. We're divorced. That is, Oscar's divorced. I'm *getting* divorced.

CECILY: Oh. Small world. We've cut the dinghy loose too, as they say.

GWENDOLYN: Well, you couldn't have a *better* matched foursome, could you?

FELIX: [*Smiles weakly*] No, I suppose not.

GWENDOLYN: Although technically I'm a widow. I was divorcing my husband, but he died before the final papers came through.

FELIX: Oh, I'm awfully sorry. [*Sighs*] It's a terrible thing, isn't it? Divorce.

GWENDOLYN: It can be—if you haven't got the right solicitor.

CECILY: That's true. Sometimes they can drag it out for months. I was lucky. Snip, cut and I was free.

FELIX: I mean it's terrible what it can do to people. After all, what is divorce? It's taking two happy people and tearing their lives completely apart. It's inhuman, don't you think so?

CECILY: Yes, it can be an awful bother.

GWENDOLYN: But of course, that's all water under the bridge now, eh? Er, I'm terribly sorry, but I think I've forgotten your name.

FELIX: Felix.

GWENDOLYN: Oh, yes. Felix.

CECILY: Like the cat.

[FELIX *takes his wallet from his jacket pocket*]

GWENDOLYN: Well, the Pigeons will have to beware of the cat, won't they?

[*She laughs*]

CECILY: [*Nibbles on a nut from the dish*] Mmm, cashews. Lovely.

FELIX: [*Takes a snapshot out of his wallet*] This is the worst part of breaking up.

[*He hands the picture to* CECILY]

CECILY: [*Looks at it*] Childhood sweethearts, were you?

FELIX: No, no. That's my little boy and girl. [CECILY *gives the picture to* GWENDOLYN, *takes a pair of glasses from her purse and puts them on*] He's seven, she's five.

CECILY: [*Looks again*] Oh! Sweet.

FELIX: They live with their mother.

GWENDOLYN: I imagine you must miss them terribly.

FELIX: [*Takes back the picture and looks at it longingly*] I can't stand being away from them. [*Shrugs*] But—that's what happens with divorce.

CECILY: When do you get to see them?

FELIX: Every night. I stop there on my way home! Then I take them on the weekends, and I get them on holidays and July and August.

CECILY: Oh! Well, when is it that you miss them?

FELIX: Whenever I'm not there. If they didn't have to go to school so early, I'd go over and make them breakfast. They love my French toast.

GWENDOLYN: You're certainly a devoted father.

FELIX: It's Frances who's the wonderful one.

CECILY: She's the little girl?

FELIX: No. She's the mother. My wife.

GWENDOLYN: The one you're divorcing?

FELIX: [*Nods*] Mm! She's done a terrific job bringing them up. They always look so nice. They're so polite. Speak beautifully. Never, "Yeah." Always, "Yes." They're such good kids. And she did it all. She's the kind of woman who— Ah, what am I saying? You don't want to hear any of this.

[*He puts the picture back in his wallet*]

CECILY: Nonsense. You have a right to be proud. You have two beautiful children and a wonderful ex-wife.

FELIX: [*Containing his emotions*] I know. I know. [*He hands* CECILY *another snapshot*] That's her. Frances.

GWENDOLYN: [*Looking at the picture*] Oh, she's pretty. Isn't she pretty, Cecy?

CECILY: Oh, yes. Pretty. A pretty girl. Very pretty.

FELIX: [*Takes the picture back*] Thank you. [*Shows them another snapshot*] Isn't this nice?

GWENDOLYN: [*Looks*] There's no one in the picture.

FELIX: I know. It's a picture of our living room. We had a beautiful apartment.

GWENDOLYN: Oh, yes. Pretty. Very pretty.

CECILY: Those are lovely lamps.

FELIX: Thank you! [*Takes the picture*] We bought them in Mexico on our honeymoon. [*He looks at the picture again*] I used to love to come home at night. [*He's beginning to break*] That was my whole life. My wife, my kids—and my apartment.

[*He breaks down and sobs*]

CECILY: Does she have the lamps now too?

FELIX: [*Nods*] I gave her everything. It'll never be like that again. Never! I—I— [*He turns his head away*] I'm sorry. [*He takes out a handkerchief and dabs his eyes.* GWENDOLYN *and* CECILY *look at each other with compassion*] Please forgive me. I didn't mean to get emotional. [*Trying to pull himself together, he picks up a bowl from the side table and offers it to the girls*] Would you like some potato chips?

[CECILY *takes the bowl*]

GWENDOLYN: You mustn't be ashamed. I think it's a rare quality in a man to be able to cry.

FELIX: [*Puts a hand over his eyes*] Please. Let's not talk about it.

CECILY: I think it's sweet. Terribly, terribly sweet.

[*She takes a potato chip*]

FELIX: You're just making it worse.

GWENDOLYN: [*Teary-eyed*] It's so refreshing to hear a man speak so highly of the woman he's divorcing! Oh, dear. [*She takes out her handkerchief*] Now you've got me thinking about poor Sydney.

CECILY: Oh, Gwen. Please don't.

[*She puts the bowl down*]

GWENDOLYN: It was a good marriage at first. Everyone said so. Didn't they, Cecily? Not like you and George.

CECILY: [*The past returns as she comforts* GWENDOLYN] That's right. George and I were never happy. Not for one single, solitary day.

[*She remembers her unhappiness, grabs her handkerchief and dabs her eyes. All three are now sitting with handkerchiefs at their eyes*]

FELIX: Isn't this ridiculous?

GWENDOLYN: I don't know what brought this on. I was feeling so good a few minutes ago.

CECILY: I haven't cried since I was fourteen.

FELIX: Just let it pour out. It'll make you feel much better. I always do.

GWENDOLYN: Oh, dear; oh, dear; oh, dear.

[*All three sit sobbing into their handkerchiefs. Suddenly* OSCAR *bursts happily into the room with a tray full of drinks. He is all smiles*]

OSCAR: [*Like a corny M.C.*] Is ev-rybuddy happy? [*Then he sees the maudlin scene.* FELIX *and the girls quickly try to pull themselves together*] What the hell happened?

FELIX: Nothing! Nothing!

[*He quickly puts his handkerchief away*]

OSCAR: What do you mean, nothing? I'm gone three minutes and I walk into a funeral parlor. What did you say to them?

FELIX: I didn't say anything. Don't start in again, Oscar.

OSCAR: I can't leave you alone for five seconds. Well, if you really want to cry, go inside and look at your London broil.

FELIX: [*He rushes madly into the kitchen*] Oh, my gosh! Why didn't you call me? I told you to call me.

OSCAR: [*Giving a drink to* CECILY] I'm sorry, girls. I forgot to warn you about Felix. He's a walking soap opera.

GWENDOLYN: I think he's the dearest thing I ever met.

CECILY: [*Taking the glass*] He's so sensitive. So fragile. I just want to bundle him up in my arms and take care of him.

OSCAR: [*Holds out* GWENDOLYN'S *drink. At this, he puts it back down on the tray and takes a swallow from his own drink*] Well, I think when he comes out of that kitchen you may have to.

[*Sure enough,* FELIX *comes out of the kitchen onto the landing looking like a wounded puppy. With a protective kitchen glove, he holds a pan with the exposed London broil. Black is the color of his true love*]

FELIX: [*Very calmly*] I'm going down to the delicatessen. I'll be right back.

OSCAR: [*Going to him*] Wait a minute. Maybe it's not so bad. Let's see it.

FELIX: [*Shows him*] Here! Look! Nine dollars and thirty-four cents worth of ashes! [*Pulls the pan away. To the girls*] I'll get some corned beef sandwiches.

OSCAR: [*Trying to get a look at it*] Give it to me! Maybe we can save some of it.

FELIX: [*Holding it away from* OSCAR] There's nothing to save. It's all black meat. Nobody likes black meat!

OSCAR: Can't I even look at it?

FELIX: No, you can't look at it!

OSCAR: Why can't I look at it?

FELIX: If you looked at your watch before, you wouldn't have to look at the black meat now! Leave it alone!

[*He turns to go back into the kitchen*]

GWENDOLYN: [*Going to him*] Felix! Can *we* look at it?

CECILY: [*Turning to him, kneeling on the couch*] Please? [FELIX *stops in the kitchen doorway. He hesitates for a moment. He likes them. Then he turns and wordlessly holds the pan out to them.* GWENDOLYN *and* CECILY *inspect it wordlessly, and then turn away sobbing quietly. To* OSCAR] How about Chinese food?

OSCAR: A wonderful idea.

GWENDOLYN: I've got a better idea. Why don't we just make pot luck in the kitchen?

OSCAR: A *much* better idea.

FELIX: I used up all the pots!

[*He crosses to the love seat and sits, still holding the pan*]

CECILY: Well, then we can eat up in *our* place. We have tons of Horn and Hardart's.

OSCAR: [*Gleefully*] That's the best idea I ever heard.

GWENDOLYN: Of course it's awfully hot up there. You'll have to take off your jackets.

OSCAR: [*Smiling*] We can always open up a refrigerator.

CECILY: [*Gets her purse from the couch*] Give us five minutes to get into our cooking things.

[GWENDOLYN *gets her purse from the couch*]

OSCAR: Can't you make it four? I'm suddenly starving to death.

[*The girls are crossing to the door*]

GWENDOLYN: Don't forget the wine.

OSCAR: How could I forget the wine?

CECILY: And a corkscrew.

OSCAR: *And* a corkscrew.

GWENDOLYN: And Felix.

OSCAR: No, I won't forget Felix.

CECILY: Ta, ta!

OSCAR: Ta, ta!

GWENDOLYN: Ta, ta!

[*The girls exit*]

OSCAR: [*Throws a kiss at the closed door*] You bet your sweet little crumpets, "Ta, Ta!" [*He wheels around beaming and quickly gathers up the corkscrew from the bar, and picks up the wine and the records*] Felix, I love you. You've just overcooked us into one hell of a night. Come on, get the ice bucket. Ready or not, here we come.

[*He runs to the door*]

FELIX: [*Sitting motionless*] I'm not going!

OSCAR: What?

FELIX: I said I'm not going.

OSCAR: [*Crossing to* FELIX] Are you out of your mind? Do you know what's waiting for us up there? You've just been invited to spend the evening in a two-bedroom hothouse with the Coo-Coo Pigeon Sisters! What do you mean you're not going?

FELIX: I don't know how to talk to them. I don't know what to say. I already told them about my brother in Buffalo. I've used up my conversation.

OSCAR: Felix, they're crazy about you. They told me! One of them wants to wrap you up and make a bundle out of you. You're doing better than I am! Get the ice bucket.

[*He starts for the door*]

FELIX: Don't you understand? I cried! I cried in front of two women.

OSCAR: [*Stops*] And they *loved* it! I'm thinking of getting hysterical. [*Goes to the door*] Will you get the ice bucket?

FELIX: But why did I cry? Because I felt guilty. Emotionally I'm still tied to Frances and the kids.

OSCAR: Well, untie the knot just for tonight, will you!

FELIX: I don't want to discuss it any more. [*Starts for the kitchen*] I'm going to scrub the pots and wash my hair. [*He goes into the kitchen and puts the pan in the sink*]

OSCAR: [*Yelling*] Your greasy pots and your greasy hair can wait. You're coming upstairs with me!

FELIX: [*In the kitchen*] I'm not! *I'm not!*

OSCAR: What am I going to do with two girls? Felix, don't do this to me. I'll never forgive you!

FELIX: I'm not going!

OSCAR: [*Screams*] All right, damn you, I'll go without you! [*And he storms out the door and slams it. Then it opens and he comes in again*] Are you coming?

FELIX: [*Comes out of the kitchen looking at a magazine*] No.

OSCAR: You mean you're not going to make any effort to change? This is the person you're going to be—until the day you die?

FELIX: [*Sitting on the couch*] We are what we are.

OSCAR: [*Nods, then crosses to a window, pulls back the drapes and opens the window wide. Then he starts back to the door*] It's *twelve* floors, not eleven.

[*He walks out as* FELIX *stares at the open window.*]

CURTAIN

ACT THREE

The next evening about 7:30 P.M. The room is once again set up for the poker game, with the dining table pulled down, the chairs set about it, and the love seat moved back beneath the windows in the alcove. FELIX *appears from the bedroom with a vacuum cleaner. He is doing a thorough job on the rug. As he vacuums around the table, the door opens and* OSCAR *comes in wearing a summer hat and carrying a newspaper. He glares at* FELIX, *who is still vacuuming, and shakes his head contemptuously. He crosses behind* FELIX, *leaving his hat on the side table next to the armchair, and goes into his bedroom.* FELIX *is not aware of his presence. Then suddenly the power stops on the vacuum, as* OSCAR *has obviously pulled the plug in the bedroom.* FELIX *tries switching the button on and off a few times, then turns to go back into the bedroom. He stops and realizes what's happened as* OSCAR *comes back into the room.* OSCAR *takes a cigar out of his pocket and as he crosses in front of* FELIX *to the couch, he unwraps it and drops the wrappings carelessly on the floor. He then steps up on the couch and walks back and forth mashing down the pillows. Stepping down, he plants one foot on the armchair and then sits on the couch, taking a wooden match from the coffee table and striking it on the table to light his cigar. He flips the used match onto the rug and settles back to read his newspaper.* FELIX *has watched this all in silence, and now carefully picks up the cigar wrappings and the match and drops them into* OSCAR's *hat. He then dusts his hands and takes the vacuum cleaner into the kitchen, pulling the cord in after him.* OSCAR *takes the wrappings from the hat and puts them in the butt-filled ashtray on the coffee table. Then*

*he takes the ashtray and dumps it on the floor. As he once
more settles down with his newspaper,* FELIX *comes out of
the kitchen carrying a tray with a steaming dish of
spaghetti. As he crosses behind* OSCAR *to the table, he
indicates that it smells delicious and passes it close to*
OSCAR *to make sure* OSCAR *smells the fantastic dish he's
missing. As* FELIX *sits and begins to eat,* OSCAR *takes a
can of aerosol spray from the bar, and circling the table,
sprays all around* FELIX, *then puts the can down next to
him and goes back to his newspaper.*

FELIX: [*Pushing the spaghetti away*] All right, how much longer
is this gonna go on?

OSCAR: [*Reading his paper*] Are you talking to me?

FELIX: That's right, I'm talking to you.

OSCAR: What do you want to know?

FELIX: I want to know if you're going to spend the rest of
your life not talking to me. Because if you are, I'm going to
buy a radio. [*No reply*] Well? [*No reply*] I see. You're not
going to talk to me. [*No reply*] All right. Two can play at
this game. [*Pause*] If you're not going to talk to me, I'm
not going to talk to you. [*No reply*] I can act childish too,
you know. [*No reply*] I can go on without talking just as
long as you can.

OSCAR: Then why the hell don't you shut up?

FELIX: Are you talking to me?

OSCAR: You had your chance to talk last night. I begged you to
come upstairs with me. From now on I never want to hear
a word from that shampooed head as long as you live. That's
a warning, Felix.

FELIX: [*Stares at him*] I stand warned. Over and out!

OSCAR: [*Gets up, takes a key out of his pocket and slams it on
the table*] There's a key to the back door. If you stick to the
hallway and your room, you won't get hurt.

[*He sits back down on the couch*]

FELIX: I don't think I gather the entire meaning of that remark.

OSCAR: Then I'll explain it to you. Stay out of my way.

FELIX: [*Picks up the key and moves to the couch*] I think you're serious. I think you're really serious. Are you serious?

OSCAR: This is my apartment. Everything in my apartment is mine. The only thing here that's yours is you. Just stay in your room and speak softly.

FELIX: Yeah, you're serious. Well, let me remind you that I pay half the rent and I'll go into any room I want.

[*He gets up angrily and starts toward the hallway*]

OSCAR: Where are you going?

FELIX: I'm going to walk around your bedroom.

OSCAR: [*Slams down his newspaper*] You stay out of there.

FELIX: [*Steaming*] Don't tell me where to go. I pay a hundred and twenty dollars a month.

OSCAR: That was off-season. Starting tomorrow the rates are twelve dollars a day.

FELIX: All right. [*He takes some bills out of his pocket and slams them down on the table*] There you are. I'm paid up for today. Now I'm going to walk in your bedroom.

[*He starts to storm off*]

OSCAR: Stay out of there! Stay out of my room!

[*He chases after him.* FELIX *dodges around the table as* OSCAR *blocks the hallway*]

FELIX: [*Backing away, keeping the table between them*] Watch yourself! Just watch yourself, Oscar!

OSCAR: [*With a pointing finger*] I'm warning you. You want to live here, I don't want to see you, I don't want to hear you and I don't want to smell your cooking. Now get this spaghetti off my poker table.

FELIX: Ha! Ha, ha!

OSCAR: What the hell's so funny?

FELIX: It's not spaghetti. It's linguini!

[OSCAR *picks up the plate of linguini, crosses to the doorway and hurls it into the kitchen*]

OSCAR: Now it's garbage!

[*He paces by the couch*]

FELIX: [*Looks at* OSCAR *unbelievingly: what an insane thing to do*] You are crazy! I'm a neurotic nut but *you are crazy!*

OSCAR: *I'm* crazy, heh? That's really funny coming from a fruitcake like you.

FELIX: [*Goes to the kitchen door and looks in at the mess. Turns back to* OSCAR] I'm not cleaning that up.

OSCAR: Is that a promise?

FELIX: Did you hear what I said? I'm not cleaning it up. It's your mess. [*Looking into the kitchen again*] Look at it. Hanging all over the walls.

OSCAR: [*Crosses to the landing and looks in the kitchen door*] I like it.

[*He closes the door and paces around*]

FELIX: [*Fumes*] You'd just let it lie there, wouldn't you? Until it turns hard and brown and . . . Yich, it's disgusting. I'm cleaning it up.

[*He goes into the kitchen,* OSCAR *chases after him. There is the sound of a struggle and falling pots*]

OSCAR: *Leave it alone!* You touch one strand of that linguini —and I'm gonna punch you right in your sinuses.

FELIX: [*Dashes out of the kitchen with* OSCAR *in pursuit. He stops and tries to calm* OSCAR *down*] Oscar, I'd like you to take a couple of phenobarbital.

OSCAR: [*Points*] Go to your room! Did you hear what I said? Go to your room!

FELIX: All right, let's everybody just settle down, heh?

[*He puts his hand on* OSCAR's *shoulder to calm him but* OSCAR *pulls away violently from his touch*]

OSCAR: If you want to live through this night, you'd better tie me up and lock your doors and windows.

FELIX: [*Sits at the table with a great pretense of calm*] All right, Oscar, I'd like to know what's happened?

OSCAR: [*Moves toward him*] What's *happened?*

FELIX: [*Hurriedly slides over to the next chair*] That's right. Something must have caused you to go off the deep end like this. What is it? Something I said? Something I did? Heh? What?

OSCAR: [*Pacing*] It's nothing you said. It's nothing you did. It's *you!*

FELIX: I see. Well, that's plain enough.

OSCAR: I could make it plainer but I don't want to hurt you.

FELIX: What is it, the cooking? The cleaning? The crying?

OSCAR: [*Moving toward him*] I'll tell you exactly what it is. It's the cooking, cleaning and crying. It's the talking in your sleep, it's the moose calls that open your ears at two o'clock in the morning. I can't take it any more, Felix. I'm crackin' up. Everything you do irritates me. And when you're not here, the things I know you're gonna do when you come in irritate me. You leave me little notes on my pillow. I told you a hundred times, I can't stand little notes on my pillow. "We're all out of Corn Flakes. F.U." It took me three hours to figure out that F.U. was Felix Ungar. It's not your fault, Felix. It's a rotten combination.

FELIX: I get the picture.

OSCAR: That's just the frame. The picture I haven't even painted yet. I got a typewritten list in my office of the "Ten Most Aggravating Things You Do That Drive Me Berserk." But last night was the topper. Oh, that was the topper. Oh, that was the ever-loving lulu of all times.

FELIX: What are you talking about, the London broil?

OSCAR: No, not the London broil. I'm talking about those two lamb chops. [*He points upstairs*] I had it all set up with that English Betty Boop and her sister, and I wind up drinking tea all night and telling them *your* life story.

FELIX: [*Jumps up*] Oho! So *that's* what's bothering you. That I loused up your evening!

OSCAR: After the mood you put them in, I'm surprised they didn't go out to Rockaway and swim back to England.

FELIX: Don't blame me. I warned you not to make the date in the first place.

[*He makes his point by shaking his finger in* OSCAR's *face*]

OSCAR: Don't point that finger at me unless you intend to use it!

FELIX: [*Moves in nose to nose with* OSCAR] All right, Oscar, get off my back. Get off! Off!

[*Startled by his own actions,* FELIX *jumps back from* OSCAR, *warily circles him, crosses to the couch and sits*]

OSCAR: What's this? A display of temper? I haven't seen you really angry since the day I dropped my cigar in your pancake batter.

[*He starts toward the hallway*]

FELIX: [*Threateningly*] Oscar, you're asking to hear something I don't want to say. But if I say it, I think you'd better hear it.

OSCAR: [*Comes back to the table, places both hands on it and leans toward* FELIX] If you've got anything on your chest besides your chin, you'd better get it off.

FELIX: [*Strides to the table, places both hands on it and leans toward* OSCAR. *They are nose to nose*] All right, I warned you. You're a wonderful guy, Oscar. You've done everything for me. If it weren't for you, I don't know what would have happened to me. You took me in here, gave me a place to live and something to live for. I'll never forget you for that. You're tops with me, Oscar.

OSCAR: [*Motionless*] If I've just been told off, I think I may have missed it.

FELIX: It's coming now! You're also one of the biggest slobs in the world.

OSCAR: I see.

FELIX: And completely unreliable.

OSCAR: Finished?

FELIX: Undependable.

OSCAR: Is that it?

FELIX: And irresponsible.

OSCAR: Keep going. I think you're hot.

FELIX: That's it. I'm finished. *Now* you've been told off. How do you like that?

[*He crosses to the couch*]

OSCAR: [*Straightening up*] Good. Because now I'm going to tell *you* off. For six months I lived alone in this apartment. All alone in eight rooms. I was dejected, despondent and disgusted. Then *you* moved in—my dearest and closest friend. And after three weeks of close, personal contact—I am about to have a nervous breakdown! Do me a favor. Move into the kitchen. Live with your pots, your pans, your ladle and your meat thermometer. When you want to come out, ring a bell and I'll run into the bedroom. [*Almost breaking down*] I'm asking you nicely, Felix—as a friend. Stay out of my way!

[*And he goes into the bedroom*]

FELIX: [*Is hurt by this, then remembers something. He calls after him*] Walk on the paper, will you? The floors are wet. [OSCAR *comes out of the door. He is glaring maniacally, as he slowly strides back down the hallway.* FELIX *quickly puts the couch between him and* OSCAR] Awright, keep away. Keep away from me.

OSCAR: [*Chasing him around the couch*] Come on. Let me get in one shot. You pick it. Head, stomach or kidneys.

FELIX: [*Dodging about the room*] You're gonna find yourself in one sweet law suit, Oscar.

OSCAR: It's no use running, Felix. There's only eight rooms and I know the short cuts.

[*They are now poised at opposite ends of the couch. FELIX picks up a lamp for protection*]

FELIX: Is this how you settle your problems, Oscar? Like an animal?

OSCAR: All right. You wanna see how I settle my problems. I'll show you. [*Storms off into FELIX's bedroom. There is the sound of falling objects and he returns with a suitcase*] I'll show you how I settle them. [*Throws the suitcase on the table*] There! That's how I settle them!

FELIX: [*Bewildered, looks at the suitcase*] Where are you going?

OSCAR: [*Exploding*] Not me, you idiot! You. You're the one who's going. I want you out of here. Now! Tonight!

[*He opens the suitcase*]

FELIX: What are you talking about?

OSCAR: It's all over, Felix. The whole marriage. We're getting an annulment! Don't you understand? I don't want to live with you any more. I want you to pack your things, tie it up with your Saran Wrap and get out of here.

FELIX: You mean actually move out?

OSCAR: Actually, physically and immediately. I don't care where you go. Move into the Museum of Natural History. [*Goes into the kitchen. There is the crash of falling pots and pans*] I'm sure you'll be very comfortable there. You can dust around the Egyptian mummies to your heart's content. But I'm a human, living person. [*Comes out with a stack of cooking utensils which he throws into the open suitcase*] All I want is my freedom. Is that too much to ask for? [*Closes it*] There, you're all packed.

FELIX: You know, I've got a good mind to really leave.

OSCAR: [*Looking to the heavens*] Why doesn't he ever listen to what I say? Why doesn't he hear me? I know I'm talking— I recognize my voice.

FELIX: [*Indignantly*] Because if you really want me to go, I'll go.

OSCAR: Then go. I want you to go, so go. When are you going?

FELIX: When am I going, huh? Boy, you're in a bigger hurry than Frances was.

OSCAR: Take as much time as she gave you. I want you to follow your usual routine.

FELIX: In other words, you're throwing me out.

OSCAR: Not in other words. Those are the perfect ones. [*Picks up the suitcase and holds it out to* FELIX] I am throwing you out.

FELIX: All right, I just wanted to get the record straight. Let it be on *your* conscience.

[*He goes into his bedroom*]

OSCAR: What? What? [*Follows him to the bedroom doorway*] Let what be on my conscience?

FELIX: [*Comes out putting on his jacket and passes by* OSCAR] That you're throwing me out. [*Stops and turns back to him*] I'm perfectly willing to stay and clear the air of our differences. But you refuse, right?

OSCAR: [*Still holding the suitcase*] Right! I'm sick and tired of you clearing the air. That's why I want you to leave!

FELIX: Okay, as long as I heard you say the words, "Get out of the house." Fine. But remember, what happens to me is your responsibility. Let it be on *your* head.

[*He crosses to the door*]

OSCAR: [*Follows him to the door and screams*] Wait a minute, damn it! Why can't you be thrown out like a decent human being? Why do you have to say things like, "Let it be on your head"? I don't want it on my head. I just want you out of the house.

FELIX: What's the matter, Oscar? Can't cope with a little guilt feelings?

OSCAR: [*Pounding the railing in frustration*] Damn you. I've been looking forward to throwing you out all day long, and now you even take the pleasure out of that.

FELIX: Forgive me for spoiling your fun. I'm leaving now—according to your wishes and desires.

[*He starts to open the door*]

OSCAR: [*Pushes by* FELIX *and slams the door shut. He stands between* FELIX *and the door*] You're not leaving here until you take it back.

FELIX: Take what back?

OSCAR: "Let it be on your head." What the hell is that, the Curse of the Cat People?

FELIX: Get out of my way, please.

OSCAR: Is this how you left that night with Frances? No wonder she wanted to have the room repainted right away. [*Points to* FELIX's *bedroom*] I'm gonna have yours dipped in bronze.

FELIX: [*Sits on the back of the couch with his back to* OSCAR] How can I leave if you're blocking the door?

OSCAR: [*Very calmly*] Felix, we've been friends a long time. For the sake of that friendship, please say, "Oscar, we can't stand each other; let's break up."

FELIX: I'll let you know what to do about my clothes. Either I'll call—or someone else will. [*Controlling great emotion*] I'd like to leave now.

[OSCAR, *resigned, moves out of the way.* FELIX *opens the door*]

OSCAR: Where will you go?

FELIX: [*Turns in the doorway and looks at him*] Where? [*He

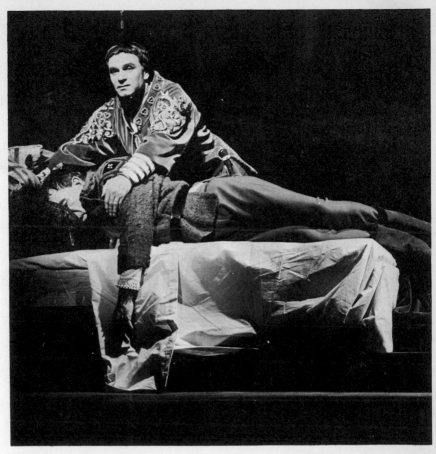

BECKET
Anthony Quinn, Sir Laurence Olivier

THE NIGHT OF THE IGUANA

l. to r. Alan Webb
       Margaret Leighton
       Bette Davis
       Patrick O'Neal

FIDDLER ON THE ROOF
The departure from Anatevka, with
Zero Mostel and Maria Karnilova
at the head of the wagon

PHILADELPHIA, HERE I COME
l. to r. Donal Donelly, Patrick Bedford
Mairin O'Sullivan

THE ODD COUPLE
Art Carney, Walter Matthau

THE ROYAL HUNT OF THE SUN
Christopher Plummer, Ben Hammer

THE KILLING OF SISTER GEORGE   PHOTO BY DOROTHY ROSS ASSOCIATES

Eileen Atkins, Beryl Reid (in background),
Lally Bowers

HADRIAN VII   PHOTO BY FRIEDMAN—ABELES
l. to r. Alec McCowen, Tom Gorman,
William Needles, Theodore Tenley

THE BOYS IN THE BAND   PHOTO BY FRIEDMAN—ABELES
Frederick Combs, Kenneth Nelson

THE GREAT WHITE HOPE
Jane Alexander, James Earl Jones,
Jimmy Pelham (rear)

PHOTO BY FRIEDMAN—ABELES

smiles] Oh, come on, Oscar. You're not really interested, are you?

[*He exits.* OSCAR *looks as though he's about to burst with frustration. He calls after* FELIX]

OSCAR: All right, Felix, you win. [*Goes out into the hall*] We'll try to iron it out. Anything you want. Come back, Felix. Felix? Felix? Don't leave me like this—you louse! [*But* FELIX *is gone.* OSCAR *comes back into the room closing the door. He is limp. He searches for something to ease his enormous frustration. He throws a pillow at the door, and then paces about like a caged lion*] All right, Oscar, get a hold of yourself! He's gone! Keep saying that over and over. He's gone. He's really gone! [*He holds his head in pain*] He did it. He put a curse on me. It's on my head. I don't know what it is, but something's on my head. [*The doorbell rings and he looks up hopefully*] Please let it be him. Let it be Felix. Please give me one more chance to kill him.

[*Putting the suitcase on the sofa, he rushes to the door and opens it.* MURRAY *comes in with* VINNIE]

MURRAY: [*Putting his jacket on a chair at the table*] Hey, what's the matter with Felix? He walked right by me with that "human sacrifice" look on his face again.

[*He takes off his shoes*]

VINNIE: [*Laying his jacket on the love seat*] What's with him? I asked him where he's going and he said, "Only Oscar knows. Only Oscar knows." Where's he going, Oscar?

OSCAR: [*Sitting at the table*] How the hell should I know? All right, let's get the game started, heh? Come on, get your chips.

MURRAY: I have to get something to eat. I'm starving. Mmm, I think I smell spaghetti.

[*He goes into the kitchen*]

VINNIE: Isn't he playing tonight?

[*He takes two chairs from the dining alcove and puts them at the table*]

OSCAR: I don't want to discuss it. I don't even want to hear his name.

VINNIE: Who? Felix?

OSCAR: I told you not to mention his name.

VINNIE: I didn't know what name you meant.

[*He clears the table and places what's left of* FELIX's *dinner on the bookcase*]

MURRAY: [*Comes out of the kitchen*] Hey, did you know there's spaghetti all over the kitchen?

OSCAR: Yes, I know, and it's not spaghetti; it's linguini.

MURRAY: Oh. I thought it was spaghetti.

[*He goes back into the kitchen*]

VINNIE: [*Taking the poker stuff from the bookcase and putting it on the table*] Why shouldn't I mention his name?

OSCAR: Who?

VINNIE: Felix. What's happened? Has something happened?

[SPEED *and* ROY *come in the open door*]

SPEED: Yeah, what's the matter with Felix?

[SPEED *puts his jacket over a chair at the table.* ROY *sits in the armchair.* MURRAY *comes out of the kitchen with a six-pack of beer and bags of pretzels and chips. They all stare at* OSCAR *waiting for an answer. There is a long pause and then he stands up*]

OSCAR: We broke up! I kicked him out. It was my decision. I

threw him out of the house. All right? I admit it. Let it be on my head.

VINNIE: Let what be on your head?

OSCAR: How should I know? *Felix put it there!* Ask him!

[*He paces around to the right*]

MURRAY: He'll go to pieces. I know Felix. He's gonna try something crazy.

OSCAR: [*Turns to the boys*] Why do you think I did it? [MURRAY *makes a gesture of disbelief and moves to the couch, putting down the beer and the bags.* OSCAR *moves to him*] You think I'm just selfish? That I wanted to be cruel? I did it for you—I did it for all of us.

ROY: What are you talking about?

OSCAR: [*Crosses to* ROY] All right, we've all been through the napkins and the ashtrays and the bacon, lettuce and tomato sandwiches. But that was just the beginning. Just the beginning. Do you know what he was planning for next Friday night's poker game? As a change of pace. Do you have any idea?

VINNIE: What?

OSCAR: A Luau! An Hawaiian Luau! Spareribs, roast pork and fried rice. They don't play poker like that in Honolulu.

MURRAY: One thing has nothing to do with the other. We all know he's impossible, but he's still our friend, and he's still out on the street, and I'm still worried about him.

OSCAR: [*Going to* MURRAY] And I'm not, heh? I'm not concerned? I'm not worried? Who do you think sent him out there in the first place?

MURRAY: Frances!

OSCAR: What?

MURRAY: Frances sent him out in the first place. *You* sent him out in the second place. And whoever he lives with next will send him out in the third place. Don't you understand? It's Felix. He does it to himself.

OSCAR: Why?

MURRAY: I don't know why. *He* doesn't know why. There are people like that. There's a whole tribe in Africa who hit themselves on the head all day long.

[*He sums it all up with an eloquent gesture of resignation*]

OSCAR: [*A slow realization of a whole new reason to be angry*] I'm not going to worry about him. Why should I? He's not worrying about me. He's somewhere out on the streets sulking and crying and having a wonderful time. If he had a spark of human decency he would leave us all alone and go back to Blanche.

[*He sits down at the table*]

VINNIE: Why should he?

OSCAR: [*Picks up a deck of cards*] Because it's his wife.

VINNIE: No, Blanche is your wife. His wife is Frances.

OSCAR: [*Stares at him*] What are you, some kind of wise guy?

VINNIE: What did I say?

OSCAR: [*Throws the cards in the air*] All right, the poker game is over. I don't want to play any more.

[*He paces around on the right*]

SPEED: Who's playing? We didn't even start.

OSCAR: [*Turns on him*] Is that all you can do is complain? Have you given one single thought to where Felix might be?

SPEED: I thought you said you're not worried about him.

OSCAR: [*Screams*] I'm not worried, damn it! I'm not worried. [*The doorbell rings. A gleeful look passes over* OSCAR's *face*] It's him. I bet it's him! [*The boys start to go for the door.* OSCAR *stops them*] Don't let him in; he's not welcome in this house.

MURRAY: [*Moves toward the door*] Oscar, don't be childish. We've got to let him in.

OSCAR: [*Stopping him and leading him to the table*] I won't give him the satisfaction of knowing we've been worrying about him. Sit down. Play cards. Like nothing happened.

MURRAY: But, Oscar . . .

OSCAR: Sit down. Everybody. Come on, sit down and play poker.

[*They sit and* SPEED *begins to deal out cards*]

VINNIE: [*Crossing to the door*] Oscar . . .

OSCAR: All right, Vinnie, open the door.

[VINNIE *opens the door. It is* GWENDOLYN *standing there*]

VINNIE: [*Surprised*] Oh, hello. [*To* OSCAR] It's not him, Oscar.

GWENDOLYN: How do you do.

[*She walks into the room*]

OSCAR: [*Crosses to her*] Oh, hello, Cecily. Boys, I'd like you to meet Cecily Pigeon.

GWENDOLYN: Gwendolyn Pigeon. Please don't get up. [*To* OS-CAR] May I see you for a moment, Mr. Madison?

OSCAR: Certainly, Gwen. What's the matter?

GWENDOLYN: I think you know. I've come for Felix's things.

[OSCAR *looks at her in shock and disbelief. He looks at the boys, then back at* GWENDOLYN]

OSCAR: Felix? My Felix?

GWENDOLYN: Yes. Felix Ungar. That sweet, tortured man who's in my flat at this moment pouring his heart out to my sister.

OSCAR: [*Turns to the boys*] You hear? I'm worried to death and he's up there getting tea and sympathy.

[CECILY *rushes in dragging a reluctant* FELIX *with her*]

CECILY: Gwen, Felix doesn't want to stay. Please tell him to stay.

FELIX: Really, girls, this is very embarrassing. I can go to a hotel. [*To the boys*] Hello, fellas.

GWENDOLYN: [*Overriding his objections*] Nonsense. I told you, we've plenty of room, and it's a very comfortable sofa. Isn't it, Cecy?

CECILY: [*Joining in*] Enormous. And we've rented an air conditioner.

GWENDOLYN: And we just don't like the idea of your wandering the streets looking for a place to live.

FELIX: But I'd be in the way. Wouldn't I be in the way?

GWENDOLYN: How could you possibly be in anyone's way?

OSCAR: You want to see a typewritten list?

GWENDOLYN: [*Turning on him*] Haven't you said enough already, Mr. Madison? [*To* FELIX] I won't take no for an answer. Just for a few days, Felix.

CECILY: Until you get settled.

GWENDOLYN: Please. Please say, "Yes," Felix.

CECILY: Oh, please—we'd be so happy.

FELIX: [*Considers*] Well, maybe just for a few days.

GWENDOLYN: [*Jumping with joy*] Oh, wonderful.

CECILY: [*Ecstatic*] Marvelous!

GWENDOLYN: [*Crosses to the door*] You get your things and come right up.

CECILY: And come hungry. We're making dinner.

GWENDOLYN: [*To the boys*] Good night, gentlemen; sorry to interrupt your bridge game.

CECILY: [*To* FELIX] If you'd like, you can invite your friends to play in our flat.

GWENDOLYN: [*To* FELIX] Don't be late. Cocktails in fifteen minutes.

FELIX: I won't.

GWENDOLYN: Ta, ta.

CECILY: Ta, ta.

FELIX: Ta, ta.

[*The girls leave.* FELIX *turns and looks at the fellows and smiles as he crosses the room into the bedroom. The five men stare dumbfounded at the door without moving. Finally* MURRAY *crosses to the door*]

SPEED: [*To the others*] I told you. It's always the quiet guys.

MURRAY: Gee, what nice girls.

[*He closes the door.* FELIX *comes out of the bedroom carrying two suits in a plastic cleaner's bag*]

ROY: Hey, Felix, are you really gonna move in with them?

FELIX: [*Turns back to them*] Just for a few days. Until I find my own place. Well, so long, fellows. You can drop your crumbs on the rug again.

[*He starts toward the door*]

OSCAR: Hey, Felix. Aren't you going to thank me?

FELIX: [*Stopping on the landing*] For what?

OSCAR: For the two greatest things I ever did for you. Taking you in and throwing you out.

FELIX: [*Lays his suits over the railing and goes to* OSCAR] You're right, Oscar. Thanks a lot. Getting kicked out twice is enough for any man. In gratitude, I remove the curse.

OSCAR: [*Smiles*] Oh, bless you and thank you, Wicked Witch of the North.

[*They shake hands. The phone rings*]

FELIX: Ah, that must be the girls.

MURRAY: [*Picking up the phone*] Hello?

FELIX: They hate it so when I'm late for cocktails. [*Turning to the boys*] Well, so long.

MURRAY: It's your wife.

FELIX: [*Turning to* MURRAY] Oh? Well, do me a favor, Murray. Tell her I can't speak to her now. But tell her I'll be calling her in a few days, because she and I have a lot to talk about. And tell her if I sound different to her, it's because I'm not the same man she kicked out three weeks ago. Tell her, Murray; tell her.

MURRAY: I will when I see her. This is Oscar's wife.

FELIX: Oh!

MURRAY: [*Into the phone*] Just a minute, Blanche.

[OSCAR *crosses to the phone and sits on the arm of the couch*]

FELIX: Well, so long, fellows.

[*He shakes hands with the boys, takes his suits and moves to the door*]

OSCAR: [*Into the phone*] Hello? Yeah, Blanche. I got a pretty good idea why you're calling. You got my checks, right? Good. [FELIX *stops at the door, caught by* OSCAR'S *conversation. He slowly comes back into the room to listen, putting his suits on the railing, and sitting down on the arm of the armchair*] So now I'm all paid up. No, no, I didn't win at the track. I've just been able to save a little money. I've been eating home a lot. [*Takes a pillow from the couch and throws it at* FELIX] Listen, Blanche, you don't have to thank me. I'm just doing what's right. Well, that's nice of you too. The apartment? No, I think you'd be shocked. It's in surprisingly good shape. [FELIX *throws the pillow back at* OSCAR] Say, Blanche, did Brucey get the goldfish I sent him? Yeah, well, I'll speak to you again soon, huh? Whenever you want. I don't go out much any more.

FELIX: [*Gets up, takes his suits from the railing and goes to the door*] Well, good night, Mr. Madison. If you need me again, I get a dollar-fifty an hour.

OSCAR: [*Makes a gesture to stop* FELIX *as he talks on the phone*]

Well, kiss the kids for me. Good night, Blanche. [*Hangs up and turns to* FELIX] Felix?

FELIX: [*At the opened door*] Yeah?

OSCAR: How about next Friday night? You're not going to break up the game, are you?

FELIX: Me? Never! Marriages may come and go, but the game must go on. So long, Frances.

[*He exits, closing the door*]

OSCAR: [*Yelling after him*] So long, Blanche. [*The boys all look at* OSCAR *a moment*] All right, are we just gonna sit around or are we gonna play poker?

ROY: We're gonna play poker.

[*There is a general hubbub as they pass out the beer, deal the cards and settle around the table*]

OSCAR: [*Standing up*] Then let's play poker. [*Sharply, to the boys*] And watch your cigarettes, will you? This is my house, not a pigsty.

[*He takes the ashtray from the side table next to the armchair, bends down and begins to pick up the butts. The boys settle down to play poker*]

CURTAIN

Peter Shaffer

Peter Shaffer was born in Liverpool, England, on May 15, 1926. His first nine years were spent in "a nice, middle-class neighborhood," and then his father, who was in real estate, moved the family of five to London in 1935. At the outbreak of World War II, to ensure the children's safety and to accommodate the sudden decentralization of the father's real estate business, there followed a whole series of moves, terminated by the enrollment of Peter and his twin brother, Anthony, at St. Paul's, a highly regarded British public school. Their studies were interrupted in 1944 when, instead of being drafted into the armed forces, the brothers were conscripted for service as coal miners. After a grueling three-year tour of duty in the mines of Kent and Yorkshire, they were released and Peter entered Cambridge University, to which he had won a scholarship.

While at Cambridge, he edited a magazine and credits this with awakening his desire to become a writer, though, in those days he had no thoughts of writing for the stage. As he explained in an interview: "There was a strange Puritanism in me that prevented me from indulging in wanting to be connected with the theatre. I believed it was the right thing to be self-supporting, to have a job, meaning an office job."

Upon his graduation from Cambridge in 1950, Mr. Shaffer sought employment in English publishing houses and when all leads failed, he decided to try his luck in America. He arrived here in 1951 and for several months worked as a salesman in a Doubleday bookshop, then took a job in the acquisitions department of the New York Public Library. During his tenure at the library, he managed to write a play about Israel called *The Salt Land* that "strove for the effect of classical tragedy in modern terms." He also began to tire of routine clerical work.

In 1954, he returned home to accept a position with the London-based music publishing firm Boosey & Hawkes. He soon proved adept at the task assigned him—assisting in publicizing symphonic sheet music—and was offered a promotion and an executive post with the company. But in 1955, encouraged by a production of *The Salt Land* on British television and by a broadcast over the B.B.C. of his radio play, *The Prodigal Father*, he quit his "job with a future" to devote all of his time to writing.

Success and financial security were not immediate. In the interim, he turned out two mystery novels (in collaboration with his twin brother), a television thriller, and served briefly as a literary and music critic for London periodicals.

It was the production of his deeply moving drama of domestic conflict, *Five Finger Exercise*, which altered the course of his life. The play, directed by Sir John Gielgud, opened at the Comedy Theatre on July 16, 1958, and London warmly welcomed Peter Shaffer as an exciting new entrant in the British theatre. He received the *Evening Standard* Drama Award for 1958 and in a poll of London newspaper reviewers, *Five Finger Exercise* was voted "the best play by a new playwright" of the 1958–59 season. The play opened in New York on December 2, 1959, and was named recipient of the New York Drama Critics' Circle Award for the best foreign play of the season.

When Mr. Shaffer's next presentation, a brace of short comedies, *The Private Ear* and *The Public Eye*, opened at the Globe in 1962, Eric Keown, the reviewer for *Punch*, wrote: "If there was ever any question of *Five Finger Exercise* being a flash in the pan, it is now dispelled. Mr. Shaffer is one of our major playwrights, of a kind we need badly." The double bill opened at the Morosco Theatre, New York, on October 9, 1963, and once again, Mr. Shaffer had achieved substantial success.

His position as a front-rank dramatist, however, was irrevocably affirmed with *The Royal Hunt of the Sun*, an epic drama dealing with Francisco Pizarro's conquest of Peru in the mid-sixteenth century. Selected by Britain's National Theatre Company as the vehicle to launch its 1964 season at the Chichester Festival, it was ingeniously staged by John Dexter and the production emerged as an exciting synthesis of all the theatre arts, and most critics were, quite frankly, stunned by it because nothing in Shaffer's previous work had prepared them for such a monumental enterprise. (His earlier plays, though undeniably well written, were comparatively small in scale.)

Critics and audiences were overwhelmed. Bernard Levin, drama critic for the London *Daily Mail*, hailed it as: "The greatest play of our generation. I do not think the English stage has been so graced nor English audiences so privileged since Shaw was in his heyday half a century ago." Peter Coe, the noted director, author and theatre essayist, in covering a 1969 revival of the play at the Theatre Royal, Bristol, wrote in *Plays and Players: "The Royal Hunt of the Sun* has a great and compelling theme or a series of themes, and it is this combination of subject, spectacle and penetrating writing that makes Mr. Shaffer's opus such a towering literary and theatrical event."

After being auspiciously introduced at Chichester, the epic drama joined the repertory of the National Theatre and played to equal acclaim as part of the company's regular season at the Old Vic in London. It opened in New York on October 26, 1965, and again there was laudation. Norman Nadel, among the laudators, concluded his newspaper critique with the statement that Shaffer's eloquent drama "might well be a masterpiece."

The play, a notable highlight in the theatre of the Sixties, appears in this collection. In reflecting upon his major work, Mr. Shaffer has noted: "Why did I write *The Royal Hunt of the Sun?* To make colour? Yes. To make spectacle? Yes. To make magic? Yes—if the word isn't too debased to convey the kind of excitement I believed could still be created out of 'total' theatre.

"The 'totality' of it was in my head for ages: not just the words, but jungle cries and ululations; metals and masks; the fantastic apparition of the pre-Columbian world and the terrible magnificence of the Conquistadors. . . . I did deeply want to create, by means both austere and rich—means always disciplined by a central aesthetic—an experience that was *entirely and only theatrical.*

"What about the words? What did I really want to write? Many things. Basically, perhaps, about an encounter between European hope and Indian hopelessness; between Indian faith and European faithlessness. I saw the active iron of Spain against the passive feathers of Peru: the conflict of two immense and joyless powers—"

After completing *The Royal Hunt of the Sun*, Mr. Shaffer wrote an hour-long farce, *Black Comedy*, for Britain's National Theatre. Immensely popular in London, the play (paired with *White Lies*, written expressly for the New York stage) later enjoyed a Broadway run of 338 performances during the 1966–67 season, followed by an extensive road tour.

The film version of *The Royal Hunt of the Sun*, filmed in Spain and the Peruvian Andes was released in the autumn of 1969. In Peter Shaffer's immediate future: a new play, *The Battle of Shrivings*, a contemporary drama, which will be produced in London in 1970 by H. M. Tennent, Ltd., with Sir John Gielgud, Celia Johnson and Patrick Magee in the principal roles.

THE ROYAL
HUNT
OF THE SUN

Peter Shaffer

The Royal Hunt of the Sun was first performed in Great Britain at the Chichester Festival on July 7, 1964. It subsequently joined the National Theatre repertory at the Old Vic, London, on December 8, 1964. The cast was as follows:

MARTIN RUIZ	Robert Lang
MARTIN RUIZ, as a boy	Roy Holder
FRANCISCO PIZARRO	Colin Blakely
HERNANDO DE SOTO	Michael Turner
FRAY VINCENTE DE VALVERDE	James Mellor
DIEGO DE TRUJILLO	Mike Gambon
SALINAS	Dan Meaden
RODAS	Trevor Martin
VASCA	Robert Russell
DOMINGO	Tom Kempinski
JUAN CHAVEZ	Christopher Timothy
FELIPILLO	Derek Jacobi
FRAY MARCOS DE NIZZA	Kenneth Mackintosh
PEDRO DE CANDIA	Frank Wylie
MIGUEL ESTETE	Peter Cellier
ATAHUALLPA	Robert Stephens
VILLAC UMU	Edward Petherbridge
CHALLCUCHIMA	Edward Hardwicke
MANCO	Neil Fitzpatrick
CHIEFTAIN	Peter John
HEADMAN	Bruce Purchase
INTI COUSSI	Louise Purnell
OELLO	Caroline John

Directed by John Dexter and Desmond O'Donovan
Scenery and Costumes by Michael Annals
Music composed by Marc Wilkinson
Movement by Madame Claude Chagrin
Lighting by John Read

The Royal Hunt of the Sun was first presented in the United States at the ANTA Theatre, New York, on October 26, 1965, by Theatre Guild Productions, Theodore Mann, Gerard Oestreicher in association with Hope Abelson. The cast was as follows:

THE SPANIARDS:

MARTIN RUIZ	*George Rose*
MARTIN RUIZ, as a boy	*Paul Collins*
FRANCISCO PIZARRO, Commander of the Expedition	*Christopher Plummer*
HERNANDO DE SOTO, Second-in-Command	*John Vernon*
FRAY VINCENTE DE VALVERDE, Dominican, Chaplain to the Expedition	*Ben Hammer*
DIEGO DE TRUJILLO, Master of the Horse	*Michael Lamont*
SALINAS, blacksmith	*Nelson Phillips*
RODAS, tailor	*Jake Dengel*
VASCA	*Tony Capodilupo*
DOMINGO	*George Sampson*
JUAN CHAVEZ	*Clyde Burton*
PEDRO CHAVEZ	*John Church*
FELIPILLO, an Indian boy employed as interpreter to Pizarro	*Gregory Rozakis*
FRAY MARCOS DE NIZZA, Franciscan Friar	*Michael Levin*
PEDRO DE CANDIA, Commander of Artillery	*Cal Bellini*
MIGUEL ESTETE, Royal Overseer	*Thayer David*

THE INCAS:

ATAHUALLPA,
    Sovereign Inca of Peru   *David Carradine*

VILLAC UMU,
    High Priest of Peru   *Mylo Quam*

CHALLCUCHIMA,
    an Inca General   *Clayton Corbin*

MANCO,
    a Messenger   *Marc Maskin*

CHIEFTAIN   *Robert Berdeen*

HEADMAN   *Judd Jones*

OELLO,
    a wife of Atahuallpa   *Sandy Leeds*

INTI COUSSI,
    step-sister of Atahuallpa   *Julie Sheppard*

PERUVIAN INDIANS: *Barry Burns, Paul Charles, Kurt Christian, Edilio Ferraro, Roy Lozano, Hector Mercado, Ken Novarro, B. J. Desimone, Don Silber*

    Directed by John Dexter
    Scenery and Costumes by Michael Annals
    Lighting by Martin Aronstein
    Mime by Madame Claude Chagrin
    Music and Sound Effects by Marc Wilkinson
    Musical Director: Herbert Harris
    Associate Producer: Don Herbert
    An ANTA presentation by arrangement with David
        Susskind and Daniel Melnick
    New York production supervised by George Jenkins
        and Ben Edwards

PLACE: *Apart from two early scenes in Spain and Panama, the play is set in the Upper Province of the Inca Empire: what is now South Ecuador and North Western Peru. The whole of Act II takes place in the town of Cajamarca.*

TIME: June 1529–August 1533

(AUTHOR'S NOTE: *Each act contains twelve sections, marked by Roman numerals. These are solely for reference, and do not indicate pauses or breaks of any kind. The action is continuous.*)

ACT I—THE HUNT

A bare stage. On the back wall, which is of wood, hangs a huge metal medallion, quartered by four black crucifixes, sharpened to resemble swords.

I

Darkness.
OLD MARTIN, *grizzled, in his middle fifties, appears. He wears the black costume of a Spanish hidalgo in the mid-sixteenth century.*

OLD MARTIN: Save you all. My name is Martin. I'm a soldier of Spain and that's it. Most of my life I've spent fighting for land, treasure and the cross. I'm worth millions. Soon I'll be dead and they'll bury me out here in Peru, the land I helped ruin as a boy. This story is about ruin. Ruin and gold. More gold than any of you will ever see even if you work in a counting house. I'm going to tell you how one hundred and sixty-seven men conquered an empire of twenty-four million. And then things that no one has ever told: things to make you groan and cry out I'm lying. And perhaps I am. The air of Peru is cold and sour like in a vault, and wits turn easier here even than in Europe. But grant me this: I saw him closer than anyone, and had cause only to love him. He was my altar, my bright image of salvation. Francisco Pizarro! Time was when I'd have died for him, or for any worship.

[YOUNG MARTIN *enters duelling an invisible opponent with a stick. He is Old Martin as an impetuous boy of fifteen*]

If you could only imagine what it was like for me at the beginning, to be allowed to serve him. But boys don't dream like that any more—service! Conquest! Riding down Indians in the name of Spain. The inside of my head was one vast plain for feats of daring. I used to lie up in the hayloft for hours reading my Bible—Don Cristobal on the rules of Chivalry. And then he came and made them real. And the only wish of my life is that I had never seen him.

[FRANCISCO PIZARRO *comes in. He is a man in late middle age: tough, commanding, harsh, wasted, secret. The gestures are blunt and often violent; the expression intense and energetic, capable of fury and cruelty, but also of sudden melancholy and sardonic humour. At the moment he appears more neatly than he is ever to do again: hair and beard are trimmed, and his clothes quite grand, as if he is trying to make a fine impression. He is accompanied by his Second-in-Command,* HERNANDO DE SOTO, *and the Dominican* FRAY VINCENTE DE VALVERDE. DE SOTO *is an impressive figure in his forties: his whole air breathes an unquestioning loyalty—to his profession, his faith, and to accepted values. He is an admirable soldier and a staunch friend.* VALVERDE *on the other hand is a peasant Priest whose zeal is not greatly tempered by intelligence, nor sweetened by any anxiety to please*]

PIZARRO: I was suckled by a sow. My house is the oldest in Spain—the pig-sty.

OLD MARTIN: He'd made two expeditions to the New World already. Now at over sixty years old he was back in Spain, making one last try. He'd shown the King enough gold to get sole right of discovery in Peru and the title of Viceroy over anything he conquered. In return he was to fit out an army at his own expense. He started recruiting in his own birthplace, Trujillo.

[*Lights up below as he speaks. Several Spanish villagers have entered, among them* SALINAS, *a blacksmith,* RODAS, *a*

tailor, VASCA, DOMINGO *and the* CHAVEZ *brothers.* PIZARRO
addresses DIEGO, *a young man of twenty-five*]

PIZARRO: What's your name?

DIEGO: Diego, sir.

PIZARRO: What do you know best?

DIEGO: Horses I suppose, if I was to name anything.

PIZARRO: How would you feel to be Master of Horse, Diego?

DIEGO: [*Eagerly*] Sir!

PIZARRO: Go over there. Who's smith here?

SALINAS: I am.

PIZARRO: Are you with us?

SALINAS: I'm not against you.

PIZARRO: Who's your friend?

RODAS: Tailor, if it's your business.

PIZARRO: Soldiers never stop mending and patching. They'll be
grateful for your assistance.

RODAS: We'll find some other fool to give it to them. I'm resting
here.

PIZARRO: Rest. [*To* YOUNG MARTIN] Who's this?

DIEGO: Martin Ruiz, sir. A good lad. He knows all his codes of
chivalry by heart. He's aching to be a page, sir.

PIZARRO: How old?

OLD MARTIN: Seventeen.

PIZARRO: Don't lie.

YOUNG MARTIN: Fifteen, sir.

[OLD MARTIN *goes off*]

PIZARRO: Parents?

YOUNG MARTIN: Dead, sir.

PIZARRO: Can you write?

YOUNG MARTIN: Two hundred Latin words. Three hundred
Spanish.

PIZARRO: Why do you want to come?

YOUNG MARTIN: It's going to be glorious, sir.

PIZARRO: Look you, if you served me you'd be Page to an old slogger: no titles, no traditions. I learnt my trade as a mercenary, going with who best paid me. It's a closed book to me, all that chivalry. But then, not reading or writing, all books are closed to me. If I took you you'd have to be my reader and writer, both.

YOUNG MARTIN: I'd be honoured, my lord. Oh, please, my lord!

PIZARRO: General will do. Let's see your respect. Greet me.

[*The boy bows*]

Now to the Church. That's Brother Valverde, our Chaplain.

VALVERDE: The blessing of God on you, my son. And on all who come with us to alter the heathen.

PIZARRO: Now to our Second-in-Command, Cavalier de Soto. I'm sure you all know the Cavalier well by reputation: a great soldier. He has fought under Cordoba! No expedition he seconds can fail. [*He takes a roll of cloth, woven with the design of a llama, from* DE SOTO] Now look at this! Indian stuff! Ten years ago standing with the great Balboa, I saw a chieftain draw this beast on the leaf of an aloe. And he said to me: Where this roams is uncountable wealth!

RODAS: Oh, yes, uncountable! Ask Sanchez the farrier about that. He listened to talk like that from him five years ago.

DIEGO: Who cares about him?

RODAS: Uncountable bloody wealth? It rained six months and his skin rotted on him. They lost twenty-seven out of fifty.

PIZARRO: And so we may again. What do you think I'm offering? A walk in the country? Jellies and wine in a basket, your hand round your girl? No, I'm promising you swamps. A forest like the beard of the world. Sitting half-buried in earth to escape the mouths of insects. You may live for weeks on palm tree buds and soup made out of leather straps. And at night you will sleep in thick wet darkness with snakes hung over your heads like bell ropes—and black men in that blackness: men that eat each other. And why should you endure all this? Because I believe that beyond this terrible place is a kingdom, where gold is as common as wood is here! I took only two steps in and found cups and pans made out of it solid.

[*He claps his hands.* FELIPILLO *comes in. He is a slim, delicate Indian from Ecuador, loaded with golden ornaments. In actuality* FELIPILLO *is a treacherous and hysterical creature, but at the moment, under his master's eye, he sways forward before the stupefied villagers with a demure grace*]

I present Felipillo, captured on my last trip. Look close at his ornaments. To him they are no more than feathers are to us, but they are all gold, my friends. Examine him. Down!

[*The villagers examine him*]

VALVERDE: Look at him well. This is a heathen. A being condemned to eternal flame unless you help him. Don't think we are merely going to destroy his people and lift their wealth. We are going to take from them what they don't value, and give them instead the priceless mercy of heaven. He who helps me lift this dark man into light I absolve of all crimes he ever committed.

PIZARRO: Well?

SALINAS: That's gold right enough.

PIZARRO: And for your taking. I was like you once. Sitting the afternoon away in this same street, drunk in the inn, to bed in the sty. Stink and mud and nothing to look for. Even if you die with me, what's so tender precious to hold you here?

VASCA: You're hissing right!

PIZARRO: I tell you, man: over there you'll be the masters— that'll be your slave.

VASCA: Well, there's a thought: talk about the slave of slaves!

DOMINGO: [*Timidly*] Do you think it's true?

PIZARRO: Do you say I lie?

DOMINGO: Oh, no, sir . . .

VASCA: Even if he does, what's to keep you here? You're a
cooper: how many casks have you made this year? That's no
employment for a dog.

PIZARRO: How about you? You're brothers aren't you?

DIEGO: That's the Chavez brothers, Juan and Pedro.

JUAN: Sir.

PEDRO: Sir.

PIZARRO: Well, what d'you say?

JUAN: I say right, sir.

PEDRO: Me too.

VASCA: And me. I'm going to get a slave or two like him.

DOMINGO: And me. Vasca's right, you can't do worse than stay
here.

RODAS: Well not me, boys. Just you catch Rodas marching through
any hissing jungle!

SALINAS: Oh, shut your ape's face. Are you going to sit here for
ever and pick fleas? He'll come sir.

PIZARRO: Make your way to Toledo for the muster. Diego, enroll
them all and take them along.

DIEGO: Sir!

[YOUNG MARTIN *makes to go off with the rest.* PIZARRO
stays him]

PIZARRO: Boy.

YOUNG MARTIN: Sir.

[*A pause*]

PIZARRO: Master me the names of all officers and men so far
listed.

YOUNG MARTIN: Oh, sir! Yes, sir! Thank you, sir!

PIZARRO: You're a page now, so act like one. Dignity at all times.

YOUNG MARTIN: [*Bowing*] Yes, sir.

PIZARRO: Respect.

YOUNG MARTIN: [*Bowing*] Yes, sir.

PIZARRO: And obedience.

YOUNG MARTIN: [*Bowing*] Yes, sir.

PIZARRO: And it isn't necessary to salute every ten seconds.

YOUNG MARTIN: [*Bowing*] No, sir.

VALVERDE: Come, my son, there's work to do.

[*They go off*]

PIZARRO: Strange sight, yourself, just as you were in this very street.

DE SOTO: Do you like it?

PIZARRO: No, I was a fool. Dreamers deserve what they get.

DE SOTO: And what are you dreaming about now?

PIZARRO: Gold.

DE SOTO: Oh, come. Gold is not enough lodestone for you, not any more to drag you back to the new world.

PIZARRO: You're right. At my age things become what they really are. Gold turns into metal.

DE SOTO: Then why? You could stay here now and be hero for a province. What's left to endure so much for—especially with your infirmity? You've earned the right to comfort. Your country would gladly grant it to you for the rest of your life.

PIZARRO: My country, where is that?

DE SOTO: Spain, sir.

PIZARRO: Spain and I have been strangers since I was a boy. The only spot I know in it is here—this filthy village. This is Spain to me. Is this where you wish me comfort? For twenty-two years I drove pigs down this street because my father couldn't own to my mother. Twenty-two years without one single day of hope. When I turned soldier and dragged my arquebus along the roads of Italy, I was so famished I was beyond eating. I got nothing and I gave nothing, and though I groaned for that once I'm glad with it now. Because I owe nothing . . . Once the world could have had me for a petty farm, two rocky fields and a Senor to my name. It said 'No'. Ten years on it could have had me for double—small estate, fifty oranges and a Sir to them. It said 'No'. Twenty years more and it could still have had me cheap: Balboa's trusty lieutenant, marched with him into the Pacific and claimed it for Spain: State Pension and dinner once a week with the local Mayor. But the world said 'No'. Said 'No' and said 'No'. Well, now it's going to know me. If I live this next year I'm going to get me a name for centuries in your ballads, out there under the cork trees where I sat as a boy with bandages for shoes. I amuse you.

DE SOTO: Surely you see you don't.

PIZARRO: Oh, yes, I amuse you, Cavalier de Soto. The old pigherd lumbering after fame. You inherited your honour—I had to root for mine like the pigs. It's amusing.

II

Lights whiter, colder.
He kneels. An organ sounds: the austere polyphony of Spanish celebration. VALVERDE *enters, bearing an immense wooden Christ. He is accompanied by his assistant,* FRAY MARCOS DE NIZZA, *a Franciscan, a man of far more serene temper and intellectual maturity. All the villagers come in also, wearing the white cloaks of chivalry and carrying banners. Among them is* PEDRO DE CANDIA, *a Venetian captain, wearing a pearl in one ear and walking with a lazy stealth that at once suggests danger.* OLD MARTIN *comes in.*

OLD MARTIN: On the day of St. John the Evangelist, our weapons were consecrated in the Cathedral Church of Panama. Our muster was one hundred and eighty-seven, with horses for twenty-seven.

VALVERDE: You are the huntsmen of God. The weapons you draw are sacred! Oh, God, invest us all with the courage of Thy unflinching Son. Show us our way to beat the savage out of his dark forests on to the broad plain of Thy Grace.

DE NIZZA: And comfort, we pray, all warriors shall be in affliction from this setting out.

OLD MARTIN: Fray Marcos de Nizza, Franciscan, appointed to assist Valverde.

DE NIZZA: You are the bringers of food to starving peoples. You go to break mercy with them like bread, and outpour gentleness into their cups. You will lay before them the inexhaustible table of free spirit, and invite to it all who have dieted on terror. You will bring to all tribes the nourishment of pity. You will sow their fields with love, and teach them to harvest the crop of it, each yield in its season. Remember this always: we are their New World.

VALVERDE: Approach all and be blessed.

[During this, the men kneel and are blessed]

OLD MARTIN: Pedro de Candia, Cavalier from Venice, in charge of weapons and artillery. These villagers you know already. There were many others of course. Almagro, the General's partner, who stayed to organize reinforcements and follow in three months. Riquelme the Treasurer. Pedro of Ayala and Blas of Atienza. Herrada the Swordsman and Gonzales of Toledo. And Juan de Barbaran whom everyone called the good servant out of love for him. And many smaller men. Even its youngest member saw himself with a following of Indians and a province for an orchard. It was a tumbled company, none too noble but ginger for wealth.

[Enter ESTETE: a stiff, haughty man, dressed in the black of the Spanish court]

And chiefly there was—

ESTETE: Miguel Estete. Royal Veedor, and Overseer in the name of King Carlos the Fifth. You should not have allowed anyone to be blessed before me.

PIZARRO: Your pardon, Veedor, I don't understand affairs of before and after.

ESTETE: That is evident. General, on this expedition my name is the law: it is spoken with the King's authority.

PIZARRO: Your pardon, but on this expedition *my* name is the law: there will be no other.

ESTETE: In matters military.

PIZARRO: In all matters.

ESTETE: In all that do not infringe the majesty of the King.

PIZARRO: What matters could?

ESTETE: Remember your duty to God, sir, and to the throne, sir, and you will not discover them.

PIZARRO: [*Furious*] De Soto! In the name of Spain our Holy country, I invest you as second in Command to me. Subject only to me. In the name of Spain our Holy country—I—I. [*He falters, clutching his side in pain. A pause. The men whisper among themselves*] Take the banners out. . . .

DE SOTO: Take up your banners. March!

> [*The organ music continues: all march out, leaving* PIZARRO *and his* PAGE *alone on the stage. Only when all the rest are gone does the General collapse. The boy is frightened and concerned*]

YOUNG MARTIN: What is it, sir?

PIZARRO: A wound from long ago. A knife to the bone. A savage put it into me for life. It troubles me at times . . . You'll start long before me with your wounds. With your killing too. I wonder how you'll like that.

YOUNG MARTIN: You watch me, sir.

PIZARRO: I will. You deal in deaths when you are a soldier, and all your study should be to make them clean, what scratches kill and how to cut them.

YOUNG MARTIN: But surely, sir, there's more to soldiering than that?

PIZARRO: You mean honour, glory—traditions of the service?

YOUNG MARTIN: Yes, sir.

PIZARRO: Dungballs. Soldiers are for killing: that's their reason.

YOUNG MARTIN: But, sir—

PIZARRO: What?

YOUNG MARTIN: It's not just killing.

PIZARRO: Look, boy: know something. Men cannot just stand as men in this world. It's too big for them and they grow scared. So they build themselves shelters against the bigness, do you see? They call the shelters Court, Army, Church. They're useful against loneliness, Martin, but they're not true. They're not real, Martin. Do you see?

YOUNG MARTIN: No, sir. Not truthfully, sir . . .

PIZARRO: No, sir. Not truthfully, sir! Why must you be so young? Look at you. Only a quarter formed. A colt the world will break for its sightless track. Listen once. Army loyalty is blasphemy. The world of soldiers is a yard of ungrowable children. They play with ribbons and make up ceremonies just to keep out the rest of the world. They add up the number of their blue dead and their green dead and call that their history. But all this is just the flower the bandit carves on his knife before shoving it into a man's side . . . What's Army Tradition? Nothing but years of Us against Them. Christ-men against Pagan-men. Men against men. I've had a life of it, boy, and let me tell you it's nothing but a nightmare game, played by brutes to give themselves a reason.

YOUNG MARTIN: But, sir, a noble reason can make a fight glorious.

PIZARRO: Give me a reason that stays noble once you start hacking off limbs in its name. There isn't a cause in the world to set against this pain. Noble's a word. Leave it for the books.

YOUNG MARTIN: I can't believe that, sir.

PIZARRO: Look at you—hope, lovely hope, it's on you like dew. Do you know where you're going? Into the forest. A hundred miles of dark and screaming. The dark we all came out of, hot. Things flying, fleeing, falling dead—and their death unnoticed. Take your noble reasons there, Martin. Pitch your silk flags in that black and wave your crosses at the wild cats. See what awe they command. Be advised, boy. Go back to Spain.

YOUNG MARTIN: No, sir. I'm coming with you. I can learn, sir.

PIZARRO: You will be taught. Not by me. The forest.

[*He stumps out*]

III

The boy is left alone. The stage darkens and the huge medallion high on the back wall begins to glow. Great cries of 'Inca!' are heard. The boy bolts off stage. Exotic music mixes with the chanting. Slowly the medallion opens outwards to form a huge golden sun with twelve great rays. In the centre stands ATAHUALLPA, sovereign Inca of Peru, masked, crowned, and dressed in gold. When he speaks, his voice, like the voices of all the Incas, is strangely formalized.

[*Enter below the Inca court:* VILLAC UMU, *the High Priest,* CHALLCUCHIMA, MANCO *and others, all masked, and robed in terracotta. They prostrate themselves*]

MANCO: Atahuallpa! God!

ATAHUALLPA: God hears.

MANCO: Manco your Chasqui speaks. I bring truth from many runners what has been seen in the Farthest Province. White men sitting on huge sheep. The sheep are red! Everywhere their leaders shouts aloud 'Here is God!'

ATAHUALLPA: The White God!

VILLAC UMU: Beware, beware Inca!

ATAHUALLPA: All-powerful spirit who left this place before my ancestors ruled you. The White God returns!

CHALLCUCHIMA: You do not know this.

ATAHUALLPA: He has been long waited for. If he comes, it is

with blessing. Then my people will see I did well to take the Crown.

VILLAC UMU: Ware you! Your mother Moon wears a veil of green fire. An eagle fell on to the temple in Cuzco.

MANCO: It is true, Capac. He fell out of the sky.

VILLAC UMU: Out of a green sky.

CHALLCUCHIMA: On to a house of gold.

VILLAC UMU: When the world ends, small birds grow sharp claws.

ATAHUALLPA: Cover your mouth. [*All cover their mouths*] If the White God comes to bless me, all must see him.

[*The Court retires.* ATAHUALLPA *remains on stage, motionless in his sunflower. He stays in this position until the end of Scene VII*]

IV

Mottled light.
Province of Tumbes. Screams and whoops of alarm imitating tropical bird cries. A horde of Indians rushes across the stage pursued by soldiers.

DE CANDIA: Grab that one! That's the chief.

[*They capture the Chieftain. At the sight of this, all the Indians fall silent and passive.* DE CANDIA *approaches him with drawn sword*]

Now, you brownie bastard, show us gold.

PIZARRO: Gently, De Candia. You'll get nothing from him in terror.

DE CANDIA: Let's see.

PIZARRO: God's wounds! Put up! Felipillo, ask for gold.

[FELIPILLO *adopts a set of stylized gestures for his interpreting, in the manner of sign language*]

CHIEF: We have no gold. All was taken by the great King in his war.

PIZARRO: What King?

CHIEF: Holy Atahuallpa, Inca of earth and sky. His Kingdom is the widest in the world.

DE SOTO: How wide?

CHIEF: A man can run in it every day for a year.

DE SOTO: More than a thousand miles.

ESTETE: Poor savage, trying to impress us with his little tribe.

PIZARRO: I think we've found more than a little tribe, Veedor. Tell me of this King. Who did he fight?

CHIEF: His brother Huascar. His father the great Inca Huayana grew two sons. One by a wife, one by a not-wife. At his death he cut the Kingdom in two for them. But Atahuallpa wanted all. So he made war, and killed his brother. Now he is lord of earth and sky.

PIZARRO: And he's the bastard?

[*All the* INDIANS *cry out*]

Answer! He's the bastard?

CHIEF: He is Son of the Sun. He needs no wedded mother. He is God.

INDIANS: [*Chanting*] Sapa Inca! Inca Capac!

PIZARRO: God?

CHIEF: God!

PIZARRO: God on earth?

VALVERDE: Christ defend us!

DE SOTO: Do you believe this?

CHIEF: It is true. The sun is God. Atahuallpa is his child sent to shine on us for a few years of life. Then he will return to his father's palace and live for ever.

PIZARRO: God on earth!

VALVERDE: Oh, my brothers, where have we come? The land of Anti-Christ! Do your duty, Spaniards! Take each an Indian and work to shift his soul. Go to them. Show them rigour! No softness to gentle idolatry. [*To the* INDIANS] The cross, you pagan dust!

[*They try to escape*]

Stay them!

[*The* SPANIARDS *ring them with swords*]

Repeat. Jesus Christ Inca!

INDIANS: [*Uncertainly*] Jesus Christ Inca!

ESTETE: Jesus Christ Inca!

INDIANS: Jesus Christ Inca!

[*The soldiers herd them off stage. Their cries punctuate the end of the scene. All go off after them, save* PIZARRO *and* DE SOTO]

ATAHUALLPA: He surely is a god. He teaches my people to praise him.

PIZARRO: He's a god all right. They're scared to hell of him. And a bastard too. That's civil war—bastards against bastards!

ATAHUALLPA: I will see him. Let no one harm these men.

PIZARRO: Let's see you, then. What's it look like to be Son of the Sun?

DE SOTO: That's something in Europe no one's ever dared call himself.

PIZARRO: God on earth, living for ever!

DE SOTO: He's got a shock coming.

[*He goes off*]

PIZARRO: Do you hear that, God? You're not going to like that! Because we've got a God worth a thousand of yours. A gentle God with gentle priests, and a couple of big cannon to blow you out of the sky!

VALVERDE: [*Off*] Jesus Christ Inca!

PIZARRO: Christ the Merciful, with his shackles and stakes! So enjoy yourself while you can. Have a glorious shine. [*He makes the sign of the cross*] Take that, Anti-Christ!

[*He runs off, laughing*]

VALVERDE: [*Off*] Jesus Christ Inca!

[INDIANS *off cry out*]

[*Enter* VILLAC UMU *and* CHALLCUCHIMA]

VILLAC UMU: Your people groan.

ATAHUALLPA: They groan with my voice.

CHALLCUCHIMA: Your people weep.

ATAHUALLPA: They weep with my tears.

CHALLCUCHIMA: He searches all the houses. He seeks your crown. Remember the prophecy! The twelfth Lord of the Four Quarters shall be the last. Inca, ware you!

VILLAC UMU: Inca, ware you!

ATAHUALLPA: [*To* CHALLCUCHIMA] Go to him. Take him my word. Tell him to greet me at Cajamarca, behind the great mountains. If he is a god he will find me. If he is no god, he will die.

[*Lights down on him. Priest and noblemen retire*]

V

[*Night. Wild bird cries.* DOMINGO *and* VASCA *on sentry duty*]

VASCA: There must be a hissing thousand of 'em, every night we halt.

DOMINGO: Why don't they just come and get us?

VASCA: They're waiting.

DOMINGO: What for?

VASCA: Maybe they're cannibals and there's a feast day coming up.

DOMINGO: Very funny . . . Six weeks in this hissing forest and not one smell of gold. I think we've been had.

VASCA: Unless they're hiding it, like the General says.

DOMINGO: I don't believe it. God-damned place. I'm starting to rust.

VASCA: We all are. It's the damp. Another week and we'll have to get the blacksmith to cut us out.

[*Enter* ESTETE *with* DE CANDIA *carrying an arquebus*]

Who's there?

DE CANDIA: Talk on duty again and *I'll* cut you out.

DOMINGO: Yes, sir.

VASCA: Yes, sir.

[*They separate and go off*]

DE CANDIA: They're right. Everything's rusting. Even you, my darling. [*The gun*] Look at her, Strozzi's most perfect model. She can stop a horse at five hundred paces. You're too good for brownies, my sweet.

ESTETE: What are they waiting for? Why don't they just attack and be done with it?

DE CANDIA: They'd find nothing against them. A hundred and eighty terrified men, nine of these and two cannon. If your King wasn't so mean we might just stand a chance out here.

ESTETE: Hold your tongue, De Candia.

DE CANDIA: Good: loyalty. That's what I like to see. The only thing that puzzles me is what the hell you get out of it. They tell me Royal Overseers get nothing.

ESTETE: Any man without self-interest must puzzle a Venetian. If you serve a King you must kill personal ambition. Only then can you become a channel between the people and its collective glory—which otherwise it would never feel. In Byzantium Court Officials were castrated to resemble the Order of Angels. But I don't expect you to understand.

DE CANDIA: You Spaniards! You men with missions! You just can't bear to think of yourselves as the thieves you are.

ESTETE: How dare you, sir!

[*Enter* PIZARRO *and* YOUNG MARTIN]

DE CANDIA: Our noble General. They say in the Indies he traded his immortal part to the Devil.

ESTETE: For what, pray? Health? Breeding? Handsomeness?

DE CANDIA: That they don't tell.

ESTETE: I daresay not. I only wonder His Majesty could give command to such a man. I believe he's mad.

DE CANDIA: No, but still dangerous.

ESTETE: What do you mean?

DE CANDIA: I've served under many men: but this is the first who makes me afraid. Look into him, you'll see a kind of death.

[*Bird cries fill the forest*]

PIZARRO: Listen to them. There's the world. The eagle rips the condor; the condor rips the crow. And the crow would blind all the eagles in the sky if once it had the beak to do it. The clothed hunt the naked; the legitimates hunt the bastards, and put down the word Gentleman to blot up the blood. Your Chivalry rules don't govern me, Martin. They're for belonging birds—like them: legitimate birds with claws trim on the perch their feathers left to them. Make no error; if I could once peck them off it, I'd tear them into gobbets to feed cats. Don't ever trust me, boy.

YOUNG MARTIN: Sir? I'm your man.

PIZARRO: Don't ever trust me.

YOUNG MARTIN: Sir?

PIZARRO: Or if you must, never say I deceived you. Know me.

YOUNG MARTIN: I do, sir. You are all I ever want to be.

PIZARRO: I am nothing you could ever want to be, or any man alive. Believe this: if the time ever came for you to harry me, I'd rip you too, easy as look at you. Because you belong too, Martin.

YOUNG MARTIN: I belong to you, sir!

PIZARRO: You belong to hope. To faith. To priests and pretences. To dipping flags and ducking heads; to laying hands and licking rings; to powers and parchments; and the whole vast stupid congregation of crowners and cross-kissers. You're a worshipper, Martin. A groveller. You were born with feet but you prefer your knees. It's you who make Bishops—Kings—Generals. You trust me, I'll hurt you past believing. [A *pause*] Have the sentries changed?

YOUNG MARTIN: Not yet, sir.

PIZARRO: Little Lord of Hope, I'm harsh with you. You own everything I've lost. I despise the keeping, and I loathe the losing. Where can a man live, between two hates?

[*He goes towards the two officers*]

Gentlemen.

ESTETE: How is your wound tonight, General?

PIZARRO: The calmer for your inquiring, Veedor.

DE CANDIA: Well, and what's your plan, sir?

PIZARRO: To go on until I'm stopped.

DE CANDIA: Admirable simplicity.

ESTETE: What kind of plan is that?

PIZARRO: You have a better? It's obvious they've been ordered to hold off.

ESTETE: Why?

PIZARRO: If it's wickedness I'm sure the crown can guess it as soon as the Army.

ESTETE: Sir, I know your birth hasn't fitted you for much civility, but remember, in me speaks your King.

PIZARRO: Well, go and write to him. Set down more about my unfitness in your report. Then show it to the birds.

[*He goes off.* ESTETE *goes off another way.* DE CANDIA *laughs and follows him*]

VI

Light brightens to morning.

Enter OLD MARTIN.

OLD MARTIN: We were in the forest for six weeks, but at last we escaped and found on the other side our first witness of a great empire. There was a road fifteen feet wide, bordered with mimosa and blue glories, with walls on both sides the height of a man. We rode it for days, six horses abreast: and all the way, far up the hillsides, were huge fields of corn laid out in terraces, and a net of water in a thousand canals.

[*Exit*]

[*Lights up on* ATAHUALLPA, *above*]

MANCO: Manco your Chasqui speaks. They move on the road to Ricaplaya.

ATAHUALLPA: What do they do?

MANCO: They walk through the field terraces. They listen to toil-songs. They clap their hands at fields of llama.

[*Enter groups of* INDIANS, *singing a toil-song and miming their work of sowing and reaping.* PIZARRO, *the* PRIESTS, FELIPILLO *and* SOLDIERS, *among them* DE SOTO, DE CANDIA, DIEGO, ESTETE *and* YOUNG MARTIN, *enter and stand watching.* YOUNG MARTIN *carries a drum*]

DE NIZZA: How beautiful their tongue sounds.

YOUNG MARTIN: I'm trying to study it but it's very hard. All the words seem to slip together.

FELIPILLO: Oh, very hard, yes. But more hard for Indian to learn Spanish.

DE NIZZA: I'm sure. See how contented they look.

DIEGO: It's the first time I've ever seen people glad at working.

DE SOTO: This is their Headman.

PIZARRO: You are the Lord of the Manor?

[FELIPILLO *interprets*]

HEADMAN: Here all work together in families: fifty, a hundred, a thousand. I am head of a thousand families. I give out to all food. I give out to all clothes. I give out to all confessing.

DE NIZZA: Confessing?

HEADMAN: I have priest power . . . I confess my people of all crimes against the laws of the sun.

DE NIZZA: What laws are these?

HEADMAN: It is the seventh month. That is why they must pick corn.

ATAHUALLPA: [*Intoning*] In the eighth month you will plough. In the ninth, sow maize. In the tenth, mend your roofs.

HEADMAN: Each age also has its tasks.

ATAHUALLPA: Nine years to twelve, protect harvests. Twelve to eighteen, care for herds. Eighteen to twenty-five, warriors for me—Atahuallpa Inca!

FELIPILLO: They are stupid; always do what they are told.

DE SOTO: This is because they are poor?

FELIPILLO: Not poor. Not rich. All same.

ATAHUALLPA: At twenty-five all will marry. All will receive one tupu of land.

HEADMAN: What may be covered by one hundred pounds of maize.

ATAHUALLPA: They will never move from there. At birth of

a son one more tupu will be given. At birth of a daughter, half a tupu. At fifty all people will leave work for ever and be fed in honour till they die.

DE SOTO: I have settled several lands. This is the first I've entered which shames our Spain.

ESTETE: Shames?

PIZARRO: Oh, it's not difficult to shame Spain. Here shames every country which teaches we are born greedy for possessions. Clearly we're made greedy when we're assured it's natural. But there's a picture for a Spanish eye! There's nothing to covet, so covetousness dies at birth.

DE SOTO: But don't you have any nobles or grand people?

HEADMAN: The King has great men near him to order the country. But they are few.

DE SOTO: How then can he make sure so many are happy over so large a land?

HEADMAN: His messengers run light and dark, one after one, over four great roads. No one else may move on them. So he has eyes everywhere. He sees you now.

PIZARRO: Now?

ATAHUALLPA: Now!

[CHALLCUCHIMA *enters with* MANCO, *bearing the image of the Sun on a pole*]

CHALLCUCHIMA: I bring greeting from Atahuallpa Inca, Lord of the Four Quarters, King of earth and sky.

ESTETE: I will speak with him. A King's man must always greet a King's man. We bring greeting from King Carlos, Emperor of Spain and Austria. We bring blessing from Jesus Christ, the Son of God.

ATAHUALLPA: Blessing!

CHALLCUCHIMA: *I* am sent by the son of God. He orders *you* to visit him.

ESTETE: Orders? Does he take us for servants?

CHALLCUCHIMA: All men are his servants.

ESTETE: Does he think so? He's got awakening coming.

CHALLCUCHIMA: Awakening?

PIZARRO: Veedor, under pardon, let my peasant tongue have a word. Where is your King?

CHALLCUCHIMA: Cajamarca. Behind the great mountains. Perhaps they are too high for you.

ESTETE: There isn't a hill in your whole country a Spaniard couldn't climb in full armour.

CHALLCUCHIMA: That is wonderful.

PIZARRO: How long should we march before we find him?

CHALLCUCHIMA: One life of Mother Moon.

FELIPILLO: A month.

PIZARRO: For us, two weeks. Tell him we come.

ATAHUALLPA: He gives his word with no fear.

CHALLCUCHIMA: Ware you! It is great danger to take back your word.

PIZARRO: I do not fear danger. What I say I do.

CHALLCUCHIMA: So. Do.

[CHALLCUCHIMA *and* MANCO *go off*]

ATAHUALLPA: He speaks with a God's tongue. Let us take his blessing.

DE SOTO: Well, God help us now.

DE CANDIA: He'd better. I don't know who else will get us out of this. Certainly not the artillery.

FELIPILLO: [*Imitating* CHALLCUCHIMA's *walk and voice*] So! Do!

DE SOTO: Be still. You're too free.

ESTETE: My advice to you now is to wait for the reinforcements.

PIZARRO: I thank you for it.

DE SOTO: There's no telling when they'll come, sir. We daren't stay till then.

PIZARRO: But *you* of course will.

ESTETE: I?

PIZARRO: I cannot hazard the life of a Royal officer.

ESTETE: My personal safety has never concerned me, General. My Master's service is all I care for.

PIZARRO: That's why we must ensure its continuance. I'll give you twenty men. You can make a garrison.

ESTETE: I must decline, General. If you go—I go also.

PIZARRO: I'm infinitely moved, Veedor—but my orders remain. You stay here. [*To his* PAGE] Call Assembly.

YOUNG MARTIN: [*Banging his drum*] Assembly! Assembly!

VII

The Company pelts on. ESTETE *goes off angrily.*

PIZARRO: We are commanded to court by a brown King, more powerful than any you have ever heard of, sole owner of all the gold we came for. We have three roads. Go back, and he kills us. Stay here, and he kills us. Go on, and he still may kill us. Who fears to meet him can stay here with the Veedor and swell a garrison. He'll have no disgrace, but no gold neither. Who stirs?

RODAS: Well, I hissing stir for one. I'm not going to be chewed up by no bloody heathen king. What do you say, Vasca lad?

VASCA: I don't know. I reckon if he chews us first, he chews you second. We're the eggs and you're the stew.

RODAS: Ha, ha, day of a hundred jokes.

SALINAS: Come on, friend, for God's sake. Who's going to sew us up if you desert?

RODAS: You can all rot for all I care, breeches and what's bloody in 'em.

SALINAS: Bastard!

RODAS: To hell with the lot of you!

[*He walks off*]

PIZARRO: Anyone else?

DOMINGO: Well, I don't know . . . Maybe he's right.

JUAN: Hey, Pedro, what do you think?

PEDRO: Hell, no! Vasca's right. It's as safe to go as stay here.

SALINAS: That's right.

VASCA: Anyway, I didn't come to keep no hissing garrison.

PEDRO: Nor me. I'm going on.

JUAN: Right, boy.

SALINAS: And me.

DOMINGO: Well, I don't know . . .

VASCA: Oh, close your mouth. You're like a hissing girl. [*To* PIZARRO] We're coming. Just find us that gold.

PIZARRO: All right then. [*To* YOUNG MARTIN] You stay here.

YOUNG MARTIN: No, sir. The place of a squire is at all times by his Knight's side. Laws of Chivalry.

PIZARRO: [*Touched*] Get them in rank. *Move!*

YOUNG MARTIN: Company in rank. Move!

[*The soldiers form up in rank*]

PIZARRO: Stand firm. Firmer! . . . Look at you, you could be dead already. If he sees you like that you will be. Make no error, he's watching every step you take. You're not men any longer, you're Gods now. Eternal Gods, each one of you. Two can play this immortality game, my lads. I want to see you move over his land like figures from a Lent Procession. He must see Gods walk on earth. Indifferent! Uncrushable! No death to be afraid of. I tell you, one shiver dooms the lot of us. One yelp of fright and we'll never be heard of again. He'll serve us like cheeseworms you crush with a knife. So come on you tattered trash—shake out the straw. Forget your village magic: fingers in crosses, saints under your shirts. You can grant prayers now—no need to answer them. Come on! Fix your eyes! Follow the pig-boy to his glory! I'll have an Empire for my farm. A million boys driving in the pigs at night. And each one of you will own a share—juicy black earth a hundred mile apiece—and golden ploughs to cut it! Get up you God-boys—March!

[MARTIN *bangs his drum. The Spaniards begin to march in slow motion. Above, masked Indians move on to the upper level*]

MANCO: They move Inca! They come! One hundred and sixty and seven.

ATAHUALLPA: Where?

MANCO: Zaran.

VILLAC UMU: Ware! Ware, Inca!

MANCO: They move all in step. Not fast, not slow. They keep straight on from dark to dark.

VILLAC UMU: Ware! Ware, Inca!

MANCO: They are at Motupe, Inca! They do not look on left or right.

VILLAC UMU: Ware! this is great danger.

ATAHUALLPA: No danger. He is coming to bless me. A god and all his priests. Praise Father Sun!

ALL ABOVE: [*Chanting*] Virchen Atix!

ATAHUALLPA: Praise Sapa Inca!

ALL ABOVE: Sapa Inca! Inca Capac!

ATAHUALLPA: Praise Inti Cori.

ALL ABOVE: Keild Ya, Inti Cori!

CHALLCUCHIMA: They come to the mountains.

VILLAC UMU: Kill them now.

ATAHUALLPA: Praise Atahuallpa.

VILLAC UMU: Destroy them! Teach them death!

ATAHUALLPA: *Praise Atahuallpa!*

ALL ABOVE: Atahuallpa! Sapa Inca! Hua-car-cu-ya-t!

ATAHUALLPA: [*Crying out*] Let them see my mountains!

[*A crash of primitive instruments. The lights snap out and, lit from the side, the rays of the metal sun throw long*]

*shadows across the wooden wall. All the Spaniards fall
down. A cold blue light fills the stage]*

DE SOTO: God in heaven!

[*Enter* OLD MARTIN]

OLD MARTIN: You call them the Andes. Picture a curtain of
stone hung by some giant across your path. Mountains set
on mountains: cliffs on cliffs. Hands of rock a hundred
yards high, with flashing nails where the snow never moved,
scratching the gashed face of the sun. For miles around the
jungle lay black in its shadows. A freezing cold fell on us.

PIZARRO: Up, my godlings. Up, my little gods. Take heart, now.
He's watching you. *Get to your feet!* [*To* DIEGO] Master,
what of the horses?

DIEGO: D'you need them, sir?

PIZARRO: They're vital, boy.

DIEGO: Then you'll have 'em, sir. They'll follow you as we will.

PIZARRO: Up we go, then! We're coming for you, Atahuallpa.
Show me the toppest peak-top you can pile—show me the lid
of the world—I'll stand tiptoe on it and pull you right out of
the sky. I'll grab you by the legs, you Son of the Sun, and
smash your flaming crown on the rocks. Bless them, Church!

VALVERDE: God stay you, and stay with you all.

DE NIZZA: Amen.

[*Whilst* PIZARRO *is calling his last speech to the Inca, the
silent King thrice beckons to him, and retires backwards
out of the sun into blackness. In the cold light there now
ensues*]

VIII

THE MIME OF THE GREAT ASCENT

As OLD MARTIN *describes their ordeal, the men climb the
Andes. It is a terrible progress; a stumbling, tortuous*

climb into the clouds, over ledges and giant chasms, per-
formed to an eerie, cold music made from the thin whine
of huge saws.

OLD MARTIN: Have you ever climbed a mountain in full armour?
That's what we did, him going first the whole way up a tiny
path into the clouds, with drops sheer on both sides into
nothing. For hours we crept forward like blind men, the sweat
freezing on our faces, lugging skittery leaking horses, and
pricked all the time for the ambush that would tip us into
death. Each turn of the path it grew colder. The friendly
trees of the forest dropped away, and there were only pines.
Then they went too, and there were just scrubby little bushes
standing up in ice. All round us the rocks began to whine with
cold. And always above us, or below us, those filthy condor
birds, hanging on the air with great tasselled wings.

[*It grows darker. The music grows colder yet. The men*
freeze and hang their heads for a long moment, before
resuming their desperate climb]

Then night. We lay down twos and threes together on the
path, and hugged like lovers for warmth in that burning cold.
And most cried. We got up with cold iron for bones and
went on. Four days like that; groaning, not speaking; the
breath a blade in our lungs. Four days, slowly, like flies on
a wall; limping flies, dying flies, up an endless wall on a rock.
A tiny army lost in the creases of the moon.

INDIANS: [*Off in echo*] Stand!

[*The Spaniards whirl round* VILLAC UMU *and his attend-*
ants appear, clothed entirely in white fur. The High Priest
wears a snow-white llama head on top of his own]

VILLAC UMU: You see Villac Umu. Chief Priest of the Sun.
Why do you come?

PIZARRO: To see the Great Inca.

VILLAC UMU: Why will you see him?

PIZARRO: To give him blessing.

VILLAC UMU: Why will you bless him?

PIZARRO: He is a God. I am a God.

VALVERDE: [*Sotto voce*] General!

PIZARRO: Be still.

VILLAC UMU: Below you is the town of Cajamarca. The great Inca orders: rest there. Tomorrow early he will come to you. Do not move from the town. Outside it is his anger.

[*He goes off with his attendants*]

VALVERDE: What have you done, sir?

PIZARRO: Sent him news to amaze him.

VALVERDE: I cannot approve blasphemy.

PIZARRO: To conquer for Christ, one can surely usurp his name for a night, Father. Set on.

IX

A dreary light.

The Spaniards fan out over the stage. DE SOTO *goes off.*

OLD MARTIN: So down we went from ledge to ledge, and out on to a huge plain of eucalyptus trees, all glowing in the failing light. And there, at the other end, lay a vast white town with roofs of straw. As night fell, we entered it. We came into an empty square, larger than any in Spain. All round it ran long white buildings, three times the height of a man. Everywhere was grave quiet. You could almost touch the silence. Up on the hill we could see the Inca's tents, and the lights from his fires ringing the valley. [*Exit*]

[*Some sit. All look up at the hillside*]

DIEGO: How many do you reckon there's up there?

DE CANDIA: Ten thousand.

DE SOTO: [*Re-entering*] The town's empty. Not even a dog.

DOMINGO: It's a trap. I know it's a trap.

PIZARRO: Felipillo! Where's that little rat? Felipillo!

FELIPILLO: General, Lord.

PIZARRO: What does this mean?

FELIPILLO: I don't know. Perhaps it is order of welcome. Great people. Much honour.

VALVERDE: Nonsense, it's a trick, a brownie trick. He's got us all marked for death.

DE NIZZA: He could have killed us at any time. Why should he take such trouble with us?

PIZARRO: Because we're Gods, Father. He'll change soon enough when he finds out different.

DE SOTO: Brace up, boy! It's what you came for, isn't it? Death and glory?

YOUNG MARTIN: Yes, sir.

PIZARRO: De Soto. De Candia. [*They go to him*] It's got to be ambush. That's our only hope.

DE SOTO: Round the square?

PIZARRO: Lowers the odds. Three thousand at most.

DE CANDIA: Thirty to one. Not low enough.

PIZARRO: It'll have to do. We're not fighting ten thousand or three. One man: that's all. Get him, the rest collapse.

DE SOTO: Even if we can, they'll kill us all to get him back.

PIZARRO: If there's a knife at his throat? It's a risk, sure. But what do worshippers do when you snatch their God?

DE CANDIA: Pray to you instead.

DIEGO: It's wonderful. Grab the King, grab the Kingdom!

DE NIZZA: It would avoid bloodshed.

PIZARRO: What do you say?

DE CANDIA: It's the only way. It could work.

DE SOTO: With God's help.

PIZARRO: Then pray all. Disperse. Light fires. Make confession. Battle orders at first light.

[*Most disperse. Some lie down to pray and sleep*]

DE NIZZA: [*To* DE CANDIA] Shall I hear your confession now, my son?

DE CANDIA: You'd best save all that for tomorrow, Father. For the men who are left. What have we got to confess tonight but thoughts of murder?

DE NIZZA: Then confess those.

DE CANDIA: Why? Should I feel shame for them? What would I say to God if I refused to destroy His enemies?

VALVERDE: More Venetian nonsense!

DE NIZZA: God has no enemies, my son. Only those nearer to Him or farther from Him.

DE CANDIA: Well, my job is to aim at the far ones. I'll go and position the guns. Excuse me.

[*He goes off*]

PIZARRO: Diego, look to the horses. I know they're sorry, but we'll need them brisk.

VALVERDE: Come my brother, we'll pray together.

[*They go too*]

PIZARRO: The cavalry will split and hide in the buildings, there and there.

DE SOTO: And the infantry in file—there, and round there.

PIZARRO: Perfect. Herrada can command one flank, de Barbaran the other. Everyone hidden.

DE SOTO: They'll suspect then.

PIZARRO: No, the Church will greet them.

DE SOTO: We'll need a watchword.

PIZARRO: San Jago.

DE SOTO: San Jago. Good.

[*The old man comes upon his page, who is sitting huddled by himself*]

PIZARRO: Are you scared?

YOUNG MARTIN: No, sir. Yes, sir.

PIZARRO: You're a good boy. If ever we get out of this, I'll make you a gift of whatever you ask me. Is that chivalrous enough for you?

YOUNG MARTIN: Being your page is enough, sir.

PIZARRO: And there's nothing else you want?

YOUNG MARTIN: A sword, sir.

PIZARRO: Of course . . . Take what rest you can. Call Assembly at first light.

YOUNG MARTIN: Yes, sir. Goodnight, sir.

DE SOTO: Goodnight, Martin. Try and sleep.

[*The boy lies down to sleep. The singing of prayers is heard, off, all around*]

PIZARRO: Hope, lovely hope. A sword's no mere bar of metal for him. His world still has sacred objects. How remote . . .

DIEGO: Holy Virgin, give us victory. If you do, I'll make you a present of a fine Indian cloak. But you let us down, and I'll leave you for the Virgin of the Conception, and I mean that.

[*He lies down also. The prayers die away. Silence*]

X

Semi-darkness.

PIZARRO: This is probably our last night. If we die, what will we have gone for?

DE SOTO: Spain. Christ.

PIZARRO: I envy you, Cavalier.

DE SOTO: For what?

PIZARRO: Your service. God. King. It's all simple for you.

DE SOTO: No, sir, it's not simple. But it's what I've chosen.

PIZARRO: Yes. And what have I chosen?

DE SOTO: To be a King yourself. Or as good, if we win here.

PIZARRO: And what's that at my age? Not only swords turn into
bars of metal. Sceptres too. What's left, De Soto?

DE SOTO: What you told me in Spain. A name for ballads. The
man of Honour has three good lives: The Life Today. The Life
to Come. The Life of Fame.

PIZARRO: Fame is long. Death is longer . . . Does anyone ever
die for anything? I thought so once. Life was fierce with
feeling. It was all hope, like on that boy. Swords shone and
armour sang, and cheese bit you, and kissing burned and
Death—ah, death was going to make an exception in my case.
I couldn't believe I was ever going to die. But once you know
it—really know it—it's all over. You know you've been cheated,
and nothing's the same again.

DE SOTO: Cheated?

PIZARRO: Time cheats us all the way. Children, yes—having children goes some steps to defeating it. Nothing else. It would
have been good to have a son.

DE SOTO: Did you never think to marry?

PIZARRO: With my parentage? The only women who would have
had me weren't the sort you married. Spain's a pile of horsedung
. . . When I began to think of a world here, something in me
was longing for a new place like a country after rain, washed
clear of all the badges and barriers, the pebbles men drop to
tell them where they are on a plain that's got no landmarks. I
used to look after women with hope, but they didn't have much
time for me. One of them said—what was it?—my soul was
frostbitten. That's a word for you—Frostbitten. How goes it,
man?

VASCA: [Off] A clear night, sir. Everything clear.

PIZARRO: I had a girl once, on a rock by the Southern Ocean. I
lay with her one afternoon in winter, wrapped up in her against
the cold, and the sea-fowl screaming, and it was the best hour

of my life. I felt then that sea-water, and bird-droppings and the little pits in human flesh were all linked together for some great end right out of the net of words to catch. Not just my words, but anyone's. Then I lost it. Time came back. For always.

[*He moves away, feeling his side*]

DE SOTO: Does it pain you?

PIZARRO: Oh, yes: *that's* still fierce.

DE SOTO: You should try to sleep. We'll need our strength.

PIZARRO: Listen, listen! Everything we feel is made of Time. All the beauties of life are shaped by it. Imagine a fixed sunset: the last note of a song that hung an hour, or a kiss for half of it. Try and halt a moment in our lives and it becomes maggoty at once. Even that word 'moment' is wrong, since that would mean a speck of time, something you could pick up on a rag and peer at . . . But that's the awful trap of life. You can't escape maggots unless you go with Time, and if you go, they wriggle in you anyway.

DE SOTO: This is gloomy talk.

[YOUNG MARTIN *groans in his sleep*]

PIZARRO: For a gloomy time. You were talking women. I loved them with all the juice in me—but oh, the cheat in that tenderness. What is it but a lust to own their beauty, not them, which you never can: like trying to own the beauty of a goblet by paying for it. And even if you could it would become you and get soiled . . . I'm an old man, Cavalier, I can explain nothing. What I mean is: Time whipped up the lust in me and Time purged it. I was dandled on Time's knee and made to gurgle, then put to my sleep. I've been cheated from the moment I was born because there's death in everything.

DE SOTO: Except in God.

[*A pause*]

PIZARRO: When I was young, I used to sit on the slope outside the village and watch the sun go down, and I used to think: if only I could find the place where it sinks to rest for the night, I'd find the source of life, like the beginning of a river. I used to wonder what it could be like. Perhaps an island, a strange place of white sand, where the people never died. Never grew old, or felt pain, and never died.

DE SOTO: Sweet fancy.

PIZARRO: It's what your mind runs to if it lacks instruction. If I had a son, I'd kill him if he didn't read his book. . . . Where does the sun rest at night?

DE SOTO: Nowhere. It's a heavenly body set by God to move round the earth in perpetual motion.

PIZARRO: Do you know this?

DE SOTO: All Europe knows it.

PIZARRO: What if they were wrong? If it settled here each evening, somewhere in those great mountains, like a God laid down to sleep? To a savage mind it must make a fine God. I myself can't fix anything nearer to a thought of worship than standing at dawn and watching it fill the world. Like the coming of something eternal, against going flesh. What a fantastic wonder that anyone on earth should dare to say: 'That's my father. My father: the sun!' It's silly—but tremendous . . . You know —strange nonsense; since first I heard of him I've dreamed of him every night. A black king with glowing eyes, sporting the sun for a crown. What does it mean?

DE SOTO: I've no skill with dreams. Perhaps a soothsayer would tell you: 'The Inca's your enemy. You dream his emblem to increase your hate.'

PIZARRO: But I feel no enemy.

DE SOTO: Surely you do.

PIZARRO: No. Only that of all meetings I have made in my life, this with him is the one I have to make. Maybe it's my death. Or maybe new life. I feel just this: all my days have been a path to this one morning.

OLD MARTIN: The sixteenth of November, 1532. First light, sir.

XI

Lights brighten slowly.

VALVERDE: [*Singing, off*] Exsurge Domine.

SOLDIERS: [*Singing in unison*] Exsurge Domine.

[*All the company comes on, chanting*]

VALVERDE: Deus meus eripe me de manu peccatoris.

SOLDIERS: Deus meus eripe me de manu peccatoris.

[*All kneel, spread across the stage*]

VALVERDE: Many strong bulls have compassed me.

DE NIZZA: They have gaped upon me with their mouths, as a lion ravening.

VALVERDE: I am poured out like water, and all my bones are scattered.

DE NIZZA: My heart is like wax, melting in the midst of my bowels. My tongue cleaves to my jaws, and thou hast brought me into the dust of death.

[*All freeze*]

OLD MARTIN: The dust of death. It was in our noses. The full scare came to us quickly, like plague.

[*All heads turn*]

The men were crammed in buildings all round the square.

[*All stand*]

They stood there shivering, making water where they stood. An hour went by. Two. Three.

[*All remain absolutely still*]

Five. Not a move from the Indian camp. Not a sound from us. Only the weight of the day. A hundred and sixty men in full armour, cavalry mounted, infantry at the ready, standing in dead silence—glued in a trance of waiting.

PIZARRO: Hold fast now. Come on—you're Gods. Take heart. Don't blink your eyes, that's too much noise.

OLD MARTIN: Seven.

PIZARRO: Stiff. Stiff. You're your own masters, boys. Not peasants anymore. This is your time. Own it. Live it.

OLD MARTIN: Nine. Ten hours passed. There were few of us then who didn't feel the cold begin to crawl.

PIZARRO: [Whispering] Send him, send him, send him, send him.

OLD MARTIN: Dread comes with the evening air. Even the priest's arm fails.

PIZARRO: The sun's going out!

OLD MARTIN: No one looks at his neighbour. Then, with the shadow of night already running towards us—

YOUNG MARTIN: They're coming! Look, down the hill—

DE SOTO: How many?

YOUNG MARTIN: Hundreds, sir.

DE CANDIA: Thousands—two or three.

PIZARRO: Can you see him?

DE CANDIA: No, not yet.

DOMINGO: What's that?—out there in front—they're doing something.

VASCA: Looks like sweeping—

DIEGO: They're sweeping the road.

DOMINGO: For him! They're sweeping the road for him! Five hundred of 'em sweeping the road!

SALINAS: God in Heaven!

PIZARRO: Are they armed?

DE CANDIA: To the teeth!

DE SOTO: How?—

DE CANDIA: Axes and spears.

YOUNG MARTIN: They're all glittering, glittering red!—

DIEGO: It's the sun! Like someone's stabbed it!—

VASCA: Squirting blood all over the sky!

DOMINGO: It's an omen!—

SALINAS: Shut up.

DOMINGO: It must be. The whole country's bleeding. Look for yourself. It's an omen!

VALVERDE: This is the day foretold you by the Angel of the Apocalypse. Satan reigns on the altars, jeering at the true God. The earth teems with corrupt kings.

DOMINGO: Oh God! Oh God! Oh God! Oh God!

DE SOTO: Control yourself.

DE CANDIA: They're stopping!

YOUNG MARTIN: They're throwing things down, sir!

PIZARRO: What things?

DE CANDIA: Weapons.

PIZARRO: No!

DIEGO: Yes, sir. I can see. All their weapons. They're throwing them down in a pile.

VASCA: They're laying down their arms.

SALINAS: I don't believe it!

VASCA: They are. They are leaving everything!

DOMINGO: It's a miracle.

DE SOTO: Why? *Why?*

PIZARRO: Because we're Gods. You see? You don't approach Gods with weapons.

[*Strange music faintly in the distance. Through all the ensuing it grows louder and louder*]

DE SOTO: What's that?

YOUNG MARTIN: It's *him*. He's coming, sir.

PIZARRO: Where?

YOUNG MARTIN: *There*, sir.

DIEGO: Oh, look, *look*. God Almighty, it's not happening! . . .

DE SOTO: Steady, man.

PIZARRO: You're coming. Come on then! *Come on!*

DE SOTO: General, it's time to hide.

PIZARRO: Yes, quick now. No one must be seen but the priests.
Out there in the middle, Fathers: everyone else in hiding.

DE SOTO: Quick! jump to it!

[*Only now do the men break, scatter and vanish*]

PIZARRO: [*To* YOUNG MARTIN] You too.

YOUNG MARTIN: Until the fighting, sir?

PIZARRO: All the time for you, fighting or no.

YOUNG MARTIN: Oh no, sir!

PIZARRO: Do as I say. Take him, de Soto.

DE SOTO: Save you, General.

PIZARRO: And you, de Soto. San Jago!

DE SOTO: San Jago! Come on.

DE CANDIA: There are seven gunners on the roof. And three over
there.

PIZARRO: Watch the cross-fire.

DE CANDIA: I'll wait for your signal.

PIZARRO: Then sound yours.

DE CANDIA: You'll hear it.

PIZARRO: [*To* FELIPILLO] Felipillo! Stand there! Now . . . now
. . . NOW!

[*He hurries off*]

XII

*The music crashes over the stage as the Indian procession
enters in an astonishing explosion of colour. The King's*

attendants—many of them playing musical instruments: reed pipes, cymbals, and giant marraccas—are as gay as parrots. They wear costumes of orange and yellow, and fantastic headdresses of gold and feathers, with eyes embossed on them in staring black enamel. By contrast, ATAHUALLPA INCA *presents a picture of utter simplicity. He is dressed from head to foot in white: across his eyes is a mask of jade mosaic, and round his head a circlet of plain gold. Silence falls. The King glares about him.*

ATAHUALLPA: [*Haughtily*] Where is the God?

VALVERDE: [*Through* FELIPILLO] I am a Priest of God.

ATAHUALLPA: I do not want the priest. I want the God. Where is he? He sent me greeting.

VALVERDE: That was our General. Our God cannot be seen.

ATAHUALLPA: I may see him.

VALVERDE: No. He was killed by men and went into the sky.

ATAHUALLPA: A God cannot be killed. See my father. You cannot kill him. He lives for ever and looks over his children every day.

VALVERDE: I am the answer to all mysteries. Hark, pagan, and I will expound.

OLD MARTIN: And so he did, from the Creation to Our Lord's ascension.

[*He goes off*]

VALVERDE: [*Walking among the Indians to the right*] And when he went he left the Pope as Regent for him.

DE NIZZA: [*Walking among the Indians to the left*] And when he went he left the Pope as Regent for him.

VALVERDE: He has commanded our King to bring all men to belief in the true God.

DE NIZZA: He has commanded our King to bring all men to belief in the true God.

VALVERDE: } [Together] In Christ's name therefore I
DE NIZZA: } charge you: yield yourself his
willing vassal.

ATAHUALLPA: I am the vassal of no man. I am the greatest
Prince on earth. Your King is great. He has sent you far across
the water. So he is my brother. But your Pope is mad. He
gives away countries that are not his. His faith also is mad.

VALVERDE: Beware!

ATAHUALLPA: Ware you! You kill my people; you make them
slaves. By what power?

VALVERDE: By this. [He offers a Bible] The Word of God.

[ATAHUALLPA holds it to his ear. He listens intently. He
shakes it]

ATAHUALLPA: No word.

[He smells the book, and then licks it. Finally he throws
it down impatiently]

God is angry with your insults.

VALDERDE: Blasphemy!

ATAHUALLPA: God is angry.

VALVERDE: Francisco Pizarro, do you stay your hand when Christ
is insulted? Let this pagan feel the power of your arm. I absolve you all! San Jago!

[PIZARRO appears above with drawn sword, and in a great
voice sings out his battle-cry:]

PIZARRO: SAN JAGO Y CIERRA ESPAÑA!

[Instantly from all sides the soldiers rush in, echoing the
great cry]

SOLDIERS: SAN JAGO!

[There is a tense pause. The Indians look at this ring of

armed men in terror. A violent drumming begins, and there ensues]

THE MIME OF THE GREAT MASSACRE

[*To a savage music, wave upon wave of Indians are slaughtered and rise again to protect their lord who stands bewildered in their midst. It is all in vain. Relentlessly the Spanish soldiers hew their way through the ranks of feathered attendants towards their quarry. They surround him.* SALINAS *snatches the crown off his head and tosses it up to* PIZARRO, *who catches it and to a great shout crowns himself. All the Indians cry out in horror. The drum hammers on relentlessly while* ATAHUALLPA *is led off at swordpoint by the whole band of Spaniards. At the same time, dragged from the middle of the sun by howling Indians, a vast bloodstained cloth bellies out over the stage. All rush off; their screams fill the theatre. The lights fade out slowly on the rippling cloth of blood*]

ACT II—THE KILL

I

Darkness. A bitter Inca lament is intoned, above.
Lights up a little. The bloodstained cloth still lies over the
stage. In the sun chamber ATAHUALLPA *stands in chains,*
his back to the audience, his white robe dirty with blood.
Although he is unmasked, we cannot yet see his face, only
a tail of black hair hanging down his neck.
OLD MARTIN *appears. From opposite,* YOUNG MARTIN *comes*
in, stumbling with shock. He collapses on his knees.

OLD MARTIN: Look at the warrior where he struts. Glory on his
sword. Salvation in his new spurs. One of the knights at last.
The very perfect knight Sir Martin, tender in virtue, bodyguard
of Christ. Jesus, we are all eased out of kids' dreams; but who
can be ripped out of them and live loving after? Three thousands Indians we killed in that square. The only Spaniard to
be wounded was the General, scratched by a sword whilst protecting his Royal prisoner. That night, as I knelt vomiting into
a canal, the empire of the Incas stopped. The spring of the
clock was snapped. For a thousand miles men sat down not
knowing what to do.

   [*Enter* DE SOTO]

DE SOTO: Well, boy, what is it? They weren't armed, is that it?
If they had been we could be dead now.

YOUNG MARTIN: Honourably dead! Not alive and shamed.

DE SOTO: And Christ would be dead here too, scarcely born. When I first breathed blood it was in my lungs for days. But the time comes when you won't even sniff when it pours over your feet. See, boy, here and now it's kill or get killed. And if we go, we betray Christ, whose coming we are here to make.

YOUNG MARTIN: You talk as if we're butlers, sent to open the door for him.

DE SOTO: So we are.

YOUNG MARTIN: No! He's with us now—at all times—or never.

DE SOTO: He's with us, yes, but not with them. After he is, there will be time for mercy.

YOUNG MARTIN: When there is no danger! Some mercy!

DE SOTO: Would you put Christ in danger, then?

YOUNG MARTIN: He can look after himself.

DE SOTO: He can't. That's why he needs servants.

YOUNG MARTIN: To kill for him?

DE SOTO: If necessary. And it was. My parish priest used to say: There must always be dying to make new life. I think of that whenever I draw the sword. My constant thought is: I must be winter for Our Lord to be Spring.

YOUNG MARTIN: I don't understand.

[PIZARRO *and* FELIPILLO *come in*]

PIZARRO: Stand up when the Second addresses you. What are you, a defiled girl? [*To* DE SOTO] I've sent de Candia back to the Garrison. Reinforcements should be there presently. Come now: let's meet this King.

II

Lights up more.
They move upstage and bow. Above, OELLO *and* INTI COUSSI *come in and kneel on either side of the Inca, who ignores the embassy below.*

My lord, I am Francisco Pizarro, General of Spain. It is an honour to speak with you. [*Pause*] You are very tall, my lord. In my country are no such tall men. [*Pause*] My lord, won't you speak?

[ATAHUALLPA *turns. For the first time we see his face, carved in a mould of serene arrogance. His whole bearing displays the most entire dignity and natural grace. When he moves or speaks, it is always with the consciousness of his divine origin, his sacred function and his absolute power*]

ATAHUALLPA: [*To* FELIPILLO] Tell him I am Atahuallpa Capac, Son of the Sun, Son of the Moon, Lord of the Four Quarters. Why does he not kneel?

FELIPILLO: The Inca says he wishes he had killed you when you first came.

PIZARRO: Why didn't he?

ATAHUALLPA: He lied to me. He is not a God. I came for blessing. He sharpened his knives on the shoulders of my servants. I have no word for *him* whose word is evil.

FELIPILLO: He says he wants to make slaves of your best warriors, then kill all the others. Especially you he would kill because you are old; no use as slave.

PIZARRO: Tell him he will live to rue those intentions.

FELIPILLO: You make my master angry. He will kill you tomorrow. Then he will give that wife [*He indicates* OELLO] to me for my pleasure.

[OELLO *rises in alarm*]

ATAHUALLPA: How dare you speak this before my face?

YOUNG MARTIN: General.

PIZARRO: What?

YOUNG MARTIN: Excuse me, sir, but I don't think you're being translated aright.

PIZARRO: You don't?

YOUNG MARTIN: No, sir. Nor the King to you. I know a little of the language and he said nothing about slaves.

PIZARRO: You! What are you saying?

FELIPILLO: General Lord. This boy know nothing how to speak.

YOUNG MARTIN: I know more than you think. I know you're lying . . . He's after the woman, General. I saw him before, in the square, grabbing at her.

PIZARRO: Is that true?

YOUNG MARTIN: As I live, sir.

PIZARRO: What do you say?

FELIPILLO: General Lord, I speak wonderful for you. No one speak so wonderful.

PIZARRO: What about that girl?

FELIPILLO: You give her as present to me, yes?

PIZARRO: The Inca's wife?

FELIPILLO: Inca has many wives. This one small, not famous.

PIZARRO: Get out.

FELIPILLO: General Lord!

PIZARRO: You work another trick like this and I swear I'll hang you. Out!

[FELIPILLO *spits at him and runs off*]

PIZARRO: Could you take his place?

YOUNG MARTIN: With work, sir.

PIZARRO: Work, then. Come, let's make a start. Ask him his age.

YOUNG MARTIN: My lord, [*Hesitantly*] how old are him? I mean 'you' . . .

ATAHUALLPA: I have been on earth thirty and three years. What age is your master?

YOUNG MARTIN: Sixty-three.

ATAHUALLPA: All those years have taught him nothing but wickedness.

YOUNG MARTIN: That's not true.

PIZARRO: What does he say?

YOUNG MARTIN: I don't quite understand, my lord . . .

[*Exit* YOUNG MARTIN]

OLD MARTIN: So it was I became the General's interpreter and was privy to everything that passed between them during the next months. The Inca tongue was very hard, but to please my adored master I worked at it for hours, and with each passing day found out more of it.

[PIZARRO *leaves, followed by* DE SOTO]

III

Re-enter YOUNG MARTIN *above.* OLD MARTIN *watches below before going off.*

YOUNG MARTIN: Good day, my lord. I have a game here to amuse you. No Spaniard is complete without them. I take half and you take half. Then we fight. These are the Churchmen with their pyxes. The Nobility with their swords. The Merchants with their gold, and the Poor with their sticks.

ATAHUALLPA: What are the poor?

YOUNG MARTIN: Those who've got no gold. They suffer for this.

ATAHUALLPA: [*Crying out*] Aiyah.

YOUNG MARTIN: What are you thinking, my lord?

ATAHUALLPA: That my people will suffer.

[Enter PIZARRO *and* DE SOTO]

PIZARRO: Good day, my lord. How are you this morning?

ATAHUALLPA: You want gold. That is why you came here.

PIZARRO: My lord—

ATAHUALLPA: You can't hide from me. [*Showing him the card of the Poor*] You want gold. I know. Speak.

PIZARRO: You have gold?

ATAHUALLPA: It is the sweat of the sun. It belongs to me.

PIZARRO: Is there much?

ATAHUALLPA: Make me free. I would fill this room.

PIZARRO: Fill?

DE SOTO: It's not possible.

ATAHUALLPA: I am Atahuallpa and I say it.

PIZARRO: How long?

ATAHUALLPA: Two showings of my Mother Moon. But it will not be done.

PIZARRO: Why not?

ATAHUALLPA: You must swear to free me and you have no swear to give.

PIZARRO: You wrong me, my lord.

ATAHUALLPA: No, it is in your face, no swear.

PIZARRO: I never broke word with you. I never promised you safety. If once I did, you would have it.

ATAHUALLPA: Do you now?

DE SOTO: Refuse, sir. You could never free him.

PIZARRO: It won't come to that.

DE SOTO: It could.

PIZARRO: Never. Can you think how much gold it would take? Even half would drown us in riches.

DE SOTO: General, you can only give your word where you can keep it.

PIZARRO: I'll never have to break it. It's the same case.

DE SOTO: It's not.

PIZARRO: Oh, God's wounds, your niceties! He's offering more than any conqueror has ever seen. Alexander, Tamberlaine, or who you please. I mean to have it.

DE SOTO: So. At your age gold is no lodestone!

PIZARRO: No more is it. I promised my men gold. Yes? He stands between them and that gold. If I don't make this bargain now he'll die; the men will demand it.

DE SOTO: And what's that to you if he does?

PIZARRO: I want him alive. At least for a while.

DE SOTO: You're thinking of how you dreamed of him.

PIZARRO: Yes. He has some meaning for me, this Man-God. An immortal man in whom all his people live completely. He has an answer for time.

DE SOTO: If it was true.

PIZARRO: Yes, if . . .

DE SOTO: General, be careful. I don't understand you in full but I know this: what you do now can never be undone.

PIZARRO: Words, my dear Cavalier. They don't touch me. This way I'll have gold for my men and him there safe. That's enough for the moment. [To ATAHUALLPA] Now you must keep the peace meanwhile, not strive to escape, nor urge your men to help you. So swear.

ATAHUALLPA: I swear!

PIZARRO: Then I swear too. Fill that room with gold and I will set you free.

DE SOTO: General!

PIZARRO: Oh, come man! He never will.

DE SOTO: I think this man performs what he swears. Pray God we don't pay bitterly for this.

[*He goes off. Enter* OLD MARTIN]

PIZARRO: My lord—[ATAHUALLPA *ignores him*]—well spoken, lad. Your services increase every day.

YOUNG MARTIN: Thank you, sir.

[*The General leaves the stage and the boy goes out of the Sun chamber, leaving* ATAHUALLPA *alone in it*]

OLD MARTIN: The room was twenty-two feet long by seventeen feet wide. The mark on the wall was nine feet high.

[*The Inca adopts a pose of command. Drums mark each name*]

ATAHUALLPA: Atahuallpa speaks! [*A crash of instruments*] Atahuallpa needs. [*Crash*] Atahuallpa commands. [*Crash*] Bring him gold. From the palaces. From the temples. From all buildings in the great places. From walls of pleasure and roofs of omen. From floors of feasting and ceilings of death. Bring him the gold of Quito and Pachamacac! Bring him the gold of Cuzco and Coricancha! Bring him the gold of Vilcanota! Bring him the gold of Colae! Of Aymaraes and Arequipa! Bring him the gold of the Chimu! Put up a mountain of gold and free your Sun from his prison of clouds.

[*Lights down above.* ATAHUALLPA *leaves the chamber*]

OLD MARTIN: It was agreed that the gold collected was not to be melted beforehand into bars, so that the Inca got the benefit of the space between them. Then he was moved out of his prison to make way for the treasure and given more comfortable state.

IV

Lights fade above, and brighten below.
Slowly the great cloth of blood is dragged off by two Indians as ATAHUALLPA *appears. He advances to the middle of the stage. He claps his hands, once. Immediately a gentle hum is heard and Indians appear with new clothing. From their wrists hang tiny golden cymbals and small bells; to the soft clash and tinkle of these little instruments his servants remove the Inca's bloodstained garments and put on him clean ones.*

OLD MARTIN: He was allowed to audience his nobles. The little loads they bore were a sign of reverence.

[VILLAC UMU *and* CHALLCUCHIMA *come in*]

He was dressed in his royal cloak, made from the skins of vampire birds, and his ears were hung again with the weight of noble responsibility.

[ATAHUALLPA *is cloaked, a collar of turquoises is placed round his neck and heavy gold rings are placed in his ears.*

*While this is happening there is a fresh tinkling and more
Indians appear, carrying his meal in musical dishes—plates
like tambourines from whose rims hang bells, or in whose
lower shelves are tiny golden balls. The stage is filled with
chimes and delicate clatter, and above it the perpetual humming of masked servants]*

OLD MARTIN: His meals were served as they always had been. I
remember his favourite food was stewed lamb, garnished with
sweet potatoes.

[*The food is served to the Inca in this manner.* OELLO *takes
meat out of a bowl, places it in her hands and* ATAHUALLPA
*lowers his face to it, while she turns her own face away
from him out of respect*]

OLD MARTIN: What he didn't eat was burnt, and if he spilled
any on himself, his clothes were burnt also. [*Exit*]

[OELLO *rises and quietly removes the dish. Suddenly* FELI-
PILLO *rushes on and knocks it violently from her hand*]

FELIPILLO: You're going to burn it? Why? Because your husband
is a God? How stupid! stupid! stupid!

[*He grabs her and flings her to the ground. A general
cry of horror*]

[*To* ATAHUALLPA] Yes, I touch her! Make me dead! You are
a God. Make me dead with your eyes!

VILLAC UMU: What you have said kills you. You will be buried
in the earth alive.

[*A pause. For a moment* FELIPILLO *half believes this.
Then he laughs and kisses the girl on the throat. As she
screams and struggles,* YOUNG MARTIN *rushes in*]

YOUNG MARTIN: Felipillo, stop it!

[VALVERDE *comes in from another side, with* DE NIZZA]

VALVERDE: Felipillo! Is it for this we saved you from Hell? Your old God encouraged lust. Your new God will damn you for it. Leave him!

[FELIPILLO *runs off*]

[*To the* INDIANS] Go!

[*A pause. No one moves until* ATAHUALLPA *claps his hands twice. Then all the servants bow and leave*]

Now, my lord, let us take up our talk again. Tell me—I am only a simple priest—as an undoubted God, do you live forever here on earth?

VILLAC UMU: Here on earth Gods come one after another, young and young again, to protect the people of the Sun. Then they go up to his great place in the sky, at his will.

VALVERDE: What if they are killed in battle?

VILLAC UMU: If it is not the Sun's time for them to go, he will return them to life again in the next day's light.

VALVERDE: How comforting. And has any Inca so returned?

VILLAC UMU: No.

VALVERDE: Curious.

VILLAC UMU: This means only that all Incas have died in the Sun's time.

VALVERDE: Clever.

VILLAC UMU: No. True.

VALVERDE: Tell me this, how can the Sun have a child?

VILLAC UMU: How can your God have a Child, since you say he has no body?

VALVERDE: He is spirit—inside us.

VILLAC UMU: Your God is inside you? How can this be?

ATAHUALLPA: They eat him. First he becomes a biscuit, and then they eat him. [*The Inca bares his teeth and laughs soundlessly*] I have seen this. At praying they say 'This is the body of our God'. Then they drink his blood. It is very bad. Here in my empire we do not eat men. My family forbade it many years past.

VALVERDE: You are being deliberately stupid.

VILLAC UMU: Why do you eat your God? To have his strength?

DE NIZZA: Yes, my lord.

VILLAC UMU: But your God is weak. He fights with no man. That is why he was killed.

DE NIZZA: He wanted to be killed, so he could share death with us.

ATAHUALLPA: So he needed killers to help him, though you say killing is bad.

VALVERDE: This is the devil's tongue.

DE NIZZA: My lord must see that when God becomes man, he can no longer act perfectly.

ATAHUALLPA: Why?

DE NIZZA: He joins us in the prison of our sin.

ATAHUALLPA: What is sin?

DE NIZZA: Let me picture it to you as a prison cell, the bars made of our imperfections. Through them we glimpse a fair country where it is always morning. We wish we could walk there, or else forget the place entirely. But we cannot snap the bars, or if we do, others grow in their stead.

ATAHUALLPA: All your pictures are of prisons and chains.

DE NIZZA: All life is chains. We are chained to food, and fire in the winter. To innocence lost but its memory unlost. And to needing each other.

ATAHUALLPA: I need no one.

DE NIZZA: That is not true.

ATAHUALLPA: I am the Sun. I need only the sky.

DE NIZZA: That is not true, Atahuallpa. The sun is a ball of fire. Nothing more.

ATAHUALLPA: How?

DE NIZZA: Nothing more.

[*With terrible speed, the* INCA *rises to strike* DE NIZZA]

VALVERDE: Down! Do you dare lift your hand against a priest? Sit! Now!

[ATAHUALLPA *does not move*]

DE NIZZA: You do not feel your people, my lord, because you do not love them.

ATAHUALLPA: Explain love.

DE NIZZA: It is not known in your kingdom. At home we can say to our ladies: 'I love you', or to our native earth. It means we rejoice in their lives. But a man cannot say this to the woman he must marry at twenty-five; or to the strip of land allotted to him at birth which he must till until he dies. Love must be free, or else it alters away. Command it to your court: it will send a deputy. Let God order it to fill our hearts, it becomes useless to him. It is stronger than iron: yet in a fist of force it melts. It is a coin that sparkles in the hand: yet in the pocket it turns to rust. Love is the only door from the prison of ourselves. It is the eagerness of God to enter that prison, to take on pain, and imagine lust, so that the torn soldier, or the spent lecher, can call out in his defeat: 'You know this too, so help me from it.'

[A *further music of bells and humming. Enter* OLD MARTIN]

THE FIRST GOLD PROCESSION

[*Guarded closely by Spanish soldiers, a line of Indian porters comes in, each carrying a stylized gold object— utensils and ornaments. They cross the stage and disappear. Almost simultaneously, above, similar objects are hung up by Indians in the middle of the sun.*]

OLD MARTIN: [*During this*] The first gold arrived. Much of it was in big plates weighing up to seventy-five pounds, the rest in objects of amazing skill. Knives of ceremony; collars and fretted crowns; funeral gloves, and red-stained death masks, goggling at us with profound enamel eyes. Some days there were things worth thirty or forty gold pesos—but we weren't satisfied with that. [*Exit*]

[*Enter* PIZARRO *and* DE SOTO]

PIZARRO: I find you wanting in honesty. A month has passed: the room isn't a quarter full.

ATAHUALLPA: My kingdom is great; porters are slow. You will see more gold before long.

PIZARRO: The rumour is we'll see a rising before long.

ATAHUALLPA: Not a leaf stirs in my kingdom without my leave. If you do not trust me send to Cuzco, my capital. See how quiet my people sit.

PIZARRO: [*To* DE SOTO] Good. You leave immediately with a force of thirty.

CHALLCUCHIMA: God is tied by his word, like you. But if he raised one nail of one finger of one hand, you would all die that same raising.

PIZARRO: So be it. If you play us false, both these will die before us.

ATAHUALLPA: There are many Priests, many Generals. These can die.

VALVERDE: Mother of God! There's no conversion possible for this man.

DE SOTO: You cannot say that, sir.

VALVERDE: Satan has many forms and there sits one. As for his advisers, it is you, Priest, who stiffen him against me. You, General, who whisper revolt.

CHALLCUCHIMA: You lie.

VALVERDE: Leave him!

[*As before they do not move until* ATAHUALLPA *has clapped his hands twice. Then, immediately, the two Indians bow and leave*]

Pagan filth.

DE SOTO: I'll make inspection. Goodbye, my lord, we'll meet in a month.

[*Exit* DE SOTO]

VALVERDE: Beware Pizarro. Give him the slack, he will destroy us all.

[*He goes out another way*]

DE NIZZA: The Father has great zeal.

PIZARRO: Oh, yes, great zeal to see the devil in a poor dark man.

DE NIZZA: Not so poor, General. A man who is the soul of his kingdom. Look hard, you *will* find Satan here, because here is a country which denies the right to hunger.

PIZARRO: You call hunger a right?

DE NIZZA: Of course, it gives life meaning. Look around you: happiness has no feel for men here since they are forbidden unhappiness. They have everything in common so they have nothing to give each other. They are part of the seasons, no more; as indistinguishable as mules, as predictable as trees. All men are born unequal: this is a divine gift. And want is their birthright. Where you deny this and there is no hope of any new love; where tomorrow is abolished, and no man ever thinks 'I can change myself', there you have the rule of Anit-Christ. Atahuallpa, I will not rest until I have brought you to the true God.

ATAHUALLPA: No! He is not true! Where is he? There is my Father-Sun! You see now only by his wish; yet try to see into him and he will darken your eyes for ever. With hot burning he pulls up the corn and we feed. With cold burning he shrinks it and we starve. These are his burnings and our life. Do not speak to me again of your God: he is nowhere.

[PIZARRO *laughs. Hurriedly* DE NIZZA *leaves*]

V

PIZARRO: You said you'd hear the Holy Men.

ATAHUALLPA: They are fools.

PIZARRO: They are not fools.

ATAHUALLPA: Do you believe them?

PIZARRO: For certain.

ATAHUALLPA: Look into me.

PIZARRO: Your eyes are smoking wood.

ATAHUALLPA: You do not believe them.

PIZARRO: You dare not say that to me . . .

ATAHUALLPA: You do not believe them. Their God is not in your face.

[PIZARRO *retreats from* ATAHUALLPA, *who begins to sing in a strange voice*]

> You must not rob, O little finch.
> The harvest maize, O little finch.
> The trap is set, O little finch.
> To seize you quick, O little finch.
>
> Ask that black bird, O little finch.
> Nailed on a branch, O little finch.
> Where is her heart, O little finch.
> Where are her plumes, O little finch.
>
> She is cut up, O little finch.
> For stealing grain, O little finch.
> See, see the fate, O little finch.
> Of robber birds, O little finch.

This is a harvest song. For you.

PIZARRO: For me?

ATAHUALLPA: Yes.

PIZARRO: Robber birds.

ATAHUALLPA: Yes.

PIZARRO: You're a robber bird yourself.

ATAHUALLPA: Explain this.

PIZARRO: You killed your brother to get the throne.

ATAHUALLPA: He was a fool. His body was a man. His head was a child.

PIZARRO: But he was the rightful king.

ATAHUALLPA: I was the rightful God. My Sky Father shouted 'Rise up! In you lives your Earth Father, Huayana the Warrior. Your brother is fit only to tend herds but you were born to tend my people.' So I killed him, and the land smiled.

PIZARRO: That was my work long ago. Tending herds.

ATAHUALLPA: It was not your work. You are a warrior. It is in your face.

PIZARRO: You see much in my face.

ATAHUALLPA: I see my father.

PIZARRO: You do me honour, lad.

ATAHUALLPA: Speak true. If in your home your brother was King, but fit only for herds, would you take his crown?

PIZARRO: If I could.

ATAHUALLPA: And then you would kill him.

PIZARRO: No.

ATAHUALLPA: If you could not keep it for fear of his friends, unless he was dead, you would kill him.

PIZARRO: Let me give you another case. If I come to a country and seize the King's crown, but for fear of his friends cannot keep it unless I kill him, what do I do?

ATAHUALLPA: So.

PIZARRO: So.

[ATAHUALLPA *moves away, offended*]

Oh, it is only a game we play. Tell me—did you hate your brother?

ATAHUALLPA: No. He was ugly like a llama, like his mother. My mother was beautiful.

PIZARRO: I did not know my mother. She was not my father's wife. She left me at the church door for anyone to find. There's talk in the village, how I was suckled by a sow.

ATAHUALLPA: You are not then . . . ?

PIZARRO: Legitimate? No, my lord, no more than you.

ATAHUALLPA: So.

PIZARRO: So.

[A *pause*]

ATAHUALLPA: To be born so is a sign for a great man.

PIZARRO: [*Smiling*] I think so too.

[ATAHUALLPA *removes one of his golden earrings and hangs it on* PIZARRO'S *ear*]

And what is that?

ATAHUALLPA: The sign of a nobleman. Only the most important men may wear them. The most near to me.

YOUNG MARTIN: Very becoming, sir. Look.

[*He hands him a dagger. The General looks at himself in the blade*]

PIZARRO: I have never seemed so distinguished to myself. I thank you.

ATAHUALLPA: Now you must learn the dance of the aylu.

YOUNG MARTIN: The dance of a nobleman, sir.

ATAHUALLPA: Only he can do this. I will show you.

[PIZARRO *sits.* ATAHUALLPA *dances a ferocious mime of a warrior killing his foes. It is very difficult to execute, demanding great litheness and physical stamina. As suddenly as it began, it is over*]

ATAHUALLPA: You dance.

PIZARRO: I can't dance, lad.

ATAHUALLPA: [*Sternly*] You dance.

[*He sits to watch. Seeing there is no help for it,* PIZARRO *rises and clumsily tries to copy the dance. The effect is so grotesque that* YOUNG MARTIN *cannot help laughing. The General tries again, lunges, slips, slides, and finally starts to laugh himself. He gives up the attempt*]

PIZARRO: [*To* ATAHUALLPA] You make me laugh! [*In sudden wonder*] You make me laugh!

[ATAHUALLPA *consults his young interpreter, who tries to explain. The Inca nods gravely. Tentatively* PIZARRO *extends his hand to him.* ATAHUALLPA *takes it and rises. Quietly they go off together*]

VI

[*Enter* OLD MARTIN]

OLD MARTIN: Slowly the pile increased. The army waited nervously and licked its lips. Greed began to rise in us like a tide of sea.

[*A music of bells and humming*]

THE SECOND GOLD PROCESSION
and THE RAPE OF THE SUN

[*Another line of Indian porters comes in, bearing gold objects. Like the first, this instalment of treasure is guarded by Spanish soldiers, but they are less disciplined now. Two of them assault an Indian and grab his headdress. Another snatches a necklace at sword's point.*
Above, in the chamber, the treasure is piled up as before. DIEGO *and the* CHAVEZ *brothers are seen supervising. They begin to explore the sun itself, leaning out of the chamber and prodding at the petals with their halberds. Suddenly*

DIEGO *gives a cry of triumph, drives his halberd into a slot in one of the rays, and pulls out the gold inlay. The sun gives a deep groan, like the sound of a great animal being wounded. With greedy yelps, all the soldiers below rush at the sun and start pulling it to bits; they tear out the gold inlays and fling them on the ground, while terrible groans fill the air. In a moment only the great gold frame remains; a broken, blackened sun]*

[*Enter* DE SOTO]

DIEGO: Welcome back, sir.

DE SOTO: Diego, it's good to see you.

DIEGO: What's it like, sir? Is there trouble?

DE SOTO: It's grave quiet. Terrible. Men just standing in fields for hundreds of miles. Waiting for their God to come back to them.

DIEGO: Well, if he does they'll be fighters again and we're for the limepit.

DE SOTO: How's the General?

DIEGO: An altered man. No one's ever seen him so easy. He spends hours each day with the King. He's going to find it hard when he has to do it.

DE SOTO: Do what?

DIEGO: Kill him, sir.

DE SOTO: He can't do that. Not after a contract witnessed before a whole army.

DIEGO: Well, he can't let him go, that's for certain . . . Never mind, he'll find a way. He's as cunning as the devil's granddad, save your pardon, sir.

DE SOTO: No, you're right, boy.

DIEGO: Tell us about their capital, then. What's it like?

[*During the preceding, a line of Indians, bent double, has been loaded with the torn-off petals from the sun. Now, as* DE SOTO *describes Cuzco, they file slowly round the stage and go off, staggering under the weight of the great gold slabs. When he reaches the account of the garden, the*

*marvellous objects he tells of appear in the treasure cham-
ber above, borne by Indians, and are stacked up until they
fill it completely. The interior of the sun is now a solid
mass of gold]*

DE SOTO: Completely round. They call it the navel of the earth
and that's what it looks like. In the middle was a huge temple,
the centre of their faith. The walls were plated with gold,
enough to blind us. Inside, set out on tables, golden platters
for the sun to dine off. Outside, the garden: acres of gold
soil planted with gold maize. Entire apple trees in gold. Gold
birds on the branches. Gold geese and ducks. Gold butterflies
in the air on silver strings. And—imagine this—away in a field,
life-size, twenty golden llamas grazing with their kids. The
garden of the Sun at Cuzco. A wonder of the earth. Look at it
now.

DIEGO: [*Rushing in below*] Hey! The room's full!

DOMINGO: It isn't!

SALINAS: It is. Look!

JUAN: He's right. It's full!

DIEGO: We can start the share-out now. [*Cheers*]

PEDRO: What'll you do with your lot, Juan, boy?

JUAN: Buy a farm.

PEDRO: Me, too. I don't work for nobody ever again.

DOMINGO: Ah, you can buy a palace, easy, with a share of that.
Never mind a hissing farm! What d'you say, Diego?

DIEGO: Oh, I want a farm. A good stud farm, and a stable of
Araba just for me to ride! What will you have, Salinas?

SALINAS: Me? A bash-house! [*Laughter*] Right in the middle of
Trujillo, open six to six, filled with saddle-backed little fillies
from Andalusia . . .

[*Enter* VASCA *rolling a huge gold sun, like a hoop*]

VASCA: Look what I got, boys! The sun! He ain't public any
more, the old sun. He's private property!

DOMINGO: There's no private property, till share-out.

VASCA: Well, here's the exception. I risked my life to get this a hundred feet up.

JUAN: Dungballs!

VASCA: I did! Off the temple roof.

PEDRO: Come on, boy, get it up there with the rest.

VASCA: No. Finding's keepings. That's the law.

JUAN: What law?

VASCA: My law. Do you think you'll see any of this once the share-out starts? Not on your hissing life. You leave it up there, boy, you won't see nothing again.

PEDRO: [*To his brother*] He's right there.

JUAN: Do you think so?

VASCA: Of course. Officers first, then the Church. You'll get hissing nothing. [A *pause*]

SALINAS: So let's have a share-out now, then!

DOMINGO: Why not? We're all entitled.

VASCA: Of course we are.

JUAN: All right. I'm with you.

PEDRO: Good boy!

SALINAS: Come on, then.

[*They all make a rush for the Sun Chamber*]

DE SOTO: Where do you think you're going? . . . You know the General's orders. Nothing till share-out. Penalty for breach, death. Disperse now. I'll go and see the General.

[*They hesitate*]

[*Quietly*] Get to your posts.

[*Reluctantly, they disperse*]

And keep a sharp watch. The danger's not over yet.

DIEGO: I'd say it had only just begun, sir.

[*He goes.* DE SOTO *remains*]

VII

Enter PIZARRO *and* ATAHUALLPA *duelling furiously;* YOUNG MARTIN *behind. The Inca is a magnificent fighter and launches himself vigorously on the old man, finally knocking the sword from his hand.*

PIZARRO: Enough! You exhaust me . . .

ATAHUALLPA: I fight well—'ye-es'?

[*From the difficulty he has with this word, it is evident that it is in Spanish*]

PIZARRO: [*Imitating him*] 'Ye-es'! . . . Like a hidalgo!

YOUNG MARTIN: Magnificent, my lord.

PIZARRO: I'm proud of you.

ATAHUALLPA: Chica!

YOUNG MARTIN: Maize wine, sir.

PIZARRO: De Soto!—A drink, my dear second.

DE SOTO: With pleasure, General, the room is full.

PIZARRO: [*Casually*] I know it.

DE SOTO: My advice to you is to share out right away. The men are just on the turn.

PIZARRO: I think so too.

DE SOTO: We daren't delay.

PIZARRO: Agreed. Now I shall astound you, Cavalier. Atahuallpa, you have learnt how a Spaniard fights. Now you will learn his honour. Martin, your pen. [*Dictating*] 'Let this be known throughout my army. The Inca Atahuallpa has today discharged his obligation to General Pizarro. He is therefore a free man.'

DE SOTO: [*Toasting him*] My lord, your freedom!

[ATAHUALLPA *kneels. Silently he mouths words of gratitude to the sun*]

ATAHUALLPA: Atahuallpa thanks the lord de Soto, the lord
Pizarro, all lords of honour. You may touch my joy.

[*He extends his arms. Both Spaniards help to raise him*]

DE SOTO: What happens now?

PIZARRO: I release him. He must swear first, of course, not to
harm us.

DE SOTO: Do you think he will?

PIZARRO: For me he will.

ATAHUALLPA: [*To the boy*] What is that you have done?

YOUNG MARTIN: Writing, my lord.

ATAHUALLPA: Explain this.

YOUNG MARTIN: These are signs: This is 'Atahuallpa,' and this
is 'ransom.'

ATAHUALLPA: You put this sign, and he will see and know
'ransom'?

YOUNG MARTIN: Yes.

ATAHUALLPA: No.

YOUNG MARTIN: Yes, my lord. I'll do it again.

ATAHUALLPA: Here, on my nail. Do not say what you put.

[YOUNG MARTIN *writes on his nail*]

YOUNG MARTIN: Now show it to Cavalier de Soto.

[*He does so.* DE SOTO *reads and whispers the word to*
ATAHUALLPA]

ATAHUALLPA: [*To the boy*] What is put?

YOUNG MARTIN: God.

ATAHUALLPA: [*Amazed*] God! . . . [*He stares at his nail in
fascination then bursts into delighted laughter, like a child*]
Show me again! Another sign!

[*The boy writes on another nail*]

PIZARRO: Tell Salinas to take five hundred Indians and melt everything down.

DE SOTO: Everything?

PIZARRO: We can't transport it as it is.

DE SOTO: But there are objects of great beauty, sir. In all my service I've never seen treasure like this. Work subtler than anything in Italy.

PIZARRO: You're a tender man.

ATAHUALLPA: [*Extending his nail to* PIZARRO] What is put?

PIZARRO: [*Who of course cannot read*] Put?

ATAHUALLPA: Here.

PIZARRO: This is a foolish game.

YOUNG MARTIN: The General never learnt the skill, my lord. [*An embarrassed pause*] A soldier does not need it.

[ATAHUALLPA *stares at him*]

ATAHUALLPA: A King needs it. There is great power in these marks. You are the King in this room. You must teach us two. We will learn together—like brothers.

PIZARRO: You would stay with me here, to learn?

[*Pause*]

ATAHUALLPA: No. Tomorrow I will go.

PIZARRO: And then? What will you do then?

ATAHUALLPA: I will not hurt you.

PIZARRO: Or my army?

ATAHUALLPA: That I do not swear.

PIZARRO: You must.

ATAHUALLPA: You do not say this till now.

PIZARRO: Well, now I say it. Atahuallpa, you must swear to me that you will not hurt a man in my army if I let you go.

ATAHUALLPA: I will not swear this.

PIZARRO: For my sake.

ATAHUALLPA: Three thousand of my servants they killed in the square. Three thousand, without arms. I will avenge them.

PIZARRO: There is a way of mercy, Atahuallpa.

ATAHUALLPA: It is not my way. It is not your way.

PIZARRO: Well, show it to me, then.

ATAHUALLPA: Keep your swear first.

PIZARRO: That I cannot do.

ATAHUALLPA: Cannot?

PIZARRO: Not immediately . . . you must see: you are many, we are few.

ATAHUALLPA: This is not important.

PIZARRO: To me it is.

[ATAHUALLPA *hisses with fury. He strides across the room and before* PIZARRO'*s face makes a violent gesture with his hand between their two mouths*]

ATAHUALLPA: [*Violently*] You gave a word!

PIZARRO: And will keep it. Only not now. Not today.

ATAHUALLPA: When?

PIZARRO: Soon.

ATAHUALLPA: When?

PIZARRO: Very soon.

ATAHUALLPA: [*Falling on his knees and beating the ground*] When?

PIZARRO: As soon as you promise not to hurt my army.

ATAHUALLPA: [*With wild rage*] I will kill every man of them! I will make drums of their bodies! I will beat music on them at my great feasts!

PIZARRO: [*Provoked*] Boy—what have I put?

YOUNG MARTIN: 'He is therefore a free man.'

PIZARRO: Continue: 'But for the welfare of the country, he will remain for the moment as guest of the army.'

DE SOTO: What does that mean?

ATAHUALLPA: What does he say?

PIZARRO: Don't translate.

DE SOTO: So it's started. My warning was nothing to you.

PIZARRO: Well, gloat, gloat!

DE SOTO: I don't gloat.

ATAHUALLPA: What does he say?

PIZARRO: Nothing.

ATAHUALLPA: There is fear in his face!

PIZARRO: *Be quiet!* . . . [*To* DE SOTO] I want all the gold in blocks. Leave nothing unmelted. Attend to it yourself, personally!

[DE SOTO *goes abruptly.* OLD MARTIN *appears in the background.* PIZARRO *is trembling*]

[*To the page*] Well, what are you staring at, Little Lord Chivalry? Get out!

YOUNG MARTIN: He trusts you, sir.

PIZARRO: Trust: what's that? Another word. Honour . . . glory . . . trust: your word—Gods!

YOUNG MARTIN: You can see it, sir. He trusts you.

PIZARRO: I told you: out.

YOUNG MARTIN: [*Greatly daring*] You can't betray him, sir. You can't.

PIZARRO: Damn you—impertinence!

YOUNG MARTIN: I don't care, sir. You just can't! [*He stops*]

PIZARRO: In all your study of those admirable writers, you never learned the duty a page owes his master. I am sorry you have not better fulfilled your first office. There will be no other.

[*The boy makes to go out*]

A salute, if you please.

[*He bows*]

Time was when we couldn't stop you.

[YOUNG MARTIN *leaves.* PIZARRO *stares after him, shaking*]

OLD MARTIN: I went out into the night—the cold high night of the Andes, hung with stars like crystal apples—and dropped my first tears as a man. My first and last. That was my first and last worship too. Devotion never came again. [*Exit*]

> [*With a moan,* PIZARRO *collapses on the floor and lies writhing in pain.* ATAHUALLPA *contemplates his captor with surprised disdain. But slowly, as the old man's agony continues, contempt in the King is replaced by a gentler emotion. Curious, he kneels. Uncertain what to do, he extends his hands, first to the wound, and then to* PIZARRO's *head, which he holds with a kind of remote tenderness. The lights go down all around them*]

PIZARRO: Leave it now. There's no cure or more easing for it. Death's entered the house you see. It's half down already, like an old barn. What can you know about that? Youth's in you like a spring of blood, to spurt for ever. Your skin is singing: 'I will never get old.' But you will. Time is stalking you, as I did. That gold flesh will cold and blacken. Your eyes will curdle, those wet living eyes . . . They'll make a mummy of your body—I know the custom—and wrap you in robes of vicuna wool, and carry you through all your Empire down to Cuzco. And then they'll fold you in two and sit you on a chair in darkness . . . Atahuallpa, I'm going to die! And the thought of the dark has for years rotted everything for me, all simple joy in life. All through old age, which is so much longer and more terrible than anything in youth, I've watched the circles of nature with hatred. The leaves pop out, the leaves fall. Every year it's piglet time, calving time, time for children in a gush of blood and water. Women dote on this. A birth, any birth, fills them with love. They clap with love, and my soul shrugs. Round and round is all I see: an endless sky of birds, flying and ripping and nursing their young to fly and rip and nurse their young—*for what?* Listen, boy. That prison the Priest calls Sin Original, I know as

Time. And seen in time everything is trivial. Pain. Good. God
is trivial in that seeing. Trapped in this cage we cry out 'There's
a gaoler; there must be. At the last, last, last of lasts he will
let us out. He will! He will!' . . . But, oh my boy, no one will
come for all our crying. [*Pause*] I'm going to kill you, Atahuallpa. What does it matter? Words kept, words broken, it
all means nothing. Nothing. You go to sleep earlier than me,
that's all. Do you see? Look at your eyes, like coals from the
sun, glowing for ever in the deep of your skull. Like my dream
. . . Sing me your little song. [*Singing*] O little finch. . . .

[ATAHUALLPA *intones a few lines of the song*]

Nothing. Nothing . . . [*In sudden anguish, almost hatred*]
O, lad, what am I going to do with you?

VIII

A red light up above.

OLD MARTIN *appears above in the Sun Chamber. Violent
music, the sound of destruction. The light fades and comes
up on stage where the soldiers assemble.*

OLD MARTIN: Nine forges were kept alight for three weeks.
The masterwork of centuries was banged down into fat bars,
four hundred and forty pounds each day. The booty exceeded
all other known in history: the sack of Genoa, Milan or even
Rome. Share-out started at once. [*Exit*]

DIEGO: General Francisco Pizarro, 57,220 gold pesos. Hernando
de Soto, 17,740 gold pesos. The Holy church, 2,220 gold
pesos.

[*Enter* ESTETE *and* DE CANDIA]

ESTETE: And a fifth of everything, of course, to the Crown.
PIZARRO: You come in good time, Veedor.
ESTETE: So it seems! Cavalier.
DE SOTO: Veedor.

PIZARRO: Welcome, de Candia.

DE CANDIA: Thank you. [*Indicating the earring*] I see the living's become soft here already. The men hung with jewels like fops at Court.

PIZARRO: You set the fashion: I only follow.

DE CANDIA: I'm flattered.

PIZARRO: What news of the reinforcements?

DE CANDIA: None.

ESTETE: I sent runners back to the coast. They saw nothing.

PIZARRO: So we're cut off, here. How's my garrison?

DE CANDIA: Spanish justice reigns supreme. They hang Indians for everything. How's your royal friend? When do we hang him?

[*Pause.* PIZARRO *tears off his earring and flings it on the floor*]

PIZARRO: Finish the share-out.

[*Violently he leaves them. The men stare after him*]

DE SOTO: Go on, Diego. Tell us the rest . . . *Go on,* man!

DIEGO: The remainder—cavalry, infantry, clerks, farriers, coopers and the like—will divide a total of 971,000 gold pesos!

[*Cheers. Enter* RODAS]

SALINAS: Well, look. Our little tailor! How are you, friend?

RODAS: Hungry. What do I get?

SALINAS: A kick up the tunnel.

RODAS: Ha, ha. Day of a hundred jokes! I got a right to a share.

DOMINGO: What for?

RODAS: I stayed behind and guarded your hissing rear, that's what for.

DE SOTO: You've no right, Rodas. As far as you cared we could all rot, remember? Well, now you get nothing; the proper wage for cowardice.

[*General agreement. The men settle upstage to a game of dice*]

[*To* ESTETE] I must wait on the General.

ESTETE: I am sorry to see him still subject to distress. I had hoped that victory would have brought him calmer temper.

DE CANDIA: I must be his new wealth, Veedor. So much, so sudden, must be a great burden to him.

DE SOTO: the burdens of the General, sir, are care for his men, and for our present situation. Let us try to lighten them for him as we can.

[*He goes off*]

DE CANDIA: Let us indeed. One throat cut and we're all lightened.

ESTETE: It would much relieve the Crown if you'd cut it.

DE CANDIA: If I . . . ? You mean I'm not Spanish, I don't have to trouble with honour.

ESTETE: You're not a subject. It could be disowned by my King. And you have none.

DE CANDIA: So the Palace of Disinterest has a shithouse after all. Look, man, you're the overseer here, so do your job. Go to the General and tell him the brownie must go. And add this from me: if Spain waits any longer, Venice will act for herself.

[*They go off. Enter* OLD MARTIN]

IX

A scene of tension and growing violence. The soldiers, now dirty almost beyond recognition, but wearing ornaments, earrings and headdresses stolen from the treasure, dice for gold. They are watched silently from above by a line of masked Indians carrying instruments for making

bird noises. A drum begins to beat. PIZARRO *stumbles in,
and during the whole ensuing scene limps to and fro
across the stage like a caged animal, ignoring everything
but his own mental pain.*

OLD MARTIN: Morale began to go fast. Day after day we watched
his private struggle, and the brownies watched us, waiting one
sign from the frozen boy to get up and kill the lot of us.

DOMINGO: Play up, then!

PEDRO: Two fours.

[JUAN *throws successfully*]

JUAN: [*Grabbing a gold bar belonging to* PEDRO] That's mine
boy.

PEDRO: No—Juan!

JUAN: Give it. [*He snatches it*]

DOMINGO: They say there's an army gathering in the mountains.
At least five thousand of them.

VASCA: I heard that too.

DOMINGO: Blas says there's some of them cannibals.

[*Bird cries*]

SALINAS: That's just stories. Hissing stupid stories. You don't
want to listen to 'em.

RODAS: I'd like to see you when they tie you to the spit.

VASCA: [*Rolling the dice*] Turn up! Turn up! Turn up!

RODAS: Come on, boys, cut me in.

VASCA: Hiss off! No stake, no play.

RODAS: Bloody bastards!

DOMINGO: They say it's led by the Inca's top general. The
brownies are full of his name.

VASCA: What is it? Rumi . . . Rumi . . . ?

DOMINGO: That's it. Ruminagui, something like that.

[*The Indians above repeat the name in a low menacing chant:* RU-MIN-Ã-GUI! *The soldiers look fearfully about them. The bird cries sound again*]

SALINAS: Come on, then, let's play.

VASCA: What for? The sun!

SALINAS: The sun!

VASCA: Turn up! Turn up! Turn up! Turn up! King and ten. Beat that!

SALINAS: Holy Mary, mother of Christ. Save my soul and bless my dice. [*He throws*] Two Kings . . . I did it! I'm sorry, lads, but that's your sun gone.

VASCA: Go on, then. Let's see you pick it up.

[SALINAS *bends and tries to shift it.* VASCA *laughs. The bird cries grow wilder*]

RODAS: He can't even lift it, but I can't play!

SALINAS: I'll settle for these.

He picks up three gold bars and walks off with them. RODAS *trips him up and he goes sprawling*]

Christ damn you, Rodas—that's the hissing last I take from you.

[*He springs at* RODAS *and clouts him with a gold bar. The tailor howls, picks up another, and a fight starts between them which soon becomes a violent free-for-all. The men shout; the birds scream; the General paces to and fro, ignoring everything. Finally* DE SOTO *rushes on just in time as* SALINAS *tries to strangle* RODAS. *He is followed by* ESTETE *and the two priests, who attend to the wounded*]

DE SOTO: *Stop this!* . . . Do you want to start it all off?

[*Silence. All the Indians rise, above. Uneasily the soldiers stare up at them*]

You—night watch. You, you go with him. You take the East Gate. The rest to quarters. Move!

[*They disperse.* ESTETE *and the priests remain*]

X

DE SOTO: [*To* PIZARRO] Mutiny's smoking. Act now or it'll be a blaze you'll not put out.

PIZARRO: What do I do?

DE SOTO: Take our chances, what else can we do? You have to let him go.

PIZARRO: And what happens then? A tiny army is wiped out in five minutes, and the whole story lost for always. Later someone else will conquer Peru and no one will even remember my name.

DE SOTO: What kind of name will they remember if you kill him?

PIZARRO: A conqueror. That at least.

DE SOTO: A man who butchered his prisoner after giving his word. There's a name for your ballads.

PIZARRO: I'll never live to hear them. What do I care? What does it matter? Whatever I do, what does it matter?

DE SOTO: Nothing, if you don't feel it. But I think you do.

PIZARRO: Let me understand you. As Second-in-Command, you counsel certain death for this army?

DE SOTO: I'll not counsel his.

PIZARRO: Then you counsel the death of Christ in this country, as you told my page boy months ago?

DE SOTO: That's not known.

PIZARRO: As good.

DE SOTO: No. Christ is love. Love is—

PIZARRO: What? *What?*

DE SOTO: Now in him. He trusts you, trust him. It's all you can do.

PIZARRO: Have you gone soft in the head? What's this chorus

now? 'Trust! trust!' You know the law out here: kill or get killed. You said it yourself. The mercies come later.

DE SOTO: Not for you. I wish to God you'd never made this bargain. But you did. Now you've no choice left.

PIZARRO: No, this is my kingdom. In Peru I am absolute. I have choice always.

DE SOTO: You had it. But you made it.

PIZARRO: Then I'll take it back.

DE SOTO: Then you never made it. I'm not playing words, General. There's no choice where you don't stick by it.

PIZARRO: I can *choose* to take it back.

DE SOTO: No, sir. That would only be done on orders from your own fear. That's not choosing.

ESTETE: May the Crown be allowed a word?

PIZARRO: I know your word. Death.

ESTETE: What else can it be?

VALVERDE: Your army is in terror. Do you care nothing for them?

PIZARRO: Well, Cavalier. Do you?

DE SOTO: I care for them. But less than I care for you . . . God knows why.

[He goes off]

ESTETE: The issue is simple. You are Viceroy here ruling in the name of the King who sent you. You have no right to risk his land for any reason at all.

PIZARRO: And what did this King ever do for me? Granted me salary if I found money to pay it. Allowed me governance if I found land to govern. Magnificent! For years I strove to make this expedition, years of scars and hunger. While I sweated your Holy Roman vulture turned away his beak till I'd shaken out enough gold to tempt his greed. If I'd failed this time he'd have cast me off with one shrug of his royal feathers. Well, now I cast him. Francisco Pizarro casts off Carlos the Fifth. Go and tell him.

ESTETE: This is ridiculous.

PIZARRO: No doubt, but you'll have to give me better argument before I give him up.

ESTETE: Perverse man, what is Atahuallpa to you?

PIZARRO: Someone I promised Life.

ESTETE: Promised life? How quaint. The sort of chivalry idea you pretend to despise. If you want to be an absolute king, my man, you must learn to act out of personal will. Break your word just *because* you gave it. Till then, you're only a pig-man trying to copy his betters.

[PIZARRO *rounds on him angrily*]

VALVERDE: My son, listen to me. No promise to a pagan need bind a Christian. Simply think what's at stake: the lives of a hundred and seventy of the faithful. Are you going to sacrifice them for one savage?

PIZARRO: You know lives have no weight, Father. Ten can't be added up to outbalance one.

VALVERDE: Ten good can against one evil. And this man is evil. His people kiss his hands as the source of life.

PIZARRO: As we do yours. All your days you play at being God. You only hate my Inca because he does it better.

VALVERDE: *What?*

PIZARRO: Dungballs to all churches that are or ever could be! How I hate you. 'Kill who I bid you kill and I will pardon it.' YOU with your milky fingers forcing in the blade. How dare you priests bless any man who goes slicing into battle? But no. You slice with him. 'Rip!' you scream, 'Tear! blind! in the name of Christ!' Tell me, soft Father, if Christ was here now, do you think he would kill my Inca? . . . Well, Brother de Nizza, you're the lord of answers: let's hear you. Do I kill him?

DE NIZZA: Don't try and trap me. I know as well as you how terrible it is to kill. But worse is to spare evil. When I came here first I thought I had found Paradise. Now I know it is Hell. A country which castrates its people. What are your Inca's subjects? A population of eunuchs, living entirely without choice.

PIZARRO: And what are your Christians? Unhappy hating men. Look: I'm a peasant, I want value for money. If I go marketing for Gods, who do I buy? The God of Europe with all its death and blooding, or Atahuallpa of Peru? His spirit keeps an Empire sweet and still as corn in the field.

DE NIZZA: And you're content to be a stalk of corn?

PIZARRO: Yes, yes! They're no fools, these sun men. They know what cheats you sell on your barrow. Choice. Hunger. Tomorrow. They've looked at your wares and passed on. They live here as part of nature, no hope and no despair.

DE NIZZA: And no life. Why must you be so dishonest? You are not only part of nature, and you know it. There is something in you at war with nature; there is in all of us. Something that does not belong in you the animal. What do you think it is? What is this pain in you that month after month makes you hurl yourself against the cage of time? . . . This is God, driving you to accept divine eternity. Take it, General: not this pathetic copy of eternity the Incas have tried to make on earth. Peru is a sepulchre of the soul. For the sake of the free spirit in each of us it must be destroyed.

PIZARRO: So there is Christian charity. To save my own soul I must kill another man!

DE NIZZA: To save love in the world you must kill lovelessness.

PIZARRO: Hail to you, sole judge of love! No salvation outside your church: and no love neither. Oh, you arrogance! . . . [Simply] I do not know love, Father, but what can I ever know, if I feel none for him?

DIEGO: [Rushing on] Sir! Sir!
Another fight broke out, sir. There's one dead.

PIZARRO: Who?

DIEGO: Blas. He drew a knife. I only meant to spit his leg, but he slipped and got it through the guts.

PIZARRO: You did well to punish fighting.

DIEGO: May I speak free, sir?

PIZARRO: What? I've got to kill him, is that it?

DIEGO: What other way is there? The men are out of their wits. They feel death all round them.

PIZARRO: So it is and let them face it. I promised them gold, not life. Well, they've got gold. The cripples have gold crutches. The coughers spit gold snot. The bargain's over.

DIEGO: No, sir, not with me. To me you're the greatest General in the world. And we're the greatest company.

PIZARRO: Pizarro's boys, is that it?

DIEGO: Yes, sir. Pizarro's boys.

PIZARRO: Ah, the old band. The dear old regiment. Fool! Look, you were born a man. Not a Blue man, or a Green man, but A MAN. You are able to feel a thousand separate loves unordered by fear or solitude. Are you going to trade them all in for Gang-love? Flag-love? Carlos-the-Fifth-love? Jesus-the-Christ-love? All that has been tied on you; it is only this that makes you bay for death.

VALVERDE: I'll give you death. When I get back to Spain a commission will hale you to the stake for what you have said today.

PIZARRO: If I let the Inca go, Father, you'll never get back to Spain.

ESTETE: You madman: see here, you put him underground by sunset or I'll take the knife to him myself.

PIZARRO: ATAHUALLPA!

[ATAHUALLPA *enters with* YOUNG MARTIN]

They ache for your death. They want to write psalms to their God in your blood. But they'll all die before you—that I promise. [*He binds* ATAHUALLPA'*s arm to his own with a long cord of rope last used to tie some gold*] There. No, no, come here. Now no one will kill you unless they kill me first.

ESTETE: De Candia!

[*Enter* DE CANDIA, *with a drawn sword*]

DE CANDIA: A touching game—gaolers and prisoners. But it's over now. General, do you think I'm going to die so that you can dance with a darkie?

[PIZARRO *pulls the sword from* YOUNG MARTIN's *scabbard.*]

DIEGO: [*Drawing*] Sorry, sir, but it's got to be done.

ESTETE: [*Drawing*] There's nothing you can do, Pizarro. The whole camp's against you.

PIZARRO: De Soto!

DE CANDIA: If de Soto raises his sword, he'll lose the arm that swings it.

PIZARRO: You'll lose yours first. Come on!

[*He rushes at* DE CANDIA *but* ATAHUALLPA *gives a growl and pulls him back by the rope. A pause*]

ATAHUALLPA: I have no eyes for you. You are nothing.

PIZARRO: I command here still. They will obey me.

ATAHUALLPA: They will kill me though you cry curses of earth and sky. [*To them all*] Leave us. I will speak with him.

[*Impressed by the command in his voice, all leave, save the General—now roped to his prisoner—and* YOUNG MARTIN]

XI

ATAHUALLPA: It is no matter. They cannot kill me.

PIZARRO: Cannot?

ATAHUALLPA: Man who dies cannot kill a God who lives forever.

PIZARRO: I wouldn't bet on it, my lord.

ATAHUALLPA: Only my father can take me from here. And he would not accept me killed by men like you. Men with no word. You may be King in this land, but never God. I am

God of the Four Quarters and if you kill me tonight I will rise at dawn when my Father first touches my body with light.

PIZARRO: You believe this?

ATAHUALLPA: All my people know it—it is why they have let me stay with you.

PIZARRO: They knew you could not be harmed . . .

ATAHUALLPA: So.

PIZARRO: Was this the meaning? The meaning of my dream? You were choosing me?

YOUNG MARTIN: My lord, it's just a boast. Beyond any kind of reason.

PIZARRO: Is it?

YOUNG MARTIN: How can a man die, then get up and walk away?

PIZARRO: Let's hear your creed, boy. 'I believe in Jesus Christ, the Son of God, that He suffered under Pontius Pilate, was crucified, dead and buried' . . . and what?

YOUNG MARTIN: Sir?

PIZARRO: What?

YOUNG MARTIN: 'He descended into Hell, and on the third day He rose again from the dead . . .'

PIZARRO: You don't believe it!

YOUNG MARTIN: I do! On my soul! I believe with perfect faith!

PIZARRO: But Christ's to be the only one, is that it? What if it's possible, here in a land beyond all maps and scholars, guarded by mountains up to the sky, that there were true Gods on earth, creators of true peace? Think of it! Gods, free of time.

YOUNG MARTIN: It's impossible, my lord.

PIZARRO: It's the only way to give life meaning! To blast out of time and live forever, *us*, in our own persons. This is the law: die in despair or be a God yourself! . . . Look at him: always so calm as if the teeth of life never bit him . . . or the teeth of death. What if it was really true, Martin?

That I've gone God-hunting and caught one. A being who can renew his life over and over?

YOUNG MARTIN: But how can he do that, sir? How could any man?

PIZARRO: By returning over and over again to the source of life—*to the Sun!*

YOUNG MARTIN: No, sir . . .

PIZARRO: Why not? What else is a God but what we know we can't do without? The flowers that worship it, the sun-flowers in their soil, are us after night, after cold and lightless days, turning our faces to it, adoring. The sun is the only God I know! We eat you to walk. We drink you to sing. Our reins loosen under you and we laugh. Even I laugh, here!

YOUNG MARTIN: General, you need rest, sir.

[*Pause*]

PIZARRO: Yes. Yes . . . yes. [*Bitterly*] How clever. He's under-stood everything I've said to him these awful months—all the secret pain he's heard—and this is his revenge. This futile joke. How he must hate me. [*Tightening the rope*] Oh, yes, you cunning bastard! Look, Martin—behold, my God. I've got the Sun on a string! I can make it rise: [*He pulls the Inca's arm up*]—or set!

[*He throws the* INCA *to his knees*]

YOUNG MARTIN: General . . . !

PIZARRO: I'll make you set forever! Two can joke as well as one. You want your freedom? All right, you're Free! [*He starts circling round* ATAHUALLPA] Walk out of the camp! They may stop you, but what's that to you? You're invulnerable. They'll knock you down but your father the Sun will pick you up again. Go on! Get up! . . . Go on! . . . Get up! . . . Go on! . . . Go on! . . . Go on! . . . Go on! . . . Go on! . . . Go on!

[*He breaks into a frantic gallop round and round the*

Inca, the rope at full stretch, ATAHUALLPA *turning with him, somersaulting, then holding him, his teeth bared with the strain, as if breaking a wild horse, until the old man tumbles exhausted to the ground. Silence follows, broken only by deep moaning from the stricken man. Quietly the Inca pulls in the rope. Then at last he speaks]*

ATAHUALLPA: Pizarro. You will die soon and you do not believe in your God. That is why you tremble and keep no word. Believe in me. I will give you a word and fill you with joy. For you I will do a great thing. I will swallow death and spit it out of me.

[Pause. This whole scene stays very still]

PIZARRO: *[Whispering]* You cannot.

ATAHUALLPA: Yes, if my father wills it.

PIZARRO: How if he does not?

ATAHUALLPA: He will. His people still need me. Believe.

PIZARRO: Impossible.

ATAHUALLPA: Believe.

PIZARRO: How? . . . How? . . .

ATAHUALLPA: First you must take my priest power.

PIZARRO: *[Quietly]* Oh, no! you go or not as you choose, but I take nothing more in this world.

ATAHUALLPA: Take my word. Take my peace. I will put water to your wound, old man. Believe.

[A long silence. The lights are now fading round them]

PIZARRO: What must I do?

[Enter OLD MARTIN*]*

OLD MARTIN: How can I speak now and hope to be believed? As night fell like a hand over the eye, and great white stars sprang out over the snow-rim of our world, Atahuallpa confessed

Pizarro. He did it in the Inca manner. He took Ichu grass and a stone. Into the Ichu grass the General spoke for an hour or more. None heard what he said save the King, who could not understand it. Then the King struck him on the back with the stone, cast away the grass, and made the signs for purification.

PIZARRO: If any blessing is in me, take it and go. Fly up, my bird, and come to me again.

> [*The* INCA *takes a knife from* YOUNG MARTIN *and cuts the rope. Then he walks upstage. All the* OFFICERS *and* MEN *enter. During the following a pole is set up above, in the sun, and* ATAHUALLPA *is hauled up into it*]

XII

OLD MARTIN: The Inca was tried by a court quickly mustered. He was accused of usurping the throne and killing his brother; of idolatry and of having more than one wife. On all these charges he was found—

ESTETE: Guilty.

VALVERDE: Guilty.

DE CANDIA: Guilty.

DIEGO: Guilty.

OLD MARTIN: Sentence to be carried out the same night.

ESTETE: Death by burning.

> [*Lights up above in the sun*]

> [ATAHUALLPA *gives a great cry*]

PIZARRO: No! He must not burn! His body must stay in one piece.

VALVERDE: Let him repent his idolatry and be baptized a Christian. He will receive the customary mercy.

OLD MARTIN: Strangling instead.

PIZARRO: You must do it! Deny your Father! If you don't, you will be burnt to ashes. There will be no flesh left for him to warm alive at dawn.

[YOUNG MARTIN *screams and runs from the stage in horror*]

You must do it.

[*In a gesture of surrender the Inca king kneels*]

OLD MARTIN: So it was that Atahuallpa came to Christ.

[*Enter* DE NIZZA, *with a bowl of water*]

DE NIZZA: I baptise you Juan de Atahuallpa, in honour of Juan the Baptist, whose sacred day this is.

ESTETE: The twenty-ninth of August, 1533.

VALVERDE: And may Our Lord and His angels receive your soul with joy!

SOLDIERS: Amen!

[*The Inca suddenly raises his head, tears off his clothes and intones in a great voice:*]

ATAHUALLPA: INTI! INTI! INTI!

VALVERDE: What does he say?

PIZARRO: [*Intoning also*] The Sun. The Sun. The Sun.

VALVERDE: *Kill him!*

[*Soldiers haul* ATAHUALLPA *to his feet and hold him to the stake.* RODAS *slips a string over his head and while all the Spaniards recite the Latin Creed below, and great howls of 'Inca!' come from the darkness, the Sovereign King of Peru is garrotted. His screams and struggles subside; his body falls slack. His executioners hand the corpse down to the soldiers below, who carry it to the centre of the stage and drop it at* PIZARRO's *feet. Then all leave save the old man, who stands as if turned to stone. A drum beats. Slowly, in semi-darkness, the stage fills with all the Indians, robed in black and terracotta, wearing the great golden funeral masks of ancient Peru. Grouped round the prone body, they intone a strange Chant of Resurrection, punctuated by hollow beats on the drums and by long, long silences in which they turn their immense triangular eyes enquiringly up to the sky. Finally, after three great cries appear to summon it, the sun rises. Its rays fall on the body.* ATAHUALLPA *does not move. The masked men watch in amazement—disbelief—finally, despair. Slowly, with hanging, dejected heads, they shuffle away.* PIZARRO *is left alone with the dead King. He contemplates him. A silence. Then suddenly he slaps it viciously, and the body rolls over on its back*]

PIZARRO: Cheat! You've cheated me! Cheat . . .

[*For a moment his old body is racked with sobs; then, surprised, he feels tears on his cheek. He examines them. The sunlight brightens on his head*]

What's this? What is it? In all your life you never made one of these, I know, and I not till this minute. Look. [*He kneels to show the dead Inca*] Ah, no. You have no eyes for me now, Atahuallpa: they are dusty balls of amber I can tap on. You have no peace for me, Atahuallpa: the birds still scream in your forest. You have no joy for me, Atahuallpa, my boy: the only joy is in death. I lived between two hates: I die between two darks: blind eyes and a blind sky. And yet you saw once. The sky sees nothing, but you saw. Is there comfort there? The sky knows no feeling, but we know them, that's sure. Martin's hope, and de Soto's honour, and your trust—your trust which hunted me: we alone make these. That's some marvel, yes, some marvel. To sit in a great cold silence, and sing out sweet with just our own warm breath: that's some marvel, surely. To make water in a sand world: surely, surely . . . God's just a name on your nail; and naming begins cries and cruelties. But to live without hope of after, and make whatever God there is, oh, that's some immortal business surely . . . I'm tired. Where are you? You're so cold. I'd warm you if I could. But there's no warming now, not ever now. I'm colding too. There's a snow of death falling all round us. You can almost see it. It's over, lad, I'm coming after you. There's nothing but peace to come. We'll be put into the same earth, father and son in our own land. And that sun will roam uncaught over his empty pasture.

OLD MARTIN: So fell Peru. We gave her greed, hunger and the Cross: three gifts for the civilized life. The family groups that sang on the terraces are gone. In their place slaves shuffle underground and they don't sing there. Peru is a silent country, frozen in avarice. So fell Spain, gorged with gold; distended; now dying.

PIZARRO: [Singing] 'Where is her heart, O little finch' . . .

OLD MARTIN: And so fell you, General, my master, whom men called the Son of His Own Deeds. He was killed later in a quarrel with his partner who brought up the reinforcements. But to speak truth, he sat down that morning and never really got up again.

PIZARRO: [Singing] 'Where are her plumes, O little finch' . . .

OLD MARTIN: I'm the only one left now of that company: land-owner—slaveowner—and forty years from any time of hope. It put out a good blossom, but it was shaken off rough. After that I reckon the fruit always comes sour, and doesn't sweeten up much with age.

PIZARRO: [Singing] 'She is cut up, O little finch. For stealing grain, O little finch' . . .

OLD MARTIN: General, you did for me, and now I've done for you. And there's no joy in that. Or in anything now. But then there's no joy in the world could match for me what I had when I first went with you across the water to find the gold country. And no pain like losing it. Save you all.

[*He goes out.* PIZARRO *lies beside the body of* ATAHUALLPA *and quietly sings to it*]

PIZARRO: [*Singing*]
> See, see the fate, O little finch,
> Of robber birds, O little finch.

[*The sun glares at the audience*]

CURTAIN

Frank Marcus

Frank Marcus joined the inner circle of modern international playwrights with his "serious" comedy, *The Killing of Sister George*, which scored heavily on both the London and Broadway stages with Beryl Reid as the formidable title figure. At its opening in 1965, *The* (London) *Times* greeted the play as "the best comedy by a new writer to appear in the West End for a long time" while the *Evening News and Star*'s distinguished first-night juror, Felix Barker, hailed the author as "a major playwright in the making."

A dexterous creator of unusual characters implicated in uncommonly provocative situations, Mr. Marcus also possesses that rare and enviable theatrical commodity: the ability to be both comic and affecting almost within the same breath. This striking characteristic is especially manifest in *The Killing of Sister George*, which also underscores Mr. Marcus' concern with the problem of illusion versus reality.

The author was born on June 30, 1928, in Breslau, Germany, and emigrated to England just before the outbreak of World War II. After completing his education and a tenure at St. Martin's School of Art, he organized the International Theatre Group, an experimental company that performed in little theatres in the area of Notting Hill Gate with Mr. Marcus functioning as actor, director and designer.

His first West End Play, *The Formation Dancers*, was presented at the Arts Theatre Club, then at the Globe in 1964. Selected and published as one of the *Plays of the Year, 1964–65*, it also brought him to the attention of producer Michael Codron. The latter invited the promising young dramatist to write a play for his production auspices with a "powerful part" for a "star" actress. The resultant *The Killing of Sister George*, written in eight weeks, won him a packet of "Best Play of the Year" awards, notably the prestigious seasonal citation from the London theatre critics.

Alerted, however, to the vagaries of the theatre, Mr. Marcus, who is married and the father of three, continued to operate a London antique silver shop (a family concern) until completely assured of the acceptance and success of *The Killing of Sister George*.

Frank Marcus' other dramatic works include *Studies in the Nude*, produced at the Hampstead Theatre Club in 1967; *Mrs. Mouse, Are You Within?*, staged in 1968 at the Theatre Royal, Bristol, later transferred to the Duke of York's, London; and *The Window*, introduced in this editor's collection, *Best Short Plays of the World Theatre: 1958–1967*, and presented by the Inter-Action Lunch-Hour Theatre Club at the Ambiance, Queensway, in 1969.

Additionally, Mr. Marcus has made new translations of three plays (including *Liebelei* and *La Ronde*) by the Austrian dramatist Arthur Schnitzler, and Ferenc Molnar's *The Guardsman* (produced at the Shaw Festival, Niagara-on-the-Lake, Ontario, 1969).

He has written several original plays for television, prepared a new screen treatment of Ibsen's *Hedda Gabler* and provided the basic theme and concept of the mimedrama *Le Trois Perruques* for his close friend Marcel Marceau, the celebrated French pantomimist.

During his "moonlighting" hours, the prize-winning playwright has contributed dramatic criticisms and essays to various publications (*The London Magazine; Plays and Players;* the New York *Times*) and since May 1968, he has officiated as drama critic for the London *Sunday Telegraph*.

THE
KILLING OF
SISTER GEORGE

Frank Marcus

The Killing of Sister George was first presented by the Bristol Old Vic at the Theatre Royal, Bristol, by arrangement with Michael Codron. It was subsequently presented at the Duke of York's Theatre, London, on June 17, 1965, by Michael Codron in association with Bernard Delfont. The cast was as follows:

ALICE "CHILDIE" MCNAUGHT	*Eileen Atkins*
JUNE BUCKRIDGE (SISTER GEORGE)	*Beryl Reid*
MRS. MERCY CROFT	*Lally Bowers*
MADAME XENIA	*Margaret Courtenay*

The Killing of Sister George was first presented in the United States on October 5, 1966, at the Belasco Theatre, New York, by Helen Bonfils and Morton Gottlieb, by arrangement with Michael Codron in association with Bernard Delfont, with the original cast, except for Madame Xenia played by Polly Rowles.

Foreign Production designed by Catherine Browne
American Production supervised by William Ritman
Directed by Val May

SYNOPSIS OF SCENES

SCENE: *The living room of June Buckridge's flat in Devonshire Street, London.*

ACT ONE

An afternoon in late September.

ACT TWO

SCENE 1: *A week later.*
SCENE 2: *The same day, evening.*

ACT THREE

Two weeks later, morning.

ACT ONE

*The living room of a West End flat in London. A bay
window at the back overlooks roofs. The furniture, an incongruous mixture of antique, nineteen-thirtyish, and modern, looks expensive but ill-assorted. There is a large radio,
bearing trophies and framed certificates; elsewhere there
are embroidered cushions in profusion, various bric-a-brac,
and Victorian dolls are on the chairs and in the corner of
a chintz-covered settee. Downstage right an arch leads to
the hall and entrance; upstage left a door leads to the bedroom; a passage off up left leads to the bathroom, and another door downstage leads to the kitchen. The Curtain
rises on an empty stage. It is a Tuesday afternoon in late
September. Presently the front door bangs, and* JUNE BUCK-
RIDGE *enters. She is a rotund, middle-aged woman, wearing
a belted white mackintosh. She is very agitated.*

ALICE: [*Calling from the kitchen*] George? . . . George, is that
you? [JUNE *opens a cigar box, finds it empty and throws it
down.* ALICE *throws up the hatch between the kitchen and the
living room.* ALICE *is a girl-woman in her thirties, looking deceptively young. She conveys an impression of pallor: her hair,
eyes and complexion are all very light. She is wearing a sweater
and jeans, with a plastic apron and orange rubber gloves, having
been in the middle of the washing up. She is very surprised*]
George, what on earth . . . ?
[JUNE *throws a doll on the floor*] George, what are you doing
at home at this time of the afternoon?

[JUNE *lights a cheroot from a box on the mantelpiece*]

JUNE: [*After a pause*] They are going to murder me.

ALICE: What—

JUNE: I've suspected it for some time.

ALICE: What?

JUNE: Will you kindly close that hatch?

ALICE: [*Closing the hatch and entering the sitting room from the kitchen*] What are you talking about?

JUNE: [*Brutally*] Shut up. You know nothing. [ALICE, *silenced, watches* JUNE *puffing nervously on her cigar*] That Australian bitch, that Sheila, let it out . . .

ALICE: The one who used to be a lady cricketer?

JUNE: [*With disgust*] Yes—the lolloping great trollop!

ALICE: So, what did she say?

JUNE: [*Very excited now*] It was in the tea-break, when she gave me a cup of tea. "I trust you're in good health," she said, with a sly wink.

ALICE: There's nothing wrong with that.

JUNE: I knew what she meant. I got the message.

ALICE: It might have been quite innocuous—

JUNE: Innocuous! They are trying to kill me, and you call that innocuous! [*Pacing up and down*] Somebody's leaked it to her—another Australian. They're everywhere: the place is rampant with them; they multiply like rabbits.

ALICE: You're imagining things.

JUNE: No not rabbits, opossums!! Dreary little pests.

ALICE: Well, anyway, what did you *do*?

JUNE: I left.

ALICE: [*Alarmed*] You walked out of rehearsal?

JUNE: [*Subdued*] I wasn't going to let some illiterate bitch wink at me . . .

ALICE: [*Biting her lip*] They won't like it . . .

JUNE: I've given six years' devoted service to that program.

ALICE: You said yourself: they don't like contract artists to have tantrums—

JUNE: [*Getting excited again*] They have no right to do this to me. I'm a senior member of the cast. If they wanted to— [*She swallows*] write me out, they should have called me to the office in the proper manner—

ALICE: Nobody wants to write you out. It's unthinkable. Applehurst couldn't survive without you . . .

JUNE: Don't you be too sure. Applehurst is more than a village, you know—it's a community, a way of life. It doesn't depend on individuals. There's many a stone in that churchyard . . .

ALICE: You talk as if it was real—

JUNE: [*Raising her voice again*] It's real to millions! It stands for the traditional values of English life—tenacity—common sense—our rural heritage—

ALICE: Oh, belt up.

JUNE: You're getting above yourself, Missy.

ALICE: But you *are* the serial! It would be nothing without you—

JUNE: Stranger things have happened. Only the other day Ronnie said: "There'll have to be some changes, you know."

ALICE: He probably meant the story line—

JUNE: No—no—it's the axe again! We're losing listeners, and they've got to have a scapegoat. It's over a year since old Mrs. Prescott was kicked by a horse . . .

ALICE: Yes, and remember the rumpus there was over that! And she was only a minor character—

JUNE: She had her following.

ALICE: She hardly had a line to say from one week to the next.

JUNE: What about the time I nursed her back to health, when she had concussion?

ALICE: That was exceptional.

JUNE: No, no, no. She had nice little bits—here and there. Remember that time she found the stray dog, and the village adopted it—[*A dark thought occurs to her*]—until it was run over by a tractor.

[*She shudders*]

ALICE: There is no comparison. Mrs. Prescott—

JUNE: [*Shouting*] Mrs. Prescott had a following.

ALICE: [*Shrugging her shoulders*] All right: Mrs. Prescott had a following.

JUNE: The subject is now closed.

[*Pause*]

ALICE: But she *was* expendable.

JUNE: [*Exploding*] Are you trying to aggravate me? Are you deliberately trying to annoy me?

ALICE: You're the most popular character in it—

JUNE: Don't screech at me. It's an ugly, grating sound.

ALICE: Well, look at your ratings.

JUNE: They are down! Four per cent last week—I'm slipping! Now do you understand?

[*Pause*]

ALICE: You still get the most fan mail, don't you?

JUNE: Only just . . . Ginger, the pubkeeper, is close on my heels. Ever since he had that win on the Premium Bonds, and lent the money to Farmer Bromley, so as they wouldn't turn his place into a factory farm—

ALICE: What about young Rosie?

JUNE: [*Conspiratorially*] Aha. [ALICE *looks puzzled*] She's preggers.

ALICE: No! You mean the actress—

JUNE: No, the character, blockhead! We reckon that'll bring back some listeners.

ALICE: [*Intrigued*] Who was responsible?

JUNE: We haven't been told yet. I think it was Lennie, her steady. If so, it'll be absolutely splendid. They can get married— everybody loves a wedding. But Arthur thinks it was Roy.

ALICE: Who's Roy?

JUNE: That soldier—from the army camp at Oakmead. He took her to that dance, remember?

ALICE: [*Concerned*] What's she going to do . . . about the baby?

JUNE: She's going to confide in me about it—in the next install-ment. Comes to me in tears; wants to get rid of it . . . [*Sighing*] Don't know what the younger generation's coming to . . .

ALICE: What do you tell her?

JUNE: What *don't* I tell her! She gets a dressing-down from me that she won't forget in a hurry! [*In her country accent*] Where is he? Mr. Clever Lad? Show me where he is, so's I can tear some strips off him, the fine young fellow. Just don't you aggravate yourself, my dear—leave it to me! My dear, who was it? Just tell me who it was!

ALICE: And does she tell you?

JUNE: No. [*Pause*] But I'll wheedle it out of her, never fear. Give me three installments and I'll do it.

ALICE: [*Tensely*] They shouldn't talk about . . . things like that.

JUNE: [*Happier now*] It's nice, though, the way they come to me . . . with their troubles . . . Oh, they know they'll get straight talking from me—no lard ever passed my lips. No, sir, fine words butter no parsnips.

ALICE: What the hell are you on about?

JUNE: They *need* me. Get that into your thick head: Applehurst needs a District Nurse. Who'd deliver the babies, who'd look after the old folk, I'd like to know?!

ALICE: Exactly! Nobody's suggesting—

JUNE: What do you mean, nobody's suggesting? Why did that woman ask about my health, then? Why did she wink at me, eh?

ALICE: Perhaps she fancies you.

JUNE: This is no time for jesting.

ALICE: How am I to know why she winked at you. Perhaps she has a nervous twitch?

JUNE: She's Australian, dunce! They're extroverts, not neurotic townsfolk like us. They come from the bloody bush!

ALICE: [*Becoming exasperated*] Well, I don't know why she winked at you!

JUNE: Oh, shut up! Stupid bitch. [*She goes to the radio and reads out one of the framed certificates*] "And in recognition of your devoted work and care for the old and sick, we name the Geriatric Ward the Sister George Ward." [ALICE *applauds slowly and ironically*] Take care, Childie, you're trailing your coat . . .

ALICE: [*Giggling*] You're the bull . . .

JUNE: [*Dangerously*] We're very cocky all of a sudden!

ALICE: [*Mock-innocently*] Who, me?

JUNE: Yes, you. Anyway, what the hell are you doing at home on a Tuesday afternoon? Why aren't you at work?

ALICE: Mr. Katz gave us the day off. It's a Jewish holiday.

JUNE: [*Suspiciously*] Oh, really. What holiday?

ALICE: I don't know. The Feast of the Contamination, or something.

JUNE: You seem to have more holidays than workdays just lately.

ALICE: Not my fault.

JUNE: [*Still suspicious*] He hasn't "had a go" at you again, your Mr. Katz, has he?

ALICE: [*Primly*] Certainly not.

JUNE: I bet he has.

ALICE: He hasn't. I'd tell you.

JUNE: I wonder. [*Self-pityingly*] Nobody tells me anything.

ALICE: That's because you always make a stupid fuss about things.

JUNE: All right, I won't make a fuss. Go on, tell me.

ALICE: There's nothing to tell.

JUNE: [*Venomously*] You expect me to believe that! After what happened last time?

ALICE: Nothing happened!

JUNE: Oh, no? A four-inch tear and three buttons off your blouse —you call that nothing?

ALICE: I told you. I got it caught in the Xerox.

JUNE: Don't lie to me, Childie.

ALICE: I'm not lying.

JUNE: Why do you avoid my eyes, then?

ALICE: Because . . . because—Oh! You're impossible, George.

[*She runs off into the bathroom*]

JUNE: Don't throw tantrums with me, young lady. [*Roaring*] Come out! Come out this instant!

ALICE: [*From the bathroom*] I shan't.

JUNE: [*Picking up one of the Victorian dolls*] Can you hear me, Childie? I've got Emmeline here, your favorite doll. [*Softly, but clearly*] And if you don't come out of the bathroom AT ONCE . . . I'll pull Emmeline's head off . . .

ALICE: [*Tear-stained, rushes into the room, tears the doll out of* JUNE's *hands, and hugs it*] Monster . . .

JUNE: There, that's better. [*Pause*] And now: apologize.

ALICE: What for?

JUNE: For causing me unnecessary aggravation.

ALICE: I'm sorry.

JUNE: You don't sound it.

ALICE: Look, I know that you're worried and everything, but that's no reason—

JUNE: Don't answer back. Don't be cheeky.

ALICE: Look, George—

JUNE: Has Mr. Katz "had a go" at you?

ALICE: [*Screaming*] No!!!

JUNE: Don't screech at me! Apologize this instant, or there'll be severe chastisement.

ALICE: I'm sorry.

JUNE: That's better. Now—down on your knees.

ALICE: Must I?

JUNE: Yes. [ALICE, *still hugging the doll, goes on her knees*] Come on—show your contrition.

ALICE: How?

JUNE: [*Pointing to the ashtray*] Eat the butt of my cigar.

ALICE: I couldn't: it would make me sick.

JUNE: [*Standing over* ALICE] Are you arguing with me?

ALICE: O.K. Hand it over.

JUNE: Good girl. Now eat it.

ALICE: Can I take the ash off?

JUNE: You may take the ash off, but you must eat the paper.

[*With an expression of extreme distaste,* ALICE *eats the cigar butt*]

ALICE: It tastes vile.

JUNE: Good. That'll teach you to be rude.

[*The telephone rings*]

ALICE: [*Rushing to answer it, relieved to be let off her punishment*] Hello, yes, this is Miss June Buckridge's flat. One moment, please.

JUNE: [*Apprehensive*] Who is it?

ALICE: I don't know.

JUNE: Why didn't you ask, fathead? [*She takes the receiver*] Hello, this is Miss June Buckridge . . . Who wants her? Yes, of course . . . Yes, I'll hold on . . . [*Putting her hand over the mouthpiece*] God Almighty, Childie, it's the BBC.

ALICE: [*Trembling*] O Lord, I hope it's nothing serious . . .

JUNE: [*On the telephone*] Hello? Hello, Mrs. Mercy, dear . . . No, of *course* not . . . Quite . . . Quite. Oh, I'm *feeling* all right . . . Yes, I . . . Well, as a matter of fact, there is something . . . Perhaps we'd better have a man-to-man—You have something to say to *me?* No, I'm not doing anything at the moment . . . Well, I'd rather not come back to BH today . . . Yes, yes, that's a *splendid* idea! Love to see you! That's right: Devonshire Street . . . top floor. You press the bell, and one of those "I speak your weight" machines answers —[*A rather forced laugh*] Yes, you know the kind of thing— [*Intoning in a deep voice*] "You are thirteen stone ten"— No, no, of course not—I wasn't implying . . . Yes, that'll be lovely . . . *any* time . . . 'Bye. [*She hangs up, wipes her brow*] She's coming round. [*Nervously lighting another cheroot*] She'll be here in a minute. God, I'm for it! *lighter*

ALICE: Who was it?

JUNE: The Assistant Head . . . Mrs. Mercy Croft—

ALICE: The one who has that weekly spot on Woman's Hour?

JUNE: "Ask Mrs. Mercy"—that's her!

ALICE: But she sounds awfully nice on the radio—at least, her advice is sort of . . . sensible.

JUNE: She is nice . . . [*Trying to convince herself*] Mrs. Mercy is a *nice woman.*

ALICE: Well, then.

JUNE: She's coming to me, you understand? At first, she asked me to see her in her office . . .

ALICE: [*After a pause*] Did she seem friendly?

JUNE: [*Tensely*] Yep.

ALICE: It'll be a good thing to clear the air—

JUNE: You don't know what you're talking about! She wants to see me on an urgent matter. We must brace ourselves for the worst—

ALICE: Will she expect some tea?

JUNE: Tea, yes of course. You must make her something special— at the double.

ALICE: There's that piece of Dundee cake that mother sent—

JUNE: That'll be absolutely first class. And make her some of your Scotch scones! And when you're serving, look cheerful, keep your shoulders back, try to make a good impression.

And if she speaks to you don't open your mouth about things you don't understand.

ALICE: I can quite easily go out.

JUNE: What, and leave me to pour tea and all that pansy stuff? Not likely. You'll stay here and do some work.

ALICE: Look, George. Try not to show how worried you are. You always get sort of . . . aggressive when you're nervous.

JUNE: Go on. Back to the kitchen where you belong!

ALICE: I wish you'd do relaxing exercises, or something.

[Exits]

JUNE: [Shouting after her] I'll do relaxing exercises on your behind, if you're not careful! Now then. [She goes to arrange the display on the radio] "Personality of the Year"—I'll put that in a prominent position . . . The English Village Preservation Society . . . The Association of British Nursing Sisters . . . The Variety Club of Great Britain . . . "Miss Humanity" nominated by the Daily Mirror . . . There's something missing . . . [Calling] Alice!

ALICE: [From the kitchen] I'm busy!

JUNE: [Imperiously] Come here! I want you.

ALICE: [Re-entering] What is it NOW? You're always interrupting . . .

JUNE: There's one missing.

[She points to the trophies]

ALICE: I haven't touched anything—

JUNE: There's one missing, isn't there? Go on—have a look! I want to hear you tell me, in your own words, which one is missing.

ALICE: [Without looking] I don't know.

JUNE: [Softly, with deadly emphasis] Where's the Honorary "Stag"?

ALICE: [*Uncertainly*] What—

JUNE: [*As before*] What have you done with it? [*No reply from* ALICE] I give you ten seconds to confess.

[*She waits, breathing heavily*]

ALICE: Let me get on with the tea. She'll be here in a minute . . .

JUNE: You've destroyed it, haven't you? [*Pause*] Where is the Honorary "Stag"?

ALICE: I threw it away.

JUNE: You . . . *what?*

ALICE: [*Slightly hysterically*] I *hated* it! A cut-off stag's head. Impaled on a pike! You had no right to keep such abominations in the house—you know I like animals!

JUNE: When did you throw it away?

ALICE: Last night.

[*She has started to cry, silently*]

JUNE: It meant a lot to me—being elected an Honorary "Stag" . . .

ALICE: [*Very contrite now*] I'll get it back; I'll get another.

JUNE: [*Tragically*] Too late.

ALICE: I'll telephone to the Town Hall—the Borough Litter Disposal Unit—

JUNE: [*Still tragically*] You mean the dustmen, don't you . . . why can't you bloody well say so . . . [*The buzzer rings*] It's her: the bitch, the cow, the plague spot, the embossed carbuncle—[JUNE *answers the buzzer*] Hello, Mrs. Mercy, dear. Expecting you. Yes, top floor. [*She switches off*] Don't stand about gawping! Blow your nose. Pull your sweater straight: you look disgusting. Now, remember: be polite and keep mum. I'll speak to you later. [*Pause*] Where the hell has she got to?

ALICE: Maybe she got stuck in the lift.

JUNE: [*Aghast*] The lift door! I think I forgot to close the door.

ALICE: [*Rushing to the door*] I'll do it!

JUNE: [*In a hoarse whisper*] Don't—it's too late! She'll either walk, or . . .

[*The doorbell rings*]

ALICE: [*Suddenly scared*] Let's not open the door!

[JUNE *throws* ALICE *a glance expressing contempt, and strides out to open the door*]

JUNE: [*Offstage*] Oh hello, Mrs. Mercy! I'm so sorry—I'd only just remembered that the lift was out of order . . .

MRS. MERCY: [*Entering, cheerfully*] Not at all—I never use the lift. [*Seeing* ALICE] Oh?

[MRS. MERCY CROFT *is a well-groomed lady of indetermi-nate age, gracious of manner, and freezingly polite. She is wearing a gray two-piece suit, matching hat and accessories, and a discreet double string of pearls round her neck. She carries a briefcase*]

JUNE: May I introduce—Miss Alice McNaught, Mrs. Croft.

MRS. MERCY: [*Extending her hand*] How do you do? [*Turning to* JUNE] Yes, I always say: we get far too little exercise these days. If we walked the stairs, instead of using lifts, those extra inches would disappear.

ALICE: [*Trying to be helpful*] I sometimes walk—

MRS. MERCY: You don't need to lose any weight, my dear—

JUNE: Alice is just preparing the tea—

MRS. MERCY: Oh, that is nice. I do hope I haven't put you to any trouble—inviting myself out of the blue.

JUNE: Rubbish.

ALICE: Not at all.

[ALICE *goes to the kitchen*]

MRS. MERCY: May I look around? I *adore* looking at other people's flats—they do reflect their occupier's personalities in an uncannily accurate way. [*Looking round*] To be perfectly honest, I imagined your home to be . . . different.

JUNE: Really?

MRS. MERCY: This charming Victoriana . . . the dolls . . . Somehow—

JUNE: [*Slightly embarrassed*] They're Miss McNaught's.

MRS. MERCY: Oh, of course, that would explain it. They just weren't *you*. I didn't know—

JUNE: [*Rather sheepishly*] Yes, I have a flatmate . . .

MRS. MERCY: [*Sympathetically*] How nice. It's so important to have . . . companionship—especially when one's an artist . . .

JUNE: These are mine—I collect horse brasses.

MRS. MERCY: How useful . . . May I look out from your window? I love overlooking things. I've always adored heights; in my young days, my husband and I often used to go mountaineering —in the Austrian Alps for preference. [*She has gone to the window*] Oh! [*A sudden yell of delight*] There's BH! You can see Broadcasting House from your window—isn't that . . . *super!* To have that reassuring presence brooding over you, seeing that you don't get into mischief!

ALICE: [*Lifting the hatch and looking into the room*] Ready in a minute.

MRS. MERCY: Oh—good!

JUNE: Would you kindly close the hatch. [ALICE *shuts the hatch*] There are times when I have an almost irresistible urge to decapitate her.

MRS. MERCY: Oh, poor Miss McNaught. I do like your settee cover—a homely pattern. I love floral design—I know it's old-fashioned, but . . .

JUNE: Childie—Miss McNaught—made them.

MRS. MERCY: Really. How clever of her—they're beautifully fitted. You're fortunate to have such a handy companion.

JUNE: [*With a bitter look at the trophies*] Yes, she's good with the needle, I'll say that for her.

MRS. MERCY: [*Lightly*] That was Sister George speaking.

JUNE: [*Self-consciously*] One can't help slipping—

MRS. MERCY: But you *are* Sister George far more than Miss June Buckridge to all of us at BH.

JUNE: Jolly nice of you to say so.

[*Motions her to sit*]

MRS. MERCY: Thank you. You have made the part completely your own—it was obvious—even at the first auditions. I remember it quite clearly, although it must be, oh—

JUNE: Almost six years ago. I was scared stiff, too.

MRS. MERCY: How charming! One can't imagine you scared stiff!

JUNE: I don't mind physical danger, I even like it. I manned an anti-aircraft during the war.

MRS. MERCY: Lovely!

JUNE: None of that sissy troop entertainment for yours truly!

MRS. MERCY: It wasn't that bad. As a matter of fact, I did a bit of organizing for ENSA myself . . .

JUNE: I'm sorry. No offense meant.

MRS. MERCY: None taken. Now Miss Buckridge—or may I call you Sister George, like everybody else?

JUNE: Certainly.

MRS. MERCY: As you know I hold a monthly Surgery in my office, when I welcome people to come to me with their problems. I've always made it a rule to be approachable. In some cases, involving matters of special importance, I prefer to visit the subjects in their own homes, so that we can talk more easily without any duress. That's why I'm here today.

JUNE: [*In her country accent*] Ah well, farmer's footsteps are the best manure!

MRS. MERCY: Quite. There's rather a serious matter I wish to discuss with you.

ALICE: [*Entering with tea*] Sorry I took so long.

MRS. MERCY: Ah, *lovely!* [*To* JUNE] We'll continue our little chat after tea.

ALICE: If you'd rather—

JUNE: You can speak quite freely, Mrs. Mercy. Miss McNaught and I have no secrets from each other.

MRS. MERCY: Well, let's all have tea first . . . [As ALICE *lays the table*] I say, what delicious-looking scones!

ALICE: They're Scotch scones.

JUNE: They're Childie's specialty. Copied from her grandmother's recipe.

MRS. MERCY: They look delish! May I try one?

ALICE: Help yourself. Here's the jam.

MRS. MERCY: They're what we used to call Girdle Scones—

JUNE: Or Drop Scones—

ALICE: It's important not to get the girdle too hot, or the outside of the scones will brown before the inside is cooked.

MRS. MERCY: They're a lovely even color . . .

ALICE: [*Very animated*] I always cool them in a towel—

MRS. MERCY: Do you?

ALICE: Yes, and I wait till the bubbles rise to the surface before I turn them over—

MRS. MERCY: They're very successful.

ALICE: I use half a teaspoon of bicarbonate of soda—

MRS. MERCY: Now you're giving away trade secrets.

ALICE: And one level teaspoon of cream of tartar—

JUNE: [*Rising*] Shut up!

[*There is a moment's silence*]

ALICE: Eight ounces of flour—

JUNE: [*Exploding*] Shut up!

ALICE: [*Softly*] And one egg.

JUNE: Shut up!!

[JUNE *hurls a cake in* ALICE's *direction*]

MRS. MERCY: [*Continuing to eat, unperturbed*] Now then, girls—temper!

ALICE: She hates me to talk about food. [*Confidentially to* MRS. MERCY] She's a wee bit overwrought—

JUNE: Overwrought, my arse!

ALICE: [*Chiding*] Now that wasn't nice—that was not a nice thing to say.

MRS. MERCY: [*Smiling indulgently*] I expect she picked it up in the army.

ALICE: She swears like a trooper—

MRS. MERCY: But she has a heart of gold.

ALICE: One day, she got into such a temper, I wrote a poem about it.

JUNE: [*Bitterly*] Yes, she fancies herself as a poetess. Goes to the City Lit. every Wednesday night, to learn about metre and things—

MRS. MERCY: What a nice hobby.

JUNE: As a poetess, she makes a good cook.

MRS. MERCY: It's still a question of mixing the right ingredients to make a tasty whole.

ALICE: That night she came back in a raging temper—

JUNE: Thank you very much, we don't want to hear anything about that—

ALICE: I wrote this poem. It began:
"Fierce as the wind
Blows the rampaging termagent . . ."

MRS. MERCY: Very expressive. [*To* JUNE] And how did you like being compared to the wind?

[JUNE *blows a raspberry*]

ALICE: [*To* MRS. MERCY] Slice of cake, Mrs. Mercy?

MRS. MERCY: Just a teeny one. Mustn't be greedy.

JUNE: Her mother made it.

MRS. MERCY: You can always tell if it's home-baked; it tastes quite different.

JUNE: You'd be surprised if you knew what Mother McNaught put into it.

MRS. MERCY: I'm not even going to ask.

JUNE: I'm delighted to hear it!

[*Laughs*]

MRS. MERCY: [*Enjoying herself*] Oh dear, this is just like a dormitory feast—all this girlish banter. [*To* JUNE] I bet you were a terror at school!

JUNE: I was captain of the hockey team and a keen disciplinarian— God help the girl I caught making me an apple-pie bed!

[*She chuckles*]

MRS. MERCY: Ah, there's Sister George again! It's wonderful how over the years the character *evolved* . . .

ALICE: Who first thought of putting her on a motorbike?

JUNE: That was because of sound effects. As long as I was on the old bike, listeners never knew whether I was static or mobile.

MRS. MERCY: A unique sound—Sister George on her motorbike, whizzing through the countryside, singing snatches of hymns—

JUNE: One day I got into trouble because I sang a hymn which sounded like "On the Good Ship Venus."

MRS. MERCY: A traditional air—?

JUNE: I've found it safer to stick to hymns. Once I tried a pop song, and d'you know, hundreds of letters came in, protesting.

MRS. MERCY: We learn from experience . . . But we don't want Applehurst falling behind the times.

JUNE: No—no—of course not.

MRS. MERCY: But we must constantly examine criticism, and if it's constructive, we must act on it. Ruthlessly.

JUNE: What sort of criticism?

MRS. MERCY: Oh, nothing in particular . . . at least . . .

JUNE: But what?

MRS. MERCY: Well, that brings me—I'm afraid—to the unpleasant part of my business . . .

ALICE: Oh dear—

MRS. MERCY: [*Rising*] But first, would you show me to the little girls' room?

JUNE: Alice, show Mrs. Mercy to the . . .

ALICE: This way, Mrs. Mercy.

JUNE: —little—girls'—

> [MRS. MERCY *exits, accompanied by* ALICE. JUNE *catches sight of her briefcase, looks round furtively, and opens it as* ALICE *returns*]

ALICE: [*Aghast*] What are you doing?

JUNE: [*Rummaging in the case*] Keep a look-out!

ALICE: You can't. You mustn't!

JUNE: [*Taking a folder*] My personal file.

ALICE: [*In a hysterical whisper*] PUT IT BACK!

JUNE: [*Perusing some papers*] Quiet! [*She takes an envelope from the file. Reads*] "Sister George. Confidential."

ALICE: She's coming!

JUNE: [*Quickly replaces the folder in the briefcase, realizes too late that she has still got the envelope in her hand: puts it behind the nearest cushion*] . . . so Emmeline said, "I don't want any Girdle Scones . . . thank you very much."

MRS. MERCY: [*Re-entering*] I got on the scales, to see if I've put on any weight.

JUNE: I don't suppose . . .

MRS. MERCY: [*Takes her briefcase, while* JUNE *and* ALICE *stand rigid with suspense*] Now then . . .

ALICE: I'll make myself scarce . . .

> [*Goes into kitchen*]

MRS. MERCY: Please sit down. [JUNE *sits*] You won't hold it against me if I speak quite plainly?

JUNE: Please do.

MRS. MERCY: It's my unpleasant duty to haul you over the coals, and administer a severe reprimand.

JUNE: Oh?

MRS. MERCY: Believe me, Sister George, I'd much rather let bygones be bygones—

JUNE: [*In a country accent*] Let sleeping dogs lie—

MRS. MERCY: Precisely . . . But I must remind you of the little chat we had just about a year ago, after that unfortunate incident in the Club . . . involving a lady colleague of mine.

JUNE: Let's not rake over old embers.

MRS. MERCY: I don't intend to. But in the light of recent events, it's difficult to forget an incident as vivid as the pouring of a glass of beer over the Assistant Head of Talks. I had hoped one black mark would have been enough for you, but this morning [*Takes a sheet of paper from the folder*] I received this memo from the Director of Religious Broadcasting. [*She hands the paper to* JUNE] I should like to have your comments.

JUNE: [*Excitedly reads the paper, flushes, and jumps up violently*] It's a lie! It's an utter, bloody lie!

MRS. MERCY: [*Firmly*] Please calm yourself, Miss Buckridge. Kindly hand me back the paper. [*As* JUNE *hands over the paper*] I take it you're not denying that you were drinking in The Coach & Horses on the night of the nineteenth?

JUNE: How the hell should I remember? [*Calling*] Alice! Come here!

ALICE: [*Enters, wide-eyed and worried*] You want me?

JUNE: Where was I on the night of the nineteenth?

MRS. MERCY: I'm sorry to involve you in this, Miss McNaught—

ALICE: [*Quietly*] That was a Wednesday: I was at the City Lit.

JUNE: You bloody well would be. [*To* MRS. MERCY] All right; it seems I was at The Coach & Horses on the night in question, having a drink with some of the boys. That's no crime.

MRS. MERCY: Miss Buckridge . . . According to this letter from the Mother Superior of the Convent of the Sacred Heart of

Jesus, you boarded a taxi stopping at the traffic lights at Langham Place—

JUNE: I thought it was empty.

MRS. MERCY: [*Reading*] A taxi bearing as passengers two novitiate nuns from Ireland who had just arrived at Kings Cross Station—

JUNE: How was I to know?

MRS. MERCY: You boarded this taxi in a state of advanced inebriation and—[*Consulting the paper*]—proceeded to assault the two nuns, subjecting them to actual physical violence!

ALICE: [*To* JUNE] You didn't really!

JUNE: No, no, no. Of course not. I'd had a few pints . . . I saw this cab, took it to be empty, got in—and there were these two black things screaming blue murder!

MRS. MERCY: Why didn't you get out again?

JUNE: Well, I'd had a very nasty shock myself! What with their screaming and flapping about—I thought they were bats, you know, vampire bats! It was *they* who attacked *me*. I remember getting all entangled in their skirts and petticoats and things . . . the taxi driver had to pull me free . . .

MRS. MERCY: A deplorable anecdote. According to the Mother Superior, one of the nuns required medical treatment for shock, and is still under sedation. She thought it was the devil.

ALICE: George, how could you!

JUNE: Don't *you* start on me! [*Clapping her hands*] Back to the kitchen! Washing up! Presto!

ALICE: [*Firmly*] No, I'm staying. This concerns me, too.

JUNE: It was all a ghastly mistake.

MRS. MERCY: No doubt, but it'll take some explaining.

JUNE: Fancy informing the Director of Religious Broadcasting. What a nasty thing to do for a holy woman!

MRS. MERCY: The Mother Superior is responsible for the nuns in her charge—

JUNE: Then she should jolly well teach them how to behave in public! I got the fright of my life, in there! Those nuns were like *mice*—albino mice—with white faces and little red eyes. And they were vicious, too. They scratched and they bit! Look—you can still see the tooth marks—[*She points to her arm*]—do you see that? I've a good mind to make a counter-complaint to the Mother Superior: they deserve to be scourged in their cells.

MRS. MERCY: [*Wearily*] I can hardly put through a report to the Controller, informing him of your allegation that you were bitten by two nuns!

JUNE: No, well, you could say—

MRS. MERCY: Let's be practical, Sister George—we're concerned with retaining the trust and respect of the public. Now people understand perfectly well that artists frequently work under great emotional stress. We do all we can to gloss over the minor disciplinary offences. But we simply cannot tolerate this sort of behavior. It's things like this which make people resent paying more for their wireless licences! Thousands of pounds spent on public relations, and you jeopardize it all with your reckless and foolish actions. Really, Sister George, we have reason to be very, very angry with you.

JUNE: [*Beaten*] What do you want me to do?

MRS. MERCY: You must write a letter immediately to the Mother Superior. You must sincerely apologize for your behavior and I suggest you offer a small donation for some charity connected with the Convent. Then you must send a copy of your letter to the Director of Religious Broadcasting, with a covering note from you, couched in suitable terms.

JUNE: You mean humbling myself.

ALICE: Don't worry, Mrs. Mercy. I'll see she does it and I'll make quite sure she doesn't get into any mischief in the future.

MRS. MERCY: There speaks a true friend. [*To* JUNE] You're very lucky to have someone like Miss McNaught to rely on. Treasure her.

JUNE: [*Bitterly*] I'll treasure her, all right!

ALICE: I'll see to it that the letters are written and sent off right away!

MRS. MERCY: [*Rising*] Good. That's what I like to hear. [*To* JUNE] I'll leave you in Miss McNaught's expert charge.

JUNE: What about Applehurst?

MRS. MERCY: [*Non-committally*] That's another, rather more complex problem . . .

JUNE: But . . . has anything been decided about the future?

MRS. MERCY: I'm afraid I can't say anything about that at the moment.

JUNE: It comes as a bit of a shock to me, you know, all this.

MRS. MERCY: It comes as a bit of a shock to me too, I assure you—especially as I understand that you often open church bazaars—

ALICE: I'll look after her—I'll keep her away from convents.

MRS. MERCY: You keep her on a tight rein, and all will be well.

ALICE: Of course I will. Between us we'll keep her in order.

MRS. MERCY: She won't have a chance, will she?

JUNE: Look here—I'm sorry—you know—if I've been a bad boy.

MRS. MERCY: [*Turning to* JUNE *and shaking hands*] Well, good-bye, dear Sister George. Keep your chin up. Things are never as bad as they seem—

JUNE: [*Listlessly, in her country accent*] Every cloud has a silver lining . . .

MRS. MERCY: That's the spirit! And—[*Whispering confidentially*] No more walk-outs at rehearsals, eh? If you have any complaints do come and see me about them.

JUNE: [*In her country accent*] Well, it's the creaking gate that gets oiled . . .

MRS. MERCY: [*Reflecting for a moment*] A somewhat unfortunate simile . . . [*To* ALICE] So nice to have met you—

ALICE: Nice to have met *you*, Mrs. Mercy. What's the subject of your talk tomorrow? Is it a secret, or are you allowed to tell?

MRS. MERCY: [*Smiling graciously*] It's family planning this week—and foundation garments next!

> [*She sails out, followed by* ALICE. JUNE *nervously lights a cheroot. There are sounds of conversation from outside, then the front door closes.* ALICE *returns and gives* JUNE *a meaningful look*]

ALICE: Well!

JUNE: [*Alarmed*] Did she say anything? Did she drop any hints behind my back?

ALICE: No. Just general comments—you know—about nuns in taxis.

JUNE: What do you mean?

ALICE: Nuns. You know, n-u-n-s. Brides of Christ.

JUNE: Oh, I see, that's what's biting you.

ALICE: [*In an outburst*] How could you! How could you make such an exhibition of yourself!

JUNE: For heaven's sake, Childie, grow up. Don't be so bloody . . . *squeamish*.

ALICE: [*Primly*] I think you owe me some sort of explanation.

JUNE: [*Chuckling*] All those petticoats . . .

ALICE: It's the sort of thing you used to do when I first knew you. In that Club in Notting Hill Gate: I remember how you used to go clomping about, without a bra, hitting girls over the head.

JUNE: Kindly keep those foul-mouthed recollections to yourself. In my young days . . .

ALICE: Your young days were spent in a cul-de-sac in Aldershot, with the Band of Hope on one side and the foot clinic on the other. You told me so yourself.

JUNE: How dare you. This is a respectable house—and don't forget who's paying the rent!

ALICE: Not much longer, perhaps.

JUNE: They wouldn't dare get rid of me because of this . . . of this trivial incident . . .

ALICE: [*Imitating* JUNE's *country accent*] We none of us know what the future holds for us.

JUNE: [*After a pause, puffing on her cigar*] I'm worried. I really am worried, Childie. Please, do me a favor . . .

ALICE: What?

JUNE: Go and ask Madame Xenia to come up. She's an expert on the future.

ALICE: She's probably got a client—

JUNE: Maybe she's between appointments. Go on.

ALICE: I can't just barge in—

JUNE: Why not? You've done it before. Remember when I was bitten by that Lakeland terrier and you thought I had the rabies! She always knows what's going to happen. Go on.

ALICE: Oh.

JUNE: This is an emergency. Extreme measures must be taken at once! Go and get her at once!

ALICE: I can't. She hates my guts.

JUNE: Madame Xenia? Why?

ALICE: She thinks I'm after her lodger. [JUNE *rises menacingly*] It's complete fantasy.

JUNE: [*Ominously, in the voice of Sister George*] There's no smoke without fire!

ALICE: Just like the last one you scared off.

JUNE: I could see which way the wind was blowing. I nipped it in the bud.

ALICE: I only helped him with his homework. He was a mere boy.

JUNE: [*Decisively*] There's nothing mere about boys . . . Now go and fetch her at once and watch your step.

ALICE: [*Going*] You've always got to have someone doing your dirty work.

JUNE: Thanks, you're a pal. [ALICE *goes.* JUNE *reads the inscription on a frame on the table*] ". . . and for your devoted work and care for the old and sick."

[*She gets out the envelope from behind the cushion. Looks at it, puts it back*]

ALICE: [*Offstage*] I'm sorry to drag you away . . .

MADAME XENIA: That's all right. I know. I know. George! [*Enter* MADAME XENIA, *a hawk-faced, elderly lady of foreign origin, henna-ed and hung with beads.* ALICE *follows*] George? Darling? What is the matter?

ALICE: Madame was in the middle of a consultation with a client—

JUNE: Oh, I *am* sorry.

MADAME XENIA: Never mind. You are my friend. Always you come first. Now, darling, what's the trouble?

JUNE: Madame Xenia, I'm worried out of my wits . . . it's the BBC. They're driving me mad—

MADAME XENIA: They will suffer for it. I will put curses on them. [*Professionally*] Sit down; make yourself at home.

JUNE: Thanks.

MADAME XENIA: I forget; I always say it to people to make them relax. Right— [*To* JUNE] Would you draw the curtains, please?

JUNE: [*Goes to draw the curtains*] Certainly.

MADAME XENIA: [*To* ALICE] And you: will you please sit facing the East?

ALICE: Which way's the East?

MADAME XENIA: [*Pointing*] There. Towards Great Portland Street.

ALICE: [*Sitting*] Yes, of course.

MADAME XENIA: [*Facing* JUNE] I require a personal possession from you—[JUNE *looks startled*]—to hold in my hand. To connect with your vibrations. Anything—a piece of jewelry—

JUNE: I don't wear jewelry. Will a hanky do?

MADAME XENIA: [*Taking* JUNE's *handkerchief*] Beautiful. Now, to work . . . First, a warning. Next week will be tough for Sagittarians. Mars is in conjunction with Venus. And I don't have to tell you what that means. [*She sits down and shuffles a pack of cards*] Cut the cards.

JUNE: [*Cutting the cards*] All right?

MADAME XENIA: Again. [JUNE *cuts again*] And once more, just for luck—

ALICE: —as the bishop said to the actress.

JUNE: [*Sternly*] We can dispense with observations from the East.

MADAME XENIA: [*Scrutinizing the cards*] A short journey to

see a friend; a pleasant surprise; unexpected money; the Queen of Spades—a woman in black you do not like?

ALICE: The Mother Superior?

JUNE: Shut up!

MADAME XENIA: Whoever it is—keep out of her way—she's no good to you.

JUNE: [Stuttering] What—what is she going to do?

MADAME XENIA: [Consulting the cards] She's asking you to a big do.

JUNE: [Incredulous] The Mother Superior?

[ALICE giggles]

MADAME XENIA: I see lots of people, lots of drink, dancing . . .

ALICE: [Brightly] I know! It's not the convent—it's the drag ball at Richmond!

MADAME XENIA: [She continues laying the cards] Maybe a slight emotional upset—nothing serious. You hear of a broken romantic association . . . You catch a cold. A very bad cold!

JUNE: [Alarmed] When?

MADAME XENIA: [Thoughtfully] Maybe it's because I'm holding your handkerchief . . . Forget the cold. What else—?

[She looks at the cards again]

JUNE: My career . . .

MADAME XENIA: I can see a red-headed man.

JUNE: Ginger the pubkeeper! What's he doing?

MADAME XENIA: I'm afraid it's not very clear . . . Ah! I see a letter—a very important letter . . .

ALICE: [Suddenly remembering] The envelope!

JUNE: [Jumping up, panic-stricken] The envelope!

ALICE and JUNE: [Gasping] The envelope . . .

MADAME XENIA: [Helpfully] It could be a postcard.

ALICE: [*Snatches the hidden letter from behind the cushion. To* JUNE] Here it is! Do you want to open it?

JUNE: [*Anguished*] No.

ALICE: Let's send it back to her, tell her she must have dropped it out of her bag.

JUNE: No, no. It's fallen into our hands; we'd better read it.

MADAME XENIA: May I see the envelope?

JUNE: Yes, of course. Do you—do you get any . . . vibrations?

MADAME XENIA: [*Carefully*] Mmm . . . It's difficult to say. It could mean one of two things . . .

JUNE: [*Squaring her shoulders*] Give it to me! I'm going to open it. [*She takes the envelope from* MADAME XENIA, *and tears it open*] What must be, must be . . . [*She glances at the contents, and collapses onto the settee*] Oh, my God!

ALICE: [*Rushing to comfort her*] George! What's the matter? George! [JUNE *remains impassive;* MADAME XENIA *has taken the letter and looks at it*] What does it say?

MADAME XENIA: "Memo from Audience Research. Latest Popularity Ratings: Sister George 64.5 per cent. Ginger Hopkins 68."

JUNE: That's the weapon they've been waiting for. Now they'll kill me.

CURTAIN

ACT TWO

SCENE ONE

A week later. It is 4 A.M. By the dim light of a table lamp JUNE *can be discerned, sitting at the table. She is wearing a dressing gown; in front of her is a tumbler and a bottle of gin. She is roused from her torpor by the ringing of an alarm clock in the bedroom.*

JUNE: [*Startled*] What . . . ? It must be morning . . . I must have dropped off . . . [*Calling*] Childie! Rise and shine— that's if you persist in this ridiculous enterprise! Childie? I'm in the living room.

ALICE: [*Dressed only in brassière and pants, carrying a bundle of clothing in her arms, comes running in. She throws her clothes on the settee, and attacks* JUNE] Pinch, punch, first of the month!

JUNE: [*Jumping up*] Are you out of your mind?

ALICE: [*Squashed*] It's the first of the month . . . October . . .

JUNE: You could have given me a heart attack.

ALICE: Sorry.

JUNE: Gawd Almighty . . . What's the time?

ALICE: Ten to four.

JUNE: When are you supposed to get there?

ALICE: There's no rush; the gang gets there at about five. Have you made out your list?

JUNE: No.

ALICE: [*Annoyed*] Well, why didn't you? Are you sure you don't want me to try for *Swan Lake*?

JUNE: Positive. I can't stand those bloody little cygnets prancing about—in their tutus—

ALICE: All right, all right. Nobody's forcing you.

JUNE: [*Rising, stretching out her arms*] My sympathy's entirely with Von Rothbart—

ALICE: I'll just try for *Giselle* then.

JUNE: Yeah, you try. And *Petrushka*; don't forget *Petrushka*.

ALICE: You told me last night you didn't want to see *Petrushka!*

JUNE: Did I? Well, I changed my mind . . .

ALICE: [*Exasperated, getting hold of the program*] Oh, you are a nuisance! I'd put a tick against *Petrushka* and then I crossed it out, and now I've got to put a tick again . . . and now I can't find it—

JUNE: You're annoying me, you know . . . Stop getting so . . . so het-up about your bloody ballet.

ALICE: It's all very well for you to talk—you'll be sitting at home. There's a big queue, and if you don't know what to ask for—

JUNE: You've got hours to decide what to ask for! You're only queuing for your queue tickets now.

ALICE: I know. But we've all got our lists. Anyway, there's no certainty that we get what we ask for: you only get so many for Fonteyn and Nureyev—

JUNE: In that case: why make a list?

ALICE: [*On the brink of hysteria*] You've got to ask for it first, even if you don't get it!

JUNE: You'll get something you're *not* asking for in a minute.

ALICE: Anyway, it wouldn't have hurt you to have come with me. You're up.

JUNE: I wouldn't be seen dead with that mob. What a collection!

ALICE: There's nothing wrong with them. They're very nice, the regulars, I've known some of them for fifteen years. Do you know: there's a woman there who follows Anya Linden everywhere . . .

JUNE: *Everywhere?*

ALICE: Oh, shut up.

JUNE: Anyway, I did come with you one day—remember? Never again. All that gossip and name-dropping—

ALICE: The only reason you didn't like it was because you were embarrassed by the lorry-driver.

JUNE: What lorry-driver?

ALICE: The one that called at you, "That's a nice pair of head-lamps."

JUNE: I had totally forgotten. Besides, he was paying me a compliment—unlike the gentleman in Soho, who suggested that you should wear a pair of sunglasses for a brassière!

ALICE: Don't be disgusting.

JUNE: [*Jeering*] You're my flatmate in more senses than one.

ALICE: [*Incensed*] George, don't drink any more.

JUNE: [*Dangerously*] Mind your own business.

ALICE: Night after night I find you sitting up—with the bottle of gin and that old press-cuttings book. And then you wonder why you're tired.

JUNE: I can't sleep.

ALICE: You don't try. You must try to relax, to unwind—

JUNE: [*Imitating her caustically*] Relax! Unwind! It's easy for you to talk—

ALICE: You've been impossible ever since that day Mrs. Mercy came to tea—

JUNE: Well, I'm more impossible since I ran into her again yesterday.

ALICE: Where?

JUNE: At BH.

ALICE: Was she friendly?

JUNE: She smiled at me—with the same expression as my old cat Tiddles had when she used to look in a goldfish bowl. Until one Sunday my parents and I came home from church, and there on the table lay the goldfish—all five of them—neatly laid out, like sardines . . .

ALICE: Did she . . . say anything to you?

JUNE: I'll show you what she did. Get up. Go on, stand up a minute. [ALICE *stands up*] You're me. I was just coming out from the studio, on my way to the canteen, when I turned a corner rather sharply, and ran slap into her. Go on—bump into me.

ALICE: No, I don't want to do that.

JUNE: Don't be soppy . . . Go on—bump into me! [ALICE *brushes against* JUNE] Oh, God help us! No, properly, stupid. Hard. Try again.

ALICE: I've got to go in a minute.

JUNE: You'll bloody well stay till I've done with you. Now then —you're coming down the corridor. [*She claps her hands*] Start!

ALICE: [*Takes a run, bumps into* JUNE, *and floors her*] Sorry!

JUNE: [*Rises*] "Oh, it's you." [*She surveys her with Mrs. Mercy's half-smile*] "Chin up, Sister George." [*She pats her arm, and walks past her*] Chin up, indeed, the lousy old cow. You noticed the way she patted my arm—as if to say: "Sorry, it can't be helped."

ALICE: You're imagining things again.

JUNE: She's been avoiding me, I tell you, and I know why . . .

ALICE: She was probably in a hurry to get somewhere. A committee meeting or something.

JUNE: They've had that. And I found out what happened.

ALICE: [*Alarmed*] What?

JUNE: I've been written out of next Tuesday's episode.

ALICE: What?

JUNE: Are you deaf? I said—

ALICE: I heard. So what—it's happened before. Every time you go on holiday—

JUNE: But I'm not going on holiday, am I? [ALICE *is silent*] Sister George is confined to her bed . . . with a bad cold . . .

ALICE: That in itself—

JUNE: [*Cutting her short*] That in itself could mean it's a dress rehearsal for my extinction.

ALICE: Nothing of the sort.

JUNE: They want to see what it sounds like without me . . . if I am expendable . . .

ALICE: What about the following episodes?

JUNE: [*Grimly*] We shall know soon. The new scripts are due in the post this morning. I can see what's going to happen. That cold's going to get worse—I can feel it in my bones. It'll turn into bronchitis, then pneumonia, and before I know where I am I shall be out like a light.

ALICE: [*Only half-convinced*] You are making a mountain out of a molehill. You've missed episodes before . . . it's nothing to lose sleep over—

JUNE: That's what you think . . . Anyway, I'm not the only one.

ALICE: What do you mean?

JUNE: Did you know that you talk in your sleep?

ALICE: I don't.

JUNE: You do. I heard you distinctly. Last night and again tonight. You woke me up.

ALICE: [*Nervously*] What did I say?

JUNE: You were tossing about, and mumbling something. And then out it came, loud and clear.

ALICE: [*Unconvinced*] What?

JUNE: [*In a plaintive, high-pitched voice*] "Take me!"

ALICE: You're lying!

JUNE: [*As before*] "Take me, Isadore!"

ALICE: That's a filthy lie, and you know it!

JUNE: The "Isadore" wasn't any too distinct: it might have been another name.

ALICE: I don't believe a word of this.

JUNE: [*More in sorrow than in anger*] You're having an affair with someone, aren't you?

ALICE: I wish I were.

JUNE: [*Crushed*] That was very . . . unkind.

ALICE: Well, you asked for it. Always nagging me. Even if I did shout "Take me" in my sleep—and I am not aware of it—

JUNE: You couldn't be: you were asleep at the time.

ALICE: All right: even if I did, it might have meant "Take me for a walk" or [*Brightly*]—"Take me to the ballet!"

JUNE: A likely story!

ALICE: You always put the nastiest interpretation on what people say.

JUNE: In nine cases out of ten it's true. [*Sipping her gin*] Are you making yourself some breakfast?

ALICE: Just a cup of coffee. I usually have a hot pie later on with the gang. In one of the workmen's cafés. It's ever such fun, really! You get the ballet crowd and the night shift from Covent Garden market all mixing together.

JUNE: Sounds scintillating.

ALICE: It's ever so lively. Why don't you get dressed and come? They'd be thrilled to see you, and everyone would ask for your autograph!

JUNE: [*High-pitched*] "Take me!"

ALICE: Oh, George!

JUNE: No, you run along and enjoy yourself . . . I'm all right where I am . . . waiting for the scripts to arrive.

ALICE: I don't know what's the matter with you just lately! You've become really . . . morbid. You used to be such fun.

JUNE: What are you talking about? We're going to the fancy dress ball tonight, aren't we? I bet it'll be you who'll be tired and wan tonight—after getting up at this unearthly hour!

ALICE: I'm glad you said that. I must take my iron pills. That'll help to keep me awake!

[*She takes a bottle from the sideboard, shakes a pill out and swallows it*]

JUNE: Let me see them.

ALICE: What for?

JUNE: [*Emphatically*] Let me see them!

ALICE: [*Handing her the bottle*] All right . . .

JUNE: [*Examining it*] Why doesn't it say what they are? [ALICE *looks nonplussed*] There's no name on the label!

ALICE: I don't know.

JUNE: [*Scrutinizing it*] All it says—[*She has difficulty in deciphering the writing in the dark*]—is 'One to be taken every day, as prescribed'. [*She sniffs the bottle*] I don't believe these are iron pills at all . . . They're those birth pills—

ALICE: Oh, really? Dr. Kunjaghari gave them to me. Why don't you go and ask him?

JUNE: [*Viciously*] Because I don't trust Dr. Kunjaghari, that's why. He's a quack. He's like those Indians who come to the door in a turban, flogging brass bangles for rheumatism!

ALICE: Perhaps you'd like to have them chemically analyzed.

JUNE: It would shake you if I did, wouldn't it?

ALICE: You can do what you like—you'd only make yourself ridiculous. Like that time you rang at the office, pretending to be Mrs. Katz.

JUNE: It served its purpose—it gave him a fright!

ALICE: It very nearly got me the sack. He knew it was you.

JUNE: He couldn't prove it.

ALICE: He's a solicitor—he could prove anything! [*Rummaging among her clothes*] Can't find my socks.

JUNE: I say—[*Regarding her benignly*] Seeing you in black pants reminds me of the army. We all had to wear regulation black woollen pants. We used to refer to them as black-outs. One day, a chap came to talk to us on the subject, "What not to do with our black-outs down." He couldn't understand why we kept giggling . . .

ALICE: [*Putting on her socks*] Found them!

JUNE: Your legs are unusually white—luminous white. Loo-minous . . . I don't think I've ever seen such white legs.

ALICE: They don't get much sun on them.

JUNE: There's something uniquely touching about white legs . . . especially when they are loo-minous white . . . You're very pale altogether. You're anaemic—you ought to take iron pills. [ALICE *throws her a meaningful glance*] I mean proper pills . . . not that muck.

[*She pours herself another gin*]

ALICE: Haven't you had enough?

JUNE: [*Quickly*] No. [*Chuckling, raising her glass*] To absent friends. Your health, albino mice!

ALICE: You *are* naughty.

JUNE: Say that again.

ALICE: What?

JUNE: What you just said.

ALICE: You *are* naughty?

JUNE: That's it. The same inflection. Takes me back years . . .

ALICE: You mean—

JUNE: When we first met—in Mrs. Goodbody's tastefully furnished bedsitters . . . I used to watch you come and go—for weeks I watched you—and never said a word to you.

ALICE: You were different then—you hadn't become famous.

JUNE: Every morning I used to watch you go to work. Punctually at ten past nine every morning. You were always in a rush.

ALICE: I had to get on the underground at twenty past—

JUNE: Often you were in such a hurry you would fall over the doorstep; or, if it had been raining, you'd come slithering out, shouting "Oops"—

ALICE: I had no idea you were watching me.

JUNE: One night, I went into the bathroom just after you'd had a bath. The mirrors were all steamed up, and the bath-mat was moist and glistening where you'd stood on it. There was a smell of talcum powder and of bath crystals—it was like an enchanted wood . . . I stood quite still on that mat —in your footsteps—and I saw that you'd left your comb behind. It was a small pink plastic comb, and it had your hairs in it. I took that comb back to my room and kept it as a souvenir . . . And all this time I'd never spoken a word to you . . .

ALICE: You soon made up for it.

JUNE: That night your boy friend saw you home . . . I knew I'd have to strike quickly.

ALICE: That was Roger. He wanted to marry me.

JUNE: [Bitterly] That's what they all said—and you fell for it, silly goose.

ALICE: Some of them meant it; Roger meant it.

JUNE: What are you talking about? Roger was already married!

ALICE: [Adamantly] He still meant it. I liked Roger; he had a ginger moustache . . .

JUNE: What a lot of rubbish. His moustache was ginger because he used to singe it with his cigarettes—you told me so yourself. You told me that being kissed by him tasted all sort of burnt and beery.

ALICE: I might have had babies . . .

[Long pause]

JUNE: [Quietly] You haven't been lonely, exactly.

ALICE: [Changing the subject] There's a performance of Petrushka on the nineteenth. I might try for that.

JUNE: [Suddenly] Shh! Shh! Was that the post?

ALICE: At this time in the morning? It won't be here for hours yet. You really ought to go to bed . . .

[There is a pause]

JUNE: [Seriously] They're driving me round the bend.

ALICE: You're driving yourself round the bend! Why don't you go to bed?

JUNE: Because I can't sleep.

ALICE: Shall I get you some hot milk?

JUNE: Urghh!

ALICE: You'll catch a cold, you know, sitting up like this.

JUNE: I've already got a cold.

ALICE: Well, keep your throat covered up, then. Put your dressing gown on properly. It's time we got you a new one—this collar is all frayed . . . come on, tuck it in . . . I'll put some new braid on it tomorrow . . . there, better?

JUNE: Thanks.

ALICE: Shall I put the bottle away?

JUNE: No, I just want to hold it for a moment.

ALICE: I ought to be going—it's half past four. Will you be all right?

JUNE: Childie, they won't do it, will they? They *can't*, after all I've done for them.

ALICE: Of course they can't, George. You must stop brooding about it, you'll make yourself ill. Why don't you go to bed and sleep it off? You can set the alarm to wake you for rehearsal.

JUNE: There's no rehearsal tomorrow.

ALICE: All right, then. Good. You can get a nice long rest. Now, George, I've got to go.

JUNE: No, wait a minute—

ALICE: Oh, George, they'll be waiting for me, I'll be at the back of the queue.

JUNE: You can't go like *that*, you know.

ALICE: Like what?

JUNE: [*Pointing to the knapsack*] You're not going on a hike, you know. Mind you: donkeys are best for loading.

ALICE: There's only a change of clothing in it, to take to the office. And a few provisions. Please, may I go now?

JUNE: Did you speak?

ALICE: Yes, I said, "May I go now?"

JUNE: [*Considering the request*] Not before you have made your obeisance to me in the proper manner.

ALICE: [*Alarmed*] What do you mean?

JUNE: [*Breathing heavily and alcoholically for a few moments*] Kiss the hem of my garment. [*With an imperious gesture*] On your knees. Go on! Down, boy, down!

[*She snaps her fingers*]

ALICE: [*Picks up her knapsack, looks at her watch, and shrugs her shoulders*] Oh, all right.

[*She goes on her knees*]

JUNE: Now repeat after me: I hereby solemnly swear—

ALICE: [*Mechanically*] I hereby solemnly swear—

JUNE: That I will not allow—

ALICE: That I will not allow—

JUNE: Anybody whosoever, including Mr. Katz, gratification of his fleshly instincts with me today or at any other time.

ALICE: [*Quickly*] All right, all right, I swear.

JUNE: Mind you remember, or may the curse of Satan fall on your head!

ALICE: [*Quickly reiterating*] That's one *Giselle*, one *Petrushka*, and no *Lac*—

JUNE: [*With enormous effort*] Rien de Lac de Cygnes. C'est juste [*Holds on to* ALICE's *scarf*] mon petit chou.

ALICE: George, let go. Let go!

JUNE: What's this?

ALICE: What?

JUNE: [*Looking at the label on scarf*] This isn't yours, is it? Where did you get it?

ALICE: George, give it back.

JUNE: Who is J. V. S. Partridge?

ALICE: A young Liberal. Satisfied?

JUNE: Far, far from satisfied. How long have you been entangled with this—youth?

ALICE: He's not a youth. He's forty-six.

JUNE: Bit long in the tooth for a young Liberal? [*Fiercely*] Who is he?

ALICE: The chap downstairs, daftie. Madame Xenia's lodger.

JUNE: Ah—I thought there was some monkey business going on.

ALICE: There is not. I've only ever seen him twice.

JUNE: How did you get his scarf, then?

ALICE: I pinched it off the hall-stand.

JUNE: D'you expect me to believe that?

ALICE: Look, George. I've never even spoken to him. It's nothing.

JUNE: That's what you said when you went off with that estate agent for a week-end in Birmingham.

ALICE: That was five years ago—

JUNE: It happened once—it can happen again—

ALICE: [*Almost screaming*] Nothing happened!

JUNE: What?

ALICE: *Nothing!*

JUNE: Well, nothing's going to happen with this one. I forbid you to speak to him again.

ALICE: You're raving mad. He's a neighbor, there's no harm in being friendly.

JUNE: [*Shouting*] I forbid you to speak to him, do you hear?

ALICE: [*Shouting back*] I'll flipping well speak to him if I want to—why shouldn't I?

JUNE: [*Venomously*] You fancy him, don't you?

ALICE: He seems perfectly agreeable—[*Sees* JUNE's *face contorted with suspicion*] Yes, I do fancy him—he's a dish. [JUNE *threatens her*] You keep away from me—you've no right to—

JUNE: I've got every right.

ALICE: I'm not married to you, you know. [*Long pause*] I'm sorry, George, but you asked for it.

JUNE: You'd better run along, you'll be late.

ALICE: Look after yourself! Don't forget the party tonight!

[*Exits*]

JUNE: [*Alone, wanders about the room. Surveys the scene for a few moments, swaying slightly. Then pulling a chair center stage*] Ah, there's my beautiful bike. Mornin', old friend! Just get you started in a minute. [*She sits astride it, and makes a purring noise to indicate the start of the engine*] Prrrrrrrrrrrrrrr —prr—prrr—[*She waves*] 'Bye Jean, 'Bye Rosie, tell your dad to look after his gammy leg! Prrrr—prrrr—[*She starts singing*] "Oh God, our help in ages past"—prr—prr—"Our hope for years to come,"—Prrr—prrrr—Morning, Ginger, morning, Vicar, you're up early today—prrr—prrr—first call old Mrs. Hinch— prrrr—prrrr—"Be thou our guard while troubles last"—prr— prr—"And our eternal"—prrr—"home."

THE CURTAIN QUICKLY FALLS

SCENE TWO

Later, the same day.
The stage is empty when the curtain rises. Laughter and shrieks can be heard from offstage.

JUNE: [*Imperiously, offstage*] Pull yourself together. Try again, and this time do it properly!

ALICE: [*Offstage*] I can't promise I'll get it right.

[*The well-known signature tune of Laurel and Hardy is heard, laboriously played on the flute.* ALICE *and* JUNE *enter, in the costume of Laurel and Hardy*]

JUNE: [*Imitating* HARDY] And what, may I ask, are you supposed to be doing?

ALICE: Nothing, Olly, just playing . . . a tune . . .

JUNE: May I suggest that you stop playing a tune . . . and get on with the next bit. A-one, a-two.

JUNE and ALICE: [*Doing a soft-shoe dance, side by side*] "By the light—dum da dum da dum—of the silvery moon—dum da dum —I used to—rum dum da dum da dum da dum—with my honey and—La da da. By the light—"

[ALICE *bumps into* JUNE]

JUNE: What was the meaning of that?

[*Hits* ALICE *with her bowler hat*]

ALICE: Nothing, Olly—I was only—practicing—

JUNE: [*Turning away in dismay, fluttering her tie*] Oh, fiddlesticks . . .

ALICE: Did you say "fiddlesticks"?

[*She rams the flute into* JUNE]

JUNE: [*Forgetting her impersonation*] Ouch, that hurt! That was not funny!

ALICE: [*Giggling*] Sorry, Olly.

JUNE: [*Giving* ALICE *a great swipe*] Sorry, Stan.

ALICE: [*As herself*] That hurt!

JUNE: [*In the best Hardy manner, dusting her hands*] Let that be a lesson to you!

[*She turns away, beaming*]

ALICE: [*Again rams the flute against* JUNE. JUNE *seizes it viciously*] Be careful, it's Miss Broadbent's—

JUNE: [*Only half acting*] A very useful instrument.

[*She hits* ALICE *over the head with it—fortunately she has the bowler on*]

ALICE: [*Squaring up to* JUNE, *making sounds of frustrated rage*] You, oh . . .

JUNE: [*Under her breath*] That's not Laurel, daftie, that's the Three Stooges!

ALICE: Sorry, Olly. [*Brightly*] Olly—

JUNE: Yep?

ALICE: Give me your hat.

JUNE: What for, Stan?

ALICE: I just want to look at something.

JUNE: [*Thrusting her hat at* ALICE] O.K. [ALICE *spits on it, and puts it on* JUNE'S *head again.* JUNE, *as herself*] What was that supposed to be?

ALICE: [*As herself*] Don't know. Just an idea. Horseplay, you know . . . We're celebrating because you're back in the series, aren't we?

JUNE: [*With an evil glint in her eye*] Just because the script-writers have cured my cold . . . there's no need to go raving, bloody mad you know.

ALICE: I thought it was funny.

JUNE: You thought it was funny?

ALICE: Yes, I thought it was funny.

JUNE: You thought it was funny. Stan.

ALICE: Yes, Olly?

JUNE: Give me your hat.

ALICE: What for?

JUNE: I just want to look at something. Look up there, Stan.

ALICE: There's nothing up there, Olly.

JUNE: Try this, then, Stan.

[ALICE *hands over her bowler:* JUNE *with a righteous nod of the head goes to the table and squirts soda into* ALICE'S *hat.* ALICE *stands, unconcernedly twiddling her thumbs.* JUNE *returns, and places the hat, brimful with soda water, on* ALICE]

ALICE: You fool—now you've spoilt my costume!

[*She attacks* JUNE, *pummelling her with her fists*]

JUNE: [*Keeping her at arm's length*] Steady, now. Steady.

ALICE: What was the point of that?

JUNE: Just an idea. Horseplay, you know.

ALICE: You are rotten. I'm all wet. Now I'll have to change.

JUNE: Nonsense, woman. A drop of good clear water never did anybody any harm.

ALICE: All right.

[*She takes some flowers out of a vase, and approaches* JUNE, *menacingly holding the vase*]

JUNE: Don't come near me! I warn you: keep away.

ALICE: I want to show you something, Olly.

JUNE: Childie, stop it. Be your age.

[*She backs away*]

ALICE: Take your punishment like a man!

JUNE: [*Shouting*] All right. [*She stands stock-still, squaring her shoulders*] Go on—what are you waiting for?

[*They laugh, and struggle with the vase*]

ALICE: [*Losing her nerve*] Never mind.

[*She puts the vase on the table*]

JUNE: Go on—I'm not afraid of a drop of water! Ugh, you're like a marshmallow.

[*The doorbell rings*]

ALICE: It's Madame Xenia, to fetch us. She's ordered a cab. She's early.

JUNE: Well, don't stand and gape. Open the door!

[*She propels* ALICE *to the door with a kick*]

ALICE: [*Offstage*] Oh! Oh, I'm sorry . . . We were expecting—

[*She ushers in* MRS. MERCY CROFT]

MRS. MERCY: I'm sorry to intrude. I do hope it's not inconvenient . . .

JUNE: [*Taken aback*] Not at all. I'm sorry we're . . .

MRS. MERCY: Playing charades?

ALICE: As a matter of fact, we were just getting ready to go out— to a fancy dress ball.

JUNE: Ball—fancy—

MRS. MERCY: Oh, I'll come back another time when it's more convenient. Perhaps Miss Buckridge could come to see me tomorrow morning, before rehearsal?

JUNE: We're not in a rush. We can talk now. Would you have a drink?

MRS. MERCY: No thank you.

ALICE: [*Cordially*] Do sit down, Mrs. Mercy.

MRS. MERCY: Thank you, dear.

JUNE: If you had telephoned a little earlier—

MRS. MERCY: *I know.* It's most remiss of me, turning up unexpectedly like this. Actually, I've come straight from a meeting —felt I had to see you personally.

ALICE: [*Anxiously*] The nuns?

MRS. MERCY: Oh, didn't the office tell you? We had a most charming communication from the Mother Superior. All is forgiven. But there's still the matter of the charity.

JUNE: What charity?

ALICE: The donation you promised to give to the convent.

JUNE: Oh, that!

MRS. MERCY: It's only obliquely mentioned in the letter—

JUNE: [*With a wry smile*] I didn't expect her to forget about it. [*To* ALICE] Remind me to send her a check tomorrow. It'll keep her Irish novices in hair shirts!

MRS. MERCY: Very nice of you, Miss Buckridge. I'm relieved to see the matter settled.

JUNE: [*Going to the cigarette box*] May I offer you a small cigar?

MRS. MERCY: Oh, no . . . no, thank you. I gave up smoking years ago.

JUNE: You don't mind if I smoke?

MRS. MERCY: Well . . .

ALICE: [*Chiding*] You smoke far too much!

JUNE: [*With a mock bow*] Thank you for your touching concern.

MRS. MERCY: Well now, I'm afraid I have some bad news for you, Miss Buckridge.

JUNE: Bad news . . . ?

MRS. MERCY: You're the first to be told. It's only just been decided; or rather, it's only just received the official stamp of approval . . .

ALICE: [*Terrified*] You can't mean—

JUNE: Be quiet, Childie.

MRS. MERCY: Yes. I'm sorry, Miss Buckridge: it's the end of Sister George.

[*There is a stunned pause*]

ALICE: [*Suddenly shouting*] But why? Why?

MRS. MERCY: Believe me, dear Miss Buckridge, the decision is no reflection on your ability as an actress. You created a character that has become a nation-wide favorite.

ALICE: [*Still incredulous*] But why kill her?

MRS. MERCY: Why do some of our nearest and dearest have to die? Because that's life. In Applehurst we try to re-create the flavor of life, as it is lived in hundreds of English villages—

ALICE: But she's the most popular character in it!

MRS. MERCY: [*Slightly uncomfortable*] I know. The BBC took
that into consideration. They felt—and I must say I concurred
—that only some dramatic event, something that would get
into the news headlines, could save Applehurst. We felt that
in their grief, robbed of one of their greatest favorites, listeners
would return again to Applehurst with a new loyalty, with a—

JUNE: [*Interrupting dully*] How?

MRS. MERCY: [*Quietly*] It's not for another fortnight. It's scheduled for the twelfth.

JUNE: But how?

MRS. MERCY: [*Smiling benignly*] It's just an ordinary morning
at Applehurst. The chaffinch on Sister George's window wakes
her up as usual and is rewarded with its daily saucerful of
crumbs—

JUNE: [*Under her breath, automatically*] Hello, Dicky . . .

MRS. MERCY: Up in the road, in the Old Mill Farm, young
Jimmy Bromley, the scamp, wakes up with a cough and
doesn't want to go to school. "We'd better get Sister George
in," says his mother—and he's up in a jiffy! Meanwhile, punctual
to the minute, Sister George finishes her breakfast and packs
a basketful of preserves and cottage cheese for old Mrs. Hinch,
in bed with bronchitis. On with her bonnet and cape, and
off she goes, striding purposefully through the autumn leaves—
sound effects here—to the bicycle shed. The bolts are pushed
back, and the door creaks open, and there's her prized possession—the motorbike.

JUNE: Good morning, old friend.

MRS. MERCY: Whiz—pop—the engine starts—and away she goes!
Pop-pop-pop-pop . . . "Hurry up, Jimmy, you'll be late for
school . . ." she calls out. "Tell Mrs. Pemberton to give you
plenty of homework to keep you out of mischief!" "I will,"
the boy calls back—adding, as she drives out of earshot—
"I don't think!"

JUNE: Cheeky little beggar!

MRS. MERCY: A chorus of greetings follow her as she heads
out into the open country—the wind billowing in her cape—
and bursts, as usual, into a snatch of her favorite hymn:

"O God, Our Help in Ages Past." Honk-honk answers her hooter in a merry descant as she turns into Oakmead Road, and then—BANG! [*She claps her hands*] Collision with a ten-ton truck.

JUNE: Oh, my God . . .

ALICE: Is it—is it . . .

MRS. MERCY: *Instantaneous.* Never regains consciousness.

ALICE: [*Has started to cry*] You can't, you can't . . .

MRS. MERCY: It so happens that your death will coincide with Road Safety Week: a cause which we know has been close to you for many years.

JUNE: [*Recovering slightly*] I've never ridden carelessly. [*Rising*] I protest—

MRS. MERCY: [*Anxious to placate her*] I know, I know. We're taking great care to establish it's the lorry driver's fault.

JUNE: [*Unconvinced*] But even so—a ten-ton truck . . .

MRS. MERCY: I'm sorry, but there it is.

JUNE: [*With dignity*] I think I have a right to a say about my own mode of death!

MRS. MERCY: [*Kindly*] Now, do leave it to us, dear Miss Buckridge. Leave it to the BBC. We know best. We've had experience in these matters.

JUNE: If I could die in the course of duty—from some infection, perhaps—an epidemic. Yes, that's it—I could go to nurse a patient somewhere up in the hills, someone suffering from some unspeakable disease . . .

MRS. MERCY: I'm sorry, Miss Buckridge, the scripts have been typed.

JUNE: But they could be altered . . .

MRS. MERCY: I'm afraid they've been officially approved.

JUNE: Then I shall take this to a higher authority—

ALICE: Yes, don't let them treat you like this. You've still got your public behind you: they won't let them kill you off!

MRS. MERCY: [*Annoyed*] I'm surprised at your attitude, Miss McNaught: I thought you'd be more sensible. I've come here of my own volition, as a gesture of courtesy to a valued and trusted colleague.

ALICE: But it's not fair!

JUNE: Shut up, Childie!

ALICE: I *won't* shut up.

MRS. MERCY: I was going to say that I'm sure the BBC will want to find *some* outlet for Miss Buckridge's talents.

JUNE: I'm still not satisfied about the—the accident.

MRS. MERCY: I'm afraid that decision is final.

ALICE: [*To* JUNE] Do you think you ought to lie down? You look awful. [*To* MRS. MERCY] She hasn't been sleeping well lately.

MRS. MERCY: Oh, I'm sorry to hear that.

JUNE: [*Pause*] Will I be buried in the churchyard?

MRS. MERCY: [*Cheerfully*] It'll be done in style! Don't you worry your head about that. There's some talk of a special memorial broadcast, with contributions from all sorts of famous people—but I shouldn't really be talking about that, as it's still in the planning stage.

JUNE: Would I be in it? In the memorial broadcast, I mean?

MRS. MERCY: Naturally. There will be lots of recorded extracts of Sister George.

JUNE: No, I meant: would I be able to tell the people how the character developed?

MRS. MERCY: Oh no! That would spoil the illusion.

JUNE: But you said just now you wanted to use me again.

MRS. MERCY: Yes, but not as Sister George.

JUNE: [*On the brink of hysteria*] What's wrong with Sister George?

MRS. MERCY: Nothing, dear Miss Buckridge. She'd be dead, that's all.

[*Pause*]

ALICE: [*To* JUNE] Come on, George, come and lie down. Come on—come on.

MRS. MERCY: In due course, I hope to discuss ideas for a new serial with you. We'll do something really exciting; I'm sure of it!

JUNE: Mrs. Mercy: I would like to thank you for coming personally to tell me of the . . . decision. I don't really feel up to discussing new ideas for serials at the moment.

MRS. MERCY: Of course you don't!

JUNE: Please don't go. Childie—Miss McNaught—will make you a cup of tea or something. I'll go and lie down for a bit, I think. I'll put that away, in the . . . cabinet.

[*Taking gin bottle*]

ALICE: Will you be all right, George?

JUNE: [*Stopping in the doorway*] What did you say?

ALICE: I said: Will you be all right?

JUNE: You called me "George" then, didn't you? You'll have to get out of that habit.

[*She exits*]

MRS. MERCY: [*Rising*] I really don't think I should stay any longer.

ALICE: Please stay, Mrs. Mercy. I'd like you to.

MRS. MERCY: Well, of course . . . if I can be of any assistance—

ALICE: [*With an awkward laugh*] Just to have somebody to talk to . . .

MRS. MERCY: I expect it hasn't been easy for you . . . recently.

ALICE: [*Quietly, with an anxious look to the door*] She's been impossible. Life's been absolute hell. You've no idea.

MRS. MERCY: I thought as much.

ALICE: Night after night I found her sitting up, drinking. Said she couldn't sleep with worry—

MRS. MERCY: Did she keep you awake?

ALICE: Some nights she made such a din—singing and, you know, reciting and things—that the neighbors complained!

MRS. MERCY: I had no idea it was as bad as that!

ALICE: It's been . . . diabolical!

MRS. MERCY: I do feel sorry for you.

ALICE: When she gets excited, or nervous, or anything, she has to take it out on somebody. Who do you think bears the brunt? Yours truly.

MRS. MERCY: I'm amazed you put up with it.

ALICE: I have no alternative.

MRS. MERCY: Oh come, there must be lots of openings for a girl with your qualifications!

ALICE: I've been with George for seven years.

MRS. MERCY: Seven years—as long as that!

ALICE: Yes, she was quite unknown when we first met.

MRS. MERCY: I expect she was easier to get on with in those days.

ALICE: She was always very jealous; wouldn't let anyone come near me.

MRS. MERCY: What a shame. Especially as it's so important for someone with literary ability to have contact with a lot of people.

ALICE: How did you know that I—

MRS. MERCY: You mentioned your interest in poetry last time we met. You attend classes, I believe?

ALICE: Yes, every Wednesday.

MRS. MERCY: I'd like to read your poems, if I may?

ALICE: Would you? Would you really? Shall I get them now?

MRS. MERCY: No, we'd better not disturb Miss Buckridge now! Give me a ring at the BBC and my secretary will fix an appointment.

ALICE: Oh, thank you. It's really nice of you . . . to take an interest.

MRS. MERCY: Have you ever thought of writing for the radio?

ALICE: It has occurred to me. You know: sometimes one hears such tripe, and one thinks—

[*She puts her hand over her mouth*]

MRS. MERCY: [*With mock reproval*] I know what you were going to say!

ALICE: Sorry.

MRS. MERCY: Never mind. We all feel the same way at times. Anyway, I'm not responsible for *all* the programs!

ALICE: I'm sure yours are by far the best.

MRS. MERCY: [*Very pleased*] Flattery—

ALICE: No, honestly. Years ago, before I knew you had anything to do with Applehurst, I listened to your talks on the wireless about people's problems and honestly, they were really . . . understanding.

MRS. MERCY: [*Touched*] I'm so glad. [*Indicating the door*] You've got a little problem on *your* hands and no mistake!

ALICE: A big problem!

MRS. MERCY: What are we going to do?

ALICE: Don't know.

MRS. MERCY: [*Quietly sympathetic*] Is she always so difficult?

ALICE: Difficult! She gets very violent—especially after she's had a few pints! You've no idea the things she gets up to!

MRS. MERCY: Really?

ALICE: Oh yes . . . [*She looks round a little wildly*] Mrs. Mercy, I'm scared. I'm scared of what will happen.

MRS. MERCY: Now don't be silly. Nothing will happen. You've been living through a rather difficult few weeks, that's all. It was the uncertainty that made her nervous. Now that she knows the worst she'll be much more bearable, you'll see.

ALICE: You don't know George! I don't know how I'll survive the next fortnight . . .

MRS. MERCY: I'll do what I can to help.

ALICE: I hope she won't get in a rage and murder me.

MRS. MERCY: [*Startled*] Are you serious?

ALICE: Dead serious. When she gets into a temper, she's capable of anything!

MRS. MERCY: Has she ever . . . attacked you?

ALICE: It happens all the time.

MRS. MERCY: But this is *outrageous!*

ALICE: She beats me, you know. She hits me with anything that comes into her hand.

MRS. MERCY: [*Horrified*] But why do you put up with it?

ALICE: [*After a pause*] I have nowhere else to go . . .

MRS. MERCY: Surely there's somewhere . . .

ALICE: I couldn't face living alone. Not any more.

MRS. MERCY: [*Overcome*] My poor girl. This is terrible . . . Look, if there's any more trouble, don't hesitate to give me a ring. Please regard me as your friend.

ALICE: Oh, you really are kind, Mrs. Mercy.

MRS. MERCY: And we must find somewhere for you to go.

ALICE: [*Gratefully*] Would you? Would you really?

MRS. MERCY: [*Squeezing* ALICE'S *arm*] Leave it to me. [*Rising*] How pretty this room looks in the evening sunlight . . . All these charming dolls—

[*She picks up Emmeline*]

ALICE: That's my favorite. Her name is Emmeline.

MRS. MERCY: [*Shaking the doll by the hand*] Hello Emmeline.

[*Pause*]

ALICE: Do you think I ought to go and see if George is all right?

MRS. MERCY: [*Speaking in a childish voice to the doll*] I should leave her where she is . . . the naughty woman . . .

ALICE: I haven't offered you a cup of tea!

MRS. MERCY: We haven't time for a cup of tea. We have to go. [*To the doll*] Good-bye, little Emmeline.

ALICE: I wish you could stay.

MRS. MERCY: So do I. But I'm glad we had a chance to have a little chat. Now remember what I told you; if there's any trouble, get straight on the telephone to me! [ALICE *puts on the bowler hat*] That's the spirit!

ALICE: [*In a Laurel voice*] Gee, I'm frightened . . .

MRS. MERCY: [*Confidentially*] Don't let her bully you.

ALICE: [*As before*] She's a devil when roused . . .

MRS. MERCY: Good-bye, dear. Must run. [*Waving from the door*] Have fun.

[*Exits*]

ALICE: [*Mechanically*] Must run . . . have fun . . . [*She looks towards the bedroom, undecided; picks up the flute and marches up to the bedroom, playing the Laurel and Hardy signature tune. No reply from* JUNE] George? George, are you all right? [*Still no reply. She hammers on the bedroom door*] George! George! [*Returning to the room pale with worry*] What am I going to do?

CURTAIN

ACT THREE

Heard in darkness before the curtain goes up is the sound of SISTER GEORGE's *motorbike, background of country noises, twittering of birds, mooing, neighing.*

SISTER GEORGE: [*Singing*] "Oh God, our help in ages past . . ."

[*Fade out. Then the monotonous sound of the engine of a heavy lorry*]

BILL: [*In a thick West Country accent*] You awake, Fred?

FRED: [*Grunts something unintelligible*]

BILL: Won't do to fall asleep now. We're nearly there.

FRED: Not up to it any more . . . this all-night driving.

BILL: There's the turning coming up now—don't miss it!

FRED: [*Sound of acceleration, and changing of gears*] Let's get there fast—I'm hungry . . .

BILL: [*Shouting*] Look out!

[*Screeching of brakes, shouting, followed by an explosion*]

BILL: [*Near hysteria*] Fred! We hit her! Fred! We hit her!

[*The sound of a car door slamming is heard*]

FRED: It weren't my fault. I braked—

BILL: Is she—? My God, she looks bad.

FRED: A nurse, by the look of her . . .

BILL: [*Calling*] Hey, there!

[*Sound of heavy footsteps, coming nearer*]

FARMER BROMLEY: [*Coming nearer*] What happened?

BILL: Bike came round the corner, fast!

FRED: I tried to brake. It weren't my fault!

FARMER BROMLEY: [*Panting*] I always did say it's a dangerous crossing. Is she badly—Holy Saints!! It's, it's Sister George!

FRED: It *were*. . . .

[*The Applehurst theme swells up. The curtain rises. Two weeks have passed. It is a sunny October morning. The room is littered with letters and telegrams, and there is an abundance of flowers.* MADAME XENIA, *discreetly dressed, is listening to Sister George's accident on a tape recorder. As the Applehurst theme swells up, she switches it off and wipes her eyes.*]

MADAME XENIA: [*Overcome*] Oi oi oi . . . poor George! [*The doorbell rings*] All right, I come! [*She goes to the front door and opens it*] . . . Yes, I will take them, but I don't know where I am going to put them . . . [*Closes door and comes in with wreaths*] Soon we shall not be able to move. [*Telephone*] They are mad. I told them we were not accepting any more calls. [*She lifts the receiver*] You are mad. I told you we are not accepting any more calls. A message from whom? The girls of your Exchange? Yes, I will convey it . . . Very nice of you . . . Charming. Miss Buckridge will be very touched. Who am I? Never you mind—I am her temporary secretary . . . No, I have nothing to do with Applehurst . . . No, I am not the old gypsy woman who stole a pig! You are beginning to make me very upset. I will not speak any more! And no more calls, if you please! [*She hangs up*] Stupid nit.

[ALICE *enters, rubbing her eyes and yawning. She is wearing baby-doll pajamas*]

ALICE: What time is it?

MADAME XENIA: [*With a black look*] Half past ten.

ALICE: Heavens—I'm going to be late for the funeral. [*Nearly trips over a wreath*] Oh, not more flowers—I shall never find my things. . . .

MADAME XENIA: [*Pointedly*] I have been working for two hours.

ALICE: [*Hunting for clothes*] Where's George?

MADAME XENIA: Out. Gone. I don't know where. I am very worried.

ALICE: Gone? When?

MADAME XENIA: Since early this morning. I came up with two wreaths and some lilies—she took one look, rushed into the lift, slammed the gate in my face and went down like a captain on a sinking ship—but not saluting—swearing.

ALICE: I hope she is not going to do something awful?

MADAME XENIA: I think she could not stand to be in the flat another moment with all this . . . [*She looks around at the flowers*] She felt claustrophobia—I must get out! It has been terrible for her since the accident—nothing but the telephone—letters—reporters.

ALICE: She ought never to have listened to the accident—it was dreadful.

MADAME XENIA: Oi oi oi, I just listened to the tape again—that beautiful hymn—the screeching brakes, then [*Claps her hands*] crash, bang, wallop!

ALICE: [*Covering her ears*] Don't!

MADAME XENIA: It was like a gas-works blowing up—horrible. [*Shudders*] I cried again.

ALICE: Ought we to ring up the police or something?

MADAME XENIA: No. We must wait. And work. Everything must be right for her when she comes back.

[*She bustles about.* ALICE *sinks into a chair*]

ALICE: I feel so exhausted—I think it's the strain.

MADAME XENIA: Nonsense—it was the farewell party last night. You have no stamina. You are a—what you call it?—a milksop.

ALICE: I've probably caught a cold. George stuffed a peach melba down the back of my dress. Really, she's getting worse and worse . . .

MADAME XENIA: Listen to this. [*Reading the inscription*] "Unforgotten, from the patients and staff of the Sister George Geriatrics Ward." Beautiful! I could cry!

ALICE: She'd like that.

MADAME XENIA: All wreaths against the wall. There. All beautifully organized.

ALICE: Honestly, Madame Xenia, you're a brick.

MADAME XENIA: Why do you say that?

ALICE: It's an expression; a friend, a help—

MADAME XENIA: I see. But I promised George I would take charge today, and I hold my promise.

ALICE: Could I look at some of the telegrams?

MADAME XENIA: If you're very careful and don't get them mixed up. One pile is personal, the other official. Over here it's doubtfuls.

ALICE: Let's see the doubtfuls.

MADAME XENIA: What I would like more than anything is a nice cup of tea . . .

ALICE: [*Looking up from a telegram*] Oh, no!

MADAME XENIA: What?

ALICE: [*Bitterly*] Trust her to get in on the act.

[*She crumples up the telegram*]

MADAME XENIA: [*Chiding*] You must not do this.

ALICE: [*Very red in the face*] How dare she send telegrams after all these years!

MADAME XENIA: From what person . . . ?

ALICE: [*Reading*] "Heartfelt condolences. Love, Liz."

MADAME XENIA: Liz?

ALICE: A friend of George's. Before my time.

MADAME XENIA: Aha.

ALICE: An absolute cow. Kept writing sarcastic little notes at first; things like "Hope you are divinely happy" and "Hope this finds you as it leaves me—guess how?"

MADAME XENIA: [*Quietly*] What I would like more than anything is a nice cup of tea . . .

ALICE: Anyway, she stole a fountain pen and a camera off George!

MADAME XENIA: Tut-tut.

ALICE: "Heartfelt condolences"—she's mocking her!

MADAME XENIA: [*Changing the subject*] Here is a nice one from my old friend the Baroness. "Shall be thinking of you today. Best wishes for a triumphant funeral. Love, Augusta." She specially put off her hairdresser so that she can listen to it this morning. And she only met George once—at my Hallowe'en party last year.

ALICE: Which one was the Baroness?

MADAME XENIA: She came as Julius Caesar. At least, that's what we *thought* she was meant to be . . .

ALICE: I hope George isn't going to be late. . . .

MADAME XENIA: I think it is a mistake for her to listen today. Psychologically it is a mistake.

ALICE: Oh, I don't know. She can't just play a character for six years, and miss her own exit.

MADAME XENIA: But it will upset her!

ALICE: All her old friends will be there—people she's worked with for years. There'll be tributes paid; there'll be a proper service! I mean to say: there's a right way and a wrong way of doing things.

[*She sits on the settee*]

MADAME XENIA: [*Shrugging her shoulders*] I do not understand you.

ALICE: Maybe in your country, people—

MADAME XENIA: [*Flaring up*] What do you mean: in my country? We had state funerals which could have taught you something: twenty-eight horses with black plumes, ha?

ALICE: [*Bitchily*] Well, you had lots of practice, didn't you? All those assassinations—

MADAME XENIA: Assassinations?

ALICE: Shooting people.

MADAME XENIA: Of course we shoot people we don't like! You send them to the House of Lords—what's the difference?

ALICE: Anyway, if you expect the BBC to lay on twenty-eight horses with black plumes, you're in for a disappointment!

MADAME XENIA: [*Furious*] Do you want me to go? Immediately I go downstairs—

ALICE: No, no—

MADAME XENIA: You can explain my absence to George when she comes back. *If* she comes back . . .

[*She moves to the door,* ALICE *runs after her*]

ALICE: No! Madame Xenia, please stay—I didn't mean to be rude. It's my nerves, I'm so worried about her—supposing she's really cracked up and thrown herself under a bus or something—what am I going to do?

MADAME XENIA: [*After a pause*] No, it is not a bus. [*Mysteriously*] I read the cards this morning . . . it is something to do with the head.

ALICE: The *head!* Oh, no, . . . I can't bear it.

MADAME XENIA: [*Suddenly*] Shh! There's somebody at the door—

ALICE: George!

MADAME XENIA: Look cheerful—she must see happy faces.

ALICE: She'll kill me if she sees me walking about like this—

[ALICE *rushes towards the bedroom, but trips over a large wreath on the way*]

JUNE: [*Shouting off*] Open the windows and let the sunshine in!

MADAME XENIA: [*Apprehensively*] We are here, my darling . . .

> [ALICE *picks up the wreath and tries to hide behind it, as* JUNE *sails in, wearing an extravagant pink chiffon hat and carrying a large parcel*]

JUNE: It's glorious out! [*To* MADAME XENIA] Darling—how sweet of you to hold the fort—I do hope you weren't pestered too much . . . [ALICE's *wreath rustles.* JUNE *sees her*] Oh God, down in the forest something stirred.

MADAME XENIA: George, we were so worried—where have you been?

JUNE: Shopping. I picked up this marvelous bargain—a Christmas Gift Hamper packed full of goodies [*Unpacking it*] Oh, two bottles of Veuve Clicquot '52.

MADAME XENIA: But—what for . . . ?

JUNE: I've decided to skip the funeral and have a celebration.

MADAME XENIA: Celebration?

JUNE: Yes, more a coming-out party, really.

MADAME XENIA: But who is coming out?

JUNE: I am!

MADAME XENIA: [*Looking at* JUNE's *hat*] I see you bought something else, as well . . .

JUNE: Do you like it?

MADAME XENIA: It is *charming!* Where did you find it?

JUNE: That little shop on the corner. Saw it in the window and couldn't resist it.

MADAME XENIA: You were absolutely right! It does something for you.

JUNE: Do you think so?

MADAME XENIA: It makes you look so young! Like eighteen years—

> [ALICE *sniggers*]

JUNE: [*Turning on* ALICE] What are you laughing at? And why aren't you dressed yet? You look indecent.

ALICE: I overslept. Bit of a hangover.

JUNE: [*Incredulous*] A hangover? After two glasses of shandy?

ALICE: I mixed it a bit.

JUNE: With what—ginger ale? [ALICE *does not reply*] Do you think it proper to entertain visitors in this—this unseemly attire?

MADAME XENIA: [*Placating*] Oh, please, please.

JUNE: Did you make Madame Xenia a cup of tea?

MADAME XENIA: It really wasn't necessary . . .

JUNE: What's the matter with you?

ALICE: Don't know.

JUNE: You should have been out and about for the last three hours. Did you do your exercises?

ALICE: [*Defiantly*] No.

JUNE: [*To* MADAME XENIA] Oh God, help us—she takes a keep-fit course. You know: knee bends, running on the spot, bicycling on her back. To judge by her condition it's been singularly ineffective! Go on—I want a cup of tea *now*. And one for Madame Xenia. And get dressed. And look sharpish about it. *Avanti!*

ALICE: [*Looking straight at* JUNE] I think your hat is a mistake.

JUNE: [*Thundering*] What? [*No reply from* ALICE] I can see this day will end in tears.

ALICE: [*Shouting*] They won't be my tears!

[*She runs off*]

JUNE: The baggage. The little baggage.

MADAME XENIA: She is upset.

JUNE: She has no business to be upset: it's *my* funeral!

MADAME XENIA: She's taking it hard. Some people—

JUNE: She's no good in a crisis. I've seen it happen again and again: people going to pieces in a crisis. During the war—

MADAME XENIA: Ah, the war! I was an air raid warden.

JUNE: I was in the army. Attached to the Commandos. It was tough, but rewarding.

MADAME XENIA: It's lucky for her she wasn't old enough.

JUNE: Childie in the army? That'd be a bit of a giggle . . . She'd have collapsed under the weight of her forage cap.

[*She laughs*]

MADAME XENIA: Would you like to go through the last tributes?

JUNE: If it's absolutely necessary.

MADAME XENIA: Look at this—from the patients and staff of the Sister George Geriatric Ward. In that hospital your name will never die.

JUNE: [*Firmly*] Her name.

MADAME XENIA: Her name, your name. It's the same thing—

JUNE: Not any longer. George and I have parted company. And do you know, I'm glad to be free of the silly bitch. [*Pause*] Honestly.

MADAME XENIA: George, what are you saying?

JUNE: I'm saying that my name is *June*. June Buckridge. I'm endeavoring to memorize it.

MADAME XENIA: You are incredible!

JUNE: Why?

ALICE: [*Entering with the tea tray*] I'm afraid one of the telegrams got crumpled up. You'd better read it.

JUNE: What telegram?

ALICE: Here. [*She serves the crumpled telegram on a bread plate*] Will there be any reply, Madam?

JUNE: [*Reads it*] Liz . . . I don't believe it!

ALICE: [*Bitterly*] I thought you'd be pleased.

MADAME XENIA: [*Attempting to mediate*] It's always nice to hear from old friends.

ALICE: [*Starts to sing "Auld Lang Syne"*] Sugar, Madame Xenia?

MADAME XENIA: No, thank you. I take it neat.

JUNE: [*Reminiscing*] She was a real thoroughbred: stringy, nervy, temperamental. I remember I used to tease her because her hair grew down her neck, like a thin mane, between her shoulder blades—[ALICE *exits, banging the door behind her*] I knew that would annoy her!

[*She chuckles*]

MADAME XENIA: She got out of bed with the left foot, this morning.

JUNE: Her behavior recently has left much to be desired. I may have to speak to her mother—

MADAME XENIA: She has her mother here?

JUNE: In Glasgow. Inoffensive old soul. Bakes cakes; minds her own business, but a terrific mumbler. Can't understand a word she says.

[*She essays a few words of high-pitched, vaguely Scottish-sounding gibberish*]

MADAME XENIA: Oh, you are a scream!

JUNE: Well, come on—let's open the Champers. [*Looks at the flowers*] Then we can clear out all the foliage . . .

[*The doorbell rings*]

MADAME XENIA: I go. Soon we shall need a greenhouse.

JUNE: It's awfully kind of you to help out today.

MADAME XENIA: My darling: for you I do anything. [*The doorbell rings*] Perhaps this one is from Buckingham Palace?

JUNE: And about time too, they've been slacking!

[JUNE *opens the champagne*]

MADAME XENIA: [*Off*] Did you want to see Miss Buckridge?

JUNE: Now then—

[*The cork pops from the bottle*]

Costume

MRS. MERCY: [*Enters. She is dressed in mourning, with a small veiled hat*] I do hope I'm not disturbing you.

JUNE: [*Surprised*] Mrs. Mercy! No, of course not . . .

MRS. MERCY: [*Handing over a bouquet*] Dear Sister George —for you—a little tribute—from all of us in admin. at BH.

JUNE: [*Nonplussed*] Oh. Thanks. Extremely decent of you. I— appreciate the thought. Would you be an angel, Madame, and put them in water? Oh, I'm terribly sorry: do you know each other? This is Madame Xenia—Mrs. Mercy Croft.

MADAME XENIA: [*Bearing down on* MRS. MERCY] What, *the* Mrs. Mercy?

JUNE: Of course, didn't you know—

MADAME XENIA: [*Softly to* MRS. MERCY] But I love you, my dear. [*Shouting*] I *adore* you!

MRS. MERCY: Have I had the pleasure?

MADAME XENIA: You don't know me from Adam, my darling, but for twenty years I have listened to you—every single week!

JUNE: How nice.

MRS. MERCY: Charming!

MADAME XENIA: [*Quite overcome*] I am—I cannot tell you —your advice is a hundred per cent. A hundred and twenty per cent! One senses—you have a heart, you have suffered—

MRS. MERCY: Well, we all have our ups and downs.

MADAME XENIA: But you have had more downs than ups—am I right?

MRS. MERCY: I shouldn't like—

MADAME XENIA: Of course I am! I knew it at once! Ask George here: am I ever wrong?

JUNE: Never. She is quite infallible. You see, Madame Xenia is a clairvoyant.

MRS. MERCY: Oh, really.

MADAME XENIA: A psychometrist.

JUNE: Oh, sorry.

MADAME XENIA: I write a syndicated column every week: star forecasts—hack work, but what-the-hell, one's got to live.

MRS. MERCY: I'm afraid I don't really believe in that kind of—

MADAME XENIA: [*Quickly*] Be careful what you do on the tenth. There's treachery around you. Don't sign any important documents before full moon—

MRS. MERCY: I'm obliged to you, but really—

MADAME XENIA: There's news from abroad—

MRS. MERCY: [*Turning to* JUNE] I thought you'd be all alone this morning. That's why I came—

JUNE: Very kind of you.

MADAME XENIA: You're inclined to suffer from digestive disorders. Don't worry, it's nothing serious—

JUNE: [*Apologetically*] Madame is helping me out today.

MADAME XENIA: A tall man doesn't like you. Avoid him.

MRS. MERCY: It would be somewhat difficult in my job to—

MADAME XENIA: An old association will be broken. Never mind: there are plenty of birds in the sky—

MRS. MERCY: [*Icily*] I think you mean fish in the sea.

MADAME XENIA: [*To herself*] Interesting. Must be born under Pisces . . . [*Cheerfully*] Oh well, I'll get some water for the flowers . . .

[*She exits*]

JUNE: She's been frightfully good: done all the organizing for me today.

MRS. MERCY: Isn't your friend—er—Miss—?

JUNE: Miss McNaught? She's not up yet! I'm afraid she's no good at times like these. No backbone. Ballast.

MRS. MERCY: [*Inspecting the wreaths*] What beautiful tributes! May I read some? I *adore* inscriptions.

JUNE: There's a whole lot more in the bathroom. As soon as Childie's dressed she can take the whole damn lot and dump them on the Cenotaph.

MRS. MERCY: But you can't do that! They're for *you*. [*Seri-*

ously] Do you know the entire Applehurst Company turned up for the recording today in black? It was quite spontaneous.

JUNE: [*Annoyed*] They must be bonkers! I can just see old Mrs. Hinch. She must have looked like The Phantom of the Opera . . . [*Sees* MRS. MERCY'S *black suit*] Oh, I beg your pardon.

MRS. MERCY: We felt we couldn't let her go without some mark of respect. After all, she has been with us . . . how long?

JUNE: Six perishing years.

MRS. MERCY: Oh, come now—you know you enjoyed every minute of it.

JUNE: [*Getting exasperated*] Yes, but it's over—I just want to forget it—

MRS. MERCY: I don't think your public will let you. [*Indicates the wreaths*] You can see how much you meant to them.

JUNE: [*Trying to escape*] Actually, I was just on the point of changing . . .

[*Takes off hat*]

MRS. MERCY: For the funeral?

JUNE: For the broadcast.

[MADAME XENIA *re-enters, brandishing a large gilded vase in the shape of a galleon bearing* MRS. MERCY'S *flowers*]

MADAME XENIA: All right?

JUNE: Wasn't there something a little more conservative?

MADAME XENIA: I can put them in a milk bottle, if you like. Or perhaps you'd prefer a bottle of gin? [*Piqued*] It is good to have one's hard work appreciated! Getting up early in the morning—

JUNE: Madame, darling—I'm eternally grateful. You've been a brick!

MADAME XENIA: Yes, so I've been told before.

MRS. MERCY: What a charming message. [*Reading*]

"Ever-present, spirit-like,
Harken! the familiar sound:
Sister George, astride her bike,
In the happy hunting ground."

[JUNE *mutters under her breath*]

MADAME XENIA: [*About to go*] Well, happy hunting, Sister George!

JUNE: You're off then, are you, dear?

MADAME XENIA: I'm afraid my client is waiting. The moment you need me, just stamp on the floor.

JUNE: Don't worry about me—I'm feeling fine. If any more flowers come, you'd better shove them in the coal-shed.

MADAME XENIA: Leave everything to me. *I am your friend!*

MRS. MERCY: [*Reading*] "Fare thee well. Go in peace, good woman."

MADAME XENIA: I can take a hint.

[*She strides out, nose in the air*]

JUNE: [*Blowing her a kiss*] Thank you, darling.

MRS. MERCY: You do have a lot of friends, don't you?

JUNE: I hope so. I like to think—

MRS. MERCY: Loneliness is the great scourge of our time.

JUNE: Too true.

MRS. MERCY: I had visions of you, sitting by your set, alone with your grief . . .

JUNE: With Miss McNaught actually, but it comes to the same thing.

MRS. MERCY: Frankly, I'm amazed you're taking it like this.

JUNE: Like what?

MRS. MERCY: So calmly. Cheerfully.

JUNE: The uncertainty was the worst. Once that was over . . .

MRS. MERCY: You have a very strong character. [*After a pause*] Will you go on listening to the program now?

JUNE: I don't know. I hadn't really thought. Probably not. I mean —it might be rather—distressing—listening to all the old voices going on without me . . .

MRS. MERCY: Isn't that a rather selfish attitude to take?

JUNE: Selfish?

MRS. MERCY: You died to save the series—surely you'll want to take an interest in its fortunes?

JUNE: Well . . .

MRS. MERCY: I think the next few episodes will be particularly fascinating. [*She warms to the subject*] Your death means an enormous re-adjustment to the whole community. It will take them weeks, even months, to get over the shock. But eventually the gap must be filled, new leaders will arise—

JUNE: Leaders? What leaders? Who?

MRS. MERCY: [*Confidentially*] Well, it's not really for release yet, but between you and me—I believe Ginger—

JUNE: [*Horrified*] Ginger? [*Slipping into country accent*] He couldn't lead a cow down Buttercup Hill. He's weak! Weak as rotten apples dropping off a tree.

MRS. MERCY: Ginger will be our anti-hero.

JUNE: An anti-hero in Applehurst?

MRS. MERCY: Contemporary appeal. Applehurst is facing up to the fact that the old values have become outdated.

JUNE: I wonder how old Mrs. Hinch is going to take that?

MRS. MERCY: [*Quickly*] Not very well, I'm afraid. She passes away.

JUNE: [*Aghast*] What!

MRS. MERCY: It's due in the second week in December.

JUNE: How?

MRS. MERCY: It'll be a cold winter in Applehurst. She gets up in the middle of the night to let the cat in . . .

JUNE: And—?

MRS. MERCY: Bronchitis. Gone in two days.

JUNE: But you can't do this! After all the care I gave that woman —why, I've nursed her from gout to gastroenteritis over the last six years.

MRS. MERCY: That's neither here nor there.

JUNE: I could have saved her—just as I saved old Mr. Burns last winter. He's three years older and look at him now, fit as a fiddle! At least he was . . .

MRS. MERCY: I'm afraid he is due for a stroke next Friday.

JUNE: But why all this carnage, all this slaughter?

MRS. MERCY: We live in a violent world, Miss Buckridge, surrounded by death and destruction. It's the policy of the BBC to face up to reality.

JUNE: Who's going to look after the survivors?

MRS. MERCY: Nurse Lawrence.

JUNE: What!

MRS. MERCY: Yes, she arrives from the District Hospital tomorrow to take over from you.

JUNE: But she's a probationer. She couldn't put a dressing on a salad! They won't stand for that, you know.

MRS. MERCY: On the contrary, Nurse Lawrence wins the trust and affection of the village, and becomes known, rather charmingly, I think, as Sister Larry.

JUNE: [Rising] You're going to make this ill-bred, uneducated slut—

MRS. MERCY: [Shouting] Contemporary appeal, Sister George! People like that do exist—and in positions of power and influence; flawed, credible characters like Ginger, Nurse Lawrence, Rosie—

JUNE: What about Rosie?

MRS. MERCY: She's pregnant.

JUNE: I know that. And as she's not married, that's about as flawed and credible as you can get!

MRS. MERCY: She's going to marry her boy friend, Lennie.

JUNE: Oh good. I'm glad . . . I'm glad about that . . . glad—

MRS. MERCY: Mind you, it's not his baby.

JUNE: Eh?

MRS. MERCY: It's Roy's from the army camp at Oakmead. She tells Lennie, makes a full confession, and he forgives her, and they live happily ever after.

JUNE: Pardon me while I vomit.

ALICE: [*Enters. She is wearing a gaily colored dress*] Oh, hello.

MRS. MERCY: [*Cordially*] Hello, dear. I was wondering where you were.

ALICE: I didn't go to work today.

MRS. MERCY: No, of course not.

ALICE: [*Sweetly, to* MRS. MERCY] Can I make you a cup of tea, Mrs. Mercy?

MRS. MERCY: I'd *adore* a cup of tea!

JUNE: [*Bitterly*] Mrs. Mercy came over to bring me the good news that I'm to be replaced by Nurse Lawrence.

ALICE: Nurse Lawrence—Nurse Lawrence? Do I know her?

JUNE: Don't be irritating. Of course you know her. That interfering busybody from Oakmead—

ALICE: [*With indifference*] Oh, her.

JUNE: Yes, her.

ALICE: [*To* JUNE] Anyway, it's not really your concern any more what happens in Applehurst. You're out of it—

JUNE: [*Bellowing*] Don't you understand? Don't you understand anything? I built it up: I made it what it is! It's not *nice* to see one's life work ruined!

MRS. MERCY: I have one piece of cheering news for you, if you can bear to hear it.

JUNE: I can bear it. Pour out a glass of gin for me, Childie, while you're over at the sideboard. Sorry, Mrs. Mercy, you were saying . . .

MRS. MERCY: It concerns your future.

JUNE: My future, yes. You are quite right: we must talk of the future. Is there still time—?

MRS. MERCY: There's still nearly an hour to go.

JUNE: Did you want to stay for the . . . the . . .

MRS. MERCY: Broadcast?

JUNE: The funeral. Yes . . .

MRS. MERCY: No, I'll have to get back to BH. We're having a little party, you know. Perhaps "party" isn't quite the right word.

ALICE: A wake?

MRS. MERCY: I suppose one could call it that. That's why I want a quick word with you, Miss Buckridge. Mrs. Coote has promised to come. You know Mrs. Coote, don't you? She's in charge of Toddler Time.

JUNE: Yes, of course I know her, a charming woman.

MRS. MERCY: Well, dear, she's very anxious to have you.

JUNE: Really?

MRS. MERCY: What I'm telling you now is strictly off the cuff. Everything's still in the planning stage. I thought I'd nip over and tell you that there's a ray of sunshine on the horizon.

JUNE: I'm all ears.

[ALICE *exits to the kitchen*]

MRS. MERCY: [*Very confidentially*] Well, dear, as you probably know, Toddler Time has been—what shall we say—a wee bit disappointing. Audience research figures—this is strictly *entre nous*, you understand—

JUNE: Yes, yes of course.

MRS. MERCY: —show a slight but perceptible slide. Mrs. Coote, I may tell you, is worried out of her mind! She hasn't slept a wink for three weeks—

JUNE: Poor love!

MRS. MERCY: The scriptwriters are running around in circles— one of them's had a nervous breakdown: the one who wrote that series about Tiddlywink, the Cockerel, which, as you know, was taken off after only three installments. Anyway, to cut a long story short, there's been some agonizing reappraisal over

Toddler Time. A completely new approach has been decided on—

JUNE: Don't tell me—marauding gollywogs, drunk teddybears and pregnant bunnies!

[ALICE *re-enters with tea*]

MRS. MERCY: [*Smiling enigmatically*] Not quite, dear. But we're preparing an absolutely super adventure serial, in which we've got loads of confidence, which will combine exciting narrative with a modern outlook. And you're being considered for the title role.

JUNE: What is it called?

MRS. MERCY: The World of Clarabelle Cow.

JUNE: [*Rising after a pause*] Am I to understand that this . . . this character is a cow?

MRS. MERCY: A very human one, I assure you: full of little foibles and prejudices—

JUNE: [*Slowly*] A . . . flawed . . . credible . . . cow?

MRS. MERCY: Credible in human terms, certainly. Otherwise the children wouldn't believe in her. Children are very discerning!

ALICE: Ought to be fun.

JUNE: I don't think I could have understood you correctly. I don't believe I really grasped the meaning of your words.

MRS. MERCY: I thought I made myself perfectly clear.

ALICE: Oh, don't be dense, George!

JUNE: [*To* ALICE] Be quiet! [*To* MRS. MERCY] Am I to take it that you have come here today—the day of the funeral of Sister George—to offer me the part of a cow?

MRS. MERCY: We've got to be practical, dear. None of us can afford to be out of work for too long.

JUNE: Childie, give me another gin! [*To* MRS. MERCY] You're not serious, are you? You're joking, aren't you?

MRS. MERCY: We don't joke about these things at the BBC, Miss Buckridge.

ALICE: [*To* JUNE] It's jolly nice of Mrs. Mercy to come over specially to tell you.

MRS. MERCY: I thought it was a brilliant idea of Mrs. Coote's.

JUNE: [*Shouting and tearing her hair*] I can't stand it! I'm going mad!

MADAME XENIA: [*Enters with another wreath*] One more for luck!

JUNE: [*Tonelessly*] From whom?

MADAME XENIA: [*Reading the inscription*] "I never thought I'd survive you. Signed: Mrs. Ethel Hinch."

MRS. MERCY: She doesn't know yet . . .

JUNE: [*Distracted*] She's going to die, Madame Xenia—in two months' time! They're going to murder her, too. An old lady of eighty-five, who's never done anyone the slightest harm!

MADAME XENIA: How terrible! Are you sure?

JUNE: [*Wildly to* MRS. MERCY] Murderess!

[*She lunges at* MRS. MERCY *and is held back by* ALICE *and* MADAME XENIA]

MRS. MERCY: Really, Miss Buckridge! Restrain yourself!

JUNE: Is your blood lust sated? How many other victims are you going to claim?

MRS. MERCY: [*Shrilly*] Control yourself!

ALICE: George, you're drunk!

MADAME XENIA: My darling is upset. She's had a shock.

JUNE: [*Making a great effort to control herself*] With reference to Toddler Time, please thank Mrs. Coote for her kind interest—

MRS. MERCY: There's no need for you to decide today—

JUNE: —and tell her I cannot possibly accept the part in question.

MRS. MERCY: Very well, I'll tell her.

[*The buzzer sounds*]

ALICE: Don't be silly, George. You can't afford to turn down—

JUNE: I'm not playing the part of a cow!

MADAME XENIA: A cow? What cow?

JUNE: [*Frantically*] I'M NOT PLAYING THE PART OF A COW!!

MRS. MERCY: I've taken your point, Miss Buckridge!

MADAME XENIA: . . . There are two nuns, to see Sister George.

JUNE: No! . . . NO!!

[*Groaning with dismay, she rushes off to the bathroom*]

MADAME XENIA: [*To* MRS. MERCY] Nuns before noon is a good omen!

MRS. MERCY: I'll take your word for it.

ALICE: [*Following* JUNE] I'd better go and see what she's doing. [*Goes to the bathroom. Offstage*] . . . George: what are you doing?

MADAME XENIA: [*Into the speaker*] I'm sorry, Sister George is getting ready for her funeral.

ALICE: [*Long pause*] George! . . . [*She re-enters*] She appears to be running a bath.

MADAME XENIA: Shall I go and speak to her?

MRS. MERCY: She won't do anything silly, will she?

MADAME XENIA: [*To* ALICE] See if she's all right! [ALICE *goes off again*] I'm so worried.

MRS. MERCY: There was bound to be a reaction.

ALICE: [*Offstage*] George? . . . I can't hear what you're saying Turn the bloody taps off!

[JUNE *mumbles offstage*]

MADAME XENIA: Oi, oi, oi.

ALICE: [*Re-entering*] Says she wants to be left alone.

MADAME XENIA: How did she sound?

ALICE: Like a walrus.

MADAME XENIA: [*Clapping her hands*] Thank God. Thank

God she's herself again. [*Tidying up confusedly*] Oi, oi, what a morning!

> [*She exits.* MRS. MERCY *and* ALICE *face each other for a few seconds. Then* MRS. MERCY *extends her arms, and* ALICE *flies to her, and bursts into tears*]

MRS. MERCY: My poor child . . . There, there . . .

ALICE: I can't stand it any more.

MRS. MERCY: I know, dear, I know. You've been under a terrible strain.

ALICE: You've no idea, Mrs. Mercy—

MRS. MERCY: I can imagine.

ALICE: She's been *terrible!*

MRS. MERCY: Hush, dear. She'll hear you.

ALICE: I was praying you'd come.

MRS. MERCY: I wasn't going to leave you alone with her today. [*She smiles*] Besides, I had promised.

ALICE: Oh, I know, but I knew how busy you were.

MRS. MERCY: First things first.

ALICE: I knew I could rely on you. I felt it the first time I met you.

MRS. MERCY: And I felt that I was speaking to a proud and sensitive person, whose personality was being systematically crushed.

ALICE: Don't!

MRS. MERCY: And with a definite literary talent.

ALICE: Honestly? Do you really think so?

MRS. MERCY: I'm being quite objective.

ALICE: Gosh. Wouldn't it be marvelous?

MRS. MERCY: What, dear?

ALICE: If I could do some work for you—writing, I mean.

MRS. MERCY: We shall see what transpires. I'll certainly give you all the help I can.

ALICE: Oh, you are nice!

MRS. MERCY: And the other offer still stands.

ALICE: Yes, well . . . I think I've almost definitely decided. I'm sorry to be so vague . . .

MRS. MERCY: Not at all.

ALICE: It's a bit of wrench, you know. I've been working for Mr. Katz for nearly four years. I'd have to give him a month's notice—

MRS. MERCY: There's no rush. I told you I'd keep the job open for a fortnight.

ALICE: And there's George.

MRS. MERCY: Yes.

ALICE: I mean: I don't know how she'd take it.

MRS. MERCY: You haven't told her, of course?

ALICE: God, no. She'd have murdered me!

MRS. MERCY: In view of what happened today, I think we were very wise—

ALICE: If she suspected I'd been to see you behind her back—

MRS. MERCY: But there was no reason why you shouldn't. You're perfectly entitled—

ALICE: Oh, I *know*. But she's so possessive. She never allows me anywhere near the BBC. I'm kept a guilty secret.

MRS. MERCY: She's shackled you to her. Anyway, you wouldn't be working for the BBC: you'd be working as my own private secretary, in my London flat.

ALICE: It sounds absolutely super. I'm sorry I'm being so slow about making up my mind.

MRS. MERCY: A thought has just occurred to me: if you're in any kind of trouble—you know, with George—you can always camp down at the flat. There's a divan—

ALICE: Oh, that'd be *wonderful!*

MRS. MERCY: It could serve as your temporary HQ. It's not luxurious, mind you.

ALICE: Never mind that. It would be an escape . . . if necessary . . .

MRS. MERCY: That's what I thought. I only ever stay there if

I've been kept late at a story conference, or something like that. I find it useful . . . I suppose it's really a place to escape for me, too . . .

ALICE: We'd be like prisoners on the run . . .

MRS. MERCY: Do you really think you can escape?

ALICE: [*After a pause*] I don't know.

MRS. MERCY: It's very difficult for you.

ALICE: It's been so long, so many years . . .

MRS. MERCY: It's hard to break the routine.

ALICE: It's little things one misses most.

MRS. MERCY: [*Smiling*] You could bring your dolls.

ALICE: [*Grabbing Emmeline*] I couldn't go anywhere without them. I even take them on holiday—and then I'm terrified they'll get lost or stolen. Sometimes George hides them—it's her idea of a joke . . .

MRS. MERCY: A very cruel joke.

ALICE: [*Clutching* MRS. MERCY] Don't let her get at me, Mrs. Mercy! Stay here—don't go away!

MRS. MERCY: I can't stay here all day, dear.

ALICE: Don't leave me alone—I'm frightened of what she will do!

MRS. MERCY: Calm yourself, Alice. No one's going to hurt you. Here, put your head on my shoulder; close your eyes . . . Relax —my goodness, you're trembling like a leaf . . .

[*She strokes* ALICE's *hair*]

ALICE: That's nice . . .

MRS. MERCY: You're my little girl. You're going to be . . . my little girl . . .

JUNE: [*Enters. She is wearing her bath robe*] What a touching sight . . .

ALICE: [*Panic-stricken, breaking away from* MRS. MERCY] George!

JUNE: [*To* MRS. MERCY] I always did say she had nice hair. That's one thing I always said for her . . .

ALICE: George, you don't understand!

JUNE: [*Grabbing the doll*] Your mummy says I don't understand. Did you see what your mummy was doing with that strange lady?

MRS. MERCY: She was overwrought, Miss Buckridge. I tried to comfort her.

JUNE: How absolutely sweet of you! And how well you have succeeded!

[ALICE *is trembling from head to toe*]

MRS. MERCY: I hope you don't think—

JUNE: [*Sweetly*] Alice, Childie: come here a minute. I want to say something to you! . . . [ALICE *looks terrified*] Come along, don't be frightened, I'm not going to hurt you.

ALICE: Why can't you tell me—in front of Mrs. Mercy?

JUNE: [*Feigning gaucheness*] Well, you know, boy's talk—

MRS. MERCY: Would you rather I left?

JUNE: Oh no, no. Whatever could have given you that idea? Come along, keep still. I only want to whisper it in your ear.

[*She whispers something*]

ALICE: [*Shouting*] No! [JUNE *whispers something else*] No, I'm not going to do it!

JUNE: Yes or no, Childie? Yes or no?

ALICE: [*Frantically*] No, no, NO!

MRS. MERCY: [*White with indignation*] What are you asking her to do, Sister George?

JUNE: The appropriate treatment, that's all. The punishment that fits the crime . . .

ALICE: [*Shrieking*] She wants me to drink her bath water!

MRS. MERCY: [*Astounded*] Her bath water?

ALICE: To humiliate me!

MRS. MERCY: [*Rising*] But this is preposterous! I've never heard of such an obscene suggestion!

JUNE: You're shut off from the world, Mrs. Mercy! "Ask Mrs.

Mercy"—all your problems answered! "Dear Mrs. Mercy, what shall I do? My flatmate is nasty to me and wants me to drink her bath water. By the time you reply to me—glug, glug, glug—it may be too late—glug—and I might have drowned!"

MRS. MERCY: [*To* ALICE] I strongly advise you to leave this house at once!

JUNE: [*To* ALICE] Well, you have had the benefit of Mrs. Mercy's expert advice. Are you going to take it?

ALICE: I'm sorry, George, I can't stay with you any longer.

MRS. MERCY: Very sensible.

JUNE: Did you hear what your mummy said, Emmeline? Your mummy wants to leave us—

MRS. MERCY: I wish you wouldn't—

JUNE: [*Dangerously*] Mind what you're saying, Mrs. Mercy: this is between Alice and myself!

ALICE: [*Pleading*] Let me have Emmeline!

JUNE: Glug, glug, glug to you.

[*She makes the doll point at* MRS. MERCY]

MRS. MERCY: I don't know how you can be so cruel. The poor child—

JUNE: "The poor child!" As you're going to see quite a lot of "the poor child," I'd better put you in the picture about her—

ALICE: George, don't! George, please!

JUNE: "The poor child" likes to pretend she's a baby, but take a close look at her!

[ALICE *bursts into tears*]

MRS. MERCY: Can't you see you're upsetting the child!

JUNE: [*Shouting*] The child? The child is a woman—she's thirty-four! [*A loud sob from* ALICE] She's old enough to have a grandchild!

MRS. MERCY: Oh, really, now you're exaggerating—

JUNE: Am I? *Am I?*

ALICE: [*Whimpering*] Don't, George . . . don't . . .

JUNE: [*With disgust*] Look at you: whimpering and pleading! Have you no backbone, can't you stand up like a man—

ALICE: [*Sobbing*] I can't . . . help it . . .

JUNE: "I can't help it!" She'll never change—feckless, self-indulgent—

ALICE: I'm going! I'm packing my bag!

[*She runs to the door, but* JUNE *bars the way*]

JUNE: Come back here!

MRS. MERCY: Let her go! Let her go!

JUNE: [*To* MRS. MERCY] You've got yourself a prize packet there, I can tell you!

ALICE: [*Screaming*] Let me go!

JUNE: She had an illegitimate child when she was eighteen. She gave it away—to strangers! She has a daughter of sixteen . . . [ALICE *collapses on the floor in a heap*] Do what you like— you make me sick!

[*She sits in an armchair*]

MRS. MERCY: Stop crying, dear. Go and pack, quickly. You needn't take everything now. Go along, hurry! I'll wait for you here . . .

[ALICE *goes into the bedroom*]

MRS. MERCY: I'm sorry Miss Buckridge, about this. It'll be all for the best, you'll see . . . I do hope you're not bearing me any grudge—[JUNE *shakes her head*] Oh, good, good. Sometimes it's best to make a clean break—it's painful, but that's the advice I always give in my program. Which reminds me: it's almost time for the broadcast. Shall I switch it on? [*She switches on the radio*] Let it give you strength, Miss Buckridge. Remember: Sister George was not killed because she was hated, but because she was loved! [ALICE *returns, tear-stained, carrying a small case*] If you study anthropology, you'll discover that in primitive societies it was always the best-loved member of the community who was selected as the sacrificial victim. By killing him they hoped that the goodness and strength of the victim would pass on to them. It was both a purge and a rededication. What you will hear in a few moments is the purge and rededication of Applehurst. Good-bye, Sister George.

[*From the radio comes the slow tolling of a bell*]

ALICE: I think she's right in what she said: Mrs. Mercy, I mean. I love you, too, George, that's why I've got to leave you. You do understand, don't you . . . I mean—[*She's starting to cry again*] All right, Mrs. Mercy, I'm coming. Good-bye, George, and—you know—thanks for everything!

[ALICE *and* MRS. MERCY CROFT *exit*]

ANNOUNCER'S VOICE: [*From the radio*] Applehurst: a chronicle of an English village. This is a sad day for Applehurst. The church bell is tolling for the funeral of Sister George, the well-beloved District Nurse, whose forthright, practical, no-nonsense manner had endeared her to the community. But death comes to the best of us, and the picturesque village is today swathed in mourning . . .

[*The church bell tolls again*]

JUNE: [*A very plaintive sound*] Moo! . . . [*Louder*] Moo! Moo!

[*A heart-rending sound*]

CURTAIN

Peter Luke

Precisely one week after the final year of the decade settled (or stormed) into place, a bolt of theatrical lightning struck the New York stage: the American première of Peter Luke's fascinating London success, *Hadrian VII*, based on the autobiographical novel (and other works) of Frederick William Rolfe who, upon occasion, called himself "Baron Corvo."

Indeed, it would be considerably more accurate to report that lightning struck *twice* on that memorable theatrical evening, for in the title role of Mr. Luke's play, star Alec McCowen gave one of the supreme performances of the Sixties. As Rolfe, a bizarre, paranoiac turn-of-the-century writer and a persistently unsuccessful candidate for holy orders with phantasmal visions of himself as Pope Hadrian VII, Mr. McCowen's virtuoso performance electrified the American theatre just as it did in Britain where he originated the role to rare and justified acclaim. (Clive Barnes, who covered both the London and New York productions for the New York *Times* counseled his readers: "If you miss Mr. McCowen in *Hadrian VII*, I solemnly assure you, you will be missing one of the most fantastically alive performances of our decade.")

The incredible real life of Frederick William Rolfe had all the built-in elements of first-rate drama. Born in 1860, at Cheapside, London, he was a gifted but erratic student, more interested in art than in conventional studies. After leaving school at fifteen, he became for a time an "unattached" student at Oxford. A diversity of fleeting jobs followed until, at the age of twenty-six, he became "overnight" a convert to Catholicism and was received into the Church of Rome. Aspiring toward the priesthood (and he never swayed from the conviction that he was born for the Church and the life of a Roman Catholic ecclesiastic), Rolfe succeeded in entering a theological seminary, but his extravagant and totally unorthodox behavior soon brought about his expulsion. Undaunted, he somehow managed to get himself into another seminary; this time the Scots College in Rome, but again he was fired on the pretext of having "no Vocation." He began to develop a strong persecution complex, which ultimately became an obsession.

During his Italianate period, he met and persuaded an old noblewoman, the Duchess of Sforza-Cesarini, to give him an allowance. He later asserted that by transferring to him certain properties in Italy she also had given him the right to a baronial title: thus, the "Baron Corvo." The Duchess' allowance eventually dried up and Rolfe struggled in self-imposed martyrdom to vindicate his wrongs and humiliations. Constantly an inch or so away from penury and almost freakishly talented, he attempted to support himself at various intervals as a schoolmaster, photographer, musician, painter of religious frescoes, inventor, astrologer and writer.

By the time he reached forty, Rolfe considered himself a full-time writer, turning out novels that were "rich, rare and bizarre in the extreme." They brought him some fame, much notoriety and no money whatsoever. In 1904, he published his now-acknowledged masterpiece, *Hadrian the Seventh*, which, for years, has been sort of an "underground classic." Rolfe described his novel as a "romance," although it was autobiographical in nature and essentially a profound study in self-justification and wish fulfillment, embracing all the bitterness and disappointments of the author's life. Before Rolfe died in extreme poverty and squalor in Venice in 1913, he declared: "One day posterity will be interested in my letters and everything I have written." Ironically, the international success of the play *Hadrian VII*, in which dramatist Peter Luke has skillfully juxtaposed reality and fantasy by framing the action of the novel within the context of Rolfe's own bizarre life, has assisted spectacularly in transforming a boast into a truism.

Peter Luke was born in England in 1919 and spent his formative years there and in Austria, Malta and Palestine. After studying painting in London and Paris, he served during World War II in Britain's Rifle Brigade. Following demobilization, he joined a wine-shipping firm where he remained for nine years. During this period, he also managed to write plays and had stories and articles published in a number of periodicals, including *The New Statesman* (& *Nation*), *The Cornhill* and *Envoy*. Subsequently, he became book critic for *The Queen*, then a play producer for the British Broadcasting Corporation. In his three-year tenure at the B.B.C., he was responsible for many acclaimed productions, notably *Hamlet at Elsinore; A Passage to India;* and *Silent Song,* the last named a winner of the 1967 Italia Prize and two other major awards. He also wrote and directed *Black Sound—Deep Song,* a film about the Spanish poet-dramatist Federico García Lorca, commissioned by the B.B.C. In that same period, two of Mr. Luke's plays—*Small Fish Are Sweet* and *Roll On, Bloomin' Death*—were staged in England, and several others were performed on television.

At present, Peter Luke is completing a new play, one that again will deal with a remarkably colorful central character, Sir Richard Burton, the nineteenth-century explorer, diplomat, author and pornographer. Production is contemplated for mid-1970; in the interim, the dramatist, who lives with his wife and their five children in a remote region of Andalusia, will be occupied with the film version of *Hadrian VII,* again to star Alec McCowen.

HADRIAN VII

Peter Luke

Based on Hadrian the Seventh *and other works by Frederick
Rolfe, "Baron Corvo"*

Hadrian VII was first staged on May 9, 1967, by the Birmingham (England) Repertory Theatre in association with Bill Freedman and Charles Kasher; Alec McCowen acted the role of Fr. William Rolfe-Hadrian VII. The production was taken to London, where it opened at the Mermaid Theatre on April 18, 1968.

The first American performance of *Hadrian VII* was presented at the Helen Hayes Theatre, New York, on January 8, 1969, by Lester Osterman Productions, Bill Freedman and Charles Kasher. The cast was as follows:

FR. WILLIAM ROLFE	*Alec McCowen*
MRS. CROWE	*Sydney Sturgess*
BAILIFFS	*William Needles, Gillie Fenwick*
AGNES	*Marie Paxton*
DR. TALACRYN, Bishop of Caerleon	*William Needles*
DR. COURTLEIGH, Cardinal-Archbishop of Pimlico	*Gillie Fenwick*
JEREMIAH SANT, F.R.S.	*Gerard Parkes*
THE CARDINAL-ARCHDEACON	*Richard Nicholls*
FATHER ST. ALBANS, Prepositor-General of the Jesuits	*Christopher Hewett*
CARDINAL RAGNA	*Louis Zorich*
CARDINAL BERSTEIN	*Truman Gaige*
RECTOR OF ST. ANDREW'S COLLEGE	*Neil Fitzgerald*
GEORGE ARTHUR ROSE	*Peter Jobin*
PAPAL CHAMBERLAIN	*John Hallow*
CARDINALS	*William A. Bush, Tom Gorman, Robert Hewitt, Arthur Marlowe, Theodore Tenley*
PAPAL GUARDS	*William Engel, Michael Stein*
ACOLYTES, SEMINARISTS, SWISS GUARDS	*B. J. DeSimone, Carl Jessop, John Kramer, James McDonald, Joseph Neal, Robert Shattuck*

Directed by Peter Dews
Settings & Costumes by Robert Fletcher
Lighting by Lloyd Burlingame

The play takes place in the early 20th century in London and Rome.

A NOTE ON THE APPEARANCE AND BEHAVIOURISMS OF ROLFE/HADRIAN

Frederick William Rolfe, when the play opens, is a smallish, spare man, of about forty. He wears his greying hair very short, is myopic and can hardly see without his plain, steel-rimmed spectacles, but he is slim, agile and erect.

His tastes are austere but he is fond of such things as goat's milk, apples, raw carrots, fresh linen and particularly water, both to drink and to wash in. He is a practical man and carries a penknife with which he prepares his apples, sharpens pencils, etc.

He smokes a lot, always rolling his own and tucking the ends in with a pencil. Cat-like, his movements are swift, lithe and silent. Likewise, there are moments when he remains utterly still. As Pope, he comports himself with extraordinary dignity when the occasion demands, though "off-duty" he reverts to his more abnormal self. In the early part of Act I and at the end of the play, Rolfe wears a threadbare clerical grey suit. During the rest of the play, Rolfe /Hadrian wears such canonical dress as may be appropriate.

ACT ONE

SCENE ONE

A corner of FREDERICK ROLFE's *bed-sitting room in London.
The room is the abode of a poor scholar of fastidious
habits and austere tastes. There is a small gas-fire right,
the meter for which is on the wall down right. Up left is
the door leading to the rest of the house. A small chest-
of-drawers is up center, and below it a wooden armchair.
Religious paintings cover the walls, and there is a small
crucifix on the wall below the fire. Next to the gas meter
is a mirror. A wooden chair is wedged beneath the door-
handle. Books lie around, and there is a bottle of ink on
the floor below the armchair.*

When the curtain rises, ROLFE *is seated in the armchair
writing a manuscript on his knees, and smoking a fat, untidy rolled cigarette which he seldom takes out of his
mouth. He is shivering with cold, and has a blanket
wrapped around him. After a moment there is a knock on
the door.* ROLFE *looks round to make sure the chair is
firmly wedged in place and smirks with satisfaction. The
knocking is repeated more peremptorily, accompanied by
rattlings of the door-handle.*

MRS. CROWE: [*Off*] Mr. Rolfe. [*She tries the handle, which
does not give*] Mr. Rolfe! [*She rattles the handle*] What's
the matter with this door? Mr. Rolfe, I know you're there.

ROLFE: Tickle your ass with a feather.

MRS. CROWE: [*Off*] What did you say?

ROLFE: Particularly nasty weather, Mrs. Crowe.

MRS. CROWE: [*Off*] Mr. Rolfe, I haven't climbed all these stairs just to be insulted. There are two gentlemen below who wish to see you.

ROLFE: [*Starting up; noticeably startled*] To see *me?*

MRS. CROWE: [*Off*] Yes, to see you.

> [ROLFE *quickly takes the fag-end out of his mouth and moves to the door to remove the barricade.* MRS. CROWE *enters furiously. She is a widow of about forty with pretentions to good looks and gentility. She succeeds only in being "genteel."* ROLFE *looks nervously past her down the staircase*]

MRS. CROWE: Ah, I thought you'd come off your high horse when you heard that.

ROLFE: [*Recovering slightly*] Oh—well, I'm very busy.

MRS. CROWE: They said it was a private matter which couldn't wait.

ROLFE: [*Attempting to bluster*] I'm not prepared to see them unless they state the precise nature of their business, Mrs. Crowe.

MRS. CROWE: If you think I'm going to run all the way up and down these stairs like a skivvy to carry your messages . . . [*Significantly*] I think you'd better see them, Mr. Rolfe.

ROLFE: Oh? Hmmmm! Very well. Please show them up, Mrs. Crowe, but let it be understood—

> [MRS. CROWE *exits, shutting the door*]

ROLFE: —that I haven't got all day. [*Crossing to the mirror*] Lascivious bitch! [*He quickly takes a stiff white collar and a plain black tie from the chest-of-drawers and puts them on. He hastily puts a packet of oatmeal out of sight in a drawer, then sits and makes notes on his manuscript*] I'm in an awful state. Calm down, calm down, buck up. [*Hearing footsteps*] Oh, my God . . .

[*There is the sound of footsteps mounting the stairs, and with a peremptory knock . . .*]

ROLFE: Come in.

[*. . .* MRS. CROWE *ushers in the two* BAILIFFS. *The* SECOND BAILIFF *is a venerable-looking old man with white hair. His colleague, the* FIRST BAILIFF, *is a tall, amiable, healthy-looking fellow in his early forties. It is suggested that they should bear a resemblance to* DR. COURTLEIGH, *Cardinal-Archbishop of Pimlico, and* DR. TALACRYN, *Bishop of Caerleon, respectively. Alternatively, the parts can be doubled to emphasise the likeness.* ROLFE *goes on making notes. After a moment he looks up*]

ROLFE: [*Turning on the charm*] Ah, good-day, gentlemen. [*With a gracious nod to* MRS. CROWE] Thank you so much, Mrs. Crowe.

[MRS. CROWE *hovers in the hope of hearing something*]

ROLFE: Please don't bother to wait. I shall see my visitors out myself.

[MRS. CROWE *exits reluctantly.* ROLFE *draws himself up to the full extent of his inconsiderable height to receive his guests. A trembling knee alone gives away his nervousness*]

ROLFE: And now, gentlemen, please tell me how I can be of service to you.

1ST BAILIFF: [*Looking at a document in his hand*] Are you Mr. Corvo?

ROLFE: [*Suspiciously*] No.

1ST BAILIFF: [*Looking at his papers*] Sorry, sir. I mean *Baron* Corvo?

ROLFE: That is not my name.

2ND BAILIFF: We're try—

1ST BAILIFF: [*Consulting his papers*] Oh. Then are you Frank W. Hochheimer?

[*The* SECOND BAILIFF *sits in the chair*]

ROLFE: [*Stiffly*] No.

1ST BAILIFF: Or Mr. F. Austin?

ROLFE: [*Icily*] I am not.

2ND BAILIFF: But you *are* Mr. Frederick William Rolfe [*He pronounces it as in "golf"*], are you not, sir?

ROLFE: That is almost correct. My name is Frederick William *Rolfe*. [*He pronounces it as in "oaf"*] And who, may I ask, are you?

1ST BAILIFF: My colleague and I are Officers of the Court—Bailiffs, you understand—and we hold a writ against you, Mr. Rolfe [*Handing the writ to* ROLFE] on behalf of certain parties—

[ROLFE *takes the writ and reads it*]

1ST BAILIFF: —claiming certain debts. Do you follow me so far, Mr. Rolfe?

ROLFE: Your brevity will assist my comprehension.

1ST BAILIFF: Quite so, sir. And I'm sure my colleague and I have no wish to remain here longer than necessary, so I will endeavour to constrict myself to the essential details, sir. The position is that, in brief, the Court has seen fit to award against you the initial sum of the debt plus the cost of the several plaintiffs versus Yourself for which a remittance must be made into Court forthwith in default of which and in consideration of a Warrant of Execution there will be no alternative but to attend at your premises and remove the contents thereof for sale by Public Auction.

ROLFE: [*Mumbling*] And then throw dice for my garments.

1ST BAILIFF: I beg your pardon?

2ND BAILIFF: 'Scuse me asking, but are you by any chance a clergyman or anything of that sort? I mean—Fr. Rolfe—it looks a bit like Father Rolfe. See what I mean?

ROLFE: My name is Frederick Rolfe. I have never taken Holy Orders. Had I done so, no doubt I should have been a bishop by now—not a mere priest.

2ND BAILIFF: [*Guffawing good-naturedly*] Ho, ho, sir. Very good.

1ST BAILIFF: Well, I think if you're quite clear as to the nature of our call, sir, we . . .

ROLFE: You leave me in no doubt as to the nature of your call.

1ST BAILIFF: [*Producing a slip of paper*] In that case perhaps you'd be good enough to sign this undertaking not to remove your furniture or effects or any part thereof from the premises until further notice.

ROLFE: You're asking me to sign this document?

1ST BAILIFF: That's right, sir. Just here.

ROLFE: I'm sorry, but that's something I never do.

1ST BAILIFF: What's that, sir?

ROLFE: Sign documents. I never sign documents.

1ST BAILIFF: Purely a formality, sir, I assure you.

ROLFE: You can assure me till the Day of Judgment, as many others have done before. Invariably their assurances were per-fervid, perfidious, casuistic and, in a word, false. Ergo, no signa-ture. Sorry.

1ST BAILIFF: Are you saying you are refusing to sign, sir?

ROLFE: I am saying in the simplest possible language that I do not intend to sign that document. Are you satisfied?

1ST BAILIFF: No, sir, I am not. If you refuse to sign this B sixty-three form here, I shall have no alternative but to apply im-mediately to the Court for a Warrant of Execution.

[*The* SECOND BAILIFF *rises and they both move upstage*]

1ST BAILIFF: You've not heard the last of this, I'm afraid, sir.

2ND BAILIFF: Good-day, sir.

[*The* BAILIFFS *exit. Alone,* ROLFE's *flippant demeanour suddenly changes to that of savage rage. He tears off his collar and tie.*

ROLFE: [*Through clenched teeth*] Someone will have to suffer for this.

[MRS. CROWE *appears at the door*]

MRS. CROWE: Are you by any chance speaking to me?

ROLFE: [*Quickly pulling himself together*] If I had heard your knock, Mrs. Crowe, I would have given myself the pleasure of addressing you, but since I did not . . . [*He sits in the arm-chair*]

MRS. CROWE: Perhaps you would be good enough to tell me who your callers were, Mr. Rolfe.

ROLFE: I'm not aware that it is part of our contract that I have to identify my visitors.

MRS. CROWE: You're in trouble again, aren't you? Were they the police?

ROLFE: No.

MRS. CROWE: [*Moving downstage a pace*] Well, why wouldn't they give their names, then? Is it money? [*After a pause*] It is, isn't it?

ROLFE: How can it be anything else? Of course it's money.

MRS. CROWE: So they were bailiffs then?

[*There is a silence while* MRS. CROWE *vacillates between her outraged feelings as a landlady and her concupiscent inclinations as a woman*]

MRS. CROWE: [*Moving above his chair; in a wheedling voice*] Why don't you let me help you? I could help you—if you wanted me to. [*She leans over him*] You know I have always wanted to be your friend. Couldn't I be now? Mr. Crowe left me quite comfortable. You know that. [*She puts her hand on his arm*]

[*In loathing at her touch* ROLFE *jumps up, and in doing so kicks over the ink bottle on the floor in front of him. He hurries to wipe up the mess*]

MRS. CROWE: [*Furious at the rejection of her advances*] There! Now look what you've done! Ink all over the floor! How do you suppose I'll ever get that out? It'll probably go right through the ceiling below.

ROLFE: [*Picking up the bottle*] I will naturally make good any damage done.

MRS. CROWE: Make good any damage! With the bailiffs hardly out of the house? [*Working herself up*] I'm not fooled by your high-falutin' talk any more. Before you do any more of your "making good" you'll kindly pay me the quarter's rent you owe. Yes, and you'll kindly pay it by the end of the week as well or I shall be obliged to give you notice to leave. As a matter of fact, I need the room for a business gentleman.

ROLFE: A business *gentleman*? Is there such a thing?

MRS. CROWE: An old friend of yours.

ROLFE: I haven't the slightest idea what you're talking about, neither have I any desire to . . . Who is this person?

MRS. CROWE: Oh, I fancy you'll remember him all right. Don't you remember Belfast?

ROLFE: Sant!

MRS. CROWE: That's right, Mr. Rolfe. Mr. Jeremiah Sant.

ROLFE: Sant and that gutter scandal-sheet of his—what is it called? The *Tory Protester?*

MRS. CROWE: I want the room.

ROLFE: What excrement is he tooting out of his Orange flute now?

MRS. CROWE: It's none of your business. It's pay up or get out.

[*She goes, deliberately not slamming the door*]

ROLFE: [*Shouting in a paroxysm of rage at the closed door*] You can't get shit from a wooden rocking-horse, you rapacious, concupiscent—female. [*After a short pause he has second*

thoughts, runs to the door, opens it, and shouts] Mrs. Crowe!
Someone will have to suffer for this.

[*There is no answer*]

ROLFE: Mrs. Crowe, I know you're listening. When you're sorry
for what you've said, don't be afraid to say so, Mrs. Crowe.
[*He closes the door and puts the blanket round his shoulders*]
Lascivious bitch. [*He rolls and lights a cigarette, holding it
cupped in his two hands for warmth*] All those curves and
protuberances—breeding, that's all they're good for. [*He sits*]
Jeremiah Sant is a gerrymandering gouger!

[*After a moment he hears footsteps on the stairs again.
He listens, wondering if it is* MRS. CROWE *coming back to
apologize. Instead, a letter is thrust under the door. He
rises, looks at it suspiciously, then picks it up and turns
it over, looking at the seal*]

ROLFE: What—what's that? Archbishop's House? [*He tears the
letter open and reads it with trembling hands. Savagely*] Hell
and damnation! Imbeciles! Owl-like Hierarchs! Degenerates!
[*After a pause*] God, if ever You loved me, hear me. They
have denied me the priesthood again. Not a chance do You
give me, God—ever. Listen! How can I serve You—[*To the
crucifix*]—while You keep me so sequestered? I'm intelligent.
So, O God, You made me. But intelligence must be active,
potent, and perforce I am impotent and inactive always; futile
in my loneliness. Why, O God, have You made me strange,
uncommon, such a mystery to my fellow-creatures? Am I such
a ruffian as to merit total exile from them? You have made
me denuded of the power of love—to love anybody or be loved.
I suppose I must go on like that to the end [*Grimly*] because
they are frightened of me—frightened of the labels I put on
them. [*He puts out his cigarette savagely*] Oh God, forgive
me smoking. I quite forgot. I am not doing well at present,
but what can I do? God, tell me clearly, unmistakably and
distinctly, tell me, tell me what I must do—and make me do

it. [*He sits*] Oh Lord, I am sick—and very tired. [*His mind is in a ferment and he cannot rest*]

[*There is a knock on the door*]

ROLFE: [*Fiercely*] Who is it?

[*He rises and moves to the door*]

AGNES: [*Off*] It's only me, sir.

ROLFE: [*Gently*] Oh! All right. Come in, Agnes.

[AGNES, *an elderly charlady, enters, wearing working clothes and an overall. She carries a tray on which is a bowl of bread-and-milk and a newspaper*]

AGNES: I brought you a little bread-and-milk. Whatever have you been saying to the Missus? Oh, well, never mind. Here you are. Eat it up whilst it's hot.

ROLFE: Thank you, Agnes. Please leave it.

[*He turns away*]

AGNES: [*Putting the tray on the chest*] My word, isn't it chilly in here? Why ever haven't you turned on the . . . [*She takes a quick look at* ROLFE, *sees that he is not paying attention, fumbles for her purse, moves down right and, taking out a coin, puts it in the meter*]

ROLFE: [*Turning and seeing her*] Agnes, I forbid you . . .

AGNES: [*Taking matches from her apron and lighting the fire*] Get along! Who d'you think you're forbidding then?

ROLFE: [*Moving over to warm himself*] You're a dear good soul, Agnes, but you shouldn't have done that.

AGNES: You can give it me back before I go to Mass Sunday.

ROLFE: But Agnes . . .

AGNES: I know you writing folk. I've had some in my time.

ROLFE: I'm trying to tell you, Agnes, that I may not be able to pay you back on Sunday.

AGNES: Sunday? I'm sure I never said *next* Sunday. Wait till the number comes up with your name on it and you can stand me a treat.

ROLFE: [*Moving to the chest*] So I will, Agnes, my word on it.

[*He picks up the tray, takes it to his chair, sits, and starts to eat hungrily*]

AGNES: I don't know why you don't go back to your painting. You had ever such a lovely touch with that.

[ROLFE *is still guzzling up the bread-and-milk when his eyes fall on the newspaper. He picks it up and starts reading it, perfunctorily at first, then with ever-increasing interest*]

AGNES: All those saints large as life. Some of them larger, I wouldn't be surprised.

[*She begins to dust the mantelpiece, then the chest*]

ROLFE: The Pope's dead.

AGNES: [*Not really listening*] Then there was your photography. I'm sure you could make a bit out of that—but you haven't got your camera now, have you?

ROLFE: Agnes, the Pope is dead.

AGNES: Yes, I know. God rest his soul. The poor old gentleman.

ROLFE: [*Reading from the paper*] "A Conclave of the Sacred College is to be convened immediately in order to elect a successor to the Holy See."

AGNES: Perhaps they'll choose our own Archbishop this time.

ROLFE: [*Continuing to read*] "In accordance with the Council of Lateran, the votes of two-thirds of the Cardinals present at the Conclave will be required for the election of the Supreme Pontiff. A Vatican expert reports, however, that with the present alignment among the various factions in the Sacred College, it is by no means easy to see how a clear two-thirds majority can be achieved. He goes on to suggest . . ."

AGNES: It's about time they had an English Pope for a change.

[ROLFE *turns to stare at her*]

AGNES: There—I've finished you now, Mr. Rolfe. See you tomorrow, then.

[AGNES *exits.* ROLFE *stares after her for a brief moment. Then he rises, replaces the tray on the chest, takes a fat-looking reference book from the mantelpiece and looks something up in the index. He sits, takes up his paper and pencil and starts to write rapidly with occasional reference to the book*]

ROLFE: English Pope. Seven-seventy-two to seven-ninety-five, Hadrian the First. Eight-sixty-nine to eight-seventy-two, Hadrian the Second. Eight-eighty-four to eight-eighty-five—not very long, that one—Hadrian the Third. Ah—here we are. Eleven-fifty-four to eleven-fifty-nine, Nicholas Breakspear, Hadrian the Fourth. Ha! Son of a monk! [*There is a pause while he flips through the reference book again*] Hadrian the Fifth, a Genoese. Hadrian the Sixth, that's right, from Utrecht. [*He continues to write, with great energy, for a moment or two*] Hadrian the Fourth . . . Hadrian the Fifth . . . Hadrian the Sixth . . . Hadrian the Seventh. In mind he was tired, worn out by years of hope deferred, of loneliness, of unrewarded toil.

[*There is a change in the lighting to a warmer hue. After a few moments,* ROLFE *is interrupted by a knock at the door*]

ROLFE: Who is it?

[MRS. CROWE *opens the door*]

MRS. CROWE: There are two gentlemen downstairs to see you.

ROLFE: Not now.

MRS. CROWE: They're clergymen.

ROLFE: Clergymen. Come in, Mrs. Crowe.

[MRS. CROWE *enters the room*]

ROLFE: What sort of clergymen?

MRS. CROWE: I couldn't really say. One's an elderly gentleman, all in red and black. The other is much younger with bits of purple.

ROLFE: His Grace the Archbishop of Pimlico, and the Bishop of Caerleon—of course.

MRS. CROWE: [*More intrigued than ever*] Oh. You were expecting them then?

ROLFE: They are not entirely unexpected. Now perhaps you would be good enough to . . .

MRS. CROWE: Yes, I'll bring them up.

> [MRS. CROWE *exits*. ROLFE *rushes to pick up his tie and collar and puts them on in front of the mirror. This done, he quickly adopts a dignified posture to receive his visitors. After a pause* MRS. CROWE *shows in* DR. COURTLEIGH *and* DR. TALACRYN]

MRS. CROWE: This way, gentlemen. I'm sorry for all the stairs. Oh dear, I'm quite out of breath myself.

ROLFE: Come in. *Thank* you, Mrs. Crowe.

MRS. CROWE: I just wondered if your guests would like some tea . . .

ROLFE: Not for the moment, thank you.

MRS. CROWE: Very well.

[MRS. CROWE *exits*]

TALACRYN: Your Eminence, may I present Mr. Rolfe . . .

> [ROLFE *ignores* COURTLEIGH, *goes straight to* TALACRYN, *kneels to him and kisses the Episcopal ring on his hand*]

ROLFE: [*To* COURTLEIGH] Your Eminence will understand that

I do not wish to be disrespectful, but the Bishop of Caerleon calls himself my friend.

COURTLEIGH: I hope, Mr. Rolfe, that you will accept my blessing as well as Dr. Talacryn's.

[ROLFE *kneels and kisses the Cardinalatial ring*]

ROLFE: Please sit down—as best you may.

[COURTLEIGH *sits center,* TALACRYN *stands left of him*]

TALACRYN: Freddy, His Eminence wishes to ask you a few questions and he thought you would not take it amiss if I were present—as your friend.

[ROLFE *acknowledges* TALACRYN'S *remark and turns to* COURTLEIGH]

COURTLEIGH: Mr. Rolfe, it has recently been brought to my remembrance that you were at one time a candidate for Holy Orders. I am aware of all the—ah—unpleasantness which attended that portion of your career; but it is only lately that I have fully realized that you yourself have never accepted or acquiesced in the verdict of your superiors.

ROLFE: I never have accepted it. I have never acquiesced in it. I never will accept it. I never will acquiesce in it.

COURTLEIGH: Quite, er . . .

ROLFE: But I nourish no grudge and seek no revenge. I am content to lead my own life, avoiding all my brother Catholics when circumstances throw them—

[COURTLEIGH *gets restive*]

ROLFE: —in my path, I don't squash cockroaches.

COURTLEIGH: And the effect upon your soul?

ROLFE: The effect upon my soul is perfectly ghastly. I have lost faith in man, and I have lost the power of loving. I have become a rudderless derelict.

COURTLEIGH: How terrible!

ROLFE: Terrible? Yes, it is indeed terrible. And, as head of the Roman Communion in this country, let the blame be upon you for the destruction of this soul.

[COURTLEIGH *raises his hands in protest*]

ROLFE: As for your myrmidons, I spit upon them and defy them and you may rest assured that I shall continue to fight them as long as I can hold a pen.

COURTLEIGH: Would you mind telling me your reasons?

ROLFE: I should have to say very disagreeable things, Eminence.

COURTLEIGH: Tell me the truth.

ROLFE: The Catholic and Apostolic Church, with its championing of learning and beauty, was always to me a real and living thing. It was with the highest hopes, therefore, that I entered Oscott College to begin my career as a Clerk in Holy Orders. I was soon obliged to leave, however, after a dispute with the Principal, who seemed to see no offence in grubs grazing on the lettuces and caterpillars cantering across the refectory table. The Archbishop of Agneda then invited me, on recommendation, to attend St. Andrew's College at Rome. I gladly went, on the assurance that my expenses would be borne by the Archbishop. They never were and, in consequence, I was several hundred pounds out of pocket.

COURTLEIGH: Dear me!

[*He looks at* TALACRYN *for confirmation.* TALACRYN *nods agreement*]

COURTLEIGH: Yes?

ROLFE: Then after four months in college, I was expelled suddenly and brutally.

COURTLEIGH: And what reason was given?

ROLFE: No reason was ever given. The gossip of my fellow students —immature cubs prone to acne and versed in dog Latin—was that I had no Vocation.

COURTLEIGH: I see. Go on.

ROLFE: Then there was the occasion in Wales when the machinations of a certain cleric, whose cloven hoof defiled the shrine of the Blessed Saint Winifred of Holywell, defrauded me of my rightful desserts for two years of arduous work undertaken at his request. Having been robed by the said priest not only of my means of livelihood, but also of health, comfort, friends and reputation, and brought physically to my knees, he then gave me the *coup de grace* by debarring me from the Sacraments. I then had no option but to leave Wales and start life from scratch. I walked to London. Two hundred and fourteen miles. It took me eighteen days.

COURTLEIGH: Good gracious! But did no one come forward to assist you at this time?

ROLFE: No one except the Bishop of Caerleon, who somewhat belatedly received me back into Communion. Eventually, others, moved no doubt by the last twitchings of their dying consciences, made tentative overtures. To these I quoted St. Matthew twenty-five, verses forty-one to forty-three.

COURTLEIGH: Now, how does that go?

[He feels in the air with his hand for the quotation]

ROLFE: From "I was hungered and ye gave me no meat" down to "Depart from me ye cursed, into aeonial fire."

COURTLEIGH: You are hard, Mr. Rolfe, very hard.

ROLFE: I am what you and your fellow Catholics have made me.

COURTLEIGH: Poor child—poor child.

ROLFE: I request Your Eminence will not speak to me in that tone. I disdain your pity at this date. The catastrophe is complete.

COURTLEIGH: My son, have you never caught yourself thinking kindly of your former friends? You cannot always be in a state of white-hot rage, you know.

ROLFE: Yes, Eminence, there are some with whom, strange to say, I would wish to be reconciled—when my anger is not dynamic, that is. *[He smiles]* But they do not come to me—as you have come.

COURTLEIGH: They probably do not wish to expose themselves to—ah—quotations from St. Matthew's gospel.

ROLFE: Did I heave china-ware at Your Lordship?

TALACRYN: You did not. [*To* COURTLEIGH] Your Eminence, I believe I understand Mr. Rolfe's frame of mind. A burned child dreads the fire.

COURTLEIGH: True. And what course did you embark on then, Mr. Rolfe?

ROLFE: I determined to occupy my energies with some pursuit for which my nature fitted me, until the Divine Giver of my Vocation should deign to manifest it to others as well as myself. I took to painting and writing. I began to write simply because, by this time, I had an imperious necessity to say certain things. [*He sits*] In any case, ultimate penury denied me access to painting materials. So literature is now the only outlet you Catholics have left me—and believe me, I have very much to say.

COURTLEIGH: You have not perhaps many kindly feelings towards me personally, Mr. Rolfe.

ROLFE: I have no kindly feelings at all towards Your Eminence, but I trust I shall never be found wanting in reverence towards your sacred purple. I am only speaking civilly to you because you are a successor to Augustine and Theodore Dunstan and Anselm, Chichele and Chichester, and because for the nonce, my friend the Bishop of Caerleon has made you my guest.

COURTLEIGH: Well, well!

ROLFE: My Lord Cardinal, I do not know what you want of me, nor why you have come.

COURTLEIGH: I wished first of all to know if you still remained Catholic.

ROLFE: If I still remained Catholic!

COURTLEIGH: People who have been denied the priesthood have been known to commit apostasy.

ROLFE: Rest assured, Eminence, I am not in revolt against the Faith, but against the Faithful.

COURTLEIGH: [*Trying not to get angry*] I am trying to determine whether or not, at the time of which we are speaking, you
formed any opinion of your own concerning your Vocation,
Mr. Rolfe.

ROLFE: No.

COURTLEIGH: No?

ROLFE: No. My opinion concerning my Vocation for the priesthood had been formed when I was a boy of fifteen. I have never
relinquished my Divine Gift.

COURTLEIGH: You persist?

ROLFE: Your Eminence, I am not a bog-trotting Fenian or one of
your Sauchiehall Street hybrids—but English and sure; born
under Cancer. Naturally I persist.

COURTLEIGH: But the man to whom Divine Providence vouch-
safes a Vocation is bound to pursue it. *You* are practising as
an author.

ROLFE: This is only a means to an end. [*Rising*] When I shall
have earned enough to pay my debts, I shall go straight to
Rome and fix the profligate priest who sacked me.

COURTLEIGH: [*Throwing up his hands*] Ssh!

TALACRYN: [*Quickly*] Your Eminence mustn't be offended by
Mr. Rolfe's satirical turn of phrase. He is not the man to
smite those who have done him ill.

ROLFE: Do not deceive yourself, My Lord. So long as we recruit
our spiritual pastors from the hooligan class, I shall smite them
with all my strength.

COURTLEIGH: Really, Mr. Rolfe!

TALACRYN: You're a little beside the point, Freddy.

ROLFE: Under the circumstances, His Eminence will indulge me.
I've had enough of being buffeted by bishops. Until I'm the
possessor of a cheque book I do not propose to start commerce
with the clergy again.

[*There is a pause while* COURTLEIGH *looks into space and*
TALACRYN *looks at his toes*]

COURTLEIGH: Frederick William Rolfe, I summon you to offer yourself to me.

ROLFE: [*After a pause: quietly*] I am not ready to offer myself to Your Eminence.

COURTLEIGH: Not ready?

ROLFE: I hoped I had made it clear that, in regard to my Vocation, I am marking time until I shall have earned enough to pay my debts which were so monstrously incurred on me.

COURTLEIGH: You keep harping on that string.

ROLFE: It is the only string you have left unbroken on my lute.

COURTLEIGH: Well, well; the money question need not trouble you.

ROLFE: But it does trouble me. And your amazing summons troubles me as well. Why do you come to me after all these years?

COURTLEIGH: It is precisely because of these years—how many was it?

ROLFE: Call it twenty.

COURTLEIGH: —that we must take your singular persistency as proof of the genuineness of your Vocation. And therefore, I am here today to summon you to accept Holy Orders with no delay beyond the canonical intervals.

ROLFE: In two years' time, when I shall have published three more books, I will respond to your summons. Not till then.

TALACRYN: But His Eminence has said that the money question need not hinder you.

ROLFE: Yes, and the Archbishop of Agneda said the same.

[COURTLEIGH *looks as if he is going to explode, and* TALACRYN *hastens to intervene*]

TALACRYN: I am witness of His Eminence's words, Freddy.

ROLFE: What's the good of that? Supposing in a couple of months His Eminence chooses to alter his mind? Could I hail a prince of the church before a secular tribunal? Would I? Could I

subpoena Your Lordship to testify against your Metropolitan
and Provincial? Could I? Would I? Would you?

[COURTLEIGH *makes as if to interject, but* ROLFE *cuts in*]

ROLFE: My Lord Cardinal, I must speak, and you must hear me.
You are offering me the Priesthood on good and legitimate
grounds, for which I thank God. But, if I correctly interpret
you, you are also offering me something in the shape of money,
and I will be no man's pensioner.

COURTLEIGH: [*Mildly*] Please understand me, Mr. Rolfe, that
the monies in question are being offered solely as restitution
for the years in which you were denied the Priesthood.

ROLFE: Oh! [*After a pause*] No, I will not take charity.

TALACRYN: Well, then, Freddy, in what form will you accept
this act of justice from us? Do make an effort to believe we
are sincerely in earnest and that in this matter we are in your
hands. [*Turning to* COURTLEIGH] I may say that, Your Eminence?

COURTLEIGH: Unreservedly.

[*There is a pause while* ROLFE *considers*]

ROLFE: [*Quietly but with determination*] I will accept a written
expression of regret for the wrongs which have been done to me
by both Your Eminence and by others who have followed
your advice, command or example.

COURTLEIGH: [*Taking a folded piece of paper from his breviary*] It is here.

ROLFE: [*At first surprised, then reading it with care*] I thank
Your Eminence. [*He tears the paper into pieces*]—and all
my brother Catholics.

COURTLEIGH: Man alive!

ROLFE: I do not care to preserve a record of my superiors' humiliation.

COURTLEIGH: [*With an effort*] I see that Mr. Rolfe knows
how to behave nobly, Frank.

ROLFE: Only now and again. But I had long ago arranged to do just that.

[*The prelates make a gesture of incomprehension to each other.* COURTLEIGH *stands.* ROLFE *kneels and receives benedictions*]

COURTLEIGH: We shall see you then at Archbishop's House tomorrow morning, Mr. Rolfe.

ROLFE: I will be there at half-past seven to confess to the Bishop of Caerleon. Your Eminence says Mass at eight and will give me to Holy Communion. Then, if it please Your Eminence, you will give me the four Minor Orders. In the meantime, I will go and have a Turkish bath and buy myself a Roman collar.

[COURTLEIGH *moves to the door.* ROLFE *goes quickly up and opens it.* COURTLEIGH *exits.* TALACRYN *is about to follow*]

ROLFE: Your Lordship doesn't happen to know the price of collars these days?

TALACRYN: [*Apologetically*] I haven't the slightest idea, I'm afraid.

ROLFE: Well then, just to be on the safe side, perhaps you wouldn't mind springing me a fiver.

TALACRYN: [*Embarrassed*] Oh, certainly. Certainly. [*He fumbles in his pockets for his wallet. Eventually he finds it and gives a banknote to* ROLFE] Thank you.

ROLFE: [*Graciously*] Not at all. See you tomorrow.

[TALACRYN *exits, leaving the door open.* ROLFE *goes to the mirror, takes off his tie and turns his collar back to front. He then gives his reflection an Episcopal blessing. Suddenly he freezes. He sees a reflection of somebody behind him. He turns round to see* JEREMIAH SANT *standing in the doorway*]

ROLFE: Sant!

SANT: Still at your play-acting, I see! What part is it this time?

ROLFE: What are you doing in here?

SANT: I've come to look at my room.

ROLFE: *Your* room?

SANT: Aye. I've been given to understand that you've got your marching orders again.

ROLFE: What do you mean?

SANT: The Order of the Boot. You're out. Just like old times, isn't it?

ROLFE: [*Changing tactics*] Yes, as a matter of fact I do have to leave here as it happens. I've been summoned for work elsewhere.

SANT: Summoned, have ye? Summonsed, more likely, from what I know of you.

ROLFE: Meanwhile this room is mine until the end of the week.

SANT: Aye, if you've paid the rent.

ROLFE: Get out of here.

SANT: Oh, aye, I'm going, but I'll be back on Saturday, so make sure you're away by then.

ROLFE: What makes you persist in hounding me?

SANT: You really want an answer? Read Revelations seventeen. Do you know how it goes?

ROLFE: I do not.

SANT: Like this: "And there came one of the seven angels, saying unto me, come hither; I will shew unto thee the judgment of the great whore that sitteth upon many waters: With whom the kings of the earth have committed fornication, and the inhabitants of the earth have been made drunk with the wine of her fornication—"

ROLFE: Orange Day rantings!

SANT: Let me finish—"So he carried me away in the spirit into the wilderness: and I saw a woman sit upon a scarlet coloured beast, full of names of blasphemy, having seven heads and ten horns . . ." As far as I'm concerned you're all seven of those heads and all ten of the horns—because you worked for me once. Remember?

ROLFE: It is not a memory I cherish.

SANT: Likely not. A fake, a liar and a cheat hardly likes to be shown up for what he really is.

ROLFE: You've no cause to say that.

SANT: Haven't I? Haven't I? You think I don't know what went on in Skene Street? You think I don't know why they carried you out into the street, in your bed for all to see?

> [ROLFE *winces at this recollection which obviously hits below the belt*]

SANT: Aye! That got ye, didn't it? "And the beast was taken, and with him the false prophet that received the mask of the beast. These were both cast alive into a lake of fire burning with brimstone!"

ROLFE: Ravings of a bog-trotting lunatic.

SANT: Lunatic, is it? Who's the biggest lunatic, you or me? When your lot go to Communion and eat that wafer, you believe it's the body, blood and bones of Jesus Christ, don't ye? That makes you a Cannibal, doesn't it?

ROLFE: Not on a Friday.

SANT: Ugh, you make me puke, you dirty Popehead.

ROLFE: Get out.

SANT: All right friend, you asked a question and I've given you the answer. [*He makes for the door*] As the Lord saith, an eye for an eye and a tooth for a tooth. I'm not finished with you yet. [*He stops with his hand on the doorhandle*] When you go leave the window wide, will ye. It's the smell of a Papish I can't abide. [*Shouting*] God save Britain from Popery! No surrender!

> [SANT *exits, leaving the door open, and singing as he goes, "The Sash My Father Wore"*]

SANT: "Our Father knew the Rome of old
And evil is thy fame.

Thy kind embrace the galling chain,
Thy kiss the blazing flame."

[ROLFE *rises and stands quite still for a moment. His*
triumphant mood has vanished and, once more, he looks
trapped and hunted. After a moment's thought he springs
into action. Pulling a holdall out from the corner up
center he puts it on the chair, takes a few effects from
the chest-of-drawers and throws them in, then goes to
the door and listens to make sure the coast is clear. Having
satisfied himself on this count he picks up the holdall
and tiptoes out, as the lights fade to a:]

BLACKOUT

SCENE TWO

A room in Archbishop's House. Seven-thirty the follow-
ing morning.
The only furniture is an upright armchair set center
and facing at an angle up left center and a thick cushion
set close left of the chair.
As the lights come up, TALACRYN *enters from an open-*
ing up right and moves to the chair. A moment later
ROLFE *enters up left.*

TALACRYN: Good morning, Freddy. I hope your new lodgings
are comfortable.

ROLFE: Compared to Broadhurst Gardens, they are as the Elysian
Fields.

TALACRYN: I never cared much for N.W.6 either. Now—shall
we get this over?

ROLFE: It may take rather a long time.

TALACRYN: All day if necessary.

[*He takes a small violet stole which he has been carry-*
ing on his arm, kisses the cross embroidered on it, and

puts it round his shoulders He then sits in the chair.
ROLFE *kneels on the cushion facing downstage, so that*
he has a three-quarter back view of the BISHOP. *He makes*
the sign of the cross. Both skip through the ritual be-
ginning and end of the confession pretty fast]

ROLFE: Bless me, Father, for I have sinned.

TALACRYN: May the Lord be in thine heart and on thy lips,
that thou with truth and humility mayest confess thy sins
[*He makes the sign of the cross*], in the name of the
Father and of the Son and of the Holy Ghost, Amen.

ROLFE: I last confessed five days ago.

TALACRYN: Since then, my son?

ROLFE: Since then I broke the first commandment by being
superstitiously silly enough to come downstairs in my socks
because I had accidentally put on my left shoe before my
right. I broke the third commandment by permitting my mind
to be distracted by the palpably Dublin accent of the Priest
who said Mass on Saturday.

TALACRYN: Is there nothing more on your conscience, my son?

ROLFE: Lots. I confess that I have broken the sixth commandment
by continuing to read an epigram in the Anthology after I
had found out that it was obscene. I have broken the third
commandment of the Church by eating dripping toast for
tea on Friday. I was hungry; it was very nice. I made a good
meal of it and couldn't eat any dinner. This was thoughtless
at first, then wilful.

TALACRYN: Are you bound to fast this Lent?

ROLFE: Yes, Father. I should now like to make a general confession of the chief sins of my life.

TALACRYN: Proceed, my son.

ROLFE: I earnestly desire to do God's will in all things, but
I often fail. I like to worship my Maker alone, unseen of all
save him. That is why I cannot hear Mass with devotion in
those churches where one is obliged to squat in a pew like
a Protestant, with other people's hot and filthy breath blowing
down my neck. My mind has a twist towards frivolity, towards
perversity. I have been irreverent and disobedient to my

superiors. For example, I said that the legs of a certain domestic prelate were formed like little Jacobean communion-rails.

[TALACRYN *reacts slightly to this last*]

ROLFE: I have told improper stories—not of the revolting kind, but those which are witty, anti-Protestant—the sort common among the clergy. Being anti-pathetic to fish, I once made an enemy sick by the filthy comparison which I used in regard to some oysters which he was about to eat. I confess that two or three times in my life I have delighted in impure thoughts inspired by some lines in Cicero's *Oration for Marcus Coelius*.

TALACRYN: I don't for the moment recall—well, never mind. Is there nothing further?

ROLFE: There is one thing which I have never mentioned in confession except in vague terms only.

TALACRYN: Relieve your mind, my son.

ROLFE: Father, I confess I have not kept my senses in proper custody. Sometimes I catch myself extracting elements of aesthetic enjoyment from unaesthetic situations.

TALACRYN: Can you be more precise, my son?

ROLFE: Yes, well, for example, I once was present at the amputation of a leg. Under anaesthetics, directly the saw touched the marrow of the thigh bone, the other leg began to kick. I was next to it, and the surgeon told me to hold it still. It was ghastly, but I did. And then I actually caught myself admiring the exquisite silky texture of the human skin. Father, I am a very sorry Christian. I confess all these sins, all the sins which I cannot remember, all the sins of my life. I implore pardon of God; and from thee, O Father, penance and absolution. [*Quickly*] Therefore, I beseech blessed Mary Ever-Virgin.

TALACRYN: My son, do you love God?

[*From silence, tardily the response emerges*]

ROLFE: I don't know. I really don't know. He is the Maker of the World to me. He is Truth and Righteousness and

Beauty. He is first. He is last. He is Lord of all to me. I
absolutely believe in Him. I unconditionally trust Him. I am
ready and willing to make any kind of sacrifice for Him. So
far I clearly see. Then in my mind, there comes a great gap—
filled with fog.

TALACRYN: Do you love your neighbour?

ROLFE: Hmm?

TALACRYN: Do you love your neighbour?

ROLFE: Oh. No. Frankly, I detest him—and her. Most people
are repulsive to me, because they are ugly in person, or
in manner, or in mind. I have met those with whom I should
like to be in sympathy, but I have been unable to get near
enough to them.

TALACRYN: Could you not love them?

ROLFE: No.

TALACRYN: Do you love yourself?

ROLFE: On the whole, I think I despise myself, body, mind
and soul. I do look after my body and cultivate my mind.
And naturally I stick up for myself, but—no, my body and
mind are no particular pleasure to me.

TALACRYN: Have you nothing else to confess, my son?

ROLFE: Nothing. Really nothing, Father. I am very tired. I long
to be at rest.

TALACRYN: That is actually the longing of your soul for God.
Cultivate that longing, my son, for it will lead you to love
Him. Thank Him with all your heart for this great gift of
longing. At the same time remember the words of Christ
our Saviour: "If ye Love Me, keep My Commandments."
Remember, He definitely commands you to love your neighbour. Serve the servants of God, and you will learn to love
God. You have tasted the pleasures of this world and they
are as ashes in your mouth. In the tremendous dignity to
which you have been called—the dignity of the priesthood—
you will be subject to fiercer temptations than those which
have assaulted you in the past. Brace the great natural strength
of your will to resist them. Begin to love your neighbour so
that you may soon consciously come to love God. My son,

the key to all your difficulties, past, present and to come, is love. For your penance, you will say—no, the penance for Minor Orders is rather long—for your penance you will say the Divine Praises with the celebrant after Mass. And now—

[*The ritual is gabbled through,* ROLFE *repeating quickly after* TALACRYN]

TALACRYN: O my God, most worthy of all love—I grieve from my heart for having sinned against Thee—And I purpose by Thy Grace—Never more to offend Thee for the time to come.

[TALACRYN *continues alone, making the sign of the cross*]

TALACRYN: Ego te absolvo in Nomine Patris et Filii et Spiritus Sancti, Amen. Go in peace and pray for me.

[ROLFE *and* TALACRYN *rise and move downstage together.* TALACRYN *resumes his informal manner*]

TALACRYN: But before you do, I have been instructed by His Eminence to inform you that you will accompany him to Rome tomorrow.

ROLFE: To Rome!

TALACRYN: You will act as his private chaplain at the Conclave which is to elect the new Pope. We will travel together, Freddy.

[ROLFE *and* TALACRYN *move upstage towards the exit right. A single bell starts to toll insistently. An echoing liturgy is distantly heard as the lights fade to a:*]

BLACKOUT

SCENE THREE

A chapel in the Vatican.
    As the lights come up, a bell tolls in the distance and the liturgy continues to be heard in some remote side chapel.

The only furnishings are two candelabra, up right center and left center. Two ACOLYTES [*boys*] *in surplices enter, from up right and up left, genuflect in unison towards the direction of the altar, and proceed to light the candelabra with long tapers. Having done so, they genuflect again, and both exit up right.*

TALACRYN *and* ROLFE *enter together up left. Their hands are folded, clasping breviaries.* ROLFE, *now in Holy Orders, wears a black soutane and biretta.* TALACRYN *wears similar garb suitable to a bishop.*

As they speak the following dialogue, they perambulate round the stage together.

ROLFE: [*Sniffing at the smell of incense*] Nothing stinks like the odour of sanctity.

TALACRYN: Now, now.

ROLFE: [*Pointing out front*] Look at those frescos. Wasn't it Mark Twain who said: "The Creator made Italy from designs by Michelangelo?"

TALACRYN: [*Distrait*] Very possibly. Their Eminences are still sitting, it seems.

ROLFE: On two addled eggs apiece.

TALACRYN: Freddy, I beg you—the whole world is waiting for the imminent announcement of a new Pope, and you make jokes in rather doubtful taste.

ROLFE: Let me assure Your Lordship that my flippancy in no way reflects my concern with the outcome of the Sacred Consistory. I've studied the form of those members of the Sacred College who could be said to be possible starters for the Supreme Pontificate, and it's my belief that the short-odds favourite . . .

TALACRYN: Short-odds favourite!

ROLFE: A sporting metaphor, indicating . . .

TALACRYN: I am acquainted with the jargon of the Turf, Freddy.

ROLFE: Then if I may continue the analogy, it's perfectly plain to a student of form that the short-odds favourite must be the present Secretary of State, Cardinal Ragna, whom God preserve.

TALACRYN: Not everyone would say "Amen" to that, I fear.

ROLFE: But then there is the malpractice called "Bumping and Boring"—

TALACRYN: —much frowned upon by the stewards—

ROLFE: —and I very much doubt whether Cardinal Ragna will be allowed to trot away with the race. Our own Archbishop, for example, would nominate the Parish Priest of Ballyjames-duff if it would keep Ragna out.

TALACRYN: Steady.

ROLFE: And I'm prepared to bet a thousand pound to a penny-halfpenny stamp that the Conclave has broken down again for the simple reason that Ragna's been nobbled.

TALACRYN: [Smiling] I wish I had it in me to be quite so irreverent as you, Freddy.

ROLFE: Perhaps, but I doubt if Your Lordship has it in him to be quite so devout either. You are a natural Christian, My Lord Bishop. I, on the other hand, am a religious maniac.

TALACRYN: You do yourself an injustice.

ROLFE: [Casually] I know I do. [Looking up at a fresco on the ceiling] Isn't that superb? [Pointing] Look at that. A little lacking in generosity in describing—[He makes a graphic gesture]—but compared to a figure like that, what can people see to admire in the female form?

TALACRYN: It's a matter of taste, I suppose.

ROLFE: [Looking at TALACRYN] What a waste!

TALACRYN: What is a waste?

ROLFE: That such a fine, upstanding man as Your Lordship should have felt inclined to accept the celibacy of priesthood.

TALACRYN: Good heavens, Freddy. If you are being serious, I can assure you that from the moment I took Orders no other thought ever occurred to me.

ROLFE: Nevertheless one has to admit that the vestigial nipples on a man are about as useful as the Pontifical pudenda. Had I been a Renaissance Pope, I should have insisted that . . .

[*A bell begins to clang insistently*]

ROLFE: Something seems to be happening.

[ROLFE *moves down left.* TALACRYN *follows to right of him*]

TALACRYN: I think they must have risen.

ROLFE: Who?

TALACRYN: The Cardinals-Compromissory.

ROLFE: Will they have reached a decision?

TALACRYN: We shall soon see. Here they come.

[*The nine* CARDINALS-COMPROMISSORY, *in full purple, led by the* BEARERS, *appear from the rear of the auditorium and move in procession down the aisles to the stage, chanting the* Christus Vincit *as they move.*

Arriving on the stage, they form an arc from right to above TALACRYN *left center. The* CARDINAL-ARCHDEACON *remains extreme right. Lastly comes an* ACOLYTE *bearing the Papal crown—the triple tiara—on a cushion. All bow in the direction of the altar, then turn inwards. As soon as everyone is in position the bell ceases*]

ROLFE: [*In a whisper to* TALACRYN] What is it? What is happening?

TALACRYN: I think God has given us a Pope.

ROLFE: Whom?

[*The litany ceases, and all turn to face* ROLFE *and* TALACRYN. *All except* ROLFE *kneel*]

CARDINAL-ARCHDEACON: Reverend Lord, the Sacred College has elected Thee to be the successor to St. Peter. Wilt thou accept pontificality?

[*Since all present are now facing towards* ROLFE *and* TALACRYN, ROLFE *assumes it is the latter who is being addressed. He turns towards* TALACRYN *with a happy smile.* TALACRYN, *however, is kneeling. Confused,* ROLFE *turns back to look at the* CARDINAL-ARCHDEACON]

CARDINAL-ARCHDEACON: [*With greater emphasis*] Reverend Lord, the Sacred College has elected Thee to be the successor to St. Peter. Wilt thou accept pontificality?

[*There is another pause.* ROLFE, *looking round to where all are on their knees facing inwards towards him, at last realizes that the awful question is addressed to him*]

ROLFE: Will *I*?

TALACRYN: [*In a whisper*] The response is *Volo*—or *Nolo*.

[ROLFE *takes a deep breath, crossing his right hand over his left on his breast*]

ROLFE: *Volo*—I will.

[*As the organ peals out:*]

THE CURTAIN FALLS

ACT TWO

SCENE ONE

When the curtain rises, MRS. CROWE *is seated upstage on the chaise-longue, with* JEREMIAH SANT *beside her. Both have drinks in their hands.*

SANT *is a member of the F.R.S.—Fellowship of Religious Segregation, an extremist group, outlawed in Ulster, dedicated to the persecution of Roman Catholics in general and the Pope in particular. He also runs a rabble-rousing newspaper called* The Troy Protestor *dedicated to the same aims.* SANT *himself is a violent and dangerous fanatic.* MRS. CROWE *is reading aloud from a newspaper.*

MRS. CROWE: Where are we? Yes, here it is— ". . . and as representatives of the Catholic world looked on, the Triple Crown was placed on the head of Frederick William Rolfe, the first English Pope to ascend the Throne of St. Peter since eleven-fifty-four when Nicholas Breakspear became Pope Hadrian the Fourth . . ."

SANT: Holy God, doesn't it make you want to puke! To think of an Englishman sinking so low. What paper is that, anyway?

MRS. CROWE: The *Daily Mirror.*

SANT: Well just listen to what the old *Protestor* has got to say. You'll have no trouble identifying the writer. [*He takes a copy of his own newspaper out of his pocket and starts to read*] "Recent sorry events in Rome must remind all True Blue Ulstermen that we will never bow down to those who are trying to sell us lock, stock and barrel to Popery. We will have no truck with the English traitor who calls himself the Pope. He may call himself Pope, but we call him the Roman anti-christ. Let us be reminded of Papist policy in Ulster. They intend to *breed* us out. But the wall of separation reaches to Highest Heaven. We will not allow the rights of the individual, nor the rights of the family, to be interfered with by a debauched priesthood. We had said 'No Surrender' before and we say 'No Surrender' again now. And we shall continue to say 'Keep the Union Jack flying for God and Ulster' " . . . That's telling 'em, hey Nancy?

MRS. CROWE: Oh, that's very good Jerry . . . but—

SANT: —but what?

MRS. CROWE: I can never understand what there is to get so excited about.

SANT: Get so excited! [*Rising and moving about*] Rome rule means Home Rule, doesn't it? But I'm thinking maybe the Papishes have cooked their own goose this time.

MRS. CROWE: How's that then?

SANT: Well, for one thing, this will queer the pitch for the Home Rulers. One false move and it could be civil war in Ireland with the Fenians cutting each other's dirty throats. And a good job too. They'll not stand for an Englishman giving orders, Pope or no.

MRS. CROWE: Oh, I'll never understand Irish politics as long as I live. Here, let me fill your glass.

SANT: Aye, you do that, sweetheart.

[*There is a pause.* SANT *has now blown off most of his steam.* MRS. CROWE *fills both glasses*]

MRS. CROWE: Looking after men—that's something I *do* understand.

SANT: True for you, Nancy. [*He sits beside her*] Never a truer word. [*He raises his glass*] Good luck!

MRS. CROWE: Here's cheers.

SANT: But there's one thing I've never been able to find out—
what you see in that abomination of desolation.

MRS. CROWE: Who?

SANT: Rolfe.

MRS. CROWE: What I see in *him?* Oh, please, Jerry. Give me
a little credit. Do you know what he used to do? No, I
don't want to talk about it. I can't bear to speak about him
any more.

[*She starts to snivel*]

SANT: Now just a moment, Nancy. Just a moment. [*He rises
and picks up the bottle from the table*] Here, give us your
glass.

MRS. CROWE: [*Upset*] Oh, no thank you, Jerry.

SANT: Come on, sweetheart. Just a half 'un.

MRS. CROWE: Oh, all right then.

[SANT *fills both glasses and sits again. They drink.* MRS.
CROWE *makes a face*]

MRS. CROWE: Oooh, this is strong.

[*She downs it in one nevertheless*]

SANT: Never mind. It'll do you good. Now, Nance, just now
you started to say something, and by-and-by you're going
to finish it. But first I'm going to tell you one or two things.

MRS. CROWE: What things?

SANT: Well, first, how would you like to come on a wee trip with
me to Rome?

MRS. CROWE: To Rome? But, Jerry, how could I? I mean . . .

SANT: Oh, don't you worry about that. We'll be properly chap-
eroned, I promise you.

MRS. CROWE: But I've got nothing to wear.

SANT: No problem at all. As you know, I am an F.R.S.

MRS. CROWE: A what?

SANT: A Senior Brother of the Fellowship of Religious Segregation, who are very disturbed by certain recent events and, as
loyal servants of the Crown, we feel it our duty to do whatever
we can to protect the Free Churches of the United Kingdom.

[*He gets up and postures round the room*]

MRS. CROWE: Yes, Jerry, but what's all this to do with you and
me going to Rome?

SANT: I'll tell ye in a minute. Now the F.R.S. are sending a
deputation to the Vatican to demand certain safeguards for
Protestants in the light of the aforesaid recent events, and I'm
heading that deputation.

MRS. CROWE: Oh!

SANT: "Sing and rejoice, O daughter of Zion: for, lo, I come,
and I will dwell in the midst of thee, saith the Lord."

MRS. CROWE: [*Impressed*] Oh, I say.

SANT: Now, you'll be asking yourself—and rightly—why I'm inviting you to come with me, and I wouldn't insult your
intelligence by trying to pretend it was just for business
reasons only . . . Here, where's your glass?

MRS. CROWE: Not another.

[SANT *refills both glasses and* MRS. CROWE *accepts without
further demur*]

SANT: As leader of this deputation I said to myself who knows
your man the Pope better than I do? Why, Nancy Crowe, of
course, and she shall come with me.

MRS. CROWE: [*Impressed and delighted*] Oh, I say!

SANT: So what do you say?

MRS. CROWE: What could I possibly say, Jerry?

SANT: You can and shall say "Yes," sweetheart. [*He raises his
glass*] Here's to us.

MRS. CROWE: Oh, Jerry! [*They clink glasses*] Oh, it *is* nice
to see you again, I must say. [*She begins to look soulful*]
Things haven't been too easy for me, one way and another.

SANT: Aye, I suspected as much when I came. And I wouldn't be surprised if it were something to do with that agent of the Whore of Babylon, the erstwhile Baron Corvo, eh?

[MRS. CROWE *does not reply, but consoles herself with another drink*]

SANT: I'm right, Nancy, aren't I?

[MRS. CROWE *nods her head*]

SANT: That little barmstick! And I'll wager he hasn't paid you the rent—sneaking out of the house the way he did.

MRS. CROWE: [*Getting maudlin*] And not even a line to say he'd got there safely. Not even a postcard.

[*She starts to snivel*]

SANT: Aye. Well, we'll soon get even with him. [*He moves back to his seat beside her, and puts his arm round her shoulders*] Now a little earlier you were going to tell me something. Now's the time. Come on, Nance.

MRS. CROWE: No, I couldn't Jerry. [*She snivels*]

SANT: [*Getting tough*] Now, Nancy, you can and you shall tell me.

MRS. CROWE: [*Content that the moment has come to give in*] Oh, Jerry, it's been going on for years. He—he wouldn't leave me alone, never. He was always—always trying to—to interfere with me, even when Mr. Crowe was alive. I've had no peace whenever he was around, Jerry, and I—I just couldn't keep him away.

[*She turns and buries her head in* SANT's *shoulder, sobbing*]

SANT: [*Surprised*] Well I'll be damned!

MRS. CROWE: Well don't sound so surprised. Aren't I attractive any more?

SANT: No, no, of course I'm not surprised, sweetheart. It's just that I always thought—anyway—I'll not stand for a respectable Protestant lady being defiled by a Papish traitor, no matter who. If I had my way I'd geld the lot of them.

MRS. CROWE: [*Quietly and viciously*] Make him squirm.

[SANT *kisses her violently on the mouth as the lights fade to a:*]

BLACKOUT

SCENE TWO

An audience chamber in the Vatican.

The only furniture is the Pontifical throne, which is set center on a small dais.

As the lights come up, CARDINAL RAGNA, *Secretary of State, an elderly, bull-like Italian,* CARDINAL BERSTEIN, *a cold, arrogant German, and* FATHER ST. ALBANS, *Prepositor-General of Jesuits, the truculent "Black Pope," an Englishman, enter together.*

ST. ALBANS: To a great extent I blame myself. I should have known what a formidable politician my compatriot, Dr. Courtleigh, was.

RAGNA: Do not tell me what is a politician. I am Secretary of State. I know what is a politician.

ST. ALBANS: [*Drily*] Do you? A pity you didn't tumble to his trick earlier then.

BERSTEIN: He is crafty like a fox, your English Cardinal.

ST. ALBANS: [*Sarcastic*] He had seen the light, he said—

RAGNA: Ha!

ST. ALBANS: —while shaving!

BERSTEIN: Ha!

ST. ALBANS: We must search afresh, he said. We must search

outside the Vatican, he said, for a man of Faith and Constancy, a man of Simplicity and Humility—he said—

RAGNA: [*Grieving*] Ay, ay, ay!

BERSTEIN: A disaster!

RAGNA: Catastrophe!

ST. ALBANS: Yes, it was a trifle unfortunate.

BERSTEIN: Psst! My lords, now that it is all over I am able to reveal to you a matter of great interest.

ST. ALBANS: Yes?

BERSTEIN: [*Proudly*] His Imperial Majesty, the Kaiser, made it known that it was his personal wish that *I* should become the successor to His late Holiness.

ST. ALBANS: Oh, really. Well I can reveal to you that the Imperial Kaiser's royal uncle, King Edward, wouldn't have been so stupid as to meddle in matters that didn't concern him.

RAGNA: And I am able to reveal to you that your German Kaiser does not know the rules of our Roman Consistory. If he did, he would know that you, as one of the nine Cardinals-Compromissory, were never eligible for election.

[BERNSTEIN *looks put out*]

RAGNA: But I will make a confession to you, My Lords. Because I thought the election of this one so improbable, I cast my vote for him, *si*, I voted for him in order to—how do you say—to throw away my vote.

BERSTEIN: Oh, really? Frankly, so did I.

[ST. ALBANS *starts a fit of suppressed giggles. The other two stare at him in amazement*]

BERSTEIN: What is it?

ST. ALBANS: Well, according to Percy van Kristen, so did Vivdi, Cacciatori and old Gintilotto. And you still think that the Archbishop of Pimlico is not an adroit politician?

BERSTEIN: It is true that he succeeded in getting this—this—

ST. ALBANS: Parvenu?

BERSTEIN: This parvenu elected Pope. But what I want to know is how.

ST. ALBANS: Any minute now someone is going to say it is the hand of God.

[RAGNA *and* BERSTEIN *give* ST. ALBANS *a sharp look*]

RAGNA: The question is not *how* but *why* . . . why, why, why?

BERSTEIN: *Ja,* why?

ST. ALBANS: It could be that Cardinal Courtleigh has a perfectly disinterested reason for placing this bomb under the skirts of [*He gestures with his hand*] you Curia die-hards. [RAGNA *and* BERSTEIN *look affronted*] He may feel that some of you lack the simplicity and humility to accede to the Throne of Peter.

BERSTEIN: [*Nettled*] So he has so much humility, this man?

RAGNA: He has the humility of a Neapolitan tenor. You remember at the Coronation when the Cardinal-Archdeacon say, "Holiness what is the Pontifical name you will choose?" he say, "Hadrian the Seventh." I said to him—you heard me, no? —"Your Holiness would perhaps prefer to be called Leo, or Pius, or Gregory, as in the modern manner." But he say—

ST. ALBANS: [*Imitating* ROLFE] "The first and previous English Pontiff was Hadrian the Fourth: the second and present English Pontiff is Hadrian the Seventh. It pleases us: and so by Our Own impulse, We command."

RAGNA: [*In disgust*] "By Our Own impulse We command." Such arrogance! Eh! But you heard what he said to me when I tell him it is very—*pericoloso*—

ST. ALBANS: Dangerous.

RAGNA: —dangerous to walk to Lateran? I said for the Holy Father to walk to Lateran through the streets of Rome today is madness.

ST. ALBANS: Why? It's only about half a mile, isn't it?

RAGNA: You English do not understand. Rome is not your Tunbridge or Cheltenham Spa. The city is full of Jews and Freemasons.

ST. ALBANS: So is Cheltenham Spa.

RAGNA: They will throw vitriol at us. It is suicide for you, and is murder for me.

ST. ALBANS: And what did he say?

RAGNA: He say, "Good. The Church is badly wanting a new martyr."

> ST. ALBANS *suppresses laughter,* BERSTEIN *tut-tuts.* COURT-LEIGH, TALACRYN *and other members of the Sacred College enter.* COURTLEIGH *is wheeled on in a bathchair. The others form a semi-circle on either side of the throne, which re-mains vacant*]

COURTLEIGH: Can anyone enlighten me as to the reason for this hasty summons?

RAGNA: [*With a gesture of resignation*] Ecco!

COURTLEIGH: Had to gobble me breakfast. Haven't even had a chance to read the *Times* yet.

ST. ALBANS: Your Eminence could hardly have done so.

COURTLEIGH: What do you mean?

ST. ALBANS: I am informed that an embargo has been placed on all newspapers within the Vatican.

COURTLEIGH: Extraordinary!

ST. ALBANS: However, I made it my business to find out the reason for this, and it appears that the embargo was placed by His Holiness prior to the publication of his Bull and Breve.

> [*There are exclamations of astonishment from several* CARDINALS]

ST. ALBANS: Further, I made it my business to obtain a copy of the text of this Bull and Breve and I think Your Eminences will be interested if I read it to you.

> [*More exclamations.* ST. ALBANS *clears his throat and pauses for effect. He then reads from a sheet of paper. The* CARDINALS *stop muttering*]

ST. ALBANS: "We, Hadrian the Seventh, Vicar of Christ, Servant of the servants of God, speak thus: We find Ourselves the sovereign of an estate to which We hold no title deeds. But Our Kingdom is not of this world. So, therefore, We, Vicar of Christ, Successor to the Throne of St. Peter, do now make Our formal and unconditional renunciation to temporal Sovereignty."

[*The* CARDINALS *gasp*]

ST. ALBANS: "Our predecessors followed other counsels and they acted in the knowledge of their responsibility to God. We, on Our part, act as We deem best. We are God's Vice-regent and this is Our will. [*Quickly*] Given at Rome, at St. Peter's by the Vatican, on this day of Our Supreme Pontificate."

[*There is a moment of utter silence*]

RAGNA: [*Shouting*] Judas! Judas! This shall not be!

ST. ALBANS: Unfortunately, Lord Cardinal, it can be—and is.

RAGNA: Am I Secretary of State or am I not Secretary of State? I am asking Your Eminences. If the Pontiff is no longer temporal sovereign, how am I Secretary of the Vatican State? You tell me I am to be dismissed by this—this clerk who has the sack from two—not one, but two—ecclesiastical colleges?

BERSTEIN: Two colleges! [*He tut-tuts*]

TALACRYN: His Holiness believes the world is sick for want of the Church. He believes, I think, that we should turn all our efforts and attention to the pursuit of non-secular matters.

RAGNA: *Va bene, va bene.* But I tell you His Holiness has very special conception of His Apostolic character. He think that is enough. It is not enough.

BERSTEIN: *Ja, ja.* It is not enough. If the temporal power is worth having, it is worth fighting for.

ST. ALBANS: I do not say that I disagree with Your Eminence.

RAGNA: Then perhaps you will make a suggestion. You say Jesuits are always very clever. Why do you not suggest we convene the Oecumenical Council? Eh?

BERSTEIN: *Ja, ja.* The Oecumenical Council only can deal with such matters.

RAGNA: I say this man is a heretic. I say he is the Anti-Pope. And I say the Sacred College must act now—before it is too late.

ST. ALBANS: And I wouldn't necessarily argue with Your Eminence, but the Oecumenical Council of the Vatican has stood adjourned since—I think I am right in saying—since eighteen-seventy. All the same . . .

RAGNA: But all the same it can be reconvened, no?

BERSTEIN: Under the circumstances it is the only thing to do. I agree.

ST. ALBANS: If the Sacred College should choose to demand . . .

RAGNA: [*Roaring*] The Sacred College *should* demand.

[*Unnoticed,* HADRIAN [ROLFE] *enters quietly. For the first time he is seen wearing the white garments of a Pope. He carries a large leather folder*]

RAGNA: If there's any anxiety or doubt in any minds the Sacred College *must* demand.

HADRIAN: [*Very quietly*] Pray, what must the Sacred College demand, Lord Cardinal?

[*All react to the sudden appearance of the* POPE. RAGNA, *taken off guard, can only work his jaw defiantly.* HADRIAN *persists in his most ominously gentle voice*]

HADRIAN: Your Eminence is free to address Us.

RAGNA: [*Recovering his truculence slightly*] I wish rather to address the Sacred College.

HADRIAN: [*Sweetly*] You have Our permission to do so.

[*He looks round the room, noting the reactions of those present*]

RAGNA: I wish to—[*He clears his throat to gain time*] I wish to . . .

HADRIAN: You wish to denounce Us as Heretic and Pseudo-

Pontiff. And to do so, you wish to convene an Oecumenical Council. Is that not correct?

[RAGNA, *his own words taken from his mouth, remains silent, his face working*]

HADRIAN: That generally is done by oblique-eyed Cardinals who cannot accustom themselves to new Pontiffs. [*Mounting the dais*] But Lord Cardinals, if such an idea should be presented to you, be ye mindful that none but the Supreme Pontiff can convoke an Oecumenical Council. We are conscious of your love and of your loathing for Our Person and Our Acts. We value the one and regret the other. But ye voluntarily have sworn obedience to Us, and We claim it. Nothing must and nothing shall obstruct Us. Let that be known. [*He sits on the throne*] Wherefore Most Eminent Lords and Venerable Fathers, let not the sheep of Christ's flock be neglected while the shepherds exchange anathemas. Try, Venerable Fathers, to believe that the time has come for taking stock. Ask yourselves whether we really are as successful as we think we are—whether in fact we are not abject and lamentable failures in the eyes of God. We have added and added to the riches, pomp and power of the Church, yet everywhere there is great wealth alongside dire poverty; there are strong nations brutally holding small ones to slavery; above all there are millions of people of goodwill looking to us for moral and spiritual leadership who get from us only dogmatic interpretations of canon law in return. If, then, we have so far failed in spreading Christ's Gospel, let us try anew. Let us try the road of Apostolic simplicity—the simplicity of Peter the Fisherman. At least let us try.

[*There is total silence*]

HADRIAN: Your Eminences have permission to retire.

[*For a moment there is silence. Then* TALACRYN *goes quickly to re-affirm his allegiance by kissing the Pontifical ring. Hesitantly at first, the others follow.* RAGNA, *still recalcitrant, makes the briefest possible acknowledgement.*

COURTLEIGH *alone is left, in his chair. Having made obeisance, the prelates move off up right, murmuring*]

HADRIAN: [*To* COURTLEIGH] We should be glad if Your Eminence could spare a few moments longer of your time.

COURTLEIGH: [*Coolly*] I am at Your Holiness's disposal. I pray Your Holiness will forgive this chair.

HADRIAN: We trust Your Eminence is not seriously incommoded.

COURTLEIGH: A very English complaint, Holy Father, a touch of the gout.

HADRIAN: Accept Our sympathy for your English complaint. We too have them, but of a different nature. We desire to establish relations with Your Eminence, chiefly because you hold so responsible a position in England, a country dear above all others to Us.

COURTLEIGH: [*Putting on his Cardinalatial mask expressive of the old and wise condescending to give ear to the young and rash*] Proceed, Most Holy Father.

HADRIAN: It is Our wish to make England's people prepared for the Lord. But we find Ourselves impeded at the outset by the present conduct of the English Roman Catholics—especially of the aboriginal English Catholics.

[COURTLEIGH *reacts sharply, then bows slightly and continues to attend.* HADRIAN *opens his folder, which contains press cuttings*]

HADRIAN: Kindly give Us your opinion of this statement, Eminence. I quote from a London newspaper whose views are not necessarily Our own. "The Roman Catholic laity resident in England are petitioning Parliament to set up some control over Roman Catholic monies and interests. It is alleged that no account is afforded by the Roman Catholic Bishops of the management or disbursement of such properties and monies." Well?

COURTLEIGH: The scandal emanated from a priest not of my Archdiocese, Holiness. We were successful in preventing it from spreading.

HADRIAN: Oh! Then there was such a petition? I was prepared to ascribe it to the imagination of one of the bright young men usually employed by the monstrous old proprietor of this newspaper. And were there many supporters of the petition?

COURTLEIGH: [*Raising a hand*] Unfortunately, there were a number.

HADRIAN: And were there any grounds for the allegations?

COURTLEIGH: Holy Father, we cannot be expected to account to every Tom, Dick and Harry for the hundreds of bequests and endowments which we administer.

HADRIAN: Why not, if your accounts are properly audited? We assume they are?

COURTLEIGH: Ah—to a great extent, yes.

HADRIAN: To a great extent? Not invariably? But do you really consider your clergy capable of financial administration?

COURTLEIGH: As capable as other men.

HADRIAN: Priests are not "as other men."

COURTLEIGH: But what would Your Holiness have?

HADRIAN: We entirely disapprove of the clergy using any secular power whatever, especially such power as inheres in the command of money. The clergy are ministers—ministers—not masters. The clergy are *more*, not *less*, human, and they certainly are not the pick of humanity.

COURTLEIGH: Even if I were to agree, I still do not precisely see Your Holiness's point.

HADRIAN: No? Then let Us take another. [*He arises, taking a small green ticket from the folder*] This does come from Your Eminence's diocese. "Church of the Sacred Heart—admit bearer to Midnight Mass—Christmas Eve—Middle Seat one shilling and sixpence." Surely not some form of discrimination?

COURTLEIGH: [*Shrugging, as if the card were of no significance*] A small attempt to prevent—ah—improper persons from attending these services.

HADRIAN: But "improper" persons should be encouraged to attend.

COURTLEIGH: [*Irritated*] And have scenes of disorder and profanation?

HADRIAN: We are determined that Our Churches be made as free to the lost as to the saved.

COURTLEIGH: May I be permitted to ask what experience Your Holiness has had in parochial administration?

HADRIAN: You could answer that question yourself, Your Eminence. But I've attended many midnight masses and heard no sign of the profanation of which you speak. Sots and harlots were undoubtedly present, but they were not disorderly. They were cowed, they were sleepy, they were curious, but they made no noise. If means of grace are obtainable in a Church, who dare deny them to those who need them most? You are here to serve—and only to serve. We especially disapprove of any system which makes access to the Church difficult— like this admission fee.

COURTLEIGH: Holy Father, the clergy must live.

HADRIAN: And so they shall. But pew-rents are abominable— and so are pews. Abolish them both.

COURTLEIGH: [*Beside himself with rage*] Your Holiness speaks as though He was not one of us.

[HADRIAN *pauses and fixes* COURTLEIGH *with a look*]

HADRIAN: Look at your Catholic Directory and see the advertisement of a priest who is prepared to pay bank interest on investments—in plain words borrow money upon usury, in direct contravention to St. Luke. Look at the Catholic Hour and see the advertisement of a priest who actually trades as a tobacconist. Look in the precincts of your churches and see the tables of the Fenian literature sellers and the seats of them that sell tickets for stage plays and bazaars. No, My Lord Cardinal, the clergy attempt too much. They may be excellent priests, but as tradesmen, stock jobbers and variety entertainers, they are catastrophes.

COURTLEIGH: [*With resignation*] But Holy Father, do think for a moment. What are the clergy to live on?

HADRIAN: The free-will offerings of the faithful.

COURTLEIGH: But suppose the faithful do not give of their free will?

HADRIAN: Then starve and go to heaven.

COURTLEIGH: [*Stung once more to defend himself*] Your Holiness will permit me to remind you that I, myself, was consecrated bishop fourteen years before you were made a Christian at baptism. It seems to me that you should give your seniors credit for having consciences of their own.

HADRIAN: My dear Lord Cardinal, if We had seen the least sign of the said consciences . . .

COURTLEIGH: I am not the only member of the Sacred College who thinks that Your Holiness's attitude partakes of—singularity —and—ah—arrogance.

HADRIAN: Singularity? Oh, We sincerely hope so. But arrogance —We cannot call it arrogance that We have attempted to show you something of Our frame of mind.

COURTLEIGH: What, then, Holy Father, would You wish me to do?

HADRIAN: We wish you to act upon the sum of Our words and conduct in order that England may have a good, and not a bad, example from English Catholics. No more than that. The Barque of Peter is way off course. Lord Cardinal, can the new Captain count on the loyal support of His Lieutenant in trying to bring her head round?

COURTLEIGH: [*Making an immense effort*] Holy Father, I assure you that You may count on me.

HADRIAN: We realize the immense effort on your part that has made you give Us this assurance and it gladdens Us to see this evidence of the Grace of your Divine Vocation.

[COURTLEIGH *bows slightly*]

HADRIAN: Well now, Lord Cardinal, to change the metaphor, let us put away the flail and take up the crook. So shall we take a little stroll in the garden and say some Office?

COURTLEIGH: [*Surprised*] Oh, well, certainly, with pleasure— that is if Your Holiness doesn't mind walking by the side of my bathchair, that is . . .

HADRIAN: Oh, but We do. It is Our invariable custom to walk *behind* bathchairs and push them.

COURTLEIGH: Oh but, Holy Father, I could not for one moment permit . . .

HADRIAN: No, but for just one hour you will submit.

COURTLEIGH: All the same, Holy Father, really . . .

HADRIAN: [*Putting his folder on* COURTLEIGH'S *lap and moving behind the bathchair*] Nonsense man, do you suppose that One has never pushed a bathchair before?

COURTLEIGH: All the same, Holy Father, it is hardly . . .

HADRIAN: Now sit quietly and open your breviary and start reading the Office.

[COURTLEIGH *obeys*]

HADRIAN: We will look over your shoulder and make the responses. [*He swivels the bathchair round*] It's awfully good exercise, you know.

[*Respectively saying and responding to the office of the day,* HADRIAN *pushes the aged* COURTLEIGH *slowly off as the lights fade to a:*]

BLACKOUT

SCENE THREE

Outside a café in Rome.
  When the lights come up, SANT *and* MRS. CROWE *are sitting at a table.* MRS. CROWE *is shielding herself with a parasol.* SANT *fans himself with a panama hat. He holds a piece of paper in his other hand.*

SANT: This is my ultimatum. Listen. [*He reads*] "Since my earlier communication in which I had the pleasure of addressing you on the aims of the Fellowship of Religious Segregation, I have been anxiously waiting the favour of an acknowledgement of same. In case the subject has slipped your memory, I should remind you that we were not adverse to give our careful consideration to any proposal you may see fit to make, financial or otherwise." That's putting it fair and square, eh?

MRS. CROWE: Yes, Jerry, but how's he going to know that you want to talk to him about the other—you know . . .

SANT: Hold your horses, woman, I haven't come to the guts of it yet. [*Continuing to read*] "But I am quite at a loss to understand on what grounds you have not yet favoured me with a reply unless there is anything on which you would like further explanation. In which case, I will be most happy to call on you per appointment for which I have been waiting at the above address here in Rome for some weeks and neglecting my business at considerable expense and inconvenience which a man in my position cannot be expected to incur and common courtesy demands should be made good."

[*The lights fade to a:*]

BLACKOUT

SCENE FOUR

The audience chamber.
As the lights come up, TALACRYN *and* HADRIAN *are entering.* TALACRYN *is reading the remainder of* SANT's *letter.* HADRIAN *is smoking a home-rolled cigarette. He moves to the throne and sits still and tense as* TALACRYN *reads.*

TALACRYN: ". . . should be made good. I therefore trust that in view of the not altogether pleasant facts that are in the possession of myself and another party well known to yourself, you will see fit to accord me a private interview at your earliest convenience. Hoping that I will not . . ."

[HADRIAN *remains rigid. His hand trembles as he removes his cigarette*]

HADRIAN: Stop! I cannot bring myself to hear any more of that illiterate filth.

TALACRYN: Forgive the presumption, but Your Holiness seems unduly upset by this impertinent nonsense.

HADRIAN: It is not His Holiness who is upset, but Frederick William Rolfe.

TALACRYN: Again forgive the presumption, but one has known Frederick William Rolfe for some years. Who are these enemies, Holy Father?

HADRIAN: Prurient scum. Pithycanthropoids and Neanderthals who beset Our path in Our previous and ghastly existence.

TALACRYN: They can be annihilated, Holiness. Surely some guillotine can be brought down that would effectively silence these . . .

HADRIAN: Blackmailers? Since Our conscience is clear, We have no desire to be so dynamic. We should not touch ordure even with a shovel.

TALACRYN: But silence is more likely to inflame such people than to quiet them. Supposing in their frustration they go to the newspapers?

HADRIAN: Then, doubtless, the Sacred College will erect their tail feathers and gobble like a flock of huge turkeycocks: "Behold the Anti-Pope!" they will say, and glare whole Inquisitions at Us.

TALACRYN: Respectfully, Holiness, the matter should not be allowed to reach such a pass. As Your Holiness rightly assumes, those within the Sacred College who were against Your accession would welcome a scandal directed at Your Person.

HADRIAN: Let them have a scandal. Let them keep aloof in their vermilion sulks. It is not Our will to move in this matter.

TALACRYN: But, forgive me if I persist, Holiness . . .

HADRIAN: [Sharply] Do not persist. [He rises, moves left center, putting out his cigarette with his foot. Changing from the Pontifical to the familiar] Frank, tell me, what have you been doing today?

TALACRYN: Today? Oh, I paid a visit, as a matter of fact, to Your old college.

HADRIAN: [*Freezing*] Oh?

TALACRYN: They cannot understand why You have not yet been to see them.

HADRIAN: Is not the Rector still the same man who once expelled me—brutally and without explanation?

TALACRYN: The Rector is an old man now, sensible to the errors of his youth, as we all are.

HADRIAN: [*To himself*] The wound goes deep. It has never properly healed.

TALACRYN: Perhaps this is the moment for cauterizing the wound, Holiness. Strangely, I forgot the horrors of my own times there after I'd visited them once or twice. Besides, the young men love to see one, and the older men—the principals— like to see the hierarchy take note of them.

HADRIAN: [*Suddenly moving to* TALACRYN] Frank, let's go to the college now. We can get there in time for lunch?

TALACRYN: [*Looking pleased*] What a good idea.

[*As* TALACRYN *and* HADRIAN *move quickly upstage, the lights fade to a:*]

BLACKOUT

SCENE FIVE

The college.
  The stage is bare.
As the lights come up we hear a distant bell, and a distant litany being chanted. Some young SEMINARISTS *in purple sopranos pass across the stage, singing. Among them is* ROSE. *When they have passed from sight,* HADRIAN *enters with* TALACRYN *and the* RECTOR. *The* RECTOR, *dressed in black, is an old man whose behaviour before the* POPE *is a mixture of self-importance and obsequiousness—the headmaster humouring a distinguished parent.*

RECTOR: This has been a great day for the College, Holy Father.

[HADRIAN *ignores the flattery*]

RECTOR: Of course, had we known Your Holiness intended to honour us, a proper reception . . .

HADRIAN: Quite unnecessary. Our children expect to see Us and We came to be seen. We now wish to know something of one student in particular.

RECTOR: Who is that, Holy Father?

HADRIAN: The somewhat older man who looks so hungry and took only bread and water at luncheon.

RECTOR: Ah, poor fellow!

HADRIAN: Now why do you say that, Monsignore?

RECTOR: Well, Holiness, I'm afraid this is not the place for him. He's very sensitive and doesn't really get on with the others.

HADRIAN: Does he quarrel with them?

RECTOR: Oh no. But he takes pains to avoid them.

HADRIAN: Perhaps he has his reasons.

RECTOR: Perhaps, but his attitude does not seem suitable in one hoping to attain Orders! He is not what I would call a good mixer.

HADRIAN: You talk as if he aspired to be a sporting parson.

RECTOR: [*Nettled*] I must tell Your Holiness that I do not feel that he has a real Vocation for the priesthood.

HADRIAN: Please know, Monsignore, that We have not come here to brag or to gloat, but We feel bound to remind you that your judgment as to Vocation has, in the past, been in error.

RECTOR: [*Shaken*] I am only too mindful—Your Holiness's personal case has for a long time been—it was a long time ago. I can only say in extenuation that to err is human.

HADRIAN: Human error is sometimes excusable. *In*human behaviour is not. Ill-considered judgment by those in authority are damnably culpable.

[*The* RECTOR *winces*]

HADRIAN: What is the name of this student who has "no Vocation?"

RECTOR: Rose, Holiness. George Arthur Rose.

HADRIAN: We wish to speak to him.

RECTOR: If it pleases Your Holiness.

HADRIAN: We will speak to him alone.

[*The* RECTOR *bows and exits*]

HADRIAN: [*To* TALACRYN, *when they are alone*] Were We too severe, Frank? The wish to smoke has made Us irritable.

TALACRYN: [*Smiling*] Your Holiness was altogether admirable. I must admit to having enjoyed the last five minutes more than a Christian should.

HADRIAN: [*Looking round and sniffing*] Still the same smell. The inevitable odour of hot boy.

TALACRYN: It seems to be the inescapable adjunct of education.

HADRIAN: Inescapable? Nonsense! We have half a mind to appoint you Protector of this College. Yes, that's right. You will give them sanitation—and sanity, for goodness sake. You might make that shrubbery into a gymnasium. And what about a swimming pool—with a lovely terrace on the top?

TALACRYN: I don't see why not.

HADRIAN: And, Frank, make friends with them and see what you can do to take that horrible secretive suppressed look out of their young eyes. You understand?

TALACRYN: I think so, Holiness.

[*The* RECTOR *returns with* ROSE, *who is dressed in the violet cassock and black soprano of a seminarist*]

RECTOR: Mr. Rose, Your Holiness.

[ROSE *observes the forms*]

HADRIAN: You will be pleased to hear, Monsignore, that We

have appointed the Bishop of Caerleon Protector of St. Andrew's College. His Lordship would be most grateful if you
would now take him on a detailed tour of the kitchens and san-
itary arrangements.

[*The* RECTOR *looks surprised, but is now totally sub-
missive*]

RECTOR: As Your Holiness pleases.

[*The* RECTOR *and* TALACRYN *exit.* ROSE *does not show
surprise but stands throughout with dignity and reserve*]

HADRIAN: Dear son, on slight knowledge We have the impression
you are one of the unhappy ones. Will you confide in Us?

ROSE: I have not complained, Sanctity.

HADRIAN: But now you may do so.

ROSE: I have no reason—I do not wish to do so.

HADRIAN: How old are you, my son?

ROSE: Twenty-nine, Sanctity.

HADRIAN: And you find your environment disagreeable?

ROSE: All environments are more or less disagreeable to me.

HADRIAN: Up to the present at least. You find that your circumstances adversely influence your conduct—prevent you from
doing yourself justice—here.

ROSE: That may be my fault.

HADRIAN: They mock you, no doubt.

ROSE: I suppose that is the case, Holiness.

HADRIAN: So was Jesus Christ mocked. But why are you?

ROSE: Because for my ablutions I carry two cans of water up two
hundred and two steps every day.

HADRIAN: No doubt they say you must be a very unclean person
to need so much washing.

ROSE: Sanctity, you are quoting the Rector.

HADRIAN: No.

ROSE: How does Your Holiness know so exactly?

HADRIAN: [*Laughing*] Have they even put a snake in your water cans?

ROSE: No, they have not done that.

HADRIAN: They did in Ours. Isn't it absurd?

ROSE: It is—and very disconcerting.

HADRIAN: But you try not to let it disconcert you?

ROSE: I try but I fail. My heart is always on my sleeve and the daws peck it. So I try to protect myself in isolation.

HADRIAN: That they call "sulkiness!"

ROSE: Yes, Your Holiness knows so exactly . . .

HADRIAN: [*Moving slowly upstage: almost to himself*] We also were never able to arrange to be loved. [*He circles slowly above* ROSE] Do you always live on bread and water?

ROSE: Yes, except for eggs.

HADRIAN: Eggs? Why eggs?

ROSE: I have been into the kitchen and seen—things. They cannot deposit sputum inside the shells of boiled eggs.

HADRIAN: [*Moving across the stage*] Do you like bread and water?

ROSE: No, but in order not to be singular I eat and drink what I can of what is set before me. But because of that, I am deemed more singular than ever.

HADRIAN: [*Moving round above* ROSE *as before*] Yet you choose to persevere, my son!

ROSE: Sanctity, I must. I am called.

HADRIAN: You are sure of that?

ROSE: It is the only thing in all the world of which I am sure.

HADRIAN: Yet you know that this college is not the place for you?

ROSE: I suppose not. But my diocesan sent me here and I intend to serve my sentence.

HADRIAN: Dear son, what is your ambition?

ROSE: Priesthood.

HADRIAN: And you *will* persevere—for however long?

ROSE: For twenty years if need be.

HADRIAN: We persevered for just that length of time.

ROSE: Then so will I.

HADRIAN: My son, it is in Our power to grant you a favour. Do you wish to ask Us for anything?

ROSE: No thank you, Sanctity.

HADRIAN: My son, do you think you are ready for priesthood?

ROSE: I am ready as soon as I may be summoned, Sanctity.

HADRIAN: You shall be summoned. Come to the Vatican tomorrow and ask for the Bishop of Caerleon. He will expect you. Your desire may soon be fulfilled. Will you pray for Us, dear son?

ROSE: Holy Father, I most surely will.

HADRIAN: Good-bye, and God bless you.

> [ROSE *kneels and* HADRIAN *gives blessing.* ROSE *exits. The* RECTOR *returns with* TALACRYN, *then crosses up right and exits*]

HADRIAN: [*To* TALACRYN] What a delicious day it has been, Frank. You persuaded Us and We are grateful.

TALACRYN: I think the walk did Your Holiness good.

HADRIAN: It was not just the walk, but something quite other —as though a curtain has been lifted, or, more exactly, as if We had been given a brief glimpse into a human heart.

TALACRYN: That is a rare and wonderful experience, Holiness.

HADRIAN: Rare? You are Our confessor. You must know that for Us the experience is unique. Frank, We have just had the first feeling of undiluted enjoyment of human society which We can ever remember.

TALACRYN: Do you remember what I said to you in London, Holiness? I said that if You could find it in Yourself to love your neighbour it would lead You to love God.

HADRIAN: Love—yes—We have recognized for the first time in

Ourselves a new and unborn power, a perfectly strange capability. Today, We have made experience of a feeling which—well, which We suppose—at any rate will pass for—Love.

[*The lights fade to a:*]

BLACKOUT

SCENE SIX

The audience chamber.
   A small chair has been set down facing towards the throne.
   When the lights come up, AGNES *is discovered sitting on the chair looking very nervous.* FATHER ROSE, *now in the cassock of an ordained priest, enters. He has a clip of papers in his hand.*

FR. ROSE: Mrs. Agnes Dixon?

AGNES: Yers?

FR. ROSE: His Holiness asked me to convey his apologies to you. He has been slightly delayed.

AGNES: That's quite all right, dear, ta.

   [FR. ROSE *nods. There is an awkward silence as they both wait for* HADRIAN]

AGNES: Been keeping busy then?

FR. ROSE: [*Slightly taken aback*] Well, as a private chaplain to His Holiness I find the days full.

AGNES: I daresay you do. He's a handful all right. When I used to look after him myself . . .

   [*Further conversation is prevented by the entrance of* HADRIAN]

FR. ROSE: Mrs. Agnes Dixon, Your Holiness.

> [AGNES *rises, trots across and flops on her knees.* HADRIAN *immediately attempts to assist her to rise*]

HADRIAN: Agnes.

AGNES: Oooh, my joints!

HADRIAN: [*Throwing off completely his cold pontifical manner*] Agnes, please sit down.

AGNES: I don't mind, sir.

HADRIAN: [*Moving her chair right of the throne*] Please, Agnes, here.

AGNES: [*Sitting*] Oooh, that's better. I've been on my feet all day, and don't these marble floors tell.

HADRIAN: [*Sitting on the throne*] I'm sorry, Agnes.

AGNES: I shouldn't be saying such things, should I, not now with you living here.

HADRIAN: Good friends are few, Agnes—particularly in the Vatican.

AGNES: These your chairs, are they?

HADRIAN: Well, I suppose they go with the job.

AGNES: Not very comfy, are they? Still—oh, there I am again! But there, I can't help but think of you still as Mr. Rolfe I used to do for.

HADRIAN: It's good to hear you say so, Agnes.

AGNES: [*Scrabbling in her capacious bag and bringing forth a packet*] Here we are, then.

HADRIAN: [*Taking it*] What is this?

AGNES: Why, the change, of course.

HADRIAN: Change?

AGNES: From the money you sent me to buy that house. I got it cheaper than we thought because it'd been empty so long.

HADRIAN: Oh, but you dear good soul, I didn't expect any change. It's all yours. Besides, you may need it to tide you over till you get the lodgers.

AGNES: Till I can get the lodgers? Why, I'm turning them away already. [*She dives in her bag again*] Oh, I nearly forgot, what with all the excitement and walking along those stone corridors with those gentlemen in their fancy get-up. One of them was ever so stuck-up, he was. I couldn't help saying, "I seen plenty more like you, my lad, at the old Holborn Empire." Oh yes, I did, but I don't think he knew what I meant. There, I knew I had it somewhere. [*She produces a jar of pickles*] It's the pickles you always had a fancy for. Made just the same as I used to. You always had a tooth for them, didn't you?

HADRIAN: Dear, good Agnes, you're kindness itself. You know, I never get anything like this nowadays. George, try one.

[*All three help themselves to a pickled onion.* FR. ROSE *gallantly tries to conceal his dislike. There is a long pause as they all munch*]

AGNES: [*With her mouth full*] Well, I must say it's good to see you again, sir, for all you've come up in the world. All the same, I shall never get used to your being Pope, never. Oh, I hope you don't think I don't know my place!

HADRIAN: [*Rising*] Your place, Agnes, is always close to Our heart.

AGNES: [*Rising*] Well, I mustn't detain you, Mr. Rolfe, so I'll be getting along just as soon as you give me a blessing and say a bit of a prayer. Thank you, sir, for all you've done and I'll say a prayer for you every day for as long as I'm spared.

[AGNES *gets, with some difficulty, to her knees and receives the Pontifical blessing*]

HADRIAN: [*Causing her to rise*] Are you going back at once, Agnes?

AGNES: Well, I was thinking of having a bit of a look-round before going back. It's silly to come all this way and not see the sights.

HADRIAN: [*Taking a card and pen from* FR. ROSE] Then take this card—[*He writes on the card*]—give it to the "fancy gentleman" who is going to take you downstairs and tell him what you want to see. Thank you.

AGNES: Will they want me to give the card up at the door?

HADRIAN: Not if you want to keep it.

AGNES: I'll keep this card till I'm laid out. God bless you, my dear.

> [*She kisses the* POPE's *ring, gets up, not without difficulty, and trots out, followed by* FR. ROSE]

HADRIAN: Filthy hypocrite! [*After a pause, he smiles gently to himself*]

> [TALACRYN *enters with unusual lack of formality. He obviously bears urgent news*]

TALACRYN: [*Moving quickly to* HADRIAN] Forgive my precipitance, Holiness, but the news I bring—is of the greatest urgency.

HADRIAN: [*Still unconcerned*] You're quite breathless, Frank. A man of your age must take care. [*He taps his heart significantly*]

TALACRYN: Holiness, please let me be serious. Calumnies have been published. Terrible things have been said.

HADRIAN: [*Freezing*] Oh? What sort of things? By whom? Who has published them?

TALACRYN: Malignant things referring to Your Holiness's secular life. Published in an Ulster newspaper, and worse . . .

HADRIAN: Yes?

TALACRYN: In a prominent journal sponsored by the Church.

HADRIAN: Who has written this? What has been said?

> [RAGNA *swirls in triumphantly, bearing a sheaf of newspapers. All the other* CARDINALS *follow him on and form an arc*]

RAGNA: Perhaps these will inform Your Holiness.

[HADRIAN *takes the papers*]

RAGNA: Your Holiness is well qualified to appreciate the validity of your English newspapers.

[HADRIAN *starts to read*]

RAGNA: These English newspapers have been to much trouble. Suddenly they find it very interesting to make study of the life of the English Pope. They find very interesting things.

HADRIAN: [*Still reading: half to himself*] Half-truth.

RAGNA: His Holiness was expelled from ecclesiastical college in Rome because he is owing everybody money. He makes friends with old Italian lady, the Duchess of Sforza-Cesarini, who is very rich.

HADRIAN: [*To himself*] Unanswerable, because it is half-truth.

RAGNA: Back in England, His Holiness becomes "Baron Corvo," a fine gentleman who inherited title from his noble Italian friend. He used title to gain influence and obtain more money.

HADRIAN: [*Still to himself*] Half-truth again. Who could have attacked with such malign ingenuity?

RAGNA: The Baron tries to buy some property, but people find he is not "Baron." He has no money to buy property. He is a fraud, an adventurer.

HADRIAN: [*Searching the column*] Anonymous! Anonymous half-truths. I should be able to recognize the filthy paw of this muck-raker.

RAGNA: So "Baron Corvo" runs away—to another town where he makes more trouble and owes more money; this time in Wales.

HADRIAN: We were not in Wales this time—but in Belfast. Yes, of course—Sant! Jeremiah Sant!

RAGNA: But in Ireland it is also the same story; he is again the great gentleman—the writer, photographer, inventor of many things, a friend of many famous people. But it is all lies. He has no money. He has no friends. He is nothing. He owes money to the people where he is living. They take him from bed and put him in the street. They throw his clothes after him so he must dress in the street.

[TALACRYN *reacts sharply at this humiliating revelation*]

HADRIAN: [*Looking at* RAGNA] Yes. We appear to be a very disreputable character, do We not. But We demand, Lord Cardinal, that you take note of certain errors.

RAGNA: Errors in Your English newspapers?

HADRIAN: Ten, eleven, twelve, thirteen, fourteen, fifteen—why should English newspapers be less corrupt than Italian? Fifteen absolute and deliberate lies, in a column and a half of print. [*He returns the newspapers and sits on the throne*] Well, Lord Cardinal?

RAGNA: [*Getting angry*] Very well, You tell me this is all lies. But today the whole world is reading these papers. What are You going to do?

HADRIAN: [*Icily*] We will ponder the matter Your Eminence has set before Us, and at a convenient time We will declare Our pleasure.

RAGNA: [*Almost apoplectic*] Convenient time, eh? Let me remind Your Holiness that I am Cardinal Secretary of State of the .Vatican, and I demand to know what You are going to do.

[*After an embarrassed pause, there is a general murmur of assent*]

COURTLEIGH: Holiness, we—that is—many of us feel that Your Holiness has been grossly misrepresented. We would appreciate a statement to refute these calumnies by the press.

HADRIAN: [*In a voice of icy reticence*] Very well. I will give to the Sacred College that statement. And when I have finished speaking I never will return to this subject. [*He leaps up and significantly draws off the Pontifical ring and puts it on the seat of the throne. He walks round and rests his hands on the back of the throne. Dropping pontifical manner*] Gentlemen, would some of you like to put Frederick William Rolfe to the question?

COURTLEIGH: Then if Your Holiness would enlighten . . .

HADRIAN: There is no Holiness here.

COURTLEIGH: [*Bowing acknowledgement*] I must confess that the question of pseudonyms is of interest.

HADRIAN: [*Moving below throne*] Pseudonyms: when I was kicked out of St. Andrew's College without a farthing or a friend I was obliged to live by my wits. Thank God who gave me wits to live by. Think of this: I was a tonsured clerk forced to earn a living by secular means, but always intending to persist in my Divine Vocation. I had a shuddering repugnance from associating my name, the name by which some day I should be known in the priesthood, with secular pursuits, so I adopted a pseudonym. But as time went on and Catholic malfeasance drove me from one trade to another, I split up my personality and carried on each trade under a separate pseudonym! Thus as Baron Corvo I wrote and painted and photographed; as F. Austin I designed decorations; as Frank Hochheimer I did journalism. There were four at least. Four entities careering round like colts in a meadow dissipating energy which, but for the imbecility of the Church, could have been canalized to fulfil its proper purpose years ago.

RAGNA: [*Tapping the newspaper*] What about the debts? Perhaps you explain the debts, please.

HADRIAN: Debts! From the moment they were first contracted with the connivance and consent of certain prelates not unknown to some of you here—

[COURTLEIGH *and* TALACRYN *show signs of embarrassment*]

HADRIAN: —debts were never off my chest for twenty years. I was foolish enough to believe that you Catholics would keep your promises and pay me for the work which I did at your order. So I accepted credit. I worked—God knows how I worked—and expected a just wage. When it was withheld, people encouraged me to hope and work on. They offered me the odd guinea to go on with. I took the filthy guinea. God forgive me for becoming so degraded. But one can't pay one's debts and lead a godly life for ever on an occasional guinea. My weakness, my fault was that I did not die—murdered at St. Andrew's College.

BERSTEIN: Perhaps you will now condescend to explain the allegations of luxurious living.

COURTLEIGH: My Lord Berstein . . .

TALACRYN: [*To* HADRIAN] Holy Father, don't say another word. [*Turning to his colleagues*] Shame on you. How can you torture the man so! Can't you see what you're doing, wracking the poor soul like this? Pulling him in little pieces all over again.

[*There are sounds of assent from several* CARDINALS]

BERSTEIN: I think it would be in the best interest if we were to hear everything.

COURTLEIGH: Surely, My Lords, we have heard enough . . .

HADRIAN: [*Mounting the dais*] But you shall hear more. They say that I gorged myself with sumptuous banquets at grand hotels. Once, after several days of starvation, I got a hard-earned begrudging and overdue fee from a magazine. I went and had an omelette at a small-town commercial doss-house which called itself "The Grand Hotel." They also say that, in my lodgings, I demanded elaborate dishes to be made from my own cookery book. Since I was beholden to my landlords I did indeed ask for special dishes—dishes of lentils and carrots— I do not touch meat—anything that was cheapest, cleanest, easiest and most filling. Each dish cost a few pence and I sometimes had one each day. And occasionally when I earned a little bit I spent a few shillings on apparatus conducive to personal cleanliness, soap, baths and so on. That is the story of my luxurious living, My Lords.

[*There is a pause, and all keep silent*]

HADRIAN: [*Moving downstage and facing up*] I have been provoked, abused, calumniated, traduced with insinuation, innuendo, misrepresentation, lies; my life has been held up to ridicule and most inferior contempt. I tell you this because, officially, I must correct an error. You may take it as an example of how your Catholics, laymen and clergy alike, can tire out and drive almost to death a man's body—perhaps even his soul. [*Moving upstage and turning*] But understand this, My Lords: by no words will I ever defend myself outside these walls. Nor do I speak in my own defence, Venerable Fathers, even to you. I, personally and of predilection, am indifferent to opinions, but it is your right to hear that which you have heard.

[*There is another silence, then* RAGNA *speaks out*]

RAGNA: [*Waving the newspapers*] An enemy hath done this!

HADRIAN: [*With candid delight*] Those are the first genuine words I have heard from Your Eminence's heart.

RAGNA: [*In a voice of thunder*] Who is it has done this evil thing?

TALACRYN: A reactionary blackmailer and a disappointed woman.

RAGNA: [*Roaring*] *Anathema sint:* Let them be smothered in the dunghill.

[*Slowly,* HADRIAN *picks up the Pontifical ring, places it on his finger, and sits*]

HADRIAN: [*In Pontifical manner*] Lord Cardinals, it is Our wish to be alone.

[*The* CARDINALS *exit.* RAGNA *is the last to leave*]

HADRIAN: Lord Cardinal.

RAGNA: [*Turning*] Holiness?

HADRIAN: [*Rising*] May We detain you a moment longer?

RAGNA: Please, Holiness.

HADRIAN: [*With warmth and charm, in contrast to his earlier manner*] We are happy to think that Your Eminence is no longer opposed to Us.

RAGNA: [*Responding warmly*] I too am happy, Most Holy Father, that God has opened my eyes to the injustices done to Your Holiness. I beg that Your Holiness will forgive me for blindness in the past.

HADRIAN: [*Deceptively docile*] Your Eminence is already forgiven. We are particularly pleased to have your Lordship's co-operation at the present time since there is a matter particularly close to Our heart on which We would welcome your advice.

RAGNA: Pray open Your heart, Most Holy Father.

HADRIAN: Very well. [*No bomb was ever dropped more gently*] By way of emphasizing the essential difference between the Church Temporal—which We have already renounced—and the Church Apostolic, We have in mind to give away the Vatican Treasure.

RAGNA: [*Shaken*] The Vatican Treasure! But has Your Holiness considered that most of the treasures are consecrated to the service of the Church?

HADRIAN: Yes. We have also considered that the Church exists for the service of God and His creatures. She does not serve either by keeping costly and beautiful things shut up in cupboards. Well, my Lord? Are you with Us or against Us?

RAGNA: [*After a pause*] Holy Father, I am with You with all my heart. Under Your inspired guidance let the Church once more meet the world in the pure missionary spirit of Her greatest days. I shall follow wherever Your Holiness may lead.

HADRIAN: God bless Your Eminence for that. To tell the truth, I was in no mood for another fight.

[*They both laugh*]

HADRIAN: Your Eminence, may I now suggest that you accompany Us to St. John Lateran?

RAGNA: *Va bene.* With great pleasure, Most Holy Father.

HADRIAN: They will be saying prayers there for those having authority in the Church. It would seem to be a suitable occasion to celebrate our reconciliation.

RAGNA: *Benissimo.* Will Your Holiness go by carriage or in the *sedia gestatoria?*

HADRIAN: Perhaps Your Eminence is in the mood to indulge Our English eccentricities even further?

RAGNA: [*Falling into the trap*] Your Holiness, with pleasure. Of course.

HADRIAN: [*With a smile*] Then we will walk.

RAGNA: [*Aghast*] Walk! But, Holiness . . .

HADRIAN: Your Eminence did say you would follow wherever We may lead.

[*He claps his hands.* FR. ROSE *enters*]

HADRIAN: My sunshade, George. Cardinal Ragna is walking with Us to Lateran.

[FR. ROSE *exits*]

RAGNA: But, Holy Father, the political situation is very, very dangerous.

[FR. ROSE *returns, with the white, pontifical sunshade with its green lining.* HADRIAN *crosses and takes it from him*]

HADRIAN: [*Smiling*] Quite. But as We mentioned to Your Eminence once before . . .

RAGNA: [*Raising his hands to heaven*] But, Holiness, I am too fat to become a martyr.

HADRIAN: [*Opening the sunshade*] My Lord Cardinal, in every fat priest, there is always a bony martyr crying out for Beatitude.

[HADRIAN *leads off, followed by the now faithful* RAGNA *crossing himself and tut-tutting, as the lights fade to a:*]

BLACKOUT

SCENE SEVEN

The audience chamber.

Two chairs have been set facing up towards the throne.

As the lights come up, a body of SWISS GUARDS *enters and take up their positions in an arc across the back of the stage. They are followed by two* CHAMBERLAINS *escorting* SANT *and* MRS. CROWE. SANT *attempts a truculent nonchalance,* MRS. CROWE *is obviously nervous.*

The SENIOR CHAMBERLAIN *escorts them to the chairs, then both* CHAMBERLAINS *retire upstage.*

There is a silence in which SANT *and* MRS. CROWE *sit awkwardly facing a ring of implacable* SWITZERS.

MRS. CROWE: [*In a stage whisper*] Oh dear, why don't they hurry up? Oh, I do wish I'd never come.

SANT: [*Also in a stage whisper*] Shut up, Nancy. Do you want them to hear you?

MRS. CROWE: I just wish it was all over, that's all.

SANT: Can't you see that's just what he wants? He wants to get us rattled. But I'll rattle him first. [*He clinks the loose change in his pocket*] Aye.

MRS. CROWE: Oh, I do hope you're right, Jerry.

SANT: Of course I am. You don't imagine I gave the papers *all* I know, do you? Not by a long chalk I didn't. Not by a very long chalk. He'll listen to me this time, or my name's not Jeremiah Sant.

[*The* SWITZERS *come to attention.* HADRIAN *enters, followed by* TALACRYN, COURTLEIGH, *another* CARDINAL *and* FR. ROSE. SANT *forgets himself and automatically makes to rise, then, remembering, sits down again insolently.*

HADRIAN *assumes the throne flanked by the* CARDINALS. FR. ROSE *stands to the right and prepares to take notes on a clipboard.*

HADRIAN *makes a gesture dismissing the* SWISS GUARDS, *who, with the* CHAMBERLAINS, *exit*]

HADRIAN: [*Frigidly, but without menace*] We have summoned you in order that ye may speak your minds to Us. But Our utterances and yours shall be recorded.

[*He indicates* ROSE]

SANT: I object. This was to be a private interview.

HADRIAN: In order to start in a conciliatory mood, We concede. [*To* MRS. CROWE] Madam, what do you want?

MRS. CROWE: Well, you know why I came here. I—er—I—er . . . [*She looks desperately to* SANT *for a lead*]

SANT: I think it would be more advantageous to all parties if I was to speak for Mrs. Crowe.

HADRIAN: We will concede this point also. Sir, we have received your questionable letter—are aware of your calumnies in the newspapers—and are now at a loss to know what more you could want of us.

SANT: [*Rising*] Want? Well, I want reparation—damages, as you might say.

HADRIAN: For what?

SANT: Why, for the loss of time while I've had to be here, and for my business which I've been obliged to neglect while I've been kept waiting.

HADRIAN: To what extent have you suffered?

SANT: To what extent? [*Walking around below the throne*] Well, that shouldn't be difficult. I've been here since last July. Say eight months, and I generally allow a pound a day expenses. But it's cost me a sight more. You can add five hundred pounds for out-of-pockets. Then there's the business: say a year with salary and commission—call it three thousand. Then there's what we'll call damages [*Significantly*] if you know what I mean. Well, including "damages" you might tot it all up together and call it—twenty thousand pounds.

HADRIAN: And your companion?

SANT: Well, better say double it. Forty thousand pounds spot cash in sterling and we'll cry quits.

[HADRIAN *takes a quick look round upon his* CARDINALS, *who return it*]

HADRIAN: You are demanding that We should pay you forty thousand pounds?

SANT: [*Sitting*] That's correct.

HADRIAN: Why do you demand this sum of Us?

SANT: Why? I should have thought I'd made my meaning plain. Do you want bells on it?

MRS. CROWE: [*Obsequiously*] Perhaps if I could have a private word with His Holiness . . .

HADRIAN: Daughter, your notorious conduct debars you from a private conversation with any clergyman except in the open confessional.

MRS. CROWE: [*Rising*] Oh, I see! So it's like that, is it? Well, I think you're going to regret what you've just said. Mr. Sant was quite right about you. You must be shown up for what you really are. [*To* SANT, *as she sits*] Jerry, you tell him.

SANT: [*To* MRS. CROWE, *gruffly*] Now just take it easy, will you? And sit down. [*Rising, to* HADRIAN] I'm afraid the lady is a wee bit upset, as well she might be. And I expect she is a wee bit embarrassed by the presence of so many people. Could we not dispense with those fine-looking gentlemen over there? [*Pointing to the* CARDINALS]

[*He sits*]

HADRIAN: [*To the* CARDINALS] Your Eminences will be so good as to retire.

COURTLEIGH: Holiness, remember you are Sovereign within these walls.

RAGNA: I will tell the Chamberlains to take these people away.

HADRIAN: No. We thank your Lordships, but We are conducting this interview. Have no fears, since We have none.

[*The* CARDINALS *leave,* RAGNA *making gestures of despair.*
FR. ROSE *remains in the background*]

HADRIAN: And now . . .

SANT: Now, sir, I should like to make an end to this matter and
I daresay you've other things to be getting on with yourself.
Suppose you make a suggestion. I don't think you'll find us
unreasonable.

HADRIAN: [*With deceptive mildness*] You ask that We should
pay you forty thousand pounds—spot cash was the term you
used—for damages which you say We have caused.

SANT: Aye, that's right.

HADRIAN: It's useless to point out to you that We did not
ask you to waste your time in Rome?

SANT: In Rome! Not likely.

HADRIAN: And that We did not force you or induce you to
neglect your business?

SANT: [*Getting angry*] No! But I daresay you were banking on
it that I'd never dare face you, weren't ye? If ye'd have had
the civility to have answered my letters and made an appointment like I suggested a while back, we'd have had this settled
and done with without all this unpleasantness.

[*He sits again*]

HADRIAN: For the credit of the human race, it must be said
that indecent exhibitions of this kind are rare. But some
men are gifted with an abnormal capacity for making fools
of themselves. Mr. Sant, does it not occur to you that you
are engaging in foolish and singularly dirty business?

SANT: [*Leaping up*] Who d'ye think you're talking to? My hands
are as clean as yours any day. Who skipped owing this lady
here her rent, aye? Well, go on . . .

[HADRIAN *turns to* FR. ROSE. FR. ROSE *produces a receipt
from the papers on his board, and moves down to* MRS.
CROWE, *who disdains it with a shrug.* SANT *snatches it*]

HADRIAN: You know, Madam, that We paid this bill the moment we were in a position to do so.

SANT: Well, if you've paid her why shouldn't you pay me?

HADRIAN: Because We owe you nothing.

SANT: So that's the way of it, is it? Then, you'll be wanting to see a bit more about yer scabby little self in the papers then?

FR. ROSE: Let me call the guard, Holiness.

HADRIAN: [*Signalling* FR. ROSE *to remain quiet*] Listen, Mr. Sant, We look upon you as a deeply injured man—

SANT: [*Sitting*] That's more like it.

HADRIAN: —injured only by himself.

SANT: What?

HADRIAN: You have suffered loss and damage only because of your persistence in doing evil things. In this you have been your own enemy.

SANT: [*Rising*] Me own *what?* You sit there and tell me . . .

HADRIAN: [*Raising his voice*] Mr. Sant, is it useless to ask you to change? You shall be helped. You will not be left alone.

SANT: [*Shouting*] I want what I come here to get—my money.

HADRIAN: If you wish honestly to earn a better living, We shall give you that opportunity.

SANT: The hell with that. What about damages for the past?

HADRIAN: [*Rising*] We promise you a chance for the future.

SANT: [*With menace*] You won't pay then?

HADRIAN: On your terms—not one farthing. But We will help you to save your soul.

SANT: [*Almost out of his mind*] You'll *save* my soul? You?

MRS. CROWE: [*Urgently*] Jerry, sit down—please.

SANT: [*To* HADRIAN] You make me sick, you dirty Taigh.

MRS. CROWE: [*Rising: desperately*] Jerry, I want to go. Please. It's no good.

SANT: [*Taking a step towards* HADRIAN] He's just a little insect. Aren't ye?

MRS. CROWE: Jerry, please . . .

FR. ROSE: [*Running right, in alarm*] Guard! Presto! Presto!

SANT: [*Quite out of his mind now, draws a revolver*] And ye know what to do with insects, don't ye? Tread them underfoot.

MRS. CROWE: [*Shrieking*] Jerry!

[SWISS GUARDS, *not knowing what is required of them, rush in shouting "Pronto! Pronto!"*]

SANT: Vengeance is mine, saith the Lord! Halleluja!

[*Before anyone can move,* SANT *fires once.* HADRIAN *stands quite still.* FR. ROSE *rushes forward. The* GUARDS' *reactions are slower, but they follow.*

SANT *fires for the second time, and* MRS. CROWE *screams.* HADRIAN *remains still, though he seems to sway.*

As SANT *fires for the third time,* FR. ROSE *tries to interpose himself between* SANT *and* HADRIAN. *He fails, but manages to catch* HADRIAN *who now slowly subsides as a patch of crimson defiles the Apostolic whiteness of his robe.*

RAGNA, TALACRYN *and other* CARDINALS *rush in. The* GUARDS *overpower* SANT, *half killing him and holding him on the floor. The* CARDINALS *surround the throne. All eyes are turned to* HADRIAN *who is supported by* TALACRYN *on one side and* RAGNA *on the other. The* GUARDS *fling* SANT *on his knees before the dying* POPE]

HADRIAN: [*Weakly*] Father, forgive them for they know not— [*He struggles for breath*]—what they . . . Venerable Fathers, Our will and pleasure is . . .

TALACRYN: Speak it, Most Holy Father.

HADRIAN: Venerable Fathers, We name you all the ministers of Our will. [*He turns towards* SANT] Son, you are forgiven. You are free.

[SANT *is dragged off by the* GUARDS. *The hysterical* MRS. CROWE *exits with him*]

HADRIAN: George, are you hurt? [*Unclasping his pectoral cross and giving it to* FR. ROSE] Dear Son, take this cross.

[FR. ROSE *takes the cross and backs away weeping.*

TALACRYN *and* RAGNA *now beckon the others to support* HADRIAN'S *body and prepare to administer final absolution. The room fills with members of the Sacred College and others*]

TALACRYN: [*In a whisper: overcome with emotion*] The profession of faith, Most Holy Lord.

HADRIAN: I believe all that which Holy Mother Church believes. I ask pardon of all men. Dear Jesus, be not to me a judge but a Saviour.

TALACRYN: Saints of God, advance to help him: Angels of the Lord, come to meet him, receiving his soul, offering it in the Sight of the Most High.

[HADRIAN *indicates his wish to be raised to his feet. He slowly raises his right hand, which can hardly bear the weight of the two huge Pontifical rings*]

HADRIAN: May God Omnipotent, [*The sign of the cross*] Father, [*The sign of the cross*] Son, [*The sign of the cross*] and Holy Ghost, bless you.

[HADRIAN *dies. A bell begins a solemn toll. Four* SWITZERS *lift up* HADRIAN'S *body and carry it slowly round the stage and off. As they do so, and the* CARDINALS *follow,* FR. ROSE *moves down center.*

The lights gradually fade until only a spot is left on him]

FR. ROSE: Prosit Quaesumus, Domine, animae famuli tui Frederick William Rolfe, Hadriane, Summi Pontificis, misericordiae tuae implorata clementia; ut ejus, in quo speravit et creditit aeternum capiat, te miserante, consortium. Per Dominum [*The sign of the cross*].

Yes, it had to happen. I suppose it was inevitable, really . . . I don't suppose it has been given to every one of you to have dissected a crab. But if you have, you will have noted that under its hard shell there lies a labyrinth of sensitive cells for the defence of which it is armed with huge ferociously snapping claws.

In just such a manner, Frederick William Rolfe, hard as adamant outside, was, within, the tenderest, the cleverest, the most unhappy, the most dreadful of all God's creatures. Yet because he knew how strong he was, he withstood the most fearful revilings and humiliations, quite careless as to what the world might say. But faced with the crass stupidity of the vulgar and obscene mob he would cast aside his self-possession and the great crookedly-curving claws, once folded and still, would come slashing and tearing with a violence that was sudden and frightful.

But the One cannot stand forever against the Many. When the air filled with the impotent howls of all who feared and therefore hated him, nothing was left in him or of him, except the desire to feel the touch of sweet white death.

And so it happened. So died Hadrian the Seventh, Bishop, Servant of the servants of God, and maybe martyr.

[As the end of the procession leaves, ROLFE, as he appeared at the beginning of Act One, walks on and watches with approval the funeral cortege. He is smoking a cigarette and carries in his arms a huge bundle of manuscript. The remaining lights start to fade]

ROLFE-FR. ROSE: [In unison] Let us pray for the repose of his soul. He was so tired.

[The lights fade to a:]

BLACKOUT

SCENE EIGHT

ROLFE's room in London as at the beginning of Act One. When the lights come up, ROLFE enters clutching his bundle of manuscript and moves to the fireplace. There is a knock at the door.

ROLFE: Come in.

[MRS. CROWE *enters*]

ROLFE: What do you want, Mrs. Crowe?

MRS. CROWE: I came up to tell you that there's the two men downstairs called to see you again.

[ROLFE *looks blank for a moment*]

ROLFE: What?

MRS. CROWE: [*With meaning*] You know.

[ROLFE *pauses in thought for a second*]

ROLFE: [*Eagerly*] Oh yes, of course. Their Lordships. Show them up, please.

MRS. CROWE: [*Dubiously*] Very well, then.

[MRS. CROWE *exits.* ROLFE *puts the manuscript on the arm-chair and tries to make himself look more respectable, then stands erect to receive his visitors. In a minute they enter. It is the two* BAILIFFS. *The younger holds a warrant of execution in his hand. The older smiles amiably*]

1ST BAILIFF: Mr. Corvo?

ROLFE: [*Scarcely audible*] No.

1ST BAILIFF: Sorry, sir, *Baron* Corvo.

ROLFE: [*Icily*] That is not my name.

1ST BAILIFF: [*Consulting his papers*] Of course, sir. You are Mr. Frederick William Rolfe.

[ROLFE *stands erect but one knee begins to tremble. The* BAILIFFS *look round the room, appraising its pitiful contents with professional eyes*]

1ST BAILIFF: You were warned, Mr. Rolfe. I did warn you, didn't I?

[ROLFE *stands rigid, saying nothing*]

1ST BAILIFF: Now I am afraid we shall be obliged to distrain your effects in accordance with this Warrant of Execution.

[*Still* ROLFE *says nothing*]

1ST BAILIFF: You do comprehend, don't you, Mr. Rolfe, that we are acting with the authority of a Warrant issued by the Court?

[ROLFE *still remains silent and immobile*]

2ND BAILIFF: A Warrant of Execution . . . [*He moves to the armchair*] I'm afraid this'll have to go too, sir.

1ST BAILIFF: [*Looking suspiciously at the pile of manuscript*] What's this then? *Hadrian the Seventh.*

ROLFE: [*Picking up the manuscript and holding it to him*] A book.

2ND BAILIFF: [*Piling books and all small items onto the chest-of-drawers*] Write books, do you?

[*He takes down the crucifix, the mirror and any other dressing and articles and puts them on the chest-of-drawers.* ROLFE *does not deign to answer*]

1ST BAILIFF: [*Helping the other*] What's it about then?

ROLFE: About? It's about a man who made the fatuous and frantic mistake of living before his time.

1ST BAILIFF: Any value?

[*The* SECOND BAILIFF *takes out the small chair and returns*]

ROLFE: It's a masterpiece and, therefore, probably not worth tuppence.

[*The two* BAILIFFS *exchange glances of incomprehension*]

ROLFE: At the same time, it is possibly beyond price. [*He passes his hands gently over the manuscript*]

[*The* BAILIFFS *look more than ever confused*]

1ST BAILIFF: [*To his colleague*] All right, then, let's get these out.

[*The* SECOND BAILIFF *takes out the armchair while the first moves the chest-of-drawers round. The* SECOND BAILIFF *re-enters and between them they take out the chest-of-drawers.*
ROLFE *stands quite still, holding his manuscript.*
After a moment the FIRST BAILIFF *returns, moves to* ROLFE, *takes the manuscript, and goes to the door*]

1ST BAILIFF: Best not to take any chances, Mr. Rolfe. After all, you could be right.

[*The* FIRST BAILIFF *exits.* ROLFE *is left all alone in the bare room, standing rigidly as he has done from the moment the* BAILIFFS *came in. As he stands there, one knee begins to tremble violently*]

CURTAIN

Mart Crowley

Toward the late 1960s, manners, mores and morals spread their wings in extraordinary and often astonishing directions and the theatre, in its classic guise and wonted way, attempted to keep pace with a period of convulsive changes.

As the decade clamorously drew to a close, sexuality—in all shapes, sizes and situations—burst forth as an unprecedentedly popular theme both on and (mainly) off Broadway. Nudity, though it did not run quite as nakedly rampant as generally believed due to some high-voltage promotion and overblown press coverage given a handful of attractions, did reveal itself on Manhattan stages. Homosexuality, male and female, was portrayed in forthright terms, no longer largely concealed by furtive shadows or relegated to subdued and circumspect interpretation. Theatrical windows blissfully were tossed open with the new permissiveness, focusing more revealing light upon age-old subjects heretofore guardedly presented in the dramatic form.

The theatre of the late Sixties came a long way indeed from the early (1926) days of Edouard Bourdet's *The Captive*, a comparatively tame though sincere treatment of lesbianism that was ruled off the Broadway boards by (of all people) Mayor James J. Walker's administration.

This courageous but judicially aborted attempt to portray on stage a subject and human condition as old as the Bible was followed, at different intervals, by a number of other cautiously molded dramas, including *The Green Bay Tree; The Children's Hour; Trio; No Exit; Tea and Sympathy,* and perhaps a parcel more, few worthy of recall.

Unquestionably, a homosexual note or hue has tinted many a modern play, some by the theatre's most distinguished contemporary authors, but no playwright within memory has so candidly or compellingly stormed the bastion of fear and clandestineness as Mart Crowley has done with his first professionally produced play, *The Boys in the Band*. Unlike the majority of his predecessors, Mr. Crowley has not circumvented the real nature of his subject and through direct and truthful confrontation has produced an intensive dramatic study of personal relationships among homosexuals.

Mart Crowley was born on August 21, 1935, in Vicksburg, Mississippi, where his father owned Crowley's Smoke House, an establishment featuring "bar, billiards, tobacco and dominoes." After studying at St. Aloysius High School in Vicksburg, Mr. Crowley departed for Washington, D.C. and Catholic University, a family compromise, for his father, "a staunch Irish Catholic and a rabid sports enthusiast," had planned on Notre Dame. At the conclusion of his second year, Mr. Crowley left for California and U.C.L.A. where he worked toward an art degree. Two years later, he was back at Catholic University to prepare for a career as a scenic designer. Fate decreed otherwise, and Mr. Crowley (flattened by a rigorous period of trying to establish himself in the New York theatre) returned to the West Coast, this time as secretary (for two years) to actress Natalie Wood, whose encouragement eventually led him into a writing career.

He journeyed back home to Mississippi and wrote a screenplay for Miss Wood based on Dorothy Baker's book, *Cassandra at the Wedding*. This soon was followed by additional screenplays, optioned and dropped, television pilots that reached no further than the projection room, and an understandable frustration that developed into a severe depression. Eventually, he pulled himself together long enough to resume sessions with his analyst who advised him, "thinking time is working time."

Sagaciously, he heeded the advice and settled down in the home of another actress friend, Diana Lynn (ostensibly to baby-sit with her children while she and her husband were away on a cruise), and within five weeks he completed *The Boys in the Band*: "I wrote the play for my own survival and personal fulfillment after years of failure. It's not a confession and it's not autobiographical, but there's a little of me in all the characters and there's a little of all the people I've known."

The author, who now resides in New York City, presently is engaged in producing the film version of *The Boys in the Band* (with the original stage cast) and participating in production plans for his new play, *Remote Asylum*, scheduled to be presented on the Broadway stage by Robert Whitehead in 1970.

THE BOYS
IN THE BAND

Mart Crowley

The Boys in the Band was first performed in January 1968, at the Playwrights Unit, Vandam Theatre, Greenwich Village.

The Boys in the Band was first produced on the New York stage by Richard Barr and Charles Woodward, Jr., at Theatre Four on April 14, 1968. The cast was as follows:

MICHAEL	Kenneth Nelson
DONALD	Frederick Combs
EMORY	Cliff Gorman
LARRY	Keith Prentice
HANK	Laurence Luckinbill
BERNARD	Reuben Greene
COWBOY	Robert La Tourneaux
HAROLD	Leonard Frey
ALAN	Peter White

Directed by Robert Moore
Designed by Peter Harvey

CHARACTERS

MICHAEL *Thirty, average face, smartly groomed*

DONALD *Twenty-eight, medium blond, wholesome American good looks*

EMORY *Thirty-three, small, frail, very plain*

LARRY *Twenty-nine, extremely handsome*

HANK *Thirty-two, tall, solid, athletic, attractive*

BERNARD *Twenty-eight, Negro, nice-looking*

COWBOY *Twenty-two, light blond, muscle-bound, too pretty*

HAROLD *Thirty-two, dark, lean, strong limbs, unusual Semitic face*

ALAN *Thirty, aristocratic Anglo-Saxon features*

The play is divided into two acts. The action is continuous and occurs one evening within the time necessary to perform the script.

ACT ONE

*A smartly appointed duplex apartment in the East Fifties,
New York, consisting of a living room and, on a higher
level, a bedroom. Bossa nova music blasts from a phonograph.*
MICHAEL, *wearing a robe, enters from the kitchen, carrying
some liquor bottles. He crosses to set them on a bar,
looks to see if the room is in order, moves toward the
stairs to the bedroom level, doing a few improvised dance
steps en route. In the bedroom, he crosses before a mirror,
studies his hair—sighs. He picks up comb and a hair dryer,
goes to work.*
The downstairs front-door buzzer sounds. A beat. MICHAEL
stops, listens, turns off the dryer. More buzzing. MICHAEL
*quickly goes to the living room, turns off the music,
opens the door to reveal* DONALD, *dressed in khakis and
a Lacoste shirt, carrying an airline zipper bag.*

MICHAEL: Donald! You're about a day and a half early!

DONALD: [*Enters*] The doctor canceled!

MICHAEL: Canceled! How'd you get inside?

DONALD: The street door was open.

MICHAEL: You wanna drink?

DONALD: [*Going to bedroom to deposit his bag*] Not until
I've had my shower. I want something to work-out today—I
want to try to relax and enjoy *something*.

MICHAEL: You in a blue funk because of the doctor?

DONALD: [*Returning*] Christ, no. I was depressed long before I got *there*.

MICHAEL: Why'd the prick cancel?

DONALD: A virus or something. He looked awful.

MICHAEL: [*Holding up a shopping bag*] Well, this'll pick you up. I went shopping today and bought all kind of goodies. Sandalwood soap . . .

DONALD: [*Removing his socks and shoes*] I feel better already.

MICHAEL: [*Producing articles*] . . . Your very own toothbrush because I'm sick to death of your using mine.

DONALD: How do you think *I* feel.

MICHAEL: You've had worse things in your mouth. [*Holds up a cylindrical can*] And, also for you . . . something called "Control." Notice nowhere is it called hair spray—just simply "Control." And the words "For Men" are written about thirty-seven times all over the goddamn can!

DONALD: It's called Butch Assurance.

MICHAEL: Well, it's *still* hair spray—no matter if they call it "*Balls*"!

[DONALD *laughs*]

It's all going on your very own shelf, which is to be labeled: Donald's Saturday Night Douche Kit. By the way, are you spending the night?

DONALD: Nope. I'm driving back. I still get very itchy when I'm in this town too long. I'm not that well yet.

MICHAEL: That's what you say every weekend.

DONALD: Maybe after about ten more years of analysis I'll be able to stay one night.

MICHAEL: Maybe after about ten more years of analysis you'll be able to move back to town permanently.

DONALD: If I live that long.

MICHAEL: You will. If you don't kill yourself on the Long Island Expressway some early Sunday morning. I'll never know how you can tank up on martinis and make it back to the Hamptons in one piece.

DONALD: Believe me, it's easier than getting here. Ever had an anxiety attack at sixty miles an hour? Well, tonight I was beside myself to get to the doctor—and just as I finally make it, rush in, throw myself on the couch, and vomit out how depressed I am, he says, "Donald, I have to cancel tonight—I'm just too sick."

MICHAEL: Why didn't you tell him you're sicker than he is.

DONALD: He already knows *that.*

[DONALD *goes to the bedroom, drops his shoes and socks.* MICHAEL *follows*]

MICHAEL: Why didn't the prick call you and cancel. Suppose you'd driven all this way for nothing.

DONALD: [*Removing his shirt*] Why do you keep calling him a prick?

MICHAEL: Whoever heard of an analyst having a session with a patient for two hours on Saturday evening.

DONALD: He simply prefers to take Mondays off.

MICHAEL: Works late on Saturday and takes Monday off—what is he, a psychiatrist or a hairdresser?

DONALD: Actually, he's both. He shrinks my head and combs me out. [*Lies on the bed*] Besides, I had to come in town to a birthday party anyway. Right?

MICHAEL: You had to remind me. If there's one thing I'm not ready for, it's five screaming queens singing Happy Birthday.

DONALD: Who's coming?

MICHAEL: They're really all Harold's friends. It's *his* birthday and I want everything to be just the way he'd want it. I don't want to have to listen to him kvetch about how nobody ever does anything for anybody but themselves.

DONALD: Himself.

MICHAEL: Himself. I think you know everybody anyway—they're the same old tired fairies you've seen around since the day one. Actually, there'll be seven, counting Harold and you and me.

DONALD: Are you calling me a screaming queen or a tired fairy?

MICHAEL: Oh, I beg your pardon—six tired screaming fairy queens and one anxious queer.

DONALD: You don't think Harold'll mind my being here, do you? Technically, I'm *your* friend, not his.

MICHAEL: If she doesn't like it, she can twirl on it. Listen, I'll be out of your way in just a second. I've only got one more thing to do.

DONALD: Surgery, so early in the evening?

MICHAEL: Sunt! That's French, with a cedilla. [*Gives him a crooked third finger, goes to mirror*] I've just got to comb my hair for the thirty-seventh time. Hair—that's singular. My hair, without exaggeration, is clearly falling on the floor. And *fast*, baby!

DONALD: You're totally paranoid. You've got plenty of hair.

MICHAEL: What you see before you is a masterpiece of deception. My hairline starts about here. [*Indicates his crown*] All this is just tortured forward.

DONALD: Well, I hope, for your sake, no strong wind comes up.

MICHAEL: If one does, I'll be in terrible trouble. I will then have a bald head and shoulder-length fringe.

[*Runs his fingers through his hair, holds it away from his scalp, dips the top of his head so that* DONALD *can see.* DONALD *is silent*]

Not good, huh?

DONALD: Not the best.

MICHAEL: It's called, "getting old." Ah, life is such a grand design—spring, summer, fall, winter, death. Who*ever* could have thought it up?

DONALD: No one *we* know, that's for sure.

MICHAEL: [*Turns to study himself in the mirror, sighs*] Well, one thing you can say for masturbation . . . you certainly don't have to look your best.

> [*Slips out of the robe, flings it at* DONALD. DONALD *laughs, takes the robe, exits to the bath.* MICHAEL *takes a sweater out of a chest, pulls it on*]

MICHAEL: What are you so depressed about? I mean, other than the usual *everything*. [*A beat*]

DONALD: [*Reluctantly*] I really don't want to get into it.

MICHAEL: Well, if you're not going to tell me, how can we have a conversation *in depth*—a warm, rewarding, meaningful friendship?

DONALD: Up yours!

MICHAEL: [*Southern accent*] Why, Cap'n Butler, how you talk!

> [*Pause.* DONALD *appears in the doorway holding a glass of water and a small bottle of pills.* MICHAEL *looks up*]

DONALD: It's just that today I finally realized that I was *raised* to be a failure. I was *groomed* for it. [*A beat*]

MICHAEL: You know, there was a time when you could have said that to me and I wouldn't have known what the hell you were talking about.

DONALD: [*Takes some pills*] Naturally, it all goes back to Evelyn and Walt.

MICHAEL: Naturally. When doesn't it go back to Mom and Pop. Unfortunately, we all had an Evelyn and a Walt. The crumbs! Don't you love that word—crumb? Oh, I love it! It's a real Barbara Stanwyck word. [*A la Stanwyck's frozen-lipped Brooklyn accent*] "Cau'll me a keab, you kr-rumm."

DONALD: Well, I see all vestiges of sanity for this evening are now officially shot to hell.

MICHAEL: Oh, Donald, you're so serious tonight! You're fun-starved, baby, and I'm eating for two! [*Sings*] "Forget your troubles, c'mon get happy! You better chase all your blues away. Shout, 'Hallelujah!' c'mon get happy . . ." [*Sees* DONALD *isn't buying it*]—what's more boring than a queen doing a Judy Garland imitation?

DONALD: A queen doing a Bette Davis imitation.

MICHAEL: Meanwhile—back at the Evelyn and Walt Syndrome.

DONALD: America's Square Peg and America's Round Hole.

MICHAEL: Christ, how sick analysts must get of hearing how mommy and daddy made their darlin' into a fairy.

DONALD: It's beyond just that now. Today I finally began to see how some of the other pieces of the puzzle relate to them. —Like why I never finished anything I started in my life . . . my neurotic compulsion to not succeed. I've realized it was always when I failed that Evelyn loved me the most— because it displeased Walt, who wanted perfection. And when I fell short of the mark she was only too happy to make up for it with her love. So I began to identify failing with winning my mother's love. And I began to fail on purpose to get it. I didn't finish Cornell—I couldn't keep a job in this town. I simply retreated to a room over a garage and scrubbing floors in order to keep alive. Failure is the only thing with which I feel at home. Because it is what I was taught at home.

MICHAEL: Killer whales is what they are. Killer whales. How many whales could a killer whale kill . . .

DONALD: A lot, especially if they get them when they were babies.

[*Pause,* MICHAEL *suddenly tears off his sweater, throws it in the air, letting it land where it may, whips out another, pulls it on as he starts down the stairs for the living room.* DONALD *follows*]

Hey! Where're you going?

MICHAEL: To make drinks! I think we need about thirty-seven!

DONALD: Where'd you get *that* sweater?

MICHAEL: This clever little shop on the right bank called Hermes.

DONALD: I work my ass off for forty-five lousy dollars a week *scrubbing* floors and you waltz around throwing cashmere sweaters on them.

MICHAEL: The one on the floor in the bedroom is vicuña.

DONALD: I *beg* your pardon.

MICHAEL: You could get a job doing something else. Nobody holds a gun to your head to be a charwoman. That is, how you say, your neurosis.

DONALD: Gee, and I thought it's why I was born.

MICHAEL: Besides, just because I *wear* expensive clothes doesn't necessarily mean they're paid for.

DONALD: That is, how you say, *your* neurosis.

MICHAEL: I'm a spoiled brat, so what do I know about being mature. The only thing mature means to me is *Victor* Mature, who was in all those pictures with Betty Grable. [*Sings à la Grable*] "I can't begin to tell you, how much you mean to me . . ." Betty sang that in 1945. '45?—'43. No, '43 was "Coney Island," which was remade in '50 as "Wabash Avenue." Yes, "Dolly Sisters" was in '45.

DONALD: How did I manage to miss these momentous events in the American cinema? I can understand people having an affinity for the stage—but movies are such garbage, who can take them seriously.

MICHAEL: Well, I'm sorry if your sense of art is offended. Odd as it may seem, there wasn't any Shubert Theatre in Hot Coffee, Mississippi!

DONALD: However—thanks to the silver screen, your neurosis has got style. It takes a certain flair to squander one's unemployment check at Pavillion.

MICHAEL: What's so snappy about being head over heels in debt. The only thing smart about it is the ingenious ways I dodge the bill collectors.

DONALD: Yeah. Come to think of it, you're the type that gives faggots a bad name.

MICHAEL: And you, Donald, *you* are a credit to the homosexual. A reliable, hard-working, floor-scrubbing, bill-paying fag who don't owe nothin' to nobody.

DONALD: I am a model fairy.

[MICHAEL *has taken some ribbon and paper and begun to wrap* HAROLD'*s birthday gift*]

MICHAEL: You think it's just nifty how I've always flitted from Beverly Hills to Rome to Acapulco to Amsterdam, picking up a lot of one-night stands and a lot of custom-made duds along the trail, but I'm here to tell you that the only place in all those miles—the only place I've ever been *happy*—was on the goddamn plane. [*Puffs up the bow on the package, continues*] Bored with Scandinavia, try Greece. Fed up with dark meat, try light. Hate tequila, what about slivovitz. Tired of boys, what about girls—or how about boys and girls mixed and in what combination? And if you're sick of people, what about poppers? Or pot or pills or the hard stuff. And can you think of anything else the bad baby would like to indulge his spoiled-rotten, stupid, empty, boring, selfish, self-centered self in? Is that what you think has style, Donald? Huh? Is that what you think you've missed out on—my hysterical escapes from country to country, party to party, bar to bar, bed to bed, hangover to hangover, and all of it, hand to mouth! [*A beat*] Run, charge, run, buy, borrow, make, spend, run, squander, beg, run, run, run, waste, waste, *waste!* [*A beat*] And why? And why?

DONALD: Why, Michael? Why?

MICHAEL: I really don't want to get into it.

DONALD: Then how can we have a conversation in depth?

MICHAEL: Oh, you know it all by heart anyway. Same song, second verse. Because my Evelyn refused to let me grow up. She was determined to keep me a child forever and she did one helluva job of it. And my Walt stood by and let her do it. [*A beat*] What you see before you is a thirty-year-old infant. And it was all done in the name of love—what *she* labeled love and probably sincerely believed to be love, when what she was really doing was feeding her own need—satisfying her own loneliness. [*A beat*] She made me into a girl-friend dash lover. [*A beat*] We went to all those goddamn cornball movies together. I picked out her clothes for her and told her what to wear and she'd take me to the beauty parlor with her and we'd both get our hair bleached and a permanent and a manicure. [A beat] And Walt let this happen. [A beat] And she convinced me that I was a sickly child who couldn't run and play and sweat and get knocked around—oh, no! I was frail and pale and, to hear her tell it, practically female. I can't tell you the thousands of times she said to me, "I declare, Michael, you should have been a girl." And I guess I should have—I was frail and pale and bleached and curled and bedded down with hot-water bottles and my dolls and my paper dolls, and my doll clothes and my doll houses! [Quick beat] And Walt bought them for me! [Beat. With increasing speed] And she nursed me and put Vicks salve on my chest and cold cream on my face and told me what beautiful eyes I had and what pretty lips I had. She bathed me in the same tub with her until I grew too big for the two of us to fit. She made me sleep in the same bed with her until I was fourteen years old—until I finally flatly refused to spend one more night there. She didn't want to prepare me for life or how to be out in the world on my own or I might have left her. But I left anyway. This goddamn cripple finally wrenched free and limped away. And here I am—unequipped, undisciplined, untrained, unprepared and unable to live! [A beat] And do you know until this day she still says, "I don't care if you're seventy years old, you'll always be my baby." And can I tell you how that drives me mad! Will that bitch never understand that what I'll always *be* is her son—but that I haven't been her baby for twenty-five years! [A beat] And don't get me wrong. I know it's easy to cop out and blame Evelyn and Walt and say it was *their* fault. That we were simply the helpless put-upon victims. But in the end, we are responsible for ourselves. And I guess— I'm not sure—but I want to believe it—that in their own pathetic, *dangerous* way, they just loved us too much. [A beat] Finis. Applause.

[DONALD *hesitates, walks over to* MICHAEL, *puts his arms around him and holds him. It is a totally warm and caring gesture*]

There's nothing quite as good as feeling sorry for yourself, is there?

DONALD: Nothing.

MICHAEL: [*À la Bette Davis*] I adore cheap sentiment. [*Breaks away*] Okay, I'm taking orders for drinks. What'll it be?

DONALD: An extra-dry-Beefeater-martini-on-the-rocks-with-a-twist.

MICHAEL: Coming up.

> [DONALD *exits up the stairs into the bath;* MICHAEL *into the kitchen. Momentarily,* MICHAEL *returns, carrying an ice bucket in one hand and a silver tray of cracked crab in the other, singing "Acapulco" or "Down Argentine Way" or some other forgotten Grable tune. The telephone rings*]

MICHAEL: [*Answering it*] Backstage, "New Moon." [*A beat*] Alan? My God, I don't believe it. How *are* you? *Where* are you? In town! Great! When'd you get in? Is Fran with you? Oh. What? No. No, I'm tied up tonight. No, tonight's no good for me. —You mean, *now?* Well, Alan, ole boy, it's a friend's birthday and I'm having a few people. —No, you wouldn't exactly call it a birthday party—well, yes, actually I guess you would. I mean, what else would you call it. A *wake*, maybe. I'm sorry I can't ask you to join us—but— well, kiddo, it just wouldn't work out. —No, it's not place cards or anything. It's just that—well, I'd hate to just see you for ten minutes and . . . Alan? Alan? What's the matter? —Are you—are you crying? —Oh, Alan, what's wrong? —Alan, listen, come on over. No, no, it's perfectly all right. Well, just hurry up. I mean, come on by and have a drink, okay? Alan . . . are you all right? Okay. Yeah. Same old address. Yeah. Bye.

> [*Slowly hangs up, stares blankly into space.* DONALD *appears, bathed and changed. He strikes a pose*]

DONALD: Well. Am I stunning?

> [MICHAEL *looks up*]

MICHAEL: [*Tonelessly*] You're absolutely stunning. —You *look* like shit, but I'm absolutely stunned.

DONALD: [*Crestfallen*] Your grapes are, how you say, sour.

MICHAEL: Listen, you won't believe what just happened.

DONALD: Where's my drink?

MICHAEL: I didn't make it—I've been on the phone.

[DONALD *goes to the bar, makes himself a martini*]

MICHAEL: My old roommate from Georgetown just called.

DONALD: Alan what's-his-name?

MICHAEL: McCarthy. He's up here from Washington on business or something and he's on his way over here.

DONALD: Well, I hope he knows the lyrics to "Happy Birthday."

MICHAEL: Listen, asshole, what am I going to do? He's *straight*. And *Square City!* ["*Top Drawer*" *accent through clenched teeth*] I mean, he's rally vury proper. Auffully good family.

DONALD: [*Same accent*] That's so important.

MICHAEL: [*Regular speech*] I mean, they look down on people in the *theatre*—so whatta you think he'll feel about this *freak show* I've got booked for dinner?

DONALD: [*Sipping his drink*] Christ, is that good.

MICHAEL: Want some cracked crab?

DONALD: Not just yet. Why'd you invite him over?

MICHAEL: He invited himself. He said he had to see me tonight. *Immediately.* He absolutely lost his spring on the phone— started crying.

DONALD: Maybe he's feeling sorry for himself too.

MICHAEL: Great heaves and sobs. Really boo-hoo-hoo-time—and that's not his style at all. I mean, he's so pulled-together he wouldn't show any emotion if he were in a plane crash. What am I going to do?

DONALD: What the hell do you care what he thinks.

MICHAEL: Well, I don't really but . . .

DONALD: Or are you suddenly ashamed of your friends?

MICHAEL: Donald, *you* are the only person I know of whom I am truly ashamed. Some people *do* have different standards from yours and mine, you know. And if we don't acknowledge them, we're just as narrow-minded and backward as we think they are.

DONALD: You know what you are, Michael? You're a *real* person.

MICHAEL: Thank you and fuck you. [MICHAEL *crosses to take a piece of crab and nibble on it*] Want some?

DONALD: No, thanks. How could you ever have been friends with a bore like that?

MICHAEL: Believe it or not, there was a time in my life when I didn't go around *announcing* that I was a faggot.

DONALD: That must have been before speech replaced sign language.

MICHAEL: Don't give me any static on that score. I didn't come out until I left college.

DONALD: It seems to me that the first time we tricked we met in a gay bar on Third Avenue during your *junior* year.

MICHAEL: Cunt.

DONALD: I thought you'd never say it.

MICHAEL: Sure you don't want any cracked crab?

DONALD: *Not yet! If you don't mind!*

MICHAEL: Well, it can only be getting colder. What time is it?

DONALD: I don't know. Early.

MICHAEL: Where the hell is Alan?

DONALD: Do you want some more club soda?

MICHAEL: What?

DONALD: There's nothing but club soda in that glass. It's not gin—like mine. You want some more?

MICHAEL: No.

DONALD: I've been watching you for several Saturdays now. You've actually stopped drinking haven't you?

MICHAEL: And smoking too.

DONALD: And smoking too. How long's it been?

MICHAEL: Five weeks.

DONALD: That's amazing.

MICHAEL: I've found God.

DONALD: It *is* amazing—for you.

MICHAEL: Or is God dead?

DONALD: Yes, thank God. And don't get panicky just because I'm paying you a compliment. I can tell the difference.

MICHAEL: You always said that I held my liquor better than anybody you ever saw.

DONALD: I could always tell when you were getting high—one way.

MICHAEL: I'd get hostile.

DONALD: You seem happier or something now—and that shows.

MICHAEL: [*Quietly*] Thanks.

DONALD: What made you stop—the analyst?

MICHAEL: He certainly had a lot to do with it. Mainly, I just didn't think I could survive another hangover, that's all. I don't think I could get through that morning-after ick attack.

DONALD: Morning-after what?

MICHAEL: Icks! Anxiety! Guilt! Unfathomable guilt—either real or imagined—from that split second your eyes pop open and you say, "Oh, my God, what did I do last night!" and ZAP, Total recall!

DONALD: *Tell* me about it!

MICHAEL: Then, the coffee, aspirin, Alka-Seltzer, Darvon, Daprisal, and a quick call to I.A.—Icks Anonymous.

DONALD: "Good morning, I.A."

MICHAEL: "Hi! Was I too bad last night? Did I do anything wrong? I didn't do anything terrible, did I?"

DONALD: [*Laughing*] How many times! How many times!

MICHAEL: And from then on, that struggle to live till lunch, when you have a double Bloody Mary—that is, if you've *waited* until lunch—and then you're half pissed again and useless for the rest of the afternoon. And the only sure cure is to go to bed for about thirty-seven hours, but who ever does that. Instead, you hang on till cocktail time, and by then you're ready for what the night holds—which hopefully is another party, where the whole goddamn cycle starts over! [*A beat*] Well, I've been on that merry-go-round long enough and I either had to get off or die of centrifugal force.

DONALD: And just how does a clear head stack up with the dull fog of alcohol?

MICHAEL: Well, all those things you've always heard are true. Nothing can compare with the experience of one's faculties functioning at their maximum natural capacity. The only thing is . . . I'd *kill* for a drink.

[*The wall-panel buzzer sounds*]

DONALD: Joe College has finally arrived.

MICHAEL: Suddenly, I have such an ick! [*Presses the wall-panel button*] Now listen, Donald . . .

DONALD: [*Quick*] Michael, don't insult me by giving me any lecture on acceptable social behavior. I promise to sit with my legs spread apart and keep my voice in a deep register.

MICHAEL: Donald, you are a real *card-carrying cunt*.

[*The apartment door buzzes several times.* MICHAEL *goes to it, pauses briefly before it, tears it open to reveal* EMORY, LARRY *and* HANK. EMORY *is in Bermuda shorts and a sweater.* LARRY *has on a turtleneck and sandals.* HANK *is in a dark Ivy League suit with a vest and has on cordovan shoes.* LARRY *and* HANK *carry birthday gifts.* EMORY *carries a large covered dish*]

EMORY: [*Bursting in*] ALL RIGHT THIS IS A RAID! EVERY-BODY'S UNDER ARREST!

[*This entrance is followed by a loud raucous laugh as* EMORY *throws his arms around* MICHAEL *and gives him a big kiss on the cheek. Referring to dish*]

Hello, darlin'! Connie Casserole. Oh, Mary, don't ask.

MICHAEL: [*Weary already*] Hello, Emory. Put it in the kitchen.

[EMORY *spots* DONALD]

EMORY: Who is this exotic woman over here?

MICHAEL: Hi, Hank. Larry.

[*They say, "Hi," shake hands, enter.* MICHAEL *looks out in the hall, comes back into the room, closes the door*]

DONALD: Hi, Emory.

EMORY: My dear, I thought you had perished! Where have you been hiding your classically chiseled features?

DONALD: [*To* EMORY] I don't live in the city any more.

MICHAEL: [*To* LARRY *and* HANK, *referring to the gifts*] Here, I'll take those. Where's yours, Emory?

EMORY: It's arriving later.

[EMORY *exits to the kitchen.* LARRY *and* DONALD's *eyes have met.* HANK *has handed* MICHAEL *his gift—*LARRY *is too preoccupied*]

HANK: Larry!—Larry!

LARRY: What!

HANK: Give Michael the gift!

LARRY: Oh. Here. [*To* HANK] Louder. So my mother in Philadelphia can hear you.

HANK: Well, you were just standing there in a trance.

MICHAEL: [*To* LARRY *and* HANK *as* EMORY *reenters*] You both know Donald, don't you?

DONALD: Sure. Nice to see you. [*To* HANK] Hi.

HANK: [*Shaking hands*] Nice to meet you.

MICHAEL: Oh, I thought you'd met.

DONALD: Well . . .

LARRY: We haven't exactly met but we've . . . Hi.

DONALD: Hi.

HANK: But you've what?

LARRY: . . . *Seen* . . . each other before.

MICHAEL: Well, *that* sounds murky.

HANK: You've never met but you've seen each other.

LARRY: What was wrong with the way *I* said it.

HANK: Where?

EMORY: [*Loud aside to* MICHAEL] I think they're going to have their first fight.

LARRY: The first one since we got out of the taxi.

MICHAEL: [*Referring to* EMORY] Where'd you find this trash.

LARRY: Downstairs leaning against a lamppost.

EMORY: With an orchid behind my ear and big wet lips painted over the lipline.

MICHAEL: Just like Maria Montez.

DONALD: Oh, *please!*

EMORY: [*To* DONALD] What have you got against Maria—she was a good woman.

MICHAEL: Listen, everybody, this old college friend of mine is in town and he's stopping by for a fast drink on his way to dinner somewhere. But, listen, he's *straight*, so . . .

LARRY: Straight! If it's the one I met, he's about as straight as the Yellow Brick Road.

MICHAEL: No, you met Justin Stuart.

HANK: I don't remember anybody named Justin Stuart.

LARRY: Of course you don't, dope. *I* met him.

MICHAEL: Well, this is someone else.

DONALD: Alan McCarthy. A very close total stranger.

MICHAEL: It's not that I care what he would think of me, really —it's just that *he's* not ready for it. And he never will be. You understand that, don't you, Hank?

HANK: Oh, sure.

LARRY: You honestly think he doesn't know about you?

MICHAEL: If there's the slightest suspicion, he's never let on one bit.

EMORY: What's he had, a lobotomy?

[*He exits up the stairs into the bath*]

MICHAEL: I was super-careful when I was in college and I still am whenever I see him. I don't know why, but I am.

DONALD: Tilt.

MICHAEL: You may think it was a crock of shit, Donald, but to him I'm sure we were close friends. The closest. To pop that balloon now just wouldn't be fair to him. Isn't that right?

LARRY: Whatever's fair.

MICHAEL: Well, of course. And if that's phony of me, Donald, then that's phony of me and make something of it.

DONALD: I pass.

MICHAEL: Well, even you have to admit it's much simpler to deal with the world according to its rules and then go right ahead and do what you damn well please. You do understand *that*, don't you?

DONALD: Now that you've put it in layman's terms.

MICHAEL: I was just like Alan when I was in college. Very large in the dating department. Wore nothing but those constipated Ivy League clothes and those ten-pound cordovan shoes. [*To* HANK] No offense.

HANK: Quite all right.

MICHAEL: I butched it up quite a bit. And I didn't think I was lying to myself. I really thought I was straight.

EMORY: [*Coming downstairs tucking a Kleenex into his sleeve*] Who do you have to fuck to get a drink around here?

MICHAEL: Will you *light* somewhere? [EMORY *sits on steps*] Or I thought I thought I was straight. I know I didn't come out till after I'd graduated.

DONALD: What about all those weekends up from school?

MICHAEL: I still wasn't out. I was still in the "Christ-was-I-drunk-last-night syndrome."

LARRY: The *what*?

MICHAEL: The Christ-was-I-drunk-last-night syndrome. You know, when you made it with some guy in school and the next day when you had to face each other there was always a lot of shit-kicking crap about, "Man, was I drunk last night! Christ, I don't remember a thing!"

[*Everyone laughs*]

DONALD: You were just guilty because you were Catholic, that's all.

MICHAEL: That's not true. The Christ-was-I-drunk-last-night syndrome knows no religion. It has to do with immaturity. Although I will admit there's a high percentage of it among Mormons.

EMORY: Trollop.

MICHAEL: We all somehow managed to justify our actions in those days. I later found out that even Justin Stuart, my closest friend . . .

DONALD: Other than Alan McCarthy.

MICHAEL: [*A look to* DONALD] . . . was doing the same thing. Only Justin was going to Boston on weekends.

[EMORY *and* LARRY *laugh*]

LARRY: [*To* HANK] Sound familiar?

MICHAEL: Yes, long before Justin or I or God only knows how many others *came out*, we used to get drunk and "horse around" a bit. You see, in the Christ-was-I-drunk-last-night syndrome, you really *are* drunk. That part of it is true. It's just that you also *do remember everything*.

[*General laughter*]

Oh God, I used to have to get loaded to go in a gay bar!

DONALD: Well, times certainly have changed.

MICHAEL: They *have*. Lately I've gotten to despise the bars. Everybody just standing around and standing around—it's like one eternal intermission.

HANK: [*To* LARRY] Sound familiar?

EMORY: I can't stand the bars either. All that cat-and-mouse business—you hang around *staring* at each other all night and wind up going home alone.

MICHAEL: And pissed.

LARRY: A lot of guys have to get loaded to have sex. [*Quick look to* HANK, *who is unamused*] So I've been told.

MICHAEL: If you remember, Donald, the first time we made it I was so drunk I could hardly stand up.

DONALD: You were so drunk you could hardly *get* it up.

MICHAEL: [*Mock innocence*] Christ, I was so drunk I don't remember.

DONALD: Bullshit, you remember.

MICHAEL: [*Sings to* DONALD] "Just friends, lovers no more . . ."

EMORY: You may as well be. Everybody thinks you are anyway.

DONALD: We never *were—really.*

MICHAEL: We didn't have time to be—we got to know each other too fast.

[*Door buzzer sounds*]

Oh, Jesus, it's Alan! Now, please everybody, do me a favor and cool it for the few minutes he's here.

EMORY: Anything for a sis, Mary.

MICHAEL: That's *exactly* what I'm talking about, Emory. *No camping!*

EMORY: Sorry. [*Deep, deep voice to* DONALD] Think the Giants are gonna win the pennant this year?

DONALD: [*Deep, deep voice*] Fuckin' A, Mac.

[MICHAEL *goes to the door, opens it to reveal* BERNARD, *dressed in a shirt and tie and sport jacket. He carries a birthday gift and two bottles of red wine*]

EMORY: [*Big scream*] Oh, it's only another queen!

BERNARD: And it ain't the Red one, either.

EMORY: It's the queen of spades!

[BERNARD *enters.* MICHAEL *looks out in the hall*]

MICHAEL: Bernard, is the downstairs door open?

BERNARD: It was, but I closed it.

MICHAEL: Good.

[BERNARD *starts to put wine on bar*]

MICHAEL: [*Referring to the two bottles of red wine*] I'll take those. You can put your present with the others.

[MICHAEL *closes the door.* BERNARD *hands him the gift. The phone rings*]

BERNARD: Hi, Larry. Hi, Hank.

MICHAEL: *Christ of the Andes!* Donald, will you bartend please.

[MICHAEL *gives* DONALD *the wine bottles, goes to the phone*]

BERNARD: [*Extending his hand to* DONALD] Hello, Donald. Good to see you.

DONALD: Bernard.

MICHAEL: [*Answers phone*] Hello? Alan?

EMORY: Hi, Bernardette. Anybody ever tell you you'd look divine in a hammock, surrounded by louvres and ceiling fans and lots and lots of lush tropical ferns?

BERNARD: [*To* EMORY] You're *such* a fag. You take the cake.

EMORY: Oh, what *about* the cake—whose job was that?

LARRY: Mine. I ordered one to be delivered.

EMORY: How many candles did you say put on it—eighty?

MICHAEL: . . . What? Wait a minute. There's too much noise. Let me go to another phone. [*Presses the hold button, hangs up, dashes toward stairs*]

LARRY: Michael, did the cake come?

MICHAEL: No.

DONALD: [*To* MICHAEL *as he passes*] What's up?

MICHAEL: Do I know?

LARRY: Jesus, I'd better call. Okay if I use the private line?

MICHAEL: [*Going upstairs*] Sure. [*Stops dead on stairs, turns*] Listen, everybody, there's some cracked crab there. Help yourselves.

> [DONALD *shakes his head.* MICHAEL *continues up the stairs to the bedroom.* LARRY *crosses to the phone, presses the free-line button, picks up receiver, dials Information*]

DONALD: Is everybody ready for a drink?

> [HANK *and* BERNARD *say,* "Yeah"]

EMORY: [*Flipping up his sweater*] Ready! I'll be your topless cocktail waitress.

BERNARD: Please spare us the sight of your sagging tits.

EMORY: [*To* HANK, LARRY] What're you having, kids?

MICHAEL: [*Having picked up the bedside phone*] . . . Yes, Alan . . .

LARRY: Vodka and tonic. [*Into phone*] Could I have the number for the Marseilles Bakery in Manhattan.

EMORY: A vod and ton and a . . .

HANK: Is there any beer?

EMORY: Beer! Who drinks beer before dinner?

BERNARD: Beer drinkers.

DONALD: That's telling him.

MICHAEL: . . . No, Alan, don't be silly. What's there to apologize for?

EMORY: Truck drivers do. Or . . . or wallpaperers. Not school teachers. They have sherry.

HANK: This one has beer.

EMORY: Well, maybe school teachers in *public* schools. [*To* LARRY] How can a sensitive artist like you live with an insensitive bull like that?

LARRY: [*Hanging up the phone and redialing*] I can't.

BERNARD: Emory, you'd live with Hank in a minute, if he'd ask you. In fifty-eight seconds. Lord knows, you're sssensitive.

EMORY: Why don't you have a piece of watermelon and hush up!

MICHAEL: . . . Alan, don't be ridiculous.

DONALD: Here you go, Hank.

HANK: Thanks.

LARRY: Shit. They don't answer.

DONALD: What're you having, Emory?

BERNARD: A Pink Lady.

EMORY: A vodka martini on the rocks, please.

LARRY: [*Hangs up*] Well, let's just hope.

[DONALD *hands* LARRY *his drink—their eyes meet again. A faint smile crosses* LARRY's *lips.* DONALD *returns to the bar to make* EMORY's *drink*]

MICHAEL: Lunch tomorrow will be great. One o'clock—the Oak Room at the Plaza okay? Fine.

BERNARD: [*To* DONALD] Donald, read any new libraries lately?

DONALD: One or three. I did the complete works of Doris Lessing this week. I've been depressed.

MICHAEL: Alan, forget it, will you? Right. Bye.

[*Hangs up, starts to leave the room—stops. Quickly pulls off the sweater he is wearing, takes out another, crosses to the stairs*]

DONALD: You must not work in Circulation any more.

BERNARD: Oh, I'm still there—every day.

DONALD: Well, since I moved, I only come in on Saturday evenings. [*Moves his stack of books off the bar*]

HANK: Looks like you stock up for the week.

[MICHAEL *rises and crosses to steps landing*]

BERNARD: Are you kidding—that'll last him two days.

EMORY: It would last *me* two years. I still haven't finished *Atlas Shrugged*, which I started in 1912.

MICHAEL: [*To* DONALD] Well, he's not coming.

DONALD: It's just as well now.

BERNARD: Some people eat, some people drink, some take dope . . .

DONALD: I read.

MICHAEL: And read and read and read. It's a wonder your eyes don't turn back in your head at the sight of a dust jacket.

HANK: Well, at least he's a constructive escapist.

MICHAEL: Yeah, what do I do—take planes. No, I don't do that any more. Because I don't have the *money* to do that any more. I go to the baths. That's about it.

EMORY: I'm about to do both. I'm flying to the West Coast—

BERNARD: You still have that act with a donkey in Tijuana?

EMORY: I'm going to *San Francisco* on a well-earned vacation.

LARRY: No shopping?

EMORY: Oh, I'll look for a few things for a couple of clients, but I've been so busy lately I really couldn't care less if I never saw another piece of fabric or another stick of furniture as long as I live. I'm going to the Club Baths and I'm not out till they announce the departure of TWA one week later.

BERNARD: [*To* EMORY] You'll never learn to stay out of the baths, will you. The last time Emily was taking the vapors, this big hairy number strolled in. Emory said, "I'm just resting," and the big hairy number said, "I'm just *ar*resting!" It was the vice!

[*Everybody laughs*]

EMORY: You have to tell everything, don't you.

[DONALD *crosses to give* EMORY *his drink*]

Thanks, sonny. You live with your parents?

DONALD: Yeah. But it's all right—they're gay.

[EMORY *roars, slaps* HANK *on the knee,* HANK *gets up, moves away.* DONALD *turns to* MICHAEL]

What happened to Alan?

MICHAEL: He suddenly got terrible icks about having broken down on the phone. Kept apologizing over and over. Did a big about-face and reverted to the old Alan right before my very eyes.

DONALD: Ears.

MICHAEL: Ears. Well, the cracked crab obviously did not work out. [*Starts to take away the tray*]

EMORY: Just put that down if you don't want your hand slapped. I'm about to have some.

MICHAEL: It's really very good. [*Gives* DONALD *a look*] I don't know why everyone has such an aversion to it.

DONALD: Sometimes you remind me of the Chinese water torture. I take that back. Sometimes you remind me of the *relentless* Chinese water torture.

MICHAEL: Bitch.

[HANK *has put on some music*]

BERNARD: Yeah, baby, let's hear that sound.

EMORY: A drumbeat and their eyes sparkle like Cartier's.

[BERNARD *starts to snap his fingers and move in time with the music.* MICHAEL *joins in*]

I wonder where Harold is.

EMORY: Yeah, where *is* the frozen fruit?

MICHAEL: [*To* DONALD] Emory refers to Harold as the frozen fruit because of his former profession as an ice skater.

EMORY: She used to be the Vera Hruba Ralston of the Borscht Circuit.

[MICHAEL *and* BERNARD *are now dancing freely*]

BERNARD: [*To* MICHAEL] If your mother could see you now, she'd have a stroke.

MICHAEL: Got a camera on you?

[*The door panel buzzes.* EMORY *lets out a yelp*]

EMORY: Oh my God, it's Lily Law! Everybody three feet apart!

[MICHAEL *goes to the panel, presses the button.* HANK *turns down the music.* MICHAEL *opens the door a short way, pokes his head out*]

BERNARD: It's probably Harold now.

[MICHAEL *leans back in the room*]

MICHAEL: No, it's the delivery boy from the bakery.

LARRY: Thank God.

[MICHAEL *goes out into the hall, pulling the door almost closed behind him*]

EMORY: [*Loudly*] Ask him if he's got any hot-cross buns!

HANK: Come on, Emory, knock it off.

BERNARD: You can take her anywhere but out.

EMORY: [*To* HANK] You remind me of an old-maid school teacher.

HANK: You remind me of a chicken wing.

EMORY: I'm sure you meant that as a compliment.

[HANK *turns the music back up*]

MICHAEL: [*In hall*] Thank you. Good night.

[MICHAEL *returns with a cake box, closes the door, and takes it into the kitchen*]

LARRY: Hey, Bernard, you remember that thing we used to do on Fire Island? [LARRY *starts to do a kind of Madison*]

BERNARD: That was "in" so far back I think I've forgotten.

EMORY: *I* remember.

[*Pops up—starts doing the steps.* LARRY *and* BERNARD *start to follow*]

LARRY: Yeah. That's it.

[MICHAEL *enters from the kitchen, falls in line with them*]

MICHAEL: Well, if it isn't the Geriatrics Rockettes.

> [*Now they all are doing practically a precision routine.* DONALD *comes to sit on the arm of a chair, sip his drink, and watch in fascination.* HANK *goes to the bar to get another beer.*
> *The door buzzer sounds. No one seems to hear it. It buzzes again.* HANK *turns toward the door, hesitates. Looks toward* MICHAEL, *who is now deeply involved in the intricacies of the dance. No one, it seems, has heard the buzzer but* HANK, *who goes to the door, opens it wide to reveal* ALAN. *He is dressed in black tie.*
> *The dancers continue, turning and slapping their knees and heels and laughing with abandon. Suddenly* MICHAEL *looks up, stops dead.* DONALD *sees this and turns to see what* MICHAEL *has seen. Slowly he stands up.* MICHAEL *goes to the record player, turns it off abruptly.* EMORY, LARRY, *and* BERNARD *come to out-of-step halts, look to see what's happened*]

MICHAEL: I thought you said you weren't coming.

ALAN: I . . . well, I'm sorry . . .

MICHAEL: [*Forced lightly*] We were just—acting silly . . .

ALAN: . . . Actually, when I called I was in a phone booth around the corner. My dinner party is not far from here. And . . .

MICHAEL: . . . Emory was just showing us this . . . silly dance.

ALAN: . . . Well, then I walked past and your downstairs door was open and . . .

MICHAEL: This is Emory. [EMORY *curtsies.* MICHAEL *glares at him*] Everybody, this is Alan McCarthy. Counterclockwise, Alan: Larry, Emory, Bernard, Donald, and Hank. [*They all mumble "Hello," "Hi"*] Would you like a drink?

ALAN: Thanks, no. I . . . I can't stay . . . long . . . really.

MICHAEL: Well, you're here now, so stay. What would you like?

ALAN: Do you have any rye?

MICHAEL: I'm afraid I don't drink it any more. You'll have to settle for gin or Scotch or vodka.

DONALD: Or beer.

ALAN: Scotch, please.

[MICHAEL *starts for bar*]

DONALD: I'll get it. [*Goes to bar*]

HANK: [*Forced laugh*] Guess I'm the only beer drinker.

ALAN: [*Looking around group*] Whose . . . birthday . . . is it?

LARRY: Harold's.

ALAN: [*Looking from face to face*] Harold?

BERNARD: He's not here yet.

EMORY: She's never been on time . . .

[MICHAEL *shoots* EMORY *a withering glance*]

He's never been on time in his . . .

MICHAEL: Alan's from Washington. We went to college together. Georgetown.

[*A beat. Silence*]

EMORY: Well, isn't that fascinating.

[DONALD *hands* ALAN *his drink*]

DONALD: If that's too strong, I'll put some water in it.

ALAN: [*Takes a quick gulp*] It's fine. Thanks. Fine.

HANK: Are you in the government?

ALAN: No. I'm a lawyer. What . . . what do you do?

HANK: I teach school.

ALAN: Oh. I would have taken you for an athlete of some sort. You look like you might play sports . . . of some sort.

HANK: Well, I'm no professional but I was on the basketball team in college and I play quite a bit of tennis.

ALAN: I play tennis too.

HANK: Great game.

ALAN: Yes. Great. [*A beat. Silence*] What . . . do you teach?

HANK: Math.

ALAN: Math?

HANK: Yes.

ALAN: Math. Well.

EMORY: Kinda makes you want to rush out and buy a slide rule, doesn't it.

MICHAEL: Emory. I'm going to need some help with dinner and you're elected. Come on!

EMORY: I'm *always* elected.

BERNARD: You're a natural-born domestic.

EMORY: Said the African queen! You come on, too—you can fan me while I make the salad dressing.

MICHAEL: [*Glaring. Phony smile*] RIGHT THIS WAY, EM-ORY!

> [MICHAEL *pushes the swinging door aside for* EMORY *and* BERNARD *to enter. They do and he follows. The door swings closed, and the muffled sound of* MICHAEL's *voice can be heard offstage*]

You son-of-a-bitch!

EMORY: [*Offstage*] What the hell do you want from me?

HANK: Why don't we all sit down.

ALAN: . . . Sure.

> [HANK *and* ALAN *sit on the couch.* LARRY *crosses to the bar, refills his drink.* DONALD *comes over to refill his*]

LARRY: Hi.

DONALD: . . . Hi.

ALAN: I really feel terrible—barging in on you fellows this way.

LARRY: [*To* DONALD] How've you been?

DONALD: Fine, thanks.

HANK: [*To* ALAN] . . . Oh, that's okay.

DONALD: [*To* LARRY] . . . And you?

LARRY: Oh . . . just fine.

ALAN: [*To* HANK] You're married?

[LARRY *hears this, turns to look in the direction of the couch.* MICHAEL *enters from the kitchen*]

HANK: [*Watching* LARRY *and* DONALD] What?

ALAN: I see you're married. [*Points to* HANK's *wedding band*]

HANK: Oh.

MICHAEL: [*Glaring at* DONALD] Yes. Hank's married.

ALAN: You have any kids?

HANK: Yes. Two. A boy nine, and a girl seven. You should see my boy play tennis—really puts his dad to shame.

DONALD: [*Avoiding* MICHAEL's *eyes*] I better get some ice. [*Exits to the kitchen*]

ALAN: [*To* HANK] I have two kids too. Both girls.

HANK: Great.

MICHAEL: How *are* the girls, Alan?

ALAN: Oh, just sensational. [*Shakes his head*] They're something, those kids. God, I'm nuts about them.

HANK: How long have you been married?

ALAN: Nine years. Can you believe it, Mickey?

MICHAEL: No.

ALAN: Mickey used to go with my wife when we were all in school.

MICHAEL: Can you believe that?

ALAN: [*To* HANK] You live in the city?

LARRY: Yes, we do. [LARRY *comes over to couch next to* HANK]

ALAN: Oh.

HANK: I'm in the process of getting a divorce. Larry and I are— roommates.

MICHAEL: Yes.

ALAN: Oh. I'm sorry. Oh, I mean . . .

HANK: I understand.

ALAN: [*Gets up*] I . . . I . . . I think I'd like another drink . . . if I may.

MICHAEL: Of course. What was it?

ALAN: I'll do it . . . if I may.

[*Gets up, starts for the bar. Suddenly there is a loud crash offstage.* ALAN *jumps, looks toward swinging door*]

What was that?

[DONALD *enters with ice bucket*]

MICHAEL: Excuse me. Testy temperament out in the kitch!

[MICHAEL *exits through the swinging door.* ALAN *continues to the bar—starts nervously picking up and putting down bottles, searching for the Scotch*]

HANK: [*To* LARRY] Larry, where do you know that guy from?

LARRY: What guy?

HANK: *That* guy.

LARRY: I don't know. Around. The bars.

DONALD: Can I help you, Alan?

ALAN: I . . . I can't seem to find the Scotch.

DONALD: You've got it in your hand.

ALAN: Oh. Of course. How . . . stupid of me.

[DONALD *watches* ALAN *fumble with the Scotch bottle and glass*]

DONALD: Why don't you let me do that.

ALAN: [*Gratefully hands him both*] Thanks.

DONALD: Was it water or soda?

ALAN: Just make it straight—over ice.

[MICHAEL *enters*]

MICHAEL: You see, Alan, I told you it wasn't a good time to talk. But we . . .

ALAN: It doesn't matter. I'll just finish this and go . . . [*Takes a long swallow*]

LARRY: Where can Harold be?

MICHAEL: Oh, he's always late. You know how neurotic he is about going out in public. It takes him hours to get ready.

LARRY: Why *is* that?

[EMORY *breezes in with an apron tied around his waist, carrying a stack of plates which he places on a drop-leaf table.* MICHAEL *does an eye roll*]

EMORY: Why is what?

LARRY: Why does Harold spend hours getting ready before he can go out?

EMORY: Because she's a sick lady, that's why. [*Exits to the kitchen.* ALAN *finishes his drink*]

MICHAEL: Alan, as I was about to say, we can go in the bedroom and talk.

ALAN: It doesn't really matter.

MICHAEL: Come on. Bring your drink.

ALAN: I . . . I've finished it.

MICHAEL: Well, make another and bring it upstairs.

[DONALD *picks up the Scotch bottle and pours into the glass* ALAN *has in his hand.* MICHAEL *has started for the stairs*]

ALAN: [*To* DONALD] Thanks.

DONALD: Don't mention it.

ALAN: [*To* HANK] Excuse us. We'll be down in a minute.

LARRY: He'll still be here. [*A beat*]

MICHAEL: [*On the stairs*] Go ahead, Alan. I'll be right there.

> [ALAN *turns awkwardly, exits to the bedroom.* MICHAEL *goes into the kitchen. A beat*]

HANK: [*To* LARRY] What was *that* supposed to mean?

LARRY: What was what supposed to mean?

HANK: You know.

LARRY: You want another beer?

HANK: No. You're jealous, aren't you? [HANK *starts to laugh.* LARRY *doesn't like it*]

LARRY: I'm Larry. *You're* jealous. [*Crosses to* DONALD] Hey, Donald, where've you been hanging out these days? I haven't seen you in a long time . . .

> [MICHAEL *enters to witness this disapprovingly. He turns, goes up the stairs.*
> *In the bedroom* ALAN *is sitting on the edge of the bed.* MICHAEL *enters, pauses at the mirror to adjust his hair. Downstairs,* HANK *gets up, exits into the kitchen.* DONALD *and* LARRY *move to a corner of the room, sit facing upstage and talk quietly*]

ALAN: [*To* MICHAEL] This is a marvelous apartment.

MICHAEL: It's too expensive. I work to pay rent.

ALAN: What are you doing these days?

MICHAEL: Nothing.

ALAN: Aren't you writing any more?

MICHAEL: I haven't looked at a typewriter since I sold the very very wonderful, very very marvelous *screenplay* which never got produced.

ALAN: That's right. The last time I saw you, you were on your way to California. Or was it Europe?

MICHAEL: Hollywood. Which is not in Europe, nor does it have anything whatsoever to do with California.

ALAN: I've never been there but I would imagine it's awful. Everyone must be terribly cheap.

MICHAEL: No, not everyone.

[ALAN *laughs. A beat.* MICHAEL *sits on the bed*]

Alan, I want to try to explain this evening . . .

ALAN: What's there to explain? Sometimes you just can't invite everybody to every party and some people take it personally. But I'm not one of them. I should apologize for inviting myself.

MICHAEL: That's not exactly what I meant.

ALAN: Your friends all seem like very nice guys. That Hank is really a very attractive fellow.

MICHAEL: . . . Yes. He is.

ALAN: We have a lot in common. What's his roommate's name?

MICHAEL: Larry.

ALAN: What does *he* do?

MICHAEL: He's a commercial artist.

ALAN: I liked Donald too. The only one I didn't care too much for was—what's his name—Emory?

MICHAEL: Yes. Emory.

ALAN: I just can't stand that kind of talk. It just grates on me.

MICHAEL: What kind of talk, Alan?

ALAN: Oh, you know. His brand of humor, I guess.

MICHAEL: He can be really quite funny sometimes.

ALAN: I suppose so. If you find that sort of thing amusing. He just seems like such a goddamn little pansy. [*Silence. A pause*] I'm sorry I said that. I didn't mean to say that. That's such an awful thing to say about *anyone*. But you know what I mean, Michael—you have to admit he *is* effeminate.

MICHAEL: He is a bit.

ALAN: A bit! He's like a . . . a butterfly in heat! I mean, there's no wonder he was trying to teach you all a dance. He *probably* wanted to dance *with* you! [*Pause*] Oh, come on, man, you know me—you know how I feel—your private life is your own affair.

MICHAEL: [*Icy*] No. I *don't* know that about you.

ALAN: I couldn't care less what people do—as long as they don't do it in public—or—or try to force their ways on the whole damned world.

MICHAEL: Alan, what was it you were crying about on the telephone?

ALAN: Oh, I feel like such a fool about that. I could shoot myself for letting myself act that way. I'm so embarrassed I could die.

MICHAEL: But, Alan, if you were genuinely upset—that's nothing to be embarrassed about.

ALAN: All I can say is—please accept my apology for making such an ass of myself.

MICHAEL: You must have been upset or you wouldn't have said you were and that you wanted to see me—*had* to see me and had to talk to me.

ALAN: Can you forget it? Just pretend it never happened. I know *I* have. Okay?

MICHAEL: Is something wrong between you and Fran?

ALAN: Listen, I've really got to go.

MICHAEL: Why are you in New York?

ALAN: I'm dreadfully late for dinner.

MICHAEL: *Whose* dinner? Where are you going?

ALAN: Is this the loo?

MICHAEL: Yes.

ALAN: Excuse me.

[*Quickly goes into the bathroom, closes the door.* MICHAEL *remains silent—sits on the bed, stares into space. Downstairs,* EMORY *pops in from the kitchen to discover* DONALD *and* LARRY *in quiet, intimate conversation*]

EMORY: What's-going-on-in-here-oh-Mary-don't-ask!

[*Puts a salt cellar and pepper mill on the table.*
HANK *enters, carrying a bottle of red wine and a corkscrew.
Looks toward* LARRY *and* DONALD. DONALD *see him, stands
up*]

DONALD: Hank, why don't you come and join us?

HANK: That's an interesting suggestion. Whose idea is that?

DONALD: Mine.

LARRY: [*To* HANK] He means in a conversation.

[BERNARD *enters from the kitchen, carrying four wine
glasses*]

EMORY: [*To* BERNARD] Where're the rest of the wine glasses?

BERNARD: Ahz workin' as fas' as ah can!

EMORY: They have to be told everything. Can't let 'em out of
your sight.

[*Breezes out to the kitchen.* DONALD *leaves* LARRY's *side
and goes to the coffee table, helps himself to the cracked
crab.* HANK *opens the wine, puts it on the table.* MICHAEL
*gets up from the bed and goes down the stairs. Down-
stairs,* HANK *crosses to* LARRY]

HANK: I thought maybe you were abiding by the agreement.

LARRY: We have no agreement.

HANK: We *did.*

LARRY: *You* did. I never agreed to anything!

[DONALD *looks up to see* MICHAEL, *raises a crab claw
toward him*]

DONALD: To your health.

MICHAEL: Up yours.

DONALD: Up my health?

BERNARD: Where's the gent?

MICHAEL: In the gent's room. If you can all hang on for five more minutes, he's about to leave.

[*The door buzzes.* MICHAEL *crosses to it*]

LARRY: Well, at last!

[MICHAEL *opens the door to reveal a muscle-bound young man wearing boots, tight Levi's, a calico neckerchief, and a cowboy hat. Around his wrist there is a large card tied with a ribbon*]

COWBOY: [*Singing fast*]
"Happy birthday to you,
Happy birthday to you,
Happy birthday, dear Harold.
Happy birthday to you."

[*And with that, he throws his arms around* MICHAEL *and gives him a big kiss on the lips. Everyone stands in stunned silence*]

MICHAEL: Who the hell are you?

[EMORY *swings in from the kitchen*]

EMORY: She's Harold's present from me and she's *early!* [*Quick, to* COWBOY] And that's not even Harold, you *idiot!*

COWBOY: You said whoever answered the door.

EMORY: But *not until midnight!* [*Quickly, to group*] He's supposed to be a *midnight cowboy!*

DONALD: He *is* a midnight cowboy.

MICHAEL: He looks right out of a William Inge play to me.

EMORY: [*To* COWBOY] . . . Not until midnight and you're supposed to sing to the right person, for Chrissake! I *told* you Harold has very, very tight, tight, black curly hair. [*Referring to* MICHAEL] This number's practically bald!

MICHAEL: Thank you and fuck you.

BERNARD: It's a good thing *I* didn't open the door.

EMORY: Not that tight and not that black.

COWBOY: I forgot. Besides, I wanted to get to the bars by midnight.

MICHAEL: He's a class act all the way around.

EMORY: What do you mean—get to the bars! Sweetie, I paid you for the whole night, remember?

COWBOY: I hurt my back doing my exercises and I wanted to get to bed early tonight.

BERNARD: Are you ready for this one?

LARRY: [*To* COWBOY] That's too bad, what happened?

COWBOY: I lost my grip doing my chin-ups and I fell on my heels and twisted my back.

EMORY: You shouldn't *wear* heels when you do chin-ups.

COWBOY: [*Oblivious*] I shouldn't do chin-ups—I got a weak grip to begin with.

EMORY: A weak grip. In my day it used to be called a limp wrist.

BERNARD: Who can remember that far back?

MICHAEL: Who was it that always used to say, "You show me Oscar Wilde in a cowboy suit, and I'll show you a gay caballero."

DONALD: I don't know. Who *was* it who always used to say that?

MICHAEL: [*Katharine Hepburn voice*] I don't know. Somebody.

LARRY: [*To* COWBOY] What does your card say?

COWBOY: [*Holds up his wrist*] Here. Read it.

LARRY: [*Reading card*] "Dear Harold, bang, bang, you're alive. But roll over and play dead. Happy birthday, Emory."

BERNARD: Ah, sheer poetry, Emmy.

LARRY: And in your usual good taste.

MICHAEL: Yes, so conservative of you to resist a sign in Times Square.

EMORY: [*Glancing toward stairs*] Cheese it! Here comes the socialite nun.

MICHAEL: Goddammit, Emory!

[ALAN *comes down the stairs into the room. Everybody quiets*]

ALAN: Well, I'm off. . . . Thanks, Michael, for the drink.

MICHAEL: You're entirely welcome, Alan. See you tomorrow?

ALAN: . . . No! No, I think I'm going to be awfully busy. I may even go back to Washington.

EMORY: Got a heavy date in Lafayette Square?

ALAN: What?

HANK: Emory.

EMORY: Forget it.

ALAN: [*Sees* COWBOY] Are you . . . Harold?

EMORY: No, he's not Harold. He's *for* Harold.

[*Silence.* ALAN *lets it pass. Turns to* HANK]

ALAN: Goodbye, Hank. It was nice to meet you.

HANK: Same here.

[*They shake hands*]

ALAN: If . . . if you're ever in Washington—I'd like for you to meet my wife.

LARRY: That'd be fun, wouldn't it, Hank.

EMORY: Yeah, they'd love to meet him—*her*. I have such a problem with pronouns.

ALAN: [*Quick, to* EMORY] How many esses are there in the word pronoun?

EMORY: How'd you like to kiss my ass—that's got two or more *essessss* in it!

ALAN: How'd you like to blow me!

EMORY: What's the matter with your *wife*, she got lockjaw?

ALAN: [*Lashes out*] Faggot, fairy, pansy . . . [*Lunges at* EM-

ORY] . . . queer, cocksucker! I'll kill you, you goddamn little mincing swish! You goddamn freak! FREAK! FREAK!

[*Pandemonium.*
ALAN *beats* EMORY *to the floor before anyone recovers from surprise and reacts*]

EMORY: Oh, my God, somebody help me! Bernard! He's killing me!

[BERNARD *and* HANK *rush forward.* EMORY *is screaming. Blood gushes from his nose*]

HANK: Alan! ALAN! ALAN!

EMORY: Get him off me! Get him off me! Oh, my God, he's broken my nose! I'm BLEEDING TO DEATH!

[LARRY *has gone to shut the door.*
With one great, athletic move, HANK *forcefully tears* ALAN *off* EMORY *and drags him backward across the room.* BERNARD *bends over* EMORY, *puts his arm around him and lifts him*]

BERNARD: Somebody get some ice! And a cloth!

[LARRY *runs to the bar, grabs the bar towel and the ice bucket, rushes to put it on the floor beside* BERNARD *and* EMORY. BERNARD *quickly wraps some ice in the towel, holds it to* EMORY's *mouth*]

EMORY: Oh, my face!

BERNARD: He busted your lip, that's all. It'll be all right.

[HANK *has gotten* ALAN *down on the floor on the opposite side of the room.* ALAN *relinquishes the struggle, collapses against* HANK, *moaning and beating his fists rhythmically against* HANK's *chest.*
MICHAEL *is still standing in the same spot in the center of the room, immobile.* DONALD *crosses past the* COWBOY]

DONALD: [*To* COWBOY] Would you mind waiting over there with the gifts.

[COWBOY *moves over to where the gift-wrapped packages have been put.* DONALD *continues past to observe the mayhem, turns up his glass, takes a long swallow.*
The door buzzes. DONALD *turns toward* MICHAEL, *waits.*
MICHAEL *doesn't move.* DONALD *goes to the door, opens it to reveal* HAROLD]

Well, Harold! Happy birthday. You're just in time for the floor show, which, as you see, is on the floor. [*To* COWBOY] Hey, you, *this* is Harold!

[HAROLD *looks blankly toward* MICHAEL. MICHAEL *looks back blankly*]

COWBOY: [*Crossing to* HAROLD]
                "Happy birthday to you,
                Happy birthday to you,
                Happy birthday, dear Harold.
                Happy birthday to you."

[*Throws his arms around* HAROLD *and gives him a big kiss.*
DONALD *looks toward* MICHAEL, *who observes this stoically.*
HAROLD *breaks away from* COWBOY, *reads the card, begins to laugh.* MICHAEL *turns to survey the room.* DONALD *watches him. Slowly* MICHAEL *begins to move. Walks over to the bar, pours a glass of gin, raises it to his lips, downs it all.* DONALD *watches silently as* HAROLD *laughs and laughs and laughs*]

CURTAIN

ACT TWO

> A *moment later.* HAROLD *is still laughing.* MICHAEL, *still at the bar, lowers his glass, turns to* HAROLD.

MICHAEL: What's so fucking funny?

HAROLD: [*Unintimidated. Quick hand to hip*] Life. Life is a goddamn laff-riot. You remember life.

MICHAEL: You're stoned. It shows in your arm.

LARRY: Happy birthday, Harold.

MICHAEL: [*To* HAROLD] You're stoned and you're late! You were supposed to arrive at this location at approximately eight-thirty dash nine o'clock!

HAROLD: What I *am*, Michael, is a thirty-two-year-old, ugly, pock-marked Jew fairy—and if it takes me a while to pull myself together and if I smoke a little grass before I can get up the nerve to show this face to the world, it's nobody's goddamn business but my own. [*Instant switch to chatty tone*] And how are *you* this evening?

> [HANK *lifts* ALAN *to the couch.* MICHAEL *turns away from* HAROLD, *pours himself another drink.* DONALD *watches.* HAROLD *sweeps past* MICHAEL *over to where* BERNARD *is helping* EMORY *up off the floor.* LARRY *returns the bucket to the bar.* MICHAEL *puts some ice in his drink*]

EMORY: Happy birthday, Hallie.

HAROLD: What happened to *you?*

EMORY: [*Groans*] Don't ask!

HAROLD: Your lips are turning blue; you look like you been rimming a snowman.

EMORY: That piss-elegant kooze hit me!

[*Indicates* ALAN. HAROLD *looks toward the couch.* ALAN *has slumped his head forward into his own lap*]

MICHAEL: Careful, Emory, that kind of talk just makes him s'nervous.

[ALAN *covers his ears with his hands*]

HAROLD: Who is she? Who was she? Who does she hope to be?

EMORY: Who knows, who cares!

HANK: His name is Alan McCarthy.

MICHAEL: Do forgive me for not formally introducing you.

HAROLD: [*Sarcastically, to* MICHAEL] Not the famous college chum.

MICHAEL: [*Takes an ice cube out of his glass, throws it at* HAROLD] Do a figure eight on that.

HAROLD: Well, well, well. I finally get to meet dear ole Alan after all these years. And in black tie too. Is this my surprise from you, Michael?

LARRY: I think Alan is the one who got the surprise.

DONALD: And, if you'll notice, he's absolutely speechless.

EMORY: I *hope* she's in *shock!* She's a beast!

COWBOY: [*Indicating* ALAN] Is it his birthday too?

EMORY: [*Indicates* COWBOY *to* HAROLD] That's your surprise.

LARRY: Speaking of beasts.

EMORY: From me to you, darlin'. How do you like it?

HAROLD: Oh, I suppose he has an interesting face and body—but it turns me right off because he can't talk intelligently about art.

EMORY: Yeah, ain't it a shame.

HAROLD: I could never *love* anyone like that.

EMORY: Never. *Who could?*

HAROLD: *I* could and *you* could, that's who could! Oh, Mary, she's *gorgeous!*

EMORY: She may be dumb, but she's all yours!

HAROLD: In affairs of the heart, there are no rules! Where'd you ever find him?

EMORY: Rae knew where.

MICHAEL: [*To* DONALD] Rae is Rae Clark. That's R-A-E. She's Emory's dike friend who sings at a place in the Village. She wears pin-striped suits and bills herself "Miss Rae Clark—Songs Tailored To Your Taste."

EMORY: Miss Rae Clark. Songs tailored to your taste!

MICHAEL: Have you ever heard of anything so crummy in your life?

EMORY: Rae's a fabulous chanteuse. I adore the way she does: "Down in the Depths on the Ninetieth Floor."

MICHAEL: The faggot national anthem.

[*Exits to the kitchen singing "Down in the Depths" in a butch baritone*]

HAROLD: [*To* EMORY] All I can say is thank God for Miss Rae Clark. I think my present is a super-surprise. I'm so thrilled to get it I'd kiss you but I don't want to get blood all over me.

EMORY: Ohhh, look at my sweater!

HAROLD: Wait'll you see your face.

BERNARD: Come on, Emory, let's clean you up. Happy birthday, Harold.

HAROLD: [*Smiles*] Thanks, love.

EMORY: My sweater is ruined!

MICHAEL: [*From the kitchen*] Take one of mine in the bedroom.

DONALD: The one on the floor is vicuña.

BERNARD: [*To* EMORY] You'll feel better after I bathe your face.

EMORY: Cheer-up-things-could-get-worse-I-did-and-they-did.

[BERNARD *leads* EMORY *up the stairs*]

HAROLD: Just another birthday party with the folks.

[MICHAEL *returns with a wine bottle and a green-crystal white-wine glass, pouring en route*]

MICHAEL: Here's a cold bottle of Pouilly-Fuissé I bought especially for you, kiddo.

HAROLD: Pussycat, all is forgiven. You can stay. No. You can stay, but not all is forgiven. Cheers.

MICHAEL: I didn't want it this way, Hallie.

HAROLD: [*Indicating* ALAN] Who asked Mr. Right to celebrate my birthday?

DONALD: There are no accidents.

HAROLD: [*Referring to* DONALD] And who asked *him?*

MICHAEL: *Guilty again.* When I make problems for myself, I go the whole route.

HAROLD: Always got to have your crutch, haven't you.

DONALD: I'm *not* leaving. [*Goes to the bar, makes himself another martini*]

HAROLD: Nobody ever thinks completely of somebody else. They always please themselves; they always cheat, if only a little bit.

LARRY: [*Referring to* ALAN] Why is he sitting there with his hands over his ears?

DONALD: I think he has an ick. [DONALD *looks at* MICHAEL. MICHAEL *returns the look, steely*]

HANK: [*To* ALAN] Can I get you a drink?

LARRY: How can he hear you, dummy, with his hands over his ears?

HAROLD: He can hear every word. In fact, he wouldn't miss a word if it killed him.

[ALAN *removes his hands from his ears*]

What'd I tell you?

ALAN: I . . . I . . . feel sick. I think . . . I'm going to . . . throw up.

HAROLD: Say that again and I won't have to take my appetite depressant.

[ALAN *looks desperately toward* HANK]

HANK: Hang on. [HANK *pulls* ALAN's *arm around his neck, lifts him up, takes him up the stairs*]

HAROLD: Easy does it. One step at a time.

[BERNARD *and* EMORY *come out of the bath*]

BERNARD: There. Feel better?

EMORY: Oh, Mary, what would I do without you? [EMORY *looks at himself in the mirror*] I am not ready for my close-up, Mr. De Mille. Nor will I be for the next two weeks.

[BERNARD *picks up* MICHAEL's *sweater off the floor.* HANK *and* ALAN *are midway up the stairs*]

ALAN: I'm going to throw up! Let me go! Let me go!

[*Tears loose of* HANK, *bolts up the remainder of the stairs. He and* EMORY *meet head-on.* EMORY *screams*]

EMORY: Oh, my God, he's after me again!

[EMORY *recoils as* ALAN *whizzes past into the bathroom, slamming the door behind him.* HANK *has reached the bedroom*]

HANK: He's sick.

BERNARD: Yeah, sick in the head. Here, Emory, put this on.

EMORY: Oh, Mary, take me home. My nerves can't stand any more of this tonight.

[EMORY *takes the vicuña sweater from* BERNARD, *starts to put it on.*
Downstairs, HAROLD *flamboyantly takes out a cigarette,*

takes a kitchen match from a striker, steps up on the seat of the couch and sits on the back of it]

HAROLD: TURNING ON! [*With that, he strikes the match on the sole of his shoe and lights up. Through a strained throat*] Anybody care to join me? [*Waves the cigarette in a slow pass*]

MICHAEL: Many thanks, no.

[HAROLD *passes it to* LARRY, *who nods negatively*]

DONALD: No, thank you.

HAROLD: [*To* COWBOY] How about you, Tex?

COWBOY: Yeah. [COWBOY *takes the cigarette, makes some audible inhalations through his teeth*]

MICHAEL: I find the sound of the ritual alone utterly humiliating. [*Takes away, goes to the bar, makes another drink*]

LARRY: I hate the smell poppers leave on your fingers.

HAROLD: Why don't you get up and wash your hands?

[EMORY *and* BERNARD *come down the stairs*]

EMORY: Michael, I left the casserole in the oven. You can take it out any time.

MICHAEL: You're not going.

EMORY: I couldn't eat now anyway.

HAROLD: Well, *I'm* absolutely ravenous. I'm going to eat until I have a fat attack.

MICHAEL: [*To* EMORY] I said, you're *not going.*

HAROLD: [*To* MICHAEL] Having a cocktail this evening, are we? In my honor?

EMORY: It's your favorite dinner, Hallie. I made it myself.

BERNARD: *Who* fixed the casserole?

EMORY: Well, *I* made the sauce!

BERNARD: Well, *I* made the salad!

LARRY: Girls, please.

MICHAEL: Please *what!*

HAROLD: Beware the hostile fag. When he's sober, he's dangerous. When he drinks, he's lethal.

MICHAEL: [*Referring to* HAROLD] Attention must *not* be paid.

HAROLD: I'm starved, Em, I'm ready for some of your Alice B. Toklas' opium-baked lasagna.

EMORY: Are you really? Oh, that makes me so pleased maybe I'll just serve it before I leave.

MICHAEL: *You're not leaving.*

BERNARD: I'll help.

LARRY: I better help too. We don't need a nose bleed in the lasagna.

BERNARD: When the sauce is on it, you wouldn't be able to tell the difference anyway.

[EMORY, BERNARD, *and* LARRY *exit to the kitchen*]

MICHAEL: [*Proclamation*] Nobody's going anywhere!

HAROLD: You are going to have schmertz tomorrow you wouldn't believe.

MICHAEL: May I kiss the hem of your schmata, Doctor Freud?

COWBOY: What are you two talking about? I don't understand.

DONALD: He's working through his Oedipus complex, sugar. With a machete.

COWBOY: Huh?

[HANK *comes down the stairs*]

HANK: Michael, is there any air spray?

HAROLD: Hair spray! You're supposed to be holding his head, not doing his hair.

HANK: *Air* spray, not *hair* spray.

MICHAEL: There's a can of floral spray right on top of the john.

HANK: Thanks. [HANK *goes back upstairs*]

HAROLD: [*To* MICHAEL] Aren't you going to say "If it was a snake, it would have bitten you."

MICHAEL: [*Indicating* COWBOY] That is something only your friend would say.

HAROLD: [*To* MICHAEL] I am turning on and you are just turning. [*To* DONALD] I keep my grass in the medicine cabinet. In a Band-Aid box. Somebody told me it's the safest place. If the cops arrive, you can always lock yourself in the bathroom and flush it down the john.

DONALD: *Very cagey.*

HAROLD: It makes more sense than where I *was* keeping it—in an oregano jar in the spice rack. I kept forgetting and accidentally turning my hateful mother on with the salad. [*A beat*] But I think she liked it. No matter what meal she comes over for— even if it's breakfast—she says, "Let's have a salad!"

COWBOY: [*To* MICHAEL] Why do you say I would say "If it was a snake, it would have bitten you." I think that's what I *would* have said.

MICHAEL: Of course you would have, baby. That's the kind of remark your pint-size brain thinks of. You are definitely the type who still moves his lips when he reads and who sits in a steam room and says things like "Hot enough for you?"

COWBOY: I never use the steam room when I go to the gym. It's bad after a workout. It flattens you down.

MICHAEL: Just after you've broken your back to blow yourself up like a poisoned dog.

COWBOY: Yeah.

MICHAEL: You're right, Harold. Not only can he not talk intelligently about art, he can't even follow from one sentence to the next.

HAROLD: *But he's beautiful.* He has *unnatural* natural beauty. [*Quick palm upheld*] Not that that means anything.

MICHAEL: It doesn't mean *everything.*

HAROLD: Keep telling yourself that as your hair drops out in handfuls. [*Quick palm upheld*] Not that it's not *natural* for one's hair to recede as one reaches seniority. Not that those wonderful lines that have begun creasing our countenances don't make all the difference in the world because they add so much *character*.

MICHAEL: Faggots are worse than women about their age. They think their lives are over at thirty. Physical beauty is not that goddamned important!

HAROLD: Of course not. How could it be—it's only in the eye of the beholder.

MICHAEL: And it's only skin deep—don't forget that one.

HAROLD: Oh, no, I haven't forgotten that one at all. It's only skin deep and it's *transitory* too. It's *terribly* transitory. I mean, how long does it last—thirty or forty or fifty years at the most—depending on how well you take care of yourself. And not counting, of course, that you might die before it runs out anyway. Yes, it's too bad about this poor boy's face. It's tragic. He's absolutely cursed! [*Takes* COWBOY's *face in his hands*] How can *his* beauty ever compare with *my* soul? And although I have never seen my soul, I understand from my mother's rabbi that it's a knockout. I, however, cannot seem to locate it for a gander. And if I could, I'd sell it in a flash for some skin-deep, transitory, meaningless beauty!

[ALAN *walks weakly into the bedroom and sits on the bed. Downstairs,* LARRY *enters from the kitchen with salad plates.* HANK *comes into the bedroom and turns out the lamps.* ALAN *lies down. Now only the light from the bathroom and the stairwell illuminate the room*]

MICHAEL: [*Makes sign of the cross with his drink in hand*] Forgive him, Father, for he know not what he do.

[HANK *stands still in the half darkness*]

HAROLD: Michael, you kill me. You don't know what side of the fence you're on. If somebody says something pro-religion, you're against them. If somebody denies God, you're against *them*. One might say that you have some problem in that area. You can't live with it and you can't live without it.

[EMORY *barges through the swinging door, carrying the casserole*]

EMORY: Hot stuff! Comin' through!

MICHAEL: [*To* EMORY] One could murder you with very little effort.

HAROLD: [*To* MICHAEL] You hang on to that great insurance policy called The Church.

MICHAEL: That's right. I believe in God, and if it turns out that there really isn't one, okay. Nothing lost. But if it turns out that there *is*—I'm covered.

[BERNARD *enters, carrying a huge salad bowl. He puts it down, lights table candles*]

EMORY: [*To* MICHAEL] Harriet Hypocrite, that's who you are.

MICHAEL: Right. I'm one of those truly rotten Catholics who gets drunk, sins all night and goes to Mass the next morning.

EMORY: Gilda Guilt. It depends on what you think sin is.

MICHAEL: Would you just shut up your goddamn minty mouth and get back to the goddamn kitchen!

EMORY: Say anything you want—*just don't hit me!*

[*Exits. A beat*]

MICHAEL: Actually, I suppose Emory has a point—I only go to confession before I get on a plane.

BERNARD: Do you think God's power only exists at thirty thousand feet?

MICHAEL: It must. On the ground, I *am* God. In the air, I'm just one more scared son of a bitch. [*A beat*]

BERNARD: I'm scared on the ground.

COWBOY: Me, too. [*A beat*] That is, when I'm not high on pot or up on acid.

[HANK *comes down the stairs*]

LARRY: [*To* HANK] Well, is it bigger than a breadstick?

HANK: [*Ignores last remark. To* MICHAEL] He's lying down for a minute.

HAROLD: How does the bathroom smell?

HANK: Better.

MICHAEL: Before it smelled like somebody puked. Now it smells like somebody puked in a gardenia patch.

LARRY: And how does the big hero feel?

HANK: Lay off, will you.

[EMORY *enters with a basket of napkin-covered rolls, deposits them on the table*]

EMORY: *Dinner is served!*

[HAROLD *comes to the buffet table*]

HAROLD: Emory, it looks absolutely fabulous.

EMORY: I'd make somebody a good wife.

[EMORY *serves pasta.* BERNARD *serves the salad, pours wine.* MICHAEL *goes to the bar, makes another drink*]

I could cook and do an apartment and entertain . . .

[*Grabs a long-stem rose from an arrangement on the table, clenches it between his teeth, snaps his fingers and strikes a pose*]

Kiss me quick, I'm Carmen!

[HAROLD *just looks at him blankly, passes on.* EMORY *takes the flower out of his mouth*]

One really needs castanets for that sort of thing.

MICHAEL: And a getaway car.

[HANK *comes up to the table*]

EMORY: What would you like, big boy?

LARRY: Alan McCarthy, and don't hold the mayo.

EMORY: I can't keep up with you two—[*Indicating* HANK, *then* LARRY]—I thought you were mad at him—now he's bitchin' you. What gives?

LARRY: Never mind.

> [COWBOY *comes over to the table.* EMORY *gives him a plate of food.* BERNARD *gives him salad and a glass of wine.* HANK *moves to the couch, sits and puts his plate and glass on the coffee table.*
> HAROLD *moves to sit on the stairs and eat*]

COWBOY: What is it?

LARRY: Lasagna.

COWBOY: It looks like spaghetti and meatballs sorta flattened out.

DONALD: It's been in the steam room.

COWBOY: It has?

MICHAEL: [*Contemptuously*] It looks like spaghetti and meatballs sorta flattened out. Ah, yes, Harold—truly enviable.

HAROLD: As opposed to you who knows so much about *haute cuisine.* [*A beat*] Raconteur, gourmet, troll.

> [LARRY *takes a plate of food, goes to sit on the back of the couch from behind it*]

COWBOY: It's good.

HAROLD: [*Quick*] You like it, eat it.

MICHAEL: Stuff your mouth so that you can't say anything.

> [DONALD *takes a plate*]

HAROLD: Turning.

BERNARD: [*To* DONALD] Wine?

DONALD: No, thanks.

MICHAEL: Aw, go on, kiddo, force yourself. Have a little *vin ordinaire* to wash down all that depressed pasta.

HAROLD: Sommelier, connoisseur, pig.

[DONALD *takes the glass of wine, moves up by the bar, puts the glass of wine on it, leans against the wall, eats his food.* EMORY *hands* BERNARD *a plate*]

BERNARD: [*To* EMORY] Aren't you going to have any?

EMORY: No. My lip hurts too much to eat.

MICHAEL: [*Crosses to table, picks up knife*] I hear if you puts a knife under de bed it cuts de pain.

HAROLD: [*To* MICHAEL] I hear if you put a knife under your chin it cuts your throat.

EMORY: Anybody going to take a plate up to Alan?

MICHAEL: The punching bag has now dissolved into Flo Nightingale.

LARRY: Hank?

HANK: I don't think he'd have any appetite.

[ALAN, *as if he's heard his name, gets up from the bed, moves slowly to the top of the stairwell.* BERNARD *takes his plate, moves near the stairs, sits on the floor.* MICHAEL *raps the knife on an empty wine glass*]

MICHAEL: Ladies and gentlemen. Correction: Ladies and ladies, I would like to announce that you have just eaten Sebastian Venable.

COWBOY: Just eaten *what?*

MICHAEL: Not *what,* stupid. *Who.* A character in a play. A fairy who was eaten alive. I mean the chop-chop variety.

COWBOY: Jesus.

HANK: Did Edward Albee write that play?

MICHAEL: No. Tennessee Williams.

HANK: Oh, yeah.

MICHAEL: Albee wrote *Who's Afraid of Virginia Woolf?*

LARRY: Dummy.

HANK: I know that. I just thought maybe he wrote that other one too.

LARRY: Well, you made a mistake.

HANK: So I made a mistake.

LARRY: That's right, you made a mistake.

HANK: What's the difference? You can't add.

COWBOY: Edward who?

MICHAEL: [*To* EMORY] How much did you pay for him?

EMORY: He was a steal.

MICHAEL: He's a ham sandwich—fifty cents any time of the day or night.

HAROLD: King of the Pig People.

[MICHAEL *gives him a look.* DONALD *returns his plate to the table*]

EMORY: [*To* DONALD] Would you like some more?

DONALD: No, thank you, Emory. It was very good.

EMORY: Did you like it?

COWBOY: I'm not a steal. I cost twenty dollars.

[BERNARD *returns his plate*]

EMORY: More?

BERNARD: [*Nods negatively*] It was delicious—even if I did make it myself.

EMORY: Isn't anybody having seconds?

HAROLD: I'm having seconds and thirds and maybe even fifths. [*Gets up off the stairs, comes toward the table*] I'm absolutely desperate to keep the weight up.

[BERNARD *bends to whisper something in* EMORY's *ear.* EMORY *nods affirmatively and* BERNARD *crosses to* COWBOY *and whispers in his ear. A beat.* COWBOY *returns his plate to the buffet and follows* EMORY *and* BERNARD *into the kitchen*]

MICHAEL: [*Parodying* HAROLD] You're *absolutely* paranoid about *absolutely* everything.

HAROLD: Oh, yeah, well, why don't you *not* tell me about it.

MICHAEL: You starve yourself all day, living on coffee and cottage cheese so that you can gorge yourself at one meal. Then you feel guilty and moan and groan about how fat you are and how ugly you are when the truth is you're no fatter or thinner than you ever are.

EMORY: Polly Paranoia. [EMORY *moves to the coffee table to take* HANK's *empty plate*]

HANK: Just great, Emory.

EMORY: Connie Casserole, no-trouble-at-all-oh-Mary, D.A.

MICHAEL: [*To* HAROLD] . . . And this pathological lateness. It's downright *crazy*.

HAROLD: Turning.

MICHAEL: Standing before a bathroom mirror for hours and hours before you can walk out on the street. And looking no different after Christ knows how many applications of Christ knows how many ointments and salves and creams and masks.

HAROLD: I've got bad skin, what can I tell you.

MICHAEL: Who wouldn't after they deliberately take a pair of tweezers and *deliberately* mutilate their pores—no wonder you've got holes in your face after the hack job you've done on yourself year in and year out!

HAROLD: [*Coolly but definitely*] You hateful sow.

MICHAEL: Yes, you've got scars on your face—but they're not that bad and if you'd leave yourself alone you wouldn't have any more than you've already awarded yourself.

HAROLD: You'd really like me to compliment you now for being so honest, wouldn't you. For being my best friend who will tell me what even my best friends won't tell me. Swine.

MICHAEL: And the pills! [*Announcement to group*] Harold has been gathering, saving, and storing up barbiturates for the last year like a goddamn squirrel. Hundreds of Nembutals, hundreds of Seconals. All in preparation for and anticipation of the long winter of his death. [*Silence*] But I tell you right now, Hallie. When the time comes, you'll never have the guts. It's not always like it happens in plays, not all faggots bump themselves off at the end of the story.

HAROLD: What you say may be true. Time will undoubtedly tell. But, in the meantime, you've left out one detail—the cosmetics and astringents are *paid* for, the bathroom is *paid* for, the tweezers are *paid* for, and the pills *are paid for!*

[EMORY *darts in and over to the light switch, plunges the room into darkness except for the light from the tapers on the buffet table, and begins to sing "Happy Birthday."* Immediately BERNARD *pushes the swinging door open and* COWBOY *enters carrying a cake ablaze with candles. Everyone has now joined in with "Happy birthday, dear Harold, happy birthday to you." This is followed by a round of applause.*
MICHAEL *turns, goes to the bar, makes another drink*]

EMORY: Blow out your candles, Mary, and make a wish!

MICHAEL: [*To himself*] Blow out your candles, *Laura.*

[COWBOY *has brought cake over in front of* HAROLD. *He thinks a minute, blows out the candles. More applause*]

EMORY: Awwww, she's thirty-two years young!

HAROLD: [*Groans, holds his head*] Ohh, my God!

[BERNARD *has brought in cake plates and forks. The room remains lit only by candlelight from the buffet table.* COWBOY *returns the cake to the table and* BERNARD *begins to cut it and put the pieces on the plates*]

HANK: Now you have to open your gifts.

HAROLD: Do I have to open them here?

EMORY: Of course you've got to open them here. [*Hands* HAROLD *a gift.* HAROLD *begins to rip the paper off*]

HAROLD: Where's the card?

EMORY: Here.

HAROLD: Oh. From Larry. [*Finishes tearing off the paper*] It's *heaven!* Oh, I just love it, Larry.

[HAROLD *holds up a graphic design—a large-scale deed to Broadwalk, like those used in a Monopoly game*]

COWBOY: What is it?

HAROLD: It's the deed to Boardwalk.

EMORY: Oh, gay pop art!

DONALD: [*To* LARRY] It's sensational. Did you do it?

LARRY: Yes.

HAROLD: Oh, it's super, Larry. It goes up the minute I get home.

[HAROLD *gives* LARRY *a peck on the cheek*]

COWBOY: [*To* HAROLD] I don't get—you cruise Atlantic City or something?

MICHAEL: Will somebody get him out of here!

[HAROLD *has torn open another gift, takes the card from inside*]

HAROLD: Oh, what a nifty sweater! Thank you, Hank.

HANK: You can take it back and pick out another one if you want to.

HAROLD: I think this one is just nifty.

[DONALD *goes to the bar, makes himself a brandy and soda*]

BERNARD: Who wants cake?

EMORY: Everybody?

DONALD: None for me.

MICHAEL: I'd just like to sleep on mine, thank you.

[HANK *comes over to the table.* BERNARD *gives him a plate of cake, passes another one to* COWBOY *and a third to* LARRY.]

HAROLD *has torn the paper off another gift. Suddenly laughs aloud*]

HAROLD: Oh, Bernard! How divine! Look, everybody! Bejeweled knee pads! [*Holds up a pair of basketball knee pads with sequin initials*]

BERNARD: Monogrammed!

EMORY: Bernard, you're a camp!

MICHAEL: Y'all heard of Gloria DeHaven and Billy de Wolfe, well, dis here is Rosemary De Camp!

BERNARD: Who?

EMORY: I never miss a Rosemary De Camp picture.

HANK: I've never heard of her.

COWBOY: Me neither.

HANK: Not all of us spent their childhood in a movie house, Michael. Some of us played baseball.

DONALD: And mowed the lawn.

EMORY: Well, *I* know who Rosemary De Camp is.

MICHAEL: You would. It's a cinch you wouldn't recognize a baseball or a lawnmower.

[HAROLD *has unwrapped his last gift. He is silent. Pause*]

HAROLD: Thank you, Michael.

MICHAEL: What? [*turns to see the gift*] Oh. [*A beat*] You're welcome. [MICHAEL *finishes off his drink, returns to the bar*]

LARRY: What is it, Harold? [*A beat*]

HAROLD: It's a photograph of him in a silver frame. And there's an inscription engraved and the date.

BERNARD: What's it say?

HAROLD: Just . . . something personal.

[MICHAEL *spins round from the bar*]

MICHAEL: Hey, Bernard, what do you say we have a little music to liven things up!

BERNARD: Okay.

EMORY: Yeah, I feel like dancing.

MICHAEL: How about something good and ethnic, Emory—one of your specialties, like a military toe tap with sparklers.

EMORY: I don't do that at birthdays—only on the Fourth of July.

[BERNARD *puts on a romantic record.* EMORY *goes to* BERNARD. *They start to dance slowly*]

LARRY: Come on, Michael.

MICHAEL: I only lead.

LARRY: I can follow.

[*They start to dance*]

HAROLD: Come on, Tex, you're on.

[COWBOY *gets to his feet, but is a washout as a dancing partner.* HAROLD *gives up, takes out another cigarette, strikes a match. As he does, he catches sight of someone over by the stairs, walks over to* ALAN. *Blows out match*]

Wanna dance?

EMORY: [*Sees* ALAN] Uh-oh. Yvonne the Terrible is back.

MICHAEL: Oh, hello, Alan. Feel better? This is where you came in, isn't it?

[ALAN *starts to cross directly to the door.* MICHAEL *breaks away*]

Excuse me, Larry . . .

[ALAN *has reached the door and has started to open it as* MICHAEL *intercepts, slams the door with one hand, and leans against it, crossing his legs*]

As they say in the Deep South, don't rush off in the heat of the day.

HAROLD: Revolution complete.

[MICHAEL *slowly takes* ALAN *by the arm, walks him slowly back into the room*]

MICHAEL: . . . You missed the cake—and you missed the opening of the gifts—but you're still in luck. You're just in time for a party game.

[*They have reached the phonograph.* MICHAEL *rejects the record. The music stops, the dancing stops.* MICHAEL *releases* ALAN, *claps his hands*]

. . . Hey, everybody! Game time!

[ALAN *starts to move.* MICHAEL *catches him gently by the sleeve*]

HAROLD: Why don't you just let him go, Michael?

MICHAEL: He can go if he wants to—but not before we play a little game.

EMORY: What's it going to be—movie-star gin?

MICHAEL: That's too faggy for Alan to play—he wouldn't be any good at it.

BERNARD: What about Likes and Dislikes?

[MICHAEL *lets go of* ALAN, *takes a pencil and pad from the desk*]

MICHAEL: It's too much trouble to find enough pencils, and besides, Emory always puts down the same thing. He dislikes artificial fruit and flowers and coffee grinders made into lamps—and he likes Mabel Mercer, poodles, and *All About Eve*—the screenplay of which he will then recite *verbatim*.

EMORY: I put down other things sometimes.

MICHAEL: Like a tan out of season?

EMORY: I just always put down little "Chi-Chi" because I adore her so much.

MICHAEL: If one is of the masculine gender, a poodle is the *insignia* of one's deviation.

BERNARD: You know why old ladies like poodles—because they go down on them.

EMORY: *They do not!*

LARRY: We could play B for Botticelli.

MICHAEL: We *could* play *Spin* the Botticelli, but we're not going to.

[*A beat*]

HAROLD: What would you like to play, Michael—the Truth Game?

[MICHAEL *chuckles to himself*]

MICHAEL: Cute, Hallie.

HAROLD: Or do you want to play Murder? You all remember that one, don't you?

MICHAEL: [*To* HAROLD] Very, very cute.

DONALD: As I recall, they're quite similar. The rules are the same in both—you kill somebody.

MICHAEL: In affairs of the heart, there are no rules. Isn't that right, Harold?

HAROLD: That's what I always say.

MICHAEL: Well, that's the name of the game. The Affairs of the Heart.

COWBOY: I've never heard of that one.

MICHAEL: Of course you've never heard of it—I just made it up, baby doll. Affairs of the Heart is a combination of both the Truth Game and Murder—with a new twist.

HAROLD: I can hardly wait to find out what that is.

ALAN: Mickey, I'm leaving. [*Starts to move*]

MICHAEL: [*Firmly, flatly*] Stay where you are.

HAROLD: Michael, let him go.

MICHAEL: He really doesn't *want* to. If he did, he'd have left a long time ago—or he wouldn't have come here in the first place.

ALAN: [*Holding his forehead*] . . . Mickey, I don't *feel* well!

MICHAEL: [*Low tone, but distinctly articulate*] My name is Michael. I am called Michael. You must never call anyone called Michael Mickey. Those of us who are named Michael are very nervous about it. If you don't believe it—try it.

ALAN: I'm sorry. I can't think.

MICHAEL: You can think. What you can't do—is leave. It's like watching an accident on the highway—you can't look at it and you can't look away.

ALAN: I . . . feel . . . weak . . .

MICHAEL: You are weak. Much weaker than I think you realize. [*Takes* ALAN *by the arm, leads him to a chair. Slowly, deliberately, pushes him down into it*] Now! Who's going to play with Alan and me? Everyone?

HAROLD: I have no intention of playing.

DONALD: Nor do I.

MICHAEL: Well, not everyone is a participant in *life*. There are always those who stand on the sidelines and watch.

LARRY: What's the game?

MICHAEL: Simply this: we all have to call on the telephone the *one person* we truly believe we have loved.

HANK: I'm not playing.

LARRY: Oh, yes, you are.

HANK: You'd like for me to play, wouldn't you?

LARRY: You bet I would. I like to know who you'd call after all the fancy speeches I've heard lately. Who would you call? Would you call me?

MICHAEL: [*To* BERNARD] Sounds like there's, how you say, trouble in paradise.

HAROLD: If there isn't, I think you'll be able to stir up some.

HANK: And who would *you* call? Don't think I think for one minute it would be me. Or that one call would do it. You'd have to make several, wouldn't you? About three long-distance and God only knows how many locals.

COWBOY: I'm glad I don't have to pay the bill.

MICHAEL: Quiet!

HAROLD: [*Loud whisper to* COWBOY] Oh, don't worry, Michael won't pay it either.

MICHAEL: Now, here's how it works.

LARRY: I thought you said there were no rules.

MICHAEL: That's right. In Affairs of the Heart, there are no rules. This is the goddamn point system! [*No response from anyone. A beat*] If you make the call, you get one point. If the person you are calling answers, you get two more points. If somebody else answers, you get only one. If there's no answer at all, you're screwed.

DONALD: You're screwed if you make the call.

HAROLD: You're a *fool*—if you screw yourself.

MICHAEL: . . . When you get the person whom you are calling on the line—if you tell them who you are, you get two points. And then—if you tell them that you *love* them—you get a bonus of five more points!

HAROLD: Hateful!

MICHAEL: Therefore you can get as many as ten points and as few as one.

HAROLD: You can get as few as none—if you know how to work it.

MICHAEL: The one with the highest score wins.

ALAN: Hank. Let's get out of here.

EMORY: Well, now. Did you hear that!

MICHAEL: Just the two of you together. The pals . . . the guys . . . the buddy-buddies . . . the he-men.

EMORY: I think Larry might have something to say about that.

BERNARD: Emory.

MICHAEL: The duenna speaks. [*Crosses to take the telephone from the desk, brings it to the group*] So who's playing?

Not including Cowboy, who, as a gift, is neuter. And, of course, le voyeur. [*A beat*] Emory? Bernard?

BERNARD: I don't think I want to play.

MICHAEL: Why, Bernard! Where's your fun-loving spirit?

BERNARD: I don't think this game is fun.

HAROLD: It's absolutely hateful.

ALAN: Hank, leave with me.

HANK: You don't understand, Alan. I can't. You can . . . but I can't.

ALAN: Why, Hank? Why can't you?

LARRY: [*To* HANK] If he doesn't understand, why don't you explain it to him?

MICHAEL: *I'll* explain it.

HAROLD: I had a feeling you might.

MICHAEL: Although I doubt that it'll make any difference. That type refuses to understand that which they do not wish to accept. They reject certain facts. And Alan is decidedly from The Ostrich School of Reality [*A beat*] Alan . . . Larry and Hank are lovers. Not just roommates, *bed*mates. *Lovers.*

ALAN: Michael!

MICHAEL: No man's still got a *roommate* when he's over thirty years old. If they're not lovers, they're sisters.

LARRY: Hank is the one who's over thirty.

MICHAEL: Well, you're pushing it!

ALAN: . . . Hank? [*A beat*]

HANK: Yes, Alan. Larry is my lover.

ALAN: But . . . but . . . you're married.

[MICHAEL, LARRY, EMORY, *and* COWBOY *are sent into instant gales of laughter*]

HAROLD: I think you said the wrong thing.

MICHAEL: Don't you love that quaint little idea—if a man is married, then he is automatically heterosexual. [*A beat*] Alan—

Hank swings both ways—with a definite preference. [A *beat*] Now. Who makes the first call? Emory?

EMORY: You go, Bernard.

BERNARD: I don't want to.

EMORY: I don't want to either. I don't want to at all.

DONALD: [*To himself*] There are no accidents.

MICHAEL: Then, may I say, on your way home I hope you *will* yourself over an embankment.

EMORY: [*To* BERNARD] Go on. Call up Peter Dahlbeck. That's who you'd like to call, isn't it?

MICHAEL: Who is Peter Dahlbeck?

EMORY: The boy in Detroit whose family Bernard's mother has been a laundress for since he was a pickaninny.

BERNARD: I worked for them too—after school and every summer.

EMORY: It's always been a large order of Hero Worship.

BERNARD: I think I've loved him all my life. But he never knew I was alive. Besides, he's straight.

COWBOY: So nothing ever happened between you?

EMORY: Oh, they finally made it—in the pool house one night after a drunken swimming party.

LARRY: With the right wine and the right music there're damn few that aren't curious.

MICHAEL: Sounds like there's a lot of Lady Chatterley in Mr. Dahlbeck, wouldn't you say, Donald?

DONALD: I've never been an O'Hara fan myself.

BERNARD: . . . And afterwards we went swimming in the nude in the dark with only the moon reflecting on the water.

DONALD: Nor Thomas Merton.

BERNARD: It was beautiful.

MICHAEL: How romantic. And then the next morning you took him his coffee and Alka-Seltzer on a tray.

BERNARD: It was in the afternoon. I remember I was worried sick all morning about having to face him. But he pretended like nothing at all had happened.

MICHAEL: Christ, he must have been so drunk he didn't remember a thing.

BERNARD: Yeah. I was sure relieved.

MICHAEL: Odd how that works. And now, for ten points, get that liar on the phone.

[*A beat.* BERNARD *picks up the phone, dials*]

LARRY: You *know* the number?

BERNARD: Sure. He's back in Grosse Pointe, living at home. He just got separated from his third wife.

[*All watch* BERNARD *as he puts the receiver to his ear, waits. A beat. He hangs up quickly*]

EMORY: D.A. or B.Y.?

MICHAEL: He didn't even give it time to find out. [*Coaxing*] Go ahead, Bernard. Pick up the phone and dial. You'll think of something. You know you want to call him. You know that, don't you? Well, go ahead. Your curiosity has got the best of you now. So . . . go on, call him.

[*A beat.* BERNARD *picks up the receiver, dials again. Lets it ring this time*]

HAROLD: Hateful.

COWBOY: What's D.A. or B.Y.?

EMORY: That's operator lingo. It means—"Doesn't Answer" or "Busy."

BERNARD: . . . Hello?

MICHAEL: One point. [*Efficiently takes note on the pad*]

BERNARD: Who's speaking? Oh . . . Mrs. Dahlbeck.

MICHAEL: [*Taking note*] One point.

BERNARD: . . . It's Bernard—Francine's boy.

EMORY: *Son,* not *boy.*

BERNARD: . . . How are you? Good. Good. Oh, just fine, thank you. Mrs. Dahlbeck . . . is . . . Peter . . . at home? Oh. Oh, I see.

MICHAEL: [*Shakes his head*] Shhhhiiii . . .

BERNARD: . . . Oh, no. No, it's nothing important. I just wanted to . . . to tell him . . . that . . . to tell him I . . . I . . .

MICHAEL: [*Prompting flatly*] I love him. That I've always loved him.

BERNARD: . . . that I was sorry to hear about him and his wife.

MICHAEL: No points!

BERNARD: . . . My mother wrote me. Yes. It is. It really is. Well. Would you just tell him I called and said . . . that I was . . . just . . . very, very sorry to hear and I . . . hope . . . they can get everything straightened out. Yes. Yes. Well, good night. Goodbye. [*Hangs up slowly.* MICHAEL *draws a definite line across his pad, makes a definite period*]

MICHAEL: Two points total. Terrible. Next! [MICHAEL *whisks the phone out of* BERNARD'S *hands, gives it to* EMORY]

EMORY: Are you all right, Bernard?

BERNARD: [*Almost to himself*] Why did I call? Why did I do that?

LARRY: [*To* BERNARD] Where was he?

BERNARD: Out on a date.

MICHAEL: Come on, Emory. Punch in.

[EMORY *picks up the phone, dials information. A beat*]

EMORY: Could I have the number, please—in the Bronx—for a Delbert Botts.

LARRY: A Delbert Botts! How many can there be!

BERNARD: Oh, I wish I hadn't called now.

EMORY: . . . No, the residence number, please. [*Waves his hand at* MICHAEL, *signaling for the pencil.* MICHAEL *hands it to him. He writes on the white, plastic phone case*] . . . Thank you. [*A beat. And he indignantly slams down the receiver*] I do wish information would stop calling me "Ma'am"!

MICHAEL: By all means, scribble all over the telephone. [*Snatches the pencil from* EMORY's *hands*]

EMORY: It comes off with a little spit.

MICHAEL: Like a lot of things.

LARRY: Who the hell is Delbert Botts?

EMORY: The one person I have always loved. [*To* MICHAEL] That's who you said call, isn't it?

MICHAEL: That's right, Emory board.

LARRY: How could you love anybody with a name like that?

MICHAEL: Yes, Emory, you couldn't love anybody with a name like that. It wouldn't look good on a place card. Isn't that right, Alan?

[MICHAEL *slaps* ALAN *on the shoulder.* ALAN *is silent.* MICHAEL *snickers*]

EMORY: I admit his name is not so good—but he is absolutely beautiful. At least, he was when I was in high school. Of course, I haven't seen him since and he was about seven years older than I even then.

MICHAEL: Christ, you better call him quick before he dies.

EMORY: I've loved him ever since the first day I laid eyes on him, which was when I was in the fifth grade and he was a senior. Then, he went away to college and by the time he got out I was in high school, and he had become a dentist.

MICHAEL: [*With incredulous disgust*] A *dentist!*

EMORY: Yes. Delbert Botts, D.D.S. And he opened his office in a bank building.

HAROLD: And you went and had every tooth in your head pulled out, right?

EMORY: No. I just had my teeth cleaned, that's all.

[DONALD *turns from the bar with two drinks in his hands*]

BERNARD: [*To himself*] Oh, I shouldn't have called.

MICHAEL: Will you shut up, Bernard! And take your boring, sleep-making icks somewhere else. Go!

[MICHAEL *extends a pointed finger toward the steps.* BERNARD *takes the wine bottle and his glass and moves toward the stairs, pouring himself another drink on the way*]

EMORY: I remember I looked right into his eyes the whole time and I kept wanting to bite his fingers.

HAROLD: Well, it's absolutely mind boggling.

MICHAEL: Phyllis Phallic.

HAROLD: It absolutely boggles the mind.

[DONALD *brings one of the drinks to* ALAN. ALAN *takes it, drinks it down*]

MICHAEL: [*Referring to* DONALD] Sara Samaritan.

EMORY: . . . I told him I was having my teeth cleaned for the Junior-Senior Prom, for which I was in charge of decorations. I told him it was a celestial theme and I was cutting stars out of tin foil and making clouds out of chicken wire and angel's-hair. [*A beat*] He couldn't have been less impressed.

COWBOY: I got angel's-hair down my shirt once at Christmas time. Gosh, did it itch!

EMORY: . . . I told him I was going to burn incense in pots so that white fog would hover over the dance floor and it would look like heaven—just like I'd seen it in a Rita Hayworth movie. I can't remember the title.

MICHAEL: The picture was called *Down to Earth*. Any *kid* knows that.

COWBOY: . . . And it made little tiny cuts in the creases of my fingers. Man, did they sting! It would be terrible if you got that stuff in your . . .

[MICHAEL *circles slowly toward him*]

I'll be quiet.

EMORY: He was engaged to this stupid-ass girl named Loraine whose mother was truly Supercunt.

MICHAEL: Don't digress.

EMORY: Well, anyway, I was a wreck. I mean a total mess. I couldn't eat, sleep, stand up, sit down, *nothing*. I could hardly cut out silver stars or finish the clouds for the prom. So I called him on the telephone and asked if I could see him alone.

HAROLD: Clearly not the coolest of moves.

[DONALD *looks at* ALAN. ALAN *looks away*]

EMORY: He said okay and told me to come by his house. I was so nervous my hands were shaking and my voice was unsteady. I couldn't look at him this time—I just stared straight in space and blurted out why I'd come. I told him . . . I wanted him to be my friend. I said that I had never had a friend who I could talk to and tell everything and trust. I asked him if he would be my friend.

COWBOY: You poor bastard.

MICHAEL: Shhhhhh!

BERNARD: What'd he say?

EMORY: He said he would be glad to be my friend. And any time I ever wanted to see him or call him—to just call him and he'd see me. And he shook my trembling wet hand and I left on a cloud.

MICHAEL: One of the ones you made yourself.

EMORY: And the next day I went and bought him a gold-plated cigarette lighter and had his initials monogrammed on it and wrote a card that said "From your friend, Emory."

HAROLD: Seventeen years old and already big with the gifts.

COWBOY: Yeah. And cards too.

EMORY: . . . And then the night of the prom I found out.

BERNARD: Found out what?

EMORY: I heard two girls I knew giggling together. They were standing behind some goddamn corrugated cardboard Greek columns I had borrowed from a department store and had draped with yards and yards of goddamn cheesecloth. Oh, Mary, it takes a fairy to make something pretty.

MICHAEL: *Don't digress.*

EMORY: This girl who was telling the story said she had heard it from her mother—and her mother had heard it from Loraine's mother. [*To* MICHAEL] You see, Loraine and her mother were not beside the point. [*Back to the group*] Obviously, Del had told Loraine about my calling and about the gift. [*A beat*] Pretty soon everybody at the dance had heard about it and they were laughing and making jokes. Everybody knew I had a crush on Doctor Delbert Botts and that I had asked him to be my friend. [*A beat*] What they didn't know was that I *loved* him. And that I would go on loving him years after they had all forgotten my funny secret. [*Pause*]

HAROLD: Well, I for one need an insulin injection.

MICHAEL: *Call him.*

BERNARD: Don't, Emory.

MICHAEL: Since when are you telling him what to do!

EMORY: [*To* BERNARD] What do I care—I'm pissed! I'll do anything. Three times.

BERNARD: Don't. *Please!*

MICHAEL: I said call him.

BERNARD: Don't! You'll be sorry. Take my word for it.

EMORY: What have I got to lose?

BERNARD: Your dignity. That's what you've got to lose.

MICHAEL: Well, *that's* a knee-slapper! I love *your* telling *him* about dignity when you allow him to degrade you constantly by Uncle Tom-ing you to death.

BERNARD: *He* can do it, Michael. *I* can do it. But *you can't* do it.

MICHAEL: Isn't that discrimination?

BERNARD: I don't like it from him and I don't like it from me— but I do it to myself and I let him do it. I let him do it because it's the only thing that, to him, makes him my equal. We both got the short end of the stick—but I got a hell of a lot more than he did and he knows it. I let him Uncle Tom me just so he can tell himself he's not a complete loser.

MICHAEL: How very considerate.

BERNARD: It's his defense. You have your defense, Michael. But it's indescribable.

[EMORY *quietly licks his finger and begins to rub the number off the telephone case*]

MICHAEL: [*To* BERNARD] Y'all want to hear a little polite parlor jest from the liberal Deep South? Do you know why *Nigras* have such big lips? Because they're always going "P-p-p-p-a-a-a-h!" [*The labial noise is exasperating with lazy disgust as he shuffles about the room*]

DONALD: Christ, Michael!

MICHAEL: [*Unsuccessfully tries to tear the phone away from* EMORY] I can do without your goddamn spit all over my telephone, you nellie coward.

EMORY: I may be nellie, but I'm no coward. [*Starts to dial*] Bernard, forgive me. I'm sorry. I won't ever say those things to you again.

[MICHAEL *watches triumphant.* BERNARD *pours another glass of wine. A beat*]

B.Y.

MICHAEL: It's busy?

EMORY: [*Nods*] Loraine is probably talking to her mother. Oh, yes, Delbert married Loraine.

MICHAEL: I'm sorry, you'll have to forfeit your turn. We can't wait. [*Takes the phone, hands it to* LARRY, *who starts to dial*]

HAROLD: [*To* LARRY] Well, you're not wasting any time.

HANK: Who are you calling?

LARRY: Charlie.

[EMORY *gets up, jerks the phone out of* LARRY'S *hands*]

EMORY: I refuse to forfeit my turn! It's *my turn* and I'm taking it!

MICHAEL: That's the spirit, Emory! *Hit that iceberg—don't miss it! Hit it! Goddamnit!* I want a smash of a finale!

EMORY: Oh, God, I'm drunk.

MICHAEL: A falling-down-drunk-nellie-queen.

HAROLD: Well, that's the pot calling the kettle beige!

MICHAEL: [*Snapping. To* HAROLD] *I am not drunk!* You cannot tell that I am drunk! Donald! I'm not drunk! Am I!

DONALD: *I'm* drunk.

EMORY: So am I. I am a *major drunk.*

MICHAEL: [*To* EMORY] Shut up and dial!

EMORY: [*Dialing*] I am a major drunk of this or any other season.

DONALD: [*To* MICHAEL] Don't you mean shut up and *deal.*

EMORY: . . . It's ringing. It is no longer B.Y. Hello?

MICHAEL: [*Taking note*] One point.

EMORY: . . . Who's speaking? Who? . . . Doctor Delbert Botts?

MICHAEL: Two points.

EMORY: Oh, Del, is this really you? Oh, nobody. You don't know me. You wouldn't remember me. I'm . . . just a friend. A falling-down drunken friend. Hello? Hello? Hello? [*Lowers the receiver*] He hung up. [EMORY *hangs up the telephone*]

MICHAEL: Three points total. You're winning.

EMORY: He said I must have the wrong party.

[BERNARD *gets up, goes into the kitchen*]

HAROLD: He's right. We have the wrong party. We should be somewhere else.

EMORY: It's your party, Hallie. Aren't you having a good time?

HAROLD: Simply fabulous. And what about you? Are you having a good time, Emory? Are you having as good a time as you thought you would?

[LARRY *takes the phone*]

MICHAEL: If you're bored, Harold, we could sing "Happy Birth-day" again—to the tune of "Havah Nageelah."

[HAROLD *takes out another cigarette*]

HAROLD: Not for all the tea in Mexico. [*Lights up*]

HANK: My turn now.

LARRY: It's my turn to call Charlie.

HANK: No. Let me.

LARRY: Are *you* going to call Charlie?

MICHAEL: The score is three to two. Emory's favor.

ALAN: Don't, Hank. Don't you see—Bernard was right.

HANK: [*Firmly, to* ALAN] I want to. [*A beat. Holds out his hand for the phone*] Larry? [*A beat*]

LARRY: [*Gives him the phone*] Be my eager guest.

COWBOY: [*To* LARRY] Is he going to call Charlie for you?

[LARRY *breaks into laughter.* HANK *starts to dial*]

LARRY: Charlie is all the people I cheat on Hank with.

DONALD: With whom I cheat on Hank.

MICHAEL: The butcher, the baker, the candlestick maker.

LARRY: Right! I love 'em all. And what he refuses to understand —is that I've got to *have* 'em all. I am *not* the marrying kind, and I never will be.

HAROLD: Gypsy feet.

LARRY: Who are you calling?

MICHAEL: Jealous?

LARRY: Curious as hell!

MICHAEL: And a little jealous too.

LARRY: Who are you calling?

MICHAEL: Did it ever occur to you that Hank might be doing the same thing behind your back that you do behind his?

LARRY: I wish to Christ he would. It'd make life a hell of a lot easier. Who are you calling?

HAROLD: Whoever it is, they're not sitting on top of the telephone.

HANK: Hello?

COWBOY: They must have been in the tub.

MICHAEL: [*Snaps at* COWBOY] Eighty-six!

> [COWBOY *goes over to a far corner, sits down,* BERNARD *enters, uncorking another bottle of wine. Taking note*]

One point.

HANK: . . . I'd like to leave a message.

MICHAEL: Not in. One point.

HANK: Would you say that Hank called. Yes, it is. Oh, good evening, how are you?

LARRY: Who the hell *is* that?

HANK: . . . Yes, that's right—the message is for my roommate, Larry. Just say that I called and . . .

LARRY: It's our answering service!

HANK: . . . and said . . . I love you.

MICHAEL: *Five points!* You said it! You get five goddamn points for saying it!

ALAN: Hank! Hank! . . . Are you crazy?

HANK: . . . No. You didn't hear me incorrectly. That's what I said. The message is for Larry and it's from me, Hank, and it is just as I said: *I . . . love . . . you.* Thanks. [*Hangs up*]

MICHAEL: Seven points total! Hank, you're ahead, baby. You're way, way ahead of everybody!

ALAN: Why? . . . Oh, Hank, why? Why did you do that?

HANK: Because I do love him. And I don't care who knows it.

ALAN: Don't say that.

HANK: Why not? It's the truth.

ALAN: I can't believe you.

HANK: [*Directly to* ALAN] I left my wife and family for Larry.

ALAN: I'm really not interested in hearing about it.

MICHAEL: Sure you are. Go ahead, Hankola, tell him all about it.

ALAN: No! I don't want to hear it. It's disgusting! [A *beat*]

HANK: Some men do it for another woman.

ALAN: Well, I could understand *that*. That's *normal*.

HANK: It just doesn't always work out that way, Alan. No matter how you might want it to. And God knows, nobody ever wanted it more than I did. I really and truly felt that I was in love with my wife when I married her. It wasn't altogether my trying to prove something to myself. I did love her and she loved me. But . . . there was always that something there . . .

DONALD: You mean your attraction to your own sex.

HANK: Yes.

ALAN: Always?

HANK: I don't know. I suppose so.

EMORY: I've known what I was since I was four years old.

MICHAEL: Everybody's always known it about *you*, Emory.

DONALD: I've always known it about myself too.

HANK: I don't know when it was that I started admitting it to myself. For so long I either labeled it something else or denied it completely.

MICHAEL: Christ-was-I-drunk-last-night.

HANK: And then there came a time when I just couldn't lie to myself any more . . . I thought about it but I never did anything about it. I think the first time was during my wife's last pregnancy. We lived near New Haven—in the country. She and the kids still live there. Well, anyway, there was a teachers' meeting here in New York. She didn't feel up to the trip and I came alone. And that day on the train I began to think about it and think about it and think about it. I thought of nothing else the whole trip. And within fifteen minutes after I had arrived I had picked up a guy in the men's room of Grand Central Station.

ALAN: [*Quietly*] Jesus.

HANK: I'd never done anything like that in my life before and I was scared to death. But he turned out to be a nice fellow. I've never seen him again and it's funny I can't even remember his name any more. [A *beat*] Anyway. After that, it got easier.

HAROLD: Practice makes perfect.

HANK: And then . . . sometime later . . . not very long after, Larry was in New Haven and we met at a party my wife and I had gone in town for.

EMORY: And your real troubles began.

HANK: That was two years ago.

LARRY: Why am I always the goddamn villain in the piece! If I'm not thought of as a happy-home wrecker, I'm an impossible son of a bitch to live with!

HAROLD: Guilt turns to hostility. Isn't that right, Michael?

MICHAEL: Go stick your tweezers in your cheek.

LARRY: I'm fed up to the teeth with everybody feeling so goddamn sorry for poor shat-upon Hank.

EMORY: Aw, Larry, everybody knows you're Frieda Fickle.

LARRY: I've never made any promises and I never intend to. It's my right to lead my sex life without answering to *anybody* —Hank included! And if those terms are not acceptable, then we must not live together. Numerous relations is a part of the way I am!

EMORY: You don't have to be gay to be a wanton.

LARRY: By the way I am, I don't mean being gay—I mean my sexual appetite. And I don't think of myself as a wanton. Emory, you are the most promiscuous person I know.

EMORY: I am not promiscuous at all!

MICHAEL: Not by choice. By design. Why would anybody want to go to bed with a flaming little sissy like you?

BERNARD: Michael!

MICHAEL: [To EMORY] Who'd make a pass at you—I'll tell you who—nobody. Except maybe some fugitive from the Braille Institute.

BERNARD: [To EMORY] Why do you let him talk to you that way?

HAROLD: Physical beauty is not everything.

MICHAEL: Thank you, Quasimodo.

LARRY: What do you think it's like living with the goddamn gestapo! I can't breathe without getting the third degree!

MICHAEL: Larry, it's your turn to call.

LARRY: I can't take all that let's-be-faithful-and-never-look-at-an-other-person routine. It just doesn't work. If you want to promise that, fine. Then do it and stick to it. But if you *have* to promise it—as far as I'm concerned—nothing finishes a relationship faster.

HAROLD: Give me Librium or give me Meth.

BERNARD: [*Intoxicated now*] Yeah, freedom, baby! Freedom!

LARRY: You gotta have it! It can't work any other way. And the ones who swear their undying fidelity are lying. Most of them, anyway—ninety percent of them. They cheat on each other constantly and lie through their teeth. I'm sorry, I can't be like that and it drives Hank up the wall.

HANK: There is that ten percent.

LARRY: The only way it stands a chance is with some sort of an understanding.

HANK: I've tried to go along with that.

LARRY: Aw, *come on!*

HANK: I agreed to an agreement.

LARRY: Your agreement.

MICHAEL: What agreement?

LARRY: A ménage.

HAROLD: The lover's agreement.

LARRY: Look, I know a lot of people think it's the answer. They don't consider it cheating. But it's not my style.

HANK: Well, *I* certainly didn't want it.

LARRY: Then who suggested it?

HANK: It was a compromise.

LARRY: Exactly.

HANK: And you agreed.

LARRY: I didn't agree to anything. You agreed to your own per-posal and *informed me* that I agreed.

COWBOY: I don't understand. What's a me . . . menaa . . .

MICHAEL: A ménage à trois, baby. Two's company—three's a ménage.

COWBOY: Oh.

HANK: It works for some.

LARRY: Well, I'm not one for group therapy. I'm sorry, I can't relate to anyone or anything that way. I'm old-fashioned—I like 'em all, but I like 'em one at a time!

MICHAEL: [*To* LARRY] Did you like Donald as a single side attraction? [*Pause*]

LARRY: Yes. I did.

DONALD: So did I, Larry.

LARRY: [*To* DONALD, *referring to* MICHAEL] Did you tell him?

DONALD: No.

MICHAEL: It was perfectly obvious from the moment you walked in. What was that song and dance about having seen each other but never having met?

DONALD: It was true. We saw each other in the baths and went to bed together but we never spoke a word and never knew each other's name.

EMORY: You had better luck than I do. If I don't get arrested, my trick announces upon departure that he's been exposed to hepatitis!

MICHAEL: In spring a young man's fancy turns to a fancy young man.

LARRY: [*To* HANK] Don't look at me like that. You've been playing footsie with the Blue Book all night.

DONALD: I think he only wanted to show you what's good for the gander is good for the gander.

HANK: That's right.

LARRY: [*To* HANK] I suppose you'd like the three of us to have a go at it.

HANK: At least it'd be together.

LARRY: That point eludes me.

HANK: What kind of an understanding do you *want*?

LARRY: Respect—for each other's freedom. With no need to lie or pretend. In my own way, Hank, I love you, but you have to understand that even though I do want to go on living with you, sometimes there may be others. I don't want to flaunt it in your face. If it happens, I know I'll never mention it. But if you ask me, I'll tell you. I don't want to hurt you but I won't lie to you if you want to know anything about me.

BERNARD: He gets points.

MICHAEL: What?

BERNARD: He said it. He said "I love you" to Hank. He gets the bonus.

MICHAEL: He didn't call him.

DONALD: He called him. He just didn't use the telephone.

MICHAEL: Then he doesn't get any points.

BERNARD: He gets five points!

MICHAEL: He didn't use the telephone. He doesn't get a god-damn thing!

[LARRY *goes to the phone, picks up the receiver, looks at the number of the second line, dials. A beat. The phone rings*]

LARRY: It's for you, Hank. Why don't you take it upstairs?

[*The phone continues to ring.* HANK *gets up, goes up the stairs to the bedroom. Pause. He presses the second-line button, picks up the receiver. Everyone downstairs is silent*]

HANK: Hello?

BERNARD: One point.

LARRY: Hello, Hank.

BERNARD: Two points.

LARRY: . . . This is Larry.

BERNARD: Two more points!

LARRY: . . . For what's it's worth, I love you.

BERNARD: Five points bonus!

HANK: I'll . . . I'll try.

LARRY: I will too.

[*Hangs up.* HANK *hangs up*]

BERNARD: That's ten points total!

EMORY: Larry's the winner!

HAROLD: Well, that wasn't as much fun as I thought it would be.

MICHAEL: THE GAME ISN'T OVER YET!

[HANK *moves toward the bed into darkness*]

Your turn, Alan.

[MICHAEL *gets the phone, slams it down in front of* ALAN]

PICK UP THE PHONE, BUSTER!

EMORY: Michael, don't!

MICHAEL: STAY OUT OF THIS!

EMORY: You don't have to, Alan. You don't have to.

ALAN: Emory . . . I'm sorry for what I did before. [*A beat*]

EMORY: . . . Oh, forget it.

MICHAEL: Forgive us our trespasses. Christ, now you're both joined at the goddamn hip! You can decorate his home, Emory—and he can get you out of jail the next time you're arrested on a morals charge. [*A beat*] Who are you going to call, Alan? [*No response*] Can't remember anyone? Well, maybe you need a minute to think. Is that it? [*No response*]

HAROLD: I believe this will be the final round.

COWBOY: Michael, aren't you going to call anyone?

HAROLD: How could he? He's never loved anyone.

MICHAEL: [*Sings the classic vaudeville walk-off to* HAROLD]
    "No matter how you figger,
        It's tough to be a nigger,

[*Indicates* BERNARD]

But it's tougher
To be a Jeeeew-ooouu-oo!"

DONALD: My God, Michael, you're a charming host.

HAROLD: Michael doesn't have charm, Donald. Michael has countercharm.

[LARRY *crosses to the stairs*]

MICHAEL: Going somewhere?

[LARRY *stops, turns to* MICHAEL]

LARRY: Yes. Excuse me. [*Turns, goes up the stairs*]

MICHAEL: You're going to miss the end of the game.

LARRY: [*Pauses on stairs*] You can tell me how it comes out.

MICHAEL: I never reveal an ending. And no one will be reseated during the climactic revelation.

LARRY: With any luck, I won't be back until it's all over. [*Turns, continues up the stairs into the dark*]

MICHAEL: [*Into* ALAN'S *ear*] What do you suppose is going on up there? Hmmm, Alan? What do you imagine Larry and Hank are doing? Hmmmmm? Shooting marbles?

EMORY: Whatever they're doing, they're not hurting anyone.

HAROLD: And they're minding their own business.

MICHAEL: And you mind yours, Harold. I'm warning you! [*A beat*]

HAROLD: [*Coolly*] Are you now? Are you warning *me*? *Me*? I'm Harold. I'm the one person you don't warn, Michael. Because you and I are a match. And we tread very softly with each other because we both play each other's game too well. Oh, I know this game you're playing. I know it very well. And I *play* it very well. You play it very well too. But you know what, I'm the only one that's better at it than you are. I can beat you at it. So don't push me. I'm warning *you*.

[*A beat.* MICHAEL *starts to laugh*]

MICHAEL: You're funny, Hallie. A laff riot. Isn't he funny, Alan? Or, as you might say, isn't he amusing. He's an amusing faggot, isn't he? Or, as you might say, freak. That's what you called Emory, wasn't it? A freak? A pansy? My, what an anti-quated vocabulary you have. I'm surprised you didn't say sodom-ite or pederast. [A *beat*] You'd better let me bring you up to date. Now it's not so new, but it might be new to you—[A *beat*] Have you heard the term "closet queen"? Do you know what that means? Do you know what it means to be "in the closet"?

EMORY: Don't, Michael. It won't help anything to explain what it means.

MICHAEL: He already knows. He knows very, very well what a closet queen is. Don't you, Alan? [*Pause*]

ALAN: Michael, if you are insinuating that I am homosexual, I can only say that you are mistaken.

MICHAEL: Am I? [A *beat*] What about Justin Stuart?

ALAN: . . . What about . . . Justin Stuart?

MICHAEL: You were in love with him, that's what about him. [A *beat*] And *that* is who you are going to call.

ALAN: Justin and I were very good friends. That is all. Unfortu-nately, we had a parting of the ways and that was the end of the friendship. We have not spoken for years. I most certainly will not call him now.

MICHAEL: According to Justin, the friendship was quite pas-sionate.

ALAN: What do you mean?

MICHAEL: I mean that you slept with him in college. Several times.

ALAN: That is not true!

MICHAEL: Several times. One time, it's youth. Twice, a phase maybe. Several times, *you like it!*

ALAN: IT'S NOT TRUE!

MICHAEL: Yes, it is. Because Justin Stuart *is* homosexual. He comes to New York on occasion. He calls me. I've taken him to parties. Larry "had" him once. *I* have slept with Justin Stuart. And he has told me all about *you*.

ALAN: Then he told you a lie. [*A beat*]

MICHAEL: You were obsessed with Justin. That's all you talked about, morning, noon, and night. You started doing it about Hank upstairs tonight. What an attractive fellow he is and all that transparent crap.

ALAN: He *is* an attractive fellow. What's wrong with saying so?

MICHAEL: Would you like to join him and Larry right now?

ALAN: I said he was attractive. That's all.

MICHAEL: How many times do you have to say it? How many times did you have to say it about Justin: what a good tennis player he was; what a good dancer he was; what a good body he had; what good taste he had; how bright he was—how *amusing* he was—how the girls were all mad for him—what close friends you were.

ALAN: We . . . we . . . were . . . very close . . . very good . . . friends. *That's all!*

MICHAEL: It was *obvious*—and when you did it around Fran it was downright embarrassing. Even she must have had her doubts about you.

ALAN: *Justin . . . lied.* If he told you that, he lied. It is a lie. A vicious lie. He'd say anything about me now to get even. He could never get over the fact that *I* dropped *him.* But I had to. I had to because . . . he told me . . . he told me about himself . . . he told me that he wanted to be my lover. And I . . . I . . . told him . . . he made me sick . . . I told him I pitied him. [*A beat*]

MICHAEL: You ended the friendship, Alan, because you couldn't face the truth about yourself. You could go along, sleeping with Justin, as long as he lied to himself and you lied to yourself and you both dated girls and labeled yourselves men and called yourselves just fond friends. But Justin finally had to be honest about the truth, and you couldn't take it. You couldn't take it and so you destroyed the friendship and your friend along with it. [MICHAEL *goes to the desk and gets address book*]

ALAN: No!

MICHAEL: Justin could never understand what he'd done wrong to make you cut him off. He blamed himself.

ALAN: No!

MICHAEL: He did until he eventually found out who he was and what he was.

ALAN: No!

MICHAEL: But to this day he still remembers the treatment—the scars he got from you. [*Puts address book in front of* ALAN *on coffee table*]

ALAN: NO!

MICHAEL: Pick up this phone and call Justin. Call him and apologize and tell him what you should have told him twelve years ago. [*Picks up the phone, shoves it at* ALAN]

ALAN: NO! HE LIED! NOT A WORD IS TRUE!

MICHAEL: CALL HIM!

[ALAN *won't take the phone*]

All right then, *I'll dial!*

HAROLD: You're so helpful.

[MICHAEL *starts to dial*]

ALAN: Give it to me.

[MICHAEL *hands* ALAN *the receiver.* ALAN *takes it, hangs up for a moment, lifts it again, starts to dial. Everyone watches silently.* ALAN *finishes dialing, lifts the receiver to his ear*]

. . . Hello?

MICHAEL: One point.

ALAN: . . . It's . . . it's Alan.

MICHAEL: Two points.

ALAN: . . . Yes, yes, it's *me.*

MICHAEL: Is it Justin?

ALAN: . . . You sound surprised.

MICHAEL: I should hope to think so—after twelve years! Two more points.

ALAN: I . . . I'm in New York. Yes. I . . . I won't explain now . . . I . . . I just called to tell you . . .

MICHAEL: THAT I LOVE YOU, GODDAMNIT! I LOVE YOU!

ALAN: I love you.

MICHAEL: You get the goddamn bonus. TEN POINTS TOTAL! JACKPOT!

ALAN: I love you and I beg you to forgive me.

MICHAEL: Give me that! [*Snatches the phone from* ALAN] Justin! Did you hear what that son of a bitch said! [*A beat.* MICHAEL *is speechless for a moment*] . . . Fran? [*A beat*] Well, of course I expected it to be you! . . . [*A beat*] How are you? Me, too. Yes, yes . . . he told me everything. Oh, don't thank *me.* Please . . . Please . . . [*A beat*] I'll . . . I'll put him back on. [*A beat*] My love to the kids . . .

ALAN: . . . Darling? I'll take the first plane I can get. Yes. I'm sorry too. I love you very much. [*Hangs up, stands, crosses to the door, stops. Turns around, surveys the group*] Thank you, Michael.

> [*Opens the door and exits.*
> *Silence.* MICHAEL *slowly sinks down on the couch, covering his face.*
> *Pause*]

COWBOY: Who won?

DONALD: It was a tie.

> [HAROLD *crosses to* MICHAEL]

HAROLD: [*Calmly, coldly, clinically*] Now it is my turn. And ready or not, Michael, here goes. [*A beat*] You are a sad and pathetic man. You're a homosexual and you don't want to be. But there is nothing you can do to change it. Not all your prayers to your God, not all the analysis you can buy in all the years you've got left to live. You may very well one day be able to know a heterosexual life if you want it desperately enough—if you pursue it with the fervor with which you annihilate—but you will always be homosexual as well. Always, Michael. Always. Until the day you die.

[*Turns, gathers his gifts, goes to* EMORY. EMORY *stands up unsteadily*]

Oh, friends, thanks for the nifty party and the super gift. [*Looks toward* COWBOY] It's just what I needed.

[EMORY *smiles.* HAROLD *gives him a hug, spots* BERNARD *sitting on the floor, head bowed*]

. . . Bernard, thank you.

[*No response. To* EMORY]

Will you get him home?

EMORY: Don't worry about her. I'll take care of everything.

[HAROLD *turns to* DONALD, *who is at the bar making himself another drink*]

HAROLD: Donald, good to see you.

DONALD: Good night, Harold. See you again sometime.

HAROLD: Yeah. How about a year from Shavuoth? [HAROLD *goes to* COWBOY] Come on, Tex. Let's go to my place.

[COWBOY *gets up, comes to him*]

Are you good in bed?

COWBOY: Well . . . I'm not like the average hustler you'd meet. I try to show a little affection—it keeps me from feeling like such a whore.

[*A beat.* HAROLD *turns.* COWBOY *opens the door for them. They start out.* HAROLD *pauses*]

HAROLD: Oh, Michael . . . thanks for the laughs. Call you to-morrow.

[*No response. A beat.* HAROLD *and* COWBOY *exit*]

EMORY: Come on, Bernard. Time to go home. [EMORY, *frail as he is, manages to pull* BERNARD'S *arm around his neck, gets him on his feet*] Oh, Mary, you're a heavy mother.

BERNARD: [*Practically inaudible mumble*] Why did I call? Why?

EMORY: Thank you, Michael. Good night, Donald.

DONALD: Goodbye, Emory.

BERNARD: Why . . .

EMORY: It's all right, Bernard. Everything's all right. I'm going to make you some coffee and everything's going to be all right.

[EMORY *virtually carries* BERNARD *out.* DONALD *closes the door. Silence.*
MICHAEL *slowly slips from the couch onto the floor. A beat. Then slowly he begins a low moan that increases in volume —almost like a siren. Suddenly he slams his open hands to his ears*]

MICHAEL: [*In desperate panic*] Donald! Donald! DONALD! DONALD!

[DONALD *puts down his drink, rushes to* MICHAEL. MICHAEL *is now white with fear and tears are bursting from his eyes. He begins to gasp his words*]

Oh, no! No! What have I done! Oh, my God, what have I done!

[MICHAEL *writhing.* DONALD *holds him, cradles him in his arms*]

DONALD: Michael! Michael!

MICHAEL: [*Weeping*] Oh, no! NO! It's beginning! The liquor is starting to wear off and the anxiety is beginning! Oh, NO!

No! I feel it! I know it's going to happen. Donald!! Donald! Don't leave me! Please! Please! Oh, my God, what have I done! Oh Jesus, the guilt! I can't handle it any more. I won't make it!

DONALD: [*Physically subduing him*] Michael! Michael! Stop it! Stop it! I'll give you a Valium—I've got some in my pocket!

MICHAEL: [*Hysterical*] No! No! Pills and alcohol—I'll die!

DONALD: I'm not going to give you the whole bottle! Come on, let go of me!

MICHAEL: [*Clutching him*] NO!

DONALD: Let go of me long enough for me to get my hand in my pocket!

MICHAEL: Don't leave!

[MICHAEL *quiets down a bit, lets go of* DONALD *enough for him to take a small plastic bottle from his pocket and open it to give* MICHAEL *a tranquilizer*]

DONALD: Here.

MICHAEL: [*Sobbing*] I don't have any water to swallow it with!

DONALD: Well, if you'll wait one goddamn minute, I'll get you some!

[MICHAEL *lets go of him. He goes to the bar, gets a glass of water and returns*]

Your water, your Majesty. [*A beat*] Michael, stop that goddamn crying and take this pill!

[MICHAEL *straightens up, puts the pill into his mouth amid choking sobs, takes the water, drinks, returns the glass to* DONALD]

MICHAEL: I'm like Ole Man River—tired of livin' and scared o' dyin'.

[DONALD *puts the glass on the bar, comes back to the couch, sits down.* MICHAEL *collapses into his arms, sobbing. Pause*]

DONALD: Shhhhh. Shhhhhh. Michael. Shhhhhh. Michael. Michael. [DONALD *rocks him back and forth. He quiets. Pause*]

MICHAEL: . . . If we . . . if we could just . . . not hate ourselves so much. That's it, you know. If we could just *learn* not to hate ourselves quite so very much.

DONALD: Yes, I know. I know. [*A beat*] Inconceivable as it may be, you used to be worse than you are now. [*A beat*] Maybe with a lot more work you can help yourself some more— if you try.

[MICHAEL *straightens up, dries his eyes on his sleeve*]

MICHAEL: Who was it that used to always say, "You show me a happy homosexual, and I'll show you a gay corpse."

DONALD: I don't know. Who was it who always used to say that?

MICHAEL: And how dare you come on with that holier-than-thou attitude with me! "A lot more work," "if I try," indeed! You've got a long row to hoe before you're perfect, you know.

DONALD: I never said I didn't.

MICHAEL: And while we're on the subject—I think your analyst is a quack.

[MICHAEL *is sniffling.* DONALD *hands him a handkerchief. He takes it and blows his nose*]

DONALD: Earlier you said he was a prick.

MICHAEL: That's right. He's a prick quack. Or a quack prick, whichever you prefer.

[DONALD *gets up from the couch, goes for his drink*]

DONALD: [*Heaving a sigh*] Harold was right. You'll never change.

MICHAEL: Come back, Donald. Come back, Shane.

DONALD: I'll come back when you have another anxiety attack.

MICHAEL: I need you. Just like Mickey Mouse needs Minnie Mouse—just like Donald Duck needs Minnie Duck. Mickey needs Donnie.

DONALD: My name is Donald. I am called Donald. You must never call anyone called Donald Donnie . . .

MICHAEL: [*Grabs his head, moans*] Ohhhhh . . . icks! Icks! Terrible icks! Tomorrow is going to be an ick-packed day. It's going to be a Bad Day at Black Rock. A day of nerves, nerves, and more nerves! [MICHAEL *gets up from the couch, surveys the wreckage of the dishes and gift wrappings*] Do you suppose there's any possibility of just burning this room? [*A beat*]

DONALD: Why do you think he stayed, Michael? Why do you think he took all of that from you?

MICHAEL: There are no accidents. He was begging to get killed. He was dying for somebody to let him have it and he got what he wanted.

DONALD: He could have been telling the truth—Justin could have lied.

MICHAEL: Who knows? What time is it?

DONALD: It seems like it's day after tomorrow.

[MICHAEL *goes to the kitchen door, pokes his head in. Comes back into the room carrying a raincoat*]

MICHAEL: It's early. [*Goes to a closet door, takes out a blazer, puts it on*]

DONALD: What does life *hold?* Where're you going?

MICHAEL: The bedroom is ocupado and I don't want to go to sleep anyway until I try to walk off the booze. If I went to sleep like this, when I wake up they'd have to put me in a padded cell—not that that's where I don't belong. [*A beat*] And . . . and . . . there's a midnight mass at St. Malachy's that all the show people go to. I think I'll walk over there and catch it.

DONALD: [*Raises his glass*] Well, pray for me.

MICHAEL: [*Indicates bedroom*] Maybe they'll be gone by the time I get back.

DONALD: Well, I will be—just as soon as I knock off that bottle of brandy.

MICHAEL: Will I see you next Saturday?

DONALD: Unless you have other plans.

MICHAEL: No. [*Turns to go*]

DONALD: Michael?

MICHAEL: [*Stops, turns back*] What?

DONALD: Did he ever tell you why he was crying on the phone—what it was he *had* to tell you?

MICHAEL: No. It must have been that he'd left Fran. Or maybe it was something else and he changed his mind.

DONALD: Maybe so. [*A beat*] I wonder why he left her. [*A pause*]

MICHAEL: . . . As my father said to me when he died in my arms, "I don't understand any of it. I never did."

[*A beat.* DONALD *goes to his stack of books, selects one, and sits in a chair*]

Turn out the lights when you leave, will you?

[DONALD *nods.* MICHAEL *looks at him for a long silent moment.* DONALD *turns his attention to his book, starts to read.* MICHAEL *opens the door and exits*]

CURTAIN

Howard Sackler

During the Sixties, the prestigious Pulitzer Prize for drama (administered by the trustees of Columbia University in accordance with terms set forth in the will of newspaper magnate Joseph Pulitzer, whose financial bequest established the annual prizes) was conferred upon just six plays. Four years were shorn of a Pulitzer Prize in the category of drama because either the trustees or its advisory board (which makes the prize recommendations) deemed that no "original American play" was worthy of the citation.

In 1969, however, there seemed to be no dissension in the hierarchy, and the decade's final Pulitzer Prize for an original American drama was awarded to Howard Sackler for *The Great White Hope*. And, on one of those magical though infrequent occasions in the theatre, the same drama also acquired the two other major seasonal awards: the New York Drama Critics' Circle citation and the Antoinette Perry (Tony) Award for best play.

Howard Sackler's sweeping chronicle of the rise and fall of an American boxer is based on the life and times of Jack Johnson (Jack Jefferson in the play), the first Negro heavyweight champion of the world, whose winning of the title in 1908 and whose subsequent uninhibited and nonconforming behavior triggered a wave of racism and provoked a nationwide cry for his defeat by "a great white hope."

A play of enormity in scale and power, *The Great White Hope* presents an affecting and tragic figure moving in the circumambiency of love, sex, bigotry, violence and the convoluted necessity of destroying any man who does not—and will not—"fit." And in his dramatic exploration of the prevailing attitudes of Johnson's

day, Mr. Sackler electrically projects them as a backdrop for our
own times.

The prize-winning drama had its world première at the Arena
Stage, Washington, D.C., on December 12, 1967. Subsidized by a
grant from the National Endowment for the Arts, the presentation
became an immediate success and attracted the attention of New
York reviewers (a growing trend in the resident and regional theatre
of the 1960s) as well as Broadway managements. The play subsequently was brought to New York by producer Herman Levin,
who wisely retained the Arena Stage's director Edwin Sherin and
its leading player, James Earl Jones, whose galvanic portrayal of
the beleaguered fighter brought him instant Broadway stardom and
numerous "best performance" awards.

While *The Great White Hope* also catapulted Howard Sackler
into the vanguard of major American dramatists of the Sixties, the
author hardly could be categorized as a "newcomer" to the theatre.
Born in New York City in 1929 and educated at Brooklyn College,
Mr. Sackler already had the distinction of seeing seven of his
earlier plays on stage. Among these: *The Pastime of Monsieur
Robert*, produced at the Hampstead Theatre Club, London, and
to be presented in 1970 by the American Conservatory Theatre,
San Francisco; *Uriel Acosta*, for which he won the Maxwell Ander-
son Award; *The Man Who Stammers* and *The Yellow Loves*,
produced by the Poets Theatre of Boston; and *Mr. Welk and
Jersey Jim*, a short play originally presented at the Actors Studio
in 1960 with Zero Mostel, and later at the Arena Stage, Washington.
The last-named play is one segment of a four-part work entitled
A Few Enquiries, scheduled for publication in 1970.

A man of diversified talent, Mr. Sackler also has functioned as a
director for nearly two hundred dramatic recordings (including
most of Shakespeare's plays) with such notables as Paul Scofield,
Sir Ralph Richardson, Rex Harrison, Dame Edith Evans, Margaret
Leighton, Flora Robson, Claire Bloom, Albert Finney, Julie Harris,
Jessica Tandy and others.

In 1961, Mr. Sackler wrote the adaptation and also directed the
English version of the Czechoslovakian film of *A Midsummer Night's
Dream*, and earlier, fashioned the original stories and screenplays
for *Killer's Kiss* and *Fear and Desire*, both directed by Stanley
Kubrick with whom he also created the documentary *Desert Padre*.

Mr. Sackler's poems have been published in *Poetry Magazine*,

Commentary, The Hudson Review, New Directions Annual and in a volume entitled *Want My Shepherd.*

The author, his wife, and two children now divide their time between London and the island of Ibiza, Spain.

THE GREAT
WHITE HOPE

Howard Sackler

The Great White Hope had its New York première on October 3, 1968, at the Alvin Theatre, under the auspices of Herman Levin. The cast was as follows:

BRADY	Gil Rogers
FRED	George Ebeling
CAP'N DAN	George Mathews
REPORTERS	Max Wright, Burke Byrnes
TRAINERS	Hector Elizondo, Lance Cunard
SMITTY	Peter Masterson
GOLDIE	Lou Gilbert
PHOTOGRAPHERS	Ed Lauter, George Curley
TICK	Jimmy Pelham
JACK JEFFERSON	James Earl Jones
ELEANOR BACHMAN	Jane Alexander
REPORTERS	Max Wright, Burke Byrnes, Bob Horen
CLARA	Marlene Warfield
ROLLER	Edward McNally
BETTOR	Joseph Hamer
TOUT	George Harris II
CRAP PLAYERS	Burke Byrnes, Ed Lauter, Michael Prince
BLACKFACE	Hector Elizondo
COLONEL COX	Dan Priest
RANGERS	Edd K. Gasper, Sean J. Walsh
WEIGHER-IN	George Curley
MEN AT FIGHT	Thomas Barbour, Jon Cypher, Marshall Efron, Lou Meyer, David Thomas, Eugene R. Wood
HANDLERS	Lance Cunard, Larry Swanson
REPORTERS	Max Wright, Bob Horen
DEACON	Garwood Perkins
YOUNG NEGRO	Woodie King
NEGRO MEN	Philip Lindsay, Jerry Laws

BOY	*Terrance Phillips*
BARKER	*David Connell*
JACK'S FRIENDS	*Lawrence Cook, Don Blakely, Dave Brown, Judy Thames, Dolores St. Amand, Verona Barnes, Joanna Featherstone, Thomas Anderson, Woodie King, Jerry Laws, Philip Lindsay, Garwood Perkins, Richard Pittman, Yvonne Southerland, Glory Van Scott, Mel Winkler, Luis Espinosa*
POLICEMEN	*George Harris II, Burke Byrnes, Ed Lauter*
CIVIC MARCHERS	*David Thomas, Christine Thomas, Thomas Barbour, Shiela Coonan, Lance Cunard, George Curley, Marshall Efron, Edd K. Gasper, Joseph Hamer, Bob Horen, Terrence O'Connor, Dan Priest, Danette Small, Larry Swanson, Sean J. Walsh, Lou Meyer*
MR. DONNELLY	*Michael Prince*
MRS. BACHMAN	*Ruth Gregory*
MR. DIXON	*Brooks Rogers*
MR. CAMERON (D.A.)	*Jon Cypher*
DETECTIVE	*Edward McNally*
CIVIC LEADERS	*Joseph Hamer, Lance Cunard, Larry Swanson, Bob Horen, Terrence O'Connor, Christine Thomas, Shiela Coonan*
A DISTINGUISHED NEGRO	*Clark Morgan*
DEPUTIES	*Edward McNally, Burke Byrnes, Edd K. Gasper, Hector Elizondo, Sean J. Walsh, Dan Priest*
SCIPIO	*Antonio Fargas*
PASTOR	*L. Errol Jaye*
MRS. JEFFERSON	*Hilda Haynes*

MEMBERS OF THE CONGREGATION	*Thomas Anderson, Philip Lindsay, Jerry Laws, Richard Pittman, Judy Thames, Joanna Featherstone, Danette Small, Yvonne Southerland, Dolores St. Amand, Verona Barnes, Dave Brown*
RUDY	*Mel Winkler*
RUDY'S TEAMMATES	*Lawrence Cook, Woodie King*
MR. EUBANKS	*Larry Swanson*
MR. TREACHER	*David Thomas*
SIR WILLIAM GRISWOLD	*Thomas Barbour*
MR. COATES	*Max Wright*
MRS. KIMBALL	*Sheila Coonan*
INSPECTOR WAINWRIGHT	*Gil Rogers*
MR. M. BRATBY	*Joseph Hamer*
MR. FARLOW	*George Curley*
OFFICIAL	*Bob Horen*
KLOSSOWSKI	*Jon Cypher*
REPORTERS	*Michael Prince, George Harris II, Edd K. Gasper*
PORTER	*Lance Cunard*
PROMOTER	*Bob Horen*
FRENCH HANDLER	*Hector Elizondo*
POP WEAVER	*Eugene R. Wood*
GERMAN OFFICERS	*Edd K. Gasper, Max Wright, Burke Byrnes, Gil Rogers*
WAITER	*George Harris II*
RAGOSY	*Marshall Efron*
AN AFRICAN STUDENT	*Don Blakely*
JUGGLER	*Lou Meyer*
STAGE HANDS	*George Curley, Ed Lauter*
MOURNERS:	*Don Blakely, Philip Lindsay, Clark Morgan, Thomas Anderson, Lawrence Cook, Garwood Perkins, Richard Pittman, Woodie King, Verona Barnes,*

	Glory Van Scott, Dave Brown, David Connell, Joanna Featherstone, Jerry Laws, Danette Small, Yvonne Southerland, Terrance Phillips, Dolores St. Amand, Judy Thames, Luis Espinosa
PHOTOGRAPHERS	Larry Swanson, Sean J. Walsh
POLICEMEN	George Harris II, Burke Byrnes, Ed Lauter
PACO	Donald Girard
EL JEFE	Hector Elizondo
GOVERNMENT AGENT	Edd K. Gasper
MEXICANS	George Harris II, Bob Horen
PAILMAN	David Connell
SIGNATURE RECORDER	Yvonne Southerland
DRUMMER	Woodie King
CONTRIBUTORS	David Connell, Garwood Perkins, Philip Lindsay, Mel Winkler, Clark Morgan, Don Blakely, Dolores St. Amand, Verona Barnes, Dave Brown, Lawrence Cook, Joanna Featherstone, Jerry Laws, Richard Pittman, Danette Small, Judy Thames, Glory Van Scott
FIRST MAN ON LADDER	Burke Byrnes
SECOND MAN ON LADDER	Dan Priest
FIGHT FANS	Lou Meyer, Joseph Hamer, Edward McNally, Gil Rogers, Thomas Barbour, Lance Cunard, Jon Cypher, Marshall Efron, George Harris II, George Curley
PINKERTON MEN	Ed Lauter, David Thomas, Bob Horen
THE KID	Sean J. Walsh
REPORTERS	Max Wright, Larry Swanson, Michael Prince
CUBAN BOY	Luis Espinosa

Directed by Edwin Sherin
Scenery by Robin Wagner
Costumes by David Toser
Lighting by John Gleason
Music Arranged by Charles Gross

TIME: *The years preceding and during the First World War.*

ACT 1

SCENE ONE/*Parchmont, Ohio: Brady's farm*
SCENE TWO/*San Francisco: a small gym*
SCENE THREE/*Reno: outside the Arena*
      CAP'N DAN
SCENE FOUR/*Chicago: a street*
SCENE FIVE/*Chicago: the District Attorney's office*
SCENE SIX/*Beau Rivage, Wisconsin: a cabin*
      SCIPIO
SCENE SEVEN/*Chicago: Mrs. Jefferson's house*

ACT 2

SCENE ONE/*London: a chamber in the Home Office*
SCENE TWO/*Le Havre: a customs shed*
SCENE THREE/*Paris: Vel d'Hiver arena*
SCENE FOUR/*New York: Pop Weaver's office*
SCENE FIVE/*Berlin: a sidewalk café*
SCENE SIX/*Budapest: Cabaret Ragosy*
      MRS. BACHMAN
SCENE SEVEN/*Belgrade: railway station*

ACT 3

SCENE ONE/*Chicago: a street*
SCENE TWO/*New York: Pop Weaver's office*
      CLARA
SCENE THREE/*Juarez: a disused barn*
      CAP'N DAN
SCENE FOUR/*United States: a street*
SCENE FIVE/*Havana: Oriente Racetrack*

[*Note*: All lines set in **boldface type** are addressed to the audience]

ACT 1

SCENE ONE

BRADY's *farm, in Parchmont, Ohio.*

Enter BRADY, *the heavyweight champion;* FRED, *his manager;* CAP'N DAN, *a champion of earlier days;* SMITTY, *a famous sportswriter; several other* PRESSMEN *and* PHOTOGRAPHERS; *a few* TRAINERS. GOLDIE, *Jack Jefferson's manager, in the background.*

BRADY: Get Burke, or Kid Foster. Big Bill Brain! I ain't gonna fight no dinge.

FRED: Now, Frank—

CAP'N DAN: Listen here to me, Franklin—

BRADY: You wouldn't fight one when you had the belt!

CAP'N DAN: Well, let's say none of them came up to it then. It wasn't that I wouldn't, I didn't have to.

FRED: He didn't have to, Frank, but you do.

BRADY: In your hat I do! I know what retired means, and that's what I am. All I have to do is dip the sheep and pay taxes.

CAP'N DAN: Hear that, boys? It's old Farmer Brown!

FRED: **Sure looks retired, don't he! Look at the arms on him.**

PRESSMAN 1: Three months back on the mill, that's all you need—

SMITTY: How long is it you put away Stankiewiez—

FRED: Not even a year! And if you smoked him in seven—

TRAINER 1: You'll get this one in five—

PRESSMAN 2: Four!

FRED: Two! They got glass jaws, right, Cap'n Dan?

BRADY: I ain't gonna fight no dinge.

CAP'N DAN: Now, Franklin, when you retired with that gold belt last summer, nobody thought it would work out like this. Everybody just thought that Sweeney'd fight Woods, and whoever won that would be the new Number One, right? So when the nigger asked could he fight Woods first we figured, what the hell, it'll keep up the interest—nobody, least of all Woods, thought he would lick him. **And then when he said he wants to try out Sweeney too, why Sweeney never puts the gloves on with a nigger, everybody knew that—besides, he was in Australia.** Nobody thought the nigger would go all that way to him, and even when he did, who would have thought he could needle old Tommy into taking him on?

SMITTY: I was down in Melbourne for the paper, Mr. Brady, and let me tell you, no paper here could print how bad it really was. He'd say, Hit me now, Tommy, and then he'd let him, grinning all the time, and then cuffing him, jabbing him, making smart-ass remarks to the crowd—wouldn't be a man and just knock him out, no, and then, when they stopped it, with Tommy there bleeding, he's still got that big banjo smile on him—Jesus.

PRESSMAN 1: You're the White Hope, Mr. Brady!

BRADY: I'm the what?

PRESSMAN 2: The White Hope! Every paper in the country is calling you that.

FRED: Frank, he lands in San Francisco tomorrow—come on!

BRADY: [To CAP'N DAN] Honest, I don't like this any more than you do.

CAP'N DAN: How're you going to like it when he claims the belt's his because you won't fight him. The heavyweight belt, son, yours and mine. He can say it's his.

SMITTY: Just grin and put it on.

CAP'N DAN: How're you going to like it when the whole damn country says Brady let us down, he wouldn't stick a fist out to teach a loudmouth nigger, stayed home and let him be Champion of the World.

SMITTY: Don't do it, Mr. Brady.

BRADY: I'll tell you the truth, Cap'n Dan. I hate to say it, but I feel too old. **I mean it, that's the truth.**

FRED: The doc says different and I do too—

TRAINER 1: **He's thinkin old because he's worried what to do—**

BRADY: Shut up. Cap'n Dan, you know what I mean.

CAP'N DAN: I know you trust me and I say you're up to it—and, Franklin, God Almighty hates a quitter! Listen here, I'll confess something to you, I had this lots of times when I was your age, every time I had a fight or a birthday.

BRADY: How'd you get rid of it?

CAP'N DAN: The one way there is: plenty of heat and nice deep massage. Now, Frank, go inside. Mrs. Brady wants to show you a letter I brought for you. I paid a call in Washington on my way out here, and even though I think it'll make you so big-headed you won't be fit to talk to, you read it, then come out here and we'll see where we stand.

[*Exit* BRADY. GOLDIE *comes forward*]

GOLDIE: Good, so it's fixed?

CAP'N DAN: **Somebody say something?**

GOLDIE: Me. I'm asking, Is it settled please, gentlemen? You tell me Yes I can maybe catch the train.

CAP'N DAN: The man's in a hurry, Fred.

FRED: What about terms?

GOLDIE: What, you expect I'm gonna yell about terms? Look, we're no babies here, you know like I know, my Jackie would fight it for a nickel, tomorrow. But it wouldn't look nice for you to take advantage, so you'll offer me low as you can get away with and I'll say OK.

FRED: Eighty-twenty, Goldie.

GOLDIE: What! **A world's championship?** You can't go twenty-five?

FRED: Eighty-twenty. That's it.

GOLDIE: Well . . . God bless America.

FRED: And Cap'n Dan to be the referee.

GOLDIE: Fred, you're kidding me?

FRED: Him or forget it. You know how it works.

GOLDIE: I don't mean no disrespect, but—

CAP'N DAN: Who'd you have in mind, friend, Booker T. Washington?

GOLDIE: All right, all right. Boy! What else?

FRED: That's all.

GOLDIE: He don't have to fight with his feet tied together?

FRED: I said that's all.

CAP'N DAN: We better set the place.

GOLDIE: Any place, name it, the Coast, Chicago—

CAP'N DAN: No big towns, Fred. You'll have every nigger and his brother jamming in there.

GOLDIE: **For my money they could have it in Iceland!**

SMITTY: How about Tulsa? Denver? Reno?

PHOTOGRAPHER 1: Hey, Reno, that's OK!

PRESSMAN 1: Small.

FRED: No—wait—

TRAINER 2: Reno—

CAP'N DAN: Why not? The good old Rockies—

FRED: Yeah—

CAP'N DAN: A white man's country!

GOLDIE: Sure, but you can find them?

FRED: They'll come from all over, it's on the main line now—

SMITTY: And it's high and dry. Mr. Brady would like that—

TRAINER 2: The drier the better! If that nigger gets a sweat up, one good whiff and Frank'll be finished.

[*Enter* BRADY *carrying the gold belt*]

BRADY: Well, he's not through yet!

CAP'N DAN: There we are—

BRADY: Want some photos, boys?

PHOTOGRAPHER 1: Sure thing, Mr. Brady—

PHOTOGRAPHER 2: With it on, OK?

[PHOTOGRAPHERS *set up cameras.* PRESSMEN *ready notebooks*]

GOLDIE: A deal?

FRED: It's a deal. [FRED *and* GOLDIE *shake hands*]

BRADY: And it's gonna be a pleasure—tell your nigger I said so!

PRESSMAN 1: Pour it on, Mr. Brady—

GOLDIE: **I should miss a train for this?**

BRADY: [*Rolling up his sleeves*] You tell Mr. Black Boy to give me that smile when he's inside those ropes—

TRAINER 1: [*To* PRESSMAN] Get it down, get it down—

BRADY: I'll appreciate it, tell him—**my eyes ain't too good these days, you understand, I like something nice and shiny to aim at**—[*Puts on belt*] OK, boys?

PRESSMAN 1: Ah!

PHOTOGRAPHER 2: Stance, please, Mr. Brady—

[BRADY *takes stance;* PHOTOGRAPHERS' *magnesium flares till end of scene*]

FRED: [*Leading* GOLDIE OFF] Don't let your boy take this nigger stuff to heart, huh? Explain how it's going to pack em in, that's all.

GOLDIE: He knows how it is. Good luck! [*Exits*]

FRED: [*Calling after him*] You're OK, Goldie!

SMITTY: [*To* CA'PN DAN, *looking at* BRADY] Well, there we are!

CAP'N DAN: Oh, he's the man all right. I just don't like the idea of calling it a Hope, I wish you boys hadn't hung that tag on him.

SMITTY: It's sure caught on, though!

CAP'N DAN: That's what bothers me, I guess.

SMITTY: Can I quote you on that?

CAP'N DAN: No, lend me a comb. **I better go stand up with him and get my picture took!**

[*Laughter and* BLACKOUT. *Thudding of a punching-bag,* then LIGHTS UP *on*—]

SCENE TWO

A *small gym, San Francisco.*

JACK JEFFERSON *shadow-boxing.* TICK, *his Negro trainer.* ELEANOR BACHMAN, *a white girl, watching.*

TICK: Mix it up, Jack honey, pace him, pace him out, hands up higher now, move, he's jabbin—don't follow them head fakes, you watch his body, there you go, jab! jab! Beauty—fake with the body, not just the head, baby—feint! jab! hook in behind it—send him the right now—no! Whut you at?

JACK: [*Continuing his movements*] Givin him a right—

TICK: An where you givin it?

JACK: Chin bone—

TICK: Sucker bone! Boy, you a worry! He groggy now, right, you jabbin his liver till he runnin outa gas an his eyes goin fishy—Why you knock on dat chin! Could be ya done whut!

JACK: Wake him up, wake him up—

TICK: Watch him! He's bobbin, he's comin to you, block it— where you gonna take dat right now?

JACK: Temple—

TICK: How!

JACK: Hook it, hook to de temple—

TICK: Why!

JACK: Softes place on his head—

TICK: Yeah! now you listenin to me, sugar! Hook him again, a beauty, three now—[JACK *stops*] Hey, whut you doin—

JACK: [*To* ELEANOR] Now, honey, you juss know you tired a sittin here, whyn't you go buy yourself a pretty or somethin—

ELLIE: No, let me stay. Unless you mind me here, Jack.

JACK: You mah Lady Luck! I don't mine you nowhere—

TICK: **Oh, long as you lookin at him, he don' mine—**

JACK: But ain't this too much rough-house for ya, honey?

ELLIE: Well—I try not to listen.

TICK: Much obliged!

ELLIE: Oh, Tick, I'm sorry—

JACK: She somethin, ain't she!

TICK: Darlin, you keep sittin there any way you like it, cause he sure workin happy. OK?

ELLIE: OK!

TICK: [*To* JACK] Now, we gonna mooch or we gonna move?

JACK: [*Moves*] Hole me dat bag! **Gonna buss it wide open, then we all go out an have a champagne lunch!**

[*Enter* GOLDIE]

GOLDIE: Four soft boiled eggs, that's what you're gonna have—

[*He does not notice* ELLIE]

JACK: Hey, Goldie!

TICK: How you doin, boss—

GOLDIE: Oy, those stairs—

JACK: Get him a chair, Tick—

GOLDIE: Cover him up first he shouldn't get ice on him.

JACK: Figured you stayin in Reno till tomorrow—

GOLDIE: What, we got it settled there—how do you feel?

TICK: [*Puts robe on* JACK] He feel like he look, boss!

GOLDIE: Not eating too quick?

TICK: No, sir, chewin good!

JACK: Ah's chewin till it hurts—

GOLDIE: **Laugh, laugh! This one you have to watch like a hawkeye!**

JACK: Come on, Goldie, when it gonna be!

GOLDIE: The Fourth of July. Now the newspaper guys—

JACK: [*Laughing*] The Fourth of July?

GOLDIE: So, it makes a difference?

JACK: No, it juss tickle mah funny-bone, dassall—

TICK: **Fourth a July an Lawd you knows why!**

GOLDIE: We should worry, listen, will we have a gate there—fifteen thousand! Jack, you know what they're callin it? Already by them it's the Fight of the Century—twenty years I never seen such a hoopla! Trains from St. Louis and Chicago, direct yet, tents they have to put up, it's a regular madhouse, and wait, from the ring they're gonna telegraph it, Jack, straight to every Western Union in the country, so like right away everybody should know, and on that we make somethin too!

TICK: Lively times, Ah kin hear you comin! Boy, you bout to win de Fight of de Century!

JACK: Yeah, or else lose an be the nigger of the minute.

GOLDIE: [*Noticing* ELLIE] Listen, come here, Jack—

JACK: Whut kina odds goin?

GOLDIE: Brady eight to five. What's the girl doin here?

JACK: Oh, she looking roun. She don't bother us none.

GOLDIE: Lookin around for what?

JACK: You be nice now, Goldie—come on over, Ellie, don't be shy now, hon—she a friend of mine, you know?

GOLDIE: Jackie, you gotta bring a girl here when you train?

JACK: Ah guess so, boss! Ah loves to dance an prance fo de wimmins!

ELLIE: How do you do.

JACK: Goldie, shake hands with Miss Ellie Bachman.

GOLDIE: Pleased to meetcha, Miss Bachman. I apologize I didn't notice you before, such a tumult we got here.

ELLIE: Oh, sure, I understand.

GOLDIE: You're a fan of Jack's, huh?

JACK: Ellie was on the same boat from Australia, she was visitin down there.

GOLDIE: Well, it's great to be home again, I bet. You can't beat Frisco!

ELLIE: Yes, I like it fine. My home is in Tacoma, though.

GOLDIE: Oh . . . it's awful damp up there, ain't it?

JACK: Mm-hmm! You know it!

ELLIE: Yes, I can't say I miss it much. [*Pause*]

TICK: Uncle of mine work up dere in a laundry once, he din like it neither . . .

JACK: Drizzle on you all the time there!

TICK: Right!

GOLDIE: Yeah, well, Miss Bachman, the guys from the papers are comin any minute, you know what I mean, so if maybe you excuse us—

JACK: She stay where she is.

TICK: **Uh-oh.**

GOLDIE: Jackie, look, what's the matter with you!

JACK: She stayin where she is.

GOLDIE: I'm gonna pass out here!

ELLIE: I'll wait in the room, Jack.

GOLDIE: In the room! Jesus Christ!

JACK: You be nice now, hear?

GOLDIE: I knew it! **Last night in my head it's like a voice—Dumbbell, go home quick, somethin's goin on with him!**

JACK: Ain't nobody's business!

GOLDIE: Grow up, for God's sake—

ELLIE: Let me go, it doesn't matter—

GOLDIE: No—please, one second—Tick, go lock the door.

[TICK *does*]

[*To* JACK]

So you don't know the score, huh? Well, I'll tell you the score, right now I'll tell you. And you should listen too, miss, I can see you're a fine serious girl, not a bum, better you should know, so there's no hard feelins here. First, Jack, they hate your guts a little bit—OK! You don't put on gloves everybody should like you. Then they hate your guts some more— still OK! That makes you wanna fight, some kinda pep it give you. And then they hate you so much they're payin through the nose to see a white boy maybe knock you on your can— well, that's more than OK, cash in, after all, it's so nice to be colored you shouldn't have a bonus? But, sonny, when they start in to hate you more than that, you gotta watch out. And that means now—Oh, I got ears, I get told things—guys who want to put dope into your food there, a guy who wants to watch the fight behind a rifle. OK, cops we'll get, dogs, that we can handle. But this on top of it, a white girl, Jack, what, do I have to spell it on the wall for you, you wanna drive them crazy, you don't hear what happens—

JACK: Whut Ah s'pose to do! Stash her in a iddy biddy hole someplace in niggertown an go sneakin over there twelve o'clock at night, carry her roun with me inside a box like a pet bunny-rabbit or somethin—

ELLIE: Jack—

JACK: Or maybe she juss put black on her face, an puff her mouth up, so's nobody notice Ah took nothin from em—

[*Knock at door*]

Let 'em wait! You know Ah done fool roun plenny, Goldie, she know it too, she know it all, but Ah ain't foolin roun now, unnerstand—[*Points to* TICK] **an if he say, "Thass whut you said lass time," Ah bust his nappy head—**

TICK: I ain't sayin nothin!

[*More knocking*]

GOLDIE: Hold on, I'm comin—Jack, I swear, I'll help you, just you shouldn't throw it in their face, Jack, I'm beggin you—

JACK: See? This whut you fell inta, darlin.

ELLIE: Do what he says.

JACK: You go along with him?

ELLIE: Along with you, any way I can.

[*More knocking*]

GOLDIE: Go, sit over there—let em in, for Chrissake—

[TICK *admits* SMITTY *and several other* PRESSMEN]

TICK: Mornin, gents—

JACK: Hiya, fellers—Hey there, Smitty—

[*Handshaking and greeting*]

GOLDIE: Just a few minutes, fellers, OK?

PRESSMAN 1: Well, you're sure looking good, Jack.

JACK: Thanks, boss!

PRESSMAN 2: Guess you know about the Fourth—

PRESSMAN 1: You starting to get jumpy?

JACK: Yeah, Ah scared Brady gonna change his mind!

SMITTY: Still think you can take him, Jack?

JACK: Well, Ah ain't sayin Ah kin take him straight off—an, anyway, dat be kina mean, you know, alla dem people, big holiday fight—how dey gonna feel Ah send em home early?

SMITTY: So your only worry is deciding which round.

JACK: Yeah, an dat take some thinkin, man! If Ah lets it go too long in dere, juss sorta blockin an keepin him offa me, then evvybody say, "Now ain't dat one shif'less nigger, why dey always so lazy?" An if Ah chop him down quick, third or fourth roun, all at once then dey holler, "No, t'ain't fair, dat po' man up dere fightin a gorilla!" **But Ah gonna work it out.**

PRESSMAN 2: What about that yellow streak Brady talks about?

JACK: [*Undoing his robe*] Yeah, you wanna see it?

GOLDIE: Don't clown aroun, Jackie—

PRESSMAN 3: Any idea, Jack, why you smile when you're fighting?

JACK: Well you know. Ah am a happy person. Ah always feel good, huh? An when Ah'm fighting Ah feels double good. So whut Ah wanna put a face on for? An you know, it's a sport, right, like a game, so Ah like whoever Ah'm hittin to see Ah'm still his friend.

PRESSMAN 2: Going to train in Chicago, Mr. Jefferson?

JACK: Yeah, Ah wanna see my little ole momma—

PRESSMAN 1: Fried chicken, Jack?

JACK: Mmm-mmh! Can't wait!

SMITTY: I believe that's Miss Bachman there, isn't it, Jack? You first met on the boat?

ELLIE: No, not exactly—

GOLDIE: Miss Bachman is my secretary, we hired her in Australia, she's from here, but she was over there and we, you know, we hired her and she came over with the boys.

SMITTY: I see—

TICK: Boss, if dey finish Ah wanna rub him down—

PRESSMAN 1: We got plenty for now, Jack—

PRESSMAN 3: Thanks—

JACK: Come again!

PRESSMAN 2: Jack, one more question?

JACK: Yeah, go head.

PRESSMAN 2: You're the first black man in the history of the ring to get a crack at the heavyweight title. Now the white folks, of course, are behind the White Hope, Brady's the redeemer of the race, and so on. But you, Jack Jefferson, are you the Black Hope?

JACK: Well, Ah'm black and Ah'm hopin.

SMITTY: Try and answer him straight, Jack.

JACK: Oh, Ah guess mah cousins mostly want me to win.

SMITTY: You imply that some don't?

JACK: Maybe some a them reckon they gonna pay a little high for that belt, if Ah take it.

SMITTY: Won't you try and change their minds, Jack, get them all behind you?

JACK: Man, Ah ain't runnin for Congress! Ah ain't fightin for no race, ain't redeemin nobody! My momma tole me Mr. Lincoln done that—**ain't that why you shot him?**

[*General laughter.* CLARA, *a Negro woman, bursts in*]

CLARA: My, oh my! It de big black rooster and de little red hen! I got you, you mother!

JACK: What you want here!

CLARA: I show you what I wants—[*Goes for* ELLIE]

ELLIE: Jack!

JACK: Hey!

TICK: [*Restrains* CLARA] You crazy, you bitch—?

GOLDIE: A little family quarrel, fellers, see you tomorrow, you know how it is—

[*They remain*]

CLARA: You leave my man be, girl, you don' leave him, Ah gonna throw you at him in chunks—

GOLDIE: You got it all wrong, Clara—

CLARA: Yeah? Ah gots it from de chambermaid at the Park Royal Hotel, Ah come all de way from Chicago to got it—

JACK: Now you got it you git you black ass outa here.

CLARA: Don't hit me!

JACK: Whut you tyin on, you evil chinch, you!

GOLDIE: Jack—fellers—

CLARA: Sing it, daddy! Let de gennumuns hear how you smirchin your wife—

GOLDIE: What do you mean?

JACK: She ain't no wife of mine—

CLARA: No which of what? **We's common law and Ah's comin home to poppa!**

JACK: Ah's common nothin! Don' you poppa me, girl, or Ah poppa you so you never forget it! Ah quit on you when you cleared out a De-troit wid Willie de pimp—

GOLDIE: Fellers, please, have a heart—Jack—

CLARA: Ah know you come after me, Ah know you was lookin—

JACK: You lucky Ah too busy to fine you, girl, selling off mah clothes, mah ring, silver brushes—

CLARA: Gimme nother chance, baby, Ah misses you awful—

JACK: Don' come on with me! You juss smelling bread, you comin here now cause you Willie's in jail—

CLARA: How you know where he at!

JACK: Ah from de jungle like you is, baby, Ah hears de drums— [To TICK] take her over to Goldie's, give her a twenty an carfare back.

TICK: Come on, Clara.

JACK: Ah tellin you once more, go way and stay there.

CLARA: You ain't closin up the book so easy, daddy—[To ELLIE] hear me, Gray Meat? Get it while you can!

TICK: Come on, out—[Drags her out]

JACK: [To ELLIE] You all right, honey?

GOLDIE: Fellers, now I'm askin you, man to man, please for everybody's good, don't write nothin about it, **if it gets out, God knows what can happen**—I mean, look, we wanna have a fight, don't we? And besides the girl has a family, what the hell—[Pause]

PRESSMAN 3: OK.

PRESSMAN 1: Don't worry, Goldie.

GOLDIE: Thanks, fellers, thanks—let's all have a drink—[Hustles THEM out; JACK has begun punching the bag]

ELLIE: Oh, Jack! It gets awful, doesn't it.

JACK: Well . . . seems to get worse and better both at once.

ELLIE: Is there anything I can do?

JACK: Yeah . . . Stick around. An don' never call me daddy.

[BLACKOUT—*sound of fireworks and band music*— LIGHTS UP *on*—]

SCENE THREE

Outside the arena, Reno.

Across the stage a banner: RENO THE HUB OF THE UNIVERSE. *Many small American flags in evidence. Stage milling with* WHITE MEN *of every sort: at the center a huge crap game, at the rear a* BLACKFACE *performer entertaining another* GROUP, *at one side a few* MEN *breaking up a fight, at the other a* MAN *supporting a singing* DRUNK, *in the foreground a* BETTOR *with a fistful of money looking for a* TOUT.

ROLLER: Ooh, six, get ready, baby from Baltimore—

PLAYER 1: Shoot em—

TOUT: [*To* BETTOR] Sure, how much you bettin—

PLAYER 2: Boxcars!

PLAYER 1: Let it ride—

BETTOR: Ninety simoleons—

TOUT: Ninety on Brady at eight to five—

BETTOR: Eight—?

ROLLER: In or out—

BETTOR: Up yours eight, mister, they're giving eleven, they're givin thirteen—

ROLLER: Who's in, who's in, who's—

BLACKFACE: [*Bursting in on the crap game*] Yassuh, yassuh, yassuh—

PLAYER 1: Hey, look who's here—

BLACKFACE: Move ovah, bredren, ole Doctuh Wishbone gwine ta roll dem cubicles—Uh oh! **Lonesome pockets!** Kin ah come in wiv a chicken laig, boss? [*Flourishes one. Laughter*]

PLAYER 3: Where's the white meat, Wishbone—

BLACKFACE: White meat? Oh, he puttin on de belt now—an dark meat, he shakin in de graby! [*Laughter, jeers.* THEY *all gather round*] **Lawd, Ah sho hopes dey's mo cullud folks den me here—**

ROLLER: Why's that, Wishbone—

BLACKFACE: Ah cain't bury all dat nigger bah mahself! [*Laughter*] Gwine ta read de sermon ovuh him, dassall—

BETTOR: Let's hear it!

BLACKFACE: "Bredren," it start, "kinely pass de plate"—no dat ain't it—[*Laughter*] "Bredren," it start, "come outer dem bushes"—no, tain't dat neether—[*Laughter*] "Bredren"—here de one—"de tex for dis po' darkie am foun in de Book ob"— well it roun bout de place where Paul git off de steamboat. "Bredren," it say, "bressed am dey dat lays down, **cause if dey ain gittin up dey mought jes's well stays down**"—[*Laughter, cheers,* SOMEONE *throws him a tambourine,* HE *sings*]
>
> Ole Marse Brady whip cullud Jack
> Come fum way down Souf,
> Hair curl on his haid so tight
> He coulden shet his mouf—

[THEY *all join in*]

> Coon, coon, coon, ah wish mah culluh'd fade,
> Coon, coon, coon, Lawd, make me a brahter shade—

[*Enter* COLONEL COX *with some* NEVADA RANGERS]

COX: All right, all right, stay where you are—

PLAYER 1: What the hell, Colonel—

PLAYER 2: Just having some fun—

COX: Boys, I got orders to confiscate all firearms—[*Protests*] **We'll give em back tonight after it's over**—

RANGER 1: [*Collecting weapons*] Let's go—

RANGER 2: Thank you!

RANGER 1: Say, that's a real old one—

PLAYER 1: [*As band strikes up nearby*] What you fraid of, Colonel, we won't have to shoot him!

BETTOR: They're comin for the weigh-in!

[*Cheering nearby*]

COX: [*To* BLACKFACE] You'd better scram, Mike.

BLACKFACE: Sure thing, Colonel—

[*Runs off; more cheering; a scale is wheeled on*]

PLAYER 1: [*Looks offstage*] That's Brady's bus—here he comes—

[MUSIC *changes to "Oh, You Beautiful Doll"*]

ROLLER: Whack that nigger, Frank—

PLAYER 2: You fix him for us—

PLAYER 1: Wipe that smile off him, boy—

[THEY *all cheer as* BRADY, *in a robe and with his hands taped, scowling, enters with* CAP'N DAN, FRED, *and entourage:* HANDLERS, PRESS, *etc.* HE *gets on the scale. Music stops*]

BRADY: Come on, it's hot as hell here. Let's go.

PRESSMAN 1: What did you have for lunch, Mr. Brady?

[*Laughter*]

BRADY: Nothin! A cuppa tea!

FRED: We'll get a statement in a minute, boys—

CAP'N DAN: Take it easy, Franklin—

WEIGHER-IN: Two hundred and four.

[*Cheers.* HE *steps off the scale, takes out a paper. Silence*]

BRADY: When I put on the gloves now and defend this here belt it's the request of the public, which forced me out of retirement. But I wanta assure them I'm fit to do my best, **and I don't think I'm gonna disappoint nobody.**

[*Applause:* JACK *enters with* GOLDIE *and* TICK: *Silence*]

JACK: **How come they's no music when I comes in?**

CAP'N DAN: How do you do, Mr. Jefferson. As you know, of course, I am your referee.

JACK: Cap'n Dan, it's a honor. Ah'm proud to shake the han whut shook the han of the Prince of Wales.

ROLLER: Don't take that lip from him! [*General "Ssh"*] Come on, boog, I'll get it over with right—[*General hubbub*]

GOLDIE: Colonel—

COX: Quiet down there!

BRADY: Get him on the scale, willya.

JACK: [*Stepping on*] Hey, Frank, how you doin? [BRADY *turns away, muttering*] **Look like Frank bout ta walk de plank!**

WEIGHER-IN: One hundred ninety-one.

GOLDIE: Brady?

WEIGHER-IN: Two hundred and four.

TICK: OK, Jack, get down—

JACK: Hey, Frank, you believe that? This man here saying Ah lighter than you!

BRADY: Yeah, very funny.

CAP'N DAN: Just your statement, please.

JACK: Huh. Oh, sure. Ah thank Mr. Brady here for being such a sport, givin me a shot at the belt today. They's been plenty a mean talk roun—[*Jeers*]

COX: Quiet, there—

JACK: But here we is, an Ah glad it come down to a plain ole scuffle. [*A few* HANDCLAPS *at the rear of the crowd, which parts to reveal a* GROUP OF NEGROES *there*] **Mercy me, it's de chillun of Isrel**—Hey, there, homefolks!

BRADY: Come on, let's clear out of here—

FRED: Right—

BRADY: Keep rootin, boys—

CROWD: All behind you, Frank—Kill the coon—Tear him apart, Frank—Find that yellow streak—

[*The* BAND *strikes up "Hot Time in the Old Town Tonight" as it follows, cheering after* BRADY *and his entourage,* PRESSMEN *and* RANGERS *behind them.* GOLDIE *and* TICK *remain.* JACK *approaches the* GROUP OF NEGROES. *Music and cheering gradually recede*]

JACK: Well, how you all today!

DEACON: Gonna be prayin fo you here, Mr. Jefferson.

JACK: Couldn't get no tickets, huh.

TICK: Bess dey don' go in dere, Jack.

JACK: Yeah, maybe so.

DEACON: That don' matter none. We juss come to pray you gonna win for us, son.

JACK: Well, if "us" mean any you wid cash ridin on me, you prayers gonna pay off roun about the fifth.

YOUNG NEGRO: No, Mr. Jefferson. He mean win for us cullud.

JACK: Oh, that what you prayin!

DEACON: May the good Lawd be guidin your hand for us, son!

ALL NEGROES: Amen, amen.

JACK: An you traipse all this way here to pray it, my, my.

YOUNG NEGRO: What the Revren mean to signify—

JACK: I know what he signify. I big but I ain dumb, hear?

YOUNG NEGRO: What you salty wif me for—

DEACON: We folks just want you to preciate—

JACK: [*To* YOUNG NEGRO] Hey, man. What my winnin gonna do for you!

YOUNG NEGRO: Huh? Oh . . . er . . .

DEACON: Give him self-respeck, that's what!

ALL NEGROES: Amen!

NEGRO 1: Tell it, brother!

YOUNG NEGRO: Yeah—Ah be proud to be a cullud man to-morrow!

NEGROES: [*General response*] Amen, that's it.

JACK: Uh huh. Well, country boy, if you ain't there already, all the boxin and nigger-prayin in the world ain't gonna get you there—

TICK: Jack, let's go—

DEACON: You look cullud, son, but you ain't thinkin cullud.

JACK: Oh, Ah thinkin cullud, cullud and then cullud, Ah so busy think cullud Ah can't see nothin else sometime, but Ah ain't think cullud-us, like you! An when you come on wid it, you know what Ah see, man? That ole cullud-us? Juss a basket-fulla crabs! Crabs in a basket—

DEACON: God send you light, son—

GOLDIE: Time to go, Jack—

JACK: Tell me you prayin here! An speck Ah gonna say Oh, thankya, Revren! You ain't prayin for me! [*"Star Spangled Banner" in the distance*] It ain't, Lawd, don't let that peck break his nose, or, Lawd, let him git outa town and not git shot at— Ah ain nothin in it but a ugly black fiss here! **They don' even push on in to see it workin!**

[COLONEL COX *reenters*]

COX: All set, Jefferson?

JACK: [*To the* NEGROES] Lay your bets, boys, you still got time.

[HE *follows the* COLONEL *out,* GOLDIE *and* TICK *behind him. Lights begin to fade very gradually*]

DEACON: Lawd, when the smoke of the battle clear away here, may this good strong man be standin up in victry. May them who keep shovin all us people down see they can't do it all the time, and take a lesson. And may us have this livin man today to show us the sperrit of Joshua. Give this to us, Lawd, we needs it, and give him light to understand why.

[*The anthem ends and a wolfish cry is heard from the* CROWD *in the stadium*]

NEGRO BOY: Revren—

DEACON: Don' worry, boy. We be all right out here.

[THEY *move back, singing, as the roar increases and the stage darkens*]

NEGROES: [*Singing unseen*]
   It's so high you can't get over it,
   It's so low you can't get under it,
   It's so wide you can't get around it,
   You must come through by the living gate.

[*The roar reaches a crescendo, suddenly—dies out* . . .
BLACKOUT.
A *match lit upstage:* CAP'N DAN *in shirt sleeves and braces, lighting a cigar*]

CAP'N DAN: [*Speaking over his shoulder*] They better throw away half those pictures they took. They'll be worse than the fight . . . [*Comes forward*] **I really have the feeling it's the biggest calamity to hit this country since the San Francisco earthquake—no, I'm serious. That one at least was only in Frisco. What kind of calamity? Hard to say it, exactly. Oh, I don't think all the darkies'll go crazy, try to take us over, rape and all that. Be some trouble, yes, but it can be managed— after all, one of em's a heavyweight champ . . . But that's it, I suppose. He is! I hold his hand up, and suddenly a nigger is Champion of the World! Now you'll say, Oh, that's only your title in sports—no, it's more. Admit it. And more than if one got to be world's best engineer, or smartest politician, or number one opera singer, or world's biggest genius at making** things from peanuts. No calamity there. But Heavyweight Champion of the World, well it feels like the world's got a shadow across it. Everything's—no joke intended—kind of darker, and different, like it's shrinking, it's all huddled down somehow, and you with it, you want to holler What's he doin up there, but you can't because you know . . . that shadow's on you, and you feel that smile . . . Well, so what do we do! Wet our pants, cry in our beer about it? No, sir, I'll tell you what we do, we beat those bushes for another White Hope, and if he's no good we find another White Hope, we'll find them and we'll boost them up till one stays—what the hell is this country, Ethiopia?

[BLACKOUT: *music—"Sweet Georgia Brown."* LIGHTS UP *immediately on—*]

SCENE FOUR

A *street, Chicago.*

Dressed-up NEGROES, *more arriving, great animation; some carry small American flags;* BARKER *among them with megaphone.* BAND *playing on stage before an enormous baroque doorway, over which is spelled* CAFE DE CHAMPION *in lights;* MAN *on ladder installing the last few bulbs,* ANOTHER *distributing yellow handbills.*

BARKER: [*Through megaphone*] Every Chicago man, woman, and chile, you all invited, tan, pink, black, yellow, and beginner brown, get along down, let's shake the han of the best in the lan in his fine new place here, celebrate the openin, come in you vehicle, come on you foot, don' bring money, just be here—

[*Auto horns and cheering offstage, then on.* JACK *enters at the wheel of an open white touring-car,* ELLIE *at his side,* TICK *and* GOLDIE *in the rear. A group of* POLICEMEN *entering with them begins pushing back the* CROWD]

JACK: Hey—hey—they all right, Mistah Offisah, leave them cullud come on—

[*Cheers as he dismounts and they mill around him, some with flowers*]

NEGROES:
God bless you, Jack—
Ah name mah baby aftuh you—
Member me, Jack?
Ah wish dey wuz ten dozen—
Reach me that han out—

[*The* CLARINETIST *aims an arpeggio at the backs of the retreating* POLICE: *laughter*]

JACK: [*His arms full of flowers*] Say . . . lookie here, thank you . . . thank you . . . oh my! . . . **Look like Rest in Peace, don't it!** [*Laughter*] Well, Ah am all rested up, an like you kin see Ah bout to make Chicago mah real home sweet home now—[*Cheers*] thass right, permint. Ah don' guess Ah'll be needin to chase aroun fo work awhile—[*Laughter*] an Ah got this joint fix up so's Ah kin visit with mah frens an git rich both at once—[*Laughter, jeers*] But wait till you see INside—

NEGRO MAN: You ain't stuck Brady's head up on the wall, man, has you? [*Hoots, laughter*]

JACK: No, but they's a picture of ole Queen Cleopattera whut'll make you set straight—[*Laughter*] an blue mirrs, big chambeliers from Germany—well, Ah ain't gonna spawl it, but say, better tell you, them jahnt silver pots on the floors, now they artistic, but they ain't juss for admirin, you know? [*Laughter. He moves toward the car*] Tick, you gimme a han with these flowuhs, you too, Ellie—[*Silence as she stands to take them, then a spatter of applause, increasing*] Yeah, evvybody say hello to mah fiancey, Ellie Bachman! [*Cheers,* ELLIE *waves, smiling.* TRUMPETER *plays a bit of "Here Comes the Bride"*] Hole on, don' jump the gun, boy—[*Laughter*] An, hey, while you at it, Gragulate mah manager here, mah fren Goldie—[*Cheers.* GOLDIE *waves*] An—

TICK: **See? You black, you juss nacheral come in lass**—[*Laughter*. TICK *springs up, flourishing the gold belt in its plush-lined case*] Brung this lil doodad, folks, to hang up ovuh de bar!

[*Whoops, cheers, drum rolls*]

JACK: OK, stash that away now—What you headin at now is a special brew a mine in there call Rajah's Peg—don' ass whut's in it, jes come inside and git it—[*Cheers*] **Yeah, open house! Les have some lively times!**

[BAND *strikes up* "Shine." *Cheering continues as* JACK, *cakewalking around the car, ceremoniously collects* ELLIE *and leads her to the doorway, where she formally cuts the ribbon across it; the* NEGROES, *all cakewalking, follow them in, the* BAND *last, continuing to play inside.* GOLDIE *and* TICK *remain*]

TICK: Come on, boss!

GOLDIE: Oh, boy. Oh, boy! You heard what he said? His fiancée? You heard him?

TICK: Yeah, but dat don' signify nothin—

GOLDIE: Nothin! With bills up in seven states against any kinda mixed-around marriages!

TICK: Boss, he only juss now say fiancey so them people don figger she a hooker, thassall—

GOLDIE: **You hear? Take a lesson how to be a gentleman!** It's all, he says. Why can't he give them a chance to boil down, what's he gotta bring her in the open, for what?

TICK: Juss did it today, boss—

GOLDIE: [*Gesturing to the car*] Right down Wabash Avenue—

TICK: **No law against dat yet**—

[*Bass drum heard in the distance—continues*]

GOLDIE: What the hell is that?

TICK: I dunno. Muss be some burial society.

[*Enter* SMITTY *and* PRESSMAN 1]

GOLDIE: Go on, take the belt in.

[TICK *goes into the Cafe; cheering, music continuing*]

SMITTY: Lively times, eh, Goldie?

GOLDIE: Yeah. Hiya.

SMITTY: Wouldn't let you in, huh?

GOLDIE: Are you kiddin?

PRESSMAN 1: He came out for some air!

[*They laugh; drum gradually approaching*]

GOLDIE: Look, what's goin on?

SMITTY: They'll be here in a minute, Goldie.

[*Drum very near*]

GOLDIE: They, who's they—? [*Looks in direction of drumming*]
What the hell is that—?

SMITTY: You know how they are about places like this. Just their
meat, Goldie.

GOLDIE: Oh, Jesus, not here, not down here, I checked it! Not in
this part of town!

SMITTY: Anywhere, Goldie. It's one big clean-up—

GOLDIE: **Oh boy!** Listen, Smitty, get the cops—

SMITTY: Always cops along, take it easy—

GOLDIE: Smitty—we'll have a riot on our hands here—

SMITTY: Really? I never thought of that.

[*They draw back as a trombone is heard, raggedly joining
the drum with "Onward, Christian Soldiers," and the*

PARADE *appears, escorted by* POLICEMEN. *The* MARCHERS *carry signs reading:*

CIVIC REFORM NOW
WOMEN'S LEAGUE FOR TEMPERANCE
SEEK YE OUT INIQUITY
AURORA BIBLE COMMITTEE
THOR WITH HIS HAMMER, NORWEGIANS AGAINST SALOONS
HEPWORTH UNION
WE HAVE BEEN TOO PATIENT
CHICAGO JOAN OF ARC CLUBS

A *lone* NEGRO *among them with a sign:*

NO SPIRITS NO VICE

The music within has stopped. Still playing their anthem, the MARCHERS *range themselves before the doorway. The* NEGROES *within have emerged and stand out before them belligerently.* JACK *comes out as the trombone and drum conclude the anthem*]

MARCHER 1:
Woe unto the keepers of the Temples of Baal!
Woe unto the swillers in the sinks of wretchedness!
Woe unto those whose delight is born of evil!

NEGRO 1: **Woe whoevuh break up a party on Division Street!**

[NEGROES *snarl agreement*]

JACK: Easy now, ace, let the man preach it—

MARCHER 2: We aren't here just to preach, Mr. Jefferson.

WOMAN MARCHER: We tell you to shut this establishment down.

NEGROES:
You what?
Who you squeakin at!
Get outa here, fishbait!
Shut me somma this!
Move—

JACK: Easy, easy—now, mistah, lookie here—

NEGROES:
Don' argue to em, Jack—
Shoo em off—

WOMAN MARCHER: Shame! Shame, Mr. Jefferson!

MARCHER 1: **Instead of offering these people an example—**

NEGRO 2: [*Squirts a soda syphon at him*] Have one on me, chesty!

POLICEMAN 1: Watch it now, you, they got their permit—

JACK: Hey—

NEGRO 2: Don't shove when you talk, man—

MARCHER 1: Drunkenness, disorder, this is what you offer—

NEGRO 3: Do somethin bout it!

MARCHER 1: We shall not allow—

NEGRO WOMAN 1: Stop beatin on de cullud, hear—

POLICEMAN 2: Look—

NEGRO 3: Hands off—

MARCHER 1: We shall not allow fresh corruption to flourish here—

NEGRO 4: I know that mother, I work for him once—

MARCHER 1: We shall not sit by—

NEGRO 3: We ain't gonna let you—

NEGRO WOMAN 1: Stop beatin on de cullud—

NEGRO 2: Show em—

POLICEMAN 3: I warn you—

NEGRO 1: Git de wimmins inside—

MARCHER 1: Sing, friends—

POLICEMAN 1: Keep back—

NEGRO 1: Juss you make one teeny noise—

[ANOTHER NEGRO *breaks through, begins wrestling with the* DRUMMER: *shouting and struggling at the police line*]

JACK: Hey, hey—

MARCHER 1: Hymn number—

NEGRO 2 : You ain't hittin no drum here—

WOMAN MARCHER: Help—

[JACK *stops the* POLICE CAPTAIN *from blowing his whistle, then restraining the* NEGRO, *beats the drum with his hand*]

JACK: Order in de court, boys, order in de court! [*Finally silence. He picks up the fallen stick and returns it to the* DRUMMER] Now, you wanta play this old drum? You play it. [*To the* MARCHERS] An you all wanta sing? Then you lean back an sing. Maybe us kin come in on it, how bout "Earth Is Not Mah Home, Ah Juss Passin Through?" [*A few* NEGROES *laugh*] **Thass my favorite.**

MARCHER 2 : We don't regard this as a frivolous matter, Mr. Jefferson.

JACK: Nossir, me neither! Cause if we kicks off a rumpus this bran new corruptions a mine here get close up! Now, I pollgize for any gritty remarks was passed, an for not bin too symbafetic on you aims—

MARCHER 1 : We are going to witness for the Lord—

JACK: OK—

MARCHER 1 : On this doorstep as long—

NEGRO 4 : Can't sweet-talk em, Jack!

NEGRO WOMAN 1 : Always beatin on the cullud!

JACK: Say, is you brains stuck, or what! These folks been layin down trouble all over, an here, we's gettin included, ain't we? Ain't that good enough? Why, it juss like whut Presden Teddy say, Square Deal for Evvybody!—come on, les treat em right, git some chairs out here, they gonna stay, OK, no use they standin, some old-timie folks long with em here—[NEGROES *begin passing chairs out into the street*] Hurry up, they been walkin plenny too, thass right, Tick, the foldin ones, yeah, thank you, set em down, couple more, here you go—if you all want some samwidges or fruit-punch or somethin, or if, you know, you jus holler out now, OK? We be right inside—

[*The intimidated* MARCHERS *have begun moving off at the appearance of the chairs, and as the* NEGROES *begin to re-*

enter the Cafe, two WHITE MEN *and a* WOMAN *enter: They approach* JACK]

DONNELLY: [*The elder of the two*] Are you Mister Jack Jefferson?

[*All movement ceases*]

JACK: Yeah, what about it?

DONNELLY: My name is Donnelly. I'm an attorney, from Tacoma. And this is Mrs. Bachman. [*Pause*]

JACK: How do you do, ma'am. Would you care to step inside?

MRS. BACHMAN: No, I would not care to step inside. Is my daughter in there?

JACK: Yes, ma'am. She is. [DONNELLY *goes in. Silence*] Ah think she be awful glad to see you, Miz Bachman. [*Long silence*] You like to sit down here fo a minute? [*Long silence*] Ellie tole me all bout her people back there . . .

[*Silence,* DONNELLY *comes out*]

DONNELLY: She refuses to leave, Mrs. Bachman. [*Pause*]

MRS. BACHMAN: [*Crying out*] Ellie! [*She crumples, weeping,* DONNELLY *supporting her*]

JACK: She all right, ma'am, she all right, Ah bring her out to ya—

MRS. BACHMAN: [*As* DONNELLY *begins drawing her away*] Ellie . . . my baby . . .

GOLDIE: Look, Mister Donnelly, where could I reach you—

DONNELLY: The Majestic—

GOLDIE: OK—

JACK: Ah see she get there—

DONNELLY: You'd better see a little further than that, sir. I strongly advise you to send that girl home.

[*The beating of the bass drum resumes, as* HE *and the* OTHER MAN, *followed by the* PRESS, *help* MRS. BACHMAN *away; the* MARCHERS *resume their withdrawal, the* NEGROES *returning to the Cafe.* JACK *is last; he turns to* GOLDIE, *now alone on the street*]

GOLDIE: Well . . . lively times.

[HE *enters the Cafe as the drumming recedes and the* LIGHTS FADE OUT]

SCENE FIVE

Office of the DISTRICT ATTORNEY, *Chicago.*

A meeting in progress. CIVIC LEADERS *facing* CAMERON, *the* DISTRICT ATTORNEY. *They include two* WOMEN *and a distinguished-looking* NEGRO. *In the background* SMITTY, *a* DETECTIVE, *and the man with* DONNELLY *in the previous scene:* DIXON.

CAMERON: No, we do not think he's a privileged character!

MAN 1: And still he carries on—

CAMERON: Now wait—[*Consults papers*] Since he opened this Cafe, as he calls it, we have made no fewer than thirteen arrests—

WOMAN 1: He wasn't arrested!

CAMERON: Madam, we have no grounds—

MAN 3: What about that shooting there—

WOMAN 1: You arrested that poor common-law wife of his—

WOMAN 2: He was involved—

CAMERON: Yes, but, madam, SHE shot at HIM! We can't prosecute him for being a target.

MAN 1: Why isn't action taken about the Bachman girl!

CAMERON: She's over the age of consent, Mr. Hewlett—

MAN 2: This—[*To the* NEGRO] Forgive me, Doctor, but I must speak my mind—This connection between them is an outrage to every decent Caucasian in America! Perhaps he thinks his victories entitle him to it, as part of the spoils—

MAN 1: **You know how niggers are—**

MAN 2: Mr. Hewlett!

MAN 1: [*To the* NEGRO] Oh, I'm sorry, sir . . .

NEGRO: We can't pretend that race is not the main issue here. And, as you imply, sir, the deportment of this man does harm to his race. It confirms certain views of it you may already hold: that does us harm. But it also confirms in many Negroes the belief that his life is the desirable life, and that does us even greater harm. **For a Negro today, the opportunity to earn a dollar in a factory should appear to be worth infinitely more than the opportunity of spending that dollar in emulation of Mr. Jack Jefferson.** But this I assert: the majority of Negroes do not approve of this man or of his doings. He personifies all that should be suppressed by law, and I trust that such suppression is forthcoming.

[*General agreement*]

MAN 2: Everyone in favor say aye—
ALL: Aye!

[THEY *rise,* CAMERON *with them*]

CAMERON: Well, I appreciate your coming here to discuss this—
MAN 2: It will not be to your benefit to let it rest here.
CAMERON: I don't intend to, sir. [*Sees* THEM *out*] Good night, good night.

[HE *shuts the door.* SMITTY, DIXON, *and* DETECTIVE *come forward*]

DETECTIVE: Like a drink?
CAMERON: Sure could use one. [*Bottle is produced,* DIXON *abstains*] Smitty?
SMITTY: I'm in training.
CAMERON: You know . . . if a good White Hope showed up and beat him it would take the edge off this.
SMITTY: Forget it, Al. The best we got around now is Fireman Riley.
CAMERON: All right, let's go to work. Bring the girl in. [DETECTIVE *leaves*] You want to question her, Dixon? It was your idea.

DIXON: No, you go ahead, Al. See what you can come up with.

SMITTY: Why don't you revoke the license on his place, that's easy enough.

CAMERON: Sure it's easy! We could close him, we could rap him on disorderly conduct, we could make a dozen misdemeanors stick, but it's all minor stuff. And you heard them. They want his head on a plate. [DETECTIVE *enters with* ELLIE] Good evening, Miss Bachman. Take a seat, please.

ELLIE: Thank you.

> [DIXON, SMITTY, *and* DETECTIVE *withdraw into the background*]

CAMERON: You understand, this is an informal inquiry, you've come at our request, but of your own free will?

ELLIE: Yes, I understand.

CAMERON: Good. Now, Miss Bachman—[*Consulting papers*] Yes, I see. You resumed your maiden name after your divorce.

ELLIE: That's right.

CAMERON: And you obtained your divorce from Mr. Martin in Australia.

ELLIE: Yes.

CAMERON: An odd place to go for a divorce.

ELLIE: I have an aunt there. I wanted to get away.

CAMERON: You hadn't met Mr. Jefferson before your trip.

ELLIE: No, I had not.

CAMERON: You did not travel there to be with Mr. Jefferson.

ELLIE: No, I did not. I met him on the boat.

CAMERON: How did he approach you?

ELLIE: He didn't. I asked the captain to introduce us.

CAMERON: May I ask why.

ELLIE: Yes. I wanted to make his acquaintance.

CAMERON: And once you had, Miss Bachman, what did he propose to you?

ELLIE: That I have dinner at his table.

CAMERON: Which you did for several evenings—

ELLIE: Yes—

CAMERON: Until you began taking your meals in his stateroom.

ELLIE: That is correct.

CAMERON: [*Consulting papers*] Where a great deal of wine and champagne was consumed.

ELLIE: You might say that.

CAMERON: Presumably he would keep filling your glass . . . ?

ELLIE: When it was empty, yes.

CAMERON: Ten times per evening? Six?

ELLIE: No, I drank very little—

CAMERON: And how often did he give you medicine or pills—

ELLIE: Never, I wasn't ill—

CAMERON: But the steward reports that you hardly left the stateroom, and that disembarking you appeared quite—

ELLIE: Well, the last day at sea we had—

CAMERON: Weren't you ill in some way? Did you feel strange, or sleepy—

ELLIE: I felt uncomfortable at how people looked at me. I wasn't used to it.

CAMERON: He took you from the boat to the hotel.

ELLIE: Yes.

CAMERON: Did you ask to be taken there?

ELLIE: No, I just went with him.

CAMERON: And what had he promised you?

ELLIE: To spend some of his time with me.

CAMERON: Nothing else?

ELLIE: Nothing that could interest you.

CAMERON: But naturally, since you were staying there with him, he provided you with money.

ELLIE: I have Mr. Martin's settlement and means of my own. He's given me presents, yes—

DIXON: Miss Bachman, your railway ticket to Chicago; did you buy it yourself? Or was it a sort of present.

ELLIE: I honestly don't remember. Yes, I believe I bought it.

DIXON: Thank you.

CAMERON: You're parrying these questions very well!

ELLIE: I didn't come here to tell lies, Mr. Cameron. I agreed to come, though Jack was against it, because I wanted to head off any notions you have of getting at him through me. I hope I've done that.

CAMERON: [*Putting away papers*] Well . . . it seems you have. And frankly I admire you for it. Not many women . . . **yes, one has to.** [*Sits on desk*] You're quite devoted to him, aren't you?

ELLIE: I love him, Mr. Cameron.

CAMERON: He's a splendid man in many ways, really. No one doubts that, you know.

ELLIE: I've never doubted it.

CAMERON: A magnificent fighter. I saw him when he—

ELLIE: That's not all he is. He's generous, he's kind, he's sensitive —why are you smiling?

CAMERON: I'm sorry. It's how you shy away from mentioning the physical attraction. I've embarrassed you, forgive me—

ELLIE: I'm not ashamed of wanting Jack for a lover. I wanted him that way.

CAMERON: Of course you did, and of course he'd want you!

ELLIE: Why, because I'm—

CAMERON: Oh no, I'm not implying—

ELLIE: He could have nearly any girl he wanted, black or—

CAMERON: Yes, I only meant that any man would be proud—

ELLIE: I'm proud that he wanted me! Is that clear!

CAMERON: Certainly—please don't be distressed, we needn't—

ELLIE: Who am I, anyway! I'm no beauty or anything or—

CAMERON: Now, now, you're being unfair to yourself—

ELLIE: Why can't they leave us alone, what's the difference— [SHE *weeps*]

CAMERON: Oh, there shouldn't be one, ideally . . . and besides, people are so blind about the physical side—a young woman, divorced, disappointed—

ELLIE: Please. If you've finished—

CAMERON: Here, here, now, you mustn't cry, Miss Bachman, it hasn't turned out all that badly, has it? You have this wonderful man now to love you—why should you cry—

ELLIE: I'll never give him up, I can't—

CAMERON: Of course not, but why be ashamed of it—

ELLIE: I'm not, I swear I'm not—

CAMERON: You seem to be, you know—

ELLIE: I'm not—

CAMERON: Well, if you say so—

ELLIE: I'm crazy for him, yes! I don't care! It's the truth! I didn't know what it was till I slept with him! **I'll say it to anyone, I don't care how it sounds**—

CAMERON: That he makes you happy that way—

ELLIE: Yes—

CAMERON: And you love him, you'd do anything for him—?

ELLIE: Yes—

CAMERON: And not be ashamed—?

ELLIE: No, never—

CAMERON: Even if it—

ELLIE: Yes—

CAMERON: Seemed unnatural or—

ELLIE: Yes—

CAMERON: And when you have, you only—

ELLIE: What—?

CAMERON: Tried to make him happy too, am I right? [SHE *freezes. Pause*] Now, Miss Bachman—

ELLIE: [*With Negro inflection*] You slimy two-bit no-dick mothergrabber. [*Pause.* SHE *rises*] If that's all.

CAMERON: Yes, I believe so—

ELLIE: Good night, then.

CAMERON: Yes. Thank you for coming in. [*See her out, shuts the door*]

SMITTY: That's that.

CAMERON: Nothing! Seduction, enticement, coercion, abduction, **not one good berry on the bush!**

DETECTIVE: Too bad, Al. Nearly did get him on five seventy-one, though.

CAMERON: Rah!

SMITTY: **Makes your hair stand up, don't it?**

DETECTIVE: Sure does. She's like a kid with a piece of chocolate cake.

CAMERON: All right! It's a rotten job . . . ! [*To* DIXON] So, what do you think? Any hope of a Federal slap here?

DIXON: I'm not sure yet, Al. I'll need to have a word with the fine-print boys. And I'd like to speak to Donnelly—OK?

[DETECTIVE *leaves*]

CAMERON: But what's there to move on? The railway ticket?

DIXON: Well, maybe not that, exactly. I doubt if we could prove he actually bought it—

CAMERON: And say you could—so?

DIXON: It's occurred to me, Al—seeing how we've just drawn a blank everywhere else—that we might just nail him with the Mann Act.

CAMERON: What? But that's for commercial ass, not this. She's not a pro!

DIXON: Yes, I know that, Al. But there is a law against "transporting a person across a state line for immoral purposes."

CAMERON: No riders, nothing about "intent to gain" or "against volition?"

DIXON: I don't believe so. [DONNELLY *enters with* DETECTIVE] Oh, good evening, Mr. Donnelly. We've spoken to your young lady—

DONNELLY: Yes? And—?

DIXON: You'll remember that our office agreed, at the outset, not to involve her in any proceedings unless it was absolutely necessary. Unfortunately, now, Mr. Donnelly, it may be, and we shall probably require certain evidence. We thought you should know this beforehand, so that you may return to Tacoma and prepare your principal.

DONNELLY: I understand, sir.

DIXON: Good. Thank you.

CAMERON: **I'll have that bastard watched day and night!**

DIXON: Don't bother, Al. We've done it right along.

[BLACKOUT. *Sound of crickets chirping.* LIGHTS UP *on*—]

SCENE SIX

A cabin, Beau Rivage, Wisconsin.

ELLIE *sitting up in bed, a sheet around her.* JACK, *wrapped in a towel, beside her. Kerosene lamp.*

JACK: Shucks, honey, it ain't cold, this the finest time for swimmin—

ELLIE: We have come to a parting of the ways.

JACK: Aw . . . big silvery moon, pine trees—

ELLIE: Snapping turtles, moccasins—

JACK: **Lawd, whut to do when romance done gone!**

ELLIE: Oh, Jack, I couldn't make it to the door.

JACK: That right? Sposin Ah carry you down there then an sorta—

ELLIE: No—

JACK: Ease you in—

ELLIE: No! No fair—Jack!—don't tickle me—

JACK: Mmm, she a reglah—

ELLIE: Please—no!—Ow!—Jack, that hurts—

JACK: Hey baby, Ah didn—

ELLIE: I know, this damn sunburn.

JACK: Aw, Ah'm sorry—here, lemme pat somethin on it—[*Takes up a champagne bottle, applies some to her back*] Yeah . . .

ELLIE: Oh, thanks . . . ooh . . . oh, yes, it's—Jack?

JACK: Don' that feel good now?

ELLIE: What are—?

JACK: Cool—?

ELLIE: Not champagne, Jack!

JACK: Well, thass alright, baby, you worth the bess.

ELLIE: All over me . . .

JACK: Get some lake on you, huh?

ELLIE: No, I—[*Peering at him*] Jack, turn around a little . . . more, this way . . . Are you feeling all right?

JACK: Ah ain't feelin no diffrunt.

ELLIE: Are you sure!

JACK: Yeah!

ELLIE: You ate all those clams, maybe you—[*Feels his head*]

JACK: Whut you doin that for, ain't got no fever—

ELLIE: Well, you look—a little peculiar, Jack.

JACK: Oh . . . ? Kinda ashy, you mean?

ELLIE: Yes, a sort of funny—

JACK: Honey, that ain't sick, that how Ah gets a sunburn. [ELLIE *tries not to laugh*] Now what you laughin at—

ELLIE: I thought—I mean—oh!—oh, Jack—

JACK: Huh?

ELLIE: I can't help it, I'm sorry—how you—oh—

JACK: Yeah—come on, that ain't nice—[HE *starts to laugh*] You thought what, honey?

ELLIE: I—I thought it just—bounces off, that's all—[BOTH *laugh uproariously*]

JACK: Bounces off—

ELLIE: Yes—

JACK: Well, Miss Medium Rare, meet Mr. Well Done! [*Gales of laughter*] **Yeah . . . lotta folks better off in de shade.**

ELLIE: Oh . . . do we have to leave tomorrow?

JACK: Shouldn't leave the place alone too long, honey.

ELLIE: I know. All right.

JACK: Case there's any fussin or—

ELLIE: Ssh, I know.

JACK: My, you do smell good though.

ELLIE: Yes?

JACK: Mm-hmm.

ELLIE: You're not tired of being alone with me, are you?

JACK: Hey. You kiddin?

ELLIE: Or tired of me asking questions like that?

JACK: Oh . . . Ah'm gettin tired of plenny . . . but, no, you ain't in there at all.

ELLIE: It's lovely to hear you say that . . .

JACK: Yeah? . . . Well, OK then . . . [*Props himself up*] How you doin for pillers?

ELLIE: Fine, darling . . . [JACK *hums a little*] Have a swim if you want to.

JACK: No, Ah'm cozy here . . . I cozy, an you rosy . . .

[ELLIE *chuckles.* JACK *turns the lamp down very low, kisses her, draws aways. Sings softly*]

> Good morning, blues
> Blues, how do you do,
> Blues say, Ah all right,
> Brother, how are you.
> Woke up dis mornin,
> Blues all round mah head,
> Look down to mah breakfas,
> Blues all in mah bread . . .
> For how long, how long,
> Ah saying, how long . . .

ELLIE: Lying in the sun I was, you know daydreaming . . . how maybe I'd stay there . . . and it would keep on burning me . . . day after day . . . oh, right through September . . . And I'd get darker and darker . . . I really get dark, you know . . . and then I'd dye my hair . . . and I'd change my name . . . and I'd come to you in Chicago . . . like somebody new . . . a colored woman, or a Creole maybe . . . and nobody but you would ever guess . . .

JACK: Won't work, honey.

ELLIE: Hm?

JACK: Evvybody know Ah gone off cullud women.

ELLIE: Oh, Jack, don't tease . . .

JACK: **Ah has, too, 'cep for mah momma.**

ELLIE: Maybe if I . . .

JACK: Ssh.

ELLIE: What will we do . . .

JACK: Ssh . . . try an sleep, honey . . . [*Turns the lamp down a little further*] Creepin up on me a little too—[*Darkness. Sings*] For how long, how long, Ah sayin . . . Always callin you honey, ain't Ah.

ELLIE: Mm.

JACK: Don' remember Ah call no woman by that. Call em by their name . . . or juss "baby," you know . . . Don' ever call you by you name, Ah guess . . .

ELLIE: Hardly ever . . .

JACK: Muss be some kinda ju-ju Ah fraid of in it . . . like if Ah says it you maybe disappear on me . . .

ELLIE: Oh . . . I don't care about my name . . .

JACK: Honey . . . hit just right . . .

ELLIE: Yes . . .

JACK: Honey fum the bees . . . [SHE *sighs*] Ever look at it real, real good awhile . . . ?

ELLIE: Can't remember . . .

JACK: Nothin like that stuff . . . Used to sit . . . Oh, long time ago, in Texas . . . we-all ud have a lil honey-treat sometime . . . whole yellah mugful . . . used to set there with it till evvybody come in . . . foolin with it, you know . . . liff up

a spoonful . . . tip it a lil bit . . . watch it start to curve up
. . . start in to sli-i-i-de ovuh . . . oh, takin its time . . . slow
. . . slow . . . honey underneath waitin . . . honey hanging
ovuh it . . . hundred years up there . . . then down . . . string-
ing down . . . down . . . tiny lil dent where it touch . . . an
then . . . [*Suddenly embracing her*] Oh, mah sweet, sweet
baby, Ah want to have it all—

ELLIE: Yes—

[*Sound of a door splintered open.* SIX MEN—*two with
lanterns—burst in. Confusion of light and bodies*]

MAN 1: On your feet, Jefferson—

ELLIE: Jack—

MAN 2: Get the window, Charlie—

MAN 3: Hey—

MAN 1: Look out—

MAN 4: Oh!

MAN 5: Grab him—

MAN 4: He's—chokin me—

MAN 1: Here, you—

[*Thud.* ELLIE *screams*]

MAN 1: Let go or I'll put a hole in you—

MAN 2: Where is he—

MAN 1: I said—

[*Thud*]

ELLIE: Stop it—

MAN 4: Jesus—

MAN 6: Light that goddamn lamp—

ELLIE: Please—

MAN 5: Sit there, lady—

MAN 1: We're the law.

[*Kerosene lamp on.* ELLIE *huddled at the head of the bed,*
JACK *crouching in a corner, grasping a chunk of firewood,
the injured* MAN *nursing his neck, the* OTHERS *facing* JACK,
*immobile—*DIXON *is among them,* ALL *breathing heavily.*
DIXON *moves forward*]

DIXON: I'm a federal marshal, Jefferson. [*Shows his badge*] Put
that down, please. [*Pause*] Come on. We don't want to
make this any worse. [*Pause.* JACK *drops wood*] At ten A.M.
this morning you drove Miss Eleanor Bachman across the
Illinois-Wisconsin state line. Having done so, you proceeded
to have relations with her. Under the Mann Act this makes
you liable and I'm therefore placing you under arrest.

ELLIE: No . . . no . . .

DIXON: Get dressed, please, Miss Bachman. We'll take you into
town.

ELLIE: Jack—

JACK: Don't worry—get dress—[*Handing her her clothes*]

MAN 2: Here.

DIXON: Hold a blanket up or something.

ELLIE: Jack . . .

JACK: Don't you fret now . . . [MAN 2 *and* MAN 3 *screen her
with a blanket. To* DIXON] Thanks, mistah.

DIXON: Sure.

JACK: [*Pulling on a sweater*] How much this carry?

DIXON: One to three.

JACK: She clear?

DIXON: Just you.

JACK: Yeah. Thanks.

MAN 1: [*Showing handcuffs*] We need these, Jim?

DIXON: No. Find him his pants and let's get out of here.

[BLACKOUT. *Soft, woeful singing in the darkness, which
continues through the following. A bizarre-looking colored
man comes forward:* SCIPIO. HE *wears a shabby purple cloak*

*fastened with a gold clasp over a shabby dark suit, a bowler
hat with a long plume hanging from it, fawn shoes, and
several large totemic-looking rings. His manner is feverish]*

SCIPIO: [*Speaking over his shoulder into the darkness*] Start
it up, thassit, brothers, singing and moanin! White man juss
drag him another away here so all you black flies, you light
down together an hum pretty please to white man's Jesus—Yes,
Lawd! [*Spits*] Waste a mah times . . . **An Ah don' care to
talk to you neither! But Ah sees two-three out there de same
blood is me, so Ah says good-evenin to em, then Ah askin em
this: How much white you up to? How much you done took
on? How much white you pinin for? How white you wanna be?
Oh, mebbe you done school youself away fum White Jesus—
but how long you evah turn you heart away frum WHITE!
How you lookin, how you movin, how you wishin an figgering—
how white you wanna be, that whut Ah askin! How white you
gaunta get—you tell me! You watchin that boy? Nothin white-y
bout him, huh? But whut he hustle after? White man's sportin
prize! Whut he gotta itch for? White man's poontang! Whut his
rich livin like? White man's nigger! Thinks he walkin and talkin
like a natchul man, don' know how he's swimmin half-drownded
in the whitewash, like they is, like you is, nevah done diffrunt,
gulpin it in evvy day, pickled in it, right at home dere—tell me
that ain't how we living! Tell me how it better you chokin on
dat whitewash then wearin a iron colluh roun you neck! Oh,
yeah, you sayin, but whut kin we do, Whut kin us or dat boy or
dem gospellers do, we passin our days in de white man's world
—well, make you own, brothers! Don' try an join em an don'
try an beat em, leave em all at once, all together, pack up! Col-
leck you wages, grab whutevah here gonna come in handy an
sluff off de ress! Time to get it goin! Time again to make us a
big new wise proud dark man's world—again! Ah says again!
Ah tellin what we had once! Nevah mine that singing—learn,
brothers, learn! Ee-gyp!! Tambuctoo!! Ethiopya!! Red 'n goldin
cities older den Jeruslem, temples an prayin to sperrits whut
stick wid us, black men carvin ivory, workin up laws, chartin
em maps for de moon an de sun, refine' cultured cullud people
hansome as statues dere when Europe an all was juss woods
fulla hairy cannibals—dat laughin don' harm us none! Five hun-**

drid million of us not all together, not matchin up to em, dat what harmin us! Dream bout it, brothers—Five hundrid million on dey own part of de earth, an not a one dere evah askin another, How much white you up to, how white you wanna be . . .

[*Glaring,* HE *makes his exit as* LIGHTS COME UP *on—*]

SCENE SEVEN

MRS. JEFFERSON's *house, Chicago.*

Surrounding MRS. JEFFERSON *in her armchair are the* PASTOR *and seven or eight* BROTHERS *and* SISTERS, *who continue singing softly, as the* PASTOR *speaks. At one side is* CLARA, *now dressed rather plainly.* MRS. JEFFERSON *wears a night-dress, with a shawl over her shoulders and another covering her legs.*

PASTOR: Lawd, we prayin longside this sick unhappy mother here, she lookin to You, Lawd, she know her boy been sinful, an she sorry about that, but she do love him, Lawd, you give him another chance she nevah ask you for anythin! She living by You Book all her days, Lawd, you seen it! We prayin you touch them judges' eyes with mercy. Let em chastise him today, Lawd, let em fine him so steep he leff withouta dime, let em scare him so hard he nevah forgit it, but, Lawd, don' let em lock this woman's boy away.

[*End singing*]

BROTHERS: Amen.

MRS. JEFFERSON: An if they does, Oh please, Lawd, let it juss be for a little.

BROTHERS: Amen.

PASTOR: We callin with you, sister.

MRS. JEFFERSON: Ah thank ya, Pastor. Wish Ah could offuh ya some lil hospitality but honess—

PASTOR: Don' fret now, sister.

MRS. JEFFERSON: Ah mean, Ah kin hardly—

SISTER 1: Nevah you mine, Tiny.

CLARA: Ah'll put on a potta fresh cawfee—[*Starts to go*]

MRS. JEFFERSON: See if Tick or somebody comin down the street firss.

[CLARA *goes to the window*]

SISTER 2: Early yet, sister.

CLARA: Juss a buncha fellers there gawnta play baseball.

MRS. JEFFERSON: [*Sighs*] Awright, Clara. Thankya.

PASTOR: [*As* CLARA *goes to kitchen*] Got a guardjin angel with that gal in you house.

BROTHER 1: Who deserve one better!

[BROTHERS *approve*]

MRS. JEFFERSON: Should've brung word by this. Caint've took this long.

PASTOR: We in de Lawd's hans, sister.

BROTHERS: Amen.

SISTER 1: You sit easy . . .

MRS. JEFFERSON: Fum when he was chile Ah knowed this day comin. Looka that, Momma, why cain't Ah, Momma, lemme lone, Momma. Nevah stop. Fidgety feet an, oh, them great big eyes, roamin an reachin, all ovuh. Tried to learn him like you gotta learn a cullud boy, Dass'nt, dass'nt, dass'nt, that ain't for you! Roll right off him. Tried to learn it to him meaner—**Mo chile you got, the meaner you go to if you lovin you chile. That plain cullud sense.** Hit him with my han, he say, So what. Hit him with my shoe, he look up an smile. Took a razor-strop to him, that make him squint but then he do a funny dance an ask me fo a nickel. Ah prayed to de Lawd put mo strenf in my arm, the worse Ah was whippin the bigger he growed, leven years old an still woulden hear nothin.

Hit him with a stick till Ah coulden hit no mo, he pull it away fum me, an bust it in two, and then he run off—

PASTOR: Sister—

MRS. JEFFERSON: Lawd fogive me treatin him so mean! Lawd fogive me not beatin on him young enough or hurtin him bad enough to learn him after, cause Ah seen this day comin—

[*Knock downstairs*]

SISTER 1: Ah let em in, Tiny. [*Goes*]

PASTOR: We hopin with you, sister. Hole onter my han now.

MRS. JEFFERSON: No, thass awright.

SISTER 1: [*Offstage*] But you all muss ain't got de right house—

RUDY: [*Offstage*] Two thirty-one?

TEAMMATE: [*Offstage*] Miz Jefferson's house, ain't it?

SISTER 1: [*Closer*] Yeah, but—hang on, whole lotta you cain't fit here—

RUDY: OK, set on de stairway, de ress of you—[SISTER 1 *backs into the room, followed by three large* YOUNG NEGROES *wearing blue satin jackets and matching baseball caps.* THEY *carry valises from which bats and other gear protrude. Their leader, and the largest,* RUDY, *takes off his cap and the* OTHERS *follow suit.* CLARA *re-enters from the kitchen*] Aftuhnoon, evvybody.

MRS. JEFFERSON: You all comin fum de courthouse?

RUDY: No ma'am. Us juss get a message—uh—askin we pay a call here. We de Blue Jays.

MRS. JEFFERSON: You de which?

RUDY: De-troit Blue Jays. You know, de cullud baseball club? **Pulvrise de Afro Giants here Sadday?**

BROTHER 2: Oh, yeah, my nephew tend dat game.

RUDY: My name Rudy Sims, ma'am.

MRS. JEFFERSON: Pleased to meet you, Mistah Sims—

CLARA: Who say you sposeta call in here?

RUDY: Well, we sorta frens with Jack—

CLARA: This here no celebratin party, you know!

MRS. JEFFERSON: Hush, Clara, if they frens with Jack—

CLARA: Why somebody sen us a baseball team here!

RUDY: Mebbe we bess wait outside in de hall, ma'am—

MRS. JEFFERSON: Nothin of the kine! Clara—

CLARA: Ah ain't never seed Jack wid no baseball frens!

[TICK *enters*]

RUDY: Well, Ah nevuh seed him wid you, so we even.

TICK: Don' let her rile you, Rudy. Thanks for comin.

RUDY: Any time, man.

TICK: Got here fass as I could, Miz Jeffson.

MRS. JEFFERSON: Well. You here . . . Come on.

TICK: It ain't good, Miz Jeffson.

SISTER 1: Lawd have mercy.

MRS. JEFFERSON: Come on. Finish up.

TICK: **Twenty-thousand-dollar fine and three years in Joliet.**

SISTER 2: Jesus above.

BROTHER 1: Three years.

CLARA: Why cain't all dem Jew lawyers do nothin! Why cain't—

TICK: Dey got a week ta try appealin on it—

BROTHER 1: Three years.

MRS. JEFFERSON: **Ah die they lock him up!**

SISTER 2: Don' take on, sister—

PASTOR: Bring me them smellin salts—

SISTER 1: Tiny—

MRS. JEFFERSON: No, Ah don' want nothin—

TICK: He do have de week out on bail, Miz Jeffson—dey set it kina heavy but we figgered dey might, an we gonna make it.

MRS. JEFFERSON: A week. Drive him crazy!

TICK: Well, we gotta try an see it don't.

CLARA: That snaky lil wax-face bitch! Where she at now! Where she bloodsuckin now! Oh, Ah'll smoke her out, an, man—

PASTOR: Sister—

CLARA: **What Ah gonna do be worth a hunnerd three yearses!**

MRS. JEFFERSON: Ain't her fault, Clara.

CLARA: She knowd this end-up comin, ain a deaf dumb bline pinhead living din know it, but, Oh, daddy, she joyin hersel so, it so good when it goin! Leave it alone? Oh, but, daddy, Ah loves you!

MRS. JEFFERSON: Could be she do love him, Clara.

CLARA: She WHAT!

MRS. JEFFERSON: **He brung her down once. She din seem too bad.**

TICK: Nice an quiet too.

CLARA: Ah ain't talkin to you! Could be she love him! Why she scat off wid her man in trouble, why she—

PASTOR: Bess unwine dat serpint from your heart, sister—

CLARA: **Love him, my black ass!**

PASTOR: Sister!

MRS. JEFFERSON: [As CLARA returns to kitchen] Poor gal been frettin so—

[JACK and GOLDIE enter]

PASTOR: Praise de Lawd an welcome.

JACK: Pastor . . . evvybody . . . good boy, Rudy.

RUDY: Ready fo ya, Jack.

JACK: Fine, no rush . . . hiya, Momma Tiny.

MRS. JEFFERSON: They din hurt you, Jack? You git nuff to eat?

JACK: Sure, Momma.

GOLDIE: **I should feel as good as he does.**

JACK: Whut about you, Momma?

MRS. JEFFERSON: Oh . . .

JACK: Still kina poorly?

MRS. JEFFERSON: It drain me out some, Ah guess.

JACK: Oh, Momma.

BROTHER 2 : Hard luck, Jack.

MRS. JEFFERSON: We been prayin an prayin here, son.

JACK: Well . . . de Lawd hear anyone he gonna hear you.

MRS. JEFFERSON: Look like he ain't this time—but He gonna put me on my feet, Ah kin feel it! An Ah gonna help Him, gonna ress up an eat good, an Ah comin down there soon, Jack—

JACK: Momma—

MRS. JEFFERSON: Often as they 'low ya to, you wait an see, bring a big ole picnic basket on my arm—

JACK: No, Momma, listen—

CLARA: [*Flinging herself upon him*] Oh, baby, baby, Ah cain't let em clap you in there—

JACK: **What she doin here!**

GOLDIE: That's all we need.

JACK: Git offa me, you! Momma, whut de hell—

MRS. JEFFERSON: Clara come roun when she hear Ah was ailin—

CLARA: Ah been doin fo you momma, Jack—

MRS. JEFFERSON: She tryna menn her ways—

TICK: [*Stealing a look out of window*] Jack.

[JACK *looks at him.* HE *nods. Pause*]

JACK: [*To* CLARA] Ah count ten fo you to beat it. One—

CLARA: No!

MRS. JEFFERSON: She been my helpmeet, Jack!

JACK: Sister fine ya a housekeeper!

CLARA: Ah keepin house, baby!

JACK: Ah up to five, girl—

TICK: [*Tense. At the window*] Let her be for now, Jack. She in here she cain't spoil it, screamin in the street or somethin.

GOLDIE: [*Mopping his face*] That's all we need.

RUDY: Soun like sense, Jack.

MRS. JEFFERSON: Spoil what? Mistah, what these boys up to?

BROTHER 1: Yeah, what goin on here?

CLARA: [To TICK at window] Whuffo you playin peekaboo wid dat dere automo-bile? [HE shoos her away]

PASTOR: [To JACK] You ain't about to make things worse, son, are you?

MRS. JEFFERSON: Jack—

JACK: Awright. I gotta truss all you folks now—

PASTOR: Son, however rough it 'pears today—

TICK: Oughta stan by the winder now, Jack. They lookin.

MRS. JEFFERSON: Who? Who lookin?

JACK: 'Tectives in that car, Momma.

MRS. JEFFERSON: Jack—

JACK: Momma, listen—

MRS. JEFFERSON: What they waitin out there for, Mistah Goldie?

GOLDIE: Well, even though Jack is out on bond, you see—

JACK: They worried Ah gonna try an jump mah bail, Momma.

GOLDIE: **They're worried. I'm in hock up to here with this.**

MRS. JEFFERSON: Jack . . . you juss got let out.

JACK: Bess time, Momma. They don' know Ah's ready.

MRS. JEFFERSON: They follerin you, but!

JACK: Thinks they is.

MRS. JEFFERSON: Jack, what if they catches you—

JACK: Won't never get near me! Now, firss thing what Ah do is take my coat off—[Does so, revealing a raspberry-colored shirt] then I stan here sorta talkin—"Why heaven sake, no foolin!"—now let em see mah face—[Looks out] "Oh, my, it look like rain . . ."—an Ah knows they seen my shirt—**Mm-mm! Don't you wish you had one!** Well, Ah goes on talkin, right? Now over there is Rudy—[RUDY looks at his watch] Uh-oh, he checkin his turnip again! They hasta hop on the train soon, you know, Blue Jays playin Montreal nex, ain't you, Rude, gainst de Canada Blacks?

RUDY: Thass right, Jack.

JACK: Less go, fellah—[RUDY *starts peeling off jacket and jersey*] He look mighty fine, ole Rude here, don' he! Not pretty is me, but he near is big an just a half shade blacker an—**Oh, mercy, he got dat shirt on too!** [RUDY *does*]

SISTER 1: Lawd proteck us!

JACK: [*Looks out*] "Yeah, it clearin up now—"

GOLDIE: Jack, listen, we should maybe talk it over more—

MRS. JEFFERSON: [*To* GOLDIE] What you trick him inter!

GOLDIE: It's his idea, believe me—

JACK: It be awright, Momma! Rudy spen de aftuhnoon by the winder an Ah go rollin cross de border with de Jays!

BROTHER 2: They fine you out, Jack—

JACK: Naw! I put on Rudy's cap an his jacket? Stick in the middle of his boys? Who all fine me! An who lookin? **You hear that sayin how all niggers look alike!** Ain't that so, team?

PASTOR: But, son, you forgittin we frens with that Canada! I mean, we's hardly a diffrunt place—

TICK: Fore they cotton to it, man, we on dat ole boat to Englin. Right?

GOLDIE: Right, right.

JACK: It all fixed, Momma!

MRS. JEFFERSON: All what fixed ain't gotta juss happen—

PASTOR: Serious offense to go floutin de law, Jack! I know they done you real hard but, son, it gonna hang ovuh you long as—

JACK: Look! What hang gonna hang but Ah ain't hangin with it! Ah done my kickin roun this country, Ah serve my one nights an my thirty days too once, an Ah ain't gonna rot like no log no three years! Or be comin out broke as Ah is now either! Ah in the prime of mah life! Ah wanna live like Ah got to, wanna make me some money again, wanna fight! **Ah got my turn to be Champeen of the World an Ah takin my turn! Ah stayin whut Ah am, wherever Ah has to do it! The world ain't curled up into no forty-eight states here!**

MRS. JEFFERSON: Praise de Lawd for lightin a way fo my boy! Fogive me Ah say Ah didden love you, Jesus!

JACK: [*Moving to her*] Thassit, Momma—

MRS. JEFFERSON: [*To* BROTHERS *and* PASTOR] Well?

BROTHERS & PASTOR: [*Worried*] Amen . . .

GOLDIE: **She could put in a word for me too, here.**

RUDY: [*Taking his place at the window*] Better move it, man.

JACK: Right. (*Pulls on* RUDY's *jersey*]

GOLDIE: Oh, boy.

JACK: You folks stay here till we gone, OK? Then start runnin in an out like, keep em busy watchin—

CLARA: Oh, take me with you, honey—

JACK: [*Pulls on a jacket*] Don't you cross me now—

CLARA: Ah go meet you, baby! Any place!

JACK: You know the score, girl.

CLARA: Please!

JACK: [*Buttoning up*] Fit awright?

GOLDIE: Yeah, beautiful.

CLARA: She comin to ya, ain't she! That where she at!

JACK: Hope you gettin to that game on time, Rudy—

CLARA: You ain't meetin that bitch! I turn you in firss—[*Runs at the door*]

TICK: Hole her—

CLARA: [*Shaking loose from him*] JACK GONNA—[*Struggles with* SISTERS *at the door*]

SISTER 1: Stop her mouf up—

CLARA: HE RUNNIN FFFF—[*Stopping her mouth,* THEY *drag her from the door, kicking*]

GOLDIE: Oh, boy—

BROTHER 1: Make some noise!

SISTER 2: Sit on her—

PASTOR: "Look ovuh, Beulah—"

BROTHER 2: Which—?

PASTOR: Ready—

MRS. JEFFERSON: No "Beulah" now, sen up a glad one—

SISTER 1: Quick, she bitin me—

MRS. JEFFERSON: Sing, chillun—

ALL: [*But* CLARA, *on whom the three largest* SISTERS *are sitting*]
> Just to talk to Jesus
> Oh, what a joy de-vine
> Ah kin feel de lectric
> Movin on de line,
> All wired up by God de Father
> For his lovin own,
> Put a call to Jesus
> On the Royal Telephone—

JACK: [*Over the singing*] Here, where that Jew's-harp—[*Finds it*] Plung on it, Rudy, it cover you face up—[*Tosses it to him.* RUDY *plays.* JACK *moves among them*] Good luck—thank you —thank you—see you soon—you too—don't worry—Thank you, Momma Tiny—Get well, darlin, try, please try—Say you come an see me—good-bye, my momma, good-bye, my sweetheart—

[MRS. JEFFERSON *nods and sings right on, clapping to the beat, and with* GOLDIE *mopping his face,* CLARA *kicking and crying,* RUDY *twanging and* ALL THE REST *in full chorus,* JACK *puts on his cap and disappears with the* JAYS]

ALL:
> Angel operators
> Waitin for you call,
> Central up in heaven,
> Take no time at all,
> Ring, and God will answer
> In his happy tone,
> Put a call to Jesus
> On the Royal Telephone.

CURTAIN

ACT 2

SCENE ONE

A *chamber in the Home Office, London.*

*Some dozen chairs facing a large desk are arranged for the
hearing about to take place. As the scene begins,* SIX MEN
and ONE WOMAN, *all middle-aged and soberly dressed, are
seating themselves. From a door opposite,* EUBANKS, *assistant to the Undersecretary, enters chatting with* TREACHER,
JACK's *solicitor. Enter* JACK, ELLIE, GOLDIE, TICK.

TREACHER: Ah, good morning—

EUBANKS: I'll go and fetch Sir William. [*Goes*]

JACK: Mornin, evvybody . . . Mornin, Miz Kimball . . . How you
today, Mac . . . ? [THEY *stare straight ahead*] **Muss be de Wax
Museum took a branch here.**

TREACHER: Over there, please, Jack.

GOLDIE: And let Mr. Treacher do the talking, understand?

TREACHER: Yes, thank you.

JACK: [*To* ELLIE] We straighten dis out, hon.

ELLIE: Well, I hope so.

JACK: Feelin kina edgy, huh.

ELLIE: [*Takes his hand*] No.

TICK: **Ah does.**

EUBANKS: [*Entering*] Sir William Griswold.

JACK: [*To* ELLIE] Hey, you breakin mah han!

> [SIR WILLIAM *enters.* GOLDIE, TICK, *and the* WOMAN *stand up*]

SIR WILLIAM: Good morning—no, no need to rise, thank you. [*Sits at desk*] Yes . . . Now, then. Allegations have been made to us concerning the possible undesirability of an alien person's continued visit here. **We have of course our own book of rules on the subject, and normally—**

COATES: With due respect, Sir William, I'm amazed that you find this necessary.

SIR WILLIAM: Mr.—?

COATES: Coates.

SIR WILLIAM: [*To* EUBANKS] Representing?

EUBANKS: British Vigilance Board.

COATES: Can you really be debating this? A convicted criminal, a fugitive from justice—

TREACHER: My client's conviction was known to the authorities. He was admitted at their discretion.

SIR WILLIAM: That is true, Mr. Coates.

COATES: And our discreet authorities are helpless to correct their initial error, is that what you imply, sir?

SIR WILLIAM: I implied nothing, I'm sure.

COATES: Your official silence indeed implies something! Like official license for breaches of the peace, for moral deficiency flaunted at the public—

JACK: Now wait—Ah ain't flung no fish at no public!

COATES: I beg your—

TICK: Jack, you hush up—

SIR WILLIAM: Gentlemen, please—

MRS. KIMBALL: [*The* WOMAN] I'll tell them what you did do, you great flash nig-nog!

EUBANKS: Madam, really—

GOLDIE: Don't you talk like that, lady—

COATES: Mrs. Kimball here—

MRS. KIMBALL: [*To* COATES] Do I speak my piece now—?

EUBANKS: Mr. Coates has the—

COATES: No, go on, Mrs. Kimball.

MRS. KIMBALL: I rented him my luxury maisonette, your honor, Ten Portman Square, and not many would rent to them, believe you me, a black and white job to boot, but I thought they at least was married, which they wasn't, and I thought she being white they'd be clean, which they wasn't, and I thought maybe them being lovebirds like they are they'd settle down early nights—nothing of the kind! Parties, champagne, nigger piano playing—mind you, I like a bit of music, but I never, all night, screaming up the stairwell. Oh, yes, I'd see them through the door when I went to shut em up, doing their dirty dances in there—**Turkey Trot and all the rest of them colored steps!**

COATES: The damage to Mrs. Kimball's flat, Sir William, was appraised at nearly four hundred pounds.

MRS. KIMBALL: Yes, that's right! Vases, chippendale, can't replace it neither—**and rubbish all over too, the filthy ape!** Undesirable!

TREACHER: The amount has been paid in full, Sir William.

SIR WILLIAM: Who is next, Mr. Coates?

COATES: Inspector Wainwright.

EUBANKS: Metropolitan Police.

WAINWRIGHT: [*Reading from notebook*] November ninth. Charged with using obscene language on Coventry Street. Fine, two pounds. November fifteenth. Charged with causing a crowd to collect. Fine, fifty shillings. Fined a further five pounds for contempt of court.

SIR WILLIAM: [*To* JACK] Why the fine for contempt, may I ask.

JACK: Well, de judge he yell, Ah fine you fifty shillins! So Ah says, Look, dat crowd's still collectin so maybe you better take a hundred off me.

WAINWRIGHT: November twenty-fifth—

SIR WILLIAM: [*To* COATES] If the police offenses are all of this nature—

COATES: You may skip to January third, Wainwright.

WAINWRIGHT: January third. Charged with assault on Mr. M. Bratby.

TREACHER: The charge has been dropped, Sir William.

COATES: Sir, when a man trained in the use of his fists—

JACK: No, Ah juss shoved him—[*To* BRATBY] Whut you tell this man, Mac?

SIR WILLIAM: You are—?

BRATBY: M. Bratby.

EUBANKS: Olympia Sporting Club.

BRATBY: Jefferson came to us proposing that we match him. We had been unwilling to associate ourselves with him—we expressed this position—he became unruly—

COATES: Attacked you, you mean!

TREACHER: The affair has been settled, Mr. Jefferson's apology—

COATES: Yes, all the affairs are settled, the popular press delightedly reports them, and nightly in the music halls they are dealt with as a joke! Is any of this desirable? This, when disruption is the order of the day, with the ground we stand on undermined by socialists, atheists, anarchists, with anarchy not merely a word but a man with a bomb in a public building—

SIR WILLIAM: Mr. Coates—

COATES: And you're amused, sir, when this lady refers to these dances coming into vogue since this man's arrival here, but read your Plato, Sir William, read your Plato—

SIR WILLIAM: I say—

COATES: "New modes of music herald upheavals of state," sir—

SIR WILLIAM: Now really, Mr. Coates, I have seen the Turkey Trot—

COATES: Let me remind you of the waltz, Sir William—

SIR WILLIAM: The waltz?

COATES: The first waltz, sir—

SIR WILLIAM : Are you asking me to dance—?

TREACHER : Sir William, may I venture—

JACK : No, Ah kin talk.

SIR WILLIAM : Yes, please. Go ahead.

JACK : Ah come over as a prizefighter, sir. Figgered Ah could fight
Billy Wells here or Jeannette, an make me mah livin here
the way Ah knows how. But we coulden git no decent match
fix up, so Ah was juss gittin fat, and kickin up and fussin
people. Now, Ah guess Ah shouldn've, cause whut Ah am, you
know, cullud Ah mean, some folks here think is a freak anyway,
but it took me some time gittin use to bein here, an Ah'm
sorry bout all these stories they brung in, an whut Ah wanna
say is, we like it here fine now, and now Lord Londsale done
set me up a match, Ah'll git trainin and fightin an we won't
have no mo rumpus.

SIR WILLIAM : Well, Mr. Coates, as I see this at the moment,
the American legalities are none of our concern, the breaches
of the peace you've cited are trivial, the man's moral character
deficient perhaps, by Queen Victoria's standards—**but she of
course is gone now**—and as to the palaver in the press and music halls these are liberties we simply have to bear—think of
them as part of the White Man's Burden. So unless Mr. Jefferson commits a crime of some sort—which I hope none of you
will tempt him to further—I do not see— You have something
to add?

COATES : I should like to correct Mr. Jefferson's assumption that he
does indeed have a match on, Sir William.

JACK : Whut you talkin bout, Ah sign up wid him dere—[*Points
to* BRATBY] **fightin Albert Lynch on March de eighteenth—**

SIR WILLIAM : Is this relevant, Mr. Coates—

COATES : Oh, I think so. Bratby?

BRATBY : Two weeks ago, at Lord Londsdale's persuasion, we
proposed this match, and Jefferson accepted. It now appears,
however, that the London County Council refuses to issue a
license for this fight. And enquiries indicate this difficulty elsewhere.

TREACHER : Refused the license on what grounds?

COATES: Mr. Farlow?

FARLOW: I should say that Mr. Coates has already expressed the Council's position.

JACK: Goldie, how the hell—

TICK: Sit easy there, baby—

COATES: This man entered England with the stated purpose of pursuing his career as a pugilist. Now, what, sir, are the grounds for his remaining in England if this career of his does simply not exist here!

[JACK *stands,* ELLIE *holds him by the hand*]

SIR WILLIAM: Please sit down, sir. [*To the others*] I shall make no comment on the principles or motives operating among you. I shall only inform you that an alien is free to change his means of livelihood, **he may take up any—**

JACK: OK. Les go.

TICK: De guy still—

JACK: Up!

[ELLIE *gets up and* TICK *gets up*]

SIR WILLIAM: [*To* JACK] It is understood, I hope, that—

JACK: Come on, Goldie—[*To* SIR WILLIAM] Ah thank you fo you time, sir, an stickin up fo me—

SIR WILLIAM: I'm really very sorry—

JACK: You scuse us now, please—[*To* TREACHER] See you, Mr. Treacher—

ELLIE: Jack—

COATES: [*To* TREACHER] Your client will be leaving the country, I take it.

JACK: Yeah, man, you take it. It's all yours.

[BLACKOUT. *Boat whistle, train whistle, another boat whistle, crowd, band playing.* LIGHTS UP *on—*]

SCENE TWO

A customs shed, Le Havre.

At one side, with the BAND, *a welcoming* CROWD: OFFICIALS, PRESS, *etc., some waving small tricolors. At the other side* TWO UNIFORMED INSPECTORS, *beyond them a sign:* DOUANE. *Some* PORTERS *hurry past them, wheeling trunks, and a cheer goes up behind them. Followed by his* ENTOURAGE, *greeting the* CROWD *with hands clasped triumphantly over his head, appears* KLOSSOWSKI, *a Polish heavyweight. The* PHOTOGRAPHERS' *flares commence, and continue through the scene. The* BAND *stops playing as* KLOSSOWSKI *meets the* OFFICIALS *and* PRESS, *shaking hands and embracing all around.*

OFFICIAL: Bienvenue encore à la France, Monsieur Klossowski!

CROWD: Bravo, Klossowski! Bienvenue! Bonne arrivée!

KLOSSOWSKI: Merci, merci, mes amis, mille mercis—

PRESSMAN 1: Alors, vous êtes prêt pour votre grand combat avec le noir Jefferson?

KLOSSOWSKI: Oho, monsieur—je suis absolument—

PRESSMAN 1: Confiant?

KLOSSOWSKI: C'est ça! **Con-fi-dent! Je m'excuse que mon français est terrible—**

CROWD: Mais non, mais non!

PRESSMAN 3: Mais vous n'êtes pas hésitant à faire la boxe avec le champion du monde? Un petit peu?

KLOSSOWSKI: Hésitant! Ha, ha, ha!

CROWD: Bravo, Klossowski!

KLOSSOWSKI: Éncoutez—Je boxai à Buenos Aires avec Paco Flores! Zut! Zut! Zut! Trois rounds, je gagne! Je boxai à Rio Pereira! Zut! Frappe! Deux rounds, je gagne! Je boxai en Afrique avec un noir gigantesque là—Zut! Boom! **Pas de con-**

teste, messieurs! Et cette Jefferson, qui c'est, qui c'est? Oh, champion du monde, oui, lalala—mais il n'a pas boxé pour longtemps! [*Miming it*] Il boit le whiskey, il fumes les cigares, il est gros, ill êtes lourde, il vit comme un—un—

PRESSMAN 1: Cochon? [*Laughter*]

KLOSSOWSKI: C'est ça! [*Laughter*] Non, messieurs, c'est pas la vie du boxeur! [*Mimes it all*] Moi, je cours chaque jour trente kilomètres, même à la bateau—oui! Je saute à la corde: cent fois! Je boxe l'ombre: une heure! Petit sac, vingt minutes! Des gymnastiques, quarante minutes, deux fois, matin et soir, et bain chaud! Douche froid! Forte massage après midi, mange bien, dix heures sommeil—[*Laughter*] Vous pensez que j'éxagère? Attendez le combat Jefferson—[*Acts it out*] et zut! Zut! Gauche à l'estomac! Droite à la tête! Gauche encore! Zut! Frappe! Boom! Dix! Voilà—**vous verrez!**

[*Cheering,* THEY *hoist him on their shoulders, the* BAND *strikes up, and he is borne off as* LIGHTS FADE: *new* CROWD *sound gradually replacing cheering, an arena* CROWD, *distant.* LIGHTS UP *on—*]

SCENE THREE

Jack's dressing room at the Vel d'Hiver arena, Paris.

JACK *is sitting on table.* TICK *taping his hands.* ELLIE. A *French* HANDLER *busy with towels, sponge, salts, etc.*

TICK: Keep breathin deep, champ, nice an slow now.

JACK: Ah knows howta breathe.

TICK: Gonna finish off dat Polack like a chicken dinner!

JACK: Hurry it up, huh.

TICK: Ain even gonna muss you wool up on him!

JACK: Don' talk like that fronna her.

ELLIE: Jack, don't be silly—

JACK: An when you start callin me "champ" anyway?

TICK: Hey, come on. See if that too tight now.

[GOLDIE *enters*]

ELLIE: Full house?

GOLDIE: Girlie, they're hangin from the rafters.

JACK: Water bottle, Tick. Wanna rinse.

GOLDIE: You OK?

JACK: Why you keep askin me?

GOLDIE: So what, so I'm askin!

JACK: You worried bout somethin? What you worrying bout!

TICK: **Man, dat Polack sure in for it tonight.**

GOLDIE: Tick, for chrissake—

TICK: [*To* HANDLER] Uh—hey, Jim, where that O bottle gone to?

HANDLER: Comment?

TICK: The O. You know, O?

HANDLER: Le—Ah—

TICK: No, the O—

HANDLER: La bouteille!

TICK: Mistah who?

JACK: Never mine—

HANDLER: Non?

TICK: Yeah, the O!

HANDLER: De l'eau! [*Produces it*]

TICK: Attaboy! **See? Juss be patient with em.**

[*Gives it to* JACK, *who gargles and spits*]

JACK: Bad tase in there, thassall.

GOLDIE: [*To* TICK] Coupla more minutes.

TICK: [*To* JACK] Put em up, baby, we better warm up some. Huh? OK?

JACK: Ah warm up inside there with the man.

TICK: Aw, be good now! Ah ain't gonna get you winded—

ELLIE: Tick!

JACK: You don' haveta tell me what wind Ah ain't got.

TICK: No, man, Ah mean—

JACK: Ah know what shape is an when Ah ain in it. Ah know when gettin in it's a waste a my good time too! **Ah don' gotta train to take no fifth-rate geechee—**

GOLDIE: Jack, who says different—

JACK: Thass who Ah fightin here, ain it!

GOLDIE: It's the best they got around here, Jack—

JACK: Hit him one an shovel up the money, right? Jump in with the big gole belt, right?

TICK: [Sings]

> Niggers is evil
> White folks too.
> So glad Ah'm a Chinaman,
> Don' know whut to do.

[PROMOTER enters]

PROMOTER: If you please, messieurs.

ELLIE: I'll go in to my seat now.

JACK: Honey—

ELLIE: [Kisses him] Good luck, darlin—

JACK: Do me a favor. Stay here.

ELLIE: Oh, Jack.

JACK: Nothin in there you wanna see.

PROMOTER: Come along, please, messieurs—[To HANDLER] vite, vite—[To JACK] But, oh, Monsieur Jefferson, the smile, the famous smile—You will not deny to our public the smile!

JACK: No, Ah got it on me.

PROMOTER: Ha, ha, very good.

TICK: **We won't be too long.**

[THEY leave. ELLIE sits. A few seconds go by and the CROWD roar increases in volume. ELLIE stands, wanders

*aimlessly, spies a newspaper, tries to read it, puts it down.
Over the* CROWD NOISES *the* ANNOUNCER'S VOICE *is heard,
incoherent.* ELLIE *folds a towel, a jersey, sits again.* SMITTY
enters]

SMITTY: Hi there, Miss Bachman.

ELLIE: Hello—

SMITTY: Smith, *Evening Mirror.* Smitty?

ELLIE: Oh, yes.

SMITTY: Mind if I—

ELLIE: Aren't you here for the fight?

SMITTY: Well, the boys'll dope me in. He's at it again, that's the
main thing.

ELLIE: Yes.

SMITTY: I've missed him, Old Jack. How is he, anyway?

ELLIE: Fine.

SMITTY: Sure is looking good! Oh, a little moody—

ELLIE: A little.

SMITTY: That'll pass, don't let it get you down. Part of it's all
this moving around.

ELLIE: Yes.

SMITTY: Once you're not, and settle in somewhere—[*A roar*]
There they go! You know what I mean?

ELLIE: Yes.

SMITTY: Makes all the difference.

ELLIE: Probably.

SMITTY: Sure—and how long can it be!

ELLIE: I don't know, really.

SMITTY: Bet you can't wait, huh? Either of you!

ELLIE: We talk about it.

SMITTY: Yeah, what a feeling—like to have a little nest here, do
you think?

ELLIE: We haven't made any—[*A roar.* SHE *shivers*]

SMITTY: Listen to em! No idea? [SHE *shakes her head*] Christ, that must be hard on you now . . . hm? [*No reply*] Well, leave that all to Jack! As long as you rest and keep your strength up—[SHE *faces him. A roar*] I've had four myself and let me tell you—

ELLIE: Go away, will you.

SMITTY: Ah, be a sport, when's it going to be?

ELLIE: It's not. Go away.

SMITTY: I mean, you were looking so peaked the other day, I had a hunch—[*A roar.* SHE *turns away*] Say, don't get sore! Look, the folks back home—

ELLIE: I told you: no!

SMITTY: **I hate to let you down, folks!**

[*A roar*]

ELLIE: Now, please—

[*A roar*]

SMITTY: Something else, maybe? Wedding bells? Homesick? Hear from your family?

[*A roar.* SHE *covers her ears, shuddering*]

ELLIE: Oh, it's never—

SMITTY: Are you feeling OK, Miss Bachman?

ELLIE: Yes—

[*A roar*]

SMITTY: He's dishing it out, he's not getting it—

ELLIE: Please—[*A roar.* SHE *bites her hand*]

SMITTY: You don't look too hot—Here, take a swallow—[SHE *shakes her head. The roaring is continuous now,* SMITTY *is nearly shouting*] How long do you think you can take it, anyway, living like this! It has to burn you out, Miss Bachman, can't you see that? Burn you out! You're not as tough as he is, you know, you can't just go on—

[*The noise has turned to angry boos and catcalls; running feet, a bell clanging. Shouts nearby: "Sauvage! Assassin!"* JACK, TICK, GOLDIE, *and the* PROMOTER *burst in, blood smears on* JACK'S *gloves and chest. Sounds of* POLICE *scuffling in the corridor*]

GOLDIE: God, why'd you keep—

PROMOTER: Quickly, please!

ELLIE: What happened—Jack—

JACK: He'll come out of it—

GOLDIE: Grab that bag—

JACK: It's all right, honey—

TICK: **Yeah—just!**

ELLIE: No—

PROMOTER: This way, please—

GOLDIE: Dress in the car, Jack—

PROMOTER: I beg of you!

JACK: Come on, honey. I'm sorry, I'm sorry.

[*Leads* HER *off,* LIGHTS *and shouts fading. Darkness*]

SCENE FOUR

Pop Weaver's office, New York.

The darkened office suite of POP WEAVER, *promoter. In the flickering light of the film they are watching sit* POP, CAP'N DAN, *and* FRED, *formerly* BRADY'S *manager.*

CAP'N DAN: How much you say he weighs, Fred?

FRED: Two thirty-seven. He's six foot five . . . watch it! Mommer!

POP: Not bad, Cap'n Dan, eh?

FRED: Wait, here's Vancouver two weeks ago—hold on—there's my boy! The one on the left.

CAP'N DAN: You couldn't exactly miss him, Fred.

FRED: Rushes straight in—there! I don't wanna brag, but when that kid first—[*The film breaks; only the beam continues*] Ah, for crying out loud!

VOICE: [*Offstage*] Won't take a minute.

FRED: So? Waddaya say! **If that's no White Hope I'm Queen Pocahontas.**

POP: He's the right stuff, Dan. Maybe a little raw yet—

FRED: Fresh, fresh is what he is! Big, clean, strong, a real farm-boy! They're waiting on their knees for something like him! [*Silence.* THEY *stare at the blank screen*]

FRED: [*Calling out*] How about it there!

CAP'N DAN: I don't think we need to see any more, Pop.

POP: Lights, please, Harry. [*The room is lit*] Well, you tell me, Dan. You want me to promote it, I'm ready to promote it, anytime, anywhere.

FRED: [*To* CAP'N DAN] Right!

POP: What do you think, Dan?

CAP'N DAN: I think he's a full-grown polar bear, myself.

FRED: Well, we have to send over somebody, don't we? The papers are hollerin, all the old bull again—**Honest, it's gettin like Remember the Maine here!**

CAP'N DAN: Oh, he fills the bill all right. But say we do send him over, and the black boy does it again, Fred. Then where are we.

POP: You won't ever have it on a plate, Dan, you know.

CAP'N DAN: Pop, Fred. Let tell you a secret. The next White Hope is the one who gets the belt back. Not means to, or almost does, or gets half-killed trying: he takes it, he finishes right on his feet, with a big horizontal nigger down for good there.

POP: What do you mean, Dan? Is it yes or no.

CAP'N DAN: I'd like you to meet a friend of mine, Pop. [*Calls*] Mr. Dixon there yet?

VOICE: [*Offstage*] Yeah!

CAP'N DAN: Come on in. [*Enter* DIXON] Pop Weaver. Fred.

POP: Have a chair, Mr. Dixon.

DIXON: [*Sits*] Thanks. [*To* CAP'N DAN] All right?

CAP'N DAN: Oh, we're hopeful, I think. [THEY *laugh*] Dixon here is with the Bureau in Washington. Like you might expect, they have Mr. Jefferson on their minds, too. I've been down there, we've had some ideas—you explain it to them, son.

DIXON: When a man beats us out like this, we—the law, that is—suffer in prestige, and that's pretty serious. How people regard the law is part of its effectiveness, it can't afford to look foolish, and this applies especially now to our Negro population. I don't mean just the ones who always flout the law, and seeing their hero doing it in style act up more than usual—those are police concerns, not ours. But though you may not be aware of it yet, a very large, very black migration is in progress. They're coming from the fields down there and filling up the slums, trouble's starting in Europe, and our mills and factories have work for them now. And I'm talking of hundreds of thousands, maybe millions soon—**millions of ignorant Negroes, rapidly massing together, their leanings, their mood, their outlook, suddenly no longer regulated by the little places they come from—situations have arisen already.** We cannot allow the image of this man to go on impressing and exciting these people.

POP: I'm only a sports promoter, Mr. Dixon.

CAP'N DAN: He read the writing on the door, Pop. Go on.

DIXON: If this position he enjoys were to be lost, through the outcome of his next engagement, let's say, the effect of this would be so much in our interest that we would be disposed to reconsider his sentence.

POP: You'd make it worth his while not to win the fight, you mean.

DIXON: I think I've said what I mean, Mr. Weaver.

CAP'N DAN: [*To* DIXON] What's the furthest you can go.

DIXON: We'd reduce it to a year, of which he'd serve six months, preferred treatment, best facilities, etcetera. **We're willing to make this as attractive as possible.**

FRED: I say my kid can beat him fair and square!

POP: Don't ride it, Fred.

FRED: Look, if you won't promote it, I'll hop on a boat with him and find someone who will!

CAP'N DAN: You don't want to do that, Fred.

FRED: What am I, a—

CAP'N DAN: Fred. I'm tellin you as a friend.

FRED: **I just don't like it.**

POP: It goes against me too, Dan.

CAP'N DAN: And against me too! I don't have to make anybody no speech here about how good I feel working something crooked! None of us like it—**we wouldn't be the men we are if we did, or be where we are! I know it's lousy!** But we got a situation here needs a little bending, the man's tried to tell you how serious it is, they're bending with it, I'm bending with it, who are you to sit there and say it goes against you, or you either, on your pedestal here!

POP: What about the champ, though, Dan?

FRED: He'll never buy it! Or my kid either, he's straight outa Sunday school, he's—

CAP'N DAN: Shut up, Fred—nobody has to tell your kid a thing! And Jack, well, after that last one, nobody there'll fight him any more, he's down to giving exhibitions, peanuts—

POP: But serving six months, Dan—

CAP'N DAN: It can't be much worse than killing the six months. And he'll step out a free man—**all that fight money! See all his pals!** Besides, his ole mammy ain't been too good, he'll want to see her before she goes. Sure he'll take it.

POP: Dan, why not ask Weiler or Michel to set it up, someone on the spot there?

CAP'N DAN: I"m asking you, Pop. [*Pause*]

POP: [*To* DIXON] You can't put that deal in writing, can you mister?

DIXON: Sorry, Pop. I wasn't even here. [*Pause*]

POP: What the hell, Fred. We'll balance it out on the one after this. Everything back on the gold standard, right?

FRED: OK, OK.

DIXON: [*Rising*] Well, thank you, gentlemen—[THEY *all rise*]

CAP'N DAN: And we thank you!

POP: I wouldn't count on results straight off, though.

DIXON: Oh, I think the country can hold up a little while. [THEY *laugh,* DIXON *waves them silent*] Excuse me—**You seem to be indignant, sir. Yes, I heard you. We have that all the time from people like you, that old Machiavelli crap. Look into it further, sir. But not in here, or at home. Give it some thought next time you're alone on the streets late at night.** [*To* CAP'N DAN] I'll be in touch with you.

[LIGHTS FADE. BLACKOUT. MUSIC: *German street band, distant.* LIGHTS UP *on*—]

SCENE FIVE

A *sidewalk café, Berlin.*

JACK, TICK, *four drunken* GERMAN OFFICERS *with them.* JACK *Indian-wrestling the largest,* OFFICER 4, *on the stein-covered table, as the other three encourage their comrade.*

OFFICER 1: Jetzt!

OFFICER 2: Kraft, Hans—

OFFICER 3: Ringe!

OFFICER 4: Kann nicht!

OFFICER 1: Nein!

OFFICER 4: Himmelsgott!

OFFICER 2: Ja!

[JACK *begins to bear his arm down*]

OFFICER 3: Aber, Hans—

OFFICER 1: Nein!

OFFICER 4: Mutter!

OFFICER 2: Halt—

OFFICER 1: Nein—

OFFICER 3: Nein, nein—

ALL: A-a-a-h!

OFFICER 1: Wunderbar! **Herrlich!** Mein herr, you are the triumph!

JACK: Well, thanks for stoppin roun, boys—

OFFICER 2: **Wir müssen die Fahne vom Regiment präsentieren!**

OFFICER 1: He says we must present to you the flag of our regiment!

JACK: Oh, cain't take that, ahma Mercan citizen—

TICK: You buy some tickets fo de show, dassall—

OFFICER 4: [*Offering his arm*] Bitte—again, please—

JACK: Tomorrow, buddy, you done wore me out.

[ALL OFFICERS *laugh*]

TICK: We see you all tomorrow, huh?

OFFICER 1: [*Picking up stein*] Kameradschaft!

[*The* OTHERS *follow suit*]

JACK: [*Standing*] Camera shaft, OK.

TICK: **Lawd, the drinkin sure hard on the feet here.**

OFFICER 4: Wir müssen ihm etwas geben!

ALL: Ja! Ja!

OFFICER 1: Mein herr, we go provide for you the suitable memento.

JACK: Great, be lookin out for ya.

TICK: Weenersane, weenersane.

ALL OFFICERS: [*Leaving*] Hop, hop, hop, hop . . .

JACK: [*Yawning and stretching*] O mah bones, whut you after.

TICK: Wanna go back to the hotel?

JACK: [*Sits*] Naw. Nothin doin there. You ready fo anuther?

TICK: Ah better pass. [*Sips*] Wonder how they make it brew up so heavy. You think they mix a egg in or whut?

JACK: Beats me, man. Puttin me to sleep, though.

TICK: Well, thass whut they does after lunch here, right?

JACK: No, man, that were someplace else.

[ELLIE *enters with* RAGOSY, *an impresario*]

RAGOSY: Ah, Meester Jafferson—

JACK: Whut you bring him for—?

RAGOSY: Such delights again to see you—

JACK: Now ain Ah tole you, mistah—

RAGOSY: Ragosy, excuse—[*Gives card*]

ELLIE: He just tagged along, Jack—

RAGOSY: I am patient rewarded!

TICK: Which one wuz he?

JACK: Huh . . . lemme think now . . . You ain't the one wanted me to team up with a circus—

RAGOSY: Please?

JACK: An it wusn't you pushin me to start a restrunt with him—

RAGOSY: No, no—

JACK: Or the artiss guy gonna hire me an do me in black cement?

RAGOSY: But you recall Ragosy!

TICK: Man, he that Hungrarian!

JACK: Oh, yeah, thassright—

[WAITER *enters*]

RAGOSY: Please, not speak additional word, I supply first champagne—[*To* WAITER] Abräumen, bitte! [*To* JACK] Wait, not to trust here, I consult myself—sit! [*Goes in*]

JACK: [*To* ELLIE] Why dinya sen him up ta Goldie, Goldie brush him!

ELLIE: He wasn't there, he had to go out.

TICK: Oh yeah? Something movin?

ELLIE: Just meeting that reporter.

JACK: Smitty?

ELLIE: Yes, he rang up.

JACK: Whut he doin here?

TICK: Must be he onna job an he sayin hello.

JACK: Nothin goin on here.

TICK: You ain't the only item in the paper, bighead.

RAGOSY: [*Reentering with champagne;* WAITER *sets glasses*] See, from my own hands! I take it the privilege—Champion, lovely friends—

TICK: **Ready wid de pumps, men.**

RAGOSY: Oh, Meester Jafferson! It pains in my heart these nights attending you. I count there the people and I make totality: **one-quarter business!** you do not divert!

JACK: Mebbe Ah oughta wear a bone through mah nose.

RAGOSY: No, no! For the true fisticuff with bleedings they come, but now you are not doing, you must look otherwise. I implore again myself, let Ragosy be devising the spectacle to you— Song! Dancing! **Sentiment!** The name is on you still like a dia-mond, my friend, only let make necessary light and then, then—

JACK: [*Leaping up: buck and wing*] **Out in San Francisco where de weather's fair Dey have a dance out dere—**

RAGOSY: Ah, aha—

JACK: **Dey call the Grizzly Bear, All your other lovin' dances don't compare—**

ELLIE: Jack, please stop it.

JACK: What?

ELLIE: Can't you just tell him no and—

JACK: Ah tell him whut Ah wants to, hon—

ELLIE: Jack, we're in the street—

JACK: An where Ah wants to an how, hear?

TICK: Baby, all she sayin—

JACK: Who ass you! [*To* ELLIE] Talk to me bout streets. If

you so goddam tetchy bout people lookin you ain't even oughta be here!

ELLIE: I don't like them looking when you're this way—

JACK: No? Well, me neither! But Ah's stuck widdit an you ain't, so any time you wanna—where you goin!

RAGOSY: [*Rising*] Oh, Madam, I sincerely—

JACK: [*To* ELLIE] Git you ass back on there! Man bought champagne—

RAGOSY: Please, Meester Jafferson—

JACK: You siddown too! [RAGOSY *does*]

ELLIE: I'll be in the room.

JACK: Yeah, then you say you sicka waitin roun hotels!

ELLIE: I never said that.

JACK: You givin out you misery so hard you don' haveta! You juss don' like nothin no more!

ELLIE: I won't answer you—

JACK: Dassit, give it out!

ELLIE: What do you want, Jack!

JACK: **Don' like nothin!**

ELLIE: [*Going*] Excuse me, please—

JACK: You siddown here, girl—

TICK: Let her go, man, she got the Fear again—

JACK: [*Calling after her*] ELLIE!

TICK: [*Following*] Ah walk her on back—

[*Noise of rhythmical clanging and shouting*]

JACK: Tell that Goldie Ah wants him, hear!

TICK: [*Looking in direction of noise*] Say—

JACK: Git! [*Holds ears*] Oh, them heavy-foot bastuds.

TICK: [*Going*] **He turnin meaner than a red hyena.**

JACK: [*Toasting* RAGOSY] Happy days, mistah—

RAGOSY: Prosit, prosit, and I eagerly to hope we—[RAGOSY *slips off as the* FOUR OFFICERS *gaily return: one is beating on dustbin*

*lid with a chair leg, two of the others frog-march between
them a very black young* NEGRO, *who struggles violently*]

NEGRO: Lassen mir! Lassen mir absteigen!

JACK: Hey—

OFFICER 1: So, we bring you as we promise—halt!

OFFICER 4: Einen Schwarzen Kameraden—[*Laughing,* THEY
dump NEGRO. JACK *helps him up*]

JACK: Here, lemme duss you off—

OFFICER 2: Is suitable, nein?

NEGRO: Mutig Soldaten spielen wie Kinder! [*Jeers and laughter*]

JACK: Don' rile em, man—

NEGRO: Again, bitte?

JACK: Whut—where the hell you from, anyway?

OFFICER 1: Where! He must ask! [*Gales of laughter*]

NEGRO: Afrika.

OFFICER 2: Boomboomboom!

OFFICER 4: Crucrucru!

OFFICER 3: **Authentick, ja!**

JACK: Oh, Jesus.

OFFICER 1: Here, you observe? [*Points to scars on* NEGRO's *face.*
JACK *gasps. More laughter*]

NEGRO: Ja. Iss tribe mark.

OFFICER 2: Walawalawala!

NEGRO: Here iss custom more large. [*Makes gesture of dueling
scar.* OFFICER 4 *goes for him*]

OFFICER 4: Scheissfarbiger Hund—

OFFICER 2: [*As other* OFFICERS *tussle with* OFFICER 4, *restraining
him*] Nein, Hans, nein—

JACK: Go siddown there, Jim—

NEGRO: Please?

JACK: [*Pushing him toward table*] Move—[*Going to struggling*
OFFICERS] Well, much obliged, fellahs, thass zackly what Ah
wanted—[OFFICER 4 *breaks away,* JACK *catches him by arm*]
Hey, Hands, you know this one? [*Stands with him toe to toe*]

OFFICERS 1, 2, 3: Ah!

OFFICER 2: Wirf ihn!

OFFICER 3: Jetzt! Jetzt!

OFFICER 1: Nun, Hans—[JACK *pulls him off balance*]

ALL OFFICERS: Bravo!

OFFICER 2: **Der schafft immer!**

OFFICER 4: [*To* WAITER] Herr Ober, Bier für uns alle!

JACK: No, Hands—[*Drawing them away*] Bess leave us darkies get quainted . . . you know, chomp a few bananas an all—

OFFICERS 3 *and* 4: [*Laughing*] Er muss eine Banane essen! Ja!

OFFICER 2: He pleases you, the new Kamerad, Herr Boxer!

JACK: [*Drawing them further*] Man, Ah'm happy as a cow with six tits. [*Shrieks of laughter.* THEY go. JACK *waves after them*] Weenersane! Donker! [*Returning*] **Wish they'd start a war up and keep them boys busy.**

NEGRO: [*Standing at table*] You forgiff I am employed in siss, please.

JACK: Thass awright, chief. Needed some ex'cise anyway.

NEGRO: I am nutt chiff. I am son from ser chiff.

JACK: Oh, yeah? Well, take a pew here with the fiel'-nigger's boy. [THEY *sit*, JACK *pours*]

NEGRO: You are ser Boxer, ja?

JACK: Thass me. When Ah workin at it.

NEGRO: From Amerika kommen.

JACK: Yeah, kommen and goin. You never been there, Ah guess.

NEGRO: Nein. I haff nutt zere ser purpose. Iss gutt?

JACK: Sometimes. Ain been there a while myself.

NEGRO: You learn zere gutt make ser laughink.

JACK: Oh, thanks.

NEGRO: Please, iss nutt uffenz. Must I learn also, I sink.

JACK: [*Laughs*] Seem like you leff it kina late.

NEGRO: Iss better, nein?

JACK: Yeah, mebbe so . . . Well, here's to us fish outa water.

[THEY *drink*]

NEGRO: Away much long iss to hurt now. You.

JACK: Might say that.

NEGRO: I am feeling. I haff in Europe sree year so.

JACK: Lawd. Lit out for good, huh?

NEGRO: Please?

JACK: Vamoose fum de ole country, Africa.

NEGRO: Ah! You sink I go for nutt be zere, nein, nein. I go so I komm zere back.

JACK: How zat?

NEGRO: Mit more knowings.

JACK: Oh! Ah gotcha.

NEGRO: Student.

JACK: Yeah. Nevah touch it myself.

NEGRO: I do nutt tell to giff shame inn.

JACK: Huh? No, Ah'm with you, man. What all you studyin?

NEGRO: Ser Law and ser Finanz and ser Chemikals-mining.

JACK: My, my, my.

NEGRO: Ja, makes ser headache!

[JACK *laughs with him*]

JACK: **Better go warn de chief bout dis one!**

NEGRO: Please? You haff choke mit ser fazzer?

JACK: Naw . . . But Ah thought Mistah White running things down there.

NEGRO: Now, ja.

JACK: They gonna letya help, huh?

NEGRO: So, I vatch.

JACK: They ain leavin go, man. No place.

NEGRO: Zumorrow, nein.

JACK: Nex Wensdy nine neither.

NEGRO: Sey make here ser war soon, ja?

JACK: So?

NEGRO: Iss like drunken peoples, Sree mann, fife mann, hitting one ozzer—you haff see, Boxer! All ser teess mit bloot, out-spitten! **Up all ser eatings, POUAH, POUAH!** Sey make so enough ser war, plack mann fly out from ser mouss. I sink.

JACK: [*Takes it in, then lifts his glass*] Here's to you an me an de "How Long Blues."

NEGRO: Please?

JACK: Drink up.

NEGRO: Ah, Boxer. Goes like you Pessimismus in Amerika all plack mann, I am fearing.

JACK: Well, don't go by me, buddy.

NEGRO: Ach, aber ja. Goes plack Champion so, goes kliene plack mann so! **Logik, nein?**

JACK: **He a bitch, ain he.**

NEGRO: Bad, stronk peoples to be so.

JACK: Oh, man, we strong on cryin there, thassall.

NEGRO: Nein, was slafe. Slafe nutt stronk, he die. Cry iss from ser life inn.

JACK: Well, it sure the wrong kina strong to git leff with when you ain slavin no more.

NEGRO: You komm gutt out. You.

JACK: Outa where.

NEGRO: Ser slafe. I see.

JACK: Ah dunno. Juss went the whole hog, man.

NEGRO: Please?

JACK: Shoot it all. You know: jump.

NEGRO: Ja, exakt. [*Points at him*] Ser bekinnink-man.

JACK: Naw, Ah ain tried ta start nothin. [NEGRO *bursts out laughing*] **What so funny bout dat?**

NEGRO: [*Rocking with laughter*] Oh, Boxer, Boxer, Boxer, ven

I am to chumping in Afrika, I hope so much nossing vill I make!

[GOLDIE *bursts in*]

GOLDIE: Jack! All over town I—oh, you busy?

[NEGRO *rises*]

JACK: Don' run off, man—

GOLDIE: Gotta talk to ya, Jack.

NEGRO: So, I go. [JACK *rises.* NEGRO *removes object from shirt*] Please, you take?

JACK: Oh, hey,—

NEGRO: Please. My fazzer giff.

JACK: [*Hesitates, then takes it*] Wish you all the luck in the worl, man, thanks.

NEGRO: Also you. You keep mit, ja?

JACK: Sure. Zat what it's for? Luck?

NEGRO: Nein. For hurt from spirits.

JACK: Yeah.

NEGRO: Gootbye, Boxer. [NEGRO *bows and goes*]

JACK: OK, I'm listenin.

GOLDIE: Well . . . we got a match.

JACK: How much Ah get for losin it?

GOLDIE: Huh?

JACK: Yeah, Ah'm listenin.

GOLDIE: **How the hell does he know!**

JACK: Mah witch-doctor tole me.

GOLDIE: Look! Lemme first explain what Smitty—

JACK: Boss, Ah know whut Smitty. They askin fo a straight fight, they ain't sendin Smitty—

GOLDIE: Whattaya gettin sore, the guy calls me up—

JACK: Nobody sore. How much it worth?

GOLDIE: Fred's got this kid, see—

JACK: Now, boss, you ain't hearin good.

GOLDIE: Eighty-twenty split. A hundred G's guarantee.

JACK: Mm, boy! **Pretty nice fo plain ole layin down, huh!**

GOLDIE: And they'll cut the rap to six months for ya.

JACK: Well! **See all folks kin do when evvybody pitch in?**

GOLDIE: Jackie, I don't blame you for—

JACK: Any special roun they like me to dive in?

GOLDIE: He says we can work all that out.

JACK: Uh huh. An whut you say?

GOLDIE: I said it stinks but I'll let him know later.

JACK: [*Pointing to champagne*] Right. Sen him a bottle a this, an tell him suck it through a straw.

GOLDIE: No thinkin it over.

JACK: How long you my manager?

GOLDIE: Five-six years.

JACK: Then why you gotta ask?

GOLDIE: Why? Cause I gotta eat, that's why! What am I managin here, for God's sake! What else you got in fronta you—

JACK: Don't try an sell me, boss.

GOLDIE: Big shot! Send him champagne! On what? The fights you have with your girl, maybe? **On a ten percent like this my enemies should live!**

JACK: Ah know it, man. Time to fine fresh meat.

GOLDIE: Well, what the hell you need me for, anyway!

JACK: Yeah, been thinkin bout that—

[*The* FOUR OFFICERS *charge in.* THEY *carry a rope*]

OFFICER 4: [*To* WAITER] Herr Ober, Bien für uns alle!

GOLDIE: Jack, let's go talk to him, they're gonna keep after you, you're getting sick here—

JACK: No, you call it right—

OFFICER 1: [*Giving* JACK *one end*] We make now to pull, Boxer?

JACK: Yeah, why not—

GOLDIE: Listen—

OFFICER 3: [*As* OFFICERS *take other end*] Erst, Hans!

JACK: There's no hard feelins, boss—

OFFICER 4: [*As* THEY *all line up*] **Nun gewinnen wir!**

GOLDIE: Jack—

JACK: Take all you need to get home on—

OFFICER 1: Prepared, mein herr?

JACK: [*Getting a grip*] Anytime! [*Tug of war:* JACK *holds*]

GOLDIE: Oh, Jackie, oh, look at what you're doin—

JACK: [*Giving ground*] It . . . ain't . . . good . . . but . . . it's . . . the . . . bess . . . Ah . . . can . . .

OFFICERS: [*Pulling him out as* LIGHTS FADE] Ho-ya! Ho-ya! Ho-ya! Ho-ya!

[BLACKOUT. *Cymbal crash, following by a tinny rendering of "Chiri-biri-bin" as* LIGHTS UP *on*—]

SCENE SIX

Cabaret Ragosy, Budapest

Small stage of a cabaret, audience unseen. A JUGGLER *in tights, working in time to the waltz, is finishing his turn. Loud applause as* HE *takes his bow;* RAGOSY, *now in evening dress and beaming, joins him on the stage and boosts the applause. Exit the* JUGGLER. RAGOSY *holds up his hand for silence.*

RAGOSY: És most, Hölgyeim es Uraim, amire mindanyian vártak! Bemutatom a Rágosy Kabaré föattrakcióját, Amerikai klasszikust "Uncle Thomas Kunyhóját." [*The saxophone begins playing "My Old Kentucky Home," and the* LIGHTING *becomes very roseate, as* TWO STAGEHANDS *position a papier-mâché weeping willow and a patch of grass.* RAGOSY *continues accordingly, describing the scene*] A jelenet a Mississippi . . . partjan jatszodik le . . . sek sek . . . Uncle Thomas és a little Éva élvezték a napkeltét . . . [*Winding up to bring them on*] Tehát bemutatjuk a világbajinokot Jack Jeffersont, elbübölö feleségével és néger barátjával!

[*Spatter of applause.* ELLIE *comes on as Little Eva, golden curls, etc.* JACK *follows her as Uncle Tom, shabby, gray wig, etc.* SHE *sits under "tree"*]

ELLIE: Here, Uncle Tom, do come and sit beside me.

JACK: Deed Ah will, Miss Eva. On dis lubly ole grassy bank.

ELLIE: See how beautiful the clouds are, Tom. And the water too.

JACK: An you right widdem, Miss Eva, you de byootifluss of all.

ELLIE: But, friend, why do you seem sad this evening?

JACK: Oh, Miss Eva, you and de Massah so kine ter Ole Tom he juss gotta cry bout it now and den.

ELLIE: Yes. We are happy here.

JACK: It like a plantation fum de Good Book, yessum. You de brightest lil sperrit Ah evah seed, Miss Eva.

ELLIE: Oh, Tom, sing about the Spirits Bright, would you?

JACK: Juss gittin set to. [*Piano gives him a chord and accompanies. Sings*]

> Ah sees a ban uh Sperrits Bright
> Dat tase de glo-ries dere—

[*Mock groan from the audience*]

> Dey are all robed in spotliss white
> As wavin palm dey bear.
> Ef Ah had wings—

[*Another mock groan, a titter, a* VOICE *saying "követ-kező";* JACK *stops, the piano stops. A moment of uncertainty*]

ELLIE: Oh, but look who has come to make us lively, Tom!

[*Enter* TICK *as Topsy, grinning and prancing*]

TICK: Hee, hee, hee!

ELLIE: Dear me, Topsy, why do you behave so!

TICK: Speck cause Ah jes plain ole wicked, Miss Eva!

JACK: What dis lil black imp done now?

TICK: Hee, hee, hee!

ELLIE: How old are you, Topsy?

TICK: Ah dunno, missy.

ELLIE: Don't you know how old you are? Who was your mother?

TICK: Ah dunno, missy. Nevah had no mother.

ELLIE: What do you mean? Where were you born?

TICK: Ah dunno, missy. Nevah wuz bo'n.

ELLIE: But Topsy, think a moment. Someone must have made you!

TICK: Nobody's Ah knows on, missy. Ah specks Ah jes growed!

ELLIE: Oh, Topsy—

TICK: Hee, hee, hee!

JACK: Awright, you shifless heathen, give us a breakdown an git back to yo stinks—

[*Piano and drums, assisted by* ELLIE, *who produces a tambourine, and* JACK, *a Jew's harp.* TICK *sings*]

TICK:
>I always think I'm up in Heaven
>When I'm down in Dixieland,
>I've got an angel of a Mammy,
>Out in Alabamy,
>Of the good old fashioned brand;
>She taught me that it's wrong,

To stay up all night long;
Go to sleep my baby,
That's Mammy's little fav'rite song.

[*Dances through the next chorus,* JACK *joining him,* ELLIE
*continuing on the tambourine. The audience seems to like
this better, but as* TICK, *breathless, resumes singing, they
again grow more and more restless*]

Everybody loves somebody
Down in dear old Dixieland,
The pretty flowers in the garden,
Keep their heads a noddin,
When you walk by hand in hand;
The gals down there are very plain—

[RAGOSY *tries to quiet audience*]

And every other lane's a lovers lane,
That's why—

[RAGOSY *pulls* TICK *from the stage, motioning to* JACK *and*
ELLIE *to continue.* ELLIE *reclines in a moribund attitude
against the tree as the saxophone commences with "Old
Black Joe"*]

JACK: Is you feelin . . . weakish agin, Miss Eva?

ELLIE: Yes. There is something I must tell you, Uncle Tom.

[*Protest from the audience*]

JACK: It can't be, Miss Eva, not yit—

ELLIE: Do not be gloomy! Look, those clouds, they are like great
gates of pearl now.

[*More protests*]

JACK: No, Miss Eva, no—

ELLIE: And I can see beyond them . . . far, far off . . .

VOICE: Gyorsan, gyorsan!

JACK: [Kneeling] Oh, Ah knows we cain't speck ta keep ya here wid us—

VOICE: Milyen unalmas!

ELLIE: Yes, I am going to a better country—

VOICE: A következö! [Laugh]

ELLIE: And I am going there before long, Uncle Tom . . . [Groan]

VOICES: Rémes! Rettentes!

JACK: Well, ef de Lawd needya back, Miss Eva—

VOICE: Hozd vissza a néger barátodat—!

JACK: Ah be hunkydory here—

VOICES: Rémes! Rémes!

[A slow handclap starts in the audience, quickly building up with foot-stamping and bottle-knocking]

ELLIE: Oh, dear Tom . . . take a tress of my . . .

VOICES: Borzasztó! Nevetséges!

[JACK rises slowly, looks out at them]

ELLIE: Take a tress of my golden hair . . . to . . . to . . . [SHE stops as the noise gets louder. RAGOSY appears at the side of the stage, trying to quiet them again, but they grow more angry at this]

VOICES:
Takaradjanak el!
Takaradjanak el!
Fogják meg!

[RAGOSY tries to speak but cannot be heard; ELLIE runs from the stage. JACK pulls the Uncle Tom wig off and stands immobile, expressionless. RAGOSY, frightened, signals desperately—for JACK to get offstage, for the saxophonist to stop playing, for the electrician to cut the lights . . . the saxophone desists, and after a few attempts the electrician

seems to find the right switch . . . as the LIGHTS DIM OUT
on JACK *the noise reaches a crescendo, then is cut off
sharply in the* BLACKOUT *as, suddenly, at the extreme opposite end of the real stage,* MRS. BACHMAN *appears, white,
pained, and haggard.* SHE *looks around at the real audience,
then speaks*]

MRS. BACHMAN: I know what most of you watching this believe
in, or think you believe in, or try to believe in. But I know
something else too, I know what Black means, and not just to
me because of my daughter, to everyone in here. All of us know,
though it might take some of you a daughter you've cared for
to make you say it, what it means, yes, means, what it is to you
truthfully—BLACKNESS!—there, feel it, what it sets off in
your heart, in the memories and words and shapes you think
with, the dark to be afraid of, pitch black, black as dirt, the
black hole and the black pit, what's burned or stained or cursed
or hideous, poison and spite and the waste from your body and
the horrors crawling up into your mind—I hate what I'm saying! As much as you do! I hate that it's so, I wish to God it
weren't! And if it was God who intended it so, and still willed
that color on a race of human beings, and brought us face to
face here, how He must hate all of us! Go on imagining that
time and justice can change it in you now, or that when it disappears in the singing of songs it's being destroyed. Tell yourselves it's only one more wrong to be righted, and that I'm a
half-mad woman, oh, making far too much of it. Wait until it
is your every other thought, like it is theirs, like it is mine. Wait
until it touches your own flesh and blood.

[*As* SHE *slowly walks off, the* LIGHTS *on her fading, a distant
rumble of artillery fire is heard, which continues throughout the next scene—*]

SCENE SEVEN

Railway station, Belgrade.

JACK *and* ELLIE *standing bedraggled in wet raincoats. Suitcases. Pools of light. Station empty.*

TICK: [*Entering*] Nothin, man. Maybe one pullin out tonight.

JACK: Anybody know whut goin on dere?

TICK: Porter say dey just practicin.

JACK: Yeah.

ELLIE: What will we do, Jack?

JACK: I dunno yet.

ELLIE: Do you think we should—

JACK: Ah said Ah dunno yet!

ELLIE: All right, I heard you.

JACK: Play cards or somethin wid her, willya?

SMITTY: [*Offstage*] Jack! [*Entering from a distance, catching his breath*] God, I'm glad I caught you . . .

JACK: Lay offa me, man.

SMITTY: It's sort of an emergency, Jack . . . back home. [*Takes out telegram*] Your mother's very low.

JACK: [*Snatching it from him*] Gimme dat. [*Reads it. Holds onto it throughout scene*]

SMITTY: I'm sorry about this, feller.

JACK: Yeah. Thanks.

SMITTY: Maybe we could work something out for you, Jack. To go straight over now and then do the rest of it. I know you want to be there. [*Pause*] You might just make it, Jack. I've hired a car and I fixed up your passage from—

JACK: [*To himself*] Button comin loose here.

ELLIE: Yes? [*Pause*]

SMITTY: Christ, deal or no deal, it's worth a try, isn't it? Even just to let her feel you're on your way, she'd be—

JACK: Thanks for comin roun, man.

SMITTY: You can't stay over here now, anyway. Jack! It's finished here. You know that. Where do you go?

JACK: Don' wan none today, man.

SMITTY: All right, don't get sore—**I really thought—**

JACK: Ah seeya sometime. [*Pause*]

SMITTY: OK . . . [*Turns to go, stops*] What the hell is it for, though, all this. I mean, you're not a Boy Scout. What the hell

THE GREAT WHITE HOPE

is it, Jack. Keeping the belt a little bit longer? Staying champ
a little while longer? I can't make you out.

JACK: Champ don' mean piss-all ta me, man. Ah bin it, all dat
champ jive bin beat clear outa me. Dat belt a yours juss
hardware, woulden even hole mah pants up. But Ah'm stuck
widdit, see, a hunk of junky hardware, but it don't let go, it
turnin green on me, but it still ain lettin go, Ah'm stuck as bad
widdit as you all stuck wid needin it offa me—shake it loose,
man! Knock me fo ten and take it, understan? Ah be much
oblige!

SMITTY: Look, you know we'd rather have it straight—

JACK: Oh, ya would, huh.

SMITTY: Sure, and, Jack, if you weren't so damned good—

JACK: [Grabbing him] Hunnerd million people ovah dere, ain'tya?

SMITTY: Yes, but—

JACK: Picked out de bess Hope ya got dere, ain'tya—?

TICK: Jack—

JACK: Ah wants a match widdim—

SMITTY: It's our way or nothing, feller—

JACK: Ah said a match widdim! An if you don' wanna gimme
one, Ah gonna makeya, same's Ah done before, see—[Releasing
him] **Ah gonna make em!** Gonna take mah funky suitcase an
mah three-four hundred dollahs, an git mahself ta Mexico,
howya like dat, man, right up nex ta ya, **gonna sit on dat line
dere an wave you crummy belt atya an sing out Here Ah is—**

SMITTY: It's not going to work, Jack—

JACK: Dassall Ah got worth tryin now—[Crumpling the telegram]
dis ain't, dis ain't, Ah know dis pass trying, Ah—

TICK: Easy—

ELLIE: Jack, I'm so sorry—

JACK: Took too much outa her, Ah guess, she musta—musta juss
—[Strikes himself a blow on the forehead, staggers]

ELLIE: Oh, Jack—

JACK: Leave me lone.

CURTAIN

ACT 3

SCENE ONE

A *street, Chicago.*

In the BLACKOUT, *at slow tempo, approaching from the distance, "How Long Blues": bass drum, clarinet, trombone. As the* LIGHTS COME UP, NEGROES *are quietly filling the stage;* THEY *arrange themselves as if lining both sides of a street. A few* POLICEMEN *station themselves among them, and a group of* PRESSMEN *is deployed at one side. The* FUNERAL PROCESSION *appears, the* BANDSMEN *first, followed by the coffin—*GOLDIE *conspicuous as a pallbearer— behind it* CLARA, *supported by* SISTER, *then the* PASTOR. *The* MUSIC *stops as the coffin is set down. The* NEGROES *close in around it and the* PASTOR *addresses them.*

PASTOR: "When thou passes through de waters Ah will be wid thee, and de rivers, dey shall not overflow thee, fo Ah am de Lawd thy God, de Holyone of Isrel."

CONGREGATION: Amen.

PASTOR: Mosta you ain present today outa respeck to Sistah Tiny here, you-all here to stan up fo son Jack. An dass fine! He got a place in you heart, de Lawd muss wan him havin it. But Bredren, make a place dere fo dis humble woman, his momma, too. Take Sistah in you heart an let her show you somethin, Bredren, Ah know you done took in what Jack bin showin you, but dis leass as good an mebbe worth more, praise de Lawd.

CONGREGATION: Amen.

PASTOR: "When thou passes through de waters Ah will be wid thee." Dis woman pass through dem all de days of her life. Born slave, like lotsa you poppas and mommas. Passed through dem waters. Passed through plain hungry waters, mean waters, cesspool-y waters. Currents like to swamp you—

CONGREGATION: Lawd!

PASTOR: Waters wid blood in em! Even passed through de waters of dat killer flood down Galveston, passin through one waters inter de nex one—

CONGREGATION: Lawd!

PASTOR: Sweatin in dem waters fum "cain't see" in de mornin till "cain't see" at night, an inter de nex one—

CONGREGATION: Jesus!

PASTOR: An when she coulden sweat no mo, passed through em juss shiverin an achin an sick—but whut wuz going long wid her!

CONGREGATION: Mah Savior!

PASTOR: Tell me dat!

CONGREGATION: Glory comin!

PASTOR: Amen! De Lawd say Ah'll be wid thee, de Lawd was passin through dem waters wid her, inter de nex one an de nex one and de nex, holdin her afloatin an liftin up de joy in her—

CONGREGATION: Hallelujah!

PASTOR: DASS whut she had, Bredren! Dass whut she show you! She din cuss dem waters—

CONGREGATION: No, Lawd!

PASTOR: She know whut evvybody know in deir heart here, **dere's ALWAYS dem waters, dere ALWAYS tribberlation, de nex one an de nex we ALWAYS passin through—**

CONGREGATION: Can't hurt me!

PASTOR: **Ah is, an you is, an you chillun gonna, an anybody's chillun till kingdom come—**

CONGREGATION: Oh, yeah!

PASTOR: She din blame de Lawd fo not partin dem waters like de ole Red Sea! She knowed He done said, "Dey shall not over-flow thee," an she TRUSTED her Lawd.

CONGREGATION: Jesus!

PASTOR: She knowed dat fifty year ago when we wuz nigh to GITTIN overflowed He give us a Moses an He did part dat sea an He took us outa bondage!

CONGREGATION: Hallelujah!

PASTOR: She knowed all de time she pine for her boy dat de Lawd workin in His own way—[CLARA *begins sobbing*] dat He ain't juss on tap evvy time we give a holler—

CONGREGATION: Oh my!

PASTOR: She felt de Lawd takin her fore she got ta see him, but she held on tight to dat—

[*Flurry of movement, photo-flashes, jostling*]

NEGRO 1: Whut gawn on dere—

PHOTOGRAPHER 1: This way, miss—

PHOTOGRAPHER 2: Excuse me—

GOLDIE: Say, can't you guys—

CLARA: [*Going for* PHOTOGRAPHER 1] Gimme dat, you mother-

PASTOR: Sistah—

NEGRO 2: Who dat—

GOLDIE: [*Checking* HER] For Godsakes—

POLICEMAN 1: No shoving there—

PASTOR: Gennulmen—

CLARA: Leggo me—

GOLDIE: Ignore em, just—

CLARA: You too, ya dirty pinkface pimp—

PASTOR: Sistah, dis ain no time—

CLARA: [*Breaking away*] Yeah, oh yeah dis de time awright! Whut he doin here, whut any of em doin here—

SISTER: Clara—

CLARA: Look at em! **Howya feelin now, folks! All dress up dere watchin de fewnral? Ain'tya bought some flowahs?**

GOLDIE: [*To* PASTOR] I'm sorry about this—

CLARA: Sho you is! You an dat white bitch an de whole pack a ya—come on ovah to de box here, sugah, see how good y'all nail de lid down—

PASTOR: Sistah—

CLARA: No! Ah seed mah Momma Tiny's heart gittin busted, Ah seed her layin dere pinin and sick till she nothin but bone, Ah heard her beggin fo Jack—Who set him runnin! Who put de mark on him! Why she die so bad! Where all her trouble fum! Dem, dem, dem, dem, an Ah wanna make juss one of em —[*Goes for the audience*]

PASTOR: Sistah—[*Struggle*]

POLICEMAN 1: [*To* PASTOR] Look, if you can't handle em—
PASTOR: Bredren—

NEGRO 2: No, let her, man—

CLARA: **Ah gonna settle wid—**

SISTER: [*Slaps* CLARA's *face*] Behave yourself!

CLARA: [*Falling on the coffin*] Oh help me, Momma Tiny, Ah wanna do right by ya, don' leave me, Momma, Momma, Ah be good, please . . .

PASTOR: Oh, brudders and sistahs! Look out when Satan start a-lightin dat hate fire! Member who de Lawd say vingeance belong ta, member he fogit not de cry a de oppressed—

SCIPIO: [*Concealed in the* CROWD] Dass right, chillun, suffer nice an easy—school em on it, boss!

PASTOR: Who talkin dere!

SCIPIO: [*Appearing*] Me—ya no-name brudder!

PASTOR: Take dat off your head here—

SCIPIO: No! Went inta buy me a hat once, boss, Man say cover you head wid a hankie and DEN try it on—

PASTOR: Shame on you!

SCIPIO: Yeah, now you sayin it—shame on me, an shame on alla us, for BEIN de oppressed, an bein it, an bein it! Shame on us moanin low two hunnerd years here! Fo needin a big White Moses fo a daddy!

NEGRO 3 : Amen, brudder!

PASTOR : Whut—

SCIPIO : Yeah! Shame on evvy Goodie-Book thumper like you! White man keep pullin de teeth outa you head an preacher here giving you de laughin-gas—

PASTOR : Ah warnin you, heathen—

SCIPIO : Ah warnin evvybody! **Warnin dat white gal an warnin dem po-lice ain nothin lass foever!**

NEGRO 2 : Tell em!

SCIPIO : **Warnin dat dead woman Jesus wuzn't swimmin! Warnin mah people dat boy juss a shadow an dey livin black men whut gotta live long—**

NEGRO 3 : Right!

SCIPIO : Don' Amen me! Makin believe you de Chillun of Isrel, fiery-furnacin an roll-on-Jordanin—you ain no Isrel! Dere— [*Points to* GOLDIE] *Dass* a Jew-man—see whut ya see! Look in de mirrah once an see whut ya see! Ah said de MIRRAH, not a lotta blue eyes you *usin* fo a mirrah, an hatin whut dey hates, de hair you got, de nose you got, de mouth you got, de—

PASTOR : Offissah, Ah'm askin you—

POLICEMAN 1 : Right—

NEGRO 3 : Whut dey doin—

SCIPIO : Hate dat woolly head, you gotta hate de man whut got it, brudders, dat man YOU—

POLICEMAN 2 : [*To* SCIPIO] Move—

SCIPIO : Don' hate it, brudders—

NEGRO 5 : Lemme through—

NEGRO 6 : Stop em—

SCIPIO : [*As* POLICE *haul at him*] Champeen in your heart, but dey ain one a you—

NEGRO 4 : Help him—

NEGRO 6 : Dey hurtin him—

NEGRO 7 : Quick—

NEGRO 8 : Dey gonna kill him—

NEGRO 4 : Let em have it—

POLICEMAN 3 : Move—

PASTOR : Bredren—

NEGRO 1 : [*Holdin back* CLARA] Sistah—

NEGRO 5 : No cuttin—

NEGRO WOMAN 1 : Help—

NEGRO 8 : Cut em—

POLICEMAN 3 : There—

NEGRO 4 : Gimme dat—

POLICEMAN 1 : Come on, call em out—!

> [*Police whistles above the pandemonium; flashing night-sticks and swinging fists; the coffin is hurried off;* LIGHTS BEGIN FADING *and hoofbeats are heard, then screams*]

NEGRO VOICES :
  Look out—
  No, dis way—
  Brudders—
  Pull em off—
  No—
  You mother—
  Here—
  Lemme git one—
  Move—
  Teddy—
  Run—
  Here—
  Mah head, mah head, mah head, mah head—

> [*Darkness. Silence.* LIGHTS UP *on—*]

SCENE TWO

Pop Weaver's office, New York.

CAP'N DAN *and* SMITTY, *followed in by* POP *and* FRED. *Newspapers.*

CAP'N DAN: Look at this, look at this—**I can't even think straight—**

SMITTY: I told you, he's out for—

CAP'N DAN: Don't tell me again! One more lousy picture of him and that belt. One more newsie sneakin down there to see him—

FRED: What about the ones on me up here, Dan'l?

CAP'N DAN: Say you can't promote it! Say he's askin too much!

FRED: After that piece in the *Journal?*

SMITTY: Here.

FRED: **Will Fight Kid for Carfare and a Watermelon.**

CAP'N DAN: Christ—

POP: Maybe we could pay him off to retire, Dan—

CAP'N DAN: **Twenty years, what I'd give for twenty years—**

POP: He wouldn't need to lay down, we'd get the belt back—

CAP'N DAN: Sure, and have a coon champ retire undefeated!

SMITTY: What if we promise him a straight fight later on if he dives on this one.

FRED: Later on.

SMITTY: You know.

CAP'N DAN: He's too goddam smart for that!

FRED: Just an idea now, but supposing we sign it, then something gets put on his sponge, or in his water . . .

SMITTY: It's worked before, Dan.

POP: I would hate to hang this on something from a drugstore.

CAP'N DAN: Jesus, listen to us, **look what that boogie's got us down to here—**

POP: Don't excite yourself, Dan—

CAP'N DAN: On the verge, I tell them! You know what I look like, stalling for months and making excuses, and all he winds up is smack on the border like a boil on the whole country's ass?

FRED: All right! Then why don't we sign it and have it, for chrissake! He'll never be in shape the way he was in Reno—

CAP'N DAN: Get it in writing—

FRED: Here, look at the gut on him—And look at that Kid—

POP: Fred—

FRED: Honest to God, he's better, every time out, listen, four KO's and three decisions since April, and I've got him with Brady now, we're giving him all kinds of angles on the nigger, like how when he smiles—

CAP'N DAN: **Do I have to hear this?**

FRED: Wait, no, I mean it—when you're doin a smile, see, your mouth's kina open and your teeth's not clenched, so you hit him when he's smilin, you can bust a guy's jaw—**That's no bull, that's from an osteopath!**

CAP'N DAN: Pop, you try, go down there yourself—

POP: Dan, I don't discourage very easy, but I'm afraid there's only one safe bet for us. It isn't ideal—

CAP'N DAN: Come on, come on—

POP: Even if he's still as good as he was, Dan, the man is no spring chicken any more. And you know what happens. Maybe not by tomorrow, or the next day either, but it will happen, Dan. The legs'll start to go, like everybody else's—**it's all downhill.**

CAP'N DAN: Two years? Three years?

POP: Whenever he's ripe we throw him in with Fred's boy—

CAP'N DAN: Pop, can't you help me?

POP: Taking this on was a real mistake, Dan. I'd like to follow through but that's the best we have.

FRED: I'd go along—

SMITTY: We could say we're waiting on account of the war—

FRED: **We could give a big play to the middleweights—**

CAP'N DAN: Pop—Jesus!

POP: We can work it, let's put it on ice—

CAP'N DAN: There ain't that much ice in this whole rotten world—

FRED: What do we do then—kill him? [*Pause*]

CAP'N DAN: How broke is he, Smitty?

SMITTY: They live in a flophouse and he trains in a barn.

CAP'N DAN: Any dough from outside?

SMITTY: Friends, a little.

CAP'N DAN: Find out who, we'll stop it—anybody sparring with him?

POP: Dan, what's the point—

SMITTY: A couple of rubes from Texas—

CAP'N DAN: Pull them out, send them home. No exhibitions, nothing, no contact, cut him off—

POP: He's not going to give, Dan—

CAP'N DAN: He made the last move he had and now we'll screw him with it, now we're gonna show him what a bad move it was, this time we ain't askin, or offerin, or tryin, or pussyfootin round this like a bunch of pansies, we got him so close we can reach out and squeeze—**we're gonna squeeze that dinge so goddam hard soon a fix is gonna look like a hayride to him!**

POP: Dan, don't get him any madder than he is—

CAP'N DAN: Start scouting out a place we can hold it—

POP: We're making us two mistakes in a row, Dan—

CAP'N DAN: Havana, maybe, the bigger the better—

POP: I mean it. Tell your people we just can't deliver.

CAP'N DAN: No, I tell them we might need a hand—

FRED: Say, wait—

CAP'N DAN: You get busy, talk to Goldie—I want all that set!

POP: We're way out over our head now, you know.

CAP'N DAN: So is he, friend. Let's see who goes under.

[BLACKOUT. *Enter* CLARA *in spotlight, as distant bell slowly chimes midnight.* SHE *clutches a flimsy stained garment to her*]

CLARA: **Do it, soon, soon, goin good now, drag him on down. Oh won'tya, fo me an mah momma an evvy black-ass woman he** turn his back on, for evvy gal wid a man longside dreamin him a piece of what HE got, fo alla his let-down secon-bess sistahs, all Mistah Number One's lil ugly sistahs—ssh!—dey's moonin fo de day you does it, dey's some sleepin an plenny itchin quiet, dey's me aholda dis, an we drawin him, drawin him. Oh, where dem rosy cheeks gonna hit him, don' never stop now, offa dat high horse an on down de whole long mud-track in fronna him, years gawnta nothin, feelin em, dere, limpin an slippin an shrinkin an creepin an sinkin right in—Call him to ya, Momma! [*Holds out the garment at full length: a nightgown, stiff with blood and excrement*] Soon, baby, soon.

[LIGHT FADES *slowly into* BLACKOUT; *thudding of a punching-bag is heard;* LIGHTS UP *on*—]

SCENE THREE

A *disused barn, Juarez.*

By *the light of a few kerosene lanterns,* JACK *pounds at a punching-bag, which is steadied from behind by* PACO, *a Mexican boy.* TICK *claps his hands in time with him.*

TICK: Slow it up, slow it up—

JACK: Whut—?

TICK: Slow it, let dat sweat out—[*Claps at a lower tempo, sings*]
    Times is very hard,
    Gimme ten-cent worth a lard,
    Gonna keep mah skillet greasy
    If Ah can, can, can,
    Gonna keep mah skillet—

[JACK *delivers a last impatient slam and turns away from it*]

Nuff?

JACK: Yeah, Ah'm pushin.

TICK: OK, Paco, dassit.

JACK: Six-thirty mañana.

PACO: Si, Campeón. We ron?

JACK: Yeah, we run.

PACO: I com for wek op?

JACK: No, Ah be up. [PACO *starts putting gear in order*]

TICK: [*Leading* JACK *to a trestle table*] Wearin us out, baby, comin on fine . . . [JACK *sits*, TICK *pulls his gloves off*] Oughta raise de bag up higher tomorrer, startya liftin em, huh? [JACK *lies down*] Yeah . . . [*Working on him*] bout a foot or so. You know, seein how big dat Kid is . . . [JACK *does 'not reply*] Sho a funny size fo a Kid, ain he? **Soun like somethin gone wrong wid his glans!**

JACK: Don't try unwindin me, man. Juss rub.

TICK: Yassuh, shine em up—

JACK: [*To* PACO, *who has picked up his gloves*] Leave dose, willya.

PACO: Si, Campeón.

TICK: You cain work out tonight no mo, Ah mean—

JACK: How much dat guy say he giveya for em.

TICK: Oh.

JACK: Fifty?

[*Barking* is heard]

TICK: You gloves, baby. [JACK *doesn't reply*]

PACO: [*Looking out*] Viene la señorita.

JACK: Put em in a piece a paper she don' see em.

TICK: Well, you kin work wid de heavy ones, time bein. Bettah fo ya, anyhow.

[*More barking.* ELLIE *enters, carrying a dish with a napkin over it.* SHE *wears sunglasses*]

PACO: Buenas noches—

TICK: Mmm-MM! Whut dat old lanlady whip up tonight?

PACO: [*At the door shooing away the dogs*] Andale! Vaya!

ELLIE: I wish they would feed their dogs around here.

JACK: You feedin yours here, ain'tya.

TICK: [*Resuming massage*] Set it down, hon—how mah gal today?

ELLIE: All right. You?

TICK: Fine! Shoulda seed him burn up dat road dis mornin, right fum de bridge to Pedrilla an up ta—

JACK: [*To* ELLIE, *not looking at her*] Gonna say it or whut.

ELLIE: No, nothing, Jack. No cables. Nothing.

JACK: Thanks.

TICK: Man, we be hearing pretty soon. Worry juss makin you tight, dass why ya ain sweatin like ya oughta—

JACK: Juss you rub, man.

TICK: Ass me, we's lucky dey ain sign it up yet! Givin us all dis good gittin-ready time?

ELLIE: Let him eat before it gets cold, Tick.

TICK : Yeah, switch you brain off a while an—

JACK: Leave it.

TICK: OK, OK. [*Long pause*]

ELLIE: Jack—

[*Train whistle*]

PACO: Tren from El Paso.

ELLIE: Yes?

TICK: Yeah . . . Whistle like dat crossin ovah.

PACO: Hasta mañana, señores.

TICK: So long, kid.

[PACO *goes*]

ELLIE: Why don't you come back and wash now, Jack. I'll wait here if you like.

JACK: Smelling pretty strong, huh?

ELLIE: You know that's not what I—

JACK: [*Sitting up*] Dass inuff, man.

ELLIE: Jack, will you talk to me?

JACK: Tick gawn ovah on a erran, you kin go walk roun dere a lil widdim—

ELLIE: No, I want to talk to you—

JACK: Mabbe git a ice-cream soda, lookit some Mericans or somethin—

ELLIE: Jack—

TICK: Not wid me, boss—**Ah ain strollin wid no white gal in no Texas!** [*To* ELLIE, *as he goes out with the package*] Hole de fort, hon, won't be too long.

[*Pause. Train whistle*]

ELLIE: Let them go ahead, Jack.

JACK: Take dem specs off. Ah cain hardly see ya.

ELLIE: [*Doing so*] I didn't think you wanted to.

JACK: You readin mah mine now?

ELLIE: Jack—

JACK: Ah toleya keep outa dis, din Ah.

ELLIE: I can't. Please, let them, you have to.

JACK: Finely battin fo de home team, huh.

ELLIE: Cable them tonight, please—

JACK: **Finely come roun to it—**

ELLIE: Jack, don't bitch me now—

JACK: Ah toleya—

ELLIE: No, I don't care! Forget what you told me! Say yes and get it over with, for God's sake! You're letting them do this to you, it's worse—

JACK: Worse fo you, mebbe—

ELLIE: Jack, it's slow poison here, there's nothing else to wait for, just more of it, you've had enough—please, you're being paralyzed—

JACK: Wid you mebbe—

ELLIE: All right, yes, with me too, with everything but hammering that stupid bag there! You're not your own man any more—

JACK: Now you rollin—

ELLIE: How can you be your own man, they have you! They do and you know it, you're theirs, at least you can buy yourself back from them—

JACK: **Sold—one-buck nigger fo de lady!**

ELLIE: Let it sound the way it is! Run when they push you and back when they pull you, work yourself sick in this hell-hole for nothing, and tell me you're not theirs—here, look at the grease you swallow for them, look at the bedbug bites on your arms, and the change in your pockets and the blotches in your eyes—

JACK: Don' leave de smell out—

ELLIE: The two of us smell! Whatever turns people into niggers —there—[*Shows her neck*] it's happening to both of us—

JACK: Wish comin true, huh—

ELLIE: No, never this, it wasn't this—

JACK: Sing it, sistah!

ELLIE: I want you there fighting them again, that's what I wish now, I want to watch when you're knocking them down for this, dozens of them, God help them, wipe it off on all of them—

JACK: How bout rooster-fightin, plenty right here—

ELLIE: Listen to me, please—

JACK: Oughta look inta dat—

ELLIE: You'd fight them and you'd be with your friends and you'd—

[JACK *crows like a rooster*]

JACK: **Somebody wanna sign me?**

ELLIE: Maybe we could live then, damn you!

JACK: Lil frame house, tree in front?

ELLIE: Anything!

JACK: Nice quiet street?

ELLIE: Anywhere! A place!

JACK: Lil cozy—

ELLIE: A kitchen!

JACK: Put de cat out? Tuck in de kids?

ELLIE: Oh, you're just hateful!

JACK: Well Ah gonna tellya whut de livin like, baby, far as Ah concern—

ELLIE: Get away from me—

JACK: Yeah, Ah put you straight on it—**an alla you, too. Ah wen into a fair once and dere wuz dis old pug, see, give anybody two bucks who stan up a roun widdim—perfessional set-up, reggerlation ring an all, cep dey had rope juss on three sides, dass right, de back side wuz de tent. So Ah watches a couple git laid out real quick in dere, but he don' look dat red-hot ta me, see, so Ah climbs in widdim. An Ah doin awright fo a youngster, when all it once he bulls me up gainss dat tent-side a de ring an SLAM, WHAM, somebody behine dere conks me, right through de canvas, musta use a two by four, an evvy time Ah stans up he shove me back agin, an SLAM, dere's anudder, down she come—good story, huh?**

ELLIE: Jack—

JACK: Dass how it go like Ah knows it, baby—

ELLIE: Sometimes, sometimes—

JACK: All de way now! dass where Ah is and dass whut Ah'm gittin, gonna git it de same sayin Yassuh, Nossuh, don' mattah whut Ah does—Ah in dere, unnerstan? An Ah don' wan you watchin, or helpin, or waitin, or askin, or hannin me jive bout livin, or anythin fromya but OUT, Ah mean OUT—

ELLIE: What—

JACK: How goddamn plain Ah gotta make it for ya!

ELLIE: Jack—if you want other girls—

JACK: Git you stuff ready, train out ten o'clock.

ELLIE: No, no, I won't, no—

JACK: When Tick come Ah sen him ovah—

ELLIE: Jack—

JACK: Bettah start movin—

ELLIE: Stop it—

JACK: Ah pologize actin so yellah up ta—

ELLIE: Wait, you have to stop it—

JACK: All Ah has to is be black an die, lady—

ELLIE: I want to stay, even if we—

JACK: Stay wid you own, lady—

ELLIE: What are you doing!

JACK: Quit dat, quit it, short an sweet—

ELLIE: I won't go—

JACK: You knowed it comin, start movin—

ELLIE: Wait—

JACK: Don' cross me now—

ELLIE: Jack, I thought we'd save something, please—

JACK: Ah said MOVE—

ELLIE: Please, I only—

JACK: MOVE! You through widdit now—

ELLIE: Jack—

JACK: No mo lousy grub you gotta puke up, no more a ya lookin
like a wash-out rag here, wid you eye twitchin alla—

ELLIE: Don't—I don't care—

JACK: Juss MOVE—

ELLIE: I'll take better—

JACK: Hangin on me, dead weight—

ELLIE: No, not for you—

JACK: Start—

ELLIE: Jack, I'll find a job, please—

JACK: Ah toleya when mah momma die, Ah toleya leave me be
a while, now—

ELLIE: Jack, I can't run any more, not by myself—

JACK: You got you people and you a—

ELLIE: No, listen—

JACK: You a young woman an you gonna—

ELLIE: Please, I'd never—

JACK: Gonna fine—

ELLIE: No one else, I'd—

JACK: Tough titty—

ELLIE: Just—

JACK: Move, or goddamn you—

ELLIE: Why can't you wait at least! Wait till you've given me a chance to make you happy—one chance, only one—**I swear I've never had one**—

JACK: Too big a order all aroun!

ELLIE: No, I won't go—

JACK: Wanna drag it out, huh—

ELLIE: I won't, I can't—

JACK: Den Ah gonna wise you up good now, you gray bitch—

ELLIE: You can't make me go, stop doing this—

JACK: Why you think Ah ain't put a han to yo fo how long, why ya think it turn me off juss lookin atya—

ELLIE: Stop it—

JACK: You stayin, stay fo it all. Ya know why? Does ya, honey-bunch? Cause evvy time you pushes dat pinch-up face in fronna me, Ah sees where it done got me, dass whut Ah lookin at, where an how come an de Numbah One Who, right down de line, girl, an Ah mean YOU, an Ah don' wanna give you NOTHIN, unnerstan? Ah cut it off firss!

ELLIE: Oh, I despise you—

JACK: Right, like alla resta ya—

ELLIE: Oh, I'd like to smash you—

JACK: Me an evvy udder dumb nigger who'd letya! Now go home an hustle one up who don' know it yet, plenny for ya, score em up—**watch out, brudders!** Oughta hang a bell on so dey hear you comin.

ELLIE: You mean this?

JACK: Look in mah purple eyes. [*Pause*]

ELLIE: You win, daddy. [SHE *turns and goes. Pauses.* JACK *takes swig from the water-bottle, gargles, spits, then walks to the punching-bag and starts to jab at it. For a few moments* HE *does not notice the entrance of a slightly shabby but imposing-looking Mexican,* EL JEFE. *Then, sensing someone behind him,* JACK *stops*]

EL JEFE: I lessen you mek beeg denuncio, Campeón. So I nut com een.

JACK: Who you, mistah?

EL JEFE: Ees nut meester, Campeón. I seet now, yes? [*Sits*]

JACK: Whut you want?

EL JEFE: [*Taking out a bottle and offering it*] You like?

JACK: No, Ah'm in trainin.

EL JEFE: Pliz?

JACK: Trainin. On a fight.

EL JEFE: Si, es terrible . . . for Negro, for peon, for avery poor peoples, **fight from meenit we out from dee modder.**

JACK: Ah astya whut you want, man.

EL JEFE: I hear, Campeón. Salud. [*Drinks*]

JACK: Look, Ah ain made no trouble wid none a you.

EL JEFE: [*Laughs a bit*] Where ees dee fadders, compadre.

JACK: De whut?

EL JEFE: Dee fadders. Dee weengs. Ees all high ovair flying like anjel, you think, no? **El hombre solo.**

JACK: Whut you after, man?

EL JEFE: Maybe you halp soon pobre black amigos. You show heem ees solo nut posible . . . Que vida, eh?

JACK: [*Moving to the door*] Man, you juss playin wid me, Ah'm gonna—

EL JEFE: [*Standing*] No, I filling to you beeg compassion, my fran. Dees Mejico my cowntry, I ongry here, I keel here, I am fugitivo lik you much times. Bot ulways to love. You cowntry you nut love her and she nut you, unly mak bad drims ich odder.

[*A car has been approaching and is heard braking*]

VOICE OUTSIDE: Han venido, Jefe.

EL JEFE: Déjanlos entrar.

[*Pause. Enter* DIXON, GOLDIE, *and a young* AGENT]

DIXON: Good evening.

EL JEFE: Señores.

GOLDIE: Hello, Jack.

JACK: Yeah. OK. Ah'm listenin.

GOLDIE: Well . . . [*To* DIXON] All right? [DIXON *impassive*] They're makin it easier, Jack. I mean it's . . . They threw in now suspended sentence.

JACK: Yeah.

GOLDIE: You fight in Havana, you hand yourself in, you go to court, one-two-three, and that's all.

JACK: Go on, boss.

GOLDIE: Well . . .

JACK: Don' be shy bout it.

GOLDIE: Jackie, it's quits now . . . [*Stops, pained*]

JACK: [*To* DIXON] Mebbe you tell me.

DIXON: Apart from your original conviction, Jefferson, which carries, you remember, up to three years, there are quite a few other violations, involving, for example: jumping bail, using the mails to bribe officials in Canada, tax irregularities, falsifying passports—

GOLDIE: They'll throw the whole book on you. Till God knows when.

JACK: Tell me de ress of it, mistah. You law up dere an Ah down here. Cain leave dat out—[*To* EL JEFE] Can he, man? You country, ain't it, man?

EL JEFE: [*Downcast*] Si, compadre.

AGENT: It is perfectly legal, once we've ascertained where a wanted man is, to request cooperation of the parties in charge there.

EL JEFE: Perdóname, Campeón, we nid from dem, comprende? **We nut like. We nid.**

JACK: Yeah.

EL JEFE: Go Habana. Ees batter.

DIXON: I would think so.

GOLDIE: Yon finish inside there, what'll you have, Jack. **An old man he'll be.**

JACK: Well . . . Ah'm far long awready, boss. Ah'm stannin here gittin older evvy minnit. An Ah'm goin right through dat door —[*Moves*]

EL JEFE: No—[*Draws pistol*] compadre! [*Steps in front of* JACK]

JACK: Use it if ya got to, man.

EL JEFE: Hombre, ivin I lat you, where now you—

JACK: Dassall up to me, man. [*Advances*]

EL JEFE: I tie weeth rope, you do theess—!

JACK: Oh, Ah killya firss, man. [*Advances*]

EL JEFE: Hijo, averyplace catch on you, I swear you, all geev you to gringos, Huerta, Obregón—

JACK: [*Advancing*] Ah goin out de door, man—

EL JEFE: Hombre . . . [*Clicks backhammer*] Hombre—

JACK: Gimme a break, fo Gawdsake.

EL JEFE: No! Who you halpeeng een your life, nadie, OSS now you halp—[JACK *advances*] Cabrón, wan more—

JACK: Well, mebbe it be doin me a favor. [*Steps around* EL JEFE, *keeps walking*]

GOLDIE: Jack—[EL JEFE *raises his pistol*]

DIXON: In the leg—

AGENT: Don't—

EL JEFE: Chíngate, gringo—[*Aims at* JACK's *back, calls*] You stuppeeng? Hombre, nut stuppeeng, I—

[JACK *at the doorway, suddenly stops, then slowly moves backward as* TICK *and* TWO MEXICANS *enter.* THEY *carry in* ELLIE's *mudsmeared and dripping body*]

MEXICAN: Se tiró en el pozo. Acabada.

EL JEFE: Díos.

JACK: Whut . . . whut . . . ?

TICK: Threw hersel down de . . .

JACK: No, no, Jesus—

TICK: **Down de well, Ah coulden—**

JACK: Git somebody, gimme de bottle—why she—

TICK: Busted her neck, man.

JACK: Honey! Honey, baby, please, sugar, no—! Whut Ah—whut Ah—whut Ah—baby, whut Ah done to ya, whut you done, honey, honey, whut dey done to us . . .

EL JEFE: [*Turns away*] No puedo mirarlo.

GOLDIE: Jack. Jack. Anything I can . . . [JACK *nods*] Anything. What, Jack.

JACK: Set dat fuckin fight up! Set it up, set it up! **Ah take it now!**

[BLACKOUT. *Sound of presses rolling.* CAP'N DAN *appears in* SPOTLIGHT: HE *smokes a cigar, wears a white carnation, carries a small valise, and is jubilant*]

CAP'N DAN: **Well, there's such a commotion on this you'd think we just organized the Second Coming! Tickets? They're going down without em, hey, honest to God, it does your heart good, songs about the Kid, pictures of the Kid stuck up in windows, stores, you pass a brick wall it has KID painted on it, people on the street saying Well, we got the Hope, Dan!—cost me two hundred in cigars already—and wait, wait, I bet you can't guess who's refereein—Brady! Oh, will they eat that up, when he's given the count and he's—what? No, he ain't in on it,**

neither is the Kid, who the hell wants that! But he's the one
who lost it, and the whole world's gonna see him take it in his
hand again, and hold it up and pass it on, like the Kid'll pass
it—[*Boat whistle interrupts him*] OK! This time we'll keep
it in the family!

[DAN *exits*]

SCENE FOUR

A *street, somewhere in the United States.*

As DAN *exits a group of* NEGROES *swarms on,* ONE *of them
rapidly beating on a bass drum,* ANOTHER *holding up a
torch in one hand and a pail in the other, a* THIRD *scrib-
bling on a long sheet of foolscap; the* OTHERS *clamorously
surround them, calling out their names and throwing
money into the pail. Drumming throughout.*

NEGRO 1 : Oscar Jones—

NEGRO 2 : Pearl Whitney—

NEGRO 3 : Jasper Smollett—

PAIL MAN : Write em down dere—throw in dem nickels—

NEGRO 4 : Charlie Webb—

NEGRO 5 : Bill Montgomery—

PAIL MAN : More! Who else here—**Sign on de telegram to Jack—
fi' cents—**

NEGRO 4 : Read out de message, man—

NEGRO 1 : Let em all hear it!

PAIL MAN : **"HELLO JACK BESS NACHUL FIGHTER IN DE
WORL—"** [*Cheers*] **"HOME FOLKS PUNCHIN RIGHT
WIDYA—SIGNED—"** [*The cheering drowns him, a* VOICE
over it sings—]

VOICE : Hot boilin sun comin ovuh—

NEGRO 6 : Waltuh Peters!

SEVERAL JOINING IN : Hot boilin sun comin ovuh—

NEGRO 2 : **We show ya!**

MORE JOINING : Hot boilin sun comin ovuh—

NEGRO 7 : **Ah'm on dere!**

ALL : [*Singing*] AN HE AIN'T A-COMIN DOWN—

[*Whooping and cheering,* THEY *run off, the sound of their* VOICES *fading into the* ROAR *of the* CROWD *as* LIGHTS COME UP *on*—]

SCENE FIVE

Oriente Racetrack, Havana.

Entrance gate. Two huge ornate wooden columns; suspended high between them, a banner featuring the simplified figures of a white boxer and a black one locked in combat. A cluster of ticketless WHITE MEN *at the barrier,* ALL *feverishly trying to follow the fight by the roars of the crowd and through* ONE *of their number perched high on a column. In the fierce heat all coats have been discarded, most shirts as well: heads are bound with handkerchiefs or covered with cheap straw hats—a few of these still left are hawked by a couple of ragged* CUBAN NEGRO BOYS.

MAN 1 : [*On column*] No, Kid—block him—you're lettin him—

[*Roar*]

MAN 2 : Again?

MAN 3 : Sounds like he—

MAN 1 : No—but the dinge caught him right in the—Kid! Christ—

MAN 4 : What—?

MAN 1 : Don't back up—

MAN 6 : [*Through paper megaphone*] Use them arms already—

MAN 7: **Ten goddam rounds, ain't took a one yet—**

[*Roar, as a* PINKERTON MAN *helps* MAN 8, *a sunstroke* victim, *through the gate*]

PINKERTON MAN 1: I toldya—leave the gate clear—

[*Roar*]

MAN 1: Another one—

MAN 4: Just keep him off you—

[POP *appears at a side door.* MAN 8 *doubles over, retching*]

PINKERTON MAN 1: Move—**it's like an oven here—**

MAN 6: Time, for chrissake—

NEGRO BOY 1: [*Shaking a gourd in* MAN 8'*s face*] Eh! Eh! Eh! Eh!

MAN 1: Kid, quit clinchin—

MAN 8: Scram, ya dirty little—

MAN 1: BELL!

MAN 9: **Thank God!**

MAN 2: How the hell can he take it!

SMITTY: [*Coming through a side door*] Jesus, Pop—

POP: You sure they got the high sign?

SMITTY: Two rounds ago!

POP: Then what—

SMITTY: Pop, I gave it four times, I know they got it, Goldie flicked the towel, Pop, we went over and over it—

MAN 4: [*To* MAN 1] How's it look—

MAN 1: He's collapsin there but so is the nigger—**puffin like a goddamn buffalo—**

MAN 2: He won't last—

MAN 6: Start sweatin blood, coon!

[FRED, *sweating and frantic, comes through side door*]

FRED: I warned you, I warned you—

POP: Get back inside—

FRED: Can'tya—

SMITTY: Ssh!

POP: They won't cross us—

FRED: They nothing, it's HIM—

MAN 1: E-leven! [*"Ooh" from* CROWD *as* FRED *rushes back in*]

MAN 1: Right off, a low one—

MAN 7: You would, ya—

MAN 5: He can't help it, the Kid's belly's five feet off the—

[*Roar*]

MAN 1: Missed him, nigger—

[*Enter the* AGENT—*heads for* POP *and* SMITTY]

[*Roar*]

MAN 1: He slipped, the nigger slipped—

[*Roar*]

Hit him, hit him again—Oh, you—

MAN 3: What—

[POP *and* AGENT *whisper*]

MAN 1: Don't just look at him!

MAN 7: No instink! No instink!

[AGENT *whispers to* SMITTY; SMITTY *runs inside*]

MAN 4: Let's get mad, Kid—

MAN 7: **A hundred and two degrees—Chalkasians ain't made for it—**

MAN 1 : Oh, them clinches—
MAN 3 : He holdin—?
MAN 1 : Come—on—

[Roar]

No, it's the nigger—! He's leanin, yeah—

MAN 4 : **He's wearin down!**
MAN 3 : **I toleya—**
MAN 1 : Break it, ref—
MAN 2 : Don't let him rest—
MAN 1 : Oh, good man—
MAN 3 : He wobblin—?
MAN 1 : Sorta—yeah! Yeah! He's backin away there, he's wipin his eyes—
MAN 6 : Go in on him—
MAN 1 : He's goin—the nigger ain't—there, he's tryna dodge him—

[Roar]

MAN 9 : Run, tar-baby, run back to your barrel—
MAN 1 : Boyoboy, yeah, **he's slowin down, he's—**
MAN 2 : Let's go—
MAN 1 : Shit—move in—

[SMITTY *re-enters with* RUDY, *the baseball player*]

AGENT : OK, Rudy—
RUDY : Who you, man—
MAN 6 : MOVE IN!
AGENT : Get your shirt off—[*To* SMITTY] get him something to carry—

[SMITTY *dashes back inside*]

RUDY: Mah whut?

AGENT: [*Tugging at the buttons*] That! Off! Like you put one on for him, remember—

MAN 1: No, Kid, chase him, he's tryna get his wind back—

RUDY: Whut de hell you—

AGENT: Get into that corner, Rudy, tell that pal of yours—

[*Roar—drowns what he says*]

MAN 1: Be care—no, jab him off ya—Christ, the nigger's all over him, pile-drivin, whalin at him—cover up, he's—duck—Oh, Jesus, the Kid just—

RUDY: [*As* SMITTY *returns with towel and bottle*] Gimme dat, you mother—[*Seizes towel and bottle, and runs inside, pulling off his shirt*]

MAN 1: Cover, Kid, turn, turn—cover, he'll cave your ribs in—

[*Roar*]

MAN 2: Stop the goddamn—

MAN 1: Wait, no, he's up—Oh the nigger's right in him, he's after it, he's—

MAN 6: Kid, don't let him—

MAN 1: All he's got, he's workin like a butcher—

MAN 2: No—

MAN 7: He's gotta—

MAN 5: Kid—Kid!—

MAN 9: Kid—

MAN 1: Hookin him, sluggin—oh, that eye—

MAN 6: Ride him out—

[NEGRO BOY *climbs up the other column to see*]

MAN 7: Kid—

MAN 6: Bust your hand, you—

MAN 1: Murder, it's murder—

MAN 4: No more—

MAN 2: Clinch him—

MAN 1: Ref—

MAN 6: Clinch him, dummox—

MAN 2: No more—

MAN 1: REF!

MAN 5: Stop it—

MAN 2: REF, YA—

NEGRO BOY: Eh! Eh! Eh! Eh!

MAN 1: He's on the ropes, he can't see, he's rollin, he's punchy—

MAN 2: How the hell does he—

[*Roar*]

MAN 6: Is he—

MAN 1: No, it's a bell, lemme down . . . lemme down . . . [*Slips down the column:* MAN 4 *is helped up to take his place*]

POP: [*To* SMITTY] Tell Fred to throw in the—

AGENT: [*To* SMITTY] Stay right here!

MAN 4: [*Looking ring-ward*] God Almighty!

MAN 1: [*To* MAN 4] They workin on the eye?

MAN 4: Yeah, but the rest of him—! **Blood, welts all over—**

MAN 5: Fifty on the coon the next—

MAN 2: Shut your hole—

MAN 6: Don't worry, Kid—

MAN 1: **That eye came up like a grape!**

POP: [*To* AGENT] Oh, Mister—

PINKERTON MAN 1: [*Offstage*] Comin through—[*Movement behind barrier*]

MAN 2: Jesus, the heat got him—

[PINKERTON MEN 1 *and* 2 *come through the gate carrying* GOLDIE *on a chair; the* AGENT *beckons to them*]

MAN 6: How you gonna fight without your Jew, spook—

GOLDIE: [*To* AGENT] Mister, it's no use, it's—

AGENT: Ssh!

MAN 4: Here they go—

[PINKERTON MEN *set* GOLDIE *down at the side door and run back inside*]

AGENT: [*To* GOLDIE] The boy get to him?

[*Roar*]

MAN 4: Nigger's slouchin in there—

GOLDIE: Mister, he don't hear, he—

MAN 4: Little stiff on his pins there—the Kid's just waiting for it—

GOLDIE: **Like it's my son, I begged him!**

MAN 4: The nigger's feelin him out—the Kid's sorta rockin there—back up, Kid—please—

[*Roar*]

The nigger roundhoused him—!

MAN 5: Here it comes—

[*Roar*]

The Kid's still up—he's still up—tryna shake his head clear—the nigger don't know where to—

[*Roar changes*]

MAN 2: Stay on your feet—

MAN 7: Kid—

MAN 4: He is! He is! The nigger can't do it—**he's hittin but he's outa juice! He's punched out!**

MAN 2: I knew it—

MAN 4: There! Nothin! Just stingin him, slappin him—

MAN 1 : Kid—

MAN 6 : He can't hurtya—

MAN 1 : He's arm-heavy—

MAN 9 : Please, Kid—

MAN 4 : Look at him—He's saggin there, just heavin at you—

MAN 6 : What the hell's he—

[*Roar*]

MAN 4 : He's hitting back! He's lashin at him—swingin there wild—

MAN 1 : **He can't see—**

MAN 2 : Kid—

MAN 4 : **The coon's givin ground—**

MAN 7 : Keep on swingin—

MAN 4 : There, the coon's lurchin round him, he's—

MAN 6 : Smell him out, Kid—

MAN 4 : There—Oh—swiped him half across the ring—

MAN 1 : [*Pulling down* NEGRO BOY] Lemme up, you goddamn—

MAN 2 : More—

MAN 3 : It's gonna happen, Kid—

MAN 4 : In on him, no, he's over—yeah—

MAN 7 : Keep swinging—

MAN 4 : Walkin in his sleep but he's after him—

MAN 6 : Press him—

MAN 4 : Just flailin them great big—

[*Roar*]

Bango!

MAN 2 : More, Kid!

MAN 7 : Wheee!

MAN 1 : [*On column*] Christ, it's like an octopus!

MAN 2 : Don't stop, Kid—

MAN 4: Ya shot it all, coon, can't hurt him!

MAN 9: Wahoo!

MAN 6: **Can't hurt nobody!**

[GOLDIE *totters to his feet and goes back inside*]

MAN 1: Kid, aim it lower—

MAN 4: Don't have to, he's reelin—

MAN 2: Lower—

MAN 7: He'll go under you—

MAN 4: No—got no legs left—

MAN 1: Bango!

MAN 2: Yippeee!

MAN 6: Give us the smile, coon—

MAN 1: He's flounderin—

MAN 2: Poleax him—

MAN 4: There—

MAN 1: Clap for that one, you—

MAN 4: Now, Kid—

MAN 2: Finish him—

MAN 1: The nigger can't hardly get his guard up—

MAN 2: Finish him—

MAN 4: It's comin—the Kid got him bulled into a corner—punchin blind—

MAN 1: The blood's in both eyes—

MAN 2: [*And* OTHERS] Now—now—now—

MAN 4: Just goin like a windmill—

MAN 7: Oh, flatten him—

MAN 2: Wipe the rotten—

MAN 4: There—the nigger's grabbin for the rope—**he's bucklin** —he's swingin with his other—

MAN 6: You're THROUGH—

MAN 4: The Kid's poundin right down on him, he's grabbin,

he's hangin, he's holdin, he can't, the Kid's drivin him down like a big black—

[*Great roar:* MAN 1 *follows the* REFEREE'*s count with his own arm; his voice barely audible*]

MAN 1 : Four—five—six—seven—eight—

[*The* CROWD'*s roar pulsates with the last two counts and pandemonium breaks loose: hugging, dancing, etc.*]

MAN 1 : [*Falling into arms below*] I love him, I love him—

[AGENT *leaves*]

MAN 2 : Wahooo—

[POP *goes inside with* SMITTY]

MAN 6 : **We got it—**
MAN 2 : Yoweee—
MAN 6 : Where's my fifty—
MAN 5 : Let's get in there—

[THEY *all push at the barrier*]

MAN 2 : What a Kid—
MAN 1 : Quit the pushing—

[*Snatches of band music from within*]

MAN 4 : They're bringin the nigger out—
MAN 2 : Who cares—
MAN 6 : Open up—
MAN 7 : We're missin all the—
MAN 6 : Break it in, for—

MAN 2 : [*As they break through*] WA-A-H-O-O-OH! [THEY

ALL *rush in except* MAN 9, *who stops to throw a coin to* NEGRO BOY 2]

MAN 9: Here, chico—buy yourself a whitewash! [HE *follows the rest and the* BOY *runs off. The sounds of jubilation within rise still higher: the remaining* NEGRO BOY *climbs the column to watch*]

PINKERTON MAN 2: [*Offstage*] Outa the way, come on, let 'em through here—

[JACK, *helped along by* TICK *and* GOLDIE *and escorted by four* PINKERTON MEN, *comes limping through the gates, the* PRESS *at his heels*]

PRESSMAN 1: Just a word, Jack—

PINKERTON MAN 2: Let's go boys—

GOLDIE: Not now—

PRESSMAN 2: Jack, in the tenth when you were—[*The music and crowd noise suddenly dwindle, and the faint but triumphant sound of the* ANNOUNCER'S VOICE *is heard.* JACK *stops*]

TICK: Les go, baby.

[JACK *stands listening*]

PRESSMAN 3: Jack—why do you think it happened? [JACK *stands listening*] I'm asking—[*The* VOICE *rises to its conclusion: great cheering: the* BOY *climbs down.* JACK *turns to* PRESSMAN 3] Why did it, Jack?

JACK: He beat me, dassall. Ah juss din have it. [*The* BOY *spits on him and darts away*] Ain't dat right, boy?

TICK: [*Moving him on*] Take it slow, nice an slow . . .

PRESSMAN 3: But why, Jack? Really.

JACK: [*Laughs, stops*] Oh, man. Ah ain't got dem reallies from de Year One . . . **An if any a you got em, step right down an say em.** [*Looks around at audience: Drum-beating begins*]

No . . . you new here like Ah is—[MUSIC: A *March Tri-umphal*] Come on Chillun! Let 'em pass by!

[*Spreading his arms,* HE *sweeps* TICK, GOLDIE, *and* 1 *or* 2 PRESSMEN *off to one side, moving slowly, as the cheering* CROWD *surges out through the gates. The* KID *rides on their shoulders: immobile in his white robe, with one gloved hand extended, the golden belt draped around his neck and a towel over his head—his smashed and reddened face is barely visible—*HE *resembles the lifelike wooden saints in Catholic processions. Joyfully his bearers parade him before the audience, and with a final cheer fling their straw hats into the air*]

CURTAIN

"*If it be true that good wine needs no bush, 'tis true that a good play needs no epilogue.*"

WILLIAM SHAKESPEARE

Here, in a single volume, are ten of the most distinguished and exciting plays of the 1960's. Ranging from hilarious comedy to stirring modern epic, from the latest work of long-established playwrights to the work of remarkably gifted newcomers, these plays—all recipients of major awards—show the depth, the diversity, and the vitality of the theatre of the sixties.

BEST PLAYS OF THE SIXTIES contains the complete text of all ten plays, each one accompanied by a preface that provides a wealth of background information on the play itself, its production, and its playwright. In addition, Stanley Richards has written a Preface to each play and a general introduction on the drama of the sixties and compiled a bibliography of other noteworthy plays of the decade.

Any theatre-lover will find here a memento of the plays he has seen, a useful reference, and hours of delightful reading.